UNDERSTANDING
THE CONTEMPORARY
MIDDLE EAST

UNDERSTANDING

Introductions to the States and Regions of the Contemporary World

Donald L. Gordon, series editor

Understanding Contemporary Africa, 3rd edition
edited by April A. Gordon and Donald L. Gordon

Understanding the Contemporary Caribbean
edited by Richard S. Hillman and Thomas J. D'Agostino

Understanding Contemporary China, 2nd edition
edited by Robert E. Gamer

Understanding Contemporary India
edited by Sumit Ganguly and Neil DeVotta

Understanding Contemporary Latin America, 2nd edition
edited by Richard S. Hillman

Understanding the Contemporary Middle East, 2nd edition
edited by Deborah J. Gerner and Jillian Schwedler

SECOND EDITION

UNDERSTANDING THE CONTEMPORARY MIDDLE EAST

edited by
Deborah J. Gerner
and Jillian Schwedler

LYNNE
RIENNER
PUBLISHERS

BOULDER
LONDON

Published in the United States of America in 2004 by
Lynne Rienner Publishers, Inc.
1800 30th Street, Boulder, Colorado 80301
www.rienner.com

and in the United Kingdom by
Lynne Rienner Publishers, Inc.
3 Henrietta Street, Covent Garden, London WC2E 8LU

Library of Congress Cataloging-in-Publication Data
Understanding the contemporary Middle East / Deborah J. Gerner and Jillian Schwedler,
   editors. — 2nd ed.
     p. cm. — (Understanding)
   Includes bibliographical references and index.
   ISBN 1-58826-062-3 (pbk. : alk. paper)
   1. Middle East. 2. Africa, North. I. Gerner, Deborah J. II. Schwedler, Jillian.
III. Understanding (Boulder, Colo.)
DS44.U473   2003
956—dc22

                          2003058575

British Cataloguing in Publication Data
A Cataloguing in Publication record for this book
is available from the British Library.

Printed and bound in the United States of America

The paper used in this publication meets the requirements
of the American National Standard for Permanence of
Paper for Printed Library Materials Z39.48-1992.

5 4 3 2

Contents

Illustrations

■ **Figure**

■ **Photographs**

Preface

This second edition of *Understanding the Contemporary Middle East* appears at a time when interest in the Middle East has expanded beyond politicians, pundits, and regional specialists to include average citizens. Since the publication of the first edition four years ago, a series of events—the outbreak of the second intifada in Israel/Palestine, the September 11, 2001, terrorist attacks on New York City and Washington, D.C., and the war that removed Saddam Hussein from power in Iraq in 2003—have propelled the Middle East and the larger Islamic world to the fore of numerous cultural, political, economic, and social debates. In North America, regional specialists have been inundated with invitations to address students, religious groups, and community organizations regarding Islam, the Arab-Israeli conflict, Iraq, and other issues related to the Middle East. At colleges and universities, professors are responding to this increased interest by adding expanded Middle East content to a wide range of courses not exclusively dedicated to Middle East studies, as well as by offering region-specific classes with greater frequency. As the U.S. government now focuses on Iran and Arab states such as Syria and Saudi Arabia in its ongoing "war on terrorism," there is a great desire on the part of students and the general public—not only in North America but throughout the world—to learn more about this critical region.

Like the first edition, this expanded and updated collection draws on the expertise of more than a dozen scholars to create a truly interdisciplinary text that is up-to-date and student friendly. Individual chapters introduce the key themes, controversies, and research within geography, history, economics, demography, politics, international relations, sociology, anthropology, gender studies, conflict resolution, religion, and literature. Although each chapter is intended to stand on its own, the authors have consciously attempted to integrate their discussion across chapters so that the book functions as a unified entity.

The introduction confronts directly the stereotypes that students often have about the Middle East and also introduces one of the themes that is woven throughout this volume: aspects of ancient and modern culture and practices that are so much a part of the region. In Chapter 2, Ian R. Manners and Barbara McKean Parmenter describe the great diversity that exists within the Middle East. They suggest that, rather than imposing on the region a single, static "geography," it is more appropriate to think about multiple geographies reflecting various types of shifting landscapes: political boundaries, physical attributes such as the presence or absence of water, and cityscapes. This approach allows for a fuller exploration of the interplay of humans and their environments and illustrates the ways that borderlessness is at least as important as borders in interpreting the Middle East.

Arthur Goldschmidt Jr. describes, in Chapter 3, the lengthy history of the region, beginning with the ancient empires of Egypt and Sumer more than 5,000 years ago. Here a central motif is the continual transformation that occurs as invaders conquer or are turned back and as the indigenous peoples resist or accommodate these outsiders. Goldschmidt gives particular attention to the creation of the Islamic Middle East as an autonomous political and social system and the challenges to that system that came from its interactions with the West in the eighteenth, nineteenth, and twentieth centuries.

Deborah J. Gerner picks up where Goldschmidt ends, discussing the domestic politics of Middle Eastern countries. In Chapter 4, she highlights several factors that have influenced the evolution of these states, such as their colonial legacy and patterns of economic development, before turning to a description of the political ideologies and forms of governmental organization that characterize the Middle East today. Gerner also elucidates a key distinction between attributes of Middle Eastern political systems that are unusual or even unique to the region and those characteristics that are more widespread globally.

These themes are also present in Chapter 5, in which Mary Ann Tétreault examines the international relations of the region. Tétreault analyzes the functioning of the Middle East as a regional subsystem, with attention given to several recent conflicts. She also illustrates how involvement with the Great Powers has frequently undercut the ability of Middle Eastern countries to act autonomously in the global arena and examines the widespread impact of the war against Iraq that began in 1991 and escalated dramatically in 2003, leading to the overthrow of the regime headed by Saddam Hussein.

Chapter 6, by Simona Sharoni and Mohammed Abu-Nimer, is unusual in two respects: it deals entirely with a single conflict, and it is jointly written by an Israeli Jew and a Palestinian citizen of Israel. This collaboration allows for a carefully nuanced discussion of the Israeli-Palestinian conflict. Sharoni and Abu-Nimer present the historical evolution of this antagonistic relationship and explain its international dimensions, then turn to a consideration of the central issues that divide many Israelis and Palestinians. Finally, they summarize past and current attempts to transform the conflict and challenge the common belief that a just and enduring settlement can only occur with the involvement of the United States and other third parties. Written from a conflict resolution perspective, their analysis provides a rich, forward-looking framework that rejects the idea that the Israeli-Palestinian conflict can never be resolved.

In Chapter 7, by Elias H. Tuma, we turn to a study of the varied patterns of economic development that Middle Eastern countries have experienced. Tuma's argument is that virtually all these countries began with a problematic developmental context—poor infrastructure, lack of a stable government, low level of technical and scientific knowledge—that has been further complicated by dominant foreign forces. Even today, Tuma writes, most Middle Eastern economies are characterized by low labor productivity, external debt, and dependent patterns of trade and investment.

The presence of petroleum is one of the most important economic factors to shape the contemporary Middle East. In Chapter 8, Mary Ann Tétreault explores the profound ways in which the discovery of oil in the early twentieth century ensured the continued and deep involvement of foreign governments and multinational corporations in regional dynamics, the creation of the Organization of Petroleum Exporting Countries, the role of oil as a substitute for military power, and the particular domestic challenges that are faced by oil-rich states. She also encourages readers to look forward by asking whether the twenty-first century will see the establishment of a new oil regime.

Building on the chapters by Tuma and Tétreault, Valentine M. Moghadam focuses in Chapter 9 on the connections among population growth, urbanization, (un)employment, poverty, and income inequality. Moghadam portrays the current labor situation with a particular sensitivity to differences between women and men in various parts of the Middle East. Her discussion is enriched by brief case studies of social and demographic trends in Morocco, Tunisia, Egypt, and among Palestinians. While confronting popular images about women in the work force, this chapter illustrates region-wide trends as well as striking differences within the Middle East.

Laurie King-Irani's analysis of kinship, class, and ethnicity in Chapter 10 adds additional texture to the complex representation of the Middle East that this book's authors create. Drawing on anthropological literature, King-Irani illustrates how differing social realities connect to each other and to various aspects of Middle Eastern life. She also provides insights into the gender and family relationships that are often a source of confusion to outsiders, stressing that many aspects of kinship, ethnicity, and class are highly adaptive in their Middle Eastern context.

This topic is continued in Chapter 11, in which Lisa Taraki situates Middle Eastern women with respect to the modern nation-state and investigates the impact of traditional norms and values on opportunities for women. In addition, she provides an extensive typology of modes of women's political participation and illustrates the diversity of experience that is a constant refrain throughout this book. Taraki's discussion of the varied and dynamic roles women play addresses stereotypes without downplaying the challenges and obstacles Middle Eastern women continue to face.

Chapter 12, by John L. Esposito, Mohammed A. Muqtedar Khan, and Jillian Schwedler, returns to two subjects addressed by several earlier chapters: the interface between religion and politics and the existence of diverse social structures within the Middle East. The authors summarize the historical role of Judaism, Christianity, and Islam in the region, then consider the myriad ways that religion, particularly in its more fundamentalist forms, continues to influence Middle Eastern politics and society. Their analysis also explores how religious questions often extend beyond state borders into a global context.

In Chapter 13, miriam cooke describes beautifully the historical and cultural underpinnings of Middle Eastern literature: poetry, short stories, novels, and plays. Literature, she shows us, does not exist in a vacuum but instead reflects and influences its environment—the cultural ferment, the impact of colonization and struggles for independence, the experience of exile and emigration—in profound ways. As the richness of Middle Eastern literature is unknown to most Westerners, this chapter also provides an introduction to numerous materials now available in English translation.

Finally, Chapter 14 presents several crucial challenges facing the region in the twenty-first century: determination of the appropriate role of religion and culture in state-society relations, the need for increased economic development, the historical legacy of colonialism and the conflicts that have arisen in its aftermath, and the widespread grassroots demand for increased political accountability.

* * *

This book could not have come into existence without the assistance of numerous individuals. Most important are our collaborators, a diverse group of dedicated educators from the Middle East and North America, all of whom have spent significant time in the region. We are fortunate for the enthusiasm and seriousness with which each undertook often extensive revisions and updating for this second edition, frequently under difficult personal or political circumstances. The opportunity to work with these top-notch scholar-teachers—to get to know them and to learn more about their disciplines—has been an honor and a privilege. That such a group of well-regarded and busy researchers care enough about education to participate in the creation and updating of this text should provide reassurance to those who would claim that scholarship and teaching are somehow incompatible.

Special thanks to Thomas Hartwell, a professional photographer based in the Middle East, whose evocative images grace many of these pages. We remain indebted to Barbara Parmenter and Ian Manners for the financial support they obtained from the University of Texas, Austin, to help cover the cost of preparing the photographs for the first edition, and to Tom for sharing his work. Chris Toensing, editor of *Middle East Report*, was extremely helpful in locating photos for the new chapter on oil. Thanks as well to Iranian artist Nasser Ovissi for permitting us to use a detail from one of his lithographs on the book's cover, and to Cheryl Rubenberg for introducing us to Ovissi's work.

This book continues to benefit from the assistance provided by Phillip Huxtable and Rajaa Abu-Jabr during preparation of the first edition. Two anonymous reviewers, as well as series editor Donald L. Gordon, provided excellent suggestions for making the original text as student friendly as possible, and we have kept their guidance in mind while preparing this updated volume. Waseem El-Rayes (University of Maryland) dedicated many hours to updating the Basic Political Data, meticulously checking the figures against multiple sources; Bradley Lewis (University of Kansas) enthusiastically provided myriad forms of assistance. Finally, the support we received from everyone at Lynne Rienner Publishers was outstanding. Lynne's enthusiastic interest and insightful guidance strengthened the book immeasurably, as did the always professional and accommodating assistance of Sally Glover, Lesli Brooks Athanasoulis, and Steve Barr.

Jillian Schwedler would like to thank Deborah J. Gerner and Lynne Rienner for inviting her to serve as coeditor for the second edition. Deborah J. Gerner would like to thank Philip A. Schrodt for joining her explorations of the Middle East in all its amazing and wonderful complexity, Jillian Schwedler for being a fabulous person to work (and play) with, and Lynne Rienner for her friendship.

Like the first volume, this second edition is dedicated to all our former professors of the Middle East, those women and men who first opened our eyes to the possibilities for research on this fascinating part of the world. We also wish to express our gratitude to the students, teachers, and other readers who have sought out this book to help them make sense of the region. *Thank you.*

—*Deborah J. Gerner,*
Jillian Schwedler

Introduction

Deborah J. Gerner

The most frequent response I receive when I tell someone I study and teach about the Middle East is: "Are you crazy? Isn't it dangerous? Don't all Muslims hate Christians and Jews? How can you be a feminist and still respect the culture 'over there'?" The mental picture of the Middle East held by most North Americans is of an area full of violent conflict, a region crawling with religious fanatics, where terrorism is endemic and women are little more than chattel.

I'm never quite sure how to respond to this reaction, for the Middle East I have come to know bears little resemblance to these stereotyped representations. *Understanding the Contemporary Middle East* challenges these popular images and presents a more nuanced portrayal of Arabs, who constitute a majority of the region's population, as well as Turks, Persians, Israelis, Berbers, and Kurds, who also live in this diverse and fascinating region.

As used in this book, the term *Middle East* refers to several distinct groups of countries covering more than 6 million square miles of deserts, mountains, and rich agricultural lands (roughly twice the area of the lower forty-eight U.S. states). There are the oil-producing countries of the Arabian Peninsula: Bahrain, Kuwait, Oman, Qatar, Saudi Arabia, the United Arab Emirates, and Yemen. These states, along with those of the Fertile Crescent region (Israel, Jordan, Lebanon, Syria, and the West Bank and Gaza Strip), are frequently viewed as the "core" Middle East. The North African countries of Algeria, Egypt, Libya, Morocco, and Tunisia are included in this region, as are the sub-Saharan states of the Comoros Islands, Djibouti, Mauritania, Somalia, and Sudan (primarily by virtue of their membership in the League of Arab States). In addition to Israel, the non-Arab states of Turkey and Iran are also important. In its earlier incarnation as the Ottoman Empire, Turkey ruled

1

virtually all of the lands of the Middle East; today the vastly smaller Turkish state straddles Central Asia, Europe, and the Middle East. Iran, too, looks in more than one direction: toward the east are Afghanistan and Central Asia, whereas to the west lies Iraq and the rest of the Arab world.

All three of the major monotheistic religions—Judaism, Christianity, and Islam—have their roots in the Middle East, and each still has significant communities of believers in the region. The imagery and lessons of the Hebrew scriptures, the New Testament, and the Quran—the ethical teachings, the stories, and the people—are an integral part of how people in the West understand the world, whether or not one is a member of any of these faith communities.

Many people use the words *Muslim, Middle Eastern,* and *Arab* interchangeably. This is quite incorrect and misleading. To begin with, not everyone who is a Muslim is an Arab. Islam is a major world religion, second in number only to Christianity, with nearly 1 billion adherents. Well over half of the worldwide Islamic community is African or Asian (including Persians, Turks, Indians, Pakistanis, Indonesians, and Chinese). Only about 20 percent of Muslims are Arab, with the remainder spread throughout the former Soviet Union, Europe, and North America. It *is* true that within the Arab world, where Islam originated, more than 90 percent of the population is Muslim. But there are also Arabs who are Christian, Druze, Bahai, and Jewish. In particular, there are a large number of Palestinian, Lebanese, and Egyptian Christians.

The interplay of the ancient and the modern affects both the world's perception of the Middle East and how the Middle East views itself. The shopkeeper standing on the stone streets within the walls of the Old City of Jerusalem—or the ancient souks (markets) of Damascus, Baghdad, or Cairo—has a more intense awareness of history than the proprietor of a Baskin-Robbins ice cream store in a Toronto strip mall. Conflict with and competition over the Middle East has figured in European history since before the time of the Roman Empire, expressing itself variously in military, religious, economic, and colonial contention. Even the early United States, seemingly isolated across a wide Atlantic Ocean, found itself engaged militarily and diplomatically in this region in the early nineteenth century as it contested the power of the "Barbary pirates" of North Africa.

Yet the contacts between the West and the Middle East have not been entirely antagonistic. European and North American cultures have been continually influenced by the Middle East, often in profound ways. During the Middle Ages, much of the Middle East was substantially more advanced than Europe in the fields of science, medicine, mathematics, architecture, literature, the visual arts, and education. Works of Greek philosophy that were lost to Western Europe survived in the Arab-Islamic world and were first reintroduced to the West through Arab intermediaries.

Some of these influences lie buried and forgotten in our everyday language. For instance, *algebra* and *alcohol* both come from Arabic originally; they became part of the English language by way of the Arab mathematical and scientific writings that helped fuel the rebirth of scientific knowledge in Europe at the end of the Middle Ages. The archaic English verb *cipher*—the act of numerical calculation—comes directly from the Arabic word for *zero;* it was through the Arabs that Europeans first learned the technique of flexibly calculating with the decimal system rather than using the awkward and limiting system of Roman numerals.

The influence of Middle Eastern culture is not limited to science and religion alone but also can be found in literature. Over the past century, various Middle Eastern poets and philosophers have risen to great literary popularity in the West. The medieval Arabic and Persian language fables and stories collected as *A Thousand and One Nights* were first translated into French in the early eighteenth century. By the late twentieth century—courtesy of the Disney corporation—modern renditions of the tales of Aladdin, Ali Baba, and Sinbad the Sailor were staples in every daycare center and preschool in the industrial world. *The Rubaiyat of Omar Khayyam* enthralled Western readers after its translation by Edward FitzGerald in the nineteenth century. In the 1960s, the "flower children" hitchhiked across the United States carrying the works of Lebanese poet Kahlil Gibran; in the late 1990s, their children placed the poetry of eleventh-century Persian mystic Jalal al-Din al-Rumi on the bestseller lists. When the Nobel Prize for literature was awarded to Egyptian Naguib Mahfouz in 1988, millions of non-Arabs suddenly discovered the social critique of *The Cairo Trilogy* and Mahfouz's numerous other writings.

The Middle East is also significant as one of several geographical regions currently undergoing the transition from a preindustrial to a postindustrial economy—from the world of the village to the world as a village. People throughout the Middle East, much like people in Africa, Latin America, and Asia, are facing tremendous challenges as they move from a rural to an urban economy, from a life based on tradition to a life based on innovation, and from a world of legends told by the dying embers of a fire to a world of satellite dishes, CNN, and Nintendo games. These changes can have a profound impact on the structure of the family, the roles of women and men, the status of religion in society, and the responsibilities of the individual to the state and of the state to the individual.

The diversity of the Middle East means that there are many different reactions to these socioeconomic transformations. For example, in response to the pressures of modernization and European influence, in the early 1920s Mustafa Kemal Atatürk and the "Young Turks" transformed Turkish society by eliminating the Islamic norms of the old Ottoman Empire and establishing a secular Turkish state. Yet just across the border from Turkey, the Iranian revolution of 1978–1979, led by the Ayatollah Ruhollah Khomeini, responded to the pressures of modernization by overthrowing a secular, Western-oriented state and reestablishing an Islamic republic based on classical Islamic norms.

As you explore various dimensions of the Middle East through this volume, you will find a world that you knew existed but about which you perhaps knew very little. These chapters will confirm some of your perceptions—but challenge many others. It is a world of immense diversity but of shared traditions; a world of extremes of wealth and poverty but of many common ideals and aspirations. This is the world of the Middle East. Enjoy.

The Middle East:
A Geographic Preface

Ian R. Manners and
Barbara McKean Parmenter

A camel caravan crossing desert dunes, oil derricks pumping thick black crude, rows of men kneeling in prayer, bearded protesters shouting slogans—more than likely these are some of the images conjured up when the outside world thinks of the Middle East. Each of us carries our own mental "geography" of the world and its places, our own way of visualizing and interpreting the earth on which we live. Professional geographers attempt to correct preconceived notions and present a broader perspective. Typically, a geographical description of the Middle East, like that of any other region, would begin with an overview of the physical environment—geology, geomorphology, climate, flora, and fauna—as a backdrop for a discussion of human activities in the region, land use, resource development, population distribution, urbanization, and political organization. Yet even the best of these descriptions often fail to convey what the Middle East is "really" like.

The Middle East cannot be easily compartmentalized into book chapters or neatly divided by border lines on a map. Sharp boundaries are blurred, discontinuities appear unexpectedly, the familiarity of everyday life surprises us in our anticipation of the exotic and dangerous. Timothy Mitchell (1988) has described how European travelers to Egypt in the nineteenth century were frequently confused by what they saw when they reached Egypt. They had seen the ancient Egyptian artifacts that had been collected and displayed in Europe's capitals, even visited the Egyptian Hall at the Exposition Universelle held in Paris; some had read the *Description de l'Egypte*, the twenty-two-volume work prepared by the French artists and scholars who had accompanied

Napoleon to Egypt, but nothing they saw or experienced quite matched up to what they had been expecting to see. There was often a palpable sense of disappointment. Where was the "real Egypt"? In a similar way, contemporary visitors to the Middle East are likely to find that their geographical knowledge has to be reformulated as they encounter a world that challenges many of their expectations.

The difficult path to understanding the Middle East in all its complexity is not traveled only by outsiders. In the Iranian film *Bashu,* director Bahram Bayza'i tells the story of a boy from the deserts of Khuzistan in southwestern Iran whose village is caught in a bombardment. Bashu understands little of the reasons for the conflict between his government and its neighbor, Iraq; he knows only that he is now both homeless and orphaned. Seeking refuge in the back of a truck, he falls asleep. When he awakes, he is bewildered to find himself in a quiet world of cool, deep-green forests, a paradise he never dreamed existed. The truck has brought him to Gilan province in northwestern Iran, where he is taken in by a peasant woman despite the disapproval of her neighbors. Bashu is of Arab descent and speaks a mixture of Arabic and Persian common to the borderlands of Khuzistan; the woman speaks Gilaki, a dialect of Persian. Unable to communicate with either his caregiver or her neighbors, Bashu struggles against their prejudices. But he is not alone in being different. The woman who has taken him in is struggling to manage the farm on her own while her husband is away fighting in the war. When her husband returns and demands that the boy be sent away, she refuses to comply. In a very real sense, the film is a small reflection of much larger issues in Middle Eastern society, exploring the ways in which people deal with differences and face changes related to environment, culture, government, religion, and gender.

Thus, although the term *Middle East* may appear to suggest a degree of homogeneity, the region is extraordinarily diverse in its physical, cultural, and social landscapes. For many, the desert seems the central physical metaphor for the Middle East, an image frequently repeated in films and novels. The sand seas of the Rub'al-Khali (the Empty Quarter) in Arabia perhaps best fit this image. Yet the landscapes of the Middle East also encompass the coral reefs that draw scuba divers to the Red Sea, permanent snowfields and cirque glaciers on the slopes of the great volcanic peaks of Mount Ararat (16,946 feet) in eastern Anatolia and Mount Damavand (more than 18,000 feet) in the Elburz Mountains of Iran, the salt-crusted flats and evaporation pans of the Dasht-e Kavir in central Iran, and the coastal marshes and wetlands of the Nile Delta. Most emphatically, and despite the vast expanses of desert and steppe, the Middle East is also very much an urban society, with more than half the population living in cities that face much the same environmental, infrastructural, and social problems of cities around the world.

There is likewise great cultural diversity in the Middle East. Much of the area came under Arab Muslim influence during and after the seventh century.

Deborah J. Gerner

The area around the ancient West Bank town of Jericho/Ariha, located 20 feet below sea level, is a mixture of hill, desert, and lush oasis.

Thomas Hartwell

Full of modern concrete, steel, and glass buildings, Riyadh is the capital of Saudi Arabia and its largest city, recently surpassing Jeddah.

At various times, Persian and Central Asian peoples and influences flowed westward into the lands around the eastern Mediterranean. Most people in the region are Muslims, but there are significant communities of Christians and Jews. The three major languages are Arabic, Turkish, and Persian, all of which are quite distinct linguistically (Arabic is a Semitic language, Persian is Indo-European, and Turkish is Ural-Altaic). Nonetheless, they have been heavily influenced by each other. Persian is written in Arabic script, as was Ottoman Turkish; only since 1928 has Turkish used a modified Latin alphabet. All three languages contain numerous words from the others, and each has a subset of distinct dialects. In addition, other peoples with their own languages are found throughout the region. There are, for example, Berber speakers in Morocco and Algeria and Baluchi speakers in southeastern Iran. Kurdish-speaking people probably constitute the fourth largest linguistic group in the region, and the revived Hebrew language has been a central integrating force among Jews in Israel.

How, then, to describe the geography of the Middle East? In this chapter we choose to present multiple geographies of the Middle East, different ways of seeing and depicting the region. In this way, we hope to present a richer description of the area than would normally be possible in a few pages, although one that is far from comprehensive.

■ Boundaries

A geography of the Middle East must first come to grips with how to define the term *Middle East*. Compared to the area portrayed in any Western atlas published in the late nineteenth century, the political landscape of the region we know today as the Middle East is virtually unrecognizable. The atlas published by the *Times of London* in 1895, for example, provides a series of maps titled "The Balkan Peninsula," "The Caucasus," "Asia Minor and Persia," and "Palestine." Nor would these places, as depicted in the atlas, have been any more familiar to those living in the region, who would have recognized no unified geographical entity but rather a mosaic of regions. "Al-Iraq" referred to the area around the Shatt al-Arab waterway, and "al-Jazira" identified the lands between the Tigris and Euphrates Rivers, including Baghdad. "Sham" indicated the area immediately around Damascus and Bilad al-Sham (or country of Sham), the larger region now comprising Syria, Lebanon, Jordan, and Palestine. Egyptians still call their country *Misr,* but originally the term referred only to the Nile Delta and its narrow valley, not to the vast territory contained within its present-day boundaries. Today's map reveals a very different geography. Almost without exception, the present sovereign states are new creations, in large measure the products of European intervention and the dismemberment of the Ottoman Empire.

The term *Middle East* is itself an unabashedly Eurocentric term. It seems to have been used first in 1902 in reference to British naval strategy in the Gulf at a time of increased Russian influence around the Caspian Sea and German plans for a Berlin-to-Baghdad railway. Largely through the columns of the *Times,* the term achieved wider circulation and came to denote an area of strategic concern to Britain lying between the Near East (another Eurocentric designation, essentially synonymous with the area remaining under the control of the Ottoman Empire), the expanding Russian empire in Central Asia, and the Indian Raj (Chirol, 1903). During World War I, the British expeditionary force to Mesopotamia was generally referred to as "Middle East Forces," as distinct from Britain's "Near East Forces," which operated from bases in Egypt. After the war, these two military commands were integrated as an economy measure, but the "Middle East" designation was retained.

With the passage of time, the name became both familiar and institutionalized, first in the military commands of World War II and later in the specialist agencies of the United Nations (UN) (Smith, 1968). Yet there remain ambiguities and uncertainties in terms of its more precise delimitation. Does the Middle East include Afghanistan to the east? With the demise of the Soviet Union, should the region be reconstituted to include the new sovereign states of Armenia and Azerbaijan? Frequently, the Maghreb states of Morocco, Tunisia, and Algeria are included in discussions of the Middle East based on the fact that they share so much of its culture and history. For similar reasons, Sudan is sometimes included despite the presence of a large non-Muslim, non-Arabic-speaking population in the southern part of the country (Blake, Dewdney, and Mitchell, 1987). In this book, we have opted for a broad interpretation by including in its discussion Turkey, Iran, and Israel, together with all the states that belong to the Arab League.

What is surprising is that the term *Middle East* is also used by people within the region. The literal Arabic translation, *al-sharq al-awsat,* and the Turkish, *orta doğu,* can be found in books, journals, and newspapers. Interestingly, the term is most widely used in discussions of geopolitical strategies in the region. Arab commentators, for example, might discuss "American policy in the Middle East" or "Israel's relationship to the Middle East." Thus it is perhaps more a reference to how others, either outside the region or outside the predominant culture, view the region and less a self-describing term.

The "map view" of a region is the most skeletal of possible geographies but is both formative and informative. Looking at a contemporary political map of the Middle East, the predominance of long, straight boundary lines stretching across hundreds of miles of desert is striking (see Map 2.1). Another revealing feature of today's map, as Bernard Lewis points out, is that the names of countries are, for the most part, restorations or reconstructions of ancient names (1989:21–22). *Syria,* for instance, is a term that first appears in Greek histories and geographies and was subsequently adopted by the

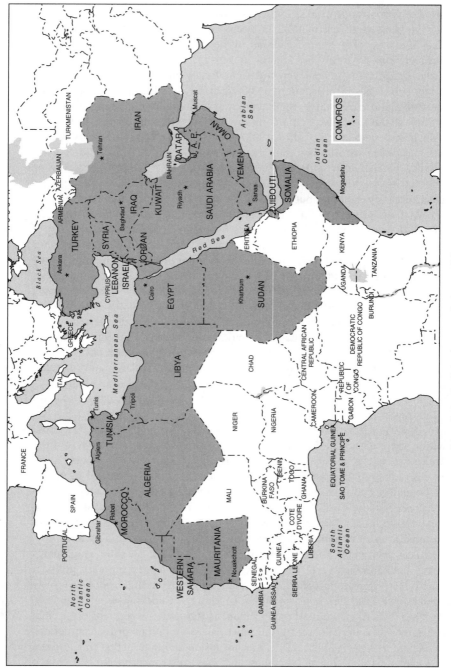

Map 2.1   Political Map of the Middle East

Romans as the name for an administrative province. But from the time of the Arab-Islamic conquest of the seventh century, the name virtually disappears from local use. Its reappearance dates from the nineteenth century, largely through the writing and influence of Western scholars. Similarly, although Europeans have been referring to the lands of Anatolia and Asia Minor as Turkey since the time of the Crusades, the inhabitants of this region did not use this name until the establishment of the Republic of Turkey in 1923.

To understand the changes that have occurred in the political map of the Middle East, it is helpful to recall that at the end of the sixteenth century the authority of the Ottoman Empire extended from the borders of Morocco in the west to the borders of Iran in the east, and from the Red Sea in the south to the northern and eastern shores of the Black Sea (see Map 2.2). In Europe the Ottomans twice laid siege to Vienna. But the eighteenth and nineteenth centuries saw a gradual retreat from these high-water marks. In the Tartar and Turkish principalities from the Crimea to the Caucasus, Ottoman sovereignty was replaced by Russian domination; in the Balkans, the Ottomans confronted growing nationalist aspirations and a concerted assault by Austria and its allies; in North Africa, the Ottomans had to deal with the expansion and imposition of colonial authority involving the French in Algeria (1830) and Tunisia (1881) and the Italians in Libya (1911).

In other areas, Ottoman power was greatly weakened by the emergence of strong local rulers. In the aftermath of Napoleon's unsuccessful invasion of Egypt, for example, an Ottoman military officer named Mehmet (Muhammad) Ali established a dynasty that made Egypt virtually independent of Ottoman rule. The bankruptcy of the Egyptian administration after efforts to modernize the country's economy and infrastructure in turn opened the way to more direct European intervention in the country's affairs through a French-British debt commission and British occupation in 1882, although the country still remained nominally under Ottoman sovereignty. In Lebanon, following a massacre of Maronite Christians by Druze in 1860 and the landing of French troops in Beirut, Britain and France forced the Ottoman sultan to establish the semiautonomous province of Mount Lebanon with a Christian governor to be appointed in consultation with European powers (Drysdale and Blake, 1985:196).

Thus, even where European powers did not control territory outright, by the end of the nineteenth century they had become deeply involved in the region's commerce and governance. The defeat of Ottoman Turkey in World War I helped create the current map of the Middle East (Fromkin, 1991). In the final dissolution of the Ottoman Empire, the remaining Arab provinces were reconstituted into the territories of Iraq, Syria, Lebanon, Transjordan, and Palestine and subjected for a brief period to direct British and French administration, albeit under the guise of a League of Nations mandate.

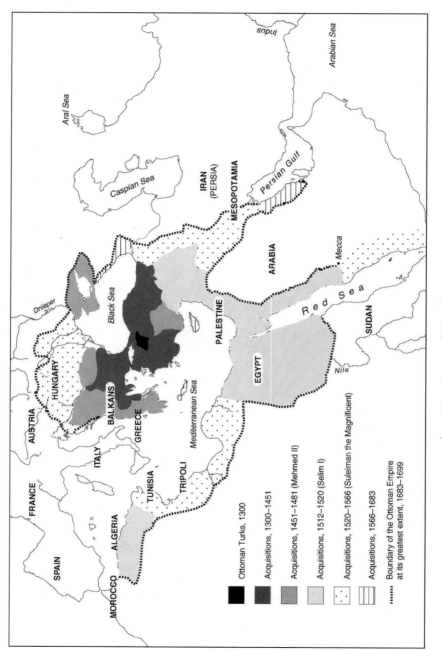

Map 2.2   Extent of the Ottoman Empire

Ottoman Turks, 1300

Acquisitions, 1300–1451

Acquisitions, 1451–1481 (Mehmed II)

Acquisitions, 1512–1520 (Selim I)

Acquisitions, 1520–1566 (Suleiman the Magnificent)

Acquisitions, 1566–1683

Boundary of the Ottoman Empire at its greatest extent, 1683–1699

The map of the Middle East, then, is both very recent and frequently a cause of conflict. From a resource perspective, the lack of correspondence between political and hydrological boundaries has complicated the development of scarce water resources. New conflicts have arisen particularly over claims to offshore resources such as oil and natural gas. In the shallow, hydrocarbon-rich waters of the Gulf, where numerous small islands, sandbanks, and reefs with contested histories of settlement and occupation provide a basis for rival claims to sovereignty, the extension of land boundaries offshore has proven to be complicated and contentious. One such dispute, between Bahrain and Qatar regarding sovereignty over the Huwar Islands and other coastal territories, became the subject of the longest arbitration case in international legal history. It was finally resolved by the International Court of Justice in The Hague in March 2001 after nine years of litigation. In its adjudication of claims that drew from long-standing family and tribal disagreements over fishing and pearling rights dating back to the nineteenth century, the Court essentially upheld a 1939 determination of boundaries by Britain, then the protectorate power in the region (Gerner and Yilmaz, 2004).

From a cultural perspective, boundaries are also problematic. The Kurds, for example, a non-Arab, predominantly Muslim people numbering several million, are spread across Turkey, Syria, Iraq, and Iran. Their quest for autonomy has at one time or another involved them in clashes with all four of these states. The distribution of Sunni and Shi'a Muslims, the two major subgroups of Islam, likewise does not adhere to national boundaries. The fault lines of this division cross the oil fields of southern Iraq and northern Arabia.

From a political perspective, the appearance, disappearance, and tentative reappearance of Palestine demonstrate that borders are still in flux. Assigned the mandate for Palestine in 1921, Britain sought to fulfill its 1917 promise to facilitate the establishment of a national home for the Jewish people while simultaneously ensuring that, as stated in the Balfour Declaration, the civil and religious rights of non-Jewish communities in Palestine were safeguarded. The establishment of Israel in 1948 realized the Zionist vision of an independent homeland in which the Jewish people could live free of persecution, a return to the land from which they had been physically separated during nearly 2,000 years of exile. A consequence of these events has been the departure, through emigration to Israel, of large numbers of Jews whose families had lived for centuries in cities and towns throughout the Middle East and the displacement of another people, the Palestinian Arabs, who fled or were forced from their homes and lands during the fighting and sought refuge in Egypt, Jordan, Syria, Lebanon, and elsewhere in the region.

In such ways have the cartographies of the region been reimagined and refashioned in the course of the twentieth century. As the century progressed, a complex body of interests grew up around the new states of the Middle East and continued into the twenty-first century. Lewis (1989:38) sees a hardening of the boundaries created by colonial administrators and the emergence of new identities based on a sense of loyalty and attachment to country. Yet the revived vitality of Islam, expressed differently in different parts of the region, is an eloquent reminder that the issue of identity is still being worked out.

Likewise, the movement of people across borders should remind us that these states are not disconnected spaces. Labor migration, for instance, has played and continues to play a major role in shaping social and economic structures throughout the area, through the remittance of foreign earnings and through the direct experience of living and working overseas. Both inter- and intraregional migrations occur: there are Turkish *gastarbeiter* (guest workers) in Germany and laborers from the Maghreb in France, and (prior to the 1990–1991 Gulf War) Egyptians, Yemenis, and Jordanians made up the majority of the labor force in Saudi Arabia and the Gulf states. Finally, some individuals cross borders more or less permanently as refugees and exiles. It is often those who are forced to leave who write most eloquently about the attachments that exist between people and places (Parmenter, 1994). In such ways, migration, whether forced or voluntary, touches on the experience of many of us and raises questions that are central to much writing in contemporary cultural geography about the nature of place and identity in the midst of globalization (Massey and Jess, 1995).

■ Aridity and Water

Imagine now that we move from our map view of the region to a closer scale. Other geographical phenomena come into focus, perhaps none so important as the presence or absence of water. Aridity is a pervasive element in land and livelihood throughout the Middle East. This is perhaps most evident during the long, hot summer drought, when only the lush greenery of irrigated fields interrupts the hazy brown landscape of bare hillsides and steppes, roads and dusty towns. Palestinian writer Laila Abou-Saif describes Cairo as "sand-colored, and the people's faces are of the same color, as if they had been sculpted and layered out of the surrounding intertwining desert. . . . Even the trees are dusty and layered with the golden sand. Cairo is always beige" (1990:6).

Yet the degree of aridity varies enormously within the region. The winter months bring rainfall to many areas, particularly the higher elevations of Asia Minor, the Zagros and Elburz Mountains of Iran, and the hills of Lebanon, Israel, and the West Bank. Heavy snowfalls can occur even as far south as Amman and Jerusalem, and the melting of winter snows has historically contributed to spring flooding in the Tigris and Euphrates River basins. In these areas, the rainfall associated with mid-latitude depressions moving through the Mediterranean basin during the winter months is prolonged, abundant, and reliable. It is sufficient for successful long-term cereal cultivation relying exclusively on dryland farming or rain-fed methods. In the more mountainous areas, poorer soils and steeper slopes may restrict the opportunities for farming, but elsewhere villages are clustered closely together and the onset of the winter rains marks the beginning of the agricultural cycle of plowing, sowing, and harvesting.

As one moves southward across the region, however, the winter storms occur less frequently. Alexandria receives an average of less than 8 inches of rainfall a year, only a fifth of that recorded at Antalya, 200 miles to the north on the Turkish coastline. Rain-fed agriculture becomes an increasingly precarious and risky proposition. In southern Jordan and in the northern desert of Saudi Arabia, rainfall is likely to be in the form of intense and highly localized storms when it does occur. Here the steppe merges imperceptibly into desert, traditionally the domain of nomadic pastoralists. In this zone, any form of agricultural activity other than herding is possible only where major rivers transport water from regions of better abundance, as in the Nile and the Tigris-Euphrates basins, or where springs and groundwater provide a supplementary supply for irrigation.

In a very immediate sense, water has been and remains the critical "life-sustaining resource." The Quran states that every living thing is made from water, and everyone from the nomadic pastoralist to the sophisticated city dweller shares an interest in its availability and distribution. Over the centuries, Middle Eastern societies developed a range of techniques for dealing with water scarcity, many of which revealed a close adjustment to the conditions of supply (Manners, 1990). Along the Nile, for instance, traditional basin irrigation permitted effective use of the river's floodwaters for millennia. Each year farmers constructed mud embankments in the river's floodplain, dividing the land into a series of basins. Drawings and paintings from Pharaonic Egypt suggest that similar methods of water management were in use as early as the fourth millennium B.C.E.[1] As the Nile rose in summer, the silt-laden floodwaters were diverted into the basins and retained there for several weeks. Once the level of the Nile dropped, surplus water could be drained back into the river and a winter crop—wheat, barley, lentils, beans, berseem (Egyptian clover)—could be cultivated in the saturated alluvial soils. Harvesting took place in March or April, after which the land lay fallow until the next flood season. By ensuring a reliable and controlled flow of water and by contributing to the maintenance of soil fertility, basin irrigation allowed for the development of a highly productive agricultural system. Equally critical from the point of view of long-term stability, the flushing action of the annual flood prevented the buildup of salts harmful to crop growth. Basin irrigation remained the dominant method of irrigation in the Nile Valley until the end of the nineteenth century, by which time the modern phase of water development had begun to take shape through the construction of barrages, annual storage reservoirs, and summer canals intended to allow for year-round irrigation and multiple cropping.

Like the basin irrigation system developed in the Nile Valley, other traditional water management devices such as the *qanats* of Iran, the *shadufs* of Egypt, and the *norias* of the Orontes River in Syria had a common purpose: to make effective use of a critical resource and thereby enable societies to survive and flourish under conditions of scarcity and uncertainty. The *qanat,* a sophisticated technique for developing, collecting, and distributing groundwater through a network of underground tunnels, may well have been in use in Iran as early as the first millennium B.C.E.: that it represented an extremely successful adaptation to a variety of local conditions is evident in the diffusion of this technique to other parts of the Middle East and North Africa, particularly during the early Arab caliphates, and from North Africa to Spain and later the "New World."

As the demand for water has grown, however, newer technologies of water development intended to make more productive use of both surface water and groundwater have frequently disrupted and displaced traditional systems. The construction of the Aswan High Dam in the 1960s, for example, enabled all of Egypt to be irrigated on a perennial basis, made possible two, and in some cases even three, crops per year, and generated power for countrywide electrification projects. These benefits came with environmental side effects, however, including serious problems of soil salinization (White, 1988).

Herein lies one of the major challenges facing the region. The burgeoning demand for water to meet agricultural, industrial, transportation, and urban needs would be difficult enough to satisfy even if water supplies were more abundant. In the Middle East the problem is greatly complicated by the

In the mountainous Dhofar region of Oman, watering troughs have been built to help the bedouin maintain strong camel herds.

Deborah J. Gerner

uneven distribution of water resources and by the lack of correspondence between political and hydrological boundaries. As a result, those countries where irrigated agriculture is of paramount importance (Egypt, Iraq, and to a lesser extent Israel, Jordan, and Syria) are unable to control the sources of water on which their populations and their economies depend. Roughly two-thirds of the water supply available to Arab countries has its source in non-Arab countries (Gleick, 1994). In Israel, by some estimates, between one-half and two-thirds of the water currently used for irrigation and domestic and industrial purposes actually originates outside the country's pre-1967 boundaries. In particular, the major aquifers that supply groundwater to municipalities and farms in Israel's coastal plains are actually recharged through rainfall occurring over the West Bank.

In such circumstances, it is hardly surprising that water rights and allocations became a key issue in the post-Oslo negotiations between the Israelis and the Palestinians over the future status of the West Bank and Gaza Strip (Wolf, 1995). Certainly it would be quite wrong to see the conflict between Israelis and Palestinians and between Israel and neighboring Arab states as primarily a struggle over water (Libiszewski, 1995; Wolf, 2000). Nevertheless, in conjunction with other imperatives, particularly national security considerations, access to water resources has been a factor in strategic thinking. In 1964, for example, the Arab states made plans to divert the flow of the Hasbani and Banias headwaters of the Jordan River away from Israel. (The Hasbani, which originates in Lebanon, was to be diverted into the Litani River and from there to the Mediterranean; and the Banias, originating in Syria, was to be diverted to a storage reservoir in Jordan on the Yarmuk River via a canal along the western edge of the Golan Heights.) These plans were brought to a halt by an Israeli attack on the construction works (Manners, 1974). And while water was not an overriding issue in the subsequent Six Day War of June 1967, the occupation by Israel of Syrian territory on the Golan Heights effectively extended Israel's hydrostrategic control over this part of the Jordan drainage basin.

More recently, in October 2002, Lebanon's completion of a pumping project involving the Wazzani Springs, an important contributor to the flow of the Hasbani particularly during the dry summer months, provoked threats of retaliatory action from Israel and resurrected old arguments and animosities over rights to use the Jordan River's waters. That a relatively minor development project intended to provide a water supply to local villages should have necessitated the dispatch of UN and U.S. mediators is perhaps an indication of the severity of the water crisis, which confronts all states in the Jordan basin. More discouraging in the long term is the extent to which efforts, begun in the aftermath of the Oslo Accords, to build trust and to create joint management institutions for equitable, sustainable use of the Jordan's waters have been undermined by the breakdown in the peace process since 2000.

The extent to which control over water resources empowers some countries at the expense of others is well illustrated in the case of the Euphrates River. The Euphrates rises in eastern Turkey, punches its way through the edge of the Anatolian Plateau in a series of dramatic gorges, then flows across the increasingly arid steppes of Syria and Iraq to a confluence with the Tigris River (which also originates in Turkey) just above Basra, Iraq. From here the two rivers flow together as the Shatt al-Arab to the Gulf. Although most of the huge drainage basin of the Euphrates is actually in Iraq, nearly 90 percent of the annual flow of the river is generated within Turkey. This means that the downstream users, Syria and Iraq, are vulnerable to Turkey's future development plans for the Euphrates River.

Iraq has long-established claims to the Euphrates; indeed, Mesopotamian power and culture was linked to effective control over the waters of these rivers (Jacobsen and Adams, 1958). The later Sassanian and Abbasid periods (fourth to twelfth centuries) were marked by a considerable expansion of the irrigation system. In the twentieth century, first during the British mandate and later after independence, the irrigation systems were rehabilitated and new control structures erected. In the 1970s Iraq began planning a major storage reservoir that, like the Aswan High Dam, was intended to provide long-term storage. Despite setbacks caused by war, Iraq's long-term plans still envision greater use of the Euphrates' waters. Syria, like Iraq, is steadily making greater use of the Euphrates' waters for irrigation development and power generation and in 1973 completed the huge Al-Thawra Dam.

But it is Turkey that holds the real key to what happens in the future, and Turkey is currently in the process of implementing a truly massive water development project in southeastern Anatolia (the Güneydoğu Anadolu Projesi [GAP]) that involves both the Tigris and the Euphrates Rivers. If fully implemented, the GAP would involve as many as twelve dams and storage reservoirs on the Euphrates and ten on the Tigris, plus additional power-generating facilities. This immense undertaking is intended to pump new life into Turkey's hardscrabble, semiarid southeast provinces, where living standards are far below the national average, but it is clearly more than just another water development project. These provinces are home to the majority of Turkey's Kurdish population. By providing people with a more secure and comfortable livelihood, the government hopes to undercut support for the Kurdish separatist movement and bring an end to a costly and bloody conflict.

In 1990, Turkey began filling the reservoir behind the Atatürk Dam, triggering protests from both Syria and Iraq. By some estimates, the Atatürk Dam and other proposed storage and diversion projects on the Euphrates could reduce downstream flows to Syria by 40 percent and to Iraq by as much as 80 percent, especially during dry years. Clearly, if all the proposed water projects are carried out, the total water demand will be well in excess of the normal flow of the river. Moreover, water quality is likely to be an issue for downstream users because an increasing proportion of the available flow will consist of return irrigation flows containing high concentrations of agricultural chemicals and salts.

Some see in this situation of growing regional competition for limited water supplies the potential for future conflict. Unfortunately, in none of the major river basins do there exist formal agreements among all riparian states (those bordering on rivers) over water rights; there is no such agreement for the Jordan River or for the Tigris and Euphrates Rivers, and legal agreements for the Nile River involve only Egypt and Sudan, to the exclusion of the seven other upstream riparian states. Boutros Boutros-Ghali's comment, when he was still Egypt's foreign minister, to the effect that "the next war in our region will be over the waters of the Nile, not politics," has been widely repeated. An alternative, more hopeful view, is that water could be a vehicle for regional cooperation. Sharing of knowledge and experience with regard to using water less wastefully, for instance through drip and subsurface irrigation systems and the recycling and reuse of wastewater, or the transfer of water from states with surpluses to states with deficits, as in the case of the proposed peace pipeline from Turkey through Syria to Jordan, the West Bank, Israel, and Gaza, are examples of cooperation that could transform regional geographies.

As Will D. Swearingen describes in *Moroccan Mirages,* for many hydraulic engineers and government administrators, the ideal vision of water development has been "not a drop of water to the sea" (1987:39). Likewise, the region's marshes and wetlands have often been targets for major hydraulic engineering projects because they are perceived as empty spaces that "waste" potentially valuable land and water resources. But water is more than just a commodity with economic value to society, a resource to be developed, its flow to be regulated on a liter-by-liter basis; water has other values and meanings to those living in the region.

People are increasingly recognizing that water sustains a range of ecological processes, which in turn support communities of fishers, hunters, reed gatherers, salt producers, and the like. The coastal lagoons of the Nile Delta, the marshes of the Shatt al-Arab, Lake Hula in Israel and Jordan's Azraq Oasis, Lake Ishkeul in Tunisia, and other wetlands scattered throughout the region were once highly productive ecosystems that provided habitat and sustenance for diverse communities of plants and animals. Those living around wetlands traditionally exploited these resources, maintaining a diverse and relatively sustainable livelihood. Wetlands are valuable for other nonconventional uses as well, including absorbing and treating human sewage and other organic wastes, recharging groundwater aquifers, and acting as vital resting and feeding sites for waterfowl and shorebirds migrating between breeding grounds in northern Eurasia and wintering grounds in Africa. In many cases, these wetlands have been drained, severely polluted, or dried out as a result of groundwater withdrawals, with devastating impacts on local communities. Fishing villages around Lake Maryut near Alexandria, Egypt, have seen livelihoods destroyed due to dumping of industrial wastes. The marshes of Azraq Oasis in Jordan have been largely drained to supplement the municipal water supply of Amman. In Iraq, the government of Saddam Hussein drained large portions of the Shatt al-Arab marshes at least in part for political reasons: to exercise greater control over the Marsh Arabs, a largely Shi'ite people opposed to Hussein's rule. Israelis drained the Hula marshes in the 1950s for agriculture, but later discovered that the high amount of fertilizers required to farm the drained and eroding peat was polluting the nearby Sea of Galilee. In the 1990s, the Jewish National Fund undertook a project to restore a portion of the marshes. Since the restoration was completed in 1998, the area has seen an increase in migratory waterfowl, including cranes and pelicans (Shapiro, 2002).

A framework for conserving the region's remaining wetlands is the Convention on Wetlands of International Importance (commonly known as the Ramsar Convention), signed in 1971. To date, fourteen of the countries covered in this book are contracting parties to the convention, protecting forty-two wetland areas totaling 1.8 million hectares, and are committed to following the convention's guidelines of wise use in the management of these sites (Ramsar Convention Bureau, 2003). These guidelines include setting up the legal framework for protection and participatory processes to involve local communities (Parmenter, 1996). What these initiatives will achieve in practice remains to be seen, but their very existence testifies to a growing awareness of the complexity of water issues.

There are connections between water and life that are crucial to any understanding of environment and culture in the Middle East. The Quran holds out to all believers the promise of a paradise that is filled with fountains and cool, shaded watercourses, "gardens beneath which rivers flow" (Schimmel, 1985). Images of gardens and water, inspired by descriptions of paradise in the Quran, have had a profound influence on Islamic art and poetry (Mac-Dougall and Ettinghausen, 1976). This promise was not limited to literary and artistic representations; it also found expression in a love of gardens that were imagined and conceived as a reflection of the beauty and serenity of paradise on earth.

This linking of the sacred and the secular, of water and life, is eloquently conveyed in a story Annemarie Schimmel relates about the puzzling question she was asked in Anatolia by an old woman, " '*Ankara'da rahmet var mı?*' [Is there mercy in Ankara?]. I wondered what the question might mean in a casual conversation with some unknown person. But it meant, 'Is there rain in Ankara?'" In Turkish, *rahmet* means both God's mercy and the blessing of rain, for it is through the blessing of rain that everything seemingly dead is made alive again (Schimmel, 1985:6).

■ Cityscapes

Closing in on our scale still further, we move from regional phenomena like water to local environments, particularly the city. In the film *Raiders of the Lost Ark,* Indiana Jones stands on a rooftop overlooking an assemblage of small, white-domed houses. His Egyptian host gestures toward the scene. "Cairo," he says. "City of the living. A paradise on earth." The scene that they are looking at is more likely a small village in Tunisia. Cairo, even in the 1930s, when the story takes place, was a large sprawling metropolis filled with apartment buildings, factories, government offices, theaters, museums, and all the other accouterments of modern urban life. The film is confirming our imaginative expectations and our own assumed position vis-à-vis this Arab city. It is exotic, alluring, and inscrutable—we gaze comfortably at this fantasy place from a high vantage point and leave it to the intrepid Indy to plunge into the labyrinthine alleyways and bazaars of Cairo itself.

The Cairo of the 1930s that the film did not show might have seemed rather mundane: a vibrant, bustling city, home at that time to just over 1 million people carrying on their daily lives in ways that were far from mysterious. But vision and imagination are powerful weapons, and Middle Eastern cities have been the object of intense imaginings over the course of their history. Nowhere in the Middle East is this more evident than in Jerusalem, a city sacred to three religions. Jews, Christians, and Muslims have struggled for centuries to make Jerusalem "their" city. "The chronicles of Jerusalem," Meron Benvenisti writes, "are a gigantic quarry from which each side has mined stones for the construction of myths—and for throwing at each other" (1996:4).

Cities have always been important in the history of the region, frequently developing as nodes connecting the well-traveled routes of armies and traders. To rulers, cities were constituted as centers of power and authority. In the eyes of travelers and traders, cities were almost literally oases of security, walled and protected, centers of commerce, learning, and entertainment. Al-Hariri, in a famous twelfth-century adventure story, *al-Maqamat* (The Assemblies), wrote admiringly of Basra in present-day Iraq: "Thy heart's desire of holy things and worldly thou findest there" (1898:164). Today the old walled cities of the region are in most cases small fractions of the larger urban fabric, which changes with each passing day. As Janet Abu-Lughod has observed, "A city at any one point in time is a still photograph of a complex system of building and destroying, of organizing and reorganizing" (1987:162). This system includes both the formal visions imposed by governors, conquerors, and administrators and the vernacular forces of ordinary citizens working to establish their own territories and routines.

Istanbul is a prime example of this dialectic between formal and vernacular. In the fourth century, the Emperor Constantine moved the seat of the

Roman Empire from Rome to the site of a former Greek settlement, Byzantium, located on a promontory bordered on one side by the Golden Horn and on the other by the Sea of Marmara. Although the city's official name was always Konstantinoupolis Nea Rome, "the city of Constantine that is the new Rome," it quickly became known as Constantinople, a name that retained currency even among Turks, whose documents and coins frequently referred to the city as Konstaniniye until the end of the Ottoman Empire (Çelik, 1986:12). Christianity enjoyed a special status in this new Rome, which was seen as a sacred city, its churches and monasteries housing a unique collection of holy relics and shrines that symbolized God's special favor. Justinian's great church of Haghia Sophia, its domed basilica rising above the city, epitomized the close relationship between the Byzantine state and the Christian church. But other buildings and monuments—palaces, walls, columns, churches, and aqueducts—remain embedded within today's urban fabric to recall more than 1,000 years of Roman-Byzantine rule.

When the Ottomans finally captured the city in 1453 after an eight-week siege, Sultan Mehmet II inherited a prized imperial city, but one in a sad state of dilapidation. The sultan initiated a massive program of repopulation and reconstruction intended to restore the city to its past grandeur and prosperity. Thousands of people were relocated to the city, since 1930 known popularly as Istanbul, from all quarters of the empire. These included skilled artisans and craftspeople to assist in the immense task of reconstruction. New palaces,

Deborah J. Gerner

Located along the Bosporus Strait, Istanbul, Turkey, symbolically links Europe and the Middle East in a single dynamic city of 9 million people.

great mosques with their schools, libraries, and charitable institutions, extensive bazaars and markets, and improved systems of water supply transformed the appearance of the city. These were the symbols of power and prosperity befitting the capital of a great empire.

In the twentieth century, with the final collapse of the Ottoman Empire, Turkish nationalists desiring to establish a secular republic along European lines made their own statement through urban planning and design. Turning their backs on Istanbul, they decided to construct a new capital in central Anatolia, hundreds of miles to the east of Istanbul, adjacent to the small town of Ankara. The design of the new Ankara was carefully planned to create an entirely different way of public life, one divorced from the Ottoman and Islamic past (Keleş and Payne, 1984). A German urban planner and architect, Hermann Jansen, was engaged to lay out a master plan for Ankara along the lines of a garden city, a scheme popular in Europe at the time and considered to embody the "rational" approach to urban planning. The plan specified separate zones for residences, businesses, and industry, separated by wide boulevards and interspersed with parks and public squares. The government encouraged new styles of architecture that were intended to give public expression to the nation's modern image (Bozdocan, 1994). These styles applied even to the design of ordinary residences, symbolizing the desire to shape not only the structure of the city but also the fundamentals of private life.

Istanbul and Ankara are only two examples of how visions backed up by political power organize and reorganize urban landscapes. Cairo was originally laid out by the Fatimid ruler Mu'izz al-Din in the tenth century to serve as a formal, ordered imperial capital next to the bustling commercial town of Fustat. Fustat itself had grown from the encampment of the Arab army that laid siege to the fortified Byzantine settlement of Babylon during the Arab conquest of Egypt in 640 C.E.[2] In her study of Cairo, Abu-Lughod relates that by one account the conquering Fatimid general "carried with him precise plans for the construction of a new princely city which Mu'izz envisaged as the seat of a Mediterranean Empire" (1971:18). The new city was named al-Qahira, "the victorious city," and its monumental architecture was to become a favorite subject of European artists.

As in other cities in the Middle East, the nineteenth and twentieth centuries saw many attempts to "modernize" and "improve" Cairo. In 1867 the ruler of Egypt, Isma'il Pasha, who already had a keen interest in urban development, attended the Exposition Universelle in Paris. There he reportedly met with Baron Georges-Eugène Haussman, the urban planner who had remade Paris into the city of broad boulevards and gardens we know today. Eager to create a modern capital before the deluge of foreign visitors who would follow completion of the Suez Canal began to arrive, Isma'il quickly translated Haussman's principles into a new plan for Cairo. With no time to waste,

Isma'il chose to leave the medieval city essentially as it was, without gas, water, sanitation, or paved streets. Instead, he concentrated on building a new European-style city to the west, complete with Haussman-style boulevards and parks, powered by steam and lit by gaslight. This was the city foreigners would see, and their only forays into the old Cairo would be as tourists viewing the scattered monuments of a distant past (Abu-Lughod, 1971:98–111).

On the other side of this dialectic between formal and vernacular is the sheer persistence and energy of ordinary citizens. Life grows up and around formal plans, through and between them like vines on a trellis. Abu-Lughod (1987:163) has noted how residential neighborhoods formed a crucial building block of cities in the Islamic world during medieval and even later times. These neighborhoods, which often housed people related to each other or with common ethnic or religious backgrounds, enjoyed a large measure of autonomy. The state was concerned primarily with regulating the commerce and ensuring the defense of the city. Thus meeting the needs and protecting the interests of the neighborhood was primarily a local community responsibility. This involved such things as cleaning and maintaining the streets, providing lighting, and supervising and sanctioning behavior. A wealthier neighborhood might have its own charitable institutions, organize its own water supply with public fountains, or appoint night watchmen for internal security, often paid for through endowments to religious foundations.

When Europeans tried to penetrate these neighborhoods, they were confused and threatened by what they saw as a chaotic warren of streets that frequently ended in cul-de-sacs. Yet the intent in the layout and structure of neighborhoods and even individual buildings was to minimize physical contact and protect visual separation. Thus Islamic building laws regulated the placement of windows, the heights of adjacent buildings, and the mutual responsibilities of neighbors toward one another so as to guard and protect privacy (Abu-Lughod, 1987:167). Of course, the majority of the urban population lived in modest circumstances that bore little resemblance to the luxurious lifestyles of the rich and powerful, and this reality was reflected in the shabby construction and cramped quarters of many neighborhoods.

Nor was urban life free of hazards. The common use of wood construction in Istanbul, for example, made the city particularly vulnerable to fires. Between 1633 and 1839 the city suffered as many as 109 major conflagrations, many of which wiped out entire neighborhoods; between 1853 and 1906 this number reached 229 as fires increasingly came to play a major role in reshaping and redesigning urban architecture (Çelik, 1986:52–53). Diseases were another harsh aspect of city life, particularly bubonic plague, which until the nineteenth century periodically reappeared to carry off large numbers of the city's population.

As in many other parts of the world, the experience in Middle Eastern cities in recent years has been one of rapid urbanization, largely as a result of the influx of rural migrants in search of employment and better living conditions. These demographic shifts have dramatically transformed not only the physical appearance of cities but also the daily lives and routines of millions of people. In 1900 perhaps 10 percent of the region's population lived in urban settlements; by the end of the twentieth century an estimated 62 percent resided in urban communities (McDevitt, 1999). The dominant impression of urban life in the region today is one of incessant construction and a struggle to deal with the consequences of unrestrained growth. Everywhere one looks there are sprawling housing projects and lines of apartment blocks alongside new ring roads; in older neighborhoods, residents add more floors to buildings, squeezing space out of places where there seems to be none available.

The most explosive phase of urban growth has occurred within the past forty years as a result of migration, but many cities in the region began to experience an increase in growth in the late nineteenth century as improvements in sanitation and hygiene were reflected in declining mortality rates. By the beginning of the twentieth century, for instance, Istanbul had already begun to spread beyond the land walls that delimited the Byzantine-Ottoman city at the head of the Golden Horn. Today the city's boundaries extend for miles along the Bosporus Strait and along the European and Asian shores of the Sea of Marmara. Villages that in the 1950s still retained a distinctive identity now remain only as names on a map, submerged beneath a tidal wave of immigrants. The construction during the 1980s of two bridges across the Bosporus Strait, linking Europe and Asia, symbolized the emergence of this new "greater" metropolitan Istanbul.

Cairo, which at the beginning of the nineteenth century had a population of around 250,000, had grown to a city of 1 million people by the mid-1930s. By 1960 the city's population had reached 3.5 million and by 1970 more than 5 million. Today there are by more conservative estimates 12 million residents and by less conservative estimates 16 million residents of greater Cairo. Put slightly differently, in the past forty years Cairo has added to its population three cities comparable to the one that existed in 1960. The boundaries of today's city extend far into the desert, and the government has constructed new "satellite" cities in a desperate attempt to keep pace with the housing and employment needs of recent immigrants. Within the city, planners have elected to build elevated highways through neighborhoods, facilitating movement between the new, upscale residential suburbs on the city's periphery and the banks, offices, and ministries in the center (Denis, 1997:9). Older neighborhoods near the center have been cleared away to make room for modern luxury apartments, conference centers, and five-star hotels, and the former residents have been relocated in public housing projects. Despite the dislocation and disruption that this entails in daily living and working arrangements, the government's efforts to transform and "improve" the appearance of the city are matched by the practices and resolve of those who have been relocated, who reconstruct the housing the state has built for them by illegally erecting partitions, adding balconies, and creating new public and private spaces to suit their needs (Ghannam, 1997:17–20).

Clearly, the pace of urbanization has overwhelmed planners. Traffic congestion, lack of services, loss of amenities and open space, air pollution, inadequate water supply, and overloaded sewage treatment systems have become an all-too-familiar experience in many cities. Perhaps only in Saudi Arabia and the Gulf states, where preexisting urban populations were smaller and where infrastructure costs and housing subsidies could be more easily absorbed, have planners been successful in imposing order on the pattern of urban growth. Elsewhere, most attempts at long-range planning have foundered as planners and politicians have tried to cope with the immediate needs of a rapidly growing population.

Even short-term government efforts to keep pace have frequently fallen short, most conspicuously in the lack of adequate low-income housing for urban migrants. Many newcomers to the cities live in "temporary" housing, often referred to as squatter settlements. By one estimate there are more than 100 *ashwa'iyyat* (spontaneous communities) housing more than 6 million people in greater Cairo (Bayat and el-Gawhary, 1997:5–6). In Turkey such spontaneous settlements are called *gecekondus*—literally, "placed there at night"—reflecting the speed with which houses are illegally erected on

The Cairo-Giza metropolis is home to between
12 and 16 million people and continues to expand rapidly.

vacant land. For those of us who see such settlements only from the outside, Latife Tekin's compelling novel *Berji Kristin: Tales from the Garbage Hills* (1996) conveys some sense of what life must be like in a squatter settlement on the edge of Istanbul, the experiences, the fears, the rumors, the wind, and the dust.

Although governments have on occasion attempted to demolish illegal settlements, a more popular approach has been periodically to offer construction pardons and provide title to land. Over time, therefore, many of these squatter settlements have acquired legal status and have become functionally and administratively integrated into the urban fabric. Makeshift houses have been replaced by more permanent residences and modest apartment blocks. Thus, temporary housing has been transformed into a more permanent feature of most large Middle Eastern cities, with numerous local variations such as Cairo's City of the Dead, where families have taken over the aboveground tombs for housing. In these new neighborhoods, where public services remain inadequate, residents often organize themselves or seek assistance from nongovernmental or religious organizations to pave streets, install water lines, organize garbage collection, establish a health clinic, or start a bus service. Neighborhood self-help and improvement associations play an important, albeit often unacknowledged role in transforming neighborhoods and nurturing a sense of community and identity among recent migrants to the city. Thus for many urban residents, the neighborhood still constitutes the most important element, both spatially and socially, in their conception of the city.

■ Conclusion

In his essay "Geography Is Everywhere," Denis Cosgrove writes about what he sees as "the real magic of geography—the sense of wonderment at the human world, the joy of seeing and reflecting upon the richly variegated mosaic of human life and of understanding the elegance of its expression in the human landscape" (Cosgrove, 1985:120). We hope that this chapter reflects that rich mosaic and conveys a sense of interconnectedness: the ways in which water links politics, economy, and religion; the ways in which cities are shaped by global practices (trading connections, colonial experiences, labor migration, flows of capital) as well as local practices and imaginings; and the ways in which species, water, people, goods, capital, and ideas move across political boundaries. We would also like to emphasize the connections that places have with their pasts. By this we mean not simply the ways in which the past is present materially in the present-day landscape of the Middle East, but the ways in which the past may be present in the memories of people and in the conscious and unconscious constructions of the histories of places (Massey, 1995:187).

All of this suggests that we need to think about borderlessness as much as we do about borders in terms of understanding people's knowledge and experience of place. The connections between past and present and the absence of boundaries are brilliantly evoked in Amitav Ghosh's novel *In an Antique Land: History in the Guise of a Traveler's Tale* (1994), in which the writer, a Hindu researcher from India, reconstructs the journey and experience of a former Indian slave who early in the twelfth century had traveled to Cairo on behalf of Abraham Ben Yiju, a Jewish trader from Tunisia living in Mangalore. At one level, the writer parallels the slave's journey, traveling to Tunisia and Egypt, living with a Muslim family in a small village outside Cairo, and learning a form of spoken Arabic that later proved helpful in reading medieval documents. At another level, the research, based on the "Geniza Documents" (letters and other items found in the *geniza,* or storeroom, of a Cairo synagogue), "bears witness to a pattern of movement so fluent and far-reaching that they make the journeys of later medieval travelers, such as Marco Polo and Ibn Battuta seem unremarkable in comparison" (Ghosh, 1994:157).

As the letters between Ben Yiju and other merchants indicate, travel between Morocco, Egypt, Syria, Yemen, and India, although not free of risk (one letter describes how a merchant had been captured by pirates off the coast of Gujarat), was frequent and regular. Here is a very different construction of the geography of the region. Looking at today's political map and the divided world of the Middle East, it is very hard for us to step back and imagine the possibility of a world in which frontiers were not clearly or precisely defined, a place where Muslims and Jews and Christians traveled freely and crossed paths frequently in the course of everyday life and commerce. S. D. Goitein describes this period, roughly from the tenth through the thirteenth centuries, as the High Middle Ages, when the Mediterranean area "resembled a free-trade community [in which] the treatment of foreigners, as a rule, was remarkably liberal" (1967:66). Goitein notes that, with few exceptions, the hundreds of documents and letters in the Geniza archive describing travels to or in foreign countries "have nothing to say about obstacles put in the way of the traveler for political reasons" (59).

Not only merchants and traders but also artisans, scholars, and craftspeople were involved in this "continuous coming and going." Add to this the many Muslims making the hajj (pilgrimage to Mecca). Until the advent of the steamship in the nineteenth century, most hajjis traveled to Mecca with one of the great overland caravans that set out each year from Cairo, Damascus, or Baghdad. But even in the fifteenth and sixteenth centuries, caravans could consist of several thousand camels, hundreds of horses, and 30,000 to 40,000 people (Peters, 1994), giving some sense of the large numbers of people involved. In earlier centuries, the round-trip journey could take several years for people from North and West Africa, China, and Southeast Asia. From India, seventeenth-century pilgrim Safi ibn Wali Qazvini spent a year traveling to and from Mecca (Pearson, 1994:45–46). Like other literate pilgrims, Qazvini wrote an account of his travels that was intended at least in part as a guide for others, providing a wealth of details about the pilgrimage route and practical information about rest stations, watering points, and the costs of purchasing supplies.

The hajj is still an extraordinary undertaking for many Muslims in terms of both logistics and financing. But for the 2 million who now make the hajj each year, the same sort of information contained in Qazvini's narrative, together with visa application forms, is to be found on the Internet. And once again, through such experiences as the hajj, local places and communities are linked to and become part of the world beyond. Tourists traveling along the Nile may be surprised to see paintings of jumbo jets adorning the mud brick walls of humble houses. Here is a poignant and elegant reminder of the significance of the hajj in the lives of these villagers, conveyed in a tradition that has evolved over the past century whereby the experience of a lifetime, circling the Ka'bah, praying at Ararat, and making a joyful homecoming, is graphically captured and portrayed in folk art and architecture (Parker and Neal, 1995).

Paintings on the outside wall of this house in
Luxor, Upper Egypt, indicate the owner has made
the hajj (pilgrimage) to Mecca, Saudi Arabia.

In contemporary atlases, the Middle East is usually divided up into a familiar mosaic of nation-states, each nation with its distinctive color like detachable pieces of a jigsaw puzzle. Benedict Anderson (1991:6–7) sees nations as "imagined political communities" in the sense that members of the nation do not know most of their fellow members yet imagine themselves part of a broader community sharing a deep sense of fraternity and comradeship. For Anderson, the "map-as-logo" contributes to this imaginative process, not least because as "this 'jig-saw' effect became normal, each 'piece' could be wholly detached from its geographic context" (175). Our desire is that this chapter will encourage people to explore what lies beneath the surface of the map, to reconnect the map with its geographic context, to ask critical questions about how our maps and knowledge of the region have been constituted, and to imagine alternative geographies.

■ Notes

We would like to express particular thanks to Kay Ebel and Zjaleh Hajibashi for their helpful comments on an early version of this chapter.

1. B.C.E., meaning "before the common era," is viewed by non-Christians as a more neutral term for marking history than B.C., meaning "before Christ."

2. C.E., meaning "of the common era," is a neutral term for A.D. *(anno Domini),* meaning "in the year of our Lord."

■ Bibliography

Abou-Saif, Laila. 1990. *Middle East Journal: A Woman's Journey into the Heart of the Arab World.* New York: Charles Scribner and Sons.

Abu-Lughod, Janet. 1971. *Cairo: 1001 Years of the City Victorious.* Princeton: Princeton University Press.

———. 1987. "The Islamic City—Historic Myth, Islamic Essence, and Contemporary Relevance." *International Journal of Middle Eastern Studies* 19:155–176.

Al-e Ahmad, Jalal. 1985. *Lost in the Crowd.* Trans. John Green. Washington, D.C.: Three Continents Press.

Anderson, Benedict. 1991. *Imagined Communities.* London: Verso Books.

Bayat, Asef, and Karim el-Gawhary (eds.). 1997. "Cairo: Power, Poverty and Urban Sprawl." *Middle East Report* 202:2–30.

Benvenisti, Meron. 1996. *City of Stone: The Hidden History of Jerusalem.* Trans. Maxine Kauffman Nunn. Berkeley: University of California Press.

Blake, Gerald, John Dewdney, and Jonathan Mitchell. 1987. *The Cambridge Atlas of the Middle East and North Africa.* Cambridge: Cambridge University Press.

Bozdocan, Sibel. 1994. "Architecture, Modernism, and Nation-Building in Kemalist Turkey." *New Perspectives on Turkey* 10:37–55.

Çelik, Zeynep. 1986. *The Remaking of Istanbul.* Seattle: University of Washington Press.

Chirol, V. 1903. *The Middle East Question, or Some Political Problems of Indian Defence*. London: John Murray.

Cosgrove, Denis. 1985. "Geography Is Everywhere: Culture and Symbolism in Human Landscapes." Pp. 118–135 in Derek R. Gregory and Rex Walford (eds.), *Horizons in Human Geography*. London: Macmillan.

Denis, Eric. 1997. "Urban Planning and Growth in Cairo." *Middle East Report* 202:8–12.

Drysdale, Alasdair, and Gerald Blake. 1985. *The Middle East and North Africa: A Political Geography*. New York: Oxford University Press.

Fromkin, David. 1991. "How the Modern Middle East Map Came to Be Drawn." *Smithsonian* 22, no. 2:132–148.

Gerner, Deborah J., and Ömür Yilmaz. 2004. *A Question of Sovereignty: Bahrain, Qatar, and the International Court of Justice*. Pew Case Studies in International Affairs. Washington, D.C.: Institute for the Study of Diplomacy, Georgetown University.

Ghannam, Fara. 1997. "Relocation and the Use of Urban Space in Cairo." *Middle East Report* 202:17–20.

Ghosh, Amitav. 1994. *In an Antique Land: History in the Guise of a Traveler's Tale*. New York: Vintage Books.

Gleick, Peter H. 1994. "Water, War, and Peace in the Middle East." *Environment* 36, no. 3:6–15, 35–42.

Goitein, S. D. 1967. *A Mediterranean Society: Economic Foundations*. Berkeley: University of California Press.

al-Hariri. 1898. *The Assemblies of al Hariri: Translated from the Arabic, with an Introduction and Notes Historical and Grammatical, by Thomas Chenery*. London: Williams and Norgate.

Jacobsen, Thorkild, and Robert M. Adams. 1958. "Salt and Silt in Ancient Mesopotamian Agriculture." *Science* 128, no. 3334:1251–1258.

Keleş, Ruşen, and Geoffrey Payne. 1984. "Turkey." Pp. 165–197 in Martin Wynn (ed.), *Planning and Urban Growth in Southern Europe*. London: Mansell.

Lewis, Bernard. 1989. "The Map of the Middle East: A Guide for the Perplexed." *American Scientist* 58, no. 1:19–38.

Libiszewski, Stephan. 1995. *Water Disputes in the Jordan Basin Region and Their Role in the Resolution of the Arab-Israeli Conflict*. Zurich: Center for Security Studies and Conflict Research.

MacDougall, Elisabeth B., and Richard Ettinghausen (eds.). 1976. *The Islamic Garden*. Washington, D.C.: Dumbarton Oaks Trustees for Harvard University.

Manners, Ian R. 1974. "Problems of Water Resource Management in a Semi-Arid Environment: The Case of Irrigation Agriculture in the Central Jordan Valley." Pp. 95–114 in B. S. Hoyle (ed.), *Spatial Aspects of Development*. London: John Wiley & Sons.

———. 1990. "The Middle East." Pp. 39–66 in Gary A. Klee (ed.), *World Systems of Traditional Resource Management*. New York: Halstead Press.

Massey, Doreen. 1995. "Places and Their Pasts." *History Workshop Journal* 39:182–192.

Massey, Doreen, and Pat Jess (eds.). 1995. *A Place in the World? Places, Cultures, and Globalization*. Oxford: Oxford University Press for the Open University.

McDevitt, Thomas M. 1999. *World Population Profile: 1998*. Washington, D.C.: U.S. Agency for International Development.

Mitchell, Timothy. 1988. *Colonising Egypt*. Cambridge: Cambridge University Press.

Parker, Ann, and Avon Neal. 1995. *Hajj Paintings: Folk Art of the Great Pilgrimage*. Washington: Smithsonian Institution Press.

Parmenter, Barbara. 1994. *Giving Voice to Stones: Place and Identity in Palestinian Literature*. Austin: University of Texas Press.

———. 1996. "Endangered Wetlands and Environmental Management in North Africa." Pp. 155–174 in Will D. Swearingen and Abdellatif Bencherifa (eds.), *The North African Environment at Risk*. Boulder, Colo.: Westview Press.

Pearson, M. N. 1994. *Pious Passengers: The Hajj in Earlier Times*. London: C. Hurst.

Peters, F. E. 1994. *The Hajj: The Muslim Pilgrimage to Mecca and the Holy Places*. Princeton: Princeton University Press.

Ramsar Convention Bureau. 2003. *Contracting Parties to Ramsar Convention on Wetlands, as of 20 January 2003: Key Documents of the Ramsar Convention*. www.ramsar.org/key_cp_e.htm (accessed January 20, 2003).

Schimmel, Annemarie. 1985. "The Water of Life." *Environmental Design* 2:6–9.

Shapiro, Haim. 2002. "For the Birds." *Jerusalem Post,* November 1, Features section, p. 20.

Smith, Gordon C. 1968. "The Emergence of the Middle East." *Journal of Contemporary History* 3, no. 3:3–17.

Swearingen, Will D. 1987. *Moroccan Mirages: Agrarian Dreams and Deceptions, 1912–1986*. Princeton: Princeton University Press.

Tekin, Latife. 1996. *Berji Kristin: Tales from the Garbage Hills*. Trans. Ruth Christie and Saliha Parker. London: Marion Boyars.

United Nations. 1992. *Demographic Yearbook*. New York: United Nations.

White, Gilbert. 1988. "The Environmental Effects of the High Dam at Aswan." *Environment* 30, no. 7:4–11, 34–40.

Wolf, Aaron T. 1995. "International Water Dispute Resolutions: The Middle East Multilateral Working Group on Water Resources." *Water International* 20, no. 3:141–150.

———. 2000. "Hydrostrategic Territory in the Jordan Basin." Pp. 63–120 in Hussain A. Amery and Aaron T. Wolf (eds.), *Water in the Middle East: A Geography of Peace*. Austin: University of Texas Press.

3

The Historical Context

Arthur Goldschmidt Jr.

History is the study of humanity's recorded past; that of the Middle East is the world's longest. In this area many staple crops were first cultivated, most farm animals were first domesticated, and the earliest agricultural villages were founded. Here, too, were the world's oldest cities, the first governments and law codes, and the earliest ethical monotheistic systems. A crossroads for people and ideas, the Middle East has sometimes contained a single political or cultural system while at other times it has split into competing fragments. During eras of internal cohesion and power, Middle Easterners controlled remote parts of Europe, Asia, and Africa. At times of dissension and weakness, however, they were invaded and ruled by outsiders. When they could not drive out the interlopers, they adjusted to them and subtly made their rulers adapt to their own ways. The interplay between invasion and accommodation is characteristic of the region. This chapter will summarize Middle Eastern history: the ancient empires, the rise of Islam and its civilization, the area's subordination to European control, and its struggle for political independence.

■ The Ancient Middle East

Environment has shaped much of the region's history. As the polar ice caps retreated, rainfall declined and hunters and food gatherers had to learn how to control their sources of sustenance. Hunting and gathering as a way of life died out in North Africa and Southwest Asia some 5,000 years ago, giving way to pastoral nomadism and settled agriculture. As Ian Manners and Barbara McKean Parmenter discuss in Chapter 2, many parts of the Middle

East receive too little rainfall to support settled agriculture. Yet archaeologists have found the world's oldest farming villages in northeastern Africa and in the highlands of Asia Minor. Many men and women migrated into the valleys of the Nile, the Euphrates, and the Tigris Rivers, where they learned how to tame the annual river floods to water their fields.

As grain cultivation spread, farmers gradually improved their implements and pottery. They needed governments to organize the building of dams, dikes, and canals for large-scale irrigation, to regulate water distribution, and often to protect farmers from invading herders. Although the nomads at times served the settled people as merchants and soldiers, they also pillaged their cities and farms. Despite the tension between the sedentary farmers and the nomadic herders, they needed each other. Without both groups, no cities, states, or civilizations would ever have arisen.

The earliest known governments arose in the oldest agrarian societies, Egypt and Sumer, more than 5,000 years ago. Starting in the third millennium B.C.E., ancient Middle Eastern peoples underwent a series of invasions from outsiders, succumbed to their rule, acquired new ideas and institutions, and eventually absorbed or expelled their conquerors. The result was a succession of ecumenical states that blended the cultures of the rulers and their subjects, culminating in the Roman Empire.

The first states based on agriculture were the kingdoms of the Upper and Lower Nile, which combined around 3000 B.C.E. to form Egypt; and the kingdom of Sumer, which had arisen a bit earlier in Mesopotamia, the land between the Euphrates and the Tigris Rivers. Both developed strong monarchies supported by elaborate bureaucracies, codes of conduct, and religious doctrines that integrated the political system into a cosmological order. Their governments marshaled large workforces to protect the lands from floods and invaders. A complex division of labor facilitated the development of writing, calculation, architecture, metallurgy, and hydraulic engineering.

▒ Semitic and Indo-Iranian Invasions

The river states were disrupted and partially transformed by outside infiltrators and invaders. Sumer was conquered by peoples who spoke Semitic languages, producing Babylonia, which reached its height during the reign of the lawgiver Hammurabi (r. 1792–1750 B.C.E.). Meanwhile, Indo-European invaders from the north mixed with local peoples in Anatolia and Persia and introduced the horse into the region. The horse-drawn chariot enabled another Semitic people to occupy the Nile Delta from 1720 to 1570 B.C.E. Whereas the Babylonians absorbed their invaders, the Egyptians expelled theirs and extended their empire into Syria.

Internal dissension and external pressures finally weakened Egypt and Babylonia, leading to a bewildering series of invasions and emerging states

Deborah J. Gerner

The Great Sun Temple of Abu Simbel was constructed along the banks of the Upper Nile, 50 miles north of the border with Sudan, during the reign of the Egyptian pharaoh Ramses II (thirteenth century B.C.E.).

around 1000 B.C.E. As the Middle East's climate grew drier, Semitic peoples, including the Phoenicians and the Hebrews, migrated from the Arabian Desert into the better-watered lands of Syria and Mesopotamia. The Phoenicians of Syria's coast became the ancient world's main mariners, traders, and colonizers. They also invented the phonetic alphabet. Under King David, who ruled in the early tenth century B.C.E., the Hebrews set up a kingdom in Palestine (which they called "the land of Israel"), with its capital at Jerusalem; this state later split and succumbed to mighty conquerors. The Hebrews developed a faith in one God, who according to the Bible appeared to Moses on Mount Sinai and later to the prophets. Elements of this ethical monotheism had existed in earlier Middle Eastern religions, but the Hebrews' ideas, crystallized in Judaism, profoundly affected the intellectual history of both the Middle East and the West.

The invention of cheap means of making iron tools and weapons led to larger and longer-lasting empires. About 1350 B.C.E., Babylonia gave way to Assyria, centered in northern Mesopotamia. This first Iron Age empire underwent several cycles of rise and decline; at its height (around 700 B.C.E.), Assyria ruled Mesopotamia, Syria, and even Egypt. Its Semitic rival and successor, Chaldea, upheld Babylon's glory for another century. Then Mesopotamia, and indeed the whole Middle East, came under the rule of Persia's King Cyrus (r. 550–529 B.C.E.).

From Cyrus's reign to modern times, the political history of the Middle East has centered on the rise and fall of successive multinational empires: Persia, Greece, Rome, the Arabs, the Seljuk Turks, the Mongols, and the Ottomans. Like Babylon, most of these empires were formed by outside invasions. External rule stirred up local resistance forces that eventually sapped the rulers' strength, leading to political fragmentation and new invasions. Often the conquerors adopted the institutions and beliefs of their Middle Eastern subjects; rarely could they impose their own uniformly.

The Persian empire of Cyrus and his heirs, the Achaemenids, was the prototype of this multinational system. Sprawling from the Indus Valley to the Nile, the empire could not make its subjects think and act alike. Instead, it tolerated their beliefs and practices so long as they obeyed its laws, paid their taxes, and sent men to the Persian army. The provincial governors were given broad civil, judicial, and fiscal powers by the Persian emperor. A feudal landownership system kept the local aristocrats loyal, and a postal system and road network—along with a uniform coinage, calendar, and administrative language—helped further unite the empire. Achaemenid Persia survived two centuries before it succumbed to Alexander the Great in the fourth century B.C.E.

■ Greek and Roman Rule

Alexander's whirlwind conquest of the Middle East between 332 and 323 B.C.E. marks a critical juncture in the area's history. For the next millennium it belonged to the Hellenistic world. Alexander wanted to fuse Greek culture with that of the Middle East, taking ideas, institutions, and administrators from the Egyptians, Mesopotamians, and Persians. This fusion did not occur in his lifetime, nor was it ever complete, but from Alexander to Muhammad the Mediterranean world and the Middle East shared a common civilization. The centers of its cultural blending were the coastal cities, of which the greatest was Alexandria. Alexander's successors in Egypt, the Ptolemies, ruled the country for three centuries. They erected monumental buildings, such as the Alexandria Lighthouse, one of the seven wonders of the ancient world, and the Museum, or academy of scholars, which housed the largest library in antiquity.

Southern Anatolia, Syria, and Mesopotamia were ruled for two centuries by the Seleucids, who were the descendants of one of Alexander's generals. In the third century B.C.E., the Seleucids lost control of their eastern lands to another dynasty descended from some of Alexander's soldiers, and they lost Persia to a Hellenized Indo-European family, the Parthians.

Meanwhile, a new state was rising farther west: Rome. Having taken Carthage, Macedonia, and Greece by 100 B.C.E., the Roman legions marched eastward, conquering Asia Minor, Syria, and Egypt. Once again most of the Middle East was united under an ecumenical empire; only Persia and part of

Located just south of Amman, Jordan, the town of Madaba is home to beautiful mosaics dating from the Byzantine era.

Mesopotamia were ruled by the Parthians. Like earlier empires, Rome absorbed much from its Middle Eastern subjects, including several religions, two of which, Mithraism and Christianity, vied for popular favor throughout the Roman Empire. Christianity finally won. After his conversion, the Emperor Constantine (r. 306–337 C.E.) moved the capital—and Rome's economic and cultural center—to Byzantium, renamed Constantinople. But the city gave its old name to Rome's successor state, the Byzantine Empire. Even now, Arabs, Turks, and Persians say *"Rum"* to mean the Byzantine Empire, its lands, and also Greek Orthodox Christianity and its adherents.

Under Roman rule, commercial cities flourished. Syrian and Egyptian merchants grew rich from the trade between Europe, Asia, and eastern Africa. Arab camel nomads, or bedouin, prospered as carriers of cloth and spices. Other Middle Easterners navigated the Red Sea, the Gulf, and the Indian Ocean. But Roman rule was enforced by a large occupying army, and grain-producing Syria and Egypt were taxed heavily. Rome's leaders did not always tolerate their subjects' beliefs. Roman soldiers destroyed the Jewish temple in Jerusalem, and many of Jesus' early followers were martyred. Christian Rome proved even less tolerant. Many Christians in North Africa and Egypt espoused heterodox beliefs that the emperors viewed as treasonous. Their efforts to suppress heresy alienated many of their Middle Eastern subjects in the fifth and sixth centuries of the common era.

One of the most impressive Roman ruins in the
Middle East is at Baalbek, in the northern Bekaa Valley of
Lebanon. This temple was completed around 150 C.E.

Rome (and later Byzantium) had one major rival: Persia. There the
Parthians gave way in the third century to the Sassanid dynasty. Bolstered by
a powerful military aristocracy and the resources of many Hellenized religious refugees from Byzantium, Sassanid Persia threatened Byzantine rule in
the Middle East. Early in the seventh century, the Sassanids briefly overran
Syria, Palestine, and Egypt. The Hellenistic era of Middle Eastern history was
coming to an end.

■ The Islamic Middle East as an Autonomous System

The revelation of Islam to an unlettered Meccan merchant in the early
seventh century, the unification of hitherto feuding Arab tribes under this new
religion, the rapid conquest of the Middle East and North Africa, the conversion of millions of Asians and Africans to Islam, and the development of
Arab-Islamic civilization under a succession of empires marked a new epoch.
Egyptians, Syrians, and Persians influenced the beliefs of their Arab conquerors just as they had transformed and absorbed earlier invaders. Yet the
rise of Islam led to new ideas and institutions, monuments and memories,
which continue to affect Middle Eastern peoples profoundly.

▨ The Arabs Before Islam

Once the camel had been domesticated around 3000 B.C.E., bands of people began roaming the Arabian Peninsula in search of water and forage for their flocks. Unable as nomads to develop architecture, sculpture, or painting, these early Arabs composed poems that embodied their code of values: bravery in battle, patience in misfortune, persistence in revenge, protection of the weak, defiance of the strong, loyalty to the tribe, hospitality to the guest, generosity to the needy, and fidelity in carrying out promises. These were the virtues people needed to survive in the desert. Their poems, recited from memory, expressed the joys and sorrows of nomadic life, hailed the bravery of their heroes, lauded their own tribes, and lampooned their rivals. Even now Arabs recite these poems and often repeat their precepts.

In Roman times the southern Arabs played a larger role in the world; they developed Yemen, colonized Ethiopia, and crossed the Indian Ocean. The northern Arabs were relatively isolated. Some adopted Judaism or Christianity, but most practiced ancestor worship or animism (the belief that every object, whether animate or inanimate, has a spirit). One of the northern tribes, the Quraysh, built a shrine, the Ka'bah, at a small desert city called Mecca on the main trade route between Syria and Yemen. Once a year, the pagan tribes of northwestern Arabia suspended their quarrels to make pilgrimages to the Ka'bah, which housed idols representing tribal deities. Some Meccans grew rich on the proceeds of the caravan trade and the annual pilgrimage.

▨ Muhammad

In Mecca, around 570, one of the world's greatest religious leaders, Muhammad, was born to a minor branch of the Quraysh. Orphaned as a child, Muhammad was reared by an uncle as a caravan trader. Upon reaching manhood, he became the agent for a rich merchant widow, Khadijah, whom he married. Until he was forty, Muhammad was simply a Meccan trader. But he was troubled by the widening gulf between the accepted Arab virtues of bravery and generosity and the blatantly acquisitive practices of Mecca's business leaders. Often he went to a hill near Mecca to meditate.

One day in the Arab month of Ramadan, Muhammad heard a voice exhorting him to recite. In awe and terror he cried, "I can't recite." The voice replied:

> Recite in the name of thy Lord, the Creator
> who created man of a blood-clot.
> Recite, for thy lord most generous
> who taught by the pen,
> taught man what he knew not.

Fearing that he had gone mad, Muhammad rushed home and asked Khadijah to wrap him in a cloak. Again the voice sounded:

> O thou enshrouded in thy mantle,
> rise and warn!
> Thy lord magnify
> thy raiment purify
> and from evil flee!

Reassured by his wife, Muhammad came to accept the voice as the Angel Gabriel's command to proclaim God's existence to the Arabs and to warn them of an imminent judgment day when all people would be called to account for what they had done. He received more revelations and began to share them in the community. Those who accepted Muhammad's divine message called themselves Muslims and their religion Islam, meaning submission to the will of God, the creator and sustainer.

Muhammad's public recitation of his revelations disturbed the Meccan leaders. Did their wealth and power not matter? If the Arabs accepted Islam, would they stop their annual pilgrimages to the Ka'bah, so lucrative to local merchants? Why did God reveal His message to Muhammad, rather than to one of the Quraysh leaders? The pagan Meccans reviled the Muslims. After Muhammad's uncle and protector died, life in Mecca became intolerable for Muslims. Finally the Arabs of Medina, a city north of Mecca, asked Muhammad to arbitrate their tribal disputes and accepted Islam as the condition for his coming there.

The *hijrah* (emigration) of Muhammad and his followers from Mecca is for Muslims the most important event in history. The Muslim calendar begins in the year it occurred, 622 C.E., and it was in Medina that Muhammad formed the Islamic *ummah* (a community ruled by a divine plan). Politics and religion are united in Islam; God, speaking to humanity through Muhammad, is the supreme lawgiver. Thus the Prophet became a political leader and, when the Meccans tried to destroy the *ummah,* a military commander as well. Buttressed by their faith, the Muslims of Medina vanquished Meccan armies larger and stronger than their own, converted most of the pagan Arab tribes, and finally converted Mecca to Islam. In 630 Muhammad made a triumphal pilgrimage to the Ka'bah, smashed its pagan idols, and declared it a Muslim shrine. Two years later, having united much of Arabia under Islam, he died.

▨ Islamic Beliefs and Institutions

Muslims believe in one God, all-powerful and all-knowing, who has no partner and no offspring. God has spoken to a succession of human messengers, of whom the last was Muhammad. To the Jewish prophets God imparted the Torah and to Jesus and his disciples the Gospels. Muslims believe that Jews and Christians corrupted their scriptures, so God sent a perfected revelation, the Quran (recitation), to Muhammad. Although Muslims regard the Quran as truer than the Bible in its present form, they do not deny any of God's prophets, honoring Abraham, Moses, and Jesus. Muslims also believe in a day of judgment, when God will assess all people and consign them to Heaven or to Hell.

Muslim duties may be summed up as the "five pillars of Islam": statement of belief in God and in Muhammad as his Prophet; ritual prayer five times daily; fasting in the daylight hours of the month of Ramadan; payment of part of one's property or income to provide for the needy; and the pilgrimage to Mecca. Muslims also abstain from drinking alcoholic beverages, eating pork, gambling, and all forms of licentious and dishonest behavior. Standards of sexual morality are strict, limiting contacts between unmarried men and women. Muslims ascribe human misdeeds to ignorance or forgetfulness and believe that God forgives those who repent.

Islam is a way of life. It prescribes how people relate to one another as well as their duties to God. Muhammad's *ummah* aspired to serve as the ideal earthly setting in which believers could prepare for the judgment day. In the centuries after Muhammad's death, Muslim scholars *(ulama)* developed an elaborate legal code, the *sharia,* to regulate all aspects of human behavior. The *sharia* was derived from the Quran, the words and deeds of the Prophet (or those actions by his followers that he sanctioned), the consensus of the *ummah,* analogical reasoning, and judicial opinion. Dynastic and doctrinal schisms soon divided the *ummah;* however, the *sharia,* upheld by the *ulama,* united Muslims of diverse races, cultures, regions, and political allegiances.

The Patriarchal Caliphs and the Early Arab Conquests

When Muhammad died, his followers needed to name a successor. No one could succeed Muhammad as the Prophet, but someone had to lead the *ummah,* and Abu Bakr was chosen as the first caliph (successor). During his caliphate the Muslims won back the rebellious tribal Arabs and deflected their energies outward against Byzantium and Persia. Under Umar ibn al-Khattab, the second caliph, these rebellious Arabs routed armies mightier than their own, wresting Syria and Egypt from Byzantine control and absorbing Sassanid Persia. The Arabs conquered most of the Middle East in a generation and much of the Old World in a century. Many Syrians, Egyptians, and Persians welcomed Arab rule as a respite from Byzantine intolerance and Sassanid exploitation. These subjects were forced neither to speak Arabic nor to become Muslims, although gradually some chose to do one or both. The new Arab rulers, often called the patriarchal caliphs, retained local administrative customs and languages and even the bureaucrats themselves; the Arabs lacked the numbers and the experience to govern their new empire unaided. Those males who did not convert were required to pay a head tax in return for exemption from military service. Jerusalem under Arab rule remained a religious center and pilgrimage site for Jews and Christians, but it became a holy city for Muslims as well.

Although Arab toleration of local customs sustained stability, the conquests strained the _ummah_ itself. The caliphs set aside some of the captured booty for charitable or communal use and put the troops on a payroll, but the sudden influx of wealth led to unrest. In 656 the third caliph, Uthman, was murdered. His friends suspected his successor, Ali (who was a son-in-law of the prophet Mohammad), of taking part in his assassination. Demanding revenge, Uthman's supporters fought Ali's backers in a battle that led to a mediation favoring Uthman's cousin, Mu'awiyah, the governor of Syria. He named himself caliph, moved the capital to Damascus, pacified the dissident Muslims, and made the caliphate hereditary in his own family, the Umayyad branch of the Quraysh tribe.

The Umayyad caliphs, who ruled in Damascus from 661 to 750, were more political than pious. They crushed their opponents and spread Arab rule to northern Africa and Spain, central Asia, and what is now Pakistan (see Map 3.1). Many Muslims resented the Umayyads. One of these dissidents was the prophet Mohammad's grandson and Ali's son, Husayn, who died during a revolt at Karbala (Iraq) in 680. Husayn's martyrdom led to a political and religious opposition movement known as Shi'ism. Even now a split remains between the Shi'ites, who accept only Ali and his descendants as rightful leaders of the _ummah,_ and the Sunnis, who recognize the caliphs who actually ruled. Sunnis now outnumber Shi'ites in most of the Muslim world, but Shi'ism is the state religion of Iran.

■ The First Islamic Empire

The Umayyads' power depended on their main fighting force, the Arab tribes, that the caliphs favored even after many non-Arabs converted to Islam. Some non-Arab Muslims turned to revolutionary movements, often pro-Shi'ite, against Umayyad rule. One such rebellion was led by the Abbasid family, who toppled the Umayyads in 750 and set up their own caliphate in Baghdad. At this point, the formal unity of the _ummah_ ended, for the Umayyads kept control over Spain. The North African Berbers, tribal peoples whose conversion from Christianity and Judaism to Islam did not mean they accepted Arab political dominance, soon cast off Abbasid rule. A Shi'ite movement, the Fatimids, took power in Tunisia and later in Egypt. Elsewhere, ambitious governors, warlords, and religious leaders carved out their own states. Most Arabs reverted to nomadism or intermarried with their conquered peoples, many of whom were now Arabized in language and culture.

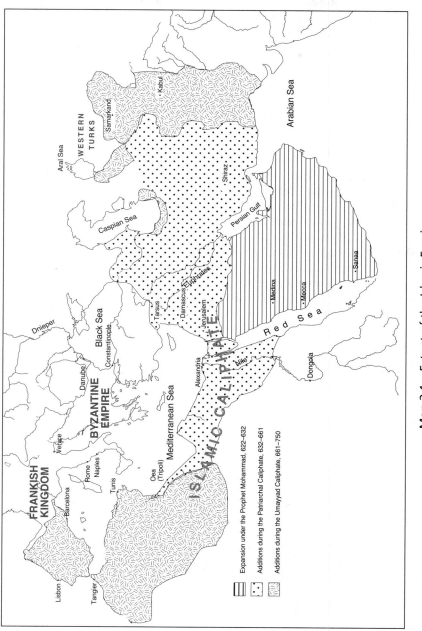

Map 3.1 Extent of the Islamic Empire

Expansion under the Prophet Mohammad, 622–632

Additions during the Patriarchal Caliphate, 632–661

Additions during the Umayyad Caliphate, 661–750

FRANKISH
KINGDOM

BYZANTINE
EMPIRE

WESTERN
TURKS

ISLAMIC CALIPHATE

Lisbon
Tangier
Barcelona
Rome
Naples
Venice
Tunis
Oea
(Tripoli)
Mediterranean Sea
Danube
Dnieper
Constantinople
Black Sea
Aral Sea
Caspian Sea
Samarkand
Kabul
Tarsus
Damascus
Jerusalem
Euphrates
Shiraz
Alexandria
Nile
Red Sea
Persian Gulf
Medina
Mecca
Sanaa
Arabian Sea
Dongola

Despite its turbulent politics, the Abbasid era (which lasted in weakened form until 1258) was one of agricultural and commercial prosperity. As industry and trade flourished, so did science and letters. Rulers competed with one another in patronizing the translation of scientific and philosophical works from Greek into Arabic, supporting court poets and historians, building mosques and palaces, and sponsoring astronomical and medical research. Thus Muslims preserved and improved their classical patrimony, which they passed on to medieval Europe, helping to spark the Renaissance.

■ Invasions from East and West

The influx of Turks from eastern Asia began in the tenth century. Many had already been imported as slave soldiers and bureaucrats for the Abbasid caliphs; others served the Abbasids or local Muslim rulers as frontier guards against non-Muslims farther east. Schooled in the arts of government and war, the Turkish *ghazi*s (border raiders) proved more reliable than the caliphs' other Muslim subjects and rose to positions of power.

One Turkish family serving a Persian dynasty received an *iqta'*—land granted for military or administrative service to the government—in Ghazna (in what is now Afghanistan) around 960. This family, the Ghaznavids, built up an empire spanning eastern Persia, central Asia, and parts of northern India. The Ghaznavids in turn gave *iqta'*s to Turkish clans from central Asia. One of these, the Seljuks, proceeded to conquer lands westward across Persia and Mesopotamia and into Anatolia, where they defeated the Byzantines in 1071. The military gains of these families attracted other Turks to serve as *ghazi*s, opening the way for large-scale immigration of Turkish tribes with their horses, two-humped camels, sheep, and goats. Soon Azerbaijan (northwestern Persia), northern Iraq, and much of Anatolia, highland areas that the Arabs had never taken, became mainly Turkish.

The Turks were devout Sunni Muslims who built new cities and refurbished old ones. They rescued the Abbasid caliph, who had been taken hostage by Shi'ite bureaucrats, and restored his authority, although not his power. For several generations the caliph ruled in Baghdad beside a Seljuk sultan (holder of power). The Turks strengthened Sunni schools, promoted Sufism (organized Islamic mysticism), and limited reinterpretation of the *sharia*. Sufism involved Muslims more deeply in their faith but caused some to withdraw from worldly pursuits. Once Sunni Muslims could not revise the *sharia,* changing social needs led rulers and subjects to bypass it, and practices diverged ever further from Islamic precepts.

As Turkish nomads poured in from the East, a different group of invaders came from the West. In 1096 the pope proclaimed a Crusade to regain the Holy Land for Christianity. Muslims had ruled Jerusalem for more than four centuries without harming Christian interests, but the Seljuk invasion of Anatolia had weakened the Byzantine Empire and threatened the Christian pilgrimage routes to the Holy City. The Crusaders helped the Byzantines to stem the Seljuk advance and then went on to take western Syria and Palestine from divided and weak Muslim rulers. For almost a century, Jerusalem, purged of its Muslim and Jewish inhabitants, was the capital of a European Christian kingdom.

Outside Jerusalem, however, the Crusaders rarely uprooted the local population, and they never took the Muslim power centers: Cairo, Damascus, Aleppo, and Mosul. Once Egypt and Syria were united under a strong Sunni Muslim ruler, Saladin, the Muslims retook Jerusalem in 1187. The Crusaders held part of coastal Syria for another century and twice invaded the Nile Delta, but Saladin's descendants, the Ayyubids, kept them in check.

Far more damaging to the Middle East were the thirteenth-century invasions by the Mongols, who came from the lands north of China. Mongol armies led by Genghis Khan (r. 1206–1227) defeated weak Muslim rulers and conquered central Asia and eastern Persia. His grandson, Hülegü, pressed farther into Persia and Mesopotamia and in 1258 took Baghdad and wiped out the Abbasid caliphate. The Mongols were not Muslims. Horse nomads accustomed to grassy steppes, they saw no need for cities or the farmers who supported them. They destroyed irrigation works in Persia, Mesopotamia, and Syria, impoverishing the land and its people. Many Muslim rulers, even Anatolia's surviving Seljuks, became Mongol vassals. But in 1260 the Mongols failed to take Palestine and Egypt, where the Ayyubids had recently been overthrown by their Turkish slave soldiers, the Mamluks. The Mamluk rulers went on to build a prosperous empire in Egypt and Syria, the bulwark of Muslim power until their conquest by the Ottoman Turks in 1516–1517. Meanwhile, Persia's Mongol rulers soon adopted Islam, accepted Persian culture, and rebuilt much of what they had earlier destroyed.

The harnessing of gunpowder by Europe in the fourteenth century altered the West's relationship with the rest of the world. Firearms and long-distance sailing ships soon enabled Europeans to explore and conquer distant lands and finally to encircle the Muslim world. States using gunpowder as their main weapon require disciplined infantries rather than the feudal cavalries of the Middle Ages. The West's adoption of firearms sparked the growth of strong monarchies, a commercial middle class, and eventually the Industrial Revolution. In the Middle East, some Muslim states learned how to use firearms on land and sea; others never did. The gunpowder revolution weakened the landowning horse soldiers there, too, but failed to stimulate European-style modernization.

■ The Ottoman Empire

The Ottoman Empire was the archetypal Muslim state built on the use of firearms. From their humble origins in the thirteenth century as Turkish *ghazi*s for the Seljuks, the Ottomans expanded their landholdings into an empire that stretched—at its height in the seventeenth century—from central Europe to the Gulf and from Algeria to Azerbaijan. Like most *ghazi*s, the early Ottomans raided peasant lands on horseback. During the fourteenth and fifteen centuries, however, they developed a disciplined corps of professional foot soldiers, the famous janissaries, who used siege cannon and lighter firearms against the Europeans or their Muslim neighbors. The Ottoman state took boys as tribute from their Christian subjects. Converted to Islam, the boys were taught Turkish and Arabic and trained as soldiers or, less often, as administrators. As Ottoman sultan's slaves, the janissaries were forbidden to marry or to own land. They lived in barracks in order to be ready to fight whenever they were needed. This system of recruitment and training was called *devshirme,* as were, collectively, the Ottoman soldiers and bureaucrats it produced.

Backed by well-equipped armies and competent administrators, the Ottoman sultans conquered the Christian peoples of the Balkans and surrounded Constantinople. In 1453 they took the city and ended the 1,000-year-old Byzantine Empire. Once the world's greatest Christian city, Constantinople (now Istanbul) became a Muslim center. During the following century, the Ottomans subdued most of their Muslim neighbors, including the Mamluks of Egypt and Syria. Only the Persians, ruled after 1501 by the Safavids, remained independent, for they, too, learned to use firearms.

Ottoman strength rested on two principles: (1) the power of the ruling class was balanced between the traditional aristocracy and the *devshirme* soldiers and administrators; and (2) the subject peoples were organized into religious communities, called *millet*s, that had autonomous control over their laws, schools, and general welfare. These internal divisions strengthened the sultan. So long as the sultan could play off the aristocracy against the *devshirme* class, both ruling groups performed their tasks as defenders and managers of the Ottoman Empire. The subject peoples were self-sufficient but geographically scattered, unable to combine against their Ottoman overlords. These subjects looked to their communal leaders—rabbis, priests, and *ulama*—whose most prominent members were named by and responsible to the sultan, to mediate between them and the government. For centuries, this approach to social and political organization endured; even now, some Middle Easterners identify themselves by their religion more than by their nationality.

Of all the factors that weakened the Ottoman Empire, the most significant was the triumph of the *devshirme* bureaucrats and janissaries over the aristocracy. This occurred during the reign of the greatest sultan, Suleiman the Magnificent (r. 1520–1566), when he appointed a series of chief ministers who had risen from *devshirme* origins. Not checked by either the weaker succeeding sultans or the declining aristocracy, these onetime slaves corrupted the Ottoman government to serve their own interests. Janissaries received per-

Deborah J. Gerner

The Blue Mosque, built in the early seventeenth century for Sultan Ahmet I, with its six minarets and numerous domes, is among the most beautiful examples of Ottoman architecture in the Middle East.

mission from the sultan to leave the barracks, marry, buy property, and enroll their sons in the corps, which stopped training and degenerated into a hereditary, privileged caste. Military failure and corrupt government ensued. Taxes rose, especially for those least able to avoid paying them. Agrarian and commercial well-being declined, partly because the trade routes between Asia and Europe shifted away from the Middle East. Once-loyal subjects rebelled against Ottoman misrule. By the late seventeenth century, the Ottoman Empire was no longer the scourge of Europe.

■ The Subordination of the Middle East to the West

During the eighteenth and nineteenth centuries the West gained military, political, and economic superiority over much of the Middle East. Whereas Arabs and Turks had once mastered the routes between Europe and Asia, by 1800 Europe sold its manufactured goods to the Middle East in exchange for raw materials and agricultural products. Europeans in Muslim lands were exempted from local taxes and legal jurisdiction; in the Ottoman Empire this exemption was guaranteed by treaties called Capitulations. Whereas once the Mediterranean Sea and the Indian Ocean were controlled by Muslim navies, now European sailing ships dominated the high seas. Whereas once the

Ottoman sultan could choose the time and place for an attack on Europe and could then dictate the peace terms, now his armies feared the mighty forces of Habsburg Austria and czarist Russia. The greatest shock came when Napoleon occupied Egypt in 1798, for France had long been an Ottoman ally.

▨ Westernizing Reforms

As early as the seventeenth century, some Ottoman sultans and their ministers saw the need for internal change. At first they regarded reform as the restoration of the institutions and practices that had made their empire strong in the past. But defeat by Western armies taught them that conditions had altered, necessitating more drastic modifications. Reforms began in the military. Sultan Selim III (r. 1789–1807) tried to set up a new army corps trained and equipped in the European fashion. The janissaries, afraid that these interlopers would take away their power, rebelled, destroyed the new corps, and deposed Selim. The conservatism of the *ulama* and trade guilds blocked reform in other aspects of Ottoman life. Even the introduction of printing was long opposed by the *ulama* and scribes, the former condemning innovation and the latter fearing the loss of their jobs.

The failure of early reform efforts taught Muslim rulers that change could not be confined to the military. Only by centering power in the state could they resist European expansion. Reform meant autocracy, not democracy. Three Middle Eastern reformers serve as examples: Mehmet (Muhammad) Ali (r. 1805–1849) of Egypt, Sultan Mahmud II (r. 1808–1839) of the Ottoman Empire, and Nasir al-Din Shah (r. 1848–1896) of Persia. Each tried to concentrate power in his own hands; each became hamstrung by European actions serving imperialist interests.

The ablest was Mehmet Ali, an Ottoman officer commanding an Albanian regiment sent to Egypt. He took control of that Ottoman province after Napoleon's forces pulled out in 1801 and proceeded to eliminate every rival for power. He massacred the Mamluks and curbed the *ulama,* who had enjoyed special power and prestige in Egypt, by exploiting their rivalries and seizing the endowments that supported them. Using French advisers and equipment, he built the region's strongest army and navy. He subordinated the rural aristocracy to the state by taking control of all farmland.

Under Mehmet Ali's rule, Egypt became the first Middle Eastern country to make the transition from subsistence to market agriculture. Tobacco, sugar, indigo, and cotton became Egypt's cash crops, earning revenues to fund his ambitious projects for industrial development and military expansion. The first non-Western ruler to recognize the Industrial Revolution, he set up textile mills and weapons factories, sent hundreds of his subjects to Europe for technical or military training, and imported European instructors to staff schools and military academies in Egypt. He even conscripted Egyptian farmers as soldiers. Officered by Turks, they became such a potent force that Mehmet Ali's son, Ibrahim, conquered Syria in 1832 and would have taken over the whole Ottoman Empire in 1839 if Britain had not intervened. Although the Ottoman Empire recognized Egypt's autonomy in 1841, Mehmet Ali felt that his ambitions had been thwarted and let his reforms lapse. However, his heirs ruled Egypt, with only nominal Ottoman control, up to the British occupation in 1882, and the monarchy remained part of Egypt's political structure until King Farouk was overthrown in 1952.

Mehmet Ali's Ottoman contemporary, Sultan Mahmud II, also tried to reform his state but first had to wipe out the janissary corps, the main obstacle to change. His efforts were hampered by the diversity and extent of his domains, local revolts, the lack of a loyal and trained bureaucracy, the Greek independence war (backed by Britain, France, and Russia), and the growing need of industrialized states to buy Ottoman raw materials and sell their own manufactures. After Mahmud's death, his son issued a reform decree that began the *tanzimat* (reorganization) era, one of intense centralization and Westernization. The *tanzimat* did not protect the Ottomans against Russian expansion in the Balkans, so Britain and France helped them defeat Russia in the Crimean War (1853–1856). The Europeans then made the Ottomans issue another decree that gave Christians and Jews legal equality with Muslims.

Persia was the only core Middle Eastern state never to fall under Ottoman rule. Its rulers' revival of ancient Persian customs preserved a national identity. This was reinforced by their adherence to Shi'ism, whereas the Ottomans were Sunni Muslims. In the sixteenth and seventeenth centuries, Persia flourished under the Safavid shahs, who adorned their capital at Isfahan and formed commercial and diplomatic ties with the European countries needing allies against the Ottoman Empire.

Persia, too, declined. The Qajar dynasty (1794–1925) resisted dissolution from within and Russian and British encroachments from without. During the first three years of Nasir al-Din Shah's reign, his energetic chief minister began a series of military, financial, and educational reforms. But in 1851 the shah executed his minister, and tribal and religious uprisings broke out. Later in his reign, Nasir al-Din began selling concessions to British investors and hiring Russian officers to train his army. Instead of reforming his government to protect Persia from foreigners, the shah let them take over. His subjects rejected his policies; a nationwide tobacco boycott made him cancel one of his most lucrative concessions, and he was finally assassinated. Later Qajar shahs proved even more submissive to foreign interference.

◼ European Imperialism in the Nineteenth Century

If European power inspired Middle Eastern reform, European policies and actions kept it from succeeding. From 1815 to 1914, European governments preserved peace among themselves by keeping a balance of power. For the Middle East, this meant that neither Britain nor Russia could let the other become supreme. Fearing that breaking up the Ottoman Empire would give Russia control of the Balkans and of the straits linking the Black Sea to the Aegean, Britain usually tried to uphold the empire's territorial integrity. Thus the British led European opposition to Mehmet Ali's threat in Ottoman Syria in 1839, Russia's occupation of the Romanian principalities in 1853, which led to the Crimean War, and Russia's frequent efforts to exploit nationalism in the Balkans. In addition, Britain backed reforms that would enable the Ottoman Empire to resist Russia, especially those during the *tanzimat* era that promised equality to non-Muslims. By contrast, Russia's expansionist aims, its claim to protect the sultan's Orthodox Christian subjects, and its support of Balkan nationalist movements served to thwart Ottoman reform efforts.

While guarding its routes to India, Britain also vied with France for power in the eastern Mediterranean; it fought to expel Napoleon from Egypt and later to remove Mehmet Ali from Syria. Britain signed treaties with tribal leaders in the Gulf and occupied Aden in order to outflank Mehmet Ali and his French allies. A British company started steamship navigation on the Euphrates River in the 1830s; another built the first railroad from Alexandria to Cairo in 1851. But it was a French diplomat, Ferdinand-Marie de Lesseps, who won a concession from Egypt's viceroy to cut a canal across the Isthmus of Suez, joining the Red Sea to the Mediterranean and slashing travel time between Europe and southern Asia. Britain tried at first to block this mainly French project, but it became the Suez Canal's main user after it was opened in 1869. France expanded across North Africa, taking Algeria in a protracted war (1830–1847) and establishing protectorates over Tunisia in 1881 and Morocco in 1912.

■ The Middle Eastern Reaction to the West

By the 1860s a number of Middle Easterners were wondering whether Westernization had gone too far. In the Ottoman Empire, many Muslims espoused pan-Islam, the idea that all Muslims should unite behind the sultan to counter outside threats and the divisive nationalist movements of non-Muslim Balkan subjects. Pan-Islam reaffirmed the tradition of Muslims uniting to defend the *ummah,* but this doctrine took on a new meaning: the Ottoman sultan claimed for himself the caliphate, hence the allegiance of all Muslims, regardless of who actually ruled them. Because Britain, France, and Russia all had Muslim subjects within their empires, Europeans soon saw the fearsome potential of pan-Islam.

Westernizing reforms, especially in education and military training, led to the growth of liberal and nationalist movements among young Egyptians, Ottomans, Arabs, Persians, and Tunisians. These new groups challenged their rulers' monopoly on power and called for constitutional government. None wholly succeeded.

The Beginnings of Egyptian Nationalism

Mehmet Ali's grandson, Isma'il (r. 1863–1879), resumed Westernizing reforms and secured Egypt's autonomy from the Ottoman Empire. He sent explorers to find the sources of the Nile River and army expeditions to conquer the Red Sea coast and the southern Sudan. Sections of Cairo and Alexandria were transformed by broad boulevards, public gardens, and huge mansions. Factories and public works built up the economy as a cotton boom caused by a drop in U.S. production during the Civil War, the growing availability of European capital, and the construction of the Suez Canal made Egypt an attractive field for investment.

Egypt's economy skyrocketed, but so did Isma'il's problems. In 1866 he set up a representative assembly to advise his government and raise revenue. Timid at first but later incited by a burgeoning press, this new body began calling for constitutional government. Isma'il borrowed vast sums from foreign banks to cover his expenditures. Unable to repay his debts, he sold his government's Suez Canal shares to Britain, accepted British and French control over Egypt's finances, and finally admitted representatives of these two creditor states into his cabinet. Egyptians resented these changes. The assembly demanded a council of ministers responsible to itself and purged of Europeans, a say in the government's budget, and an end to the budget cuts that harmed many Egyptians. In 1879 Isma'il dismissed his "European cabinet" and named one that heeded the assembly's call for constitutional government, whereupon the European powers ordered the Ottoman sultan to replace Isma'il with his son, Tawfiq.

Obeying his European advisers, Tawfiq Pasha purged the dissidents from his regime and tried to pay back some of his father's debts. But many Egyptians, harmed by European meddling, called for independence. Their main backers were some Egyptian army officers led by Colonel Urabi, who wanted Egypt freed from both Turks and Europeans. In 1881, Urabi's troops surrounded the palace and called for a new cabinet responsible to an elected parliament. Tawfiq gave in, and soon Egypt had a constitution. Nationalism's triumph was brief; its leaders were split, the Europeans threatened to intervene, and Tawfiq turned against the nationalists in 1882. The British landed in Alexandria, invaded the Suez Canal, and marched into Cairo. Urabi yielded, ending Egypt's first constitutional era.

When Britain occupied Egypt, it promised to pull its troops out as soon as order was restored to the country. It was easy to defeat the nationalists and prop up Tawfiq on his throne, but it was harder to remedy the causes of Egypt's disorder: huge debts, a peasantry burdened by high taxes, and a revolt in Sudan. The longer Britain stayed on to tackle Egypt's problems, the harder it was to leave. A talented administrator, Lord Cromer, became Britain's diplomatic representative in Cairo. Backed by British troops, he reformed Egypt's finances and administration and gradually emerged as its ruler in all but name.

Although the country prospered, British advisers sapped the authority of the Egyptian ministers. The British claimed to be preparing the Egyptians for self-rule, but in fact Egypt became a training ground for British colonial administrators. They often forgot that Egypt was not a British colony; rather it was an autonomous Ottoman province under temporary occupation. The extension of irrigation under British rule was not paralleled by expanded education or industrial development. Cromer became autocratic and spiteful in undercutting Tawfiq's son, Abbas II. When Abbas succeeded Tawfiq in 1892, he gathered a cabal of young Egyptians to help him thwart Cromer's power. Their spokesman, an articulate lawyer named Mustafa Kamil, founded the National Party. The Nationalists urged Britain to withdraw its forces from Egypt and later demanded a new constitution. Cromer ignored them, but his successor promised to hasten Egypt's progress toward self-rule. Unfortunately for the Nationalists, Mustafa Kamil died prematurely in 1908, and his followers split. A more repressive British policy forced the leading Nationalists into exile. At the outbreak of World War I, the British declared a protectorate, deposed Abbas, and severed Egypt's ties with the Ottoman Empire.

▓ Liberalism and Nationalism Within the Ottoman Empire

As the *tanzimat* era wound down, a group of Westernized intellectuals and army officers known as the New Ottomans called for a more liberal regime, which to them meant a constitution. In 1876, amid Balkan revolts, growing state indebtedness to Europe, and threats of a Russian invasion, a military coup placed a liberal sultan on the throne. He was soon replaced by Abdülhamid II, who issued a constitution in December of that year to forestall a Russian attempt to break up his empire. For about a year, the Ottoman Empire had a popularly elected parliament, but as Russia attacked anyway and advanced on Istanbul, Abdülhamid shut it down and suspended the constitution. For thirty years the sultan further centralized state control and stifled nationalist and liberal movements. A group of Westernized students and army officers, convinced that the empire could be saved only by restoring the 1876 Constitution, formed the Committee of Union and Progress, or the Young Turks. In 1908 they forced the sultan to restore the constitution and hold elections; in 1909, after an abortive countercoup, they deposed him. But the Young Turk regime soon became a military junta. As Balkan revolts and Western imperialism took one Ottoman province after another, the leaders increasingly adopted Turkish nationalism, offending those subjects who did not identify with Turkish culture.

Among the Ottoman subjects who resisted Turkish nationalism were those who spoke Arabic. Long divided by local, sectarian, or family rivalries, the people of Syria, Mesopotamia, and Arabia began to view themselves as one Arab nation. Arabic-speaking lawyers, teachers, students, and army officers formed nationalist societies in the main Ottoman cities. Some wanted internal autonomy and equal status with the Turks as Ottoman subjects; others demanded Arab independence from Turkish rule. Some called for restoring the caliphate to an Arab ruler. Although Arab nationalism had only a few adherents at first, its ideas helped spark the Arab Revolt during World War I.

▪ Persian Constitutionalism

Persia's Qajar shahs were autocratic and weak. They could not protect the farmers and city dwellers from nomadic tribes, nor could they stop Russian military incursions or the commercial ascendancy of the British and other Europeans. In reaction, the idea of constitutional government arose within three groups: merchants, Shi'ite *ulama,* and Westernized intellectuals. The merchants resented the shahs' concessions to foreign companies, which threatened their livelihood; the *ulama* feared that Westernization would undermine Islam generally and their own influence in particular; and the intellectuals, influenced by Western liberalism and nationalism, viewed the shah, backed by foreign advisers and money, as an obstacle to reform.

These groups wanted different things. United by nationalism, however, they engineered the 1892 tobacco boycott and a national revolution in 1906. The shah responded to the latter with a constitution that provided for a popularly elected parliament *(majlis),* but in 1907 his successor called in Russian troops to suppress the *majlis* and its revolutionary backers. But outside the capital the Constitutionalists continued their struggle. A prominent tribal leader helped them retake Tehran, and they replaced the shah with a more docile relative.

Once in power, the Constitutionalists failed to implement their reform program. Their political revolution did not change social and economic conditions, they were split into factions, and outsiders exacerbated their problems. The British government mainly sought to protect commerce and defend India. For Russia, expansion into Persia was a continuation of its policy of taking Central Asia. Meanwhile, a British firm received a concession to explore southern Persia for oil. The first major discovery came in 1908, and the Anglo-Persian Oil Company was formed the next year. Soon it built a refinery at Abadan, and when Britain's fleet switched from coal to oil in 1912, Persia's new role as an oil producer made it central to British imperial strategy.

Britain and Russia had agreed in 1907 to define spheres of influence within Persia. Russia's sphere covered the country's northern third, including Tehran. Britain, whose area bordered on northwestern India, allowed the Russians to tighten their grip on Persia's government before and during World War I. Even the 1917 Bolshevik Revolution and the consequent withdrawal of Russian troops only briefly interrupted their efforts to control Persia.

▦ World War I, the Ottoman Jihad, and the Arab Revolt

World War I completed the continuing subordination of Middle Eastern peoples to Western domination. Since the eighteenth century, Russia had won control over the lands north of the Black Sea, the Caucasus Mountains, most of the Caspian Sea coast, and vast stretches of Muslim Central Asia. Persia was virtually a Russian protectorate. The czarist regime hoped to gain Istanbul and the Bosporus and Dardanelles Straits in the war. France ruled North Africa. Britain held Egypt, the strategic Mediterranean island of Cyprus, and Aden at the southern entrance to the Red Sea; it also had treaties requiring it to protect most of the Gulf rulers. British and French capitalists had huge investments in Middle Eastern land, buildings, factories, railroads, and utilities. In 1914, Germany was the likely protector of the remnants of the Ottoman Empire; a German military mission was reorganizing its army, and German capital was financing construction of a rail line from Istanbul to Baghdad, raising its influence in the Ottoman interior.

Istanbul's decision to enter World War I as Germany's ally sealed the fate of the Ottoman Empire. The Ottoman proclamation of jihad (struggle for Islam) failed to rally the Muslims under Allied rule to rise in rebellion. As Britain repulsed Turkish attacks on the Suez Canal and sent expeditionary forces into Mesopotamia and Palestine, the Arabs' loyalty to the Ottoman sultan waned. Husayn ibn Ali, the emir (prince) of Mecca and sharif (leading descendant of Muhammad) of the prestigious Hashemite family, negotiated secretly with Sir Henry McMahon, Britain's high commissioner in Egypt, who pledged British support for Arab independence if Husayn rebelled against the Turks. He reserved Baghdad and Basra for separate administration, however, and excluded Mersin, Alexandretta, and "portions of Syria lying to the west of the districts of Damascus, Homs, Hama, and Aleppo" from the areas to be granted independence. These terms fell short of the nationalists' dream of independence for all the Arabic-speaking Ottoman lands. Although Husayn was disappointed, the Ottoman government's repression of the Arabs in Syria enraged him and led him to proclaim the Arab Revolt in 1916. Together, the Arabs and the British drove the Turks from Palestine and Syria, while Anglo-Indian troops took Mesopotamia (Iraq). The Ottoman Empire surrendered in October 1918.

Because the Arabs predominated in Palestine, Syria, and Iraq, their leaders expected Britain to grant them independence in return for their support during the Arab Revolt. U.S. president Woodrow Wilson urged autonomy for these former Ottoman lands in the twelfth of his Fourteen Points, which Britain and France accepted as the basis for making peace. According to the Husayn-McMahon correspondence, confirmed in 1918 by new British and French assurances to the Arabs, the Fertile Crescent and the Hejaz were to be ruled by Sharif Husayn's family, the Hashemites.

But this was not to be. During the war Britain had made conflicting commitments to other interested parties. In a series of secret pacts, the Allies had agreed that the Bosporus and Dardanelles Straits, Istanbul, and eastern Anatolia were to go to czarist Russia, portions of western Anatolia to the Greeks and the Italians, and most of the Arab lands to Britain and France. The 1916 Sykes-Picot Agreement designated part of the Syrian coast for direct French control and a larger zone of French influence in the Syrian hinterland as far east as Mosul. Britain was to govern lower Iraq and to have a sphere of influence over the rest of Iraq and Palestine, except that the Christian holy places would be under an international administration. Only in the desert were the Arabs to be free from Western rule.

Meanwhile, there was another group, the Jewish nationalists, or Zionists, who were pressing the Western powers to recognize their claim to Palestine, or Eretz Yisrael. Beginning in the 1880s (in part due to the Russian pogroms against Jews), some European Jews settled in Palestine, which was still under Ottoman rule and inhabited mainly by Arabs. During World War I, Chaim Weizmann, a distinguished chemist and Zionist leader living in England, made his views known to the cabinet, which authorized Foreign Secretary Sir Arthur Balfour to declare the British government's support for the establishment in Palestine of a national home for the Jewish people. He cautioned that nothing should be done to prejudice the civil and religious (but not political) rights of Palestine's "existing non-Jewish inhabitants," who then comprised over nine-tenths of its population. The 1917 Balfour Declaration was a major victory for the nascent Zionist movement.

▧ The Postwar Peace Settlement

All of these contradictory commitments were aired at the 1919 Paris Peace Conference. Sharif Husayn's son, Faisal, spoke for the Arab provisional government that the Hashemites had set up in Damascus. Seeking to learn what Arabs in Syria and Palestine wanted, President Wilson sent out the King-Crane Commission, which found that the Arabs opposed French rule and Zionist colonization and strongly desired independence. Its report was ignored. The British let the French troops enter Beirut and later acceded to

French control over Syria, including Lebanon but not Palestine. Arab nationalists in Damascus declared Syria's independence in March 1920 and vowed to resist, but the French defeated their forces in July and toppled the Arab provisional government.

By this time, the Allies had agreed on how to divide and rule the conquered Ottoman provinces. Respecting President Wilson's principle of self-determination, Britain and France did not annex these territories, as earlier conquerors had done. Rather, under the League of Nations Covenant, Ottoman lands captured during the war were designated as countries that had developed enough so that their independence could be provisionally recognized, subject to a brief period of foreign tutelage under League supervision. Accordingly, France became the mandatory power in Syria and Lebanon and Britain in Iraq and Palestine. In principle, the mandatory powers were to administer these mandates to benefit the inhabitants and to prepare them for self-rule. In practice, the mandates benefited mainly Britain and France, not their new and resentful subjects.

France split Syria into smaller administrative units to ensure its control, thus embittering the nationalists. Faisal, ousted from Damascus, was crowned in Baghdad in 1921 as the British tried to suppress a general revolt in the new state of Iraq, a hastily cobbled combination of the Ottoman provinces of Mosul, Baghdad, and Basra, minus the emirate (principality) of Kuwait. For Faisal's brother Abdullah, who had been promised the throne in Iraq, the British created the emirate of Transjordan, a desert land inhabited by bedouin tribes. Britain helped Abdullah weld his new state into a cohesive unit by forming the Arab Legion, a camel corps made up of men from most of the tribes and led by British officers. The Zionists protested that Abdullah's kingdom was not open to Jewish colonization, and Arab nationalists decried the fragmentation of what they felt should have been a unified Syria. Abdullah himself hoped that, once the French left Syria, he could move from dusty Amman to historic Damascus.

■ The Middle East Since World War I

When Europe's armies laid down their weapons at the war's end, Britain seemed to dominate the Middle East. Its troops patrolled western Arabia, Palestine, Syria, Iraq, some of Persia, parts of the Caucasus long under czarist rule, and the Turkish straits. But the rise of nationalism limited Britain's ability to rule the Middle East. Egypt and Iraq were soon convulsed by nationwide revolutions against the British occupying forces. The Arabs rioted in Palestine against the Jewish immigrants and in Syria against the French colonists, for they viewed both groups as serving British imperial interests.

Deserted by its Young Turk leaders, the defeated Ottoman government let the British and French occupy the straits, but Ottoman attempts to demobilize the Turkish army as Greek forces invaded western Anatolia set off a mutiny led by its ablest general, Mustafa Kemal (later named Atatürk, "Father of the Turks"). Soon Kemal's followers set up in Ankara a nationalist government that replaced and then abolished the Ottoman sultanate. The new Republic of Turkey rejected the 1920 Treaty of Sèvres, imposed by the Allies, and negotiated with them three years later at Lausanne to gain a more acceptable treaty.

In Persia, Britain drafted a treaty with the Qajar rulers that would have turned their country into a British protectorate, but the *majlis* rejected the pact and revolts broke out in various parts of Persia. In 1921 an officer in the shah's guard, Reza Khan, took control and set up a military dictatorship, reducing Britain's role to protecting its oil fields in southwest Persia.

Western Imperialism in the Arab Lands

After the war, the British managed to keep their communication links across the region to India. Egypt's revolutionaries did not win the independence they had sought in 1919, but the British did promise in 1922 to end the protectorate and let the Egyptians draw up a formal constitution, creating a parliament that would vie with the king for power. British troops remained to guard Cairo, Alexandria, the Suez Canal, and such vital infrastructure as airports and radio transmitters. Sudan remained under a formal Anglo-Egyptian condominium, but the British held almost all the power. London also reserved the right to defend Egypt against outside aggression and to protect foreigners and minorities from nationalists or Muslim extremists. Under the new constitution, the Egyptians held parliamentary elections in 1923, and their former delegation (in Arabic, *wafd*) to the Paris Peace Conference turned into the overwhelmingly popular Wafd Party.

Palestine came under the direct control of Britain's Colonial Office, with a high commissioner governing in Jerusalem. The Jewish community had a Jewish Agency and an elected assembly to manage its internal affairs. The Muslim and Christian Arabs had no such organizations, and their leaders rejected a proposed legislature in which they would not have been given majority control reflective of their population. Jews and Arabs spoke different languages, lived in distinct villages or separate neighborhoods, and related as little as possible to each other as communities, although some got along well on the individual or family level. Jewish immigrants from war-torn revolutionary Russia or central Europe viewed local Arabs as threatening brigands, greedy landlords, or backward peasants. The Palestinian Arabs feared that the Zionist movement would dispossess them of their lands and their homes. Jews and Arabs, both having long memories of powerlessness, showed scant sympathy for each other as they began their contest for Palestine.

The French accepted control over Syria but resented having to forgo Palestine and oil-rich western Iraq. France was determined to parlay its League of Nations mandate over Syria into a colony. Soon after French troops had driven out the Arab nationalists, France divided the country into districts: Damascus, Aleppo, the north Mediterranean coast for the Alawis (a breakaway Shi'i sect), the highlands south of Damascus for the Druze (also a past offshoot of Shi'ism), and a special Republic of Lebanon.

This last-named state, the only one of these fragments to outlive the French mandate, was the enlarged version of the Ottoman province of Mount Lebanon, which had enjoyed autonomy under European protection between 1860 and 1914. Mount Lebanon's inhabitants had been mostly Maronite Christians (who had broken away from Greek Orthodoxy and later entered into communion with Roman Catholicism). The French hoped that, by enlarging Lebanon, they could preserve a Maronite plurality large enough to give them effective control over its other inhabitants, be they Druze, Sunni or Shi'i Muslim, Greek Orthodox, or adherents of other Christian sects. The Republic of Lebanon, which in the 1920s had a slight Christian majority, soon won substantial autonomy under Maronite leadership. French rule in Syria benefited farmers and merchants, as the mandatory regime invested in roads and other public works, but did not allay the chagrin of the nationalists who had craved Arab independence.

In North Africa, the French treated Algeria as an integral part of France. European settlers held most of the cultivable land, dominated political life, and controlled Algiers and the other major cities. The Algerian Muslims, mainly Berber but including many Arabs, had no political rights and only belatedly formed a secular nationalist party. A Muslim bey (governor) ruled in Tunisia and had Muslim ministers, but real power was held by the French governor-general and his advisers. The presence of European settlers was less visible than in Algeria, however, and opposition to French rule came from an emerging professional class, which formed the Destour (Constitution) Party.

Morocco, which unlike the rest of North Africa had never been under Ottoman rule, was now divided between a Spanish enclave in the north, the international city of Tangier, and a French protectorate over most of the country. A French governor-general advised the sultan and his ministers, who normally obeyed. A large-scale rural rebellion was suppressed in 1925 only with great difficulty. Although Morocco's urban nationalists formed the Istiqlal (Independence) Party, the French invested heavily in agriculture and mining, expecting to remain. Italy, which had seized Tripolitania from the Ottoman Empire in 1911, slowly took Cyrenaica and the Fezzan as well, creating what is now Libya. Its administration was especially brutal. Efforts to colonize Libya with Italians displaced many Arabs but attracted few settlers.

▉ Independence in Turkey, Iran, and the Arabian Peninsula

It is one of the great ironies of Middle Eastern history that most of the Arabs, who had thrown in their lot with the Allies during World War I, did not achieve their political goals after 1918, whereas the Turks, who had joined the Central Powers and shared in their defeat, managed to retain their independence once the war was over. The Turkish-speaking lands of Anatolia and Thrace could have been divided among Britain, France, Greece, Italy, and possibly even the United States. The Treaty of Sèvres might have awarded some eastern areas to Armenians and Kurds. Instead, Kemal led a nationwide revolt that gradually won the support of the Union of Soviet Socialist Republics (USSR), France, and Italy, expelled the Greek invaders who had occupied much of western Anatolia, and persuaded the British to withdraw their troops from the Bosporus and Dardanelles Straits. The new treaty signed at Lausanne in 1923 freed Thrace and Anatolia (with no special enclaves for the Armenians or the Kurds) from foreign rule and accepted Turkey's abolition of the Capitulations that had long exempted European expatriates from Ottoman control.

Kemal also abolished the sultanate and the other political institutions of the moribund Ottoman Empire in 1923. Ankara became the capital of Turkey, the first republic in the modern Middle East. More drastic reforms followed, as Kemal ended the Islamic caliphate and dismantled Turkey's Muslim institutions, including its *sharia* courts and schools, its dervish and Sufi orders, and even its holidays. The Arabic alphabet, in which Turkish had been written for a thousand years, was replaced by the Roman one. The Gregorian calendar and Western clocks became standard, as did the metric system of weights and measures. Kemal discouraged women from veiling their faces and ordered men to wear hats with brims in place of the fezzes that had become the customary head covering for Muslim officers and officials. The *ulama* lost most of their power as judges and educators. Kemal wanted to wrest Turkey out of the Middle East and make it a part of Europe. Because he had saved his country from a hated Allied occupation, most Turks adored and obeyed him.

Kemal had an imitator in Persia, the country now called Iran. Reza Khan had taken power in 1921. When civilian politicians proved too quarrelsome and the shah incompetent, Reza took power into his own hands. Crowning himself as the new shah in 1925, he founded the Pahlavi dynasty and declared that Persia should be called Iran (meaning land of the Aryans). Like Kemal, Reza Shah weakened the *ulama* and secularized their courts, schools, and welfare institutions. He outlawed the veiling of women and required both sexes to wear European-style clothing. The new shah also curbed the nomadic tribes that had dominated most of rural Persia by forcing them to settle down as farmers. Trying to strengthen state control over the countryside, he extended the telegraph lines and road network and decreed the construction of the Trans-Iranian Railway. The presence of the Anglo-Iranian (formerly Anglo-Persian) Oil Company, owned and managed by the British, limited Iran's economic sovereignty, but Reza Shah did manage to renegotiate its concession to the host country's benefit. As oil output expanded, more and more Iranians went to work for the company. As nationalist feelings spread, many Iranians began to ask why such a vital resource should be controlled by foreigners.

Petroleum exploration began in other Middle Eastern countries as well. British companies found new deposits in Iraq and Kuwait, as did U.S. companies operating in Bahrain. A coalition of U.S. firms that became the Arabian American Oil Company (ARAMCO) prospected for oil in the deserts of Arabia. This peninsula had long been dominated by feuding Arab tribes, but in the early twentieth century a remarkable military leader named Abdul Aziz ibn Saud took over much of Arabia. Having subdued most of the tribes in central and eastern Arabia, Ibn Saud managed to take Mecca and Medina from the Hashemites in 1925. After conquering Asir, Ibn Saud proclaimed the Kingdom of Saudi Arabia in 1932. His country remained poor until ARAMCO struck oil; it was only much later that Saudi Arabia evolved into an economic giant.

Yemen remained a separate state under a hereditary dynasty of Zaydi Shi'i imams (religious leaders), mountainous and colorful but lacking education, healthcare, industry, and oil. To the south of Yemen, where the Red and Arabian Seas meet, lay the British colony of Aden. The tribal shaikhs near the coasts of the Arabian Sea and the Gulf had made treaties that placed them under British protection. Oman, which in previous centuries had been an autonomous actor in regional affairs, had also become a British protectorate. Oil was found in some of these areas, too, but no significant amounts were extracted or sold until the 1960s.

▨ The Retreat of Western Imperialism

With the spread of education and communications, nationalism grew among the Arabic-speaking peoples under British and French control. This feeling was expressed either as Arab nationalism, the idea that all people who speak Arabic should be united in one nation-state, or as a more localized patriotism. As more Arabs attended schools and colleges and as a burgeoning press fueled their desire for independence and unity, they openly attacked the British and French mandates in the Fertile Crescent and the prolonged British domination over Egypt and Sudan. Indeed, the British themselves wanted to prepare Iraqis, Transjordanians and Palestinians, Syrians and Lebanese, and Egyptians and Sudanese for self-rule and eventual independence, but as separate countries, not as a single united state (as Arab nationalists wanted).

Leading the Arabs' march to independence was the Kingdom of Iraq. Although its subjects were less advanced than the Syrians or Egyptians, the British were prepared to certify that Iraq was ready for sovereign statehood. In 1932 Iraq achieved formal independence and was admitted to the League of Nations. The next year King Faisal I died suddenly and was succeeded by his minor son. A rebellion by the Assyrians (Nestorian Christians) was suppressed by Iraqi troops, who massacred many villagers. Other ethnic minorities (mainly non-Arab Kurds and Turcomans living in the north, who made up one-fifth of Iraq's population, but also Jews in Baghdad) were barred from power. Most of Iraq's Arab Muslims were Shi'a, who also suffered from discrimination.

Iraq's parliament was dominated by landowning tribal leaders, and certain aristocratic families monopolized cabinet posts. A series of military coups brought various army officers to power, culminating in an Arab nationalist government that was toppled in 1941 by a British military intervention in 1941, leaving a legacy of anti-Western hostility that would resurface under such leaders as Abd al-Karim Qasim (1958–1963) and Saddam Hussein (1979–2003).

The brother of Iraq's King Faisal I, Abdullah, managed to unite Transjordan, which became formally independent in 1946. Its most viable institution, the Arab Legion, had helped the British suppress riots in Palestine west of the Jordan, the area subject to the Jewish-Arab struggle for the "twice-promised land."

The Zionist movement had hoped to persuade enough Jews to immigrate to Palestine to form a Jewish state. During the 1920s, however, few came, lulling the Arab majority. But in 1929 a quarrel at the Western Wall sparked large-scale rioting in which many Arabs and Jews were killed or injured. The British government sent out an investigating commission, which reported that sales of Arab-owned lands to Jewish settlers were taking many Palestinian Arab farmers' tenancy rights and hence their livelihoods. The Jewish settlers blamed Arab violence for the riots and claimed they had brought prosperity to Palestine.

The Nazi takeover in Germany speeded up Jewish immigration in the 1930s, fueling Arab fears that they would soon become a minority. In 1936 the Arab political parties, hitherto divided on family and religious lines, united as the Arab Higher Committee, which organized a general strike against the mandate. A three-year civil war ensued. A British commission of inquiry visited Palestine in 1937 and recommended forming separate enclaves in Palestine for Jewish immigration and settlement. Palestine's Arabs, backed by newly independent Iraq and Egypt, opposed the partition, as did a meeting of the Zionist Congress, albeit for different reasons. The British revised their proposal and then, anxious about their strategic bases in Egypt and Iraq in case war with Germany broke out, issued the May 1939 White Paper, which

Jennifer A. Smith

The sign, in English and Hebrew, reads: "This market was built on Jewish property stolen by Arabs after the 1929 massacre." It hangs on the wall of a controversial Jewish settlement building in the West Bank city of Hebron/Khalil. The area was previously part of a Palestinian market.

restricted Jewish immigration and land purchases in Palestine. The Zionists felt betrayed, for Europe's Jews were in mortal peril and no other country would admit them. Palestinian Arabs, for their part, doubted British promises of independence, even though they constituted a majority in Palestine, and argued that Zionism was another manifestation of Western imperialism.

If the British were distrusted in Palestine, the Arabs hated France's mandates in Syria and Lebanon. Only the Maronites wanted the French presence; most other Christians and virtually all Muslims in Syria wanted Arab unity and independence. During an interval when a leftist government held power in Paris, the French offered independence, only to retract it when a more conservative cabinet took over. France's sudden defeat by Nazi Germany in 1940 enabled Britain and the United States to pressure the anti-Nazi Free French to recognize the independence of Syria and Lebanon in 1943, but it was another three years before the last French troops left.

At the end of World War II, Egypt was the most populous Arab state. It had the most newspapers and magazines, the leading universities, the largest cinema and record companies, and the most influential writers. Yet it lagged behind the other Arab countries in gaining independence. While the Wafd and other political parties vied for popular support in parliamentary elections, King Fu'ad I used his influence with the *ulama*, the army, and sometimes the village leaders to increase his own power. Both contended with the continued

British occupation of Egypt and Sudan. Only in 1936 did Britain and Egypt come to terms because both feared Italy's rising power in Libya and Ethiopia, countries that bordered on Egypt and Sudan. The British agreed to limit their forces to the Suez Canal zone, Cairo, and Alexandria, reducing them to 10,000 men in peacetime. Sudan, claimed by Egypt, remained under an Anglo-Egyptian condominium.

Egypt's King Fu'ad died in 1936 and was succeeded by his teenaged son, Farouk, who was initially adored by his subjects. But he lost popular support in 1942 when the British made him appoint a cabinet that would back their presence in Egypt during World War II. Egypt was occupied by even more British imperial troops during World War II than during World War I, as Fascist Italy and Nazi Germany invaded from Libya, and the Suez Canal had to be defended at all costs. Antidemocratic groups such as pro-Fascist Young Egypt, the Communists, and the Muslim Brothers vied for Egyptian support. The Wafd and other parliamentary parties seemed outdated. Once the war ended, Egyptians demanded that British troops leave their country, including Suez and Sudan.

▨ The Struggle Between Arab Nationalism and Zionism

The idea of Arab unity won growing support in the Fertile Crescent, Egypt, and the Arabian Peninsula during World War II. Arabs had decried the division of the Fertile Crescent into British and French mandates and hoped that independence would soon lead to unification. Nuri al-Said, Iraq's prime minister, proposed a union of Syria, Lebanon, Transjordan, and Palestine with his own country. But King Farouk of Egypt and King Ibn Saud of Saudi Arabia also wanted to lead the Arabs. Egypt, therefore, called for a looser organization for all sovereign Arab states. The Arabs accepted the latter alternative, and the Arab League came into being in 1945, with its headquarters in Cairo and an Egyptian as its secretary-general. The Arab countries also joined the United Nations (UN) that same year. Although Arab peoples still craved unity, their governments went their separate ways.

The issue that seemed to unite all Arabs was Palestine. Europe's Jews, decimated by the Nazi *Shoah* (Holocaust), sought a safe haven, but Palestine's Arab majority feared a flood of refugees who would demand statehood at their expense. As the British continued to enforce the immigration restrictions in their 1939 White Paper after World War II, some Jews resorted to terrorism. The British government became ever more hostile to Zionism and to Jewish settlement, and fighting intensified among Jews, Arabs, and British troops.

In 1947 Britain announced that it could no longer govern its mandate and submitted the Palestine issue to the United Nations. The UN General Assembly set up a special committee, which went to Palestine to look into the problem and recommended that its lands be divided into seven parts, three for the

Jews and three for the Arabs, leaving Jerusalem and Bethlehem as a separate area under the control of the United Nations. The Arab states opposed this plan, which awarded more than half the territory (including the fertile coastal area) to the Jews, who had only a third of the population and owned about 7 percent of the land. Pressured by the United States, more than two-thirds of the General Assembly voted for the partition proposal.

Despite threats by Egypt, Iraq, and the other Arab states to intervene militarily against partition, British troops prepared to pull out of Palestine, and the UN debated how to restore order. On May 14, 1948, when the British left Jerusalem, the Jewish Agency met in Tel Aviv to declare the independent State of Israel within the lands that they controlled. The United States and the USSR recognized the Jewish state, even as the Arab states sent their armies to destroy it.

Israel's creation was a revolutionary event for both Jews and Arabs. There had been no Jewish state for millennia; now one existed as an enclave in an overwhelmingly Arab region. As the armies of Egypt, Iraq, Syria, Lebanon, and Transjordan failed to take Palestine, most Palestinian Arabs fled to the neighboring states, driven either by the fatuous hope that the Arab armies would bring them back or by the realistic fear that the Israelis would drive them out. The result was the emergence of more than 750,000 Arab refugees, who were placed in camps in those areas of Palestine—the West Bank and the Gaza Strip—not captured by the Israelis or in the neighboring countries, mainly Syria, Lebanon, and Jordan. These Palestinian refugees refused assimilation into the Arab countries and demanded the right under international law to return to their homes. Israel offered to readmit a few of these refugees, but only as part of a general peace settlement. The Arab states signed separate armistice agreements with Israel in 1949 but did not recognize the new state. Israel declared that all Jews had the right to become citizens, took in survivors of the *Shoah,* and gave refuge to Jews from Arab lands.

▪ Political Changes in the Arab Countries

The defeat of the Arab armies in the 1948 Palestine war was one of the causes of the army coups that afflicted some Arab countries, starting in 1949 with three successive revolts in Syria. Arab monarchies were toppled in Egypt in 1952, Iraq in 1958, Yemen in 1962, and Libya in 1969. The demand for greater popular participation and for a fairer distribution of each country's resources probably did more to cause these revolutions than the Palestine problem, but the general trend was toward government by an officer corps coming from middle-class (as opposed to landowning) backgrounds and committed to reform. The presence of Palestinian refugees reminded Arabs in many countries of their old regimes' failure to defend them against Zionism and imperialism. The Palestinians themselves, although lacking the economic advantages and political rights of their Arab hosts, became increasingly educated and politicized. They often pressed the Arab governments to restore their rights by fighting Israel.

Revolutionary Arab regimes espoused socialism, a policy viewed as neutral between the communism of the USSR and the capitalism of the West, and Arab unification. The leading proponent of these policies was Egyptian president Gamal Abdul Nasser. Nasser had led the officers' conspiracy that ousted King Farouk in 1952, but his emergence as the Arabs' champion was gradual. He negotiated a new pact with Britain in 1954 securing the latter's evacuation of the Suez Canal zone. He also renounced Egypt's claims to rule Sudan, which became independent in 1956.

Nasser resisted Western efforts to draw him into an anti-Communist alliance in 1955 but agreed instead to buy $200 million worth of arms from the Soviet bloc, a move that aroused Western fears of Communist gains in the Arab world. The U.S. government, working with Britain and the World Bank, offered to lend Egypt the money to build a new dam near Aswan that would control the Nile floodwaters and greatly increase the country's farmland and hydroelectric generating capacity, but it later retracted its offer in order to punish Nasser for his pro-Communist policies. Nasser responded in July 1956 by nationalizing the Suez Canal Company. The British and French governments denounced the seizure and conspired with Israel to attack Egypt. Although the attackers retook the canal, they were opposed by nearly every UN member, including the United States. Ultimately, they had to withdraw, and Nasser emerged as an Arab hero for standing up to the West.

Early in 1958, Egypt acceded to Syria's request to form an organic union of the two countries, which they called the United Arab Republic (UAR). Many nationalists hoped that other Arab states would join the new political entity. Instead, Jordan and Iraq formed their own federation, which soon foundered when a coup overthrew the Iraqi monarchy. A civil war broke out in Lebanon between Arab nationalists (mainly Muslim) who sought closer ties with the UAR and Lebanese particularists (mainly Christian) who wanted independence from the Arabs. U.S. troops occupied Lebanon in July 1958 and helped restore order.

The general trend seemed to be toward pan-Arabism, as north Yemen federated with the UAR, the army seized power in Sudan, and even Saudi Arabia replaced a weak king with a brother who was thought to favor Nasser. Not only was Arab unity strong in the late 1950s, but many governments followed Nasser's lead in redistributing large estates to hitherto landless farmers, nationalizing companies owned by foreign or local capitalists, and expanding public education and welfare institutions. The watchwords of the day were "neutralism" and "Arab socialism."

Like the eastern Arab world, North Africa was also emerging from colonialism. Libya, ruled by Italy up to World War II, was the first to gain independence, in 1951. France gave up its protectorates over both Tunisia and Morocco in 1956, but hesitated in Algeria. More than 1 million European settlers wanted to keep Algeria a part of France, but a nationalist revolt broke out in 1954 and continued for eight years. The French government and army grew tired of fighting rearguard colonial wars, and in 1962 President Charles de Gaulle granted independence to Algeria. Its leaders soon declared their support of Nasser and Arab socialism.

■ The Northern Tier

As stated in the introduction to this book, not all Middle Eastern states are Arab. Turkey and Iran, although predominantly Muslim, are proud of their distinctive cultures and heritages. Both managed to stand up to the British and kept their independence after World War I. Both bordered on the USSR and had to come to terms with it. Although the Soviets helped Turkey to resist the Greeks and the British during the rise of Mustafa Kemal Atatürk in the 1920s, the Turks resumed the Ottoman policy of opposing Russian imperialism. Ismet Inönü, who had succeeded Atatürk as president, kept Turkey out of World War II and prevented the Allies from using the Bosporus and Dardanelles Straits to supply the USSR. Stalin's postwar demand to station Soviet troops on the straits led the United States to back Turkey in the 1947 Truman Doctrine.

In 1952, Turkey joined the North Atlantic Treaty Organization (NATO), having committed troops to defending South Korea against the Communists. Inönü's government even allowed a rival political party to form, only to oust it from power in 1950. Turkey has continued to industrialize its economy and modernize its society, but its recent history has been punctuated by military coups and by challenges from militant Marxists, Muslims, and Kurdish separatists. Turkey remains a bridge between the West and the Middle East and has become a link to the former Soviet republic of Azerbaijan and to Central Asia.

Iran also had to protect its independence from the USSR. Even though the two countries had signed a pact that authorized the Soviets to enter Iran whenever it was occupied by troops hostile to the USSR, Reza Shah's government sought to limit the Soviet Union's influence. In the 1930s, Iran drew close to Nazi Germany, whose doctrines of Aryan supremacy appealed to local pride and offered a means to fight Anglo-Russian control. When the Nazis invaded the USSR in 1941, the Soviet and British governments demanded the expulsion of German advisers from Iran and seized control of the Trans-Iranian Railway to ship Western munitions to the beleaguered Soviets. Reza abdicated in favor of his son Mohammad and went into exile. At the war's end, British troops left Iran, but the Soviets tried to set up puppet regimes in Kurdistan and

Azerbaijan. It took a general UN condemnation, U.S. threats, and clever Iranian diplomacy to oust the Soviet army.

But Britain still controlled Iran's oil, and in 1951 a cabinet headed by Mohammad Mosaddeq nationalized the Anglo-Iranian Oil Company. Iran's nationalists were elated, but Western countries supported Britain by refusing to buy any oil from Iran. In 1953 an army coup, engineered in part by British and U.S. intelligence agencies, overthrew Mosaddeq's government. The shah, who had fled the country during the turmoil, regained his throne. He began a policy of concentrating control in his own hands at the expense of Iran's landowners, merchants, and *ulama*. He also signed an anti-Communist alliance with Turkey, Pakistan, Britain, and Iraq. Britain and the United States saw Iran, Turkey, and Pakistan as a bulwark against a possible Soviet drive toward the oil-rich Gulf. The West sold vast quantities of weapons to these countries, but skeptics wondered whether those arms would just be used to keep their regimes in power.

▧ The Intensification of the Arab-Israeli Conflict

In the late 1950s and early 1960s, Israel's conflict with its Arab neighbors seemed to die down as Arab states tried to unite and leaders struggled for power. The United Arab Republic lapsed when Syria broke away in 1961. A popular nationalist movement, the Ba'th Party, committed to Arab unification and socialism, seized power successively in Iraq and Syria early in 1963. The Ba'th tried to form a new Arab union with Egypt, but the talks broke down. An army coup had ousted the Yemeni monarchy in 1962, but the new republican regime sought Egyptian military aid and troops to stay in power, while Saudi Arabia began backing tribes loyal to the ousted imam. A draining civil war ensued in Yemen.

What brought the Arabs back together was Israel's completion of a development scheme that took large quantities of water from the Jordan River to irrigate new agricultural lands within the Jewish state. Early in 1964, Nasser invited the other Arab heads of state to Cairo to discuss ways of countering the Israeli scheme, which would deprive Jordan and other Arab states of fresh water needed for their irrigation projects. The Arabs agreed to prepare for future action against Israel and formed the Palestine Liberation Organization (PLO) to unite the Palestinian Arabs politically. Meanwhile, Fatah, led by Yasser Arafat, launched commando raids inside Israel. Although abetted by Syria, these attacks tended to come from the West Bank, which was controlled by Jordan. To deter future raids, Israel's army attacked West Bank villages late in 1966, yet some Israelis blamed Syria.

An aerial dogfight broke out between Israel and Syria in April 1967. The USSR told Egypt that Israeli troops were massing for an attack on Syria.

Nasser, anxious to remain the champion of Arab nationalism, ordered the UN to withdraw its peacekeeping forces, which had patrolled the Sinai and the Gaza Strip since the 1956 war. As Israel mobilized its reserves, Egypt declared a blockade in the Gulf of Aqaba against Israeli shipping. Arab governments, their press and radio stations, and their people all called for defeating Israel and restoring the Palestinians to their homes.

Although many in the United States and Western Europe favored Israel, their governments hoped to avoid war by taking the issue to the UN. Israel, fearing an Arab offensive, decided to launch a preemptive strike. On June 5, 1967, Israeli fighter planes struck at Egypt's military airfields and wiped out most of the Egyptian air force. Before the Arabs could hit back, the Israelis bombed the other Arab air forces. They invaded the Egyptian Sinai, Gaza, the Jordanian-ruled sector of Jerusalem and the West Bank, and finally Syria's Golan Heights. In six days, using its superior technology, organization, and mastery of the air, Israel defeated Egypt, Syria, and Jordan, tripling the area under its control.

Although the Arab states agreed to UN-mediated cease-fires, they refused to make peace. At a summit held in Khartoum, Sudan, the Arab leaders agreed not to negotiate with Israel, but to rearm and regain their lost lands by force. The PLO tried but failed to mobilize the Palestinians of the Gaza Strip and the West Bank, numbering more than 1 million people under Israeli military rule, to rebel. After five months of debate, the UN Security Council unanimously passed Resolution 242, which called on Israel to withdraw from lands occupied in the recent war but also ordered all countries to recognize the right of "every state in the area" to exist "within secure and recognized boundaries." Israel, Egypt, Jordan, and Syria, as UN members, were all bound under the UN Charter to accept Security Council resolutions, but each made its own interpretation of this one, to which all member states have paid lip service since 1967. Resolution 242 did not mention the Palestinians, who felt that neither the major powers nor the Arab governments really cared about their interests.

In 1969, Arafat was elected chairman of the PLO, the umbrella group for most Palestinians. Some became guerrillas and resorted to acts of violence against not only Israel but also any Arab government that worked closely with the West, notably Jordan and Lebanon. Palestinian guerrilla groups seemed to resist Israel more effectively than had the armies of Egypt, Syria, and Jordan in 1967. Despite Israeli-inspired propaganda attacks against "Arab terrorism," most Arabs flocked to support the PLO.

Nasser launched his 1969 War of Attrition against Israel's troops in the Sinai partly to counter Palestinian claims to military leadership. Israel's counterattacks obliged Egypt to seek more military aid from the USSR, leading to aerial dogfights over the Suez Canal. U.S. secretary of state William Rogers proposed a peace plan that would halt the War of Attrition and set up indirect talks to bring Egypt and Israel to a peace settlement based on Resolution 242.

Nasser accepted the Rogers Peace Plan but indirectly undercut it by moving Soviet missiles up to positions near the Suez Canal. Meanwhile, Palestinian guerrillas threatened to take over Jordan, but the Jordanian army, loyal to King Hussein, crushed them. Nasser's efforts to restore peace among the Arabs contributed to his fatal heart attack on September 28, 1970. His funeral in Cairo inspired demonstrations of grief all over the Arab world because of his heroic stand against Western imperialism. Nasser's successor, Anwar Sadat, vowed to continue the fallen leader's policies of Arab nationalism, opposition to Israel, nonalignment, purchases of Communist arms, and socialism. Soon, however, Sadat began liberalizing Egypt's economy and society and ordered most Soviet advisers to leave the country in 1972.

The Rogers Peace Plan collapsed in 1971 as both Israel and the Arabs refused to make the necessary concessions. Sadat threatened to renew the war against Israel if it did not withdraw from the Sinai and recognize Palestinian political rights. He also tried to cement a union with Syria, Libya, and Sudan. Neither his threats nor his union scheme worked. Palestinian commando groups carried out terrorist actions against civilian Israelis and foreigners, hoping to convince Israel and its backers that the Arab lands captured in 1967 were not worth keeping. But Israel believed that it had to retain the territories until the Arabs were willing to negotiate for peace. As the Arabs quarreled among themselves and Egypt distanced itself from its erstwhile Soviet backers, Israel and its backers became overconfident.

Israel's complacency was shaken on October 6, 1973, when Egypt and Syria attacked Israeli positions in the Sinai and the Golan Heights. Although poorly prepared, the Israelis called up their reserve soldiers and brought them to both fronts. By the second week, Israel was driving back the Syrians and Egyptians. The Soviet Union and the United States rushed to rearm their Middle Eastern clients on a massive scale. Then the Arabs decided to unsheathe an economic weapon. In 1960, the leading nonindustrialized oil producers had created the Organization of Petroleum Exporting Countries (OPEC), which tried to limit oil supplies and set common prices. OPEC had begun to affect the world oil market in 1971, and the October 1973 war gave it a pretext to drive up prices 400 percent. The Arab members of OPEC announced that they would sell no oil to the United States and the Netherlands and would reduce supplies to other oil importers until Israel pulled out of all occupied lands and recognized the Palestinians' political rights. So vital had Arab oil become to Europe and Japan that many countries made political promises to ensure winter supplies. The UN Security Council adopted Resolutions 338 and 340, calling for a cease-fire and for immediate negotiations between Israel and the Arabs.

The Israelis had won the war, but as other governments turned against them, they felt that they had lost politically. U.S. secretary of state Henry Kissinger worked to disentangle the Egyptian and Israeli armies and to set up a general peace conference that met briefly in Geneva in December 1973. Kissinger began flying between Jerusalem and Cairo, dealing with Egypt's and Israel's leaders separately. Finally they agreed to separate the Israeli and Egyptian armies by creating demilitarized zones between them. After that, tensions lessened and the oil embargo ended. Kissinger engineered a similar agreement between Israel and Syria. Both agreements enabled the Arab states to regain some of the lands Israel had taken in 1967 or 1973. Both sides took steps that, it was hoped, would lead toward future peace talks.

A second agreement between Egypt and Israel in 1975, also brokered by Kissinger, led to a further Israeli pullback and to an Egyptian renunciation of force to settle the Arab-Israeli conflict. Both sides feared political deals: the Israelis might jeopardize their security by conceding too much to the Arabs; Egypt and Syria feared making concessions that might anger other Arabs, especially the Palestinians. In 1974, the Arabs agreed that only the PLO could speak for the Palestinians, but Israel refused to talk to what it viewed as a terrorist group. When an ultranationalist coalition, led by Menachem Begin (who had played an active role in the underground paramilitary group Irgun Zvai Leumi up to 1948), won Israel's 1977 election, the country seemed to be on a collision course with the Arabs. U.S. president Jimmy Carter wanted to reconvene the Geneva Conference (with the Soviet Union) and to include Palestinians in the new talks, to Israel's dismay.

Then Egyptian president Anwar Sadat surprised everyone by announcing that he would go to Jerusalem to parley with Israel's government. Although startled, Begin agreed to receive him and a new peace process began, leading to U.S. mediation and finally to an extraordinary summit held at Camp David, with Carter as host and Sadat and Begin as chief negotiators. A tentative agreement was reached for peace between Egypt and Israel, and the three leaders signed the pact in September 1978. Diplomats ironed out the details, and the final Egyptian-Israeli peace treaty was signed in March 1979. The treaty provided for Israel's phased withdrawal from the Sinai, full diplomatic relations between Jerusalem and Cairo, and ongoing negotiations about the status of Palestinians under Israeli occupation. The other Arab states and the PLO denounced Sadat's policy, broke diplomatic ties with Egypt, and vowed to continue their opposition to Israel.

▓ The Islamic Revolution in Iran

While the West watched the Egyptian-Israeli peace talks, a revolution was brewing against the government of Mohammad Reza Shah Pahlavi, who had ruled Iran for almost thirty-seven years. The United States and most European countries had long backed the shah as a bulwark against Soviet expansionism and pan-Arabism, selling Iran billions of dollars worth of Western arms. Iran's surging income caused by the oil price hikes in 1973 drew U.S. and European investors to Tehran, where the shah proclaimed grandiose development schemes. These plans, run from the top down, gave little attention to what the Iranian people needed. They stressed showcase projects instead of making basic changes in the villages where most Iranians lived or in the factories or on the farms where most Iranians worked. The shah tolerated no opposition to his policies; a large intelligence bureau, Sazman-e Ettelaat va Amniyat-e Keshvar (SAVAK), spied on dissidents and jailed or tortured his critics.

Opposition to the shah came from nationalists who had backed Mosaddeq in 1951–1953, Marxists, labor leaders, intellectuals, and students. None of these groups was strong enough to withstand threats of imprisonment, torture, or even death at the hands of SAVAK agents. The best-organized and most popular opposition came from Muslim leaders, in part because Iran is a Shi'ite country, and Shi'ism empowers its *ulama* to reinterpret Islamic law. One such inspiring leader was the Ayatollah Ruhollah Khomeini, who inveighed in his sermons and writings against the shah's tyranny and U.S. interference in Iranian affairs. Exiled from Iran in 1964, Khomeini continued to stir up opposition from Iraq and later from Paris. His sermons were smuggled into Iran and passed from hand to hand; some were even read aloud in the mosques.

An attack on Khomeini in the Iranian press sparked popular demonstrations early in 1978, and government efforts to suppress them led instead to larger protests. Growing numbers of Iranians turned against the shah's government and demanded the civil liberties and human rights advocated by President Carter. Even many in the United States doubted that the regime could survive and called for a nationalist government that would unite the Iranian people. The shah, stricken with cancer and cut off from the people, appointed a nationalist premier and left Iran in January 1979, expecting the United States to restore his regime as it had done in 1953. This did not occur.

The Iranian people, elated at the shah's departure, staged demonstrations to bring back the ayatollah. In February Khomeini returned, the shah's army defected to the ayatollah's side, and the government turned over its power to the revolutionaries. A cabinet whose members held opinions ranging from nationalist to Marxist to ultra-Islamic temporarily took charge of Iran, and revolutionary *komiteh*s (committees) rounded up SAVAK agents and the shah's supporters, trying many and jailing and executing some of them. A popular plebiscite backed Khomeini's demand that Iran become an Islamic republic.

The Iranian revolution was a turning point in modern Middle Eastern history. A government committed to rapid Westernization was toppled by a popular regime dedicated to making Islam the basis of its policies and the guide for its economy, society, and culture. The new regime vowed to export its revolution throughout the Muslim world. The emirates and shaikhdoms of the Gulf, with their vast oil revenues and wide disparities between rich and poor, were vulnerable. Some had large and oppressed Shi'i populations. Iran's seizure of the U.S. embassy and the taking of fifty-two hostages outraged Westerners, but it also empowered Muslims to criticize Washington and other Western governments viewed as hostile to Islam.

U.S. diplomatic and military efforts to secure the release of the hostages failed. Soviet troops, observing U.S. weakness after the Iranian revolution, occupied Afghanistan in December 1979. Military aggression seemed to be in fashion, as Iraqi president Saddam Hussein renounced a treaty he had signed with the shah's government in 1975 letting Iran share control with Iraq over the confluence of the Euphrates and Tigris Rivers, the Shatt al-Arab waterway, and proceeded to invade Iran in 1980. This dispute was a pretext for deeper antagonisms between the two countries: Iraq wanted to replace Egypt as the Arabs' leader; Iran called on all Muslims, especially Shi'a, to replace their secularized regimes with Islamic republics. Iraq attacked Iran's southwestern province, which contains most of its oil and has Arab inhabitants who might have rallied to Saddam's Arab nationalism.

Iraq made huge inroads into Iran at first, but the Iranians fought back and eventually regained the captured lands and even managed to take some strategic islands near Iraq's second largest city, Basra. Neither the Shi'i majority in Iraq nor the Arab minority in Iran rebelled against its government, but each state spent huge sums on weapons and suffered heavy losses of personnel and equipment, as well as destruction of oil refineries, homes, shops, and factories. Both sides drafted what males they could find, even foreign workers and young boys, into their armies to replenish their fallen soldiers. Both, especially Iraq, fired missiles at the enemy's cities and used poison gas in combat.

Iran soon realized that it would have to release the U.S. hostages to gain international support for its war effort. Algerian diplomats mediated the dispute and secured the release of all fifty-two hostages after 444 days in captivity. Although U.S. president Ronald Reagan's administration seemed to favor Iraq, it sold U.S. missiles and spare parts to Iran for secret funds that could later be used to finance anti-Communist rebels in Nicaragua. When Iran and Iraq attacked each other's oil tankers in the Gulf and then started firing on the ships of other countries, the U.S. government took to reflagging Kuwaiti tankers and using its warships to escort them. In 1988, the United States and Iran almost went to war with each other when a U.S. naval officer accidentally shot down an Iranian passenger plane over the Gulf, but Tehran found that almost no country would back it. The UN Security Council had passed a resolution calling for a cease-fire between the warring states. Iraq had already accepted the resolution, and in July 1988 Iran reluctantly followed suit.

The Iranian revolution had many repercussions beyond the war with Iraq. Between 1979 and 1987, Tehran tried to foment revolts throughout the Muslim world, using its Islamic Republican Party to export revolutionary ideas. Iranian guerrillas set up training camps for revolutionary groups as remote as the Moros in the Philippines and the Polisario rebels opposing Moroccan control of the Western Sahara. Especially important, however, was Iran's aid to Lebanon's Shi'a, once poor and unheeded but emerging in the 1980s as a major player in that country's civil war.

■ Lebanon: Cockpit of Middle Eastern Rivalry

Ever since independence, Lebanon had presented one face to the West: that of a democratic, urbane society, the "Switzerland of the Middle East." To many of its own inhabitants, and certainly to other Arabs, however, it showed another face: one of unfair privileges enjoyed by its Christians at the expense of Lebanon's Muslims (both Sunni and Shi'i) and the Druze. As more Lebanese moved to the cities, where disparities of wealth and power were clearer, and as the Muslim percentage of Lebanon's population rose relative to that of the Christians, discontent mounted. Economic and social conditions improved after the 1958 civil war, but Lebanese Muslims and Palestinian refugees still resented their inferior status. Skirmishes sometimes broke out between Muslims and Christians or between Palestinians and Lebanese. Usually they were settled quietly, but in 1975 Sunni Muslim and Maronite Christian militias started fighting in earnest, the PLO soon joined in, and a major civil war began. In 1976, the Lebanese government invited Syria into the country to help suppress Muslim and Palestinian militias. Syrian troops did indeed buttress the Maronite-dominated government in 1976, but they stayed in Lebanon and soon shifted to the Muslim side. Early in 1978, Israel invaded southern Lebanon, partly to keep the Syrian army away from their northern border, but withdrew after the UN stationed a buffer force in the parts of Lebanon bordering Israel.

But low-intensity conflict dragged on. Ignoring the UN buffer, Palestinian commandos sometimes raided northern Israel; Israeli troops bombed suspected PLO bases in Lebanese villages and even Beirut neighborhoods. In 1982 Israel invaded southern Lebanon, repulsed the Syrian army and PLO militias, bypassed the UN force, and besieged Beirut. Lebanon's parliament elected a Maronite president aligned with Israel against the Palestinians and their Arab backers. When he was killed in an explosion, Israel's troops invaded Beirut. While they were there, Maronite militias invaded the mainly Palestinian neighborhoods of Sabra and Shatilla, where they killed hundreds of old men, women, and children. Appalled by the massacre, which Israel's army seemed to abet, the Western powers sent a multinational force into Lebanon.

Washington hoped to persuade Syria and Israel to leave Lebanon and the various militias to hand over their arms and their powers to a reconstituted Lebanese government. Instead, the Israelis and the multinational force angered not just the Sunni Muslims and Palestinians but also Lebanon's hith-

Deborah J. Gerner

In 2002, a significant number of buildings in central Beirut, Lebanon, remained in a state of total disrepair, a visual reminder of the intermittent war that engulfed the country for more than two decades.

erto quiet Shi'i citizens. Soon Lebanese Shi'a, trained by Iranian revolutionaries, were driving trucks loaded with explosives into Western embassies, the barracks of the foreign armies, and Maronite strongholds, killing or injuring hundreds. These suicide squads wrought such havoc among the European, U.S., and Israeli forces that they withdrew, although Israel continued to occupy southern Lebanon for fifteen more years. Their success in ousting at least some foreign troops from Lebanon enhanced the prestige of these Muslim militants.

■ The Iraq-Kuwait Crisis and Israeli-Arab Negotiations

Iraq has long suffered from always being the number two Arab state, whether subordinate to Egypt as the Arabic cultural center or second to Saudi Arabia as the area's largest oil producer. Iraq's own potential has gone unrealized, and its war against Iran in the 1980s left it heavily indebted to Saudi Arabia and other Arab Gulf states. Iraqis also believe that Kuwait was created by British imperialism, a dynastic enclave that serves the interests of Western oil importers. At times Iraq has tried to annex Kuwait, hoping to enlarge its coastline and become the leading power on the Gulf. In July 1990, Iraq accused Kuwait of "slant-drilling" for oil under Iraqi territory and of demanding repayment of loans it had made to Iraq during the war against Iran. Other

Arab governments tried to mediate the dispute, but Saddam ordered Iraqi troops to occupy Kuwait on August 2, 1990.

Iraq failed to foresee that U.S. president George H. W. Bush would fiercely oppose its annexation of Kuwait. Once Arab pressure had failed to make the Iraqis withdraw, the Bush administration began an intense campaign to liberate Kuwait, initially by diplomacy and later by sending troops and matériel to Saudi Arabia in what came to be called Operation Desert Shield. Economic sanctions backed by increasingly strident UN Security Council resolutions warned Iraq to remove its troops from Kuwait. Kuwaitis who escaped to other Arab lands called for military measures instead of economic sanctions. Saudi Arabia, hitherto opposed to any concentration of foreign troops in its territory, which includes the two holiest Muslim cities, became a base for a U.S.-led coalition of Arab and foreign forces opposed to Iraq's action.

Far from being intimidated, Saddam warned that any attempt to dislodge the Iraqis from their reclaimed province would lead to the torching of Kuwait's oil fields. Nevertheless, the coalition attacked Iraq on January 16, 1991, launching Operation Desert Storm. When six weeks of intense allied bombing did not lead to Iraq's retreat from Kuwait, the coalition forces began a ground war that succeeded, within 100 hours, in expelling Iraq's forces. Bush then stopped the hostilities, even as the allied coalition was entering southern Iraq. Some critics argue that the troops should have occupied Baghdad and deposed Saddam, but the UN resolutions called only for the liberation of Kuwait.

Shi'a in the south and Kurds in the north revolted against Iraq's central government, but the help that they needed from the United States and its allies never came. Both uprisings were suppressed. Any dissident officers in the Iraqi army who sought to topple their leader were killed, jailed, or driven from Iraq. The UN sanctions remained in effect, keeping Iraq from importing consumer goods for its people, but Saddam stymied the UN inspectors who could have certified the destruction of his nuclear, chemical, and biological weapons. It was a hollow victory for the allied coalition.

As he had promised (to gain Arab support for the war against Iraq), the Bush administration did convene a conference, initially in Madrid and later in Washington and then Moscow, at which Israeli and Arab delegations met to talk peace. Although Israel refused direct talks with the PLO, representatives from the Occupied Territories were admitted into a joint Jordanian-Palestinian delegation. While public talks dragged on, representatives of Israel and the PLO met secretly in Oslo and hammered out an agreement that surprised everyone when it was first announced in 1993. The public signing of a Declaration of Principles by Israel and the PLO in the presence of President Bill Clinton led to intense negotiations, focused initially on the withdrawal of Israeli troops from Gaza and Jericho.

After many delays, Israel reached an agreement in May 1994 with Palestine's "self-governing authority," enabling Arafat to return to Gaza. Israel could still manipulate the supposedly autonomous Palestinians by retaining troops in Gaza and the West Bank and by barring Palestinian workers from entering Israel during times of crisis. Few jobs were available to them in the autonomous areas. Some frustrated Palestinians forsook the PLO for more radical movements such as Hamas. Jordan and Israel signed a peace treaty in October 1994, and several North African and Gulf states entered into diplomatic or commercial relations with the Jewish state. Israel reached a further agreement with the PLO in September 1995, providing for troop withdrawals from major West Bank population centers, but Jerusalem's status was left for future negotiations, and most Palestinian lands remained under Israel's control. Prime Minister Yitzhak Rabin was murdered by an Israeli who believed that his government had already given up too much to the Arabs. A new government, headed by Benjamin Netanyahu, was elected in 1996. It stepped up Jewish settlements in the West Bank and repressive policies against Palestinians. Only intense U.S. pressure made Netanyahu give up part of Hebron in 1997 and a few other occupied lands in 1998. His fragile coalition eventually collapsed, forcing him to call for early elections.

In 1999, the Labor Party leader, Ehud Barak, won by a narrow margin. He offered to cede most of the West Bank and Gaza to Yasser Arafat during negotiations at Camp David and Sharm al-Shaikh in 2000, but the Palestinians could not accept a deal that would have obliged them to give up their right of return to other lands now part of Israel. Palestinians and Israelis both stepped up attacks on each other, and a new Palestinian uprising broke out in September 2000. The hawkish general, Ariel Sharon, accused of fomenting the 1982 Palestinian massacre at Sabra and Shatilla, defeated Ehud Barak in a special election in 2001 and spearheaded an Israeli drive to intimidate the Palestinians by reoccupying most of the West Bank and Gaza.

In 2002, the European Union, the United Nations, and the governments of Russia and the United States proposed a "road map to peace." By mid-2003, however, the plan had foundered on the intransigence of the Jewish settlers in the Occupied Territories; Israel's construction of a "security fence" on the West Bank, its "targeted killings" (assassinations) of Palestinians, and its armed incursions into Palestinian-controlled areas; and the inability of the Palestinian Authority to curb ongoing attacks on Israeli civilians by Palestinian "suicide bombers."

▨ Terrorism in the Middle East (and Elsewhere)

Terrorism became the last resort of increasingly desperate Arabs, who sent suicide bombers into Israel to kill civilians, blew up U.S. embassies in Kenya and Tanzania in 1998, damaged a U.S. Navy warship in Yemen, and on September 11, 2001, launched a dramatic hijacking of four U.S. civil airliners to attack New York's World Trade Center and the Pentagon in Washington,

D.C. The group behind these attacks was Al-Qaida (The Base). Its headquarters was in Afghanistan, from which it had expelled the Soviet forces in the late 1980s, but its members were mainly Arab and its leader, Osama bin Laden, came from Saudi Arabia. Indeed, the nineteen hijackers involved in the September 11 attacks were all Arabs, mostly citizens of Egypt and Saudi Arabia. They protested U.S. favoritism toward Israel, U.S. influence over many Arab regimes, and the domination of U.S. culture in many parts of the Muslim world. U.S. president George W. Bush declared a "war against terrorism" and directed U.S. forces to bombard and occupy Afghanistan to capture bin Laden and destroy Al-Qaida.

His administration identified Iraq as a major supporter of terrorism and demanded that it fulfill the UN Security Council's Gulf War resolutions to destroy its weapons of mass destruction: nuclear, chemical, and biological. If the Iraqi government failed to prove that it had done so, and the UN inspectors could not verify their absence, the U.S. armed forces, aided if possible by its allies, would invade Iraq and oust Saddam's government. On March 20, 2003, the United States and Britain attacked Iraq, bombarded and occupied the country, and drove Saddam's regime out of power. Yet in the months following, the United States and Britain found it difficult to restore stability or to ensure supplies of gasoline, food, and medicine to most Iraqis. Creating a new government to represent Iraq's diverse mix of Sunni and Shi'i Muslim Arabs, Kurds, Turcomans, and Christians took longer than expected; meanwhile, dissidents launched assaults on foreign troops and exploded a number of bombs aimed at both local and foreign targets.

■ Conclusion

The peoples and the countries of the Middle East are not at peace, either with one another or, indeed, with themselves. Secular nationalism competes with Islam as the leading ideology for many Middle Eastern Arabs, Iranians, and Turks. The breakup of the Soviet Union has drawn some Middle Eastern countries into competition over the new republics of the Caucasus and Central Asia. The Cold War may have ended, but Washington articulates its Middle East policy goals not by diplomacy, but by force. Borders between countries, drawn mostly by Western imperialists for their own interests, rarely reflect natural frontiers and are often violated by the armies of strong states preying upon weaker ones. Many Middle Eastern peoples have moved into burgeoning cities, acquired years of schooling, and been exposed to radio and television propaganda, swelling their ambitions beyond what their societies actually have to offer. Young adults feel especially frustrated, a feeling often enhanced by their migration from countries of high population and little oil (such as Egypt) to others that are poor in labor but rich in oil (such as Saudi

Arabia), separating them from their parents, spouses, children, and friends. Other chapters will show that no other area poses so great a danger to world peace as the volatile Middle East.

■ Bibliography

Abun-Nasr, Jamil M. 1987. *A History of the Maghrib in the Islamic Period*. New York: Cambridge University Press.

Cleveland, William L. 2001. *A History of the Modern Middle East*. 2nd ed. Boulder, Colo.: Westview Press.

Daniel, Elton. 2001. *The History of Iran*. Westport, Conn.: Greenwood Press.

Fisher, Sydney Nettleton, and William Ochsenwald. 1997. *The Middle East: A History*. 5th ed. 2 vols. New York: McGraw-Hill.

Goldschmidt, Arthur, Jr. 2002. *A Concise History of the Middle East*. 7th ed. Boulder, Colo.: Westview Press.

Hodgson, Marshall G. S. 1974. *The Venture of Islam*. 3 vols. Chicago: Chicago University Press.

Hourani, Albert. 1991. *A History of the Arab Peoples*. Cambridge: Harvard University Press.

Issawi, Charles. 1982. *An Economic History of the Middle East and North Africa*. New York: Columbia University Press.

Julien, Charles-André. 1970. *History of North Africa from the Arab Conquest to 1830*. Trans. John Petrie. Ed. C. C. Stewart. New York: Praeger.

Lapidus, Ira M. 2002. *A History of Islamic Societies*. 2nd ed. New York: Cambridge University Press.

Lewis, Bernard. 2002. *What Went Wrong? Western Impact and Middle Eastern Response*. New York: Oxford University Press.

Perry, Glenn E. 1997. *The Middle East: Fourteen Islamic Centuries*. 3rd ed. Upper Saddle River, N.J.: Prentice-Hall.

Saunders, J. J. 1965. *A History of Medieval Islam*. New York: Barnes and Noble.

Zürcher, Erik J. 1997. *Turkey: A Modern History*. Rev. ed. London: I. B. Tauris.

Middle Eastern Politics

Deborah J. Gerner

Syria Watches Nervously as Rival Baath Party Next Door in Iraq Is Dissolved . . . Israel Seals Gaza Strip . . . Mass Grave Discovered in Iraq's Holy Shiite City . . . Iran's President Arrives for Talks in Lebanon . . . Algeria Says It Frees 17 Missing European Tourists in Commando Raid . . . Four Explosions Rock Riyadh . . . Deadly Suicide Attacks Stun Morocco . . . Turkey to End Travel Ban on Greek Cypriots . . . Qatar's Emir Gives Bush Arab View on Iraq

—*Associated Press, May 2003*

Viewed from the perspective of daily headlines, politics in the Middle East appear confused, chaotic, and often violent. When asked why they are interested in taking a course in Middle Eastern politics, students often say they want to be able to understand the news stories they listen to or read but don't know where to begin. This chapter focuses on the current political situation of the Arab world, Iran, Israel, and Turkey. It first describes several general factors that influence the contemporary Middle East, such as its colonial legacy, the evolving international context, and the level of economic development, and then reviews a variety of political institutions and ideologies that function in the region. Particular attention is given to clarifying those characteristics of Middle Eastern domestic politics that are relatively unusual, for example, the prevalence of ruling monarchies, from those attributes that are more common, such as close relations between the state and the military establishment. The critically important issue of gender, which is only touched on here, is treated more comprehensively in Chapters 9, 10, and 11.

■ The Colonial Legacy

Domestic politics in the Middle East are influenced by a paradox: this ancient region, with a history that dates back to the earliest years of human settlements, has only recently been organized politically into modern states, that is, centralized political units with sovereignty over a fixed territory and population. In Chapter 3, Arthur Goldschmidt describes the paths these countries took to reach the end of the twentieth century. This section briefly summarizes one of the most significant aspects of that history for understanding contemporary politics: the impact of European imperialism in the region.

The term *imperialism* refers to the establishment of political and economic control by one state or empire over a foreign territory. In the context of the Middle East, the involvement of European powers, particularly Britain and France, was highly interventionist and, from the perspective of regional history, often arbitrary. At the same time, there was considerable variation in the extent and nature of European control, both between subregions (e.g., North Africa versus the Arabian Peninsula) and also between adjacent areas within a single region (e.g., Syria versus Jordan). Decisions made during the colonial era had effects that persist until today and continue to influence the Middle East's political development well after the formal colonial systems have disappeared.

In contrast to the Americas, sub-Saharan Africa, and Asia, which were subjected to colonial exploitation after being "discovered" by Europeans, the geographical extent and the resources of the Middle East were known to the political powers of Europe for more than a thousand years. Prior to the middle of the nineteenth century, however, widespread colonial activity by Europe was blocked by the military power of the Ottoman Empire. When Europeans did begin to assert their authority, opportunistically as Ottoman control weakened, it occurred in the context of existing European imperial systems. The pattern of a single colonizer exercising control over a large contiguous territory—as with the British in North America and southern Asia or the Spanish in Latin America—did not occur, and so the colonial experience of states in the Middle East varied substantially across time and place.

Egypt provides an illustration of the political complexities of colonialism. At the beginning of the nineteenth century, Egypt was occupied by Napoleonic France. French forces were defeated by the British, who restored Ottoman control of Egypt; however, Ottoman rule was soon challenged by Mehmet (Muhammad) Ali—a soldier originally appointed by the Ottomans to administer Egypt—who began to develop Egypt as a powerful and autonomous state. Although they attempted to rule as monarchs, Ali's successors were unable to continue this independence and, in conjunction with construction of the Suez Canal, the country fell into deep debt to European financiers. These financial problems provided the pretext for a British invasion in 1882 and the consolidation of forty years of direct British control. In 1923, Britain granted nominal independence to Egypt but maintained the pro-British monarchy and reserved the right to station troops in the country (which it did during World War II as Germany sought to gain control of the Suez Canal). Even after the British-imposed monarchy was overthrown in 1952, Britain and France briefly invaded Egypt in 1956 in a final attempt to reassert European authority over the canal.

Although the details vary, similar intensity and intricacy of colonial involvement can be found in most of the major countries of the region. Most significant, British and French colonial interests competed throughout the region. On occasion this caused conflict between the European states, as with the Fashoda dispute in Sudan in 1898; at other times Britain and France agreed to sweeping divisions of authority, as with the Sykes-Picot Agreement in 1916, which divided up former Ottoman districts into modern-day Syria, Lebanon, Iraq, Jordan, Israel, and the Palestinian territories. Algeria was actually made an administrative part of France and won independence only through a long and costly war; Tunisia, too, was colonized by the French but its freedom came more easily. Europe and the United States considered the Gulf region peripheral during most of the period—allowing Abdul Aziz ibn Saud to assemble an independent state on the Arabian Peninsula without external interference—but it became important to the West in the 1930s with the discovery of oil. Although Britain and France were responsible for most of the colonial activity in the region, other European states—notably Italy in Libya and Russia in Iran—also exercised substantial influence.

These diverse colonial interactions left a patchwork of widely differing political circumstances. Probably the most extreme example can be found by comparing the experiences of Israel, Jordan, and Lebanon. The heavily populated parts of these countries occupy a small geographical area that, in the absence of borders, could be easily driven around by car in a day. But in the second half of the twentieth century, the experiences of the three countries could not be more different. Lebanon—in the French sphere of influence under the Sykes-Picot division—developed as a confessional parliamentary democracy that attempted to balance Muslim and Christian interests while maintaining the dominant position of the latter. Modern Israel developed out of a League of Nations mandate for Palestine—itself a relic of the Ottoman Empire—that under British control was promised as a "homeland" to the Zionist movement in the 1917 Balfour Declaration. Jordan was forged from another area under British control and politically constituted as an Arab monarchy ruled by a family from the Arabian Peninsula to whom Britain owed a favor. At the beginning of the twenty-first century, still another political entity—some form of Palestinian state between Israel and Jordan and between Egypt and Israel—struggles to emerge. Three (and potentially four) very different states have been established in an area that for most of its history was intertwined economically, culturally, and religiously.

As this example shows, the colonial experience, although relatively short-lived in the context of the entire history of the Middle East, has been critically important in determining the contemporary political environment. Differences between the North African states of Morocco, Algeria, Libya, and Egypt reflect (at least in part) the fact they were, respectively, under Arab, French, Italian, and British authority during the early twentieth century. When British prestige in the Gulf waned, it was smoothly replaced with U.S. influence, whereas the Algerian political system was strongly influenced by the bloody war for independence from France. A few countries—Morocco, Turkey, Saudi Arabia, and Oman—escaped direct European domination almost entirely (although they were still profoundly affected by the threat of this control), whereas others—Djibouti, for instance, or the Western Sahara, whose referendum on independence has been delayed repeatedly—are among the last areas in the world to achieve political sovereignty. As was true in Africa, the boundaries imposed by European powers often had little correspondence to the distribution of ethnic groups on the ground—most notably in the division of the Kurdish region between Turkey, Iraq, and Iran—or created states whose legitimacy could be called into question, as with Iraq's claims on Kuwait or Syria's claims on Lebanon. The colonial empires are gone, yet their effects not only linger but have substantial influence.

■ A Changing International Context

Following European decolonization during the 1940s, 1950s, and 1960s, the foreign affairs of the Middle East have been dominated by three major conflicts: the Cold War, the Arab-Israeli dispute, and the long-term war against Iraq. The first of these has now disappeared, but the second and third continue to have implications for the region's domestic politics.

The end of the Cold War and the dissolution of the Soviet Union had profound effects on Soviet allies such as Syria, Iraq, Libya, and the former People's Democratic Republic of Yemen (PDR Yemen). Those countries can no longer count on the former superpower for military or economic assistance (although Russia will still gladly sell arms for hard cash), nor is Russia interested in providing the preferential trade arrangements that were often used by the Soviet Union to secure alliances. Allies of the United States face an equally difficult situation. Opposing Communism was not a difficult agenda to sell to a Muslim population, although U.S. efforts under the Reagan administration in the 1980s to convince Arab states that their main enemy was the Soviet Union rather than Israel was a dismal failure. In the absence of the

"Communist threat," governments that are seen as too dependent on U.S. support may find that this policy generates significant domestic opposition, as both Egypt and Saudi Arabia have learned.

In contrast to the Cold War, the Arab-Israeli conflict continues, primarily between Palestinians and Israel. Egypt and Jordan have officially normalized relations with Israel, and visitors can now pass freely, if not easily, among these three countries. In 2000, Israel withdrew from southern Lebanon, ending nearly two decades of occupation. Syria, economically disadvantaged and deprived of Soviet support, can refuse negotiations on the Israeli-occupied Golan Heights, but it cannot force the issue militarily. With the Oslo Agreement of 1993, the election of Israeli prime minister Ehud Barak in May 1999, and the resumption of Israeli-Palestinian talks a few months later, there was a brief period when a genuine rapprochement between Palestinians and Israelis appeared likely. The disastrous Camp David talks in 2000, the subsequent outbreak of the second intifada (sparked by Ariel Sharon's provocative visit to the Haram al-Sharif/Temple Mount in September 2000), the failure of the Taba talks of January 2001, and the election of Ariel Sharon all contributed to the collapse of peace talks. As of September 2003, Israel had reoccupied much of the land it ceded to the Palestinians as part of the Oslo peace process and had begun to build a twenty-four-foot-high wall to separate West Bank Palestinians both from Israel and from their ancestral farm lands and water resources. (Mary Ann Tétreault, in Chapter 5, and Simona Sharoni and Mohammed Abu-Nimer, in Chapter 6, explore this issue more fully.)

The implications of these changes in the Arab-Israeli political landscape are likely to be profound in Israel. A common saying in Israel is that once its number one problem—relations with its neighbors—is resolved, then it will have to confront its number two problem: the nature of the Jewish state. Israelis face the challenge of violent Jewish fundamentalist movements, the rise of ethnically defined political parties, and heated debates on the extent to which the government should legislate religious practices (Kyle and Peters, 1993; Sprinzak and Diamond, 1993; Evron, 1995; Dowty, 1998). Ironically, as Israel is being reluctantly accepted in parts of the Arab world, its political problems are also coming to resemble those of its neighbors.

Jordan and Egypt, and perhaps someday Lebanon and Syria, must also accommodate the transformation of Israeli-Arab relations. With the Israeli threat removed, these states have more difficulty justifying politically the large militaries that absorb unemployed young males and provide patronage for political allies. At the same time, there has been little in the way of an economic "peace dividend": Israel markets its products globally, not locally, and joint economic ventures have been largely confined to tourism and a few conspicuous demonstration projects. Although an end of the Arab-Israeli conflict might bring peace to the region, it seems less likely to bring prosperity, at least initially.

In the long run—perhaps in another fifty years—the situation could prove more promising. A U.S. expatriate who spent most of his life in Ramallah, a town located just north of Jerusalem in the West Bank, loved to tell stories of the years before 1967, when he could go to Beirut for the weekend, and friends who lived in Jerusalem commuted daily to work in Amman. Those of us who have only lived in the era of a politically divided Middle East forget that the great cities of the Levant—Beirut, Damascus, Amman, Jerusalem, and Jaffa–Tel Aviv—are all within about a fifty-mile circle centered on the Sea of Galilee. If appropriate roads were in place and border controls removed, each could be reached easily in a morning's drive, much as Europeans can now move among Paris, Brussels, Bonn, and Amsterdam.

■ Economic Development

Like all decolonized areas, the states of the Middle East confront the problem of economic development. This issue will be covered in detail in Chapters 7, 8, and 9; here I point out several aspects that are most salient to domestic politics. (See Richards and Waterbury, 1996, for an extensive treatment of the Middle East's political economy through the mid-1990s; and Rivlan, 2001, for more recent analysis.)

Any discussion of economics must deal separately with states that have significant oil revenues and those that do not. The oil wealth of the era of the Organization of Petroleum Exporting Countries (OPEC) made possible policies of almost unimaginable extravagance—such as growing wheat in the desert using desalinated water—and the subsequent decline in the price of oil to pre-1973 levels (when adjusted for inflation) leaves a series of new political problems for the petroleum-based economies. In contrast, states that have little or no oil face a fairly conventional set of development issues, similar to those of any newly industrializing country.

The drop in oil revenues has created several sources of domestic instability. The most obvious issue is that governments have fewer funds available to deal with potential opponents of the regime, either by co-opting them or paying for the coercive power required to suppress them. (This is further complicated in the Arab monarchies because the line between state and private ownership is blurred and individual economic problems can have political implications.) These constraints occur when many states have had to reduce social services and subsidy programs, potentially decreasing support for the ruling elites. In a number of countries, economic restructuring programs mandated by the International Monetary Fund (IMF) in the 1980s and 1990s led to civil unrest as governments began eliminating food and gasoline subsidies on which poorer citizens relied.

A more subtle political change could also be under way. When oil revenues were abundantly available, most oil-rich states relied heavily on expatriate workers not only for menial labor but also for professional services such as banking, engineering, and education. Because they were foreigners, these individuals had no say in the politics of the host country. As citizens replace these expatriate professionals, a growing indigenous middle class will be created. If the Middle East follows the pattern of numerous other countries, pressures for greater democratic openness will follow. This has not yet occurred to a significant degree, but the potential is clearly present.

Outside the oil-rich states, the political problems of development differ little from those found elsewhere in the world. On average, the Middle East is neither unusually wealthy nor unusually poor, although there are extremes on either end: Turkey and Israel have achieved economic growth comparable to that of the successful Asian newly industrializing countries, whereas resource-poor Djibouti, Mauritania, Sudan, and Somalia have very limited prospects

Thomas Hartwell

More than 2 million people have been killed by fighting and famine during the civil war that has engulfed eastern and southern Sudan since the early 1980s. Millions more have lost their homes and must live in makeshift shelters like this one.

for development. International war has disrupted economic expansion in Iran, Iraq, and Kuwait; civil war has had the same effect in Lebanon and Algeria.

■ Informal Structures of Power

To fully understand the processes of Middle Eastern politics, one must look beyond the formal structures of governance—kings, emirs, parliaments, presidents, and prime ministers—which are discussed below. Of particular importance are the informal structures of family and social networks: the average citizen in the Middle East, whether Arab, Israeli, Turk, or Persian, finds these far more important in influencing political loyalties than would typically be the case for a citizen of North America or Western Europe.

The word that many Western analysts have attached to these networks is *tribes,* but this term is not particularly accurate since Middle Eastern political networks frequently do not differ in language, religion, or cultural traditions, attributes that are distinguishing characteristics of a tribe as the word is commonly used. (When such distinctions do exist, however—for instance, with the complex religious differences within Lebanon or the linguistically distinct Kurds—they usually translate into politically important alignments.) Instead, as Laurie King-Irani discusses in Chapter 10, the networks are usually based on extended families and geographical connections to a region or village.

Within these networks, linkages are first and foremost social or economic and only then political. However, as politics become more local, the strength of the existing social networks increases. As a consequence, political control can change at the top of the system with relatively little change at the bottom: Egypt was under foreign political control for 2,284 years—from the defeat of the last Pharaonic dynasty by Alexander the Great in 332 B.C.E. to the overthrow of British-supported King Farouk in 1952—yet in the villages of the Nile Delta or the neighborhoods of Cairo, a distinctly Egyptian style of local politics persisted. The Ottoman Empire recognized this aspect of Middle Eastern life and guaranteed local control of local issues through its *millet* system (which placed each religious community under the jurisdiction of its own religious authorities for most legal, social, and cultural affairs). In contrast, the efforts by European colonial powers to develop centralized and uniform governance frequently caused chaos.

At the same time, the old systems of social networks are less pronounced today than a century ago. Within the Middle East, rapid urbanization has disrupted and weakened centuries-old alliances based in isolated villages. Although immigrants to major cities such as Cairo, Istanbul, and Tehran are still influenced by family and village, new loyalties and affiliations challenge the older bonds. These traditional loyalties are further eroded by the migration of many expatriate workers—often the best and brightest young people of a generation—to jobs in the Gulf, Europe, or North America, where the old ties are difficult to maintain, particularly for an immigrant's daughters and sons born in a distant land.

Consequently, the contemporary Middle East sees a mix of traditional and modern political structures. King Fahd of Saudi Arabia and King Abdullah of Jordan, for instance, still base much of their power—particularly in the military and security services—on traditional systems of loyalty based on family and village. Most of former Iraqi leader Saddam Hussein's inner circle of advisers and administrators came from his home village of Tikrit; desert bedouins, not the Palestinians who form the majority of the population, dominate the Jordanian monarchy's security services and tribal groupings put forth political candidates to represent their distinct interests. In contrast, the economic elites of Beirut and Istanbul are more likely to follow a European model of social relationships, and some may, in fact, feel more comfortable in European circles than in Arab or Turkish social groups. This spills over into politics: these countries have large, European-style bureaucracies, flexible political patronage systems, and substantial (if interrupted) periods of parliamentary government.

However, the two systems can coexist. Within Israel, the Labor Party, which tends to attract individuals whose parents or grandparents immigrated to Israel from Europe, has a European-style system of flexible loyalties based on ideology. In contrast, the Shas Party, which emerged in the 1990s as a major player in Israeli politics, attracts voters from the ethnically Arab Jewish communities who immigrated from Morocco, Yemen, and Iraq. Shas places far greater importance on traditional relationships and political guidance from conservative rabbinical leaders. This tension between various styles of political organization is likely to be a pervasive factor in Middle Eastern politics for the foreseeable future.

■ The Myth of Political Instability

Early on, any discussion of the domestic politics of the Middle East that is directed to a Western audience must confront one of the most pervasive—but at the same time most conspicuously untrue—myths about the region: that governments in the Middle East are precarious and extremely changeable. Nothing could be further from the truth. In the past several decades, many have been extraordinarily stable. (This leaves open the question of whether the form this stability takes is or is not desirable.) Indeed, a meeting of Arab leaders held today would feature several of the same men who were in power in 1970: Muammar Qaddafi of Libya, Oman's Sultan Qaboos, Shaikh Zayid al-Nuhayyan of the United Arab Emirates (UAE), and Palestinian leader Yasser Arafat. Until his death from cancer in 1999, King Hussein of Jordan was the longest-ruling leader in the region, having served as king for nearly five decades. King Hassan II, who also died in 1999, had governed Morocco since 1961. Djibouti has had only two leaders since gaining independence in 1977: Hassan Gouled Aptidon, president until April 1999, and his nephew Isma'il Omar Guelleh, who was elected to succeed him. Saudi Arabia's King Fahd, Kuwait's Jabir al-Sabah, Yemen's Ali Abdallah Salih, and Egypt's Hosni Mubarak have each been in power for more than twenty years. A meeting of today's European leaders, in contrast, would have no individuals in common with a similar gathering held in 1970.

In addition, both Egypt and Saudi Arabia have handled transfers of power smoothly under the difficult conditions of assassination; Jordan, Oman, and Tunisia have replaced, more or less gracefully, leaders whose mental or physical condition had deteriorated; Syria, Qatar, and Bahrain each dealt with the death of a longtime leader and the transition to a new generation with apparent ease. The political system established in Turkey in the 1920s has survived to the present day and has been far more stable than the governments of European Mediterranean states such as Spain, Italy, Yugoslavia, and Greece during the same seventy-year period, notwithstanding three coups by the Turkish military. Significant revolutionary transformations have occurred—conspicuously, in Iraq (1958), Libya (1969), and Iran (1979) with the overthrow of Western-imposed monarchies—but even these changes were arguably no more dramatic than those that occurred in Eastern Europe and the Soviet Union in the late 1980s and early 1990s. Furthermore, the resulting governments have been substantially more stable than those in most of the successor states of the former Soviet Union.

To be sure, there are military interventions, irregular transfers of power, and internal political intrigues in the Middle East, but no more so than in Latin America or Southeast Asia and less so than in much of Africa. The Middle East probably did experience an unusual number of political upheavals in the years immediately following decolonization (as did almost every other newly independent region), but the norm since the mid-1960s has been continuity.

Although the political systems in the Middle East have generally been firmly established since the early 1970s, the region is currently facing a series of challenges brought on by political and economic changes in the global system. These occur at the same time that a number of the leaders in the region are growing old and facing health problems, most notably Fahd, Zayid, and Arafat. This natural aging of the postcolonial leadership—combined with a very large population of adolescents who have been exposed to the economic, political, and cultural currents of the global political economy—could lead to substantial changes in the coming decades; a prospect welcomed by some and feared by others. Indeed, this has already begun to occur: Jordan's King Abdullah, Bahrain's King Hamad ibn Isa al-Khalifah, Emir Hamad al-Thani of Qatar, and King Mohammed VI of Morocco are significantly younger than their fellow monarchs, as is Syrian president Bashar al-Assad.

■ Prospects for Democratization

With the virtual demise of Marxist-Leninist governments around the world, liberal democracy, characterized by the regular, open, honest electoral competition of political parties and protection of rights to organize politically, has become the dominant ideological basis for legitimizing political power. (The one possible competitor, the "Confucian capitalist" model of Asia, has no intrinsic appeal or cultural support in the Middle East.) The term *liberal democracy* reflects the union of two related processes: political liberalization and political democratization. Rex Brynen, Bahgat Korany, and Paul Noble explain:

> *Political liberalization* involves the expansion of public space through the recognition and protection of civil and political liberties, particularly those bearing upon the ability of citizens to engage in free political discourse and to freely organize in pursuit of common interests. *Political democratization* entails an expansion of political participation in such a way as to provide citizens with a degree of real and meaningful collective control over public policy.
>
> The distinction is an important one, since it is possible to have elements of one without the other. Political repression can be relaxed without expanding political participation. . . . Conversely, some political systems may claim widespread popular participation (for example, revolutionary regimes that empower previously marginalized groups) while restricting political freedoms (for example, repressing those deemed counterrevolutionary). (1995:3–4)

In contrast to many areas of the world that have successfully adapted Western liberal democratic structures and norms to local conditions (Japan, India, and Latin America, for instance), democratization poses several problems in the Middle East. Perhaps the most fundamental challenge lies in the preexistence of many democratic—but not *liberal* democratic—institutions in the region. The successful monarchies have maintained and expanded extensive traditional consultative structures and in Jordan, Kuwait, and Morocco have even established liberal democratic institutions, albeit with highly constrained powers. The revolutionary regimes base their legitimacy on mass political party structures, even though these have deteriorated into mere shells. Most countries in the region also hold regular elections for a nationally elected assembly. The importance of these "representative" institutions for governance varies considerably from state to state, but in countries as diverse as Morocco, Lebanon, Turkey, Bahrain, Iran, and Yemen—just to name a few—citizens remain willing to stand in long lines to cast their ballots on polling day.

Consequently, much of the Middle East, although not liberal democratic, is not totally devoid of structures for political participation (in contrast, for instance, to the military regimes of Latin America in the 1970s). The claim of a regionally constructed "Arab democracy" has some credibility. Nevertheless, the existing Middle Eastern models for liberal democracy all have significant flaws. The extreme secularism of Mustafa Kemal Atatürk's constitution for Turkey is not acceptable in the current environment of Islamic revivalism and is challenged even in Turkey itself. Lebanon's initial attempts at confessional democracy—a system that assumes religious affiliation is the primary factor in how society is organized politically and constitutionally ensures the power of various groups—led to a devastating civil war. As a non-Islamic state, and in the eyes of much of the region an illegitimate one, Israel does not appeal as a model.

However, the major liberal democratic powers have done little to encourage democracy in the region, notwithstanding U.S. rhetoric in the wake of the

In 1997, men waited in long lines in Sana'a to vote in
parliamentary elections, Yemen's second since unification.

2003 military campaign against Iraq. In the mid–twentieth century, Britain left absolute monarchies in place as it retreated. The United States has consistently tolerated undemocratic policies in its allies, including the monarchies of Saudi Arabia and Oman, the police state of Reza Pahlavi (the shah of Iran), and the single-party rule of Egypt. France's experiment in Lebanon failed, and France has been accused of complicity in the cancellation of elections in Algeria in 1992.

Given this set of circumstances, why should one expect that democratization would even be an issue in the Middle East? At least three factors suggest that it will be. First, the creation of a literate, urbanized middle class has consistently, in a variety of cultures, led to prodemocratic political movements. Second, the most dynamic economies of the region—Turkey, Israel, and pre–civil war Lebanon—have been democratic, a fact that has not gone unnoticed. Third, many of the conditions that supported and legitimized nondemocratic regimes—including postcolonial politics, the Cold War competition, and oil wealth—are declining in importance.

Most contemporary democratic theory (notably Putnam, 1993) emphasizes the importance of the institutions of "civil society" in buttressing liberal democracy. As Egyptian sociologist Saad Eddin Ibrahim explains:

> While there are a variety of ways of defining [the concept of civil society], they all revolve around *maximizing volitional, organized, collective participation in the public space between individuals and the state*. In its institutional form, "civil society" is composed of nonstate actors or nongovernmental organizations (NGOs), including political parties, trade unions, professional associations, community development associations, and other interest groups. Normatively, "civil society" implies values and behavioral codes of tolerating—if not accepting—others and a tacit or explicit commitment to the peaceful management of differences among individuals and collectivities sharing the same "public space"—that is, the polity. (1995:29)

Traditional Middle Eastern society already has a rich set of institutions and nonstate actors, including labor unions and political parties, that mediate between public and private space. These often exist in the nondemocratic context of the mosque, family, or clan but are not less valid (nor less valuable) for that reason. Informal arrangements also serve many of the same functions as formal civic institutions. A farmer does not need to form a cooperative when his village has been sharing in the task of the olive harvest for generations; a mother has less interest in forming a parent-teacher association when her child's instructor is a cousin she has known since birth. Transplanting Western institutions of civil society into the Middle East—an objective of many North American and European development projects—is like trying to pour coffee into a cup that is already full: very little new coffee will remain in the cup, and in the meantime one has created a mess.

Nonetheless, there will be challenges. Clearly any liberal democratic movement will need to accommodate Islam explicitly in some form. According to Arab democratic theorists, this presents few problems: many interpretations of Islamic theology are at least as sympathetic to democratic ideals as is Christianity (and are more so than the Hinduism of India, where nonetheless a thriving liberal democracy has been established). However, many of the most politically powerful trends in contemporary Islam are highly conservative, appealing to traditional institutions and seeking to institute antidemocratic cultural norms (for example, regarding the role of women).

Furthermore, any democratic movement must deal with the issue of ethnonational and religious minorities, an unresolved issue in Turkey, Iran, Iraq, Lebanon, Israel, and elsewhere. In addition to indigenous groups such as the Egyptian Coptic Christians and the Kurds, many of the smaller states have very large populations of "foreign" workers, some of whom have been resident for generations. Establishing the rights and roles of minorities is a problem even for established democracies, as the experiences of the United States, France, and Germany illustrate; it is more difficult still in states for which political independence is relatively new and liberal democracy is an experiment some already regard with skepticism.

■ The Role of the Military

Throughout the Middle East, the military has played (and continues to hold) a critical role in both the construction and the implementation of domestic policy; furthermore, the region is the most highly militarized in the world. Several factors, some specific to the area, others more generally applicable to newly independent states, explain why "the balance between governmental institutions of administration and coercion, on the one hand, and political structures, on the other" is tipped so strongly in favor of the former (Bill and Springborg, 1994:228).

First, neither the period of European colonization and occupation nor the political situation immediately after independence was conducive to the establishment of formal civic groups. Colonial powers, intent solely on exploiting the resources of the region, discouraged or suppressed indigenous institutions for fear that these would be used as centers of opposition to colonial rule. Many of these policies continued after independence, particularly when rulers had been installed by the departing European power or were supported through the anti-Communist agenda of the United States. When states were allied with the Soviet Union, the opposite problem occurred: most grassroots civic activity was channeled into officially recognized, state-controlled institutions, leaving little room for independent action.

Thus, the focus of social organization was on rapid modernization and the creation of a military capable of addressing internal and external threats to the fragile regimes. In both Turkey under Atatürk and in Iran under the Pahlavi dynasty, the government claimed its authoritarian rule was necessary to the economic development of the country. Elsewhere, civil and international conflicts—the Iran-Iraq War, the invasion of Kuwait, long-standing Arab-Israeli tensions, civil war in Sudan, Kurdish autonomy movements, and so on—provided a justification (some would argue an excuse) for a massive buildup of military forces throughout the region.

In 1999, the Middle East (including North Africa), with just over 5 percent of the world's population, accounted for more than 13 percent of the world's armed forces with 2.8 million soldiers (U.S. Department of State 2002:5). Countries like Oman, Qatar, and Saudi Arabia spend 10 percent or more of gross national product (GNP) on military expenditures. Through the 1980s and 1990s, the region accounted for an astonishing 40 percent of global arms imports, although most of these purchases were concentrated in a small number of countries: Saudi Arabia, Egypt, Israel, Kuwait, Iran, and the UAE. Saudi Arabia was by far the largest arms importer during this period, followed by Israel (which also has an indigenous arms industry). By the end of the 1990s, Middle East arms imports had declined somewhat, but still accounted for over 26 percent of total world imports in 1999 (U.S. Department of State 2002:9). Table 4.1 illustrates the overall military expenditures of Middle Eastern countries. The budgetary priority granted to defense spending in the Middle East has given greater political influence to the military, even in the domestic arena, than in countries in which the military establishment accounts for a much smaller portion of central government spending.

Second, military power frequently played a key role in the origins of the ruling regimes, resulting in a significant intertwining of the political and military elites. For instance, the unification of the central Arabian territory into the state of Saudi Arabia during the first three decades of the twentieth century can be attributed almost entirely to the military prowess of Abdul Aziz ibn Saud (although Ibn Saud also deserves credit for the political consolidation of the areas he conquered). In Algeria, the eight-year war of independence left the country virtually demolished, with the National Liberation Front (FLN) the one political-military institution that was intact and able to rule. Muammar Qaddafi came to power in Libya in 1969 through a military coup, and the military remains an important source of power for this leader.

During Israel's early years, the military was clearly associated with the Mapai (which later evolved into the Labor Party); thus the political and the military were inextricably associated. In recent years, the military has become more autonomous (especially with the decline in Labor's political dominance), but it is still quite powerful. The common military experience of vir-

Table 4.1   Military Expenditures of Middle Eastern Countries, 1999

Country	Total Expenditures (U.S.$ millions)	As % of GNP	Per Capita (U.S.$)	Armed Forces (per thousand people)
Algeria	1,830	4.00	60	3.9
Bahrain	415	8.06	666	14.5
Djibouti	23[a]	4.36	51[a]	18.0
Egypt	2,390	2.66	36	6.4
Iran	6,880	2.92	106	7.1[a]
Iraq	1,250	5.51	57	19.1
Israel	8,700	8.81	1,510	30.1
Jordan	725	9.15	150	21.1
Kuwait	2,690	7.73	1,410	11.0
Lebanon	653	3.96	185	16.4
Libya	n/a	n/a	n/a	17.0[a]
Mauritania	37	4.00	14	4.2
Morocco	1,450	4.26	49	6.6
Oman	1,780	15.34	726	15.5
Qatar	1,060	10.00	1,470	16.7
Saudi Arabia	21,200	14.93	43	8.9
Sudan	424	4.81	12	3.1
Syria	4,450	6.97	280	19.5
Tunisia	357	1.79	38	3.7
Turkey	9,950	5.32	154	12.2
United Arab Emirates	2,180[a]	4.07	935[a]	27.9
Yemen	374	6.05	22	4.1
United States	281,000	3.03	1,030	5.4

Source: U.S. Department of State, Bureau of Verification and Compliance, 2002:tab. 1.
Notes: a. Estimate.
n/a indicates data not available.

tually all Jewish Israeli citizens has left an indelible mark on that country's politics: high rank, preferably in a selective army unit, and combat experience in one or more of Israel's many wars are important attributes for success in the political arena, and all recent prime ministers have impressive military credentials.

Finally, in a number of countries, elite military units, combined with effective secret intelligence forces (in Arabic, *mukhabarat*), are essential in securing the regime against political opposition. This was certainly the case in Iraq under Saddam Hussein; some sixteen divisions of military intelligence, with varying degrees of power, were each responsible for a specific type of crime (Makiya, 1993:339). Admittance into the military academies required membership in the Iraqi Ba'th Party; once accepted, military personnel were expected to show absolute commitment to Iraq and to the dictates of the president. In the aftermath of the Gulf War, following Iraq's invasion of Kuwait in 1990, reports emerged of mutinies and high-level defections from the elite Republican Guard. However, the *mukhabarat* and other security services continued to function efficiently, which minimized organized opposition to the regime.

Often, a leader will assign relatives or long-term allies to handle critical security functions. Within the Saudi military establishment, close family members hold all the significant positions: the minister of defense is King Fahd's full brother Sultan, Sultan's deputy is his brother Turki, the minister of the interior is another full brother, and the National Guard is headed by Crown Prince Abdullah. Similarly, in Jordan an overwhelming majority of the military officers are from East Bank families with links to the royal family that go back to the earliest days of the state and before.

The implications of extensive military involvement in the governance of Middle Eastern countries are profound. When a regime must rely on the military to protect it from opposition movements, terrorism, or civil unrest, that regime becomes vulnerable to praetorianism, a situation in which "the civil authorities face constant threats from powerful military forces who try to shape all kinds of political decisions while remaining formally out of government" (Wilson, 1996:135). The repeated ultimatums given by the Turkish military in 1997 to force the resignation of Prime Minister Necmettin Erbakan, head of the Islamic Refah Party, illustrate how these pressures operate. Furthermore, "once they begin to perform the functions typically associated with parties, legislatures, and interest groups, . . . militaries render those political institutions irrelevant" (Bill and Springborg, 1994:235), which makes political liberalization all the more difficult.

Female soldiers participate in a military parade in Algiers, Algeria.

■ Political Ideologies and Institutions

As is true for most newly independent countries, the basic political challenge for the Middle East in the post–World War II era has been the task of state building: the creation of governments that are legitimate, stable, and capable of acting autonomously both regionally and globally (Hudson, 1977; Luciani, 1990). For a variety of reasons, this has not been easy. First, the current political structures of many Middle Eastern countries were imposed by outside powers, rather than resulting from a gradual, internally driven process. Thus the governments of these newly independent countries often lacked the political, economic, and social institutions and the widespread legitimacy that would have existed had the state-building activity begun at the grassroots level. In many countries, the presence of powerful multinational corporations (notably international petroleum companies) meant that the new states were immediately drawn into the global political economy without having the opportunity to determine the type of relationship that would be of greatest benefit to their own development. This, too, has made the tasks of governance more difficult.

A further complication has been "the blurred boundaries between [the] state and [the] collective, supra-state identity inspired by common Arab-Islamic culture, history, and vision" (Sela, 1998:4). As a result, there is a significant tension between the utopian dream of a united pan-Arab nation with a shared history, culture, and sense of common identity stretching from the Strait of Hormuz to the Atlantic and the practical dictates of more than twenty politically sovereign Arab states. In a different world, a single Arab nation-state might have emerged. The region is at least as ethnically cohesive as India, Russia, or Indonesia and is comparable in size. However, European colonial involvement and the competing interests of both indigenous and international elites prevented this outcome. Nonetheless, some Arabs view the existing political divisions as illegitimate and reject, for instance, the separation of Lebanon from Syria. In this context, they believe it is perfectly appropriate for one state to intervene in the internal affairs of another, since all are part of the greater Arab nation. From the Arab perspective, the contemporary nation-state model may always be a shoe that doesn't fit quite right, creating a blister or sore in one place or another.

■ Sources of Governmental Legitimation

Throughout the 1950s and 1960s, Arab leaders attempted to gain legitimacy in a variety of ways and with considerable ideological innovation (e.g., Ba'thism), balancing state-based claims with the aspirations of the Arab nation as a whole. By the early 1970s, two forms of governance—conservative monarchies and military or single-party revolutionary republics—dominated the political landscape. The traditional monarchies, such as those of the Arabian Peninsula, were strongly patriarchal, with the king or emir taking on the role of domineering yet benevolent father doing what he believes is best for his family. Constitutional monarchies like those of Jordan, Morocco, and Iran under the shah maintained the monarch as the ultimate political authority but also established elected legislatures with modest amounts of authority and developed significant governmental bureaucracies.

In contrast, some of the revolutionary states functioned under authoritarian personalistic leadership (most notably Libya, Syria, and Iraq), whereas others (e.g., Algeria, Egypt, Mauritania, Tunisia, and PDR Yemen) relied on the strength of a dominant political ideology, as expressed through a single political party, to provide support and legitimacy for the state leadership. The distinctions between these models should not be overstated, however; in the Middle Eastern context there are a variety of ways in which they overlap (see Anderson, 1991). Lebanon stands out as the one Arab country that had neither a king nor revolutionary leadership in the twentieth century. Its creation as an explicitly Christian-dominated Arab state, codified in the 1943 National Pact, made it unique.

Turkey, Iran, and Israel also do not fit neatly into either a monarchical or a revolutionary model. Yet they reflect the same pressures of political development and the struggles for governmental legitimacy that have influenced the entire region. The governments of both Turkey and Israel are products of late-nineteenth-century and early-twentieth-century liberal European ideologies such as nationalism that were superimposed onto a background of more traditional societies. In the creation of their political structures, both countries were inspired by Western-style political modernization approaches (in the case of

Guards hold back the crowds at a state rally in Tripoli, Libya. The large posters picture Qaddafi.

Turkey, due to its proximity to Europe; in Israel, as a consequence of its initial origins as a diaspora nationalist movement) rather than by the family-oriented, personalistic style of rule present in much of the region. Consequently, the Israeli and Turkish regimes are based on secular and formally democratic norms—although without the political integration of ethnic or religious minorities—and accept the principle of public accountability for the political leadership. In the 2000s, however, both countries were dealing with substantial challenges from groups seeking to radically redefine the role of religion within these states, as well as to challenge their liberal democratic nature.

▓ Political Islam

The political patterns established in the initial years of independence continue to exist today, although with some modifications in response to pressures for increased political liberalization (Norton, 1995). At the same time, in recent decades a new model—the Islamic republic—has mounted an increasingly significant challenge to the secular, nationalist ideologies used to legitimize both existing regimes and opposition movements in the revolutionary states. (John Esposito, Mohammed Muqtedar Khan, and Jillian Schwedler explore this issue in greater detail in Chapter 12.) This should not surprise us, for it mirrors two more globally general patterns.

First, people who see their world changing and feel that the values they hold dear are threatened, and believe that the government is not responding to their concerns, often turn to religion as a source of tradition and stability. Religious expression thus becomes a way to articulate frustration with the existing political structures. For instance, the twentieth-century founder of the Muslim Brotherhood, Hassan al-Banna (1906–1948), argued that the colonial domination of the region in the nineteenth and twentieth centuries was a direct result of the declining importance of Islam in the lives of ordinary people; a return to Islam would allow for an improved political situation. Second, individuals often focus on the political dimensions of religion when they perceive themselves as oppressed by the existing secular government. In the Middle East, there are a number of countries with "brutal and all-pervasive internal security structures" that create an atmosphere conducive to Islamic opposition movements (Bulliet, 1999:192).

Both elements were present in Iran under the rule of Pahlavi leader Mohammad Reza Shah. The shah combined extreme repression of opponents and claims of a historical right to rule with strongly Western-oriented modernization policies such as the White Revolution. A few years before the Iranian revolution that led to the establishment of the Islamic Republic, the shah held an incredibly expensive celebration linking his rule to that of the ancient Persian empire. This was regarded with great skepticism by the majority of the Iranian population and, in retrospect, illustrated the fragility of the shah's position. Unlike the Turkish and Israeli systems, the Iranian model ultimately proved unstable.

Although the first and most successful contemporary implementation of political Islam occurred at the edge of the Arab world, in Iran, the Islamic model has subsequently been applied in Sudan and Mauritania, presents a major challenge in Algeria, and has influenced political dynamics across the entire region, including among Palestinians, in Egypt, and in previously Christian-dominated Lebanon. While it may not dominate at the national level, political Islam's impact at the local level has been profound in many countries (Ismail, 2001). Islam's grounding in the impressive history of the region, its emphasis on the socioeconomic equity and justice promised but not achieved by the nationalist revolutionary ideologies, its comprehensive belief system, which gives guidance on virtually all aspects of life, and its extensive critique of Western goals and values are all crucial to understanding Islam's success as an instrument of political action.

▓ A Framework for Grouping Countries

As suggested above, governments in the Middle East can be roughly classified into one of four groups: nationalist revolutionary republics, monarchies, Islamic states, and conditional democracies. Nationalist revolutionary republics such as Algeria, Libya, Egypt, Syria, and Iraq are generally characterized by single-party rule with a strongly institutionalized state structure. Monarchies, whether traditional or parliamentary, include Jordan, Morocco, Saudi Arabia, and a number of small Gulf states. Turkey, Israel, and Lebanon are generally classified as democratic states, although each has elements that may call this into question, whereas Iran, Mauritania, and Sudan have labeled themselves Islamic republics (notwithstanding that Iran has significant democratic elements).

Of course, any such effort at classification is a static, imperfect reflection of reality; most countries' political institutions have elements of several different systems. For instance, the Islamic Republic of Iran holds regular and contested elections, and Islam plays a significant role in several of the revolutionary republics. This categorization does, however, provide a convenient way to discuss the diversity of forms that Middle Eastern governments take (see Table 4.2).

■ Nationalist Revolutionary Republics

For much of the twentieth century, the nationalist revolutionary state was one of the most important political models for the Middle East. Although the region suffered from its proximity to Europe by experiencing two centuries of

Table 4.2 Formal Political Participation in the Middle East, 2003

Country (year of independence)	Executive, Legislative System	Political Parties Legal?	Date of Female Political Suffrage	Date Females First Represented in Parliament
Algeria (1962)	President, National People's Assembly	yes	1962	1962
Bahrain (1971)	Absolute monarchy, appointed Consultative Council	no	2002	—
Comoros (1975)	Military coup, May 1999	no	1956	1993
Djibouti (1977)	President, Chamber of Deputies	yes	1946	2003
Egypt (1922)	President, prime minister, National Assembly	yes	1956	1957
Iran (1925)	Supreme religious leader, president, Islamic Consultative Assembly	no	1963	1963
Iraq (1932)	President, National Assembly	yes	1980	1980
Israel (1948)	President, prime minister, National Assembly	yes	1948	1949
Jordan (1946)	King, prime minister, National Assembly	yes	1974	1989
Kuwait (1961)	Emir, National Assembly	no	a	a
Lebanon (1943)	President, prime minister, Chamber of Deputies	yes	1952	1991
Libya (1951)	General, General People's Assembly	no	1964	n/a
Mauritania (1960)	President, prime minister, Parliament	yes	1961	1975
Morocco (1956)	King, prime minister, National Assembly	yes	1963	1993
Oman (1951)	Absolute monarchy, partially elected Consultative Council	no	2003	2000[b]
Palestinian Territories[c]	President, prime minister, Legislative Council	yes	1996	1996
Qatar (1971)	Emir, elected advisory Municipal Council	no	1999	—
Saudi Arabia (1932)	Absolute monarchy, appointed Consultative Council	no	d	d
Somalia (1960)	National Assembly	e	e	e
Sudan (1956)	President, National Assembly	no	1964	1964
Syria (1946)	President, People's Council	yes	1953	1973
Tunisia (1956)	President, prime minister, Chamber of Deputies	yes	1959	1959
Turkey (1923)	President, prime minister, Grand National Assembly	yes	1934	1935
United Arab Emirates (1971)	Federation of emirates	no	d	d
Yemen (1990)[f]	President, National Assembly	yes	1967[g]	1990

Source: UNDP, 1998:168–169, 194; data on executive and legislative systems—except for Comoros, Djibouti, Qatar, Somalia, and the United Arab Emirates—from Levine, 1998:16.

Notes: a. Women do not have suffrage or the right to stand for election. In 1999, the emir of Kuwait issued a decree giving women full political rights, but it has not yet been ratified by parliament.

b. Women were appointed to a nonelected consultative council before they received formal suffrage.

c. Not yet recognized as independent.

d. Neither women nor men have suffrage or the right to stand for election.

e. After many years of civil war, Somalia now has an interim government. It is unclear what form the government will take, but women were originally granted suffrage in 1956.

f. Date refers to unification of the Yemen Arab Republic and PDR Yemen.

g. Refers to the former PDR Yemen.

n/a indicates data not available.

colonial intervention and interference in the development of regional politics, this proximity provided at least one possible compensating advantage: intense exposure to the intellectual currents that accompanied the consolidation of the modern industrialized state in Europe, notably nationalism, political liberalism, and socialism.

As Arthur Goldschmidt outlines in Chapter 3, the "Arab awakening" (Antonius, 1946) began in the early to middle 1800s and culminated in a series of independence and self-determination movements in the twentieth century. Due to the constraints of colonialism, few of these ideas could be implemented prior to the 1950s, but the intellectual groundwork existed, at least some of the relevant political writings were in Arabic, and the literature spoke to the region's history (Khalidi, 1991; Tibi, 1997). In this respect the Middle East was in a quite different situation than Asia or sub-Saharan Africa, which were relatively isolated from European political developments by the sheer impact of physical distance in the days before telecommunications.

The first successful twentieth-century nationalist movement in the Middle East, that of Atatürk following the end of World War I, shows the effects of these influences. Atatürk's single most dramatic innovation—the secularization of Turkey—was completely consistent with liberal revolutionary movements from the U.S. and French Revolutions forward. Although Atatürk was reluctant to share power, he did support the adoption of European political forms, such as a parliamentary system with a prime minister and cabinet chosen from the unicameral Grand National Assembly. This meant that the necessary structures for participatory government were in place after Atatürk's death.

In contrast, early efforts by the intelligentsia and the middle classes in Iran to limit the power of the Qajar monarchy and give control to an elected assembly failed. By the mid-1920s, Reza Khan, who founded the relatively short-lived Pahlavi dynasty, had replaced the Qajar ruler. Reza Khan and his son Mohammad Reza Pahlavi combined social, economic, and military modernization with repression and authoritarian rule. Little was done to nurture the nascent parliament or develop other democratic institutions (Halliday, 1979).

Another three decades passed before the process of state building commenced in the Arab Middle East, but when decolonization began in earnest in the 1950s, significant ideological movements were ready and waiting to challenge the immediate postcolonial political structures imposed by Britain, France, and the United States. Thus the 1950s and 1960s saw a proliferation of alternative political approaches, often incorporating Islamic political values and histories into a formally secular framework. Much to the distress of the former colonizers, most of these new ideologies drew as much from the theories of Karl Marx and V. I. Lenin as on those of Thomas Jefferson and John Locke. As a consequence, they emphasized a strong, centralized, and bureaucratized state, a characteristic that persists to this day even in countries that have in other ways moved away from this approach.

When viewed in the context of the 1950s and 1960s, there are several reasons for the appeal of progressive and centralized approaches to politics, none of which have anything to do with "Arab exceptionalism" or a distinctly Middle Eastern respect for strong leadership. First, the consolidation of state power was consistent with the prevailing Western political trends in government. During the previous two decades, the liberal democracies of Western Europe and North America had increasingly centralized authority, initially to counter the effects of the Great Depression and then to mobilize their economies for World War II. Both Marxists and progressive political theorists argued that such an expansion in central governmental authority was necessary to counter the economic power of industrialized capitalism.

Second, elements of the Soviet Union's Communist model were initially quite attractive. In a mere twenty-five years, the Soviet Union had gone from a quasi-feudal society to an industrialized power capable of withstanding the military assault of one of the most advanced European economies during World War II. It had survived the Great Depression, which had devastated most of the capitalist world, and in the 1950s the toll that Stalin's brutal policies had extracted from the Soviet people was not widely known or understood. Thus, varieties of socialism were appealing not just in the Arab world but in every area undergoing decolonization (e.g., China, Vietnam, Cuba, and parts of Africa). It is likely that socialism would have been implemented even more widely than it actually was if not for the efforts of the U.S. Central Intelligence Agency (CIA) and other Cold War agents of containment.

Finally, it was the political left rather than the right that had consistently opposed colonialism. As discussed below, the monarchies, without exception, allied themselves with the colonial powers or their successor, the United States. Even in the era of colonialism, progressive and socialist groups had provided greater assistance in the anticolonial cause than had the liberal democracies. Two of the most conspicuous of the European liberal democracies—Britain and France—had been the two most conspicuous meddlers in Arab affairs. Although the United States might have been able to exploit its anticolonial policies to promote a liberal democratic agenda (as it did during the 1956 Suez crisis), it consistently subordinated such a goal to the pursuit of a simple anti-Communist agenda. The CIA overthrow of Iran's Mohammad Mossadeq in 1952, anti-Nasserist policies following the Suez crisis, the 1958 military intervention in Lebanon, and the deepening U.S. military activity in Indochina by the mid-1960s ended any anticolonial credibility the United States might once have had.

A full discussion of the diverse intellectual currents in Arab political thought during this period would fill several dozen books (and has). Here I will summarize the tenets of two ideological approaches that had a significant impact in the Middle Eastern political arena—Ba'thism and Nasserism—before turning to a brief discussion of the contemporary situation of three of the nationalist revolutionary republics: Egypt, Tunisia, and Syria.

Ba'thism

The Ba'th Party is one of the only political movements that is truly indigenous to the Arab world. In the 1940s the Arab Ba'th Party was founded by two Syrians, Greek Orthodox Michael Aflaq (who was the group's intellectual leader) and Sunni Muslim Salah al-Din al-Bitar (who served as the political strategist). This group merged in 1953 with a second organization, the Arab Socialist Party, to create the Arab Socialist Resurrection Party, also known as the Ba'th Socialist Party. The first members of the Ba'th Party came primarily from the intellectual elite, but the Ba'th quickly gained support among disadvantaged groups and established itself as a mass movement.

The basic Ba'thist ideology embraced a set of principles that drew on both traditional and modern sources of legitimacy in the Arab world: history, religion, nationalism, development, freedom, and socialism. Most important, Ba'thism called for social reform and economic justice, to be achieved through Arab socialism. In his writings, Aflaq resisted the temptation to rely exclusively on European socialist thinkers, with their emphasis on class struggle. Instead, he emphasized that the Ba'thist economic model was neither capitalist nor Communist: it was a middle way that was the product of the Arab world's unique history. A second key element of Ba'thism was its emphasis on pan-Arab unity, which was understood to involve the unification of existing Arab states into a single political entity as a replacement for patriotism centered on a specific state. Third, Ba'thism was anti-imperialist and anti-Zionist; it stressed the achievement of true Arab independence from all forms of colonialism.

Finally, Ba'thism called for a toleration of religious minorities within an overall Arab-Islamic political framework that included representative government and civil rights. Aflaq maintained that Islam was a "historically formative force but one with no specific contemporary ideological or political role" (Bill and Springborg, 1994:73). As a result, Ba'thism could appeal both to the majority Muslim population and to Christians who would be left out of a more explicitly Islamic formulation of nationalism. The Ba'th Party is the dominant political actor in Syria, remains important in post-Saddam Iraq, and plays a more minor role in Jordan, Lebanon, and elsewhere.

Nasserism

Gamal Abdul Nasser was part of the Free Officers group who engineered the 1952 coup in Egypt that overthrew King Farouk. By the end of 1954,

Nasser had begun to consolidate his position as president, prime minister, and head of the Revolutionary Command Council, which controlled Egyptian political life. To maintain power, the charismatic Nasser created a strong state bureaucracy and a variety of nationalist institutions, such as the Arab Socialist Union (ASU), that he could dominate. Nasser's pan-Arab ideals and increasing interest in leftist ideologies evolved into a political and socioeconomic doctrine that came to be known as Nasserism.

Nasser maintained that socialism had to be adapted to the specific needs of Egypt rather than following the antireligious Marxism of the European states. In part as a way of responding to the Muslim Brotherhood, Nasser attempted to root his economic approach in the Islamic ideal of equitable economic distribution: "The Islamic ideal meant a society without injustice, which meant freedom from hunger, want and exploitation, which in turn implied common ownership of the means of production and a planned society. Within the framework of national unity all would be encouraged to cooperate for the national good" (Hopwood, 1985:100).

Unlike Ba'thism, however, "Nasserism was not a well-conceived thesis by one or more ideologues, but emerged as an ideology out of a series of practical responses to the problems, domestic and foreign, that Egypt . . . faced as it tried to consolidate its newly won political and economic independence" (Hiro, 1996:217). Thus its impact as a political movement declined after Nasser's death, and many of the Nasserist parties that had been established outside of Egypt collapsed.

■ States Dominated by a Single Party

Very few countries in the Middle East have genuine multiparty political systems. Instead, many have a single "government" party that dominates the political landscape and a set of ineffectual, often restricted, opposition parties that have little ability to influence the political direction of the country.

In this sense, Egypt is the quintessential model of a single-party bureaucratized state. Egypt's 1971 Constitution, as amended in 1990, identifies the country as a democratic, socialist Arab republic. It calls for a strong president, supported by a National Assembly of at least 350 people (currently there are 444 elected and 10 appointed representatives). The Egyptian National Assembly nominates the president; that name is then put to the general population in a national referendum. The person is declared president if the nomination is approved by a simple majority of those voting. Originally the constitution stipulated that the president could hold only two six-year terms, but President Anwar Sadat had this article amended to state that the president could be reelected for an unspecified number of terms. In 1999, Hosni Mubarak was "elected" for a fourth six-year term.

During the period between Egypt's independence in 1922 and the Free Officers' coup in 1952, a limited multiparty system was put in place. For the next twenty-five years, the ASU was the only legal political party. When it was dissolved in 1977, shortly after Sadat announced Egypt would return to a multiparty system, it was replaced by the National Democratic Party (NDP), which has continued to dominate Egyptian politics (see Korany, 1998). In 1984, multiparty elections were held for the first time, and there are now more than ten recognized groups in addition to the ruling NDP. However, opposition representation in the assembly is trivial; all the opposition parties together won only fourteen seats in the November 1995 national elections, which were marred by boycotts and widespread accusations of fraud and intimidation. In the 2000 elections, independents and opposition parties did better, receiving ninety-one seats; however, this still represented only a negligible challenge to the dominance of the NDP. Furthermore, the government consistently represses efforts at founding an Islamic political party.

The Egyptian political system has survived two crises that might well have led to its demise: the death of the charismatic Nasser three years after Egypt's disastrous military defeat by Israel in 1967 and the assassination of Sadat in 1981. The highly bureaucratized nature of the state, the combination of co-optation and control of opposition parties, extremely limited moves toward political liberalization, and economic liberalization (the relaxation of state controls on the economy so that markets can play a greater role) have kept the governmental system established by Nasser essentially intact, even though Nasserism as an ideology has faded. The question is whether Egypt is

Egyptian president Hosni Mubarak has been in power since 1981.

in the midst of a democratic transition, or if, as Eberhard Kienle (1998) argues, it is in the process of deliberalization and has actually become less democratic than it was in the 1980s.

Tunisia provides another example of a formally multiparty state in which a single party completely dominates politics. As in Egypt, Tunisia's first leader after independence and the abolition of the monarchy was a strong, authoritarian figure who was able to set the direction for the country. President Habib Bourguiba claimed he "invented" Tunisia, and indeed his impact over three decades was enormous. According to the 1959 Constitution, Tunisia is a "presidential republic" in which the president has much more power than the elected National Assembly. Under Bourguiba, Tunisia implemented a secular, Western-style legal system and, until the 1970s, pursued socialist-style economic development. Grassroots political participation was channeled through what was for many years Tunisia's only legal political party: the Neo-Destour Party and its successor, the Destour Socialist Party.

In the 1980s, serious economic difficulties brought on by economic liberalization led to riots and instability in Tunisia. Advisers urged Bourguiba to open up the political process, but he refused and instead became highly repressive, directing particular attention to leaders of the opposition Islamic Tendency Movement (MTI). Eventually, the situation became so serious that Prime Minister Zine Abidine Ben Ali overthrew Bourguiba in a bloodless coup that took advantage of a part of the Tunisian Constitution specifying that if the head of state is incapacitated, the prime minister should perform the job:

> Ben Ali's November 7, 1987, coup inaugurated the heady period of political reform that swept across the Middle East and North Africa in the 1980s. The new president promised to establish the rule of law, to respect human rights, and to implement the kind of democratic political reforms that Habib Bourguiba had steadfastly refused. Along with Algeria, Jordan and Yemen, Tunisia rode the leading edge of what many hoped would be a wave of democratic transitions in the region. (Alexander, 1997:34)

President Ben Ali, who was elected to a five-year term in 1989 and reelected in 1994 and 1999, publicly committed himself to introducing genuine political pluralism in Tunisia. However, this has not occurred. Tunisia does have a multiparty political system, with at least five opposition political parties that have been approved to compete for limited representation in the National Assembly; however, significant repression of Islamic political groups remains. Hizb al-Nahdha (Party of the Renaissance), the successor to the MTI, is widely described as reformist rather than revolutionary and has indicated its willingness to work within the rules of a competitive, representative democracy; despite this, it continues to be excluded from the electoral process. On several occasions, opposition groups have boycotted national elections, arguing that the electoral system is heavily biased in favor of the government. Electoral results tend to support this contention. Thus Tunisia, like Egypt, remains de facto a single-party state, despite its formal multiparty label.

■ Personalistic Systems

The distinction between single-party and personalistic states is not sharp, as James A. Bill and Robert Springborg make clear in their description of personalism:

> Middle Eastern societies and political systems grew out of tribal constellations, and the personalism that prevailed in the family and the clan has had a pervasive and protracted influence. The Middle Eastern leader has led by virtue of his personal relations with his followers. Formal organizations and institutions have seldom effectively intervened. Even when institutions such as formal bureaucracies have developed, the real business of ruling and political decision making has resided in personal networks. (1994:160)

Current examples of this style of rule include Syria, Libya, and Iraq under Saddam Hussein, all with strong leaders who govern as dictators despite the formal presence of legislative bodies.

Until recently, Syria's political system combined Ba'thism and a cult of personality around President Hafez al-Assad. Syria gained independence as a republic in 1946 after twenty-six years under a mandate granted to France by the League of Nations. With little experience as a modern autonomous entity, Syria experienced tremendous political instability: between 1949 and 1954 there were four military coups. After Syria's short-lived and disastrous merger with Egypt between 1958 and 1961, the Ba'thists achieved a dominant position within the Syrian government as a result of the March 1963 military coup and have remained in control ever since. Hafez al-Assad assumed power in 1970 in a bloodless coup and became president in 1971, holding that position until his death on July 17, 2000. His son Bashar succeeded him and the ubiquitous posters with Hafez al-Assad's smiling face that once filled shop windows throughout Syria have been replaced by equally ubiquitous posters featuring Hafez and Bashar together, Bashar alone, or the two and Basel, Hafez's favorite son who was killed in a car accident.

According to the 1973 Constitution, Syria is a socialist and democratic republic with a strong president and legislation based on Islamic law. Presidential elections are held every seven years; however, only one candidate appears on the ballot. There is some involvement of the population in governance of the country through a 250-person People's Assembly that approves the national budget and responds to laws issued by the Ba'th Central Committee. In recent years, several minor political parties have served as a token "loyal opposition" to the dominant Ba'th Party and are represented in the assembly.

Syria has been relatively stable for the past three decades, especially when compared with its early years of independence. This stability can be attributed to a number of factors, including "the fact that Syria was dominated by only one all-powerful political faction with a highly reliable and effective security apparatus" (Van Dam, 1996:137). The severe economic crisis of the 1980s, with its potential for political repercussions, was alleviated somewhat by the transition away from a statist economy and toward economic liberalism (Melhem, 1997; see also Kienle, 1994). Nevertheless, there are several serious potential challenges to the legitimacy of the regime, particularly from the Muslim Brotherhood, which has attempted to overthrow the regime on several occasions, most dramatically in an uprising in the city of Hama in 1982. Furthermore, the same continuity of leadership that has lent stability to the regime could create difficulties in the future since few of the political and military elite are young.

■ Traditional and Parliamentary Monarchies

The Middle East is the only area of the world where traditional monarchies (as distinct from constitutional monarchies, which exist in parts of Europe) have persisted in a number of states. At times, this has been used to label the domestic politics of the region "medieval" or even "primitive." A closer look suggests that the monarchical regimes might better be characterized as an adaptation of established forms of patrimonial leadership to the contemporary nation-state system (see Weber, 1947). Drawing on a variety of traditional sources of legitimacy such as custom, a history of family governance, ancestral ties to the prophet Muhammad, a leader's personal attributes, and the royal family's role as a symbol of nationalism, the current Arab monarchies have proved remarkably resilient.

This persistence is particularly striking when we recall that in the 1950s and 1960s six monarchies were unable to survive the critical postcolonial period and were removed from power: Egypt, 1952; Tunisia, 1956; Iraq, 1958; Yemen, 1962; South Arabia (which became PDR Yemen), 1967; and Libya, 1969. Yet since 1969 only a single additional monarchy—the Pahlavis of Iran—has been overthrown, suggesting that the remaining royal rulers have found ways to repress democratic sentiment, co-opt opposition movements, or otherwise adapt their rule to address, at least minimally, popular pressures for political reform.

Thus the challenge for the Arab monarchies today is less one of validating the legitimacy of their political control through tradition and more one of "establishing a linkage with modernity," as Michael C. Hudson argued nearly thirty years ago (1977:230). Sociopolitical structures such as the *diwan* (informal gatherings in the homes of elites at which there is wide-ranging discussion regarding contemporary issues), along with the Islamic concept of *shura* (consultation), have allowed for a fair amount of grassroots input without moving to a liberal-democratic model. "Institutional flexibility and inclusiveness," among other attributes, have aided the Arab monarchies in the process of state formation (Anderson, 2000:55). Furthermore, significant economic resources have made it possible in some instances to buy off the opposition (Gause, 1994, 2000). In addition, all of these states have chosen to align themselves politically with the West. In the name of anticommunism (originally) or anti–Islamic revivalism (currently), the United States in particular has been willing to supply the Arab ruling elites with whatever weapons and expertise they require to maintain internal security.

In four countries—Bahrain, Kuwait, Morocco, and Oman—the same extended family has held political power for more than 200 years. The current ruling family in Oman has governed the coast of the country (although not the interior) since 1749; Sultan Qaboos became the leader in 1970 when he overthrew his father in a bloodless coup that was supported by the British. The Sabah family of Kuwait trace their rule back to the early 1700s, when a group of formerly nomadic clans settled along the northeastern Arabian coast; the related al-Khalifah family established its authority in Bahrain in 1782 after defeating the Iranians who had previously controlled the islands.

The most enduring Arab regime is found in the kingdom of Morocco. Monarchical government in that country dates back twelve centuries. The Alawi family, which traces its roots to the prophet Muhammad, came to power in the 1660s and consolidated its control over virtually all of modern-day Morocco in the early 1700s. Unlike most of the Arab world, Morocco escaped both European and Ottoman colonialism. After a brief period of Spanish and French control in the early twentieth century, Morocco regained its independence in 1956 and is now governed by King Mohammed VI, who succeeded his father, King Hassan II, in July 1999. The Moroccan regime consequently fits into a small set of states in which a long-standing monarchy has been able to resist the inroads of colonialism and emerge intact in the postcolonial period. (Ethiopia, prior to the overthrow of Haile Salassie, and Siam/Thailand are two other examples of this unusual pattern.)

The other Arab monarchies are either the result of twentieth-century consolidations of power, as in the case of Saudi Arabia, or are relatively recent "dynasties" that gained their political position either in part (Qatar, the UAE) or entirely (Jordan) from the assistance of the retreating colonial powers. In the 1800s the British signed treaties with a variety of local leaders in the Gulf, adopting a policy of indirect rule and support for the specific families with whom they negotiated agreements. This served to reinforce the position of the Gulf's ruling families and convert them into "royalty," who then took over full control of the newly independent countries when the British withdrew from the Gulf.

Some of these artificially created dynasties failed due to incompetence, as in Iraq, where neither of the two successors to King Faisal I were able to hold the country's diverse population together. Others, such as the Idris regime in Libya, were never accepted by the population on whom they were imposed and could not survive in power once European support was withdrawn. In non-Arab Iran, the Pahlavi dynasty, which replaced the Qajar dynasty in a bloodless coup in the 1920s, maintained control only with the support of the CIA and was eventually overthrown.

Aspects of Arab Kingship

The Arab concept of kingship differs significantly from the European model. Hudson notes that "the ideal Arab monarchy, perfectly legitimized, . . . would be an Islamic theocracy governed by the ablest leaders of a tribe tracing its lineage to the Prophet." Legitimacy in general must be earned by capable leadership, and "there are no strongly legitimized succession procedures—neither inheritance nor election—in Arab culture" (1977:167).

These criteria lead to two significant differences between the European and Arab institutions of monarchy. First, the conflict between the monarchy and the political power of the church that characterized so much of the European feudal system has no counterpart in the Arab world. The authority of an Arab monarch still can be challenged on religious grounds, as occurred with the revolt in Arabia of the religiously fundamentalist Ikhwan (brethren) against Abdul Aziz ibn Saud in the late 1920s. But there is no Islamic "pope" (or Confucian bureaucracy) to whom a monarch can appeal for legitimacy independent of his own religious authority, or conversely, who can threaten a monarch by withholding approval.

Second, the absence of a widely recognized succession procedure limits the development of the extended family dynasties such as the Hapsburgs in Austria (r. 1282–1918) and the German-English House of Hanover. The status of sharif—a descendant of the prophet Muhammad—enhances the legitimacy of a ruler, but at any given point there are hundreds or thousands of potential leaders with this designation. Consequently, being a sharif does not carry the same power as being the eldest son of a king would in Europe, and marriage into such a family does not by itself guarantee that someone can claim political control.

As a result, Arab monarchies do not generally show the pattern—common in Europe—of a weak or decadent leader (for example, George III of Great Britain or Louis XVI of France) being kept in power in order to preserve the traditions that also legitimize the power of organized religion and the lower nobility. An ineffective or otherwise problematic ruler can be replaced by a family member—as happened in modern times in Oman and Qatar—without threatening the legitimacy of the entire regime.

Furthermore, because the ruler must demonstrate leadership and piety, he must be accessible to the population through a wide range of traditional institutions. For instance, shortly after he became king in 1999, Abdullah II of Jordan disguised himself as a taxi driver, left behind his bodyguards, and drove around Amman listening to ordinary citizens complain about the government. This unusual action, reminiscent of Abdullah's father, King Hussein, in the early years of his reign, was widely acclaimed and echoed the legends of great Arab monarchs in classical times who would leave their palaces disguised as beggars and roam the streets and marketplaces to assess public opinion. The "absolute" power of the Bourbons of France or the Romanovs of Russia— who ruled in nearly complete isolation from the populations of their territories—has no counterpart in Arab tradition. (This is of particular note because "Orientalist" images often ascribe to the Arab monarch greater unfettered power than that found in European monarchies.)

One disadvantage of this system is that Arab monarchies are potentially more vulnerable than European monarchies to leadership crises upon the death of a ruler because the line of succession may be less well established. Furthermore, because the system is entirely patrilineal, half the population is excluded from direct power. Although the Arab system has avoided weak kings such as George III of England and Nicholas II of Russia, it has also never produced strong queens such as Elizabeth I and Victoria of England or Catherine the Great of Russia.

■ Saudi Arabia

Among the Gulf states, Saudi Arabia is clearly the most powerful; it is "also the most inscrutable" to non-Saudi "researchers and reporters [who are] all but barred from the country while American soldiers and oil company staff live inside fenced compounds" (Carapico, 1997:1). Widespread restrictions on civil rights and political freedoms further limit knowledge about the kingdom. Officially, King Fahd, the fourth son of the country's founder Abdul Aziz ibn Saud, serves as monarch and rules Saudi Arabia. Due to Fahd's extensive health problems, however, his half brother, Crown Prince Abdullah, has taken on increasing responsibilities in recent years.

Drawing on its considerable political and economic resources, the Saudi leadership has consistently argued that it has pursued domestic policies in support of modernization and development with an emphasis on cooperation, negotiation, and compromise that is consistent with the Quran. Nonetheless, the royal family has not been immune to criticism and threats to its political legitimacy. Opponents of the regime—whether secular or religious—maintain that the oil wealth has been used to enrich the Saudi family more than the country as a whole, that the government is corrupt, and that the refusal of the House of Saud to share power is non-Islamic. There is also dissatisfaction among many with the close ties between Saudi Arabia and the United States.

Shortly after the Gulf War, a group of Western-educated intellectuals tried to persuade the king to introduce democratic reforms in Saudi Arabia: the creation of a constitutional monarchy, greater respect for human rights, and the opportunity for political parties and universal suffrage. In response, a number of religious leaders urged Fahd instead to transform Saudi Arabia into a fully Islamic state along the lines of Iran. In an attempt to quell this nascent dissent, in February 1992 King Fahd announced the establishment of a sixty-man *majlis al-shura* (consultative council) whose appointed members were drawn from the professional, academic, religious, business, and retired military elites of the country. In July 1997, the king appointed a new *majlis* and expanded its membership from sixty to ninety persons. In the current *majlis,* 37 percent are academics (from both religious and secular institutions), 43 percent are bureaucrats and professionals, and 20 percent are businessmen, police, diplomats, and military personnel (Dekmejian, 1998:209). The council can propose legislation; however, its actions have no binding force.

At the same time that the initial consultative council was created, Fahd also reorganized the provincial system of government and proclaimed a new Basic Law that, among other changes, provided a revised procedure that makes the grandsons as well as the sons of Abdul Aziz eligible for royal succession. The latter was extremely important, given that there are no clear rules for how power is passed within any of the Gulf's ruling families. Crown Prince Abdullah is only two years younger than King Fahd, and it is not at all clear who will be named crown prince when Abdullah becomes king.

■ States of the Arabian Peninsula

The remaining monarchies of the Arabian Peninsula have several attributes in common. They are all relatively small in terms of both land and population, with little arable land; each has a significant expatriate population that is responsible for much of the economic activity; and all rely on petroleum and natural gas for a significant portion of their export revenue. The rulers of each country face internal pressures for political liberalization; most have chosen to respond cautiously by lifting some restrictions on speech and the media, decentralizing the government and giving greater power to individual ministries, establishing elected or appointed consultative councils, and introducing constitutions. At present, however, none of the Gulf states permits political parties.

Qatar, Oman, and the UAE. Similar to Saudi Arabia in some ways, Qatar is a religiously conservative, traditional emirate, ruled by Hamad ibn Khalifah ibn Hamad al-Thani, who ousted his father, Khalifah, in a nonviolent coup on June 27, 1995. In this wealthy emirate, the decisions of the monarch are binding, and members of the al-Thani family hold many of the significant political positions: the prime minister is Hamad's brother Abdullah, the deputy prime minister is another of Hamad's brothers, and the foreign minister is his cousin and brother-in-law. Hamad, who is significantly younger than the other Gulf leaders (except for Bahrain's Hamad ibn Isa al-Khalifah), sees himself as a modernizing ruler. He has allowed for increased political debate in the public arena and has begun to enfranchise the population: on March 8, 1999, some 23,000 Qatari women and men voted in the first-ever elections for a twenty-nine-member advisory Municipal Council. (The number of voters is small because individuals who are in the military or police and those who have been Qatari citizens for less than fifteen years were ineligible to participate, as was the more than 75 percent of the population that is expatriate.) Six women were among the more than 200 candidates, although none were elected. The Municipal Council has a term of four years, after which Qatar is expected to establish an elected parliament that will have genuine, although limited, legislative authority. On April 29, 2003, Qataris overwhelmingly approved Qatar's first written constitution.

Oman, too, has begun to move slowly toward constitutional rule and limited popular political participation. In September 2000, Oman held elections for an eighty-two-person Consultative Assembly. Both men and women were granted suffrage rights and close to two dozen women were among the more than 550 individuals who stood for office (two women were elected). Previously, membership in the council was determined by Sultan Qaboos and he still exercises some control over who is permitted to run. The assembly advises the government, reviews legislation, and provides a formal means for community leaders to provide input to the government. The sultan also appoints a smaller State Council. A new Basic Law, implemented in November 1996, addressed the critical question of leadership continuity in Oman (given that Sultan Qaboos has no heir). Article 5 of the Basic Law indicates that Qaboos's successor must be "a Muslim, judicious, of sound mind and [a] legitimate son of Omani Muslim parents" (quoted in O'Reilly, 1998:83); he must also be a descendant of Sayyid Turki ibn Said ibn Sultan (Sultan Qaboos's great-great-grandfather, who ruled Oman between 1871 and 1888).

The third of the small, traditional Gulf states is the UAE, a union of seven shaikhdoms formed when Britain withdrew from the Gulf in the early 1970s. Independence was to be followed by the creation of a permanent constitution and elections, but this never occurred. Thus, although the UAE is technically a republic, in reality it is a federation of emirates with no suffrage and no political parties. Governance of the 3 million residents (only about 20 percent of whom are indigenous to the area) is by the Supreme Council, composed of the leader of each emirate and headed by Shaikh Zayed of Abu Dhabi. There is also a forty-person Federal National Assembly, whose membership reflects the power distribution of the UAE: Abu Dhabi and Dubai have eight representatives each; Sharjah and Ras al-Khaimah have six each; and Umm al-

Quaiwan, Fujairah, and Ajman have only four each. Periodically, tensions erupt among the emirates over the dominance of Abu Dhabi and Dubai, however, because these are the largest and wealthiest regions, the federation could not easily exist without their involvement and criticism is constrained.

Bahrain and Kuwait. The constitutions of both Bahrain and Kuwait call for a legislative body; however, until recently in the multi-island country of Bahrain, parliamentary rule was a legal fiction. The thirty-person National Assembly, partially elected by a small number of male Bahraini citizens in 1973, was suspended in 1975 after it "balked at endorsing a broadly-written decree that would enable the government to detain critics and opponents at will for 'statements' or 'activities' deemed to threaten the country's 'internal or external security'" (Stork, 1997:34). Emir Isa ibn Salmon al-Khalifah, who ruled Bahrain from independence until his death on March 6, 1999, then suspended the constitution and dismissed the parliament. In place of the parliament, the emir created an appointed Consultative Council in December 1992; however, this "largely cosmetic emblem of democratic reform" (Fakhro, 1997:175) did little to quell popular desires for greater political participation.

More than two-thirds of the Bahraini population is Shi'a, and over the years there have been allegations of Iranian-supported plots to overthrow the Sunni-controlled government. Demands of the opposition members include political rights for women, the restoration of the constitution and parliament, and more economic opportunities. The response of Emir Isa's government was to increase political repression: detaining dissidents without charge, using torture, and increasing restrictions on freedom of expression (Human Rights Watch, 1997). Government policy changed significantly with the accession of Hamad ibn Isa al-Khalifah in 1999. The new emir called for a national plebiscite and in February 2002 Bahrain became a constitutional monarchy. The first elections for the parliament were held on October 24, 2002.

Of all the Gulf states, Kuwait has arguably been the most successful in preempting revolutionary pressures. This is due in large part to

> the massive and successful program of the al-Sabah dynasty . . . to preserve its power by building the region's first modern welfare state. . . . For decades, the Kuwaiti government has lavishly subsidized everything from electricity to housing, has underwritten travel abroad for those seeking education or medical treatment, and has created comfortable, well-paying, white collar jobs for 96 percent of its working citizens. (Sadowski 1997:7)

Between the dramatic decline in worldwide oil prices and the cost of reconstructing Kuwait after the Iraqi invasion, however, Kuwait's ability to buy off dissent has declined, creating a potentially unstable situation.

At present, Kuwait is the only Middle Eastern country in which men but not women are permitted to vote. Until 1996, suffrage was granted only to adult males who were residents of Kuwait prior to 1920 and their male descendants; now male descendants of the (very few) naturalized citizens can also vote, but the electorate is still tiny compared with the total population. The fifty-person National Assembly has a checkered history: it was dissolved in 1975, reconstituted in 1981, and suspended again in July 1986. At the time, the Sabah family argued that Kuwait could not afford the divisiveness that democracy encouraged. Under popular pressure to revive the legislature, the royal family created an advisory national council in June 1990. The council was suspended during the war with Iraq but was restored in July 1991 and remained in place until the National Assembly began operation again in 1992.

The 1992 election was heavily contested, and its results were a shock to the Kuwaiti royal family: opposition candidates won thirty-one seats, defeating many progovernment candidates. Sixteen of these were associated with various Islamic factions; the remainder were liberal or leftist figures, many of whom were quite critical of the Sabah family. Three Islamist parties are also well represented in the current assembly, which was elected in 1996; however, secular opposition figures were less successful than they had been in 1992, reflecting popular dissatisfaction with the 1992 assembly. In May 1999, Shaikh Jabir al-Sabah dissolved the parliament and called for early elections after legislators strongly criticized a cabinet member. A few weeks later, the emir announced his desire that women be permitted to vote and run for office beginning in 2003; however, the parliamentary elections held on July 5 of that year excluded women.

▓ Jordan and Morocco

The role of parliaments in Jordan and Morocco is more substantial than in the other Middle Eastern monarchies: they are popularly elected, and political parties are permitted to function, although in Morocco the fundamentalist "Justice and Charity" movement is not recognized.

Jordan, the only royal kingdom remaining in the Levant, has been a constitutional monarchy since the 1928 Constitution established an elected legislative council (although ultimate responsibility still rested with the Hashemites). A new constitution promulgated in February 1947 called for a bicameral National Assembly, with an eighty-person lower house elected by popular vote and a smaller upper house appointed by the king. From 1953 to 1999, King Hussein, the grandson of King Abdullah and the great-grandson of Sharif Husayn ibn Ali of Mecca, ruled the country. Upon Hussein's death, the throne passed to his son Abdullah II.

The October 1956 elections brought to power a leftist government that challenged the young King Hussein, whose response was to declare martial law and ban all political parties, although elections continued to be held. After the Six Day War with Israel and the Israeli occupation of the West Bank, which Jordan still claimed, King Hussein suspended the parliament entirely. Eventually, in 1984, an amendment to the constitution allowed for a reconvening of the ninth parliament (in place in 1967) with by-elections to replace the deceased deputies. Four years later, Hussein formally gave up administrative responsibility for the West Bank, thus necessitating a restructuring of the electoral districts to distribute seats on the East Bank only. At the same time, the government adopted an IMF economic restructuring program that proved extremely unpopular, as the value of the Jordanian dinar was halved and government subsidies for basic foodstuffs began to be lifted. In the wake of riots through the country in April 1989, King Hussein decided to reliberalize the political system, allowing nonpartisan parliamentary elections in November 1989—the first in more than two decades.

In reopening the political process slightly, Hussein was attempting "to pre-empt a crisis [and] to find a political balance—one which gives his people the reformed political system . . . that they want, and which guarantees the future of Hashemite rule" (Yorke, 1989:18). Faced with a strong Islamic movement, the king chose to integrate Islamists into the government rather than banning them, as occurred in Algeria, Egypt, and Tunisia. In fact, Jordan's Islamists had long been allies of the monarchy, not only in the conflict with leftists in the 1950s and 1960s, but also during the events of Black September in 1970. After reliberalization in the early 1990s, Islamist ministers sought (mostly unsuccessfully) to introduce laws restricting activities such as the consumption of alcohol or requiring gender separation in public swimming pools and sports facilities. At the same time, participation in the government required the Islamists to compromise and forge alliances with other political entities (Ahmad, 1997).

Subsequent multiparty elections were held in 1993, 1997, and on June 17, 2003. In 1993, some two dozen parties reflecting a diversity of views contended for representation. By the November 1997 elections, however, there was a serious reversal in Jordan's moves toward democratization. Prior to the elections, Human Rights Watch reported with dismay that there was "a clear intent to discourage Jordanians from organising and participating in public discussion of political issues that segments of the civil society deem to be of national importance" and questioned whether, under these circumstances, any elections could be considered free and fair (cited in Andoni, 1997:19). In addition, changes in the election law clearly strengthened the position of traditional regime loyalists at the expense of opposition groups. As a result, nine opposition parties, including the large Islamic Action Front, boycotted the election, leaving the field wide open for progovernment candidates to gain a substantial majority in the lower house. The 2003 elections, held more than eighteen months late, also returned a progrovernment assembly. Although Islamists and other political parties competed, additional changes in the election law disadvantaged the opposition.

As is true of a number of states, the Kingdom of Morocco has attempted to address political dissent through a new, slightly more liberal constitution. However, just as in Kuwait and Jordan, the king can dissolve the parliament at will and indeed did so for more than a decade beginning in 1965. Under the 1996 Constitution, the king maintains significant political control: he must approve all members of the cabinet and can override the parliament at will.

At present, Morocco has a two-tiered legislative body: a 325-member Chamber of Representatives, which is directly elected for a five-year term, and a Chamber of Councilors, which is indirectly elected by local councils, professional organizations, and labor groups for staggered nine-year terms. Both women and men have suffrage. In the November 1997 elections, the opposition (which is dominated by the Istiqlal Party and the Socialist Union of Popular Forces [USFP]) gained a plurality of seats in the lower chamber. The new coalition government included twenty-two members of the opposition out of a total of forty-one ministers; USFP leader Abderrahmane Youssoufi became Morocco's prime minister.

The electoral code was revised in early 2002 in preparation for Morocco's September 2002 parliamentary elections, the first since Muhammed VI took the throne in 1999. In what observers called the freest elections in Morocco's history, the governing coalition of the USFP (50 seats) and the nationalist Istiqlal Party (48 seats) maintained control, but with a diminished number of seats from the previous parliament. The Islamist Justice and Development Party tripled its representation by winning 42 of 325 seats, making it the third largest party in parliament. Despite this, when the king announced the new government in November 2002, he did not grant the Islamists any cabinet positions. The biggest winners in the elections were women, whose share of seats increased from 2 to 34. The king launched a strong campaign to increase women's participation in the legislature, and parties responded by putting forth a dramatically increased number of female candidates.

■ Democracies and Conditional Democracies

As discussed above, a few states in the Middle East—Israel, Lebanon, Turkey, and perhaps Iran—can be considered at least nominally democratic. These countries developed political arrangements along the lines of the European powers, with parliamentary (rather than presidential) systems of governance. Yet even these countries are not fully "liberal." Instead, due to the emphasis on religion and ethnicity that is inherent in their political structures, all four might better be labeled "conditional" democracies. To a certain extent, the first three countries used the liberal democratic model—adopting European norms and appealing for European assistance—to make the best of a bad situation (Turkey to recover what it could from the remains of the Ottoman Empire, Lebanon because it was small and divided, and Israel because it was considered illegitimate by its Arab neighbors). But because of the institutional distinctions that exist between groups of citizens, there are important differences between the democracy found in these states and the liberal democratic tradition of Europe and North America.

A comparison between Turkey and Iran is particularly interesting. Neither, I would argue, is a fully consolidated democracy. In both cases, sovereignty is divided, with an elected president and legislature constrained by either the military (in the case of Turkey) or religious authorities (in Iran). To make this function requires an incredibly detailed constitution, which both countries have, and an active judiciary to interpret the laws while following a clear ideological position. As illustrated below, Israel and Lebanon face a different set of challenges having to do less with divided sovereignty and more with attempting to maintain certain positions of privilege for a portion of the population based on religion.

■ Turkey

In Turkey, formal power rests with the 550 members of the Grand National Assembly, whose terms run for five years. The president, who is elected by the assembly for a seven-year term, may call for earlier elections if the assembly is deadlocked and unable to function. Political parties are permitted; however, the government consistently denies the right of Kurds to organize an ethnically based political party and attempts to limit their power as a distinct ethnic group through a high electoral quota that makes it difficult for a Kurdish-oriented party to join the Assembly. The government's position is that Kurds may have full civil rights as Turks but cannot express these in the context of Kurdish self-determination. In addition, Turkey has moved to restrict political expression by Islamic movements, most recently (as discussed earlier) by forcing the Refah Party out of the assembly despite its position as part of the governing coalition at the time. The repeated, although short-lived, interventions by the military to preserve the Atatürk model, as well as long-term suppression of the civil liberties of the Kurds, also weaken Turkey's democratic credentials.

Over the years, a variety of political parties have been represented in the Grand National Assembly. These have included the strongly secular Demokratik Sol Partisi (Democratic Left Party), which gained a plurality (22 percent) of the votes in the April 1999 elections; the far right-wing Milliyetci

Hareket Partisi (Nationalist Action Party), which took second place in 1999 with 18 percent of the vote; the center-right Anavatan Partisi (ANAP, or Motherland Party), with 13 percent; and the moderate-right Dogru Yol Partisi (True Path Party), with slightly fewer votes. The repeated creation of Islamic-identified parties that are then banned reflects both the growing interest in this approach to Turkish politics and the efforts of governmental structures to keep Turkey a secular state. The first explicitly Islamist party, the Milli Nizam Partisi (MNP, or National Order Party), was founded in 1970 by Necmettin Erbakan. It was short-lived, however; the Turkish Constitutional Court banned the MNP the following year. This led Erbakan to form the Milli Selemet Partisi (MSP, or National Salvation Party), which gained representation in the assembly until it, too, was banned after the 1980 military coup. The Refah Partisi (RP, or Welfare Party) picked up where the MSP left off. It, too, was established by Erbakan and was part of the ruling coalition after the December 1995 elections, in which it received a plurality of the votes. Erbakan's relations with the Turkish military were poor, however, resulting in a series of government-military confrontations in January and February 1997 over Rafah's support for *sharia* law; these tensions eventually led Erbakan to step down. Rafah was banned in 1998 but reorganized as the Fazilet Partisi (Virtue Party) and stood for election in 1999. In 2001 it, too, was banned by the Constitutional Court (Habibi, 2003).

At this point, Islamist politicians split into two groups. Some of the members created Saadet Partisi (Felicity Party), led by Islamist stalwort Erbakan. The more reformist-oriented members of the banned Virtue Party joined with other reform-minded political figures to establish the Adalet ve Kalkinma Partisi (Justice and Development Party), headed by former mayor of Istanbul Recep Tayyip Erdogan. While the Felicity Party had no significant impact on the November 2002 elections, the Justice and Development Party achieved an impressing victory, receiving 34 percent of the popular vote and gaining a strong majority of seats in the Grand National Assembly. Turkey's oldest political party, the left-of-center, social democratic Cumhuriyet Halk Partisi (Republican People's Party), which failed to reach the 10 percent electoral threshold in 1999, received 19.4 percent of the vote and was awarded 178 seats.

As the new Islamist-led government came to power in 2003—just as the United States was pushing for a military intervention to change the Iraqi regime—its leaders demonstrated a very moderate stance that was not anti-Western, as many had feared. The government continues to prioritize Turkey's gaining membership to the European Union and worked closely with the United States to reach an agreement over the stationing of troops in Turkey to facilitate attacks along Iraq's northern border. While Turkey's Islamist leaders came to a tentative agreement with Washington, the Turkish parliament voted against the presence of the foreign troops. Nevertheless, the process by which that decision was taken illustrates not only the functioning of democratic institutions in Turkey, but also that Islamists will not necessarily take an anti-Western position on all issues.

▧ Israel

For its Jewish citizens, Israel is the most open political system in the Middle East. Its founding principle of maintaining the Jewish character of the state and its failures in dealing with the political rights of the Palestinians, both within Israel, where there is systematic legal and budgetary discrimination (Ghanem, 2001), and particularly in the Occupied Territories, limit the extent to which it can be called fully "liberal." Furthermore, in the 1990s a substantial challenge to democratic norms by "Jewish revivalism" emerged.

Israel's political system is based directly on democratic norms. Most of the Zionist leaders who helped found Israel were advocates of democratic socialism, and Israel has had liberal democratic institutions from the very beginning. Although military service is critical to advancing a political career, the Israeli military has never intervened to overthrow a government, and non-Jewish citizens—notably the sizable Palestinian minority within Israel—are permitted to vote and stand for election, although non-Jewish members of the Israeli parliament (Knesset) were not included in governing coalitions until quite recently.

The structure of power in Israeli politics has gone through three distinct phases. In the early years of the state, politics were dominated by a single party, Labor, whose leadership consisted almost entirely of individuals of European descent. The Labor Party exercised control not only through the legislative mechanisms of the Knesset but also through interlocking control of the labor unions and state enterprises, which provided ample opportunities for patronage.

In 1977, the Labor Party's dominance was challenged by a group of conservative parties that coalesced under the name Likud. In addition to providing alternatives to Labor policies—for example, Likud was interested in restraining the Labor-dominated state enterprises—Likud appealed to a number of Jewish voters who had emigrated from Arab countries such as Morocco, Yemen, and Iraq. Likud broke the Labor monopoly on political control of Israel and held power for a number of years, either alone or in "national unity" coalitions with Labor.

The third phase began with a change in electoral laws—effective in 1996—that provided for the direct election of a prime minister. Prior to this, the leader whose party gained a plurality of votes in an election was given the first opportunity to negotiate with other party leaders to create a ruling coalition. If successful, that person became the prime minister; if not, the president would turn to the party with the second highest number of votes and give that leader the same chance to form a government.

Although intended to make the prime minister less dependent on the unstable parliamentary coalitions within the Knesset, the direct election of the prime minister had the unexpected effect of encouraging the growth of a number of small, single-interest parties in the elections of 1996 and 1999. Both Labor and Likud lost substantial numbers of seats to new, ethnically oriented parties, notably Israeli B'Aliyah, which primarily represents recent Russian emigrants, and Shas, which now has the fourth largest number of seats in the Knesset. Partly for that reason, Labor and Likud both supported a repeal of the Direct Election Law in February 2001 and the country returned to a more traditional parliamentary system in which the prime minister is the head of the party that is able to form a government after single-ballot general elections. The Knesset election on January 28, 2003, gave Likud a plurality of the seats and the right to form the new government.

In addition to the potential parliamentary instability caused by the proliferation of small parties, the liberal character of Israeli democracy is also openly questioned by some of the religious parties, who wish to see much more power granted to religious authorities. For example, the relative domains of secular and religious courts are being sharply contested, despite the fact that religious councils already have considerably greater power in Israel than they have in most other liberal democracies. Consequently, Israel is confronting many of the same issues of balancing secular and religious power that Muslim states in the region are facing.

■ Lebanon

The situation in Lebanon is complicated. Constitutionally, Lebanon is a parliamentary republic with an elected 128-member Chamber of Deputies reflecting a convoluted confessional division with at least eighteen separate entities designed to create a form of sectarian proportional representation. By law and tradition, the president is a Christian, while the prime minister is a Muslim. The cabinet is chosen by the prime minister in consultation with members of the parliament and the president. The 1989 Taif Accords attempted to modify the balance of political power within the parliament to reflect more accurately the various ethnoreligious communities; however, it did not fundamentally modify the notion of defining people by their political-religious affiliation.

The return to democracy after fifteen years of civil and international conflict has not been easy. In September and October 1992, Lebanon held its first general elections in twenty years. Many Lebanese, especially Christians, boycotted because they said the electoral framework was unfair; others, however, argued that the real issue was that Lebanese Christians were no longer given the drastically disproportionate representation they had held in the past.

Due in part to the boycott but also reflecting both Lebanese preferences and Lebanese pragmatism, pro-Syrian candidates and Islamic groups aligned with Iran won a number of the seats. The new prime minister, who also served as the finance minister, was Rafiq al-Hariri, a Sunni and Lebanese-Saudi national born in Lebanon. Hariri, a billionaire who made his money in the construction industry, had the support of both Syria and Saudi Arabia (which was essential). The parliament chose Christian Elias Hrawi to be the new president. Top cabinet leadership reflected the continuing use of family ties and confessional distinctions in the allocation of positions of power. Nabih Berri, head of the Syrian-backed Shi'a party Amal (Hope), became the speaker of the parliament. President Hrawi's son-in-law, Fares Buwayz, was named foreign minister, and the minister of defense was Mohsen Dalloul, a Shi'a who had ties to Syria.

The second, post–Taif Accords parliamentary elections were held in August and September 1996, under a new election law passed the previous July. Opponents maintained that the revised law violated the Taif Accords in ways that benefited government supporters; however, they were unable to stop the law's passage. During the campaign season, an informal alliance of the Lebanese government, represented by Hariri, Nabih Berri of Amal, and Druze leader Walid Jumblatt, joined together to minimize the electoral success of Hezbollah, a position consistent with Syria's desire to support the more secular Amal. When the votes were tallied, Hariri's cross-confessional coalition had won a bloc of twenty seats, as had Amal's cross-confessional coalition. Ten seats went to the Druze and their Christian allies; Hezbollah and its allies received nine seats.

The most recent elections were held in 2000. In general, these were judged to be genuinely fair, although critics maintained that the complicated election laws do not permit voters to express their true preferences. Certainly it is accurate to say that Lebanese politics remain dominated by the various sects, with little movement toward a nonsectarian system. What *has* changed is that the parliament more closely matches the composition of the population, although the numbers are still skewed in favor of the Christians. Muslim candidates received 57 percent of the vote (of which Sunnis received 25 percent, Shi'a 25 percent, Druze 6 percent, and Alawite less than 1 percent) but gained only half the seats in the Chamber of Deputies. Christian candidates, on the other hand, received only 43 percent of the vote but were also allotted half the seats in the legislature.

Under the new election law, a presidential election was to be held in fall 1995 to replace Elias Hrawi, since a president is only permitted to serve a single six-year term. However, the parliament ignored this requirement and on October 19, 1995, voted to extend Hrawi's term for an additional three years. The move angered many Lebanese, who saw it as a blatant attempt to curry favor with the Syrians. Three years later, in October 1998, Emile Lahoud was elected president, a position he continued to hold in 2003.

■ An Islamic Quasi-Democracy

In February 1979, following months of increasingly widespread civil unrest, the staunchly pro-Western, authoritarian Pahlavi regime in Iran was overthrown. Much to the surprise of Western observers—although not to many in the region—the government that eventually gained control came not from Iranian elites, nor from leftist movements that the shah had brutally suppressed, but from a conservative Islamic movement led by Ayatollah Ruhollah Khomeini, a prominent Shi'a cleric who returned from exile in Paris. With the success of the Iranian revolution, a new era of political Islam was born.

Khomeini's "Islamic Republic" was a radical departure from the earlier revolutionary movements in the Middle East. In contrast to Nasserism and Ba'thism, which combined a variety of anticolonial, Western, and Arab ideas, Khomeini and his followers implemented a conservative political agenda that derived almost entirely from traditional Islamic thought and practice. Although the details of the nature of "Islamic" governance are complex and hotly debated (including—in fact, particularly—within the Islamic Republic itself), three characteristics distinguish it.

The first is the use of Islamic law—*sharia*—in place of various systems of civil law. This went directly against the twentieth-century tendency in the Middle East and other postcolonial regions to replace, at least in part, traditional legal systems based on religion and custom with uniform secular legal codes, often derived from the legal systems of former colonial powers. In practice, the implementation of *sharia* also involves the imposition of additional conservative social norms that are not actually addressed in the Quran, most conspicuously regarding restrictions on the behavior of women.

Second, the Islamic Republic of Iran placed the supreme authority of the state in the hands of religious councils. These councils also chose a supreme religious leader, a post held by Khomeini until his death in 1989. However, the remaining familiar structures of a modern state—a president, popularly elected parliament, court system, and so forth—remained intact and play an important role in ruling the state. The religious authorities can overturn the decisions of these secular structures, but such decisions must be made on the basis of Islamic law and tradition rather than personal whim. Candidates for election to the secular government require approval from the religious authorities, and during his lifetime Khomeini retained absolute authority on issues regarding war and other foreign policy matters, although he often chose not to exercise his power.

Finally, Khomeini followed an approach to Islam that placed a high priority on missionary efforts. Consequently, the Islamic Republic saw itself in the vanguard of an international revolution and immediately sought to export its model of conservative political Islam to other states. (In this regard, the agenda of Iranian fundamentalism appeared to the West to be very similar to that of international communism, despite some notable differences, and was treated similarly.) Iran has had only limited success in its effort to promote political Islam, but the concept of a conservative Islamic state following *sharia* has had tremendous influence throughout the Middle East.

Twenty-five years after Khomeini's triumphant return to Iran, the experiment of the Islamic Republic can be regarded as a mixed success. Contrary to the predictions of many skeptics who expected an early end to a "medieval" governing structure imposed on an industrializing, urbanizing state, the Islamic Republic has survived, has been generally stable, and has thus far successfully coped with several major difficulties, including a devastating war with Iraq, the collapse of the price of oil, and substantial refugee inflows from Iraq and Afghanistan. Over time, the power of the religious authorities has weakened, although it remains significant, and Iran has a number of attributes of a state making the transition to democracy.

The key is that, in contrast to many depictions in the West, the Iranian model is not one of a totalitarian religious state. A functioning secular government remains in place, both for theological reasons (Islam emphasizes the importance of the *ummah,* the Muslim community as a whole, and not merely the *ulama,* the religious elites) and presumably because the Shi'i clerics have little interest in taking on the responsibility for filling potholes and collecting garbage. These secular political institutions provide a natural source of opposition to the power of the religious authorities, particularly in urban areas. Furthermore, the religious authorities themselves derive their power from the approval and respect of their followers, not from any intrinsic "divine right." Khomeini had very broad support within Iran and therefore could mobilize millions of people, but no leader of Khomeini's stature has emerged since his death, and competition for leadership within the religious councils weakened their control somewhat. The February 2000 parliamentary elections were revealing in this regard. The elections were extremely competitive, with 6,000 candidates vying for one of the 270 seats, and ended with a major victory for the leftist, reform-oriented Islamic Participation Front. Despite its apparent mandate, the sixth parliament has been constrained by the Council of Guardians, which has limited its ability to implement the types of changes that its supporters had hoped to see (Rezaei, 2003).

■ Conclusion

At the dawn of a new millennium in the Christian calendar, the states of the Middle East are confronting several major political challenges. First, the region is undergoing a generational change in both its leaders and its political issues: the faces and agendas that dominated the last three decades of the twentieth century seem unlikely to be as critical in the first decades of the twenty-first century. As noted earlier, most governments in the Middle East have been remarkably stable, with individual leaders remaining in power for decades. However, many pivotal figures in the region are elderly and are likely either to die or to become incapacitated in the near future. Even when successors have been clearly designated, the new leaders will not have the experience or outlook of their predecessors. When succession is unclear—as in Egypt, Oman, the UAE, Libya, or the Palestinian Authority—substantial periods of instability are possible.

As the leaders of the elder generation are fading, so are many of the older issues. The Cold War, during which the superpowers both used and were used by many states in the region, ended at the beginning of the 1990s. The revolutionary secular ideologies of the postcolonial period—Nasserism and Ba'thism—have faded and no longer inspire serious intellectual debate. The future agenda appears unlikely to mirror the past. In place of these concerns, a new issue clearly dominates: the often competing pressures for either democratic or religious governance that would provide increased popular involvement in government. This has affected the full range of states, including countries such as Turkey and Israel, which have strong parliamentary traditions, and the Arab Gulf states, several of which have recently established consultative councils and held elections. Such moves toward greater democratization are consistent with trends in most of the world.

Tensions involving Israel and its neighbors remain a second critical concern. This may at first appear to be a matter for international relations scholars rather than those looking at the politics *within* states, as this chapter has done. The impact of this conflict on the internal politics of the parties involved is massive, however, and justifies its mention here. While aspects of the Arab-Israeli conflict have been addressed successfully (most notably the Egyptian-Israeli and Jordanian-Israeli peace treaties and Israel's withdrawal from southern Lebanon), relations between Israelis and Palestinians are worse than any time since the Israeli occupation of the West Bank and Gaza Strip began in 1967. Massive violations of human rights occur daily as people attempt to maintain a normal life in the midst of Israeli targeted assassinations and other attacks, Palestinian suicide bombings, and the long-term ghettoization of Palestinian cities and villages (due to Israeli military closures, roadblocks, the "security wall," and Jewish-only housing settlements, among other factors), which have left the economy in tatters and nongovernmental organizations warning of a possible humanitarian disaster if the situation does not change. Neither Palestinians nor Israelis perceive of themselves as secure and the sense of deep despair among peace activists is palpable.

In an interview in June 2002, Naomi Chazan, then deputy speaker of the Knesset and a member of the leftist Meretz Party, commented sadly:

> Both societies are totally traumatized. Palestinians are traumatized and justifiably. Israelis are traumatized, and justifiably. People are scared and jittery and they smoke too much and they are jumpy and they do things they would usually consider unacceptable. . . . [The violence has] brought out the absolute worst in both peoples. The absolute worst. On the Israeli side, fascism and racist statements have become common place. What is said against

Arab members [of the Knesset] is absolutely horrendous. . . . I get home sometimes and I can weep. What is said about Arabs in the Knesset I would not accept to be said about Jews. . . . Each society is allowing things to be said in its name that it would never accept under other circumstances. It is making us ugly. The extremes have taken over.

With such a tense and violent situation, where mutual trust is all but nonexistent, one might be tempted to conclude that this conflict will never be resolved. However, people feared the same dire future for South Africa, which is now a vibrant pluralist society despite the horrific legacy of apartheid. The conflict between Israeli Jews and Palestinians is extremely difficult, to be sure, but there is no inevitability to its continuance.

Finally, governments are under increasing pressure to implement policies that will improve economic performance and respond to a global economy that does not place a premium on oil. With the decline in oil revenues, there will be greater pressure on Middle Eastern regimes to industrialize and diversify their economies. The professional class of accountants, engineers, and doctors who once lived as politically powerless expatriates is likely to demand a greater share of political power. The Middle East will also need to reassess its role in the global economy to decide, for instance, whether or not to pursue regional integration, link with the more developed economies of Europe, or join with the less developed economies of Africa and southern and Central Asia. These will be difficult questions for the new generation of Arabs, Iranians, Israelis, and Turks in the twenty-first century.

■ Note

An earlier version of this chapter benefited enormously from the comments of Donald L. Gordon and Gwenn Okrulick. Jillian Schwedler and several outside reviewers made excellent suggestions for this revision. None of the above should be held responsible for whatever errors of fact or interpretation remain despite their wise counsel.

■ Bibliography

Ahmad, Mumtaz. 1997. "Political Islam: Can It Become a Loyal Opposition?" *Middle East Policy* 5, no. 1:68–74.
Alexander, Christopher. 1997. "Authoritarianism and Civil Society in Tunisia." *Middle East Report* 27, no. 4:34–38.
Al-Haj, Abdullah Juma. 1996. "The Politics of Participation in the Gulf Cooperation Council States: The Omani Consultative Council." *Middle East Journal* 50, no. 4:559–571.
Anderson, Lisa. 1991. "Absolutism and the Resilience of the Monarchy." *Political Science Quarterly* 106, no. 1:1–15.

————. 2000. "Dynasts and Nationalists: Why Monarchies Survive." Pp. 53–69 in Joseph Kostiner (ed.), *Middle East Monarchies: The Challenge of Modernity*. Boulder, Colo.: Lynne Rienner.

Andoni, Lamis. 1997. "Jordanian Elections: Setback for Democratisation." *Middle East International*, December 5, p. 19.

Antonius, George. 1946. *The Arab Awakening: The Story of the Arab National Movement*. New York: G. P. Putnam's Sons.

Arnold, Guy. 1997. *The Maverick State: Qaddafi and the New World Order*. London: Cassell.

Bill, James A., and Robert Springborg. 1994. *Politics in the Middle East*. 4th ed. New York: HarperCollins.

Brynen, Rex, Bahgat Korany, and Paul Noble. 1995. "Introduction: Theoretical Perspectives on Arab Liberalization and Democratization." Pp. 3–27 in Rex Brynen, Bahgat Korany, and Paul Noble (eds.), *Political Liberalization and Democratization in the Arab World*, vol. 1: *Theoretical Perspectives*. Boulder, Colo.: Lynne Rienner.

Bulliet, Richard. 1999. "Twenty Years of Islamic Politics." *Middle East Journal* 53, no. 2:189–200.

Carapico, Sheila. 1997. "From the Editors." *Middle East Report* 27, no. 3:1, 24.

Chazan, Naomi. 2002. Interview conducted at the YWCA in East Jerusalem, June 23.

Dekmejian, R. Hrair. 1998. "Saudi Arabia's Consultative Council." *Middle East Journal* 52, no. 2:204–218.

Dowty, Alan. 1998. *The Jewish State: A Century Later*. Berkeley: University of California Press.

El-Kikhia, Mansour O. 1997. *Libya's Qaddafi: The Politics of Contradiction*. Gainesville: University of Florida Press.

Evron, Boas. 1995. *Jewish State or Israeli Nation?* Bloomington: Indiana University Press.

Fakhro, Munira A. 1997. "The Uprising in Bahrain: An Assessment." Pp. 167–188 in Gary G. Sick and Lawrence G. Potter (eds.), *The Persian Gulf at the Millennium: Essays in Politics, Economy, Security, and Religion*. New York: St. Martin's Press.

Gause, F. Gregory, III. 1994. *Oil Monarchies: Domestic and Security Challenges in the Arab Gulf States*. New York: Council on Foreign Relations.

————. 2000. "The Persistence of Monarchy in the Arabian Peninsula: A Comparative Analysis." Pp. 167–186 in Joseph Kostiner (ed.), *Middle East Monarchies: The Challenge of Modernity*. Boulder, Colo.: Lynne Rienner.

Gerner, Deborah J., and Ian S. Wilbur. 2000. *Semantics or Substance? Showdown Between the United States and the Palestine Liberation Organization*. Pew Case Studies in International Affairs. Washington, D.C.: Institute for the Study of Diplomacy, Georgetown University.

Ghanem, As'ad. 2001. *The Palestinian-Arab Minority in Israel, 1948–2000*. Albany: State University of New York Press.

Goldstein, Joshua S., Jon C. Pevehouse, Deborah J. Gerner, and Shibley Telhami. 2001. "Dynamics of Middle East Conflict and U.S. Influence, 1979–97." *Journal of Conflict Resolution* 45, no. 5:594–620.

Habibi, Sahar. 2003. *Religious Participation in Democratic Societies: The Case of Turkey's Islamist Party*. Honors thesis, University of Kansas.

Halliday, Fred. 1979. *Iran: Dictatorship and Development*. 2nd ed. New York: Penguin Books.

————. 1997. "*Arabia Without Sultans* Revisited." *Middle East Report* 27, no. 3:27–29.

Hiro, Dilip. 1996. *Dictionary of the Middle East*. London: Macmillan.

Hopwood, Derek. 1985. *Egypt: Politics and Society 1945–1984*. 2nd ed. London: Allen and Unwin.

Hudson, Michael C. 1977. *Arab Politics: The Search for Legitimacy*. New Haven, Conn.: Yale University Press.

Human Rights Watch. 1997. *Routine Abuse, Routine Denial: Civil Rights and the Political Crisis in Bahrain*. New York: Human Rights Watch.

Husain, Mir Zohair. 1995. *Global Islamic Politics*. New York: HarperCollins College.

Ibrahim, Saad Eddin. 1995. "Liberalization and Democratization in the Arab World: An Overview." Pp. 29–57 in Rex Brynen, Bahgat Korany, and Paul Noble (eds.), *Political Liberalization and Democratization in the Arab World*, vol. 1: *Theoretical Perspectives*. Boulder, Colo.: Lynne Rienner.

Ismail, Salwa. 2001. "The Paradox of Islamist Politics." *Middle East Report* 221 (Winter):34–39.

Khalidi, Rashid (ed.). 1991. *The Origins of Arab Nationalism*. New York: Columbia University Press.

Kienle, Eberhard (ed.). 1994. *Contemporary Syria: Liberalization Between Cold War and Cold Peace*. New York: St. Martin's Press.

———. 1998. "More Than a Response to Islamism: The Political Deliberalization of Egypt in the 1990s." *Middle East Journal* 52, no. 2:219–235.

Korany, Bahgat. 1998. "Restricted Democratization from Above: Egypt." Pp. 39–69 in Bahgat Korany, Rex Brynen, and Paul Noble (eds.), *Political Liberalization and Democratization in the Arab World,* vol. 2: *Comparative Experiences*. Boulder, Colo.: Lynne Rienner.

Kyle, Keith, and Joel Peters (eds.). 1993. *Whither Israel: The Domestic Challenges*. New York: I. B. Tauris.

Levine, Mark. 1998. "National Elections in the Middle East and the Arab World Since 1980." *Middle East Report* 209:16.

Luciani, Giacomo (ed.) 1990. *The Arab State*. Berkeley: University of California Press.

Makiya, Kanan. 1993. *Cruelty and Silence: War, Tyranny, Uprising, and the Arab World*. New York: W. W. Norton.

Melhem, Hisham. 1997. "Syria Between Two Transitions." *Middle East Report* 27, no. 2:2–7.

Norton, Augustus Richard (ed.). 1995. *Civil Society in the Middle East*. Vol. 1. Leiden: E. J. Brill.

Omaar, Rageh. 1997. "Jordan: A Changed Landscape." *Middle East International,* December 5.

O'Reilly, Marc J. 1998. "Omanibalancing: Oman Confronts an Uncertain Future." *Middle East Journal* 52, no. 1:70–84.

Penrose, Edith. 1993. "From Economic Liberalization to International Integration: The Role of the State." Pp. 3–25 in Tim Niblock and Emma Murphy (eds.), *Economic and Political Liberalization in the Middle East*. London: British Academic Press.

Putnam, Robert D. 1993. *Making Democracy Work: Civic Traditions in Modern Italy*. Princeton: Princeton University Press.

Rezaei, Ali. 2003. "Last Efforts of Iran's Reformists." *Middle East Report* 226 (Spring):40–46.

Richards, Alan, and John Waterbury. 1996. *A Political Economy of the Middle East*. 2nd ed. Boulder, Colo.: Westview Press.

Rivlan, Paul. 2001. *Economic Policy and Performance in the Arab World*. Boulder, Colo.: Lynne Rienner.

Sadowski, Yahya. 1997. "The End of the Counterrevolution? The Politics of Economic Adjustment in Kuwait." *Middle East Report* 27, no. 3:7–11.

Schrodt, Philip A., and Deborah J. Gerner. 2000. "Using Cluster Analysis to Derive Early Warning Indicators for the Middle East, 1979–1996." *American Political Science Review* 94, no. 4:803–818.

Sela, Avraham. 1998. *The Decline of the Arab-Israeli Conflict: Middle East Politics and the Quest for Regional Order.* Albany: State University of New York Press.

Simons, Geoff. 1996. *Libya: The Struggle for Survival.* 2nd ed. New York: St. Martin's Press.

Sprinzak, Ehud, and Larry Diamond. 1993. *Israeli Democracy Under Stress.* Boulder, Colo.: Lynne Rienner.

Stork, Joe. 1997. "Bahrain's Crisis Worsens." *Middle East Report* 27, no. 3:33–35.

Tibi, Bassam. 1997. *Arab Nationalism: Between Islam and the Nation-State.* 3rd ed. New York: St. Martin's Press.

UNDP (United Nations Development Programme). 1998. *Human Development Report 1998.* New York: Oxford University Press.

U.S. ACDA (U.S. Arms Control and Disarmament Agency). 1997. *World Military Expenditures and Arms Transfers 1996.* Washington, D.C.: U.S. Government Printing Office.

U.S. Department of State, Bureau of Verification and Compliance. 2002. *World Military Expenditures and Arms Transfers 2000.* Washington, D.C.: U.S. Government Printing Office.

Van Dam, Nikolaos. 1996. *The Struggle for Power in Syria: Politics and Society Under Asad and the Ba'th Party.* London: I. B. Taurus.

Weber, Max. 1947. *The Theory of Social and Economic Organization.* New York: Oxford University Press.

Wilson, Frank L. 1996. *Concepts and Issues in Comparative Politics: An Introduction to Comparative Analysis.* Upper Saddle River, N.J.: Prentice-Hall.

Yorke, Valerie. 1989. "Hussein's Bid to Legitimise Hashemite Rule." *Middle East International,* November 17.

International Relations

Mary Ann Tétreault

■ **Sovereignty in the Middle East**

All the bounded areas on modern world maps are called *nation-states,* but their qualities as political communities are not alike. Many barely qualify as *nations,* usually defined as a population "sharing [a] historic territory, common myths and historical memories," a common economy, and a popular culture (Smith, 1991:14; also Connor, 1994). Some also fail the test for *states,* compulsory political organizations claiming a monopoly on the legitimate use of force to execute orders over a specific territory (Weber, 1978; Jackson, 1990). Whatever their failings when viewed from within, however, the post–World War II order inaugurated an era during which nation-states were seen from without as equally sovereign members of the international community. Nation-state members of international organizations as varied as the United Nations (UN), the Organization of Petroleum Exporting Countries (OPEC), and the Arab League claim equal formal status. Sometimes called *negative sovereignty* (Jackson, 1990:27), this status stems from the principle that every state has the same rights under international law, including the right to be free from external interference in its internal affairs.

Negative sovereignty is not always fully observed. But as compared to the status of most of the world prior to World War II, this norm truly defined a new era in international relations. Earlier, nation-states were only one among several forms of political organization, and few among them were sovereign in this sense. European governments and their agents—not only armies and navies but also privateers and for-profit corporations such as the British East India and West India Companies—freely pursued imperial ventures of various types, mostly outside Europe (Doyle, 1986; Polanyi, 1944). By the late nineteenth century, the "state ideal"—the desire to have a state of one's own—had spread. Opposition to imperialism became more common, and nationalist movements blossomed. European imperialists countered, justifying their continued control of foreign territories as fulfilling a "civilizing mission" that required them to bear the "white man's burden," which was to rule nations "unfit" to govern themselves (Jackson, 1990:71; also Said, 1993).

This justification wore thin during World War I. The U.S. government, led by President Woodrow Wilson, declared "self-determination" or the right of a people to choose its own government to be an important goal of the war. Afterward, however, this principle was applied only in central and eastern Europe, where the imperialists formerly in charge were on the losing side and the residents of former colonies were white Europeans. Imperialist winners of World War I did not want self-determination in Asia and the Middle East, where nonwhite local populations were regarded as inferior people (Ahmed, 1992:esp. chap. 8; Christison, 2000:27). Just as important, the winners themselves either were the colonial powers in those regions (see, e.g., Antonius, 1946; Moynihan, 1993) or else wanted the stability of colonial rule by friendly governments to safeguard direct foreign investments by their citizens (Bromley, 1994).

The Middle East was a strategic and economic crossroads linking Europe to Asia. The Suez Canal and Palestine were important way-stations on the route to India, explaining some of Britain's reluctance to relinquish control over the region (Fromkin, 1989:281–283). The French also had imperial interests in the Middle East, including dependencies in North Africa and a long-standing patronage of the Christian community on Mount Lebanon. Both Britain and France desired privileged access to territories such as Iraq, rumored to be rich in petroleum reserves. The U.S. government, with plenty of U.S. investors' interests to protect, also wanted colonial domination of the Middle East to continue (Bromley, 1994). British and U.S. leaders were especially reluctant to apply the principle of self-determination to Palestine, where both supported establishing a homeland for Jews in a land where the vast majority of the population was Arab (Christison, 2000).

Keeping alive the Ottoman Empire—the "sick man" of Europe—had been a concern of European foreign offices for decades. European leaders feared that if the Ottoman Empire were to collapse, their own countries would fight over which would get the choicest pieces of its carcass. This picture changed when Britain and France became allies, their German rival was defeated in World War I, and revolution and the consequent preoccupation with internal consolidation that took Russia out of the "great game" (imperial competition with Britain in western Asia) altered the balance of power in Europe. Now the "sick man" could be allowed to die because the wartime victors were confident that they could control the "successor states" without having to go to war. The victors never intended to give up their imperial "burdens"; the new "states" remained vulnerable to European insistence that some states were simply too "immature" to be fully sovereign.

This is why colonial possessions such as Algeria remained colonies after the war. Protectorates and bonds, the "special relationships" that allowed Britain to control the foreign policies of the small Gulf states, remained in effect (Anscombe, 1997). In addition, the League of Nations, the forerunner of today's United Nations, granted "mandates" allowing Britain and France to control nominally independent states created from territories that previously were part of the Ottoman Empire. Leaders and populations throughout the Middle East felt cheated of their Wilsonian right of self-determination, and negative sovereignty became a cherished goal of their political regimes. At the same time, however, the persistence of "traditional ideas on the privileges and vulnerability of states and a substantial amount of confusion between the national state apparatus and those who are manipulating it [resulted in] twenty-two . . . weak Arab states in a highly integrated world system" (Salamé, 1990:31).

This untidy situation came about in part because of how the aftermath of World War I shaped the foreign and domestic relations of Middle Eastern states. As we have seen in previous chapters, the formal boundaries defining many of these states were products of postwar, Great Power politics. Rather than conforming to local interests and traditions, territories and peoples were divided and combined to satisfy the state interests of the major powers and to weaken potential local challengers to their imperial domination. Large parts of Syria, the heart of the Arabs' hoped-for independent state, were sheared off by European imperialists or appropriated by ambitious locals. An independent Lebanon was carved from Syria to suit the French and their Maronite Christian protégés. In consequence, Syria became smaller, less viable economically, and therefore more dependent on France. Syria lost ground also against the founder of modern Turkey, Mustafa Kemal. Known after 1933 as Atatürk (father of the Turks), Mustafa Kemal refused to accept the victorious powers as the sole arbiters of the boundaries defining the postwar Middle East. Instead, he extended the territory of Turkey through military conquest, adding a piece of greater Syria to the area under his new government's control.

When the European mapmakers redrew the boundaries of Syria, they were oblivious to the consequences their exercise would have for Lebanon's integrity. The core of the new state, the community of Mount Lebanon, had evolved over 400 years under Ottoman rule as a politically pluralist, multicultural community (Harik, 1990:13–14). The new state of Lebanon also was multicultural, incorporating substantial populations of Muslims and Druze along with the French-favored Maronite Christians. Their minority status increased the dependence of the Maronites on their French protectors. With French backing, the Maronites squeezed constitutional concessions from non-Christian groups, giving Christians the lion's share of political authority in the new state. Even when their relative proportion of the Lebanese population declined, the Maronites resisted allowing others to enjoy the same political rights as themselves. This undermined the legitimacy of the state and, beginning in 1958, led to recurrent civil war (Maktabi, 2000).

The fate of the Hashemite dynasty offers another example of initiatives by postwar mapmakers that sabotaged the sovereignty of Middle Eastern states. As detailed by Arthur Goldschmidt in Chapter 3, the British divided their Palestine mandate to create the kingdom of Transjordan, partly motivated by the need to reward Abdullah ibn Hussein with a land to rule. Faisal ibn Hussein, Abdullah's brother and the local leader most closely identified with the Arab Revolt, was proclaimed king of Syria in 1920. Postwar Syria was far from the "Arab state" that Faisal had dreamed of leading and, as things turned out, he did not get to lead it for long. A British protégé like his brother Abdullah, Faisal was ousted from Syria by France, the new mandatory power there. In 1921 Faisal became king of Iraq, a British mandate.

Iraq presents one of the clearest examples of the perversity of boundary drawing and state building under the mandates described by Ian Manners and Barbara McKean Parmenter in Chapter 2. Iraq was assembled from large segments of what used to be three Ottoman districts: Baghdad, with its majority of Sunni Muslim Arabs; Basra, where the majority of the population is Shi'i Arab; and Mosul, where Iraqi oil was first discovered on the territory of primarily Sunni Muslim Kurds (Marr, 1985). Iraq's chronic problems with "state building" are rooted in its troubled history as a trinational state (Makiya, 1996). Yet a number of scholars, chief among them Michael Hudson (1977), argue that Iraq's problems are not unique. They believe that "positive sovereignty"—popular legitimacy plus the capacity to govern—is lacking throughout the Middle East.

The transition from an international system where only the most powerful states enjoyed negative sovereignty to one where negative sovereignty was declared a right of every state coincided with modern state formation in the Middle East. There it helped to produce mostly small, weak, and externally dependent regimes with a diminished capacity both to govern independently and to mobilize the support and loyalty of their citizens (Salamé, 1990). Citizen-nationalists and governments alike tended to blame their countries' problems on Western imperialism. Leaders and populations of Middle Eastern states constructed national ideologies—"state ideas"—incorporating strong opposition against external interference. Yet all around the world, wherever states were too weak to prevent it, external intervention by major powers continued (Weber, 1995). In today's rapidly changing international system, the Middle East, like the Balkans, is a favored target of those seeking to extend the authority of dominant states over the internal politics of regions where they have economic and strategic interests (Havel, 1999; Rogers, 2002; Zanoyan, 2002).

External intervention also brought selective advantages to states whose oil and gas reserves were discovered and developed by foreign companies, many based in Britain or the United States. Their incomes at first were limited to royalties and fees, but they grew at astronomical rates following the oil revolution of the early 1970s, which forced crude oil prices upward and transferred control of oil and gas reserves from foreign companies to national governments (Tétreault, 1985). As discussed in detail in Chapter 8, however, oil has been a mixed blessing to its owners (Amuzegar, 1982). Although it gave them more choices and greater leverage in foreign policy, it also insulated state-building elites from domestic demands for political participation. Democratization was halted and even reversed, and the development of institutions that form the bedrock of state capacity to preside over a self-sufficient society and economy was retarded (e.g., Crystal, 1990; Gasiorowski, 1991; Zanoyan, 2002). Hydrocarbon resources allowed oil-exporting regimes to take the easy way out. They supported both a strategy of economic development that offered ample room for corruption—but little support for a vibrant private sector (see Luke, 1983, 1985)—and a strategy of political and social development based on paying off disgruntled citizens rather than accommodating their demands for autonomous participation in national life (Beblawi, 1990; Tétreault, 2000; Zanoyan, 2002).

Oil reserves are unevenly distributed among the states of the Middle East, but oil income affects nearly all of them. Especially before the collapse of oil prices in 1986, oil-exporting states spent large amounts on foreign aid (Hallwood and Sinclair, 1982), salaries paid to imported workers (Ibrahim, 1980), and direct foreign investments in neighboring countries (Stephens, 1976; Tétreault, 1995). As oil incomes shot upward beginning in 1970, a sizable proportion of this money was spent on arms (Dawisha, 1982–1983; Nitzan and Bichler, 2002). It is no secret that having money of one's own brought with it more choice and freedom. As foreign aid donors and arms buyers, Middle Eastern states could exercise independent leverage abroad. Saudi aid to Islamist groups allowed Saudi Arabia to influence populations in other Arab states, while in Central Asia, Saudi money (along with U.S. arms) nourished the most radical Islamist factions, including the Taliban (Rashid, 2001). But the oil and arms circuit also left them vulnerable to foreign governments able to use their strategic dependence to extort lucrative contracts for arms purchases (Clawson, 1995; Nitzan and Bichler, 2002).

■ Local Challenges to State Sovereignty

The arbitrary nature of state boundaries in the Middle East provided a focus of activism for those who wanted political integration to match the common religious, historical, and linguistic roots that they saw as uniting this region (Dawisha, 2003). Movements that transcend ethnic divisions—such as Arab nationalism and Islamism—along with "historic missions" that transcend state boundaries—examples include defeating imperialism, liberating Palestine, reconstructing Eretz Yisrael, achieving Arab unity, and defending religious and cultural values (Salamé, 1994:87; Dawisha, 2003)—were used to justify territorial encroachment and intervention in the domestic affairs of Middle Eastern states by their ambitious neighbors.

In addition to these rather grandiose claims, simple boundary disputes also plagued the region. In the Gulf, borders were left poorly defined by the colonial powers while a long history during which various empires, states, and tribes controlled oases, rivers, and ports at different times made plausible claims that a piece of territory within the boundaries of one state "really" belonged to another. In recent years, however, several disputed boundaries between Saudi Arabia and Oman, Yemen, and Qatar have been resolved. An interstate boundary was drawn to divide the former Neutral Zone, a jointly controlled territory established under the 1922 Treaty of Uqair to accommodate the migration of bedouin tribes between Saudi Arabia and Kuwait (Dickson, 1956). Oman and its other neighbors also have resolved most of their boundary disputes. Perhaps the most notable of these relatively peaceful resolutions of border conflicts ended a long dispute between Qatar and Bahrain. Disputes over the Hawar Islands and Fasht al-Dibel rocks, which were controlled by Bahrain and claimed by Qatar, and Zubarah, which was controlled by Qatar and claimed by Bahrain, persisted after decades of unsuccessful mediation efforts. In 1991, Qatar petitioned the International Court of Justice (ICJ) in The Hague to rule on this matter. The ICJ gave its decision in March 2001, using several different principles not only to allocate the disputed lands but also to construct a maritime boundary between the two states through an area thought to contain oil and gas resources (N.A., 2001). This dispute between Bahrain and Qatar had almost led to war in 1986, and both governments were relieved when what the Court had called the longest case in its history was finally settled (Gerner and Yilmaz, 2004).

A long-standing boundary dispute with imperialist roots centers on the Western Sahara, a former Spanish colony located on the Atlantic coast of Africa. Parts of this territory were claimed by Morocco and Mauritania, which sent armies to occupy it in 1975 when Spanish imperial authority was waning under the pressure of a national liberation movement that had evolved into an armed insurgency. Encroachment by neighboring Morocco and Mauritania forced thousands of Saharawis into exile in Algeria. There they live in refugee camps that are "surprisingly well organized" and led by native administrators under the direction of a popular council with an elected president (Berke, 1997:3). The remaining insurgents forced Mauritania to relinquish its claims in 1979, but Morocco continues its occupation and insurgents continue to oppose it, although military activity is low-level and sporadic. Mediation efforts have so far not even succeeded in forcing Morocco to meet with representatives of the government-in-exile and a proposed referendum on the political future of the area has been delayed repeatedly.

The Western Sahara conflict aggravates relations between Morocco and its other neighbors: Algeria, which supports the government-in-exile, and Spain, which still occupies two islands off the Moroccan coast. Morocco attempted to seize one of them, Parsley Island, in the summer of 2002, but pressure from the European Union forced Morocco to withdraw its troops. The tension created by more than a quarter century of dispute over the Spanish Sahara destabilizes the whole western Mediterranean and, like the dispute between Bahrain and Qatar, shows the potential of conflicts over sovereignty to explode into war. Boundary conflicts between Iran and Iraq, and Iraq and Kuwait, along with Israel's occupation and annexation of Arab territories, have led to full-scale wars. Some of these boundary conflicts will be discussed in subsequent sections of this chapter.

■ The Middle East and the Great Powers

As Deborah Gerner discusses in Chapter 4, most areas of the Middle East began the twentieth century as clients or dependencies of one or another European power. Even modern Turkey, the core of the old Ottoman Empire, had been an economic colony of its European creditors since the establishment of the Ottoman Debt Commission in 1881 (Polanyi, 1944). The Turkish state idea incorporated elements of what Atatürk saw as the greatest strengths of the West: modernization, secularization, and state-centered nationalism. His goal was to make Turkey an equal of the Great Powers, not a dependency of them. He pursued that goal successfully on the battlefield, wresting control of far more territory than the victors of World War I had intended to leave for the rump Turkish state they had envisioned as emerging from the shambles of empire.

North African communities were among the most eager to avoid or overthrow European rule. Examples of bitter and protracted anticolonial conflict include the bloody conquest of what is now Libya by the forces of Fascist Italy, and the vicious eight-year war that ended 130 years of French control of Algeria. The Algerian war was exemplary in its brutality (Talbott, 1980). It included widespread terrorist violence by both sides, and the systematic torture, execution, and assassination of thousands of Algerian women and men by the French military (Shatz, 2002). French forces had been disgraced by their nonperformance against Germany in the "phony war" of 1940 and, in May 1954, by having been beaten at Dien Bien Phu, the battle that ended their nine-year attempt to crush the anticolonial movement in Vietnam. Chillingly depicted in Gillo Pontecorvo's 1966 film *The Battle of Algiers,* what historian John Talbott (1980) called "the war without a name" brought France itself to the verge of civil war, while the philosopher of Algerian liberation, Franz Fanon, glorified revolutionary violence in his 1961 book *The Wretched of the Earth* as the only way to restore a culture with a degraded and degrading past.

A far from purifying violence erupted across Algeria during the still smoldering civil war that began in 1992. The uprising was ignited when the Algerian military, representing the forces that had controlled the country since liberation in 1962, canceled parliamentary elections that they feared would mean the victory of their Islamist rivals. The ensuing civil war, with its own toll of tens of thousands of tortured, executed, and assassinated Algerians on both sides, is both legacy and echo of the long and ugly war against the French.

Although many Middle Eastern leaders fought against European intervention, others sought it out. Toward the end of the nineteenth century, Emir Mubarak of Kuwait (r. 1896–1915) actively angled for British protection. He hoped both to prevent his country from being attached to the Ottoman Empire by an energetic Turkish governor (Anscombe, 1997; al-Ebraheem, 1975) and to get some assistance first to consolidate his own power and then to ensure that his lineal descendants would rule Kuwait after his death (Anscombe, 1997; Rush, 1987). Abdul Aziz ibn Saud manipulated British officials to help him acquire more than half the territory of Kuwait in 1922 (Dickson, 1956). Until the conclusion of World War II, he relied on British and U.S. gold to help him consolidate his conquests on the Arabian Peninsula and keep the leaders of subordinate tribes firmly in his camp (Anderson, 1981; Salamé, 1990). Nearly every Middle Eastern government was ready to welcome foreign-owned companies willing to pay for the right to prospect for oil. In consequence, external intervention by the Great Powers or their agents was neither always nor uniformly condemned by Middle Eastern political leaders, although citizen nationalists often saw things differently.

Nationalists protested the grave burdens that imperialism imposed on most of the region. Along with strategic interests such as protecting the route to India, imperial powers used their colonies and dependencies primarily to make themselves rich (Wolf, 1982). Local economies were truncated by drawing national boundaries through areas and populations that were parts of larger trading and commercial markets. Colonies and economic dependencies were bled for the benefit of settlers and overseas investors. Oil companies took the lion's share of profits from their often wasteful exploitation of the region's petroleum reserves (see, e.g., Penrose, 1968; Rand, 1975; Tétreault, 1995). Foreign occupiers violated local customs with impunity, and belittled the religion, society, and culture of the populations they were milking (see, e.g., Ahmed, 1992; Lazreg, 1994; Tétreault, 1995). Zionist immigration into Palestine, which had begun years before the Balfour Declaration of 1917 pledged British support for a Jewish homeland there, threatened communities and the livelihoods of the native population. All these political, economic, and psychological burdens were aggravated by the imperialists' practice not only of playing social groups within countries against one another to enhance their political control (Migdal, 1988; al-Naqeeb, 1990) but also of pitting one country against others in situations such as negotiations for oil concessions, to increase the colonizers' economic returns (e.g., Chisholm, 1975).

■ Dependency

Dependency is a relationship of inequality between a developing and a developed country (Caporaso, 1978). Creating dependency is a conscious aim of colonization and imperialism. During the eighteenth century, when the American states were colonies of Britain, the British passed laws such as the Navigation Acts that required the colonies to sell raw materials to Britain and then buy British products. Britain benefited both from the trade itself and also from processing the raw materials purchased from the colonies. Both provided jobs for British workers and tax revenues for the government. Colonial trade was a relationship of exchange, but the exchange was unequal in the present and was intended to remain unequal in the future. The American colonies had to win a war of independence to throw off the crippling yoke of British imperialism.

During the nineteenth and twentieth centuries, imperialism enabled first Europe and then the United States to gain similar preferential access to raw materials located in the Middle East. Governments signed exclusive contracts with British and U.S. oil companies to develop local hydrocarbon industries. Oil companies purchased supplies and equipment from their home countries and imported all but the most menial workers. Oil development also distorted local economies. In oil-rich Hasa in Saudi Arabia, agriculture was destroyed to accommodate pipelines and pumping stations (Munif, 1989). Most of the oil was sold overseas as a raw material that was both processed and consumed outside the countries where it had originated.

Foreign oil companies no longer own all of the Middle East's oil and gas reserves. However, the way these reserves were developed and the way the domestic economies of oil-exporting countries were constructed around oil production and sales tied the economies of these states to global markets and made them economically dependent even after governments nationalized these industries in the early 1970s. When oil prices fall, for example, there is little that one or even several oil exporters can do to bring them back up and keep them there. OPEC had some success stabilizing oil prices in the 1960s and raising them in the 1970s. However, that success was ephemeral, enhanced by circumstances such as the closing of the Suez Canal by the 1967 Arab-Israeli war and surging U.S. oil demand for the Vietnam War. Within a few years, structural changes, such as the discovery and development of new oil fields outside OPEC countries, brought world oil prices back down. Oil prices fell to historically low levels in the mid-1980s, creating economic hardship and domestic conflict in many oil-exporting countries (Hunter, 1986).

The domestic economies of the wealthiest oil-exporting countries were organized to spend oil revenues rather than to produce a wide range of goods and services to satisfy local needs and wants. Rivers of cash from oil sales, along with growing demand for foreign products from tanks and machine guns to cars and television programs, created consumption patterns that depended on imported goods. Oil exporters expanded production capacity to ensure that they could continue to buy what they wanted from overseas. As global capacity expanded, some exporters were compelled to increase oil production, not only to justify their investment but also to support growing populations. But producing more oil glutted markets, pushing prices down and encouraging even more production to keep income levels up. This vicious circle came around again in the late 1990s, but talk of structural reform never turned into action. When oil prices went back up, incentives for exporting country governments to make fundamental changes to reduce dependency disappeared. Despite these ups and downs in the oil market, the Middle East remains dependent on oil and gas sales as a primary source of government revenues.

▓ Cliency

Cliency is a strategic relationship between a major power seeking a local base and a less powerful state whose assets are compatible with the needs of the major power (Gasiorowski, 1991; Tétreault, 1991). The client's stock in trade can include geographic location, port and basing facilities, and a regime willing to act on behalf of the major power. In return for one or more of these assets, the major power patron transfers arms, military training and equipment, and other types of military and economic assistance to the less powerful client. Both sides gain from cliency, but unlike dependency, cliency offers the government of the smaller state proportionately more than it offers the larger partner. Indeed, as the client becomes embedded in the foreign policy strategies of its patron, the dependence of a patron on a client's strategic assets may grow at the same time that patron leverage against the client government declines. Meanwhile, the extranational assets it receives from its patron allows the client government to protect itself against external and internal challenges by buying off foreign and domestic enemies or using patron-supplied force against them.

The Cold War increased the importance of cliency in the relationships of Middle Eastern states with major outside powers. The superpowers were interested in economic gains, especially from their relations with oil-exporting states, but strategic concerns were primary. A large portion of foreign aid from the superpowers took the form of military assistance. Nearly all of it imposed obligations in the form of services required of Middle Eastern client states: diplomatic and military support and preferential access by the patron state and its agents to the client's domestic resources (Gasiorowski, 1991). Sometimes resources provided by patron states were used by rebellious military officers against weak and unpopular client governments. One example is the 1969 overthrow of King Idris in Libya (Bill and Springborg, 1994). Some were used by client governments against their own populations, which occurred in Iran (Gasiorowski, 1991).

International politics changed during the Cold War and dependency relations changed as well. Competition increased in the market for Middle Eastern oil concessions, most markedly in Libya but also in Iran and the Arabian Peninsula states (Penrose, 1968). As detailed in Chapter 8, these changes helped to shift control of oil from foreign multinational oil companies to host governments. Another apparent benefit of the Cold War era was that imperialism was replaced by at least the rhetoric of negative sovereignty. The accepted convention, that all states were autonomous and could freely choose their own allies and partners, meant that the superpowers sometimes could be brought to bid for client allies, a situation that Egypt used to great advantage in financing its Aswan Dam project in the 1950s (Mosley, 1978).

Too close an alliance with either superpower risked retaliation from disgruntled nationalists against overly compliant regimes. Strong leaders were able to preserve some autonomy from Cold War patrons. In 1955, Egypt's Gamal Abdul Nasser, along with leaders of other developing countries, held a conference in Bandung, Indonesia, whose main product was the "nonaligned movement." Nonalignment was a declaration of independence from a permanent relationship to either superpower and was seen as a guarantee of the negative sovereignty of developing states. Yet despite declarations of nonalignment and promises of mutual support from other nominally nonaligned states, very few countries in the Middle East were successful at finding a middle ground between the superpowers.

One success story was Kuwait, the role model for other small Gulf emirates seeking to orchestrate a balance of power among potential patrons (Anscombe, 1997). Initiated as part of the state-building strategy of Mubarak al-Sabah, Kuwait's first twentieth-century emir (al-Ebraheem, 1975; Anscombe, 1997; Assiri, 1990; Tétreault, 1991), a century of persistence in courting a panoply of external partners paid off for Kuwait when it was invaded by Iraq in 1990. Influential foreign nationals associated with Kuwaiti-owned companies argued the Kuwaiti case to world leaders before their views and policies were fully formed, and European governments hosting large Kuwaiti investments moved rapidly to protect Kuwaiti assets (Tétreault, 1995). Thanks to the collapse of the Cold War's rigid alliances and to a history of cordial relations with the Soviet Union, including generous Kuwaiti assistance following a major earthquake there in 1989, a multinational coalition including both the United States and the Soviet Union was rapidly assembled to roll back the Iraqi invasion. Despite strong support for Iraq among the populations of nearly every state in the Middle East, the unity of their U.S. and Russian patrons, together with positive incentives ranging from debt forgiveness to promises of future economic assistance from Kuwait, pulled nearly all of these states into the Kuwaiti camp (Tétreault, 1992).

Unlike Kuwait, most Middle Eastern states found that a nonaligned strategy was difficult to sustain in practice. Saudi Arabia proclaimed itself to be nonaligned. However, religious militancy and oil interests ensured that it was almost entirely oriented toward the West even though the United States and other Western governments were strong supporters of Israel (Korany, 1991; Quandt, 1981). A structurally similar set of pressures upset the efforts of the so-called confrontation states (those engaged militarily against Israel) to remain nonaligned. Syria, Iraq, and Egypt drifted into the Soviet orbit to obtain military support for their wars against U.S.-backed Israel. As the region's total oil income increased, however, the Arab confrontation states found they could get foreign military assistance from their Arab oil-exporting neighbors (Dawisha, 1982–1983).

■ Middle East Regionalism

Regionalism was a movement that began during the latter part of World War II and attracted people who wanted to build postwar regimes that would foster peaceful international relations. Regionalists recommended that countries joined by proximity, culture, and common interests establish international organizations for functional purposes such as economic development or military security. The League of Arab States (Arab League) was founded in 1945, among the first of these new organizations. The Great Powers of World War II, like the great powers of today, refused to accept the Arab League's "strong" definition of regionalism, which insisted that security be a matter wholly internal to participating states rather than subject to intervention by the larger world community (MacDonald, 1965:9–11). Even so, the Arab League was recognized by the United Nations and, at its inception, was regarded as a building block of the new postwar order.

Along with regional organizations like the Arab League, functional organizations such as OPEC and the Organization of Arab Petroleum Exporting Countries (OAPEC) also were established and charged with advancing the common economic interests of their members (Tétreault, 1981). OPEC is a multiregional organization; OAPEC is both monoregional and monoethnic. An important goal of both is consensus building, the development of joint positions based on a perception of shared interests sufficiently strong to keep members together even when they come under pressure.

Regional and functional organizations in the Middle East, like Arab nationalism and pan-Islam, promote group identification that goes beyond the state. Yet unlike mass movements, regional and functional organizations are creatures of the state. Their spread aided the practical implementation of negative sovereignty by legitimating agreements and structures that are both interstate and limited in membership. Theoretically, regionalism also could restrict negative sovereignty by assigning formal responsibility for particular policies to the international organization. However, many such organizations, including most in the Middle East, follow decision rules requiring consensus. This affirms the authority of the individual member to veto policies it does not like, preserving sovereignty but also discouraging compromise and inhibiting collective action.

The ability to mobilize a consensus on any issue declines as the membership or the issue slate of an organization expands. New members may have core interests that are marginal to those of the founders. The Arab League was unable to progress beyond a very low level of regional integration as it grew from a group of five closely neighboring states, four of which were strongly Arab nationalist (Egypt, Syria, Iraq, and Lebanon—the fifth founding member was Jordan), to a large organization with more than twenty members from two continents, many with vastly different histories, economies, and political cultures. The same problems afflict OPEC, whose five founding members (Venezuela, Iran, Iraq, Kuwait, and Saudi Arabia) had the petroleum and financial resources to exercise market power collectively through production restraint. By adding small producers such as Gabon and Ecuador and desperate ones such as Nigeria and Indonesia prevented OPEC from developing effective production restraint strategies. New members with different economic goals aggravated already endemic political conflicts within the group (Mikdashi, 1972). OPEC's founders also had conflicting interests, and the organization's charter made consensus decisions mandatory so each could protect itself against the others. As OPEC grew, members also devised informal conventions freeing them from having to be bound by collective decisions under certain conditions (Tétreault, 1981:42). These conditions allowed OPEC to pursue a limited range of common interests, but it continues to have problems preventing members from pursuing independent interests even when their actions visibly harm the common good.

A decrease in common interests and purposes among the members of an international organization also can be triggered by changes in member governments and regimes. OAPEC was formed in 1968 to give its three founders, Libya, Kuwait, and Saudi Arabia, a base from which to resist demands by Arab radicals that they apply the "oil weapon" regardless of their financial situations or their ability to deliver public services to their populations. But when King Idris of Libya was overthrown in 1969 by a group of military officers led by Colonel Muammar Qaddafi, the new regime in Libya suddenly introduced into the heart of the organization the very militancy that OAPEC had been established to avoid.

Organizational cohesion is very sensitive to the preservation of close similarity among the structural and ideological interests of group members. Concerns in this regard led the founders of the Gulf Cooperation Council (GCC—Kuwait, Saudi Arabia, Qatar, Oman, Bahrain, and the United Arab Emirates) to exclude Yemen because it "did not share 'identical systems, identical internal and foreign policies, identical ideologies, identical aspirations and identical human, social, and political problems' [with] the Arab gulf littoral states" (Lawson 1997:15; Lawson, 2000). The GCC was established in 1981 to replace bilateral security arrangements with a regional security regime and also to promote economic integration among its members. Reflecting Iraq's status as a belligerent in the Iran-Iraq War, the GCC also excluded Iraq from membership (Peterson, 1988).

Despite significant economic integration, GCC collective security measures have consistently fallen short. Some were conceptually defective, such as Saudi policies for centralizing police records and permitting police forces of member states to cross the border into another member state in cases of hot pursuit. Sometimes members simply failed to carry out their GCC obligations. The GCC members refused to assist Kuwait following liberation when, with a conflagration in its oil fields, it asked for a loan of up to 1 million barrels of oil per day to meet the requirements of its overseas refineries. This refusal exposed the hollowness of GCC institutions; the council had adopted an oil-sharing agreement just four years earlier precisely to deal with production shortfalls in a member state (Tétreault, 1995:147). The record of the GCC shows that even where founding members perceive themselves as virtually "identical," regional organizations in the Middle East are hard-pressed to overcome the shortsighted attachment of their members to narrow definitions of negative sovereignty.

■ Moving Toward Regional Autonomy or a New Imperialism?

The end of the Cold War initiated a global realignment that also affects the international relations of the Middle East. During the era of the most intense East-West confrontation, "hot wars" in the Middle East were widely viewed as proxy conflicts between superpower clients. As Soviet power weakened in the late 1980s, Soviet capacity to intervene abroad also declined. At first, local issues became more prominent in regional conflicts. This was reflected in the realignments among regional actors during the Gulf War (1990–1991) and shifts in support for the principals in the Arab-Israeli conflict. In 2001, a far less accommodating international system began to move against the interests of the Arab states and Iran, but how they will respond to this new situation, individually and collectively, remains unclear.

Within a few days, the 1990 invasion of Kuwait by Iraq pushed the United States from a tacit alliance with Iraq to demanding that Iraq withdraw completely from Kuwait (Sciolino, 1991; Smith, 1992; Urquhart, 2002). Working through the UN Security Council, the United States spearheaded a series of resolutions condemning Iraq and imposing severe economic sanctions against it. The Soviet Union was a prominent part of the anti-Iraq coalition. Although it preferred a negotiated settlement, the Soviet government remained part of the coalition throughout the nearly six weeks of war (Melkumyan, 1992). Soviet cooperation was critical in the UN Security Council, the formal venue for the coordination of the coalition against Iraq. Had the Soviet Union chosen to use its Security Council veto, neither the economic sanctions nor the large multinational military operation that was launched in January 1991 could have been achieved. Soviet participation also muted, although it could not entirely quell, criticism of U.S. policy by those sympathetic to Iraq or opposed to unilateral military activities by the United States on the Arabian Peninsula.

Even before the end of the Cold War, the Soviet Union had softened its stance toward Israel, for example, by allowing Soviet Jews to emigrate. In

Kuwaiti troops, operating out of Saudi Arabia, prepare to liberate Kuwait in 1991. After a month-long bombing campaign, the ground war lasted just one hundred hours.

consequence, the United States became the predominant extraregional power involved in the Israeli-Palestinian conflict, but its pro-Israeli bias discouraged Palestinians, whose offers of compromise were repeatedly treated as new floors for the next round of negotiations (Ashrawi, 1995). The post–Cold War realignment offered an opportunity for other external partners to alter the environment of those negotiations. The Norwegian government initiated talks that allowed Israelis and Palestinians to engage simultaneously in public negotiations in Madrid and secret negotiations in Oslo. The agreement that they hammered out was signed in September 1993 in Washington, D.C.

The end of the Cold War appeared to reduce the ability of the United States to pry support from reluctant allies for policies they believed to be unwise, unnecessary, or contrary to their own national interests. Doctrines such as "dual containment," under which the United States justified demands that other countries isolate both Iran and Iraq, did not have the widespread support among U.S. allies that the original containment policy against the Soviet Union had enjoyed. France was the only major Western ally pursuing a notably independent foreign policy toward the Middle East during most of the Cold War (Wood, 1993), but during the 1990s the Oslo Accords were only one example of growing foreign policy autonomy among several countries that had been part of the U.S. bloc during the Cold War. As I discuss below, the United States moved to reverse this trend after George W. Bush became president.

■ The Middle East as a Foreign Policy Subsystem

When Iraq invaded Kuwait in August 1990, a common refrain among Arabs was that such an event had never occurred before: Arab countries did not attack one another militarily. But this was not exactly true. Iraq had both threatened and invaded Kuwait several times previously. Although far from the same scale as in 1990, Iraq had sent military forces to take, hold, and occupy part of northern Kuwait in the mid-1970s (Assiri, 1990). It also used "salami tactics" to acquire territory from Kuwait, periodically sending troops to the frontier to inch the border southward (Tétreault, 1995:123–124).

Other inter-Arab conflicts also are forgotten by those professing to be shocked by Iraq's 1990 invasion of Kuwait. Egypt conducted extensive military operations in Yemen in the mid-1960s during its proxy war against Saudi Arabia and has engaged for years in recurrent border clashes with Libya. As I discussed earlier, Libya and Algeria oppose Morocco by assisting nationalists in the Western Sahara in their struggle to create a "Saharawi nation" in Spanish Morocco. The government of King Hussein mounted a strong military offensive against a semisovereign Palestinian enclave in Jordan during the "Black September" of 1970; Syria intervened militarily in Lebanon during the civil war and its military forces continue to occupy part of Lebanon today. Arabian Peninsula border clashes were common through most of the twentieth century, while boundary conflicts and covert operations involving non-Arab Iran remain a problem.

Among the most persistent axes of conflict in the region are those in which non-Arabs are belligerents. Examples include confrontations between Israel and various Arab opponents, conflicts in which Kurds are active participants, and hostilities between Iraq and Iran. These three sets of conflicts intersect with and amplify one another, and frequently attract involvement by one or more outside powers. At the same time, the Middle East is the home of countless regional governmental and nongovernmental organizations (NGOs) that reflect common economic, cultural, and policy interests. Some, such as OPEC, include both non-Arab and extraregional partners. Others, like the inclusive Arab League and the exclusive OAPEC and GCC, are all-Arab.

I count myself among those who are generally pessimistic about what these various attempts to promote community among Middle Eastern states have accomplished. However, I also believe that continuing these efforts both normalizes the concept of common interests and supports the gradual growth of institutions that could embody what now are mostly formulaic assertions of "brotherhood" among states in this region. As Iran and the Arab states find themselves increasingly pressed by a hostile U.S. administration, the advantages of closer cooperation could overshadow their long-standing reluctance to sacrifice some cherished autonomy to protect national and regional interests.

The Arab-Israeli Conflict

The Arab-Israeli conflict is discussed more fully by Simona Sharoni and Mohammed Abu-Nimer in Chapter 6, but here I want to emphasize two elements in this century-long struggle: its large external dimension and the role of the Palestinians in international relations in the Middle East generally. When Zionist leaders declared Israel to be a state in 1948, both the United States and the Soviet Union rushed to recognize it. At that time, Israeli institutions such as the army and the labor movement were more socialist than liberal (Bill and Springborg, 1994:261). Even so, as Cold War positions hardened, Israel grew increasingly identified with the United States. At first, this reflected Israeli economic dependence on support from the U.S. Jewish community as much as or more than any strategic dependence on the U.S. government (Nitzan and Bichler, 2002).

Israel's ties to the U.S. government strengthened following the Six Day War in June 1967. Then France, formerly Israel's primary foreign source of armaments, shifted toward the Arab states because of French concerns about the long-term security of oil supplies (Weisberg, 1977). Although the Israelis had bombed a U.S. intelligence vessel, the *Liberty,* to keep their war preparations from discovery, domestic politics pushed the United States to support Israel during the 1967 war (Bamford, 2001; Christison, 2000). U.S. support included coordinating measures to defeat the first systematic application of the Arab "oil weapon" against Israel's allies (Sankari, 1976; Tétreault, 1981).

The October 1973 Arab-Israeli war was deeply embedded in Cold War politics. Following as it did the 1972 migration of Egypt out of the Soviet and into the U.S. orbit, the war put the Nixon administration in the difficult situation of having a foreign policy victory that threatened its domestic political position. Although U.S. officials had received a series of explicit warnings beginning in spring 1973 that war between Israel and the Arab states was imminent (Tétreault, 1985:34), Arab attacks on Israeli positions took the U.S. government by surprise. Initial Arab victories alarmed the United States, prompting a massive airlift of supplies to Israel that reversed most of the Arab gains. The war also provided an opportunity for the Soviet Union to recoup some of its diplomatic losses in the region. When Israel violated the UN-brokered cease-fire agreement of October 22, 1973, the Soviet Union announced that it would send in troops. It also approached the United States about forming a joint U.S.-Soviet peacekeeping force. U.S. president Richard Nixon, fearful of his domestic standing in the midst of the Watergate investigation, was afraid to engage in any action in the Middle East that could be construed as aiding the Arabs. Instead, he put U.S. military forces on alert, making any joint U.S.-Soviet action in the Middle Eastern war impossible (Kissinger, 1979:552–611).

The threat of global conflict during the 1973 war was ratcheted to a high level by policymakers in different countries trying to juggle fundamentally incompatible domestic, regional, and global demands. National leaders in powerful countries acted in their own interests without worrying about how their actions would affect their allies. This echoes the cavalier behavior of European powers in the Middle East during and after World War I, the history of the British mandate in Palestine, and Cold War maneuvering in the region before and after the October 1973 war. Thus the 1977 decision of Anwar Sadat to go to Jerusalem, an extraordinary gesture toward resolving the Arab-Israeli conflict, can be seen as a gamble whose potential benefits included the removal of a magnet for superpower confrontation, as well as an end to the balance of terror between Arabs and Israelis and a chance to resolve the problem of what to do about the Palestinians.

Following the Israeli victory in the 1948 war and the consequent expulsion of thousands of Palestinians from their homes (Christison, 2000; Morris, 1989), the Palestinian diaspora fanned out across the region. Large numbers of Palestinians were concentrated in refugee camps and enclaves. Rising oil revenues generated job opportunities, and Palestinians also formed resident communities of workers and families in oil-rich states such as Kuwait (see, e.g., Ghabra, 1987). Palestinians formed an essential element in the Arab nationalist amalgam. A reminder of the ineffectiveness of Arab armies against

Israeli armies in the field, the Palestinians evoked shame, guilt, and a sense of obligation in other Arabs and their governments. Arab leaders such as Egypt's Gamal Abdul Nasser (Nasser, 1955), Libya's Muammar Qaddafi (Zartman and Kluge, 1991), Syrian president Hafez al-Assad (Seale, 1988), and Iraqi president Saddam Hussein (Ahmad, 1991) conceived regional historic missions that included restoring Palestinian national territory as a primary goal.

The Arab states recognized the Palestine Liberation Organization (PLO) as the legitimate government—the "state-in-exile"—of the Palestinians but, for many different reasons, virtually every Arab government resisted absorbing any significant number of Palestinian refugees into its own population. "Jordan was the only Arab country to grant them citizenship," but some Palestinians still live in camps even there (Elon, 2003:6). Instead, the Arab states supported positive sovereignty for the PLO even though the PLO's lack of territory made negative sovereignty impossible. PLO embassies operated in many Arab capitals, and Arab governments in the Gulf deducted PLO taxes from Palestinian workers' paychecks. Along with regular elections to the Palestinian National Council, these tax payments, large infusions of Arab foreign aid, and the myriad informal institutions of Palestinian society nourished the development of a distinctive Palestinian identity despite the absence of a Palestinian territorial state (see Gerner, 1994; Peretz, 1990).

The separate peace agreement signed by Egypt and Israel in 1979 caused the other confrontation states to lose interest in military intervention to help the Palestinians. In 1991, the dissolution of the Soviet Union erased the status of the Arab-Israeli conflict as a cockpit of the Cold War, further reducing the political salience of the Palestinians and their plight. The first intifada (uprising), which began in December 1987, expressed the despair of Palestinians who, after twenty years of increasingly brutal occupation, were enraged at the indifference of the rest of the world (Elon, 2002). It also highlighted the main structural change from the Egyptian-Israeli peace agreement—the Arab-Israeli conflict had become an Israeli-Palestinian conflict (Ben-Yehuda and Sandler, 2002).

At first, the intifada was highly successful in crystallizing a coherent, disciplined, mostly nonviolent resistance movement. As it went into its third year, however, the intifada started to flag, a result of unrelenting Israeli opposition and the exhaustion of Palestinian resources (Gerner, 1991, 1994; Hunter, 1993). Yasser Arafat's support of the Iraqi invasion of Kuwait was a response to Saddam Hussein's proposal to coordinate efforts to liberate Palestine through an Arab National Charter, and Saddam's acceptance of PLO positions on what that liberation would entail (Ahmad, 1991; Christison, 2000). But Arafat's apparent endorsement of the invasion also provided a rationale for other Arab governments to reorient their stance toward Palestinians. Gulf governments, short of cash thanks first to a decade of shrunken oil revenues and second to the billions needed to for the liberation of Kuwait (Tétreault,

1992), found Arafat's gesture a convenient pretext for halting foreign aid to the PLO. Palestinians working in Gulf countries were expelled as security risks, drastically reducing their financial contributions to families living in the West Bank and Gaza. Palestinians also lost diplomatic recognition and suffered other forms of retaliation. Thus, although extremists on both sides of the Israeli-Palestinian conflict engaged in increasingly blatant terrorist tactics to retard the peace process, the loss of external support made accommodation an attractive option to Palestinians.

After the Oslo Agreement was signed, Israeli and Palestinian radicals stepped up their opposition while the Israelis dragged their feet on implementing interim provisions of the Oslo Accords. Even prime ministers declaring their commitment to a permanent resolution of the confict permitted settlements to expand in number and size (Agha and Malley, 2001; Elon, 2002). Meanwhile, the Palestinian National Authority, under Yasser Arafat, proved to be both antithetical to democratization and riddled with corruption. The failure of U.S.-brokered negotiations in the summer of 2000 between Arafat and than–Israeli prime minister Ehud Barak, who had staked his political career on the achievement of a settlement, prompted new threats and confrontations by opponents on both sides (Agha and Malley, 2001; Malley and Agha, 2002; Morris, 2002). A highly publicized intrusion by Israeli general Ariel Sharon, accompanied by a thousand Israeli troops, at the al-Aqsa Mosque in Jerusalem, became the casus belli for Palestinian radicals already determined to derail the peace agreement. They launched a second, "al-Aqsa" intifada, one that never even pretended to be nonviolent.

Despite ups and downs, the administrations of George H. W. Bush and Bill Clinton played active roles as they tried to keep the peace process on track. This changed in 2001 with the inauguration of President George W. Bush, a man already committed to the program of the Israeli right wing. His domestic constituency base was dominated by two strongly pro-Israel/anti-Palestinian groups: radical neoconservative hard-liners and the "Christian Coalition," both committed to Israel's retention of the Occupied Territories. Terrorist attacks on the United States in September 2001 moved the U.S. president even closer to Israeli prime minister Ariel Sharon. As the situation on the ground deteriorated, the intifada and Israel's military reoccupation of land that formerly had been relinquished to the Palestinian Authority under the provisions of the Oslo Agreement generated high rates of civilian casualties, hardening the hearts of populations on each side against compromise with the other (Elon, 2002).

◼ The Kurdish Conflict

The Kurds, like the Palestinians, are a nation without a state (McDowell, 1996). As detailed by Arthur Goldschmidt in Chapter 3, Kurds were promised

During the second intifada, Israel blocked numerous roads, such as this one from Birzeit to Ramallah, forcing Palestinians to leave their cars and walk across a rocky path. In mid-2003, numerous towns and villages were only accessible by foot.

an autonomous territory by the European powers under the Treaty of Sèvres following World War I. However, a large slice of "Kurdistan," the Kirkuk area, was among the first oil-producing regions in the Middle East. Because of the oil, the British wanted Kirkuk attached to Iraq, one of their mandates (Marr, 1985). Subsequently the territory of the Kurds, a non-Arab, non-Turkic people, was divided among five adjoining states: Iran, Iraq, Turkey, Syria, and the former Soviet Union (now Azerbaijan). Kurdish ethnic enclaves persist because high mountains separate communities, tribal leaders exercise strong authority over local populations, and internal Kurdish disagreements as well as tensions between Kurds and the governments of the affected states produce repeated conflicts. These struggles are more than a set of civil wars; they also feature strife among Kurds and their host governments.

Oil and separatist politics coincide in Iraq, where one of the elements holding the Kurds together was their long insistence on local autonomy and rights to a share of Iraqi oil revenues. Iraqi Kurds engaged in repeated uprisings against the central government from the earliest years of the Iraqi state. During the 1930s and 1940s, Kurdish guerrillas led by Mullah Mustafa Barzani fought an intermittent civil war in Iraq. Iranian Kurds also refused to resign themselves to assimilation. During World War II, assisted by Soviet troops, Iranian Kurds established a short-lived independent republic called

Mahabad. Despite rivalry among Kurdish tribal leaders, Kurds often assist one another in wars against the states. For example, Barzani led several thousand Iraqi Kurdish fighters into Iran to help defend Mahabad against Iranian troops.

After Mahabad fell, Barzani went into exile in the Soviet Union, but following the 1958 revolution he was permitted to return to Iraq. The postrevolutionary Iraqi regime released Kurdish political prisoners and also appointed Kurds to important government posts. The common bond between Kurds and Iraq's new leader, Abd al-Karim Qasim, was opposition to Arab nationalism. This alliance ended when the Iraqi government rejected Kurdish demands for autonomy as secessionist. The civil war in Iraq resumed in 1961.

Just as Kurds sometimes are willing to cooperate with one another against a state, they also form temporary alignments with one state against another state or against another Kurdish faction. Kurdish rebels in Iraq receive periodic assistance from the Iranian government, and Iraqi and Iranian troops have fought one another in the Kurdish region during uprisings. During the early 1970s, Iraqi Kurdish rebels were aided both by Iran and, through Iran, by the United States. Negotiations between representatives of the Iraqi government and the Kurds produced compromises on many issues dividing the two sides. However, it was not until 1975, when the Iranian government and the United States agreed to halt military support of Iraqi Kurds in exchange for moving the boundary between Iraq and Iran, that this phase of the fighting ended (Ahmad, 1991).

Following the Iranian revolution in 1979, Iraqi Kurds became a target of Iranian political manipulation once again. During the Iran-Iraq War (1980–1988), Saddam Hussein saw the Kurdish region as a point of strategic vulnerability. Fighting took place not only between Iraq and Iran but also between Iraqis and Kurds in both countries. In violation of international treaties, the Iraqi military used chemical weapons against both Iranian troops and Iraqi Kurdish villages, including Halabja, and razed hundreds more Kurdish villages to the ground (Makiya, 1993). After the Gulf War (1990–1991), Iraqi Kurds rose up against the government of Saddam Hussein, but brutal repression by Iraqi troops led to a massive outflow of refugees into Iran and Turkey. Britain, France, Holland, and the United States created "safe havens" for the Kurds, including a no-fly zone policed by British and U.S. aircraft deployed from bases in Turkey.

Within the safe haven, a Kurdish administration located in Erbil was established by two often-warring Kurdish factions, the Kurdistan Democratic Party (KDP) under Massoud Barzani (son of KDP founder Mullah Mustafa Barzani), and the Patriotic Union of Kurdistan (PUK) under Jalal Talabani. However, the economic isolation of the safe haven and its almost complete dependence on resources from outside brought the two factions into repeated conflict (Barkey, 1997). Their competition for scarce resources aggravated differences in the assumptions and goals of their leaders, and these divisions were played up by the governments of Iran, Turkey, and Iraq. U.S. forces continued to protect the Kurds for their opposition to Saddam, and residents of the no-fly zone became accustomed to their autonomy and what some touted as a model democracy for the region (for example, see Salih, 2002). Kurds were among the strongest proponents of U.S. intervention to topple Saddam's regime, although given Turkish opposition to a Kurdish free state and perhaps even to what the Kurds see as their political "bottom line"—an autonomous Kurdish province in a postwar federalized Iraq—their position in Iraq and in the region as a whole remains anything but assured.

Turkey is ambivalent about Iraq's Kurds because it has problems with its own. The long history of Kurdish separatism in Turkey violates the keystone of the Turkish state idea of state-centered nationalism. Atatürk's image of Turkey as an integrated nation-state governed by a uniform civil law was linked to the end of the Ottoman *millet* system that had permitted minority communities a significant degree of self-government in matters affecting personal status. Pressure on all citizens of the new Turkey to conform to Atatürk's secular, modernist, and national norms was intense and often violent, but Atatürk also made efforts to co-opt Kurds into supporting the state idea rather than simply repressing or killing them.

As in Iraq and Iran, rebellious outbursts in Turkey's Kurdish region were entangled in national and regional political movements. During a period of severe internal conflict in Turkey in the mid-1970s, a Marxist-Leninist organization, the Kurdistan Workers Party (PKK), emerged from the leftist movement. In 1984, the PKK launched an armed insurrection that killed more than 20,000 people in about a dozen years. Efforts to suppress the rebellion are estimated to cost Turkey about 3 percent of its gross domestic product (GDP) every year, and tie down about 250,000 Turkish troops and security personnel (Barkey, 1997; also McDowell, 1996).

Turkey's conflicts with its Kurdish minority also feature intervention by neighboring states. Syria and Iran have backed the PKK, which established military bases in the safe haven in Iraq. Until fall 1998, Syria provided a safe haven to PKK rebels. Relations between Turkey and Syria deteriorated alarmingly, however, and under strong Turkish pressure, the Syrians expelled PKK exiles, including PKK leader Abdullah Öcalan. The following year, Öcalan was captured by Turkish agents and jailed. His 1999 trial, at which he was found guilty and sentenced to death, was widely covered in the press. Non-Kurdish Turks welcomed the death sentence because they believe that Öcalan masterminded terrorist acts that killed large numbers of Turkish people.

Turkey's actions to suppress Kurdish opposition complicate its bid for membership in the European Union (EU). Human rights issues constitute the primary public rationale for European resistance to Turkey's acceptance, although reasons far less acceptable (such as dislike of Turkey's Muslim culture) also are responsible. Turkey has made efforts to improve its human rights record and bring its laws into line with EU practice on such issues as the death penalty. These changes are good news to Turkish Kurds, a population suffering extensive human rights abuses at the hands of the state. In August 2002, the government passed laws that abolished the death penalty and made it legal for Kurds to broadcast and teach in their own language. The status of the approximately twenty persons then awaiting execution, including Abdullah Öcalan, remained in doubt; but on October 3, 2002, Öcalan's sentence was commuted and the others also are likely to be spared. Just as the lure of eventual accession to the EU hastened the opening of repressive regimes in Spain and Greece, it also improves the civil rights and liberties for all Turkish citizens, including Turkey's Kurds.

▓ The Conflict Between Iran and Iraq

Both the Israeli-Palestinian conflict and the Kurdish conflict intersect the conflict between Iran and Iraq. Iran is not an Arab country and did not participate in the Arab boycott against Israel mounted to protest its establishment and to undermine its survival (Losman, 1972). In consequence, Iran was free to sell oil to Israel and increase oil production during anti-Israel Arab oil embargoes in 1967 and 1973, undercutting the effectiveness of the Arab "oil weapon" (Tétreault, 1981). Iran and Israel, aspiring regional military powers, both became U.S. clients and partners during the Cold War. Their cliency relationships with the United States were enhanced under the Nixon Doctrine, which advocated greater U.S. reliance on regional proxies to further U.S. Cold War interests (Tétreault, 1985; Elon, 2002). Thus it is not surprising that during the Iran-Iraq War the Reagan administration would initiate illegal sales of weapons to Iran in exchange for money to aid the contras in Nicaragua through the agency of an Israeli intermediary (Draper, 1991).

Unlike Iran, Iraq was a prominent defender of the Palestinians, in part because Iraqi leaders wanted to lead the Arab nationalist movement. In 1967, Iraq spearheaded radical demands for an Arab oil embargo against Israel's allies in the Six Day War. The resulting income losses pushed three other Arab oil-exporting countries to establish OAPEC in January 1968 to block future Iraqi demands (Tétreault, 1981). Iraq fought beside Syria in the October 1973 war, despite the strong rivalry between these two Ba'thist regimes and their quarrels over issues ranged from Euphrates River water rights to oil pipeline transit fees. Iraq's role as a champion of the Palestinian cause remained untarnished even when it refused to participate in the 1973–1974 oil embargo against Israel's allies (Tétreault, 1981). Before the Egyptian-Israeli peace treaty was signed in March 1979, Iraq led a drive at the Baghdad summit meeting of Arab states in November 1978 to retaliate against Egypt should it take that step (Ahmad, 1991).

Iraq's differences with Iran can be traced back through hundreds of years of rivalry between various Arab and Persian empires, but the modern roots of this conflict are another legacy of the cavalier attitudes of the imperialists responsible for shaping post–World War I territorial settlements. Territorial struggles also draw the Kurds into this conflict:

> The borders between the two countries, arranged for the most part by out-siders, have never been firmly accepted by either side. . . . Iraqi fear of Per-sian hegemony was, in their minds, based on gradual Iranian encroachment on "Arab" land, including the Arab territory of Khuzistan (formerly al-Muhammarah) in 1925, the incorporation of the waters around Khur-ramshahr in 1937, and the 1975 treaty that gave Iran half of the Shatt al-Arab. (Marr, 1985:291)

Successful maneuvering by Iran in the Iraqi-Kurdish dispute in the mid-1970s had moved the border between the two from the Iranian side of the Shatt al-Arab to the "thalweg," an imaginary line down the middle of the waterway. Iran's victory reduced Iraq's access to the Gulf and increased its dependence on pipelines crossing Syria and Turkey to carry its oil to markets.

Following the successful 1978–1979 Islamist revolution in Iran, the new government's leaders challenged Iraq by stirring antigovernment sentiments among Iraqi Kurds in the north and making religious appeals to Iraqi Shi'a in the south. In September 1980, Saddam Hussein invaded Iran, thinking he could take advantage of the domestic turmoil caused by internal struggles among the clergy and other supporters of the revolution over who would con-trol the postrevolutionary regime (Keddie, 1981; Moghissi, 1994). Saddam also wanted to end Iranian propaganda campaigns and border clashes chal-lenging Iraqi sovereignty. Iraqis expected a quick victory and a postwar set-tlement that would reverse decades of territorial gains by Iran. They were sur-prised at the resistance they encountered and the lack of support from ethnic Arab citizens of Iran. The conflict bogged down into a war of attrition similar to the trench warfare that claimed so many casualties on the western front dur-ing World War I.

The Iran-Iraq War had a significant oil dimension. As it ground on, Iran's far larger population base erased the strategic advantage Iraq had seized by its surprise attack. Each side sought to devastate not simply the enemy's soldiers but the capacity of the enemy to wage war at all. Iraq successfully mobilized wealthy Arab oil exporters to support its "Arab war" against Iran in spite of their membership in the new Gulf Cooperation Council. In consequence, when Iran bombed Iraq's pipelines to cripple Iraq's capacity to earn oil rev-enues to buy more arms, crude production earmarked by Kuwait and Saudi Arabia to be sold "on Iraq's account" kept oil income flowing into Iraq any-way. The oil-rich Arab Gulf states sent Iraq additional cash and also supplied it with arms. Kuwait imported war matériel destined for Iraq and even constructed a highway from Shuwaikh port to the Iraqi border to carry it north more efficiently. When Iran retaliated by bombing Kuwaiti oil tankers, the Kuwaitis appealed to the Soviet Union, the United States, and other naval powers for protection, resulting in the reflagging of Kuwaiti ships to discourage Iranian attacks (Assiri, 1990). The United States also assisted Iraq directly with "intelligence, economic aid, helicopters, and licenses for exports that were crucial to [Saddam's] development of, among other things, the chemical weapons that he later used with great success to blunt Iranian counterattacks and to subdue the Kurds of northern Iraq" (Urquhart 2002:16).

Perhaps the most important component of the oil war was the expansion of oil production by Saudi Arabia that began in 1985. This flood of oil raised money for the states financing the war, but it depressed oil prices worldwide to their lowest level (in constant dollars) since the 1960s. Arab Gulf exporters with excess production capacity could compensate to some degree for the loss of income from lower prices by increasing production. But Iran, already producing at full capacity and denied other sources of foreign exchange as the result of U.S. sanctions, suffered a sharply reduced capacity to rearm. The oil war counterbalanced Iran's advantages in manpower, and helped to prevent an Iranian victory. Even so, it was not enough to allow Iraq to win the shooting war, which ended in a stalemate in 1988.

By then, conditions in the belligerent countries were far from what they had been before the war began. Despite the largesse of its Arab neighbors,

In the 1980s, young Iraqi women were
trained to fight in the war against Iran.

Iraq was forced to borrow money from Western banks. By the end of the war, Iraq owed U.S.$15 billion to nonconcessional lenders (Tétreault, 1993:96). Meanwhile, the Iraqi people, who had lived under miserable conditions throughout the war, expected the peace to live up to all the promises their leader had made during the war (al-Khafaji, 1995). But Saddam Hussein could not satisfy both the banks and his population, especially given the depression in oil prices ensured by continued overproduction.

Tim Niblock (1982) sees a link between Iraqi conflicts with Iran and Iraqi assaults on Kuwait. He notes that Iran has repeatedly challenged Iraqi sovereignty and usually with success. Iraq's inability to win against Iran leads it to turn against Kuwait, which is much smaller and weaker but against which it has very weak claims. Even so, before 1990, every Iraqi challenge to Kuwait was rewarded with money, land, or leverage on the domestic and foreign policies of Kuwait (Assiri, 1990).

That things turned out so differently in 1990 reflects changes in the external environment that made intervention by a coalition of extraregional states against Iraq possible, though not inevitable. Indeed, some Kuwaiti aid and investment recipients supported Iraq. Jordan violated UN sanctions against Iraq by transporting military supplies off-loaded in the Gulf of Aqaba to the Iraqi border; Yemen supported the Iraqi position in most UN Security Council votes. Yet the majority of Arab governments lined up behind Kuwait. Whether, like the governments of other GCC states, they fought in their own interests, or like Syria, because they detested the Iraqi regime, or like Egypt, because they were lured by the prospect of debt forgiveness and a new infusion of economic aid, many defied large and vocal segments of their own populations by that choice.

In the West, the differences between Kuwait and Iraq seemed clear. In the Middle East, the choice was far less obvious. Saddam Hussein's prominence as an Arab nationalist and his loud proclamations of support for the Palestinians, vast and obvious differences in wealth between Kuwaiti tourists and the masses of impoverished citizens in Egypt, Morocco, and other far less wealthy countries, and the association of the most prominent members of the anti-Iraq coalition with past imperialism and present dependency prompted many Arab citizens to support Iraq rather than Kuwait. This was true not only for the common person in the "Arab street" but also for intellectuals like Moroccan sociologist Fatima Mernissi (1992). The diplomatic and economic isolation of Iraq following the liberation of Kuwait, despite Saddam Hussein's decision to set fire to Kuwaiti oil wells (Tétreault, 2000), repress with exemplary brutality a Shi'i intifada in the south (al-Shahristani, 1994; al-Khafaji, 1994), and crush a Kurdish uprising in the north (Kakai, 1994), only increased widespread sympathy for Iraq throughout the Arab world.

Following the end of the Gulf War, Saddam Hussein engaged in cat-and-mouse games with UN inspection teams sent to monitor the dismantling of

Iraq's chemical and biological weapons. In many of these encounters, he had the political support of some Arab governments and most Arab populations. When the Iraqi government accused U.S. nationals on the UN arms inspection teams of spying and then expelled them late in 1997, no Arab government, not even Kuwait, supported military retaliation against Iraq. However, when all the remaining UN inspectors were withdrawn by Richard Butler, the head of the inspections organization, the UN Special Commission, in December 1998, six Arab governments, including Egypt and Syria, reprimanded Iraq. The return of UN arms inspectors in December 2002 also evoked mixed reactions. On the one hand, despite energetic efforts, the inspectors did not uncover a "smoking gun"; on the other hand, U.S. insistence that weapons were there, coupled with the growing conviction that the administration would go to war whether weapons were found or not, raised concerns about the whole enterprise.

The George W. Bush administration had stated months before the resumption of inspections that "regime change" in Iraq was its primary goal. The rationale for mounting military attacks on countries whose regimes the United States wishes to change was laid out in a redefined *National Security Strategy of the United States of America,* published on September 20, 2002. In this document, the United States announced an intention to launch preemptive wars in pursuit of its national interests, and to do so unilaterally, that is, whether or not other countries joined or even acquiesced in such efforts. The inexorable march toward war took place amid leader ambivalence and popular dissent (*Middle East Report,* 2003). Saddam's neighbors were not unhappy at the prospect of seeing him go, but they were uneasy about the ultimate aims of the United States in the region, and worried about domestic reaction to another U.S. war on Iraq. This perspective held even in Iran. Despite long-standing antagonism between Iraq and Iran, the war fed into a renewed struggle between conservative clerics who control the several undemocratic organs of government, and a coalition of liberals and moderates (which also includes clerics) whose base lies in the popular majorities that twice elected Mohammad Khatami president. After U.S. president George W. Bush declared victory on May 1, 2003, Iran's external security, along with the delicate balance among contending domestic forces, was challenged by the intense interest of factions within the U.S. government in taking what they viewed as a successful policy "on the road," perhaps to Tehran. The rapid fall of Saddam Hussein's regime also initiated a flood of practical problems. Several center on Iraqi Kurds. More than 70,000 were armed by U.S. forces and they fought with distinction. Their importance was enhanced by the refusal of Turkey's parliament to grant U.S. ground forces permission to operate from Turkey during the war.

The collapse of security and order within Iraq following Saddam's departure left a fluid situation in which large numbers of armed Iraqi Kurds, many of whom have not given up the dream of an independent Kurdistan, can consider their options from a stronger position than they would have had otherwise. Thanks to the safe haven, they have a government in which cooperation among the various factions is relatively strong. In view of the conflict and chaos in the rest of the country, it should not be surprising that the Kurds are reluctant to relinquish their local autonomy and the democratic institutions they constructed so carefully in favor of a state enterprise whose outlines are obscure and whose future is uncertain. At the same time, they are very grateful to the United States, whose protection and support underwrote their governance project. The Kurds in their enclave enjoy the only functioning political regime in post-Saddam Iraq, but U.S. and Turkish interests both will determine whether and how it will survive.

The return of extraregional powers to the Middle East, especially those ready to wage war to change regimes they do not like, evokes the same fear and rage that met earlier great power interventions, which, as we have seen, also imposed and deposed regimes. The irony is that the states of the Middle East were global pioneers in regionalism and, by this time, should have been able to present a united front to these outsiders. Instead, they have been unable to progress much beyond establishing international organizations and assigning them very limited tasks. In consequence, the region is still so fragmented that these states remain unable to protect their sovereignty or their common interests from the great powers of the day, as well as from terrorist assaults. The combination of external intervention and domestic insecurity and unrest have created the worst of all possible worlds for the vulnerable nation-states of the Middle East.

■ Conclusion

The international relations of the Middle East are deeply influenced by legacies of imperialism, particularly the persistence of external intervention and its perverse effects on local regimes. The region is noted both for its authoritarian rulers, supported if not actually installed by foreign patrons near and far, and for their ineptitude in foreign policy, domestic policy—and sometimes both (Zanoyan, 2002). This legacy has convinced leaders and populations alike that their own efforts to change things for the better continue to be jeopardized by the whims of manipulative neighbors and the interests of the reigning great powers. Another imperialist legacy is a deficiency in state capacity reflected in the marginal legitimacy of domestic regimes. The resulting lack of positive sovereignty, joined to "a nationalist anti-imperialism nowadays degenerating into chauvinism and xenophobia" (Salamé, 1994:18), keeps many Middle Eastern countries "quasi-states" whose status depends almost entirely on norms of negative sovereignty. Repeated efforts to create strong intraregional and extraregional alliances have failed just as repeatedly. One reason is the exaggerated prominence of negative sovereignty as a cherished principle. National leaders are unwilling to compromise until problems turn into crises that only heroic efforts can conceivably reverse. Even organizations such as OPEC, established to protect the chief economic resource of the region, have faltered time and again over the refusal of members to compromise their individual differences in the general interest (see, e.g., Mikdashi, 1972; Skeet, 1988; Tétreault, 1985). Instead, national leaders distract their populations with ambitious historic missions that in themselves create excuses for intraregional intervention and often extraregional intervention as well.

The end of formal imperialism did not end outside interest in the Middle East or external intervention into its affairs. Hydrocarbon resources add to the geostrategic value of the region, attracting continued economic and strategic intervention by Great Powers in their own national interests or in pursuit of their own global historic missions (Renner, 2003). One such historic mission, winning the Cold War, promoted contests between the United States and the Soviet Union for Middle Eastern clients. These contests, along with rising oil incomes, fueled a transfer of arms from all over the world to the Middle East and its many conflicts.

The interstate boundaries drawn by departing imperial powers left other legacies. Among these are festering nationalist conflicts such as in Israel-Palestine and in imaginary Kurdistan, with its far from imaginary wars and rebellions. Other time bombs exploded in recurring outbursts, such as those between Iraq and its neighbors, Iran and Kuwait. These conflicts repeatedly have attracted external intervention that itself caused or aggravated intraregional, civil, and interstate wars.

The end of the Cold War inaugurated a new global strategic era initially premised on collective security and international cooperation. The revival of the United Nations during the Gulf War (1990–1991) encouraged world leaders to imagine intervention differently, as an openly chosen course of action aimed at ensuring security and human rights. But the lack of military response by the UN and its most powerful members to vicious conflicts in places like Bosnia and Rwanda, where oil was not among the interests to be advanced, called the new interventionism into question (Havel, 1999; Tétreault, 1995). Deployment of peacekeepers during both of those conflicts merely showed how little could be achieved without highly focused intervention by sufficient forces to stop the violence and then keep the peace. Whether the disintegration of Iraq is repaired through such a focused and limited multinational intervention or proves to be just another example of self-interested great power politics whose outcome sets the stage for a new generation of conflict is important far beyond the Middle East.

Another agent of intervention is the multinational corporation. Often regarded as arms of their home governments, multinationals under globalization pursue foreign policies to suit their own interests, sometimes in accord

Thomas Hartwell

World leaders gathered in Sharm el-Sheikh, Egypt, for an antiterrorism conference. Front row, from left to right: Yasser Arafat, Boris Yeltsin, Hosni Mubarak, Bill Clinton, Shimon Peres, and King Hussein.

with and sometimes against the stated positions of political leaders in their home or host countries. One example is pipeline politics. The rush of private investment in oil and gas development in Central Asia touched off controversy regarding the number and location of pipelines required to bring these new hydrocarbon supplies to market. For political reasons, the U.S. government first advocated a new pipeline through Turkey and then, following the defeat of the Taliban, one through Afghanistan. For economic reasons, oil companies such as Chevron and Total preferred a plan that would put a pipeline through Iran.

Indeed, oil company executives, along with academic observers, are among the most active advocates of reintegrating Iran into the international community, and their concerns are far broader than the simple issue of where to locate a pipeline. Investors have interests in the long-term stability of the region as a whole, and few believe that stability can be achieved if Iran remains marginalized and impoverished. Consequently, large corporations with Middle Eastern investments are active in seeking to end the relative isolation of Iran imposed by the government of the United States.

Extraregional intervention in the Middle East by dominant countries, international organizations, and financial and economic actors is likely to increase in response to the defeat of Saddam Hussein and collapse of Iraq. Although such intervention does not have to be either one-sided or negative in its impact, the 2003 war in Iraq does not offer reasons for optimism. Globalization, with its promise of expanding the joint benefits of investment and economic development across many nations, appeared to offer autonomous participation by Middle Eastern states and firms in the world economy. Yet strategic problems from other kinds of globalization—weapons proliferation and terrorism—along with well-documented human rights violations, offer a steady stream of excuses for direct involvement by foreign governments and NGOs in the domestic politics and foreign policies of Middle Eastern states. What if the war on terrorism actually aggravates domestic and regional conflict by suppressing concerns for human rights and civil liberties, causing external constraints on abusive governments and belligerent leaders to disappear? If strategic intervention were to be "globalized" through organizations like the United Nations, would it be less destabilizing and more effective than military intervention by major powers? Multilateral intervention would limit the state-to-state cliency relationships so destructive to domestic and regional peace in the Middle East, and could transform dependency into mutual relationships by giving all sides a stake in the outcome.

Complicating all of these scenarios is the persistent incapacity of so many Middle Eastern regimes to manage domestic conflicts peacefully. This problem has grown along with economic distress and the rise of religiously based opposition groups that, although they have increased domestic political participation, also have made it more abrasive and violent. During the Cold War, some of these groups were viewed as foils against secular opposition groups and enjoyed the tacit and occasionally even the open protection of conservative governments (see Tétreault, 2000). Their domestic revolutionary potential was revealed in Iran and Afghanistan, but their capacity to inflict damage outside the region was not appreciated for some years. Since the September 2001 attacks on the United States by Osama bin Laden's organization, however, the so-called war on terrorism has become the primary rationale for external intervention in the Middle East. Thus, as Vahan Zanoyan (2002) notes, the ability of Middle Eastern states to retain any significant autonomy depends critically on their ability to get their domestic houses in order. This includes taking regional approaches to strengthening their private sectors as a means of reducing dependency and opening their regimes to citizen participation.

A substantial reduction in conventional forms of external intervention also would be welcome. If nothing else, it would leave some space in which the nations of the Middle East could move forward with the business of creating positive sovereignty. Success would produce states with the capacity to protect and support populations who, in turn, would protect and support them.

■ Bibliography

Agha, Hussein, and Robert Malley. 2001. "Camp David: The Tragedy of Errors." *New York Review,* August 9. www.nybooks.com/articles/14380 (accessed January 3, 2003).

Ahmad, Ahmad Yousef. 1991. "The Dialectics of Domestic Environment and Role Performance: The Foreign Policy of Iraq." Pp. 186–215 in Bahgat Korany and Ali E. Hillal Dessouki (eds.), *The Foreign Policies of Arab States: The Challenge of Change.* 2nd. ed. Boulder, Colo.: Westview Press.

Ahmed, Leila. 1992. *Women and Gender in Islam.* New Haven, Conn.: Yale University Press.

al-Ebraheem, Hassan Ali. 1975. *Kuwait: A Political Study.* Kuwait: Kuwait University.

al-Khafaji, Isam. 1994. "State Terror and the Degradation of Politics." Pp. 20–31 in Fran Hazelton (ed.), *Iraq Since the Gulf War: Prospects for Democracy.* London: Zed Books.

———. 1995. "War as a Vehicle for the Rise and Demise of a State-Controlled Society: The Case of Ba'thist Iraq." *Amsterdam Middle East Papers* no. 4 (December).

al-Naqeeb, Khaldoun Hasan. 1990. *Society and State in the Gulf and Arab Peninsula: A Different Perspective.* Trans. L. M. Kenny. London: Routledge.

al-Shahristani, Hussein. 1994. "Suppression and Survival of Iraqi Shi'is." Pp. 134–140 in Fran Hazelton (eds.), *Iraq Since the Gulf War: Prospects for Democracy.* London: Zed Books.

Amuzegar, Jahangir. 1982. "Oil Wealth: A Very Mixed Blessing." *Foreign Affairs* 60, no. 4:814–835.

Anderson, Irvine H. 1981. *Aramco, the United States, and Saudi Arabia: A Study of the Dynamics of Foreign Oil Policy, 1933–1950.* Princeton: Princeton University Press.

Anscombe, Frederick F. 1997. *The Ottoman Gulf: The Creation of Kuwait, Saudi Arabia, and Qatar.* New York: Columbia University Press.

Antonius, George. 1946. *The Arab Awakening: The Story of the Arab National Movement.* New York: G. P. Putnam's Sons.

Ashrawi, Hanan. 1995. *This Side of Peace.* New York: Simon and Schuster.

Assiri, Abdel Reda. 1990. *Kuwait's Foreign Policy: City-State in World Politics.* Boulder, Colo.: Westview Press.

Bamford, James. 2001. *Body of Secrets: Anatomy of the Ultra-Secret National Security Agency from the Cold War Through the Dawn of New Century.* New York: Doubleday.

Barkey, Henri J. 1997. "Kurdish Geopolitics." *Current History* 96 (January):1–5.

Beblawi, Hazem. 1990. "The Rentier State in the Arab World." Pp. 85–98 in Giacomo Luciani (ed.), *The Arab State.* Berkeley: University of California Press.

Ben-Yehuda, Hemda, and Shmuel Sandler. 2002. *The Arab-Israeli Conflict Transformed: Fifty Years of Interstate and Ethnic Crisis.* Albany: State University of New York Press.

Berke, Shari. 1997. "Sahara Dispute and Environment." Trade and Environment Database, Case no. 24. www.american.edu/ted/ice/sahara.htm (accessed May 16, 2003).

Bill, James A., and Robert Springborg. 1994. *Politics in the Middle East*. 4th ed. New York: HarperCollins.

Bromley, Simon. 1994. *Rethinking Middle East Politics*. Austin: University of Texas Press.

Caporaso, James A. 1978. "Dependence, Dependency, and Power in the Global System: A Structural and Behavioral Analysis." *International Organization* 32, no. 1 (Winter):13–43.

Chisholm, Archibald H. T. 1975. *The First Kuwait Oil Concession Agreement: A Record of Negotiations, 1911–1934*. London: Frank Cass.

Christison, Kathleen. 2000. *Perceptions of Palestine: Their Influence on U.S. Middle East Policy*. Berkeley: University of California Press.

Clawson, Patrick. 1995. "U.S.-GCC Security Relations II: Growing Domestic Economic and Political Problems." *Strategic Forum*, August.

Connor, Walker. 1994. *Ethnonationalism: The Quest for Understanding*. Princeton: Princeton University Press.

Crystal, Jill. 1990. *Oil and Politics in the Gulf: Rulers and Merchants in Kuwait and Qatar*. Cambridge: Cambridge University Press.

Daniels, John. 1971. *Kuwait Journey*. Luton, UK: White Crescent Press.

Davidson, Basil. 1992. *The Black Man's Burden: Africa and the Curse of the Nation-State*. New York: Random House.

Dawisha, Adeed. 2003. *Arab Nationalism in the Twentieth Century: From Triumph to Despair*. Princeton: Princeton University Press.

Dawisha, Karen. 1982–1983. "The U.S.S.R. in the Middle East: Superpower in Eclipse?" *Foreign Affairs* 61, no. 4:438–452.

Dessouki, Ali E. Hillal. 1991a. "The Global System and Arab Foreign Policies: The Primacy of Constraints." Pp. 25–48 in Bahgat Korany and Ali E. Hillal Dessouki (eds.), *The Foreign Policies of Arab States: The Challenge of Change*. 2nd ed. Boulder, Colo.: Westview Press.

———. 1991b. "The Primacy of Economics: The Foreign Policy of Egypt." Pp. 156–185 in Bahgat Korany and Ali E. Hillal Dessouki (eds.), *The Foreign Policies of Arab States: The Challenge of Change*. 2nd ed. Boulder, Colo.: Westview Press.

Dickson, H. R. P. 1956. *Kuwait and Her Neighbours*. London: George Allen and Unwin.

Doyle, Michael W. 1986. *Empires*. Ithaca: Cornell University Press.

Draper, Theodore. 1991. *A Very Thin Line: The Iran-Contra Affairs*. New York: Touchstone Books.

Elon, Amos. 2002. "No Exit." *New York Review*, May 23, pp. 15–16, 18, 20.

———. 2003. "An Unsentimental Education." *New York Review*, May 29, pp. 4, 6–7.

Fromkin, David. 1989. *A Peace to End All Peace: The Fall of the Ottoman Empire and the Creation of the Modern Middle East*. New York: Avon Books.

Gasiorowski, Mark J. 1991. *U.S. Foreign Policy and the Shah: Building a Client State in Iran*. Ithaca: Cornell University Press.

———. 1993. "The Qarani Affair and Iranian Politics." *International Journal of Middle East Studies* 25, no. 4:625–644.

Gause, F. Gregory III. 1994. *Oil Monarchies: Domestic and Security Challenges in the Arab Gulf States*. New York: Council on Foreign Relations.

Gerner, Deborah J. 1991. "Palestinians, Israelis, and the *Intifada:* The Third Year and Beyond." *Arab Studies Quarterly* 13, nos. 3–4:19–60.

———. 1994. *One Land, Two Peoples: The Conflict over Palestine*. 2nd ed. Boulder, Colo.: Westview Press.

Gerner, Deborah J., and Ömür Yilmaz. 2004. *A Question of Sovereignty: Bahrain, Qatar, and the International Court of Justice.* Pew Case Studies in International Affairs. Washington, D.C.: Institute for the Study of Diplomacy, Georgetown University.

Ghabra, Shafeeq N. 1987. *Palestinians in Kuwait: The Family and the Politics of Survival.* Boulder, Colo.: Westview Press.

Hallwood, Paul, and Stuart Sinclair. 1982. *Oil, Debt and Development: OPEC in the Third World.* London: George Allen and Unwin.

Havel, Václav. 1999. "Kosovo and the End of the Nation-State." Trans. Paul Wilson. *New York Review,* June 10, pp. 4, 6.

Harik, Iliya. 1990. "The Origins of the Arab State System." Pp. 1–28 in Giacomo Luciani (ed.), *The Arab State.* Berkeley: University of California Press.

Hopwood, Derek. 1985. *Egypt: Politics and Society, 1945–1984.* 2nd ed. Boston: Unwin Hyman.

———. 1988. *Syria, 1945–1986: Politics and Society.* Boston: Unwin Hyman.

Hudson, Michael C. 1977. *Arab Politics: The Search for Legitimacy.* New Haven, Conn.: Yale University Press.

Hunter, F. Robert. 1993. *The Palestinian Uprising: A War by Other Means.* Revised and updated edition. Berkeley: University of California Press.

Hunter, Shireen T. 1986. "The Gulf Economic Crisis and Its Social and Political Consequences." *Middle East Journal* 40, no. 4 (Autumn):593–613.

Ibrahim, Saad Eddin. 1980. "The Negative Effects of Difference of Income Among Arab Countries on Development in Countries with Low Per Capita Income: The Case of Egypt." In Organization of Arab Petroleum Exporting Countries (OAPEC), *Sources and Problems of Arab Development.* Kuwait: OAPEC.

Jackson, Robert H. 1990. *Quasi-States: Sovereignty, International Relations and the Third World.* Cambridge: Cambridge University Press.

Kakai, Falaz al-Din. 1994. "The Kurdish Parliament." Pp. 118–133 in Fran Hazelton (ed.), *Iraq Since the Gulf War: Prospects for Democracy.* London: Zed Books.

Kaufman, Burton I. 1978. *The Oil Cartel Case: A Documentary Study of Antitrust Activity in the Cold War Era.* Westport, Conn.: Greenwood Press.

Keddie, Nikki R. 1981. *Roots of Revolution: An Interpretive History of Modern Iran.* New Haven, Conn.: Yale University Press.

Kissinger, Henry. 1979. *White House Years.* Boston: Little, Brown.

Korany, Bahgat. 1991. "Defending the Faith Amid Change: The Foreign Policy of Saudi Arabia." Pp. 310–353 in Bahgat Korany and Ali E. Hillal Dessouki (eds.), *The Foreign Policies of Arab States: The Challenge of Change,* 2nd ed. Boulder, Colo.: Westview Press.

Kutschera, Chris. 2002. "The Kurds' Secret Scenarios." *Middle East Report* 225 (Winter):14–21.

Lawson, Fred H. 1997. "Dialectical Integration in the Gulf Co-Operation Council." Occasional paper no. 10. Abu Dhabi: Emirates Center for Strategic Studies and Research.

———. 2000. "Theories of Integration in a New Context: The Gulf Cooperation Council." Pp. 7–31 in Kenneth P. Thomas and Mary Ann Tétreault (eds.), *Racing to Regionalize: Democracy, Capitalism, and Regional Political Economy.* International Political Economy Yearbook, Volume 11. Boulder, Colo.: Lynne Rienner.

Lazreg, Marnia. 1994. *The Eloquence of Silence: Algerian Women in Question.* New York: Routledge.

Losman, Donald L. 1972. "The Arab Boycott of Israel." *International Journal of Middle East Studies* 3 (April):99–115.

Luke, Timothy W. 1983. "Dependent Development and the Arab OPEC States." *Journal of Politics* 45, no. 4:979–1003.

———. 1985. "Dependent Development and the OPEC States: State Formation in Saudi Arabia and Iran Under the International Energy Regime." *Studies in Comparative International Development* 20, no. 1:31–54.

MacDonald, Robert W. 1965. *The League of Arab States: A Study in the Dynamics of Regional Organization*. Princeton: Princeton University Press.

Makiya, Kanan. 1993. *Cruelty and Silence: War, Tyranny, Uprising, and the Arab World*. New York: Norton.

———. 1996. "The Politics of Betrayal." *New York Review*, October 17, pp. 8–12.

Maktabi, Rania. 2000. "State Formation and Citizenship in Lebanon: The Politics of Inclusion and Exclusion in a Sectarian State." Pp. 146–178 in Nils A. Butenschøn, Uri Davis, and Manuel Hassassian (eds.), *Citizenship and the State in the Middle East: Approaches and Applications*. Syracuse, N.Y.: Syracuse University Press.

Malley, Robert, and Hussein Agha. 2002. "Camp David: The Tragedy of Errors," *New York Review,* June 13, 46–49.

Marr, Phebe. 1985. *The Modern History of Iraq*. Boulder, Colo.: Westview Press.

Maxwell, Gavin. 1983. *Lords of the Atlas*. London: Century.

McDowell, David. 1996. *A Modern History of the Kurds*. London: I. B. Tauris.

Melkumyan, Yelena. 1992. "Soviet Policy and the Gulf Crisis." Pp. 76–91 in Ibrahim Ibrahim (ed.), *The Gulf Crisis: Background and Consequences*. Washington, D.C.: Center for Contemporary Arab Studies.

Mernissi, Fatima. 1992. *Islam and Democracy: Fear of the Modern World*. Trans. Mary Jo Lakeland. Reading, Mass.: Addison Wesley.

Middle East Report (MERIP). 2003. "Dissent." No. 226 (Spring).

Migdal, Joel S. 1988. *Strong Societies and Weak States: State-Society Relations and State Capabilities in the Third World*. Princeton: Princeton University Press.

Mikdashi, Zuhayr. 1972. *The Community of Oil Exporting Countries*. Ithaca: Cornell University Press.

Moghissi, Haideh. 1994. *Populism and Feminism in Iran*. New York: St. Martin's Press.

Morris, Benny. 1989. *The Birth of the Palestinian Refugee Problem, 1947–1949*. Cambridge: Cambridge University Press.

———. 2002. "Camp David and After: An Exchange (1. An Interview with Ehud Barak)," *New York Review,* June 13, pp. 42–45.

Mosley, Leonard. 1978. *Dulles: A Biography of Eleanor, Allen, and John Foster Dulles and Their Family Network*. New York: Dial Press.

Moynihan, Daniel Patrick. 1993. *Pandemonium: Ethnicity in International Politics*. New York: Oxford University Press.

Munif, Abdulrahman. 1989. *Cities of Salt*. New York: Vintage International.

N.A. 2001. "The Bahrain-Qatar Border Dispute: The World Court Decision," pt. 2. *The Estimate* 13, no. 7 (April 6). www.theestimate.com/public/040601.html (accessed January 2, 2002).

Nasser, Gamal Abdel. 1955. *Egypt's Liberation: The Philosophy of the Revolution*. Washington, D.C.: Public Affairs Press.

Niblock, Tim. 1982. "Iraqi Policies Towards the Arab States of the Gulf, 1958–1981." Pp. 125–149 in Tim Niblock (ed.), *Iraq: The Contemporary State*. New York: St. Martin's Press.

Nitzan, Jonathan, and Shimshon Bichler. 2002. *The Global Political Economy of Israel*. London: Pluto Press.

Penrose, Edith T. 1968. *The Large International Firm in Developing Countries: The International Petroleum Industry.* Cambridge: MIT Press.

Peretz, Don. 1990. *Intifada: The Palestinian Uprising.* Boulder, Colo.: Westview Press.

Peterson, Erik. 1988. *The Gulf Cooperation Council.* Boulder, Colo.: Westview Press.

Polanyi, Karl. 1944. *The Great Transformation.* New York: Farrar and Rinehart.

Quandt, William. 1981. *Saudi Arabia in the 1980s.* Washington, D.C.: Brookings Institution.

Rand, Christopher T. 1975. *Making Democracy Safe for Oil.* Boston: Little, Brown.

Rashid, Ahmad. 2001. *Taliban: Militant Islam, Oil, and Fundamentalism in Central Asia.* New Haven, Conn.: Yale University Press.

Renner, Michael. 2003. "Post-Saddam Iraq: Linchpin of a New Oil Order." *FPIF Policy Report,* January. www.fpif.org/papers/oil_body.html (accessed January 3, 2003).

Rogers, Paul. 2002. "Iraq: Consequences of a War." Oxford Research Group Briefing Paper. October.

Rush, Alan. 1987. *Al-Sabah: History and Genealogy of Kuwait's Ruling Family, 1752–1987.* London: Ithaca Press.

Said, Edward W. 1993. *Culture and Imperialism.* New York: Alfred A. Knopf.

Salamé, Ghassan. 1990. "'Strong' and 'Weak' States: A Qualified Return to the Muqaddimah." Pp. 29–64 in Giacomo Luciani (ed.), *The Arab State.* Austin: University of Texas Press.

——— (ed.). 1994. *Democracy Without Democrats? The Renewal of Politics in the Muslim World.* London: I. B. Tauris.

Salih, Barham. 2002. "A Kurdish Model for Iraq." *Washington Post,* December 9, p. A23.

Sampson, Anthony. 1975. *The Seven Sisters: The Great Oil Companies and the World They Shaped.* New York: Viking Press.

Sankari, Farouk. 1976. "The Character and Impact of Arab Oil Embargoes." Pp. 265–278 in Naiem A. Sherbiny and Mark A. Tessler (eds.), *Arab Oil: Impact on the Arab Countries and Global Implications.* New York: Praeger.

Sciolino, Elaine. 1991. *The Outlaw State: Saddam Hussein's Quest for Power and the Gulf Crisis.* New York: John Wiley and Sons.

Seale, Patrick. 1988. *Asad: The Struggle for the Middle East.* London: I. B. Tauris.

Shatz, Adam. 2002. "The Torture of Algiers." *New York Review* 49(18), November 21: 53–57.

Shwadran, Benjamin. 1955. *The Middle East, Oil and the Great Powers.* New York: Praeger.

Skeet, Ian. 1988. *OPEC: Twenty-five Years of Prices and Politics.* Cambridge: Cambridge University Press.

Smith, Anthony D. 1991. *National Identity.* Reno: University of Nevada Press.

Smith, Jean Edward. 1992. *George Bush's War.* New York: Henry Holt.

Stephens, Robert. 1976. *The Arabs' New Frontier.* London: Temple Smith.

Talbott, John. 1980. *The War Without a Name: France in Algeria, 1954–1962.* New York: Alfred Knopf.

Tétreault, Mary Ann. 1981. *The Organization of Arab Petroleum Exporting Countries: History, Policies, and Prospects.* Westport, Conn.: Greenwood Press.

———. 1985. *Revolution in the World Petroleum Market.* Westport, Conn.: Quorum Books.

———. 1991. "Autonomy, Necessity, and the Small State: Ruling Kuwait in the Twentieth Century." *International Organization* 45, no. 4:565–591.

——. 1992. "Kuwait: The Morning After." *Current History* 91:6–10.

——. 1993. "Independence, Sovereignty, and Vested Glory: Oil and Politics in the Second Gulf War." *Orient* 34, no. 1:87–103.

——. 1995. *The Kuwait Petroleum Corporation and the Economics of the New World Order.* Westport, Conn.: Quorum Books.

——. 2000. *Stories of Democracy: Politics and Society in Contemporary Kuwait.* New York: Columbia University Press.

Urquhart, Brian. 2002. "The Prospect of War." *New York Review,* December 19, pp. 16, 18, 20, 22.

Weber, Cynthia. 1995. *Simulating Sovereignty: Intervention, the State, and Symbolic Exchange.* New York: Cambridge University Press.

Weber, Max. 1978. *Economy and Society.* Eds. Guenther Roth and Claus Wittich. Berkeley: University of California Press.

Weisberg, Richard C. 1977. *The Politics of Crude Oil Pricing in the Middle East, 1970–1975.* Berkeley: University of California Press.

Wolf, Eric. 1982. *Europe and the People Without History.* Berkeley: University of California Press.

Wood, Pia Christina. 1993. "France and the Israeli-Palestinian Conflict: The Mitterrand Policies." *Middle East Journal* 47, no. 1:21–40.

Zanoyan, Vahan. 2002. *Time for Making Historic Decisions in the Middle East.* Strategic and Future Series no. 1. Kuwait: Center for Strategic and Future Studies, November.

Zartman, I. William, and A. G. Kluge. 1991. "Heroic Politics: The Foreign Policy of Libya." Pp. 236–259 in Bahgat Korany and Ali E. Hillal Dessouki (eds.), *The Foreign Policies of Arab States: The Challenge of Change.* 2nd ed. Boulder, Colo.: Westview Press.

6

The Israeli-Palestinian Conflict

Simona Sharoni and Mohammed Abu-Nimer

The Arab-Israeli conflict, and especially its Israeli-Palestinian dimension, has been at the heart of Middle Eastern politics in the twentieth century. Indeed, the Israeli-Palestinian conflict provides a unique opportunity to examine a host of concepts important to understanding Middle Eastern politics and world politics more generally. These concepts include national identity and self-determination, security dilemmas, the role of religion, the increasing importance of nonstate actors, the relative impotence of international law and international organizations such as the United Nations (UN) in dealing with complicated conflicts, Great Power involvement, globalization and economic interdependence, and forms of violent and nonviolent conflict resolution. Given the theoretical and political significance of these issues, it is not surprising that the Israeli-Palestinian conflict is among the most researched topics across academic disciplines as well as in applied settings; it also receives regular and prominent coverage in the media. Yet despite the growing body of literature and media accounts of the conflict, many people still view it either in a simplistic, one-dimensional manner or as distant and too complex to be grasped by ordinary people.

This chapter is designed to provide a framework for understanding the Israeli-Palestinian conflict and the prospects for its resolution. Our analysis is interdisciplinary in scope, grounded primarily in our academic training in conflict resolution. Uniquely, this chapter is coauthored by two conflict resolution scholars: a Jewish Israeli and a Palestinian who holds Israeli citizenship. Our academic expertise notwithstanding, we have both been actively involved for the past two decades in attempts to bring about a just and lasting solution to the conflict.

All too often, media accounts and academic scholarship on the Israeli-Palestinian conflict have fallen into a trap of false symmetry. Typically, the conflict has been presented as an intractable struggle between two national movements with competing claims over the same territory. Such an interpretation obscures the asymmetrical power relations between Israeli Jews and Palestinians, both in the past and in the present. For example, it is seldom recognized that the creation of the State of Israel in 1948, which affirmed the national aspirations of the Jews, came at the expense of Palestinians, whose desire for self-determination and territorial sovereignty remains largely unfulfilled (see Nakhleh and Zureik, 1980; Said, 1980; Abu-Lughod, 1982; Quigley, 1990; Aruri, 1995). We choose to stress this point from the start not to glorify one party or vilify the other. Rather, we do so because we believe that a successful resolution of this conflict depends to a great extent on the recognition of these structured inequalities and the ability to devise a framework to transform these power relations.

Toward this end, we draw both on conflict resolution literature and on our own experience and familiarity with the region to illustrate the complexity of this conflict and highlight possible venues for its resolution. As with any other conflict, a comprehensive analysis should begin with a careful examination of the parties involved and of the historical turning points that marked its escalation and de-escalation. Keeping in mind that history in general and histories of protracted conflicts in particular are never simple or objective and always reflect particular political positions, we choose to begin our analysis with a description of the parties to the conflict to provide a context for understanding their contending interpretations of history. After an overview of central turning points and crucial dynamics throughout the history of the conflict, we examine the core issues and points of contention. Finally, we offer a framework to examine past and present attempts to resolve the conflict and identify the conditions and processes that we deem essential to a just and lasting resolution.

■ The Parties: Two Peoples— Palestinians and Israeli Jews

The Israeli-Palestinian conflict has shaped the lives of at least three generations of Israelis and Palestinians. The Arab-Israeli conflict, particularly its Israeli-Palestinian dimension, has played a central role not only in the daily lives of people throughout the Middle East but also in the lives of Palestinians and Jews living outside Israel and the Occupied Territories, many of whom see their existence as inseparable from political developments in the region (see Kelman, 1982; Segal, 1989; Heller and Nusseibeh, 1991; Rothman, 1992; Gerner, 1994; Tessler, 1994). Many scholarly and media accounts, however, tend to overlook this fact, presupposing the existence of two cohesive and unified parties locked into a conflict. Little or no attention is devoted to the composition of the parties themselves, that is, to differences not only between but also within the Palestinian and Israeli-Jewish collectivities.

To come to terms with the Israeli-Palestinian conflict requires a more complex analysis of the parties involved. Such an analysis ought to approach the parties as diverse and often fragmented communities and must take into account how the parties define themselves and how they are viewed by others. It is important to note, however, that the meanings assigned to particular notions of identity and community change over time. Thus a careful examination of Palestinian and Israeli-Jewish collectivities should underscore the changes in their composition, self-image, and perceptions of and interactions with one another (Kimmerling and Migdal, 1993; Sharoni, 1995b).

Indeed, the Palestinian-Israeli conflict has played a central role in shaping the collective identities of Palestinians and Jews, for the most part in direct opposition to one another, and until recently each reflected denial of the legitimacy of the other party's identity claims (Kelman, 1982; Moses, 1990; Volkan, 1990). The terms *Palestinians* and *Israelis,* which are presently used to describe the conflict both in media and scholarly accounts, were once in themselves a topic of contention. In fact, until the mid-1970s many Jews in Israel and elsewhere as well as numerous politicians, scholars, and media analysts worldwide did not use the term *Palestinians,* thus failing to acknowledge Palestinians' rights to self-determination and territorial sovereignty (Hajjar and Beinin, 1990). Only since the 1980s has the term *Palestinians* been integrated into the mainstream discourse on the conflict, and it has been used almost exclusively (including in Israel) in both scholarly and popular references to the conflict. A similar trend has occurred in recent years, following the signing of the Oslo Accords and the establishment of the Palestinian National Authority (PNA), with the term *Palestine* beginning to replace other formulations such as *the territories* and *the West Bank and Gaza Strip* (see Usher, 1995a; Suleiman, 1995).

The extensive use of the term *Israelis* is relatively new as well, dating to the establishment of the State of Israel on May 15, 1948, when the collective reference to *Jews* was replaced by the term *Israelis.* Although large segments of the international community immediately adopted the term, until the 1990s the Arab countries and a handful of sympathizers with the Palestinian cause, including several national liberation movements, avoided the use of the term *Israelis,* using instead such terms as *Jews* or *Zionists.*

The prevalent use of the terms *Palestinians* and *Israelis* underscores the view that the Israeli-Palestinian conflict is first and foremost an intractable conflict between two national movements who claim the same piece of land. In addition, the gradual acceptance and normalization of these terms signals more than a mere semantic shift; it points to a growing recognition of the legitimacy of both parties' identity claims and opens up space for a possible reformulation of these claims in ways that are not mutually exclusive (Fernea and Hocking, 1992).

Palestinians

The term *Palestinians* refers to the Arabs—Christian, Muslim, and Druze—who have lived in Palestine for centuries. The number of Palestinians worldwide is estimated at more than 5 million, and they are usually divided into three major subgroups: Palestinians who live in the West Bank and Gaza Strip, those who live inside Israel's pre-1967 borders and hold Israeli citizenship, and those who live in the diaspora. The Palestinian diaspora is a direct result of the creation of the State of Israel, which resulted in the destruction of Palestinian Arab society, dispersing hundreds of thousands of Palestinians to lives in exile or as refugees. Almost 70 percent of the inhabitants of the Gaza Strip and 15 percent of the inhabitants of the West Bank have lived in refugee camps since 1948 (Said et al., 1990; Yahya, 1991).

The experience of displacement and the context of a national liberation struggle have contributed to a high level of politicization among all sectors of Palestinian society. The Palestine Liberation Organization (PLO) played a central role in the process of politicization and in the consolidation of a collective Palestinian identity (Cobban, 1984; Nassar, 1991). The PLO was established in 1964 by the Arab League but gradually gained considerable independence from the Arab regimes and came to serve as the umbrella organization for different political factions with varying ideological orientations and operative strategies. The major factions included Fatah, the largest group, headed by Yasser Arafat, the Popular Front for the Liberation of Palestine (PFLP), the Democratic Front for the Liberation of Palestine (DFLP), and the Palestine Communist Party (PCP). The differences between these political factions notwithstanding, most Palestinians have long regarded the PLO as their "sole legitimate representative."

A careful analysis of Palestinian collectivity ought to pay attention to the social, economic, and religious makeup of the society as well as to political differences. For Palestinians in the West Bank and Gaza Strip and in Israel, the place of residence often reflects their socioeconomic status. Working-class Palestinians in the West Bank and Gaza Strip—many of whom worked until recently in Israel—reside in refugee camps and in villages; the villages are also home to peasants, whereas the elites and the petit-bourgeois class, which includes merchants, traders, and professionals, can often be found in the urban centers (Hiltermann, 1990). Another crucial social sphere that is affected by social class is education. The educational experience of Palestinians varies, depending on the geographical location as well as on the historical and political context. For example, during the Palestinian uprising that began in 1987, known as the intifada, Palestinians' access to education in the West Bank and Gaza Strip was restricted due to the widespread closure of educational institutions by the Israeli military and the arrest, imprisonment, or expulsion of both professors and students (al-Haq, 1988:419–434). It is seldom acknowledged that despite these difficult circumstances, Palestinians have the highest per capita rate of university graduation in the Arab world and one of the highest worldwide (Said et al., 1990).

Another fact that is often overlooked is that not all Palestinians are Muslims; Palestinian Christians live as a minority in both the West Bank and Israel (Abu-Lughod, 1987). Nevertheless, due to specific historical and political challenges that have confronted Palestinians, religious differences within Palestinian society have by and large been set aside as Palestinians sought unity under the banner of national liberation and self-determination. In recent years, however, political Islam has come to play a more prominent role within Palestinian society and politics (Taraki, 1989; Legrain, 1990; Usher, 1995a, 1995b). The early months of the first Palestinian intifada saw the emergence of the Islamic Resistance Movement (which is better known by its acronym, Hamas) in the West Bank and Gaza Strip. By the close of the 1980s, Hamas became part of the Palestinian political scene, regularly polling second only to Arafat's Fatah movement in professional and student elections across the West Bank and especially in the Gaza Strip. Since the signing of the Oslo Accords in September 1993, Hamas has established itself as the single largest political opposition group in Palestinian society (Usher, 1995b).

The redeployment of Israeli troops in some parts of the West Bank and Gaza Strip and the establishment of the PNA inevitably brought change to Palestinian society and politics. In the middle to late 1990s, Palestinians achieved limited self-rule, held general elections, and began to establish social and political institutions such as security services, a legal system, a Palestinian supreme court, and a house of representatives called the Palestinian Council. These accomplishments notwithstanding, many Palestinians are growing impatient with the flaws and limitations of the current state-building process and with the failure of the "peace process" to improve their daily lives, let alone to lead to Palestinian self-determination and statehood (Usher, 1995a; Rabbani, 1996; Guyatt, 1998).

Israelis

The term *Israelis,* which has been in use only since the establishment of the state in 1948, invokes biblical references to the people of Israel and to the ancient Israelites. Yet many scholars have pointed out numerous inconsistencies in the theses that suggest that the Jews who presently reside in Israel are the descendants of the ancient Israelites (see Evron, 1995; Shahak, 1995). Most scholarly and media accounts of the conflict use the term *Israelis* because they assume a natural overlap between the state and its citizens. However, this usage is highly misleading because one-sixth of Israel's population consists of Palestinians who hold Israeli citizenship (Rekass, 1989; Rouhana, 1989; Smooha, 1989, 1992). The terms *Israeli Jews* or *Jews who live in Israel,* which we use in this chapter, more accurately describe this party to the conflict.

Israeli-Jewish society identifies itself as a Zionist society, morally, politically, and technically. The moral aspect of this identification is grounded in the presupposition that Jews can never hope to achieve equality of rights as religious or cultural minorities in Gentile societies. The political aspect of this identification has been predicated upon two correlative elements: (1) the mobilization of Jews throughout the world to immigrate to Palestine; and (2) the establishment of a Jewish state in Palestine, namely the State of Israel, and the mobilization of moral and material support from Jews and non-Jews worldwide for the continued existence of Israel as a Jewish state. Finally, Israel is a Zionist society technically in that its legal structure and the routine of its everyday life are determined in every domain by the distinction between Jews and non-Jews (Davis, 1986:176–177).

Divisions do exist, however, not only between Jews and non-Jews but also within the Israeli-Jewish population, which comprises more than 80 percent of Israel's overall population (Reich, 1985). Israeli-Jewish society is quite heterogeneous, composed of immigrants from numerous countries and reflecting a variety of ethnic and linguistic groups; religious preferences; and cultural, historical, and political backgrounds. The two main ethnic groupings are the Ashkenazi Jews, who originated mostly in Europe and North America, and the Mizrachim, whose origins can be traced mainly to North Africa and the Middle East. The term *Mizrachim* (Orientals in Hebrew) is gradually replacing other terms, such as *Sephardim,* previously used to refer to this segment of Israel's population (Shohat, 1988; Swirski, 1989). Another term that has been in use recently in reference to this group is *Arab Jews,* a term that highlights the sociocultural similarities between Jews from the Middle East and North Africa and their fellow Arabs. The Israeli establishment sought to suppress these similarities, using the Arab-Israeli conflict as an excuse (Alcalay, 1993), and the same excuse was used to downplay the disparities in power and privilege between Ashkenazi and Mizrachi Jews. These disparities have remained largely unaddressed as the Israeli establishment utilized the salience of the Israeli-Palestinian conflict to establish unity in the face of the enemy and construct a strong sense of national identity (Sharoni, 1995a). The centrality of the conflict has also shaped the Israeli political system and the leading political parties.

At present, the Israeli political map includes seventeen parties (some of which comprise several smaller parties) with representation in the Israeli parliament, the Knesset. Historically, the two principal political parties in Israel have been Labor and Likud. The Labor Party, which is predominantly Ashkenazi and secular, controlled Israeli politics between 1948 and 1977. Its original ideology has undergone significant transformations in recent years as it attempted to reconcile the tensions between Zionism, socialism, and democratic practices (Kimmerling, 1983; Shapira, 1992). Over the years, the party's positions and policies on the Israeli-Palestinian conflict have been mixed. Officially, the party supports a "land for peace" solution, and therefore it is generally perceived to be more moderate and willing to compromise than Likud. At the same time, the Labor Party encouraged the construction of settlements in the West Bank and Gaza Strip after 1967, was tough in dealing with the intifada, and for many years opposed the establishment of an independent Palestinian state alongside Israel. More recently, however, the Labor Party and especially Shimon Peres and Yitzhak Rabin were credited with making a significant step toward peace with the signing of the Oslo Accords.

The Likud Party, which came to power for the first time in 1977, is more conservative economically and religiously than Labor and enjoys more support among Mizrachi and working-class Jews. The party has traditionally taken a more hard-line stance on the Arab-Israeli conflict in general and the Palestinian issue in particular. Its original platform claimed Jewish sovereignty over all territories occupied by Israel in 1967, with the exception of the Sinai, which was returned to Egypt following the signing of the Camp David Accords in 1979 (Lesch and Tessler, 1989; Saunders, 1985). Likud and Labor have been alternating in power since 1984, with the Likud Party headed by Benjamin Netanyahu defeating Labor in the May 1996 elections. Although Likud initially opposed the Oslo Accords and the subsequent agreements and vowed to derail their implementation, its position was somewhat modified due to both internal and international pressure. Nevertheless, the policies of the Netanyahu government led to a major stalemate in the negotiations between Israel and the Palestinians, one of many factors that resulted in early elections in May 1999, with the new Labor leader, Ehud Barak, replacing Netanyahu as prime minister.

But Barak's tenure was short lived. He lost the 2000 elections to Ariel Sharon, the Likud's candidate after the outbreak of the second Palestinian uprising, known as the al-Aqsa intifada. The massive propaganda about the far-reaching concessions that Barak had supposedly offered and the Palestinians rejected, contributed a great deal to Sharon's victory (Hiro, 1999; Thomas, 1999; Reinhart, 2002). Despite Sharon's failure to deliver Israelis the security he promised in his election platform and the collapse of his coalition government in late 2002, he was reelected in January 2003 by a landslide with the Labor Party suffering the most significant loss in its history. But analysts argue that Sharon's reelection does not represent an unwillingness of the part of Israelis to reach a negotiated solution with the Palestinians. Rather, it calls into question the Israeli political system, which fails to represent the majority of Israelis (Reinhart, 2002).

■ The History and Dynamics of the Conflict

The conventional view among conflict resolution scholars and diplomats in the West is that dwelling on the history of conflicts in general and of the Palestinian-Israeli conflict in particular is counterproductive, mainly because the parties' interpretations of history often appear irreconcilable. At the same time, history played a central role in shaping people's collective identities, perceptions of one another, and general attitudes toward the conflict and the prospects for its resolution. According to this view, if history is ignored, it would be extremely difficult to establish the framework and conditions for a just and lasting peace. Thus the question is not whether to deal with history, but rather how to approach history so that its examination contributes to both the analysis of the conflict and the exploration of new venues for its resolution. Toward this end, we review some of the history of the conflict that Arthur Goldschmidt presents in Chapter 3, identify a number of significant turning points in that history, and examine their contributions to the escalation or de-escalation of the conflict. In our discussion, we give particular attention to the differences and similarities in Palestinians' and Israelis' perceptions of these events.

▢ Modern Zionism and the Partition of Palestine

The first turning point of the conflict involves the emergence of Zionism and the beginning of Jewish immigration to and settlement in Palestine in the 1880s. The Zionist movement emerged in the late nineteenth century in Europe in response to the rise of European nationalism and anti-Semitism. During and after the Holocaust, which increased the flow of Jewish immigrants to Palestine, the Zionist movement gained significant international recognition and support.

There is no single definition for the term *Zionism*. As with many other contested terms, the meanings and practices associated with Zionism depend on the particular standpoint of the person or group defining it. Although there are different strands of Zionism (socialist or nonsocialist, religious or secular), for most Jews, Zionism is a movement for Jewish national self-determination designed to restore their right to live in the land of their ancestors (Herzberg, 1962). Palestinians and many others, however, view Zionism as an exclusive ideology that underlies the settler-colonial movement responsible for the occupation of Palestine and the dispossession and exploitation of its indigenous population (Said, 1980; Abdo, 1992; Zunes, 1994).

The divergent interpretations of this turning point by Palestinians and Jews lie not only in their differing views of Zionism both as an ideology and as a political project but also in their different perspectives regarding the origins of the conflict. According to prevalent Jewish interpretations, the conflict is centuries old, and Zionism was an attempt to ensure the return of Jews to the land of Israel, Eretz Yisrael, which God promised to Abraham and his "seed" (Sachar, 1964; Parkes, 1964; Grayzel, 1968; Tessler, 1994). According to Palestinian interpretations, the Palestinian-Israeli conflict is a modern phenomenon whose origins lie not in the Bible but rather in Zionist ideology and its implementation in Palestine through policies that are reminiscent of other settler-colonial projects around the world (Khalidi, 1971; Muslih, 1992; Kimmerling and Migdal, 1993; Lustick, 1993, Finkelstein, 1995; Greenstein, 1995).

Many conventional accounts of the conflict overlook the fact that Palestine was not "a land without people for the people without a land," as the Zionist slogan proclaimed; it had an existing indigenous population who sought independence first from the Ottoman rulers and later from the British. Thus, Jewish immigration to Palestine precipitated a century-old clash between two national movements struggling for self-determination and territorial sovereignty. From the start, Palestinians were placed in a disadvantageous position. According to Palestinian historians, the root cause of the Palestinians' disadvantage lies in two political decisions made in Europe. The first decision was made in 1897 by the World Zionist Organization, which met in Basel, Switzerland, and resolved to establish a Jewish state in Palestine. The second decision, known as the Balfour Declaration, was made by the British in 1917, undermining the rights of the indigenous Palestinian population and promising to support the establishment of a Jewish national home in Palestine (Muslih, 1992).

Given this context, the collision between Zionism and Palestinian nationalism was almost inevitable and escalated into violent confrontations in 1920 in Jerusalem, in 1921 in Tel Aviv–Jaffa and the surrounding areas, and in 1929 in Jerusalem and Hebron. One of the most dramatic escalations of the conflict occurred during the Arab Revolt, which lasted from 1936 to 1939. This revolt was the longest-running Palestinian protest against Jewish national aspirations in Palestine prior to the establishment of the State of Israel. This mostly grassroots movement involved both violent and nonviolent dimensions such as strikes, nonpayment of taxes, and other forms of civil disobedience (Khalidi, 1971; Hirst, 1984).

The first period of the revolt ended at the request of the newly formed Arab Higher Committee for Palestine (AHC), which urged Palestinians to wait for the outcome of deliberations by the Palestine Royal Commission, known as the Peel Commission, which was set up by Britain to investigate the situation. The revolt's second stage was sparked by the Peel Commission report recommending the partition of Palestine into two states in order to accommodate the competing claims of Palestinians and Jews, which resulted in further escalation of the situation, with Zionist, Palestinian, and British forces fighting for control. Given the fierce resistance to the plan among both Palestinians and Jews, Britain was eventually forced to abandon the 1937 partition plan.

Nevertheless, partition plans continued to surface; these became particularly popular and gained international legitimacy in the aftermath of World
War II and the Holocaust, which resulted in the near destruction of the Jewish
people in Europe, as well as Gypsies, homosexuals, disabled persons, and others deemed "undesirable" by the Nazis. The best-known is the 1947 United
Nations partition plan, also known as UN Resolution 181, which called for the
creation of a Jewish state and an Arab state in Palestine (see Map 6.1). The
plan, which indicated that the British mandate over the area was to end on
May 15, 1948, "gave the new Jewish state 57 percent of Palestine, including
the fertile coastal region." Palestinians viewed this proposal as fundamentally
flawed and unjust since "at the time Jews represented only about 33 percent
of the population and owned only 7 percent of the land." Indeed, UN estimates suggest that the division of territory spelled out in the 1947 partition
plan would have given the Jewish state economic revenues three times as
great as those of the Palestinian state. On November 29, 1947, the UN General Assembly voted in favor of this particular plan (Gerner, 1994:43).

The Zionist response to UN Resolution 181 was to endorse it with reservations, insisting that the "Jewish homeland" be distinctively Jewish rather than
religiously and ethnically pluralistic. At the same time, Zionist leaders did not
abandon the conviction that eventually all of Palestine should come under Jewish control. From the Palestinian perspective, the UN partition plan was an illegal and illegitimate attempt to divide Palestine. Moreover, Palestinians feared
that the establishment of two states would result in the expulsion of Palestinians
who lived in areas that fell within the designated territory of the Jewish state.
But contrary to common representations of this event that tend to portray Palestinians as rejectionists unwilling to compromise, the Arab leadership in and outside Palestine did not simply reject the partition plan; it endorsed the alternative
proposal of the UN Special Committee on Palestine, which called for a single,
unified state in Palestine that would be democratic and secular and grant equal
rights to all its citizens (see Flapan, 1987; Finkelstein, 1995).

The UN vote on partition sparked an unprecedented wave of violence,
which escalated into a full-fledged war following the establishment of the
State of Israel on May 14, 1948. The differences in the interpretations of history by Palestinians and Jews have been most evident in the ways in which
they refer to this war. Jews refer to it as a war of independence, marking the
fulfillment of their national aspirations with the establishment of the State of
Israel. For Palestinians, however, the 1948 war (known as El-Nakbah, which
means "the catastrophe") meant disaster and destruction. In the course of the
war, the Palestinian community was virtually destroyed. Approximately
780,000 Palestinians became refugees as a direct result of Israel's establishment. Some Palestinians fled, others were driven out by force, and 418 Arab
villages were destroyed or depopulated (Morris, 1988, 1990). The war ended
with the establishment of Israel on roughly 77 percent of the total area of

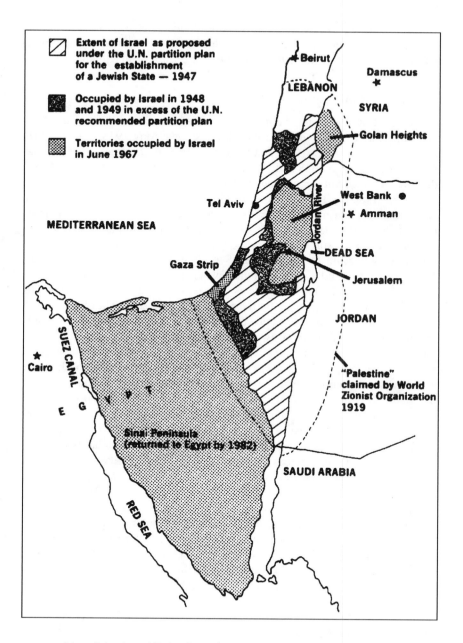

Map 6.1 Israel/Palestine, Showing the 1947 Partition Plan, 1948 Boundaries, and Borders After the 1967 War

Palestine. The remaining 23 percent was divided between Jordan, which gained control over the West Bank (including East Jerusalem), and Egypt, which took upon itself the administration of the Gaza Strip (Muslih, 1992).

■ International Conflicts

In most literature on the conflict, the years since the establishment of the State of Israel are often divided into three periods: May 1948 to June 1967, June 1967 to December 1987, and December 1987 to the present. During the first period, between 1948 and 1967, Palestinians were in a state of shock and despair. The difficult circumstances and the lack of political leadership and economic resources forced them into a state of dependency on neighboring Arab states. As a result, until 1967, with the exception of the establishment of the PLO in 1964, Palestinian nationalism was for the most part muted; resistance to Israel was expressed primarily by Arab leaders residing outside Palestine. Meanwhile, on the other side of the Palestinian-Israeli divide, Israeli Jews worked to build a Western-style Jewish state in the middle of the Arab world. Consequently, the Palestinians who remained in Israel after the 1948 war were viewed as a problem for the evolving Jewish state. They were placed under military rule until 1966 and subjected to a slew of discriminatory regulations under the pretext of Israel's "national security" (Gerner, 1994:47, 57–58; Lustick, 1980; Zureik, 1979).

The June 1967 war, also referred to as the Six Day War, is one of the most significant turning points in the history of the conflict. It dramatically changed the map of the Middle East, resulting in Israel's occupation of the West Bank and Gaza Strip, the Sinai, and the Golan Heights. Contrary to conventional Israeli interpretations, however, which have insisted that Israel occupied these territories in a war of self-defense, ample evidence illustrates that Israel initiated the war under the pretext of a "preemptive attack" (Zilka, 1992). At the conclusion of the war, Israel's conquest appeared to be just temporary. In fact, on June 19, 1967, the Israeli cabinet voted unanimously to give back the Sinai to Egypt and the Golan Heights to Syria in return for demilitarization and peace. With regard to Jordan, Israel demanded border adjustments, citing security reasons, but the status of Jerusalem was considered nonnegotiable; the city was unified and declared an indivisible part of Israel (Zilka, 1992:33). But despite UN Resolution 242, which was unanimously adopted on November 22, 1967, and called for Israeli withdrawal from the territories occupied during the war, Israel objected to a complete withdrawal and refused to withdraw from any territory before a peace treaty was signed. Syria rejected the resolution altogether, and Egypt and Jordan refused to sign a peace treaty prior to Israel's withdrawal.

Israel's victory in the Six Day War and its conquest of the remaining 23 percent of Palestine left Egypt, Syria, and Jordan shocked and humiliated and

Deborah J. Gerner

This woman and child live in Bureij Camp, one of twenty-seven overcrowded refugee camps in the West Bank and Gaza Strip that are home to half a million displaced Palestinians.

turned Palestinians' hopes to a deep sense of despair. Those Palestinians who were not forced to flee (many for the second time) and become refugees in the surrounding Arab countries were subjected to harsh military laws imposed by Israel. In addition, large amounts of land were confiscated to build Jewish settlements in the West Bank and Gaza Strip, which Israeli officials started referring to by the biblical names of Judea and Samaria. Jewish settlement construction in the Occupied Territories began within six months and had massive government support.

The 1973 war represents yet another significant turning point in the history of the Israeli-Palestinian conflict, marking the last war between Israel and an allied Arab force. The war began on October 6, 1973, with a coordinated attack launched by Egypt and Syria. But after a massive airlift of advanced military equipment from the United States, Israel was able to turn things around. On October 24, at the conclusion of the war, Israel recaptured most of the Sinai territory from which it had had to retreat and solidified its hold over the Golan Heights. This military victory notwithstanding, the 1973 war was politically costly for Israelis; it ended the collective sense of euphoria created in the aftermath of the 1967 war and shattered the illusion of military invincibility, clearing the way for a more realistic and critical assessment of Israeli society and politics and especially of the Arab-Israeli conflict. For Palestinians, the 1973 war marked yet another chapter in their growing disillusionment with the ability of Arab states to lead the struggle over Palestine.

As a result of the 1967 war and especially in the aftermath of the 1973 war, Palestinians sought their independent representation through the national resistance movement led by the PLO. Yasser Arafat's election as chairperson of the organization in 1969 represented an important milestone in the Palestinians' struggle for self-determination, and international recognition of the PLO as the sole representative of the Palestinian people. By 1974, Palestinians were able to alert the international community to the plight of the Palestinian people; achieve independent representation in many international bodies, including the UN and its related organizations; and gain recognition on the world stage. Yet throughout this period, Israel refused to recognize Palestinians' existence and right of self-determination (Kimmerling and Migdal, 1993:209–239).

The civil war in Jordan in 1970, which was characterized by daily violent confrontations between Palestinians and the Jordanian regime, was a major setback in the Palestinian efforts to strengthen the national movement outside Palestine. The months of buildup escalated into eleven days of bloodshed, often referred to as Black September, which resulted in the killing of thousands of Palestinians and Jordanians, spoiled the relationship between the Palestinian leadership and the Jordanian regime, and destroyed the political and military infrastructure established by the PLO in Jordan (Tessler, 1994:460–462). Following these events, the PLO began building its bases in Lebanon. Meanwhile, the Palestinian resistance movement in the territories was growing. Its strength and organization were reflected in the results of the first municipal elections in the West Bank in 1976. But when Likud came to power in 1977, Israel moved against these elected mayors and the newly elected municipal councils, appointing instead people who were considered more "moderate" and easy to control (Gerner, 1994:91).

Contrary to the gloomy predictions of many analysts, the unexpected victory of the right-wing Likud Party in the 1977 elections resulted in a temporary de-escalation of the Arab-Israeli conflict. A few months after Likud came to power, Egyptian president Anwar Sadat surprised the Israeli government and public, as well as the Arab world and the international community, when he became the first Arab head of state to visit Jerusalem. Another event that both reflected and contributed to the de-escalation of the conflict was the emergence of a distinct peace movement in Israel: Peace Now. The group, founded in 1978 by reserve officers and soldiers, argued that the Israeli government was not doing enough to bring about peace with Egypt (Bar-On, 1985; Wolfsfeld, 1988). Although Peace Now could not take much credit for this development, the Israeli and Egyptian governments began direct negotiations that year, and in 1979 Israel signed a formal peace treaty with Egypt, often referred to as the Camp David Accords.

The Camp David Accords have been viewed as significant in the history of the Palestinian-Israeli conflict because of the problematic manner in which they addressed the Palestinian dimension of the Arab-Israeli conflict and because they enabled the United States to establish itself as a major "peace broker" in the region and thus increase its sphere of power and influence. The accords contained two documents; the one titled "A Framework for Peace in the Middle East" attempted to address the Palestinian problem. With its vague formulation regarding the nature of Palestinian autonomy and its failure to recognize the PLO as the official representative of the Palestinian people and thus as a party to the negotiations, the document provoked strong negative reactions from the Palestinians (Lesch and Tessler, 1989).

It soon became clear that the government of Menachem Begin had no intention of allowing the Camp David Accords to lead to an Israeli withdrawal from the West Bank and Gaza Strip. To the contrary, in the 1980s Israel pursued its plan to lay the foundation for the permanent retention of the Occupied Territories. The government expanded settlement construction, applied Israeli laws to Jews residing in these areas, and took additional steps in such areas as transportation, communication, and economic activity to link the West Bank and Gaza more closely to Israel and to blur the 1967 border, often referred to as "the Green Line" (Tessler, 1994:519–521). For Palestinians, this period has been characterized by harsh economic conditions and growing dependency on Israel, a shortage of adequate housing, a crisis in education and deteriorating school facilities, and many other problems that have become more acute as a result of the Israeli occupation (Nakhleh, 1980; Tamari, 1980).

Its reservations regarding the Camp David Accords notwithstanding, during this period the PLO began to signal its readiness for a political settlement. Israel refused to acknowledge, let alone act upon, the softening in the PLO's public statements and political agenda; instead, it took actions to remove the remaining elected Palestinian leaders in the West Bank and Gaza Strip and to set up instead the Village Leagues, whose Arab members were appointed by Israel and thus lacked credibility among Palestinians. These actions prompted fierce resistance by Palestinians, resulting in serious clashes between Palestinians and Israeli soldiers in March, April, and May 1982. Another significant event during this period was the emergence of the popular committees, including women's groups and labor unions, across the West Bank and Gaza Strip. These local committees, most of which were affiliated with the various factions of the PLO, were established to address the service needs of the Palestinian community.

The Israeli invasion of Lebanon in 1982 marked a serious escalation of the Israeli-Palestinian conflict. The Israeli government's decision to inflict damage on the PLO's political and military bases in Lebanon stemmed directly from the insistence of most members of the Israeli government at the time that the PLO was the source of unrest and troubles in the West Bank and Gaza Strip. Nevertheless, the Israeli government's previous attempt, in 1978, to destroy the PLO's headquarters and bases in Lebanon not only failed but triggered the escalation of Israeli-Palestinian hostilities across the Israeli-Lebanese border and heightened tensions between Israel and the Arab states (Gerner, 1994:124–128; Tessler, 1994:568–599). In June 1982, Israeli troops invaded Lebanon for the second time, instigating what became the most controversial war in Israel's history.

The officially stated Israeli goals were to move Palestinian fighters out of range of northern Galilee and to eliminate the PLO's political and military infrastructure in Lebanon. Yet Israeli troops proceeded into Lebanon beyond the twenty-five miles initially announced, encircling and bombing Beirut in an effort to force the evacuation of Arafat and the PLO (Schiff and Ya'ari, 1984). Israel agreed to stop the bombing only after the completion of the PLO's evacuation in late August.

The cease-fire did not last long. In mid-September 1982, following the assassination of Beshir Gemayel, the newly elected Lebanese president, Israeli troops returned to Beirut, occupying the entire city and sealing off the Sabra and Shatilla refugee camps, home to many Palestinians and poor Lebanese. These actions precipitated one of the most tragic events in the history of the conflict: the Sabra and Shatilla massacre. The massacre was carried out by Lebanese Maronite Christians, who were known for their hatred of Palestinians, with Israeli knowledge and according to some accounts even tacit approval. Forty hours later, when the camps were finally unsealed, the body count reached 700–800 people, according to Israeli estimates, the majority of whom were civilians, including many women and children. Contending accounts indicated that the number of people murdered was perhaps as high as 1,500 or 2,000 (Schiff and Ya'ari, 1984; Tessler, 1994:590–599).

The Israeli invasion of Lebanon reinvigorated existing Israeli peace groups such as Peace Now and the Committee for Solidarity with Bir Zeit University (which decided to rename itself the Committee Against the War in Lebanon). In addition, the invasion triggered the emergence of new protest groups such as Parents Against Silence, Women Against the Invasion of Lebanon, and Yesh Gvul (literally, "There is a limit") (Kaminer, 1996; Sharoni, 1995a:106–109). Questioning the legitimacy and morality of the war, Yesh Gvul called upon Israeli soldiers to refuse to serve in Lebanon. Not only did hundreds of soldiers sign petitions declaring that they were prepared to take this course of action, but also a significant number of soldiers were sent to jail for their "refusal to carry out an order" (Kaminer, 1996:36–38).

For the first time in Israel's history, Israeli citizens not only questioned their government's policies but also took to the streets to voice their discontent. From the beginning of the invasion, a flurry of protest activities included vigils and demonstrations in the streets and on university campuses, antiwar petitions, and letters to the editors. The first national demonstration against the war on June 26, 1982, drew approximately 20,000 Israelis, who demanded the immediate withdrawal of their country's army from Lebanon. A few months later, in response to the Sabra and Shatilla massacre, Israel witnessed its largest demonstration ever; according to Peace Now and media reports, about 400,000 people participated. Political protest intensified following the publication of the report by the Kahan Commission, a special inquiry commission set up to investigate Israeli involvement in the Sabra and Shatilla massacre (Kaminer, 1996:34–36). The commission's report and the public debates it triggered, coupled with the widespread antiwar demonstrations (which lasted until the partial Israeli withdrawal from Lebanon in 1985), signaled a gradual erosion of the Israeli consensus regarding issues of peace and security.

For Palestinians, the defeat of the PLO in Lebanon resulted in internal fragmentation and disputes among the different PLO factions as well as among the Arab countries that supported them. At the same time, the internal Palestinian leadership had been growing and organizing against the Israeli occupation. In fact, the destruction of the PLO infrastructure in Lebanon contributed to the emergence of a more organized grassroots, autonomous resistance movement in the West Bank and Gaza. This resistance movement gained prominence on the world's stage with the outbreak of the intifada in December 1987.

■ The 1987 Palestinian Uprising

The popular uprising was precipitated on December 8, 1987, "when an Israeli army tank transporter collided with a line of cars filled with Palestinian workers waiting at the military checkpoint at the north end of the Gaza Strip" (Gerner, 1994:97). The accident left four Palestinians dead and seven seriously injured, and rumors began to spread that the collision was not an accident but rather a deliberate act carried out by Israel in retaliation for the killing of an Israeli salesperson in Gaza a few days earlier. The funerals of the dead turned into a massive demonstration; Palestinians continued to protest the following day, and the demonstrations and resistance rapidly spread from the Gaza Strip to East Jerusalem and the rest of the West Bank. Although the accident is often viewed as the catalyst for the uprising, analysts agree that the conditions under which Palestinians lived resembled a pressure cooker, and thus an explosion was imminent.

The literal meaning of the Arabic word *intifada* is "shaking off." For Palestinians, this word has symbolized not only their determination to shake off the Israeli occupation but also their disillusionment with external forces—

the United Nations, the United States, and the Arab states and Arab League—
and their resolve to take matters into their own hands. Palestinian mobilization was unprecedented not only in scope and magnitude but in organization
as well. People who took part in the mostly nonviolent actions that characterized the intifada—from street demonstrations, tax resistance, and commercial
strikes to the establishment of agricultural cooperatives and alternative education centers—were extremely disciplined and came from various socioeconomic backgrounds, political affiliations, and all walks of life. Within weeks,
the focus of the conflict and the world's attention turned to scores of Palestinians in the West Bank and Gaza Strip, led by an indigenous leadership (the
Unified National Leadership of the Uprising) who demanded the withdrawal
of the Israeli military from their occupied land and a just and lasting solution
to the conflict (Nassar and Heacock, 1991; Gerner, 1990; Brynen, 1991;
Hunter, 1991).

On the other side of the Palestinian-Israeli divide, the Israeli government,
which the intifada had caught by surprise, was trying with great difficulty to
formulate a response to the uprising and at the same time to launch a public
relations campaign designed to redeem Israel's image worldwide. Indeed, the
intifada marked a significant shift in power relations between Israel and the
Palestinians. Although in strategic terms the advantage still lay with the Israeli
side, Palestinians had the moral high ground. For the first time in the history
of the conflict, the David versus Goliath analogy was used in scholarly analyses and media reports, describing Israel as Goliath, the mighty aggressor, and
the Palestinians as David, the underdog who is determined to win against all
odds because his cause is just (Lockman and Beinin, 1989; Schiff, 1990;
Perez, 1990).

But Palestinians were well aware that in order to fulfill their aspirations
for self-determination, they needed to establish their own social, political, and
economic infrastructure, a project prevented by the Israeli occupation. Toward
this end, Palestinians established five principal popular committees to deal
with agriculture, education, food storage, health care, and security. These
committees, which operated both nationally and locally, soon became the
most practical mechanism for political mobilization and for the preservation
of the community. For many Palestinians, the committees represented the
infrastructure of the future Palestinian state, or at least transient democratic
institutions designed to govern the community during the intifada. Palestinian
women were actively involved in the establishment and operation of all the
popular committees, which resembled the women's committees that had been
active in the West Bank and Gaza Strip for more than a decade (Jad, 1990;
Hiltermann, 1991; Sharoni, 1995a:72–73).

During the first two years of the intifada, the general atmosphere within
the Palestinian community was extremely positive. The sense of purpose and
self-reliance, coupled with the ability to forge unity within and mobilize inter-

national support for the Palestinian cause, empowered Palestinians and filled many with pride and hope that a diplomatic solution was in sight. Indeed, analysts agree that the intifada enabled Palestinians to renounce the armed struggle, recognize Israel's right to exist, and resolve to establish a Palestinian state in the West Bank and Gaza Strip alongside Israel (Tessler, 1994:717–725). This dramatic transformation became evident in November 1988, when Yasser Arafat formally and publicly endorsed the two-state solution and proclaimed the independent state of Palestine in the West Bank and Gaza Strip.

For the most part, the Israeli government ignored the significance of the 1988 declaration, and efforts to achieve a political solution foundered. Instead, the Israeli government and military continued to respond to the uprising with repression and intransigence. As happened during the 1982 invasion of Lebanon, the government's actions were met with growing public criticism and protest. Although the main currents in the Israeli peace camp had already acknowledged the destructive effects of the occupation on Israeli society long before the intifada began, the uprising was a watershed for political mobilization on the Israeli left. Women and groups who were previously involved in solidarity work with Palestinians led the struggle, which centered around one or more of the following messages: end the occupation, negotiate peace with the PLO, and create two states for two peoples (Kaminer, 1996:41–48). Although the peace movement was fairly successful in mobilizing public opinion, its efforts fell short of changing the Israeli government's policies. By late 1990 the Palestinian-Israeli conflict had settled into a grim war of attrition as the world's attention was diverted to the crisis in the Gulf (Hajjar and Beinin, 1990; Gerner, 1991).

▓ Palestinians and Israeli Jews in the 1990s

The Gulf crisis, which began on August 2, 1990, with the Iraqi invasion of Kuwait and escalated into a war in January 1991, represents another turning point in the history of the conflict (Bennis and Moushabeck, 1991; Sifry and Cerf, 1991; Hiro, 1992). Contrary to the common view among scholars and media analysts that Palestinians made a poor political choice by siding with Saddam Hussein, the Palestinian position was far more complex (Andoni, 1991). Throughout the crisis, the official Palestinian position underscored two principles: denunciation of the Iraqi occupation and opposition to a military solution to resolve the crisis (Ashrawi, 1991:191). But like many other societies, Palestinian society is not monolithic; there were Palestinians who expressed sympathy with Saddam Hussein for standing up to the Gulf states, the United States, and the West more generally and especially to Israel. Nevertheless, regardless of their view on the Gulf crisis, Palestinians criticized the explicit double standard of the international community that utilized the UN and appeals to international law to demand Iraq's immediate withdrawal from Kuwait but failed to apply the same measures to the Israeli occupation of the West Bank and Gaza Strip (Ashrawi, 1991:192–195).

The Gulf crisis and war contributed to the escalation of tension between Israeli Jews and Palestinians. When the U.S.-led air attacks on Iraq began, Israel imposed a twenty-four-hour curfew on Palestinians in the West Bank and Gaza Strip, which lasted a full month and a half. Iraq responded to the air attack with largely ineffective but frightening Scud missile attacks on Saudi Arabia and Israel. Although only two Israelis died directly as a result of those attacks, the country was in a state of panic, and thousands of Israelis fled from the urban areas to the countryside to avoid a possible missile attack. Israelis' sense of helplessness was compounded by the fact that they were asked not to retaliate against Iraq because the United States feared that an Israeli attack might break the already fragile coalition (Schiff, 1990). At the same time, on the other side of the Palestinian-Israeli divide, 1.5 million Palestinians were under total curfew, many on the verge of starvation, with no warning sirens against Scuds and no gas masks to protect them against the possibility of an airborne chemical attack (Strum, 1992:59–78; Sharoni, 1995a:82–83).

In addition to its effects on Israel and on Palestinian-Israeli relations, the Gulf War had grave implications for Palestinians both in the West Bank and Gaza Strip and in the Gulf. The long curfew caused great economic hardship, which intensified when Palestinians who had worked in Israel before the war discovered that their employers had replaced them with recent Jewish immigrants. Palestinians in the Occupied Territories were also affected by the fate of relatives who had been working and living in the Gulf. Close to 400,000 Palestinians living in Kuwait lost their livelihoods and were forced once again to flee and look for refuge elsewhere. Since most of these people had been supporting family members in the West Bank and Gaza Strip, their unexpected displacement translated into a direct loss of income for many families. Moreover, external contributions from the Gulf states to the PLO and to Palestinian institutions such as hospitals, schools and universities, and social welfare organizations stopped almost instantly (Andoni, 1991).

In the aftermath of the Gulf War, the Arab-Israeli conflict was back on the agenda of U.S. Middle East policy. In October 1991, after months of intense and systematic shuttle diplomacy efforts carried out by U.S. secretary of state James Baker, an international peace conference was convened in Madrid, Spain, under joint sponsorship of the United States and the Soviet Union (Gerner, 1992). The conference's participants included Egyptian, Syrian, Lebanese, and Israeli delegations, and a joint Jordanian-Palestinian delegation because the Israeli government refused to accept an independent Palestinian delegation led by the PLO. These peace talks continued throughout 1992 and the first half of 1993 in Washington, D.C., and elsewhere on two parallel tracks: bilateral and multilateral. Despite the fact that no agreements were reached during that period and that by mid-1993 negotiations on the Palestinian-Israeli track had reached a total stalemate, some analysts contend that the very fact that Palestinian and Israeli-Jewish officials were engaged in face-to-face negotiations was a major step forward in Palestinian-Israeli relations (Tessler, 1994:748–750).

The victory of the Labor Party in the 1992 Israeli elections triggered for many hopes for progress in the peace process. Another encouraging sign in this direction was the new government's introduction of a bill removing the ban on unauthorized meetings with members of the PLO. These developments notwithstanding, the situation in the West Bank and Gaza Strip continued to be tense, escalating into occasional violent clashes. Then in late August 1993 the world learned that secret negotiations between Israeli government officials and official representatives of the PLO had been taking place in Norway for many months. The announcement that the two parties had signed a joint Declaration of Principles (also known as the Oslo Accords) was both surprising and encouraging. Soon thereafter the world witnessed PLO president Yasser Arafat and Israeli prime minister Yitzhak Rabin shaking hands after signing the Declaration of Principles at the White House in Washington, D.C.

On July 1, 1994, after twenty-seven years in exile, Arafat set foot on Palestinian soil, greeted by hundreds of thousands of Palestinians. Soon thereafter he formed the Palestinian National Authority, and the first democratic Palestinian elections were held in January 1996. Initially, the Oslo Accords enjoyed public support on both sides of the Palestinian-Israeli divide. Ordinary people, fed up with the cycle of violence that characterized the conflict, were eager to reap the benefits of peace promised to them by their leaders. But as negotiations dragged on and living conditions failed to improve, support

Palestinian National Authority, Central Photographic

Palestinian president Yasser Arafat has also served as leader of the Palestine Liberation Organization since 1969.

for the agreement, and the peace process in general, declined. Moreover, the stalemate in the process and the failure of the leadership on both sides to keep the public informed about the dynamics and points of contention, coupled with the lack of improvement in Palestinians' living conditions, precipitated a new wave of violence.

The atmosphere of crisis strengthened the opposition to the Oslo Accords and exposed internal divisions and conflicts within both Palestinian and Israeli societies. These divisions, which became clearer following the signing of the Oslo Accords, involve questions of identity and community and contending views not only about the boundaries between Israel and Palestine and the relationship between them but also about the social and political character of each society. The sharp political divisions within Israeli society became evident in November 1995 following the assassination of Yitzhak Rabin by a fellow Jew who opposed Rabin's notion of peace.

But contrary to common perceptions, the Oslo Accords were not a peace treaty. Rather, they constituted an agenda for negotiations covering a five-year "interim period," which was expected to lead to a permanent settlement based on UN Security Council Resolutions 242 and 338. The accords called for a transitional period during which Israel would gradually withdraw its troops from major Palestinian centers in the Occupied Territories, beginning with Gaza and Jericho (Aruri, 1995; Usher, 1995a). In May 1994, nearly five months behind schedule, following the signing of the Cairo agreement that was designed to ratify the Declaration of Principles, the Israeli military began its redeployment as the Palestinian police began to move into the newly autonomous areas.

At the end of the 1990s, the Palestinians had full autonomy in 27 percent of the Occupied Territories (Area A; 6.6 percent of the territory of historical Palestine). In the West Bank, this translated into 3 percent of the total surface area, whereas in Gaza the PNA controlled 60 percent of the territory. In the West Bank villages (Area B), however, the PNA had only civil and police powers; Israel remained responsible for "internal security," the meaning of which was open to interpretation (see Map 6.2). Furthermore, because the towns and villages are mostly noncontiguous and Israel remained in command of the road network connecting them, all movement of goods and persons into and out of these enclaves as well as between them could be interdicted at will (Rabbani, 1996:4).

Further complicating the already delayed implementation of the Oslo Accords was the unexpected victory of the Likud Party, led by Benjamin Netanyahu, in Israel's May 1996 elections. Netanyahu argued, and many analysts agreed, that his policies of settlement expansion and the "judaization" of East Jerusalem merely followed those set by earlier Labor governments. Nevertheless, the blunt and uncompromising manner in which Netanyahu carried out these policies resulted in a serious escalation of Palestinian-Israeli relations and another major setback in, if not total collapse of, the peace process.

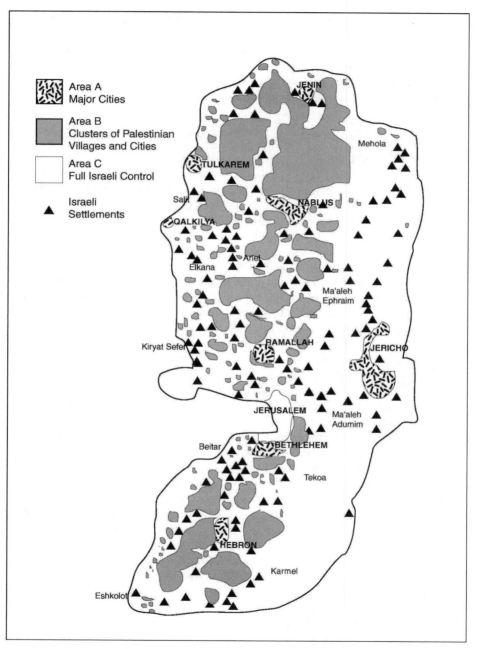

Map 6.2   Areas A, B, and C Within the West Bank

The main disputes have revolved around two central issues: Jewish settlements and Jerusalem. Both of these issues, along with the questions of Palestinian refugees and final borders, were not addressed in the Oslo Accords but rather left to be discussed during final status negotiations, which were originally set to begin in September 1998 but had not started when the five-year Oslo transition period ended in May 1999.

▓ The Al-Aqsa Intifada

The present Palestinian uprising, also referred to as the second intifada, started on September 28, 2000, following a provocative visit by Likud leader Ariel Sharon, accompanied by hundreds of soldiers to the Haram-al-Sharif (Dome of the Rock) in Jerusalem, one of the holiest Muslim sites. Unlike the first intifada, which was by and large an unarmed popular revolt, Palestinian armed men led the al-Aqsa intifada right from the start. The Israeli military tried to suppress the movement with massive force. More than 7,000 Palestinians were reported injured in the first five weeks of the uprising, with many suffering injuries in the head and upper body (Reinhart, 2002). In addition to further restricting the free movement of Palestinians between the West Bank and the Gaza Strip and within towns and villages in the West Bank, the Israeli military gradually but systematically invaded areas that had been handed over to the Palestinian Authority (PA) as stipulated in the Oslo Accords. Moreover, Sharon started a political assassination campaign, targeting key leaders and activists of all Palestinian factions.

Palestinian militants responded with intensified shootings directed at Israeli settlements, especially around Jerusalem, and a growing number of suicide bombings targeted Israeli cities and towns. Israeli forces and policymakers utilized these attacks as a pretext to launch massive retaliation operations into densely populated Palestinian areas in West Bank and Gaza. The uneven nature of this violent confrontation is reflected in an ever-increasing death toll; as of September 2003, at least 2,468 Palestinians and 870 Israelis had been killed in this second intifada, a ratio of three Palestinians for each Israeli (Palestine Red Crescent Society, 2003; Israeli Foreign Ministry, 2003).

The terrorist attacks against the United States on September 11, 2001, had grave implications for the already deteriorating situation in the West Bank and Gaza Strip. Despite the fact that Palestinian leadership have continuously and unequivocally denounced the attacks and offered to help the United States in its efforts against terrorism, the coordination and cooperation between the U.S. and Israeli governments have strengthened. Backed by the U.S. administration, Sharon declared that Arafat was irrelevant, and that there would be no negotiation until he was removed or replaced by another leader. To materialize this objective, the Israeli army twice besieged Arafat's compound and destroyed it, leaving him with a single building and isolated from the international community.

Various leaders around the world criticized Israel's systematic humiliation of Arafat. Nevertheless, by June 2002, Arafat and the Palestinian leadership more generally were isolated and in serious crisis. The PA had lost all its security forces and its ability not only to control but also to move from town to town. In addition, the economic situation reached an all-time low with unprecedented unemployment rates and the utter collapse of all economic development plans. This crisis has contributed to the rising influence and support for Hamas and Islamic Jihad ideology in the Palestinian streets (Mansour, 2002; Abu-Nimer, 2003) as well as for secular militant groups.

■ One Land, Two Peoples: Central Issues and Points of Contention

As the previous section illustrates, the dynamics of the conflict, the range of solutions, the role of outside actors, and the political positions of both Palestinians and Jews have dramatically changed throughout the course of the conflict. At the same time, the central issues underlying the conflict have not been dramatically transformed. One such set of issues involves the competing claims of two national movements for the same piece of land.

The Israeli-Palestinian conflict has served as both the catalyst and the touchstone for the consolidation of particular notions of national "imagined community" for Palestinians and for Israeli Jews. For Palestinians, the imagined community came to be seen as a future sovereign Palestinian state. Apart from differences concerning the territorial boundaries and the political and social character of their future state, there is a broad consensus among Palestinians that the principles of national self-determination and territorial sovereignty are inseparable and crucial to the survival of the Palestinian people. A consensus around the same principles has served as the basis for the Israeli-Jewish imagined community. Although Jews realized their dream and established a Jewish state, this has come at the expense of Palestinians, whose desire to fuse national self-determination with territorial sovereignty remains unfulfilled. This turn of events has in many ways formed the basis for the present conflict.

The principles of national self-determination and territorial sovereignty underlie the early conflicts between Zionist settlers and the indigenous Palestinian population. The dynamics and intensity of the Israeli-Palestinian conflict and its significant military component over the years have contributed to the escalation of the conflict and reinforced sharp distinctions between "us" and "them." The establishment of the State of Israel further exposed the differences between Palestinian and Israeli nationalisms: first, the difference between institutionalized state nationalism and the nationalism of a liberation movement, and second, the disparities in power relations between an occupying state and a population struggling to rid itself of that state's rule.

The emerging Jewish state has placed a special emphasis on its national security. For Palestinians, however, national liberation has emerged as the most important focus of their collective identity, especially following the Israeli occupation of the West Bank and Gaza Strip in 1967 and the emergence of the PLO as a vehicle of national aspirations. Within Israeli-Jewish society, the constant invocation of Israel's security concerns has helped reinforce an overt and covert militarization of people's lives. But for Palestinians, the centrality of the conflict has manifested itself in the privileging of national liberation not only as the primary ideology of struggle against Israeli occupation but also as the principle discourse that shapes certain ideas and ways of thinking about Palestinian identity and community.

National security and national liberation doctrines are similar in that they view the potency and unity of the nation as superior to issues raised by private citizens and various social groups within that nation. As a result of the primary emphases on national security and national liberation, different social and economic problems within both communities have been put on the back

Deborah J. Gerner

Israeli troops confront Palestinian demonstrators in the
highly contested West Bank city of Hebron/Khalil. The Palestinians
were protesting their lack of access to the Mosque of Ibrahim,
known to Jews as the Cave of Machpelah, where the
prophet Abraham, Sarah, and their children are believed to be buried.

burners until the Israeli-Palestinian conflict is resolved. Nevertheless, the differences between Israeli-Jewish and Palestinian nationalisms, which are often overlooked, are far greater than the similarities. They involve fundamental differences in the history and social context of the two national movements and, most particularly, striking disparities of power and privilege between the two communities.

In order to formulate a solution to this long-standing conflict that would be acceptable to both Palestinians and Jews, one should first identify the central issues for each party. During this process, it is important to pay attention to the changes that occurred in the parties' framing of issues over the years as well as to similarities and differences in the parties' perceptions of central issues. Following is a preliminary list of some of the issues that analysts view as central to a just and lasting resolution of the conflict:

- Fixed, agreed-upon borders between Israel and its neighbors.
- The assurance of mutual security for all states and peoples in the region.
- The status of Jerusalem.
- Jewish settlements in the West Bank and Gaza Strip.
- Compensation for Palestinians who were forced to leave their homes and property as a direct result of the Israeli-Palestinian conflict.
- The political, civil, and national status of Palestinians who live in Israel and hold Israeli citizenship.
- The economic viability of Israel, Palestine, and the other states in the region and the economic relations among them.
- The allocation of resources such as water among the states of the region.
- The role of the international community in peacekeeping, peacemaking, and peacebuilding.

These points are not listed in any particular order. In fact, if Palestinians and Israeli Jews were asked to prioritize them, they would most likely come up with very different lists. Moreover, many of these issues are interrelated, and some have been addressed at least partially within the framework of the Oslo Accords. Other issues, however, such as settlements, final borders, the fate of Palestinian refugees, and the status of Jerusalem, have been identified as topics to be discussed during final status negotiations.

On these particular issues, it is interesting to note the difference between the official Israeli and Palestinian positions. For Palestinians, these are the main issues presently underlying the Israeli-Palestinian conflict. Concerned (for good reason) that the process would break down before these issues could be discussed, Palestinians wanted to place these issues on the agenda from the start. Israel, however, preferred to defer the discussion of these four issues primarily because the resolution of any one of them would have been impossible without an Israeli concession. Although the decision to delay the discussion of these four critical issues was presented to the parties as a compromise, a careful study of the Israeli position reveals that Israel, the more powerful party in the negotiations, was able to impose its will on the Palestinians with the help of a third party who wanted to keep the peace process on track.

These same issues and power dynamics continued to haunt the Palestinian-Israeli negotiators in their last round of direct negotiation in Camp David II. With the intensive and direct intervention of President Bill Clinton, who was in his last few months in office and under pressure to deliver a major political gain to seal his presidency and long involvement in the Israeli-Palestinian peace process, Barak offered the Palestinian authority control over 95 percent of Palestinians in the West Bank and Gaza Strip. Palestinians rejected the offer, arguing that the proposed settlement would prevent the creation of a viable Palestinian state due to the lack of territorial contiguity and the fact that the West Bank was to be divided into three main sections by Israeli highways designed to connect Jewish settlements. For its part, Israel did not fully accept the terms put forth in the Clinton plan, although Arafat's reservations and rejection of Barak's offer overshadowed Israel's own numerous objections.

Another bone of contention involved the question of Palestinian refugees. According to Palestinian negotiators, the number of 1948 refugees who would be allowed to return was too low; Palestinian negotiators asked for half a million, while the Israeli negotiators offered 25,000. Moreover, Barak's proposal did not grant sovereignty on the Haram-Al-Sahrif area. Regardless the details of the Camp David offer, as of mid-2003 it was clear that the same issues that had been postponed by the Oslo Accords in 1993 remained unresolved. Such an outcome is not surprising given that by the time Arafat and Barak arrived at Camp David, the level of trust among Palestinian and Israeli leaders and their faith in reaching an agreement was far lower that the euphoria of the historical breakthrough in Oslo in 1993 (Barak and Arafat did not meet face-to-face during any of the Camp David sessions).

Regardless of when the next phase of negotiation occurs, there is little hope that these two populations will reach any sustainable and just resolution without addressing the root causes of the conflict. Among the most critical issues that must be addressed are the physical and psychological insecurity of Palestinians and Israelis, the indiscriminate killing of Israeli and Palestinian civilians, the lack of viable Palestinian statehood, the right of return for refugees, the economic deterioration (60–70 percent unemployment rate is estimted in Gaza during the second intifada), the massive collective punishment through curfews and closures, and the continued expansion of settlements.

Another point to keep in mind in examining changes that occurred in the parties' positions over time involves the question of political representation. More specifically, the changes occurred mostly in Israel's position, and they center mainly on Israel's willingness to finally accept the PLO as the legitimate representative of the Palestinian people. The negotiations that led to the signing of the Camp David Accords in 1978 did not treat the Palestinians as an autonomous party, nor did they acknowledge the PLO as their sole representative. At the time, many elected officials in Israel publicly denied the existence of a Palestinian people. This situation changed dramatically with the outbreak of the 1987 intifada. Yet until summer 1993, the Israeli government refused to negotiate with the PLO. This policy was particularly evident in the period preceding the Madrid conference in 1992, when the Israeli government vetoed certain Palestinian delegates because of their suspected affiliation with the PLO. Moreover, the Israelis refused to accept an independent Palestinian delegation and insisted on a joint Jordanian-Palestinian delegation instead. According to many analysts, the Oslo Accords were signed because Israeli officials who took part in the secret meetings with PLO officials realized that if Israel were serious about peace, it would have to negotiate directly with the PLO.

Ironically, ten years after Oslo, Israelis and Palestinians remained embroiled in a debate over whom to negotiate with. The Israeli government (backed by the United States) declared that it would not negotiate with the Palestinian leadership as long as Arafat was heading the Palestinian Authority. As a result, the Palestinians came under enormous international pressure to make amendments to their political system and introduce the position of a prime minister. The Palestinian leadership maintained that Sharon was not a serious partner for negotiation and had no political offer or agenda for resolution except the declaration that he would accept a Palestinian state on 42 percent of the territories. However, his policy on the ground is contrary to any intention to reach a peaceful resolution. Nevertheless, several Palestinian leaders, such as Mahmoud Abbas (Abu Mazin) and Ahmad Qura'i (Abu Ala), met with Sharon on various occasions during 2003. At the same time, Palestinian opposition groups and nongovernmental organizations (NGOs) continued to call for political and economic reforms and refused to accept Arafat's removal as Sharon's condition for negotiation.

The "Road Map" initiative was developed by the Quartet—the United States, the European Union, Russia, and the United Nations—to promote a resumption of negotiations, the implementation of a cease-fire, and reformation of the Palestinian political system (including the removal of Arafat from direct day-to-day governance) in a way that would be politically palatable to both parties. Under European and U.S. influence, Arafat appointed Mahmoud Abbas, one of the architects of Oslo, to a newly created prime minister post in early 2003. After less than a year Abbas resigned, indicating that the unclear division of authority made his position untenable. He was replaced by Ahmad Qura'i. In addition, the Palestinian Legislative Council intensely debated a new Palestinian constitution that would be the basis for a modified governing system. These actions met the Quartet's "Road Map" conditions for resumption of negotiations and declaration of a Palestinian state by 2005 as declared by President George W. Bush in an address to the United Nations.

In spite of completing these political revisions, the Palestinians continue to live under full Israeli reoccupation of the territories (Israeli forces have reoccupied the majority of the areas that they handed to the PA under the various terms of the Oslo Accords) and without functioning authority. Thus the social welfare, health, education, and other basic services are addressed neither by Israel nor by the Palestinian Authority. In addition, many Palestinians and political analysts share a growing fear and suspicion that the Israeli government and military establishment have planned a major population expulsion and transfer to take place in the aftermath of the 2003 U.S.-led war against Iraq, while world attention is focused elsewhere.

There are also speculations that, after a reconstruction of the Iraqi regime, the United States will turn to the Israeli-Palestinian issue in order to ensure the settlement of long-standing political conflicts in the region. This pattern would be more similar to what occurred after the 1990–1991 war against Iraq.

Finally, once the parties agree on a preliminary agenda and on who will be involved in the negotiations, they must address a set of very important procedural issues: when, where, and for how long negotiations will take place, whether the process requires a third party to mediate issues, and, if so, who that party should be. Before the parties meet at the negotiation tables, delegates must study the issues, prepare position papers, and review past attempts to resolve the conflict. A careful analysis of past and present conflict resolution attempts, their success (or failure), and the ways in which they were perceived in both communities may inspire new thinking and creative ideas for the resolution of the conflict.

■ The Rocky Road to Peace: Past and Present Attempts to Resolve the Conflict

Since the turn of the twenty-first century, numerous attempts at resolution have been carried out separately and jointly by Palestinians, Jews, and various members of the international community. Following is a partial list of some of the major scenarios that have been proposed by various actors over the years:

- Two states for two people: a Palestinian state alongside Israel, in the West Bank and Gaza Strip.
- Greater Israel: a Jewish state that would annex the West Bank and Gaza Strip and "transfer" the Palestinian population to Jordan and other Arab countries.

- Greater Palestine: a Palestinian state on all the territory of historical Palestine, with no Israeli Jews except those whose families lived in Palestine before 1948.
- Greater Israel: a Jewish state in all the territory of historical Palestine with Palestinians as citizens.
- Greater Palestine: a Palestinian state in all the territory of historical Palestine with Israeli Jews as citizens.
- A partial autonomy, more or less according to the terms described in the Oslo Accords: Palestine controls the civic affairs and internal security in its cities and villages, and Israel administers external security and controls the land and natural resources.
- Return to the pre-Oslo situation: Israel continues to control the territories.
- A binational state on the land of Palestine/Israel.

It is important to distinguish between those attempts that have addressed primarily the needs and aspirations of one party to the conflict (Jews or Palestinians) and those that have sought to take into account the needs, aspirations, and preferred solutions of both Palestinians and Jews. According to some analysts, to come to terms with the contending resolution perspectives on the Israeli-Palestinian conflict, it may be useful to place them along a continuum bounded by the terms *exclusivist* on one end and *accommodationist* on the other (Vitalis, 1992:290). This continuum clearly reflects the dominant view, according to which the conflict stems from competing claims of two peoples to the exclusive right of national self-determination and sovereignty rights on the same piece of land. According to this view, the single-state solutions—whether Jewish or Palestinian—are exclusivist in nature since they undermine the other party's vision and claims.

There is a tendency, especially among scholars writing about resolution of the conflict, to view the transition from exclusivist scenarios to accommodationist ones as a combination of historical progression and rational choice. Thus the Zionist state-building project in Palestine, which led to the establishment of the Jewish state in 1948 by completely undermining the existence of the indigenous Arab population, is often compared with the attempts in the 1950s and 1960s of Palestinians supported by Arab leaders to liberate their homeland.

According to this interpretation, with time and the impact of particular political developments, as both Israeli Jews and Palestinians concluded that their vision of an exclusive homeland was not likely to lead to peace, they gradually began to explore accommodationist scenarios. These scenarios reflected some willingness to compromise and acknowledge, although with many reservations, the other party's national aspirations and right to the land. This acknowledgment, which is particularly evident in such proposals as the two-state solution and the binational state, is praised in the literature as a "win-win solution" and presented as the best scenario for a peaceful resolution of the conflict (Kelman, 1982; Vitalis, 1992). However, such scenarios overlook the grave power differentials between Palestinians and the State of Israel, which are crucial to the understanding of the transition from exclusivist to accommodationist visions within both communities.

Another common continuum of analysis is that between violent and nonviolent attempts to resolve the conflict. Like the exclusivist-accommodationist categorization, this continuum has been inspired by a combination of rational choice theories with some historical analysis. Accordingly, over time, most Palestinians and Israeli Jews came to the conclusion that the conflict could not be resolved through military might and that diplomacy might be a better venue. Still, in most media accounts of the conflict, there has been a tendency to present Palestinians as more prone to violence and more reluctant to accept diplomatic solutions. This tendency also manifests itself in differential treatment of violence carried out by Palestinians, which is usually referred to as "terrorist attacks," whereas violence carried out by the State of Israel is said to be done in the name of "national security."

The debate over the use of suicide bombing campaigns carried out by Hamas and Islamic Jihad during the second intifada and the excessive use of the military and "target assassination" by Israeli security forces further illustrates the impact of such differences in power relations. Many Palestinian leaders, including Arafat, have consistently criticized the use of suicide bombing. Those Palestinians who do not denounce the use of this tactic have consistently argued that the cycle of violence stems from the occupation itself. Furthermore, systematic research on the use of suicide bombing suggests a link between the Israeli leader's policies and the suicide bombings. More specifically, some argue that Sharon's policies have significantly contributed, as a matter of course and in some cases deliberately, to the persistence of suicide bombings (Sharoni, 2002; Niva, 2003).

As critical scholarship on terrorism has underscored, rather than blaming the underdog in a conflict for resorting to violent means, we must examine the conditions under which certain groups see no other alternative but violence to achieve their goal. By pursuing this line of thinking, we do not condone violence but instead look beneath the surface for its root causes in an attempt to propose a more comprehensive and long-lasting solution (see Rubenstein, 1987). Thus in the context of the Palestinian-Israeli conflict, as the PLO achieved legitimacy on the world's stage and especially after it was recognized by Israel and the United States as the official representative of the Palestinian people, it appears to have gradually and willfully moved away from military struggle to pursue diplomatic means for the resolution of the conflict.

It is important to note that neither Palestinian nor Israeli collectivities are homogeneous; both communities have individuals and groups who still refuse to move away from exclusivist and militant solutions to the conflict. From a conflict resolution perspective, characterizing these people as simply "enemies of peace" and therefore suppressing their activities would be a mistake. Rather, we must examine the impetus behind the behavior of these individuals and groups and their contending solutions to the conflict.

What could further complicate the dynamics of the conflict and the prospects for its resolution is the role of outside parties, with their own agendas and definitions of peace. The United States has a long and complex history of vested economic and political involvement in the Middle East. Most U.S. administrations agree that a resolution of the Israeli-Palestinian conflict is crucial to achieving a comprehensive peace in the Middle East. Peace is viewed as synonymous with stability, which is necessary for continued U.S. hegemony in the region. To further this end, the United States has assumed the role of referee and principal negotiator.

Yet despite its self-portrayal and peacemaking initiatives, the United States hardly fits the role of an impartial third party. In fact, some analysts have argued that in the Middle East, as in many other parts of the world, the United States has acted more as a cobelligerent than as a peacemaker. This has been the case especially after September 11, 2001 (Abu-Nimer, 2003). As Israel's chief ally and protector, the United States was simply unable to discharge its self-assigned mission as a catalyst for peace; the tensions between such roles as mediator and those of Israel's chief diplomatic backer, bankroller, and military supplier have surfaced quite often (Aruri, 1995:19–21). Moreover, due to the largely unchallenged U.S. insistence that it is the only party that can act as a mediator between Palestinians and Israeli Jews, the services of other potential third parties have been ignored or relegated to backstage initiatives. Even in the Quartet, the United States remains the overwhelmingly dominant player. This trend has resulted in the marginalization of the United Nations as a potential peacemaker and in the abandonment of the once popular idea of convening a UN-sponsored international peace conference (Bennis, 1996:211–232).

When discussing past and present attempts to resolve the conflict, most media accounts, like much of scholarly literature on the conflict, tend to focus on the activities of elected officials, thus overlooking attempts by citizens on both sides of the political divide to bring about a peaceful resolution to the conflict. Some scholars have distinguished between peace-from-above and peace-from-below, or top-down and bottom-up conflict resolution attempts (Falk, 1994:189; Sharoni, 1996). In the context of the Israeli-Palestinian conflict, top-down conflict resolution takes place primarily around negotiation tables, usually outside the region, and is often characterized by attempts to apply generic, universal models of conflict resolution. Bottom-up peace initiatives, however, tend to emerge from the "inside," from within Palestinian and Israeli societies and struggles. According to those who emphasize bottom-

Deborah J. Gerner

Israeli peace activists such
as Uri Avnery of Gush Shalom
play an important but
often ignored role in
promoting strategies for
conflict resolution.

up solutions, social movements, protest, and grassroots activism are viewed as crucial venues for peacemaking and conflict resolution (Sharoni, 1996).

Indeed, long before the much-celebrated handshake between Arafat and Rabin, Palestinians and Israelis at the grassroots level had launched both separate and collaborative initiatives designed to bring about a just and lasting solution to the conflict. Despite their absence from the negotiation table, Palestinian and Israeli-Jewish women have played a significant role in the struggle to end the Israeli occupation of the West Bank and Gaza Strip (Hiltermann, 1991; Strum, 1992; Sharoni, 1995a; Emmett, 1996). Other examples of conflict resolution initiatives at the grassroots level include such groups as Israeli-Palestinian Physicians for Human Rights, which provides medical attention and services to Palestinians in need, and joint educational projects and dialogue groups designed to counter stereotypes and fear and establish conditions for coexistence between Palestinians and Israeli Jews (Abu-Nimer, 1993; Hurwitz, 1992; Fernea and Hocking, 1992; Rosenwasser, 1992; Kaminer, 1996).

Such activities even continued during the second intifada, although on a much smaller scale than during the first uprising. The majority of the Israeli peace groups associated with the Zionist left and center stopped their joint activities and peace protests with the intensified Israeli campaign in the West Bank and Gaza Strip and with the suicide bombings inside Israel. Besieged by Sharon's policy and the suicide bombings, only few groups, such as Taayush, Rabbis for Human Rights, the Israeli Committee Against House Demolitions, and certain local women initiatives, remained active. On the Palestinian side, in response to the lack of condemnation of the Israeli military campaign against the PA, most of the NGOs responded to direct instructions from the PA in November 2000 and suspended all contacts with their Israeli counterparts. However, the PA and the NGOs resumed their cooperation and joint work in the late summer of 2001. In early 2003, the Israeli peace movement and joint Palestinian-Israeli cooperation for peace began to increase again. More demonstrations and protests were staged in Israeli cities and towns and Palestinian-Israeli meetings again occurred, both inside and outside the Middle East (Abu-Nimer, 2003).

These initiatives clearly demonstrate that the expertise for resolving conflicts peacefully does not reside solely with official government personnel or procedures. Rather, citizens and groups from a variety of backgrounds and with a variety of skills can play an important role in peacemaking and conflict resolution processes. Moreover, there is a growing realization among conflict resolution experts and ordinary citizens alike that formal, government-to-government official interactions between instructed representatives of sovereign nations are not sufficient to secure international cooperation or resolve deep-rooted conflicts. Even if the parties to the conflict sign a peace agreement, its successful implementation depends on the support of grassroots constituencies on both sides of the political divide (Sharoni, 1996). In fact, one of the major shortcomings of the Oslo Accords was in the failure of both Palestinian and Israeli-Jewish officials to draw on the experience and expertise of peace and community activists on both sides of the Palestinian-Israeli divide. This rupture in the relationship between official and unofficial peacemakers may have its roots in different definitions of peace that inform the groups' practices and affect their relations with one another.

Indeed, one more way to examine various peace and conflict resolution initiatives is by focusing on the definition of peace that informs them. One of the most popular distinctions in the field of peace and conflict resolution studies is that between negative peace and positive peace (Barash, 1991:529–590). Negative peace is defined merely as the absence of war or direct violence, whereas positive peace requires the eradication of all forms of violence, including structural violence, and a transformation of society grounded in the principles of equality, social justice, and nonviolence. In the case of the Palestinian-Israeli conflict, it seems that official representatives of the two collectivities viewed peace mostly as the absence of war and direct violence (negative peace), whereas grassroots activists within both communities envisioned peace as a transformative process grounded in the presence of justice (positive peace). The advantage of this distinction is that it enables us to come to terms with competing sets of values, experiences, and political discourses that inform various definitions of peace.

For example, peace has been defined and envisioned differently by Israeli Jews and Palestinians both before and after the signing of the Oslo Accords. Peace for Jews has primarily meant peace with security, although since the signing of the Oslo Accords this formulation has been used interchangeably with terms such as *peace and stability* or *peace and prosperity*. For Palestinians, however, references to peace have almost always been accompanied by invocation of such terms as *justice, equality, liberation,* and *self-determination* (Sharoni, 1995b:400–401). The significant differences between them notwithstanding, these definitions are not mutually exclusive but rather interdependent. Both the two-state solution and the binational-state option can accommodate these contending visions of peace.

The main challenge, however, is not only for each collectivity to recognize the validity of the other party's vision. Because of the asymmetrical nature of the conflict, the fulfillment of these interdependent visions appears to depend on the willingness of the stronger party to the conflict, the Israeli government, to take the first step and recognize the Palestinians' right of self-determination. To win the support of its electorate for such an act, the Israeli government must introduce it not as a unilateral concession but rather as an essential step toward long-lasting peace in the region. In accepting the two-state solution and recognizing Israel's right to exist, Palestinians have demonstrated their realization that the fulfillment of their national aspirations depends on Israel's sense of security. It is imperative now that Israeli Jews understand and publicly acknowledge that their quest for security, stability, and prosperity will not materialize as long as Palestinians' quest for justice, equality, and national self-determination remains unfulfilled.

Israeli and Palestinian peace activists often
participate jointly in political demonstrations.

■ Conclusion

In the 1990s, the Palestinian leadership and Israeli government moved away from exclusivist military solutions to the conflict to more accommodationist diplomatic ones; however, this shift did not last. The two national collectivities continue to hold very different definitions of peace, informed to a great extent by the power disparities between them that the Oslo Accords failed to address. This asymmetry in power relations has been reinforced by the failure of past and present conflict resolution attempts to successfully address the two central issues at the heart of the Palestinians' struggle—national self-determination and territorial sovereignty. Most Palestinians feel that they have already made a serious concession by giving up the dream to reclaim historical Palestine and instead accepting the two-state formula, that is, a Palestinian state in the West Bank and Gaza Strip, alongside Israel.

The implementation of the two-state solution, however, depends on a complete Israeli withdrawal from the territories it occupied in 1967 in violation of international law. So far, the Israeli government has refused to comply and return to the pre-1967 borders. The Oslo Accords offered a temporary cover-up of the situation by highlighting Israel's willingness to negotiate directly with the PLO and grant Palestinians limited autonomy to govern their internal affairs. With the collapse of the Oslo Accords, Israel remains in control of most of the contested land, and Jewish settlements continue to expand. As a result, Palestinians across the West Bank and Gaza Strip who have seen very little improvement in their daily lives since the signing of the Oslo Accords in 1993 are growing more and more impatient. The Israeli government has continued to use its national security as a precondition for peace, failing to recognize that Israelis will not be secure until Palestinians fulfill their national aspirations through a political solution they deem just.

Rather than subsume alternative visions of what peace might look like under the narrow formulations of those presently in power, we ought to treat more seriously the divergent positions of the people—Palestinians and Israeli Jews—whose lives have been entangled in the conflict. Such voices and perspectives often point out that the Israeli-Palestinian conflict is more than simply an intractable territorial dispute between two national collectivities; it also involves contending visions concerning the resolution of the conflict and the future of the Middle East that have been the subject of heated political debates and contestations within both Palestinian and Israeli-Jewish communities.

Finally, as citizens of the Middle East and as conflict resolution scholars, we would like to voice our skepticism regarding conflict resolution initiatives carried out by such interested third parties as the United States or a myriad of conflict resolution experts. Far from being neutral or impartial facilitators, these outside parties, whose intentions are sometimes noble, tend to marginalize or altogether ignore the hopes and fears of ordinary people in the region while imposing their own conflict resolution frameworks and visions of peace. In contrast, we believe that Palestinians and Israeli Jews, if not their present leaders, hold the key to a just and lasting resolution of the conflict. The role of Middle Eastern scholars and conflict resolution experts, or the international community more generally, is not to bring peace to the Middle East, but rather to empower and support those people in the region who have long been involved in the elusive search for peace.

■ Bibliography

Abdo, Nahla. 1992. "Racism, Zionism, and the Palestinian Working Class, 1920–1947." *Studies in Political Economy* 37, no. 2:59–93.

Abu-Lughod, Ibrahim (ed.). 1982. *Palestinian Rights: Affirmation and Denial*. Wilmette, Ill.: Medina Press.

Abu-Lughod, Janet. 1987. "The Demographic Transformation of Palestine." Pp. 139–164 in Ibrahim Abu-Lughod (ed.), *The Transformation of Palestine*. Evanston, Ill.: Northwestern University Press.

Abu-Nimer, Mohammed. 1993. "Conflict Resolution Between Arabs and Jews in Israel: A Study of Six Intervention Models." Ph.D. diss., George Mason University, Fairfax, Va.

———. 2002. "Dialogue in the Second Intifada: Between Despair and Hope." *Global Dialogue*, 4, no. 3:130–143.

———. 2003. "September 11 and Palestinian Reaction: No Win." In Rashied Omar (ed.), *Multiple Voices: Opportunities and Challenges for Islamic Peacebuilding After September 11*. Notre Dame: Notre Dame University Press.

Alcalay, Ammiel. 1993. *After Jews and Arabs: Remaking Levantine Culture*. Minneapolis: University of Minnesota Press.

Al-Haq. 1988. "Repression of Education." Pp. 419–448 in Al-Haq, *Punishing a Nation: Human Rights Violations During the Palestinian Uprising*. Ramallah, West Bank: Al-Haq.

Andoni, Lamis. 1991. "The PLO at the Crossroads." *Journal of Palestine Studies* 81:54–65.

Aruri, Naseer. 1995. *The Obstruction of Peace: The U.S., Israel, and the Palestinians*. Monroe, Maine: Common Courage Press.

Ashrawi, Hanan Mikhail. 1991. "The Other Occupation: The Palestinian Response." Pp. 191–198 in Phyllis Bennis and Michel Moushabeck (eds.), *Beyond the Storm: A Gulf Crisis Reader*. Brooklyn: Olive Branch Press.

Barash, David. 1991. *Introduction to Peace Studies*. Belmont, Calif.: Wadsworth.

Bar-On, Mordechi. 1985. *Peace Now: The Portrait of a Movement*. In Hebrew. Tel Aviv: Hakibbutz Hameuchad.

Bennis, Phyllis. 1996. *Calling the Shots: How Washington Dominates Today's UN*. Brooklyn: Olive Branch Press.

Bennis, Phyllis, and Michel Moushabeck (eds.). 1991. *Beyond the Storm: A Gulf Crisis Reader*. Brooklyn: Olive Branch Press.

Brynen, Rex (ed.). 1991. *Echoes of the Intifada: Regional Repercussions of the Palestinian-Israeli Conflict*. Boulder, Colo.: Westview Press.

Cobban, Helena. 1984. *The Palestinian Liberation Organization: People, Power, and Politics.* Cambridge: Cambridge University Press.

Davis, Ury. 1986. "Israel's Zionist Society: Consequences for Internal Opposition and the Necessity for External Intervention." Pp. 176–201 in Ejaz Eaford (ed.), *Judaism or Zionism: What Difference for the Middle East?* London: Zed Books.

Eisenberg, Laura Zittrain, and Neil Caplan. 1998. *Negotiating Arab-Israeli Peace: Patterns, Problems, Possibilities.* Bloomington: Indiana University Press.

Emmett, Ayala. 1996. *Our Sisters' Promised Land: Women, Politics, and Israeli-Palestinian Coexistence.* Ann Arbor: University of Michigan Press.

Evron, Boas. 1995. *Jewish State or Israeli Nation?* Bloomington: Indiana University Press.

Falk, Richard. 1994. "World Order Conceptions and the Peace Process in the Middle East." Pp. 189–196 in Elise Boulding (ed.), *Building Peace in the Middle East: Challenges for States and Civil Society.* Boulder, Colo.: Lynne Rienner.

Fernea, Elizabeth Warnock, and Mary Evelyn Hocking (eds.). 1992. *The Struggle for Peace: Israelis and Palestinians.* Austin: University of Texas Press.

Finkelstein, Norman. 1995. *Image and Reality of the Israel-Palestine Conflict.* London: Verso.

Flapan, Simha. 1987. *The Birth of Israel: Myths and Realities.* New York: Pantheon Books.

Gerner, Deborah J. 1990. "Evolution of the Palestinian Uprising." *International Journal of Group Tensions* 20, no. 3:233–265.

———. 1991. "Palestinians, Israelis, and the *Intifada:* The Third Year and Beyond." *Arab Studies Quarterly* 13, nos. 3–4:19–60.

———. 1992. "The Arab-Israeli Conflict." Pp. 361–382 in Peter J. Schraeder (ed.), *Intervention in the 1990s: U.S. Foreign Policy in the Third World.* Boulder, Colo.: Lynne Rienner.

———. 1994. *One Land, Two Peoples: The Conflict Over Palestine.* 2nd ed. Boulder, Colo.: Westview Press.

Grayzel, Solomon. 1968. *A History of the Jews.* New York: New American Library.

Greenstein, Ran. 1995. *Genealogies of Conflict: Class, Identity, and State in Palestine/Israel and South Africa.* Hanover: Wesleyan University Press.

Guyatt, Nicholas. 1998. *The Absence of Peace: Understanding the Israeli-Palestinian Conflict.* London: Zed Books.

Hajjar, Lisa, and Joel Beinin. 1990. *Palestine and Israel: A Primer.* Washington, D.C.: Middle East Research and Information Project.

Heller, Mark, and Sari Nusseibeh. 1991. *No Trumpets, No Drums: A Two-State Settlement of the Israeli-Palestinian Conflict.* New York: Hill and Wang.

Herzberg, Arthur (ed.). 1962. *The Zionist Idea: A Historical Analysis and Reader.* New York: Doubleday.

Hiltermann, Joost. 1990. "Work in Action: The Role of the Working Class in the Uprising." Pp. 143–158 in Jamal Nassar and Roger Heacock (eds.), *Intifada: Palestine at the Crossroads.* New York: Praeger.

———. 1991. *Behind the Intifada: Labor and Women's Movements in the Occupied Territories.* Princeton: Princeton University Press.

Hiro, Dilip. 1992. *Desert Shield to Desert Storm: The Second Gulf War.* London: HarperCollins.

———. 1999. *Sharing the Promised Land: A Tale of Israelis and Palestinians.* Brooklyn: Olive Branch Press.

Hirst, David. 1984. *The Gun and the Olive Branch: The Roots of Violence in the Middle East.* 2nd ed. London: Faber and Faber.

Hunter, Robert. 1991. *The Palestinian Uprising.* Berkeley: University of California Press.

Hurwitz, Deena (ed.). 1992. *Walking the Red Line: Israelis in Search of Justice for Palestine.* Philadelphia: New Society.

Israeli Foreign Ministry. 2003. www.israel.org/mfa/go (accessed September 14, 2003).

Jad, Islah. 1990. "From Salons to the Popular Committees: Palestinian Women 1919–1989." Pp. 125–142 in Jamal Nassar and Roger Heacock (eds.), *Intifada: Palestine at the Crossroads.* New York: Praeger.

Kaminer, Reuven. 1996. *The Politics of Protest: The Israeli Peace Movement and the Intifada.* Sussex, UK: Academic Press.

Kelman, Herbert C. 1982. "Creating the Conditions for Israeli-Palestinian Negotiations." *Journal of Conflict Resolution* 26:39–75.

Khalidi, Walid. 1971. *From Haven to Conquest: Readings in Zionism and the Palestine Problem Until 1948.* Beirut: Institute for Palestine Studies.

Kimmerling, Baruch. 1983. *Zionism and Territory: The Socio-Territorial Dimensions of Zionist Politics.* Berkeley: University of California Press.

Kimmerling, Baruch, and Joel Migdal. 1993. *Palestinians: The Making of a People.* New York: Macmillan.

Legrain, Jean-François. 1990. "The Islamic Movement and the Intifada." Pp. 175–189 in Jamal Nassar and Roger Heacock (eds.), *Intifada: Palestine at the Crossroads.* New York: Praeger.

Lesch, Ann M., and Mark Tessler (eds.). 1989. *Israel, Egypt, and the Palestinians: From Camp David to the Intifada.* Bloomington: Indiana University Press.

Lockman, Zachary, and Joel Beinin (eds.). 1989. *Intifada: The Palestinian Uprising Against Israeli Occupation.* Boston: South End Press.

Lustick, Ian. 1980. *Arabs in the Jewish State: Israel's Control of a National Minority.* Austin: University of Texas Press.

———. 1993. *Unsettled States, Disputed Lands: Britain and Ireland, France and Algeria, Israel and the West Bank and Gaza.* Ithaca: Cornell University Press.

Mansour, Camille. 2002. "The Impact of 11 September on the Israeli-Palestinian Conflict." *Journal of Palestine Studies* 31, no. 2:5–18.

Morris, Benny. 1988. *The Birth of the Palestinian Refugee Problem, 1947–1949.* Cambridge: Cambridge University Press.

———. 1990. *1948 and After: Israel and the Palestinians.* Oxford: Oxford University Press.

Moses, Rafael. 1990. "Self, Self-View, and Identity." Pp. 47–55 in *The Psychodynamics of International Relationships,* vol. 1. Lexington, Mass.: Lexington Books.

Muslih, Muhammad. 1992. "History of the Israeli-Palestinian Conflict." Pp. 62–79 in Elizabeth Warnock Fernea and Mary Evelyn Hocking (eds.), *The Struggle for Peace: Israelis and Palestinians.* Austin: University of Texas Press.

Nakhleh, Emile (ed.). 1980. *A Palestinian Agenda for the West Bank and Gaza.* Washington, D.C.: American Enterprise Institute.

———. 1988. "The West Bank and Gaza: Twenty Years Later." *Middle East Journal* 42:209–226.

Nakhleh, Khalil, and Elia Zureik (eds.). 1980. *The Sociology of the Palestinians.* New York: St. Martin's Press.

Nassar, Jamal R. 1991. *The Palestine Liberation Organization: From Armed Struggle to the Declaration of Independence.* New York: Praeger.

Nassar, Jamal, and Roger Heacock (eds.). 1991. *Intifada: Palestine at the Crossroads.* New York: Praeger.

Niva, Steve. 2003. "A Predictable Cycle of Violence." *Al-Ahram Weekly* no. 627 (February 27–March 5, 2003). weekly.ahram.org.eg/2003/627/op192.htm (accessed May 28, 2003).

Palestine Red Crescent Society. 2003. www.palestinercs.org (accessed September 14, 2003).

Parkes, James. 1964. *A History of the Jewish People*. Baltimore: Penguin Books.

Perez, Don. 1990. *Intifada: The Palestinian Uprising*. Boulder, Colo.: Westview Press.

Quigley, John. 1990. *Palestine and Israel: A Challenge to Justice*. Durham, N.C.: Duke University Press.

Rabbani, Mouin. 1996. "Palestinian Authority, Israeli Rule: From Transitional to Permanent Arrangement." *Middle East Report* (October–December):2–6.

Reich, Bernard. 1985. *Israel: Land of Tradition and Conflict*. Boulder, Colo.: Westview Press.

Reinhart, Tanya. 2002. *Israel/Palestine: How To End the War of 1948*. New York: Seven Stories Press.

Rekass, Elie. 1989. "The Israeli Arabs and the Arabs of the West Bank and Gaza: Political Affinity and National Solidarity." *Asian and African Studies* 23, nos. 2–3:119–154.

Rosenwasser, Penny. 1992. *Voices from a "Promised Land": Palestinian and Israeli Peace Activists Speak Their Hearts*. Willimantic, Conn.: Curbstone Press.

Rothman, Jay. 1992. *From Conflict to Cooperation: Resolving Ethnic Conflict and Regional Conflict*. Newbury Park, Calif.: Sage.

Rouhana, Nadim. 1989. "The Political Transformation of the Palestinians in Israel: From Acquiescence to Challenge." *Journal of Palestine Studies* 3:38–59.

Rubenstein, Richard. 1987. *Alchemists of Revolution: Terrorism in the Modern World*. New York: Basic Books.

Sachar, Abram Leon. 1964. *A History of the Jews*. New York: Knopf.

Said, Edward. 1980. *The Question of Palestine*. New York: Vintage.

Said, Edward, Ibrahim Abu-Lughod, Janet Abu-Lughod, Muhammad Hallaj, and Elia Zureik. 1990. *A Profile of the Palestinian People*. Chicago: Palestine Human Rights Campaign.

Saunders, Harold. 1985. *The Other Walls: The Politics of the Arab-Israeli Peace Process*. Washington, D.C.: American Enterprise Institute for Public Policy Research.

Segal, Jerome. 1989. *Creating the Palestinian State: A Strategy for Peace*. Chicago: Lawrence Hill Books.

Schiff, Ze'ev. 1990. *Intifada: The Palestinian Uprising—Israel's Third Front*. New York: Simon and Schuster.

Schiff, Ze'ev, and Ehud Ya'ari. 1984. *Israel's Lebanon War*. New York: Simon and Schuster.

Shahak, Israel. 1995. *Jewish History, Jewish Religion: The Weight of Three Thousand Years*. London: Pluto Press.

Shapira, Anita. 1992. *Land and Power: The Zionist Resort to Force, 1881–1948*. New York: Oxford University Press.

Sharoni, Simona. 1995a. *Gender and the Israeli-Palestinian Conflict: The Politics of Women's Resistance*. Syracuse, N.Y.: Syracuse University Press.

———. 1995b. "Peace as Identity Crisis." *Peace Review* 7, nos. 3–4:399–407.

———. 1996. "Conflict Resolution and Peacemaking from the Bottom Up: The Roles of Social Movements and People's Diplomacy." Paper prepared for the fourth seminar of the International University of People's Institutions for Peace (IUPIP), Rovereto, Italy.

———. 2002. "Sharon's War Threatens Israel's Security." www.alternet.org/story. html?storyID=12768 (accessed August 2, 2003).

Shohat, Ella. 1988. "Sephardim in Israel: Zionism from the Standpoint of Its Jewish Victims." *Social Text* 19, no. 10:1–35.

Sifry, Micah, and Christopher Cerf (eds.). 1991. *The Gulf War Reader*. New York: Times Books/Random House, 1991.

Smooha, Sammy. 1989. *Arabs and Jews in Israel*. Vol. 1: *Conflicting and Shared Attitudes in a Divided Society*. Boulder, Colo.: Westview Press.

———. 1992. *Arabs and Jews in Israel*. Vol. 2: *Change and Continuity in Mutual Tolerance*. Boulder, Colo.: Westview Press.

Strum, Philippa. 1992. *The Women Are Marching: The Second Sex and the Palestinian Revolution*. New York: Lawrence Hill Books.

Suleiman, Michael (ed.). 1995. *U.S. Policy in Palestine: From Wilson to Clinton*. Normal, Ill.: AAUG Press.

Swirski, Shlomo. 1989. *Israel: The Oriental Majority*. London: Zed Books.

Tamari, Salim. 1980. "The Palestinians in the West Bank and Gaza Strip: The Sociology of Dependency." Pp. 84–111 in Khalil Nakhleh and Elia Zureik (eds.), *The Sociology of the Palestinians*. New York: St. Martin's Press.

Taraki, Lisa. 1989. "The Islamic Resistance Movement in the Palestinian Uprising." Pp. 171–177 in Zachary Lockman and Joel Beinin (eds.), *Intifada: The Palestinian Uprising Against Israeli Occupation*. Boston: South End Press and the Middle East Research and Information Project.

Tessler, Mark. 1994. *A History of the Israeli-Palestinian Conflict*. Bloomington: Indiana University Press.

Thomas, Baylis. 1999. *How Israel Was Won: A Concise History of the Arab-Israeli Conflict*. Lanham, Md.: Lexington Books.

Usher, Graham. 1995a. *Palestine in Crisis: The Struggle for Peace and Political Independence After Oslo*. East Haven, Conn.: Pluto Press in association with the Transnational Institute and the Middle East Research and Information Project.

———. 1995b. "What Kind of Nation? The Rise of Hamas in the Occupied Territories." *Race and Class* 37, no. 2:65–80.

Vitalis, Robert. 1992. "The Palestinian-Israeli Conflict: Options and Scenarios for Peace." Pp. 285–313 in Elizabeth Warnock Fernea and Evelyn Hocking (eds.), *The Struggle for Peace: Israelis and Palestinians*. Austin: University of Texas Press.

Volkan, Vamik. 1990. "An Overview of Psychological Concepts Pertinent to Interethnic and/or International Relationships." Pp. 31–46 in Vamik D. Volkan, Demetrios A. Julius, and Joseph V. Montville (eds.), *The Psychodynamics of International Relationships,* vol. 1. Lexington, Mass.: Lexington Books.

Wolfsfeld, Gadi. 1988. *The Politics of Provocation: Participation in Protest in Israel*. Albany: State University of New York Press.

Yahya, Adil. 1991. "The Role of the Refugee Camps." Pp. 91–106 in Jamal Nassar and Roger Heacock (eds.), *Intifada: Palestine at the Crossroads*. New York: Praeger.

Zilka, Avraham. 1992. "History of the Israeli-Palestinian Conflict." Pp. 7–61 in Elizabeth Warnock Fernea and Mary Evelyn Hocking (eds.), *The Struggle for Peace: Israelis and Palestinians*. Austin: University of Texas Press.

Zunes, Steve. 1994. "Zionism, Anti-Semitism, and Imperialism." *Peace Review* 6, no. 1:41–49.

Zureik, Elia. 1979. *The Palestinians in Israel: A Study in Internal Colonialism*. London: Routledge and Kegan Paul.

The Economies of the Middle East

Elias H. Tuma

The economies of the Middle East have come a long way since individual countries acquired statehood and became free of foreign occupation.[1] Some have achieved development and wealth, whereas others remain relatively poor; however, all face significant challenges as they proceed into the twenty-first century. There are twenty-four sovereign states in the Middle East and one potential state, Palestine, whose political status is still in limbo. These states vary widely in area, population, resource endowments, levels of economic and human development, political and economic regimes, and the ability to integrate into the global economy. Economists classify most of them as middle-income countries, although the range of per capita incomes is extremely wide.

Several important features of this diversity may be gleaned from the available quantitative data. First, the natural and human resources available for mobilization vary from state to state. In terms of population, for example, the tiny country of Bahrain has a little over half a million inhabitants, while Egypt, Turkey, and Iran each has over 63 million people. Virtually all have an extremely high rate of population growth that is due at least in part to immigration, whether temporary, as in laborers working in the Gulf states, or permanent, as in Israel's effort to gather-in Jews from around the world. Their land endowments also vary immensely, as Table 7.1 shows.

The largest country, Sudan, with more than 250,000 hectares of land, is more than 3,000 times larger than the smallest country, Bahrain, which has only 69,000 hectares. (For comparison, 1 hectare is equal to 2.47 acres; 1 square mile contains 259 hectares.) Virtually all the Middle Eastern countries have predominantly arid environments and limited arable land. For instance, less than 2 percent of the total territory of Bahrain and Kuwait is suitable for agriculture; Iran has 17,300,000 hectares of arable land, or just over 10 per-

Table 7.1   Agricultural Resources, 1999

Country	Population (millions, 2000)	Land Area (thousand hectares)	Arable Land + Permanent Crops (thousand hectares)	Arable land (thousand hectares)	Permanent Crops (thousand hectares)
Algeria	30.40	238,174	8,215	7,700	515
Bahrain	0.69	69	6	3	3
Comoros	0.56	223	118	78	40
Djibouti	0.66	2,318	0	0	0
Egypt	64.00	100,145	3,300	1,834	466
Iran	63.70	162,200	19,265	17,300	1,965
Iraq	23.30	43,737	5,540	5,200	340
Israel	6.20	2,062	440	351	89
Jordan	4.90	8,893	387	244	143
Kuwait	2.00	1,782	7	6	1
Lebanon	4.30	1,023	308	180	128
Libya	5.30	17,594	2,150	1,815	335
Mauritania	2.70	102,522	500	488	12
Morocco	28.70	44,630	9,445	8,500	945
Oman	2.40	21,246	77	16	61
Qatar	0.59	1,100	21	18	3
Saudi Arabia	20.70	214,969	3,785	3,594	191
Somalia	8.80	62,734	1,065	1,043	22
Sudan	31.10	250,581	16,900	16,700	200
Syria	16.20	18,378	5,502	4701	801
Tunisia	9.60	15,536	5,100	2,850	2,250
Turkey	65.30	76,963	26,672	24,138	2,534
United Arab Emirates	2.90	8,360	134	82	52
Yemen	17.50	52,797	1,668	1,545	123

Sources: Population figures from World Bank, 2002a, except for Bahrain, Comoros, Djibouti, and Qatar, from World Bank, 2002b. Land data from FAO, 2002.

cent of its total area. Turkey is the only country with a large portion of cultivable land, approximately one-third of its total, while Syria and Tunisia each have a little less than one-third in arable land. However, when measured as arable land per capita, Iran, Morocco, Syria, Tunisia, Iraq, and Turkey each has more arable land per capita than the United Kingdom. Five of these countries have about half as much arable land per capita as the United States. The more limiting factor in agriculture is water.

Water resources are both scarce and unequally distributed. As Ian Manners and Barbara Parmenter discuss in Chapter 2, Iraq's and Syria's water sources originate in Turkey and are shared by all three countries, not always amicably. Iraq's water from the Tigris and Euphrates Rivers needs better management to avoid salinity and exploit the rivers' tremendous potential for energy generation. In addition, some parts of Iraq are flooded swamps, whereas other areas are desert. The other significant river, the Nile, is Egypt's, Sudan's, and Ethiopia's main water source for domestic and industrial/agricultural use. It is indispensable for growing cotton, sugar cane, and vegetables and is a major source for fisheries, recreation, and power generation. But the Nile is suffering from overuse and pollution.

Many Middle Eastern countries are able to exploit mineral deposits and other natural resources for economic development, as Table 7.2 illustrates. Some countries are able to attract foreign tourists and their much-needed hard currency. Israel, Palestine, and Saudi Arabia have holy places that attract

Table 7.2   Natural Resources

Country	Natural Resources	Principal Industries
Algeria	oil, natural gas, iron, zinc, mercury	petroleum, light industries, natural gas
Bahrain	oil, natural gas, fisheries	petroleum, aluminum, ship repair
Comoros	agriculture	perfume, tourism
Djibouti	none	port and maritime support, construction
Egypt	oil, natural gas, iron, copper, manganese, phosphates	textiles, food processing, chemicals
Iran	oil, natural gas, sulfur, iron, copper, coal, lead, zinc	petroleum, textiles, cement
Iraq	oil, natural gas, phosphates	petroleum, petrochemicals, textiles
Israel	copper, phosphates, bromide, potash	food processing, diamond cutting, textiles
Jordan	phosphates, potash	phosphates, petroleum, cement
Kuwait	oil, fisheries	petroleum, petrochemicals, desalination plants
Lebanon	limestone, iron, copper, coal	food processing, cement, petroleum
Libya	oil, natural gas	food processing, petrochemicals, textiles
Mauritania	iron, gypsum, fisheries	iron and gypsum mining, fish processing
Morocco	phosphates, iron, manganese, zinc, coal, silver, lead	mining, mineral processing, food processing
Oman	oil, natural gas, coal, copper, chromite	petroleum, fisheries, copper smelting
Qatar	oil, natural gas, fisheries, iron	petroleum, natural gas, fisheries
Saudi Arabia	oil, natural gas, iron, gold	petroleum, petrochemicals, cement
Somalia	uranium, timber, fisheries	sugar refining, tuna and beef canning, textiles
Sudan	oil, iron, copper	textiles, cement, cotton ginning
Syria	oil, natural gas, phosphates, iron	petroleum, mining, manufacturing
Tunisia	oil, phosphates, iron, copper, zinc, coal	mining, petroleum, olive oil
Turkey	coal, chromite, copper, iron, manganese, mercury	textiles, food procesing, mining
United Arab Emirates	oil, natural gas, cement aggregate	petroleum, light manufacturing
Yemen	oil, natural gas, gold, salt, limestone, silica	oil refining, food processing, textiles

Sources: Data for natural resources from Spencer, 1998, and Ramsay, 1997. Data on principle industries from FAO, 2003.

many religious pilgrims. Egypt, Syria, Turkey, Iraq, Jordan, and Israel/Palestine have major historical sites that attract tourism and form an important economic resource. However, the attractions for foreign capital have been severely constrained in recent years because of terrorism and insecurity for both tourism and investment. Except for the countries with large oil reserves, the only significant potential source of wealth for most Middle Eastern countries is embodied in the still-to-be-developed abundant human capital.

The Middle Eastern countries vary widely in the extent to which they have been able to develop their economies. Middle Eastern economies range in gross domestic product (GDP) from U.S.$200 million a year in Comoros, to nearly U.S.$200 billion in Turkey in 2000. As Table 7.3 illustrates, these countries also exhibit wide extremes of wealth per person. Djibouti, Somalia, Sudan, and Yemen each have a per capita GDP of less than U.S.$1,000 a year, whereas countries such as Bahrain, Israel, Kuwait, Qatar, and the United Arab

Table 7.3   Indicators of Development

Country	GDP (U.S.$ millions)	GDP per Capita (U.S.$)	% Urban	% Literate	HDI Score
Algeria	53,306	5,063	60	67	0.693
Bahrain	5,300	13,688	92	87	0.824
Comoros	200	1,429	33	59	0.510
Djibouti	500	800	83	63	0.447
Egypt	98,725	3,420	45	55	0.635
Iran	104,904	5,531	62	76	0.714
Iraq	73,848	3,388	77	n/a	n/a
Israel	110,386	18,440	91	96	0.893
Jordan	8,340	3,955	74	89	0.714
Kuwait	37,783	13,976	98	82	0.818
Lebanon	16,488	4,705	90	86	0.758
Libya	31,661	5,930	88	79	0.766
Mauritania	935	1,609	58	42	0.437
Morocco	33,345	3,419	56	48	0.596
Oman	14,962	5,946	84	70	0.747
Qatar	10,460	18,065	92	82	0.801
Saudi Arabia	137,287	10,815	86	76	0.754
Somalia	1,631	177	28	n/a	n/a
Sudan	11,516	305	36	57	0.439
Syria	16,984	4,454	55	74	0.700
Tunisia	19,462	5,957	66	70	0.714
Turkey	199,937	6,380	75	85	0.735
United Arab Emirates	46,481	18,612	86	75	0.809
Yemen	532	806	25	45	0.468

Sources: GDP data are for 2000 and are taken from World Bank, 2002b, except for Iraq, Libya, Qatar, and Somalia (all 1998), from UN, 2001, and Bahrain, Comoros, and Djibouti (1999), from UNDP, 2001. GDP per capita data for Djibouti, Iraq, Kuwait, Libya, Oman, Qatar, Somalia, and Sudan are for 1998 and are from UN, 2001. Data on urbanization for Bahrain, Comoros, Djibouti, and Qatar are from UNDP, 2002. The Human Development Index data are from UNDP, 2001. All other data are for 1999 and are from World Bank, 2002a, 2002b.

Note: n/a indicates data not available.

Emirates (UAE) have a per capita GDP comparable to those of Western European countries. Other indicators of development, such as adult literacy rates and proportion of the population in urban areas, also exhibit considerable variation among countries.

In recent years, much criticism has been aimed at the use of income as a measure of economic conditions. For instance, the per capita GDP dollar value tends to underestimate the purchasing power of income. When prices in the individual countries are taken into consideration, the value of the GDP per capita tends to go up significantly. Purchasing power parity (PPP) shows how much one has to pay in the United States for what a dollar buys in the specific country. For example, Algeria's GDP per capita of U.S.$3,480 in 1999 had a PPP of U.S.$5,063, and Egypt's U.S.$2,490 GDP per capita in 1999 had a PPP of U.S.$3,420. This means that the quality of life is better than indicated by the estimated dollar value of GDP.

As a substitute for the flawed per capita GDP measure, the United Nations has devised an index of human development to measure a country's achievement in improving the quality of life for its people. The Human Development Index (HDI) ranks countries on a scale from 0 to 1 using three indicators: life expectancy, an education index that includes the adult literacy rate and school enrollments, and a measure of per capita income adjusted to reflect purchasing power. The 1999 HDI ranks 162 countries. The lower the rank, the better the quality of life in the respective country. For example, the United States ranked sixth after Norway, Australia, Canada, Sweden, and Belgium. By comparison, several Middle Eastern countries ranked below 100; only Israel (22), Bahrain (40), Kuwait (43), the UAE (45), and Qatar (48) are in the top 50 countries (UNDP, 2001). Overall, the HDI rankings indicate that Middle Eastern countries are well below international averages in achieving a decent quality of life for their citizens.

Given the wide diversity among the states of the Middle East, why, then, do we treat these countries as a unit, as is often the case in literature, world affairs, and this book? Perhaps the most obvious reason is intellectual inertia: as discussed by Ian Manners and Barbara McKean Parmenter in Chapter 2, the region has long been treated as a unit in academic, foreign policy, and journalistic writings. There are, however, more valid reasons for considering these states together. First, they share numerous historical experiences, including (in most cases) rule by the Ottoman Empire. Common features of language, religion, colonial legacy, and proximity to each other are also important. Furthermore, with the possible exception of Turkey, these countries consider themselves parts of the Middle East. However, the implied unity of the region is deceiving since most countries follow their own interests. Even members of the Arab League rarely coordinate their policies effectively. (For a discussion of the economic experiences of individual countries, see Niblock and Murphy, 1993; Lavy and Sherrer, 1991; and Chaudhry, 1997.)

The conceptual framework that I employ here to analyze the economies of the Middle East is represented in the schematic analysis of economic and political change shown in Figure 7.1. The basic idea is that development policy emanates from the philosophy, or doctrine, on which the economic system is based. The philosophy guides the establishment of institutions that reflect and sustain it, and in turn these institutions guide the creation of administrative machinery that will formulate and implement policies. The administration supervises the fieldworkers, who also must be in favor of the policy for it to

Figure 7.1   Schematic Analysis of Economic and Political Change

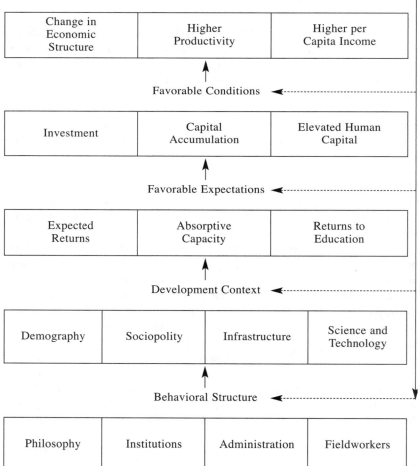

succeed. Thus, a favorable behavioral structure leads to the creation of a favorable development context: favorable population policy, stable and reliable government, an efficient infrastructure, and a favorable level of science and technology. A favorable development context promotes favorable expectations, which in turn encourage investment, capital accumulation, and elevation of the quality of human capital. This dynamic process allows for changing the economic structure, raising productivity, and improving per capita income. In contrast, failure to create favorable conditions at any level of this scheme can cripple the process of development and prevent a country from realizing its potential.

In light of this framework, a few observations will suggest the argument of this chapter. First, Middle Eastern countries entered the twentieth century with unfavorable structures and developmental contexts, with the exception of a favorable demographic context. Given this, one could hardly have expected highly successful results from the economic development strategies pursued in the Middle East. Second, economic change in the twentieth century was discontinuous primarily because of extra-economic forces: foreign domination by one power or another, hot and cold international wars, the oil price revolution, and intraregional and civil wars.

Because of the importance of historical patterns of development for understanding contemporary Middle Eastern economies, this chapter is organized by chronological phases or subperiods that are separated by recognizable benchmarks: 1918–1939 (initial conditions); the years of World War II, 1939–1945 (change of focus); 1945–1982 (postwar expansion and oil boom); and 1982 to the present (reassessment and change of direction). In my concluding remarks, I suggest explanations for the differences among Middle Eastern states in terms of their current conditions and prospects for economic development in the future. In Chapter 8, Mary Ann Tétreault elaborates the critical role that petroleum has played in some parts of the region, and in Chapter 9, Valentine Moghadam further develops several aspects of Middle Eastern economies at the turn of the millennium.

■ Initial Conditions, 1918–1939

The defeat of the Ottoman Empire and its replacement by Britain, France, and Italy as colonial powers in the Middle East opened windows to the developed industrial world. This change had the potential to enhance economic development, transfer technology, and integrate regional economies into the international economy. The initial conditions, however, were somewhat restrictive, and the colonial powers showed little interest in promoting development.

The economies of the pre–World War II Middle East were strongly characterized by dualism, in which two economies, one developed and the other underdeveloped, existed simultaneously. In the modern sector, wages are relatively high, high-skill occupations are common, and modern technology is employed. For most of the population, however, work is done through low-productivity techniques and poverty is ubiquitous. This economic duality continues to act today as a barrier to development in most Middle Eastern countries, although to a lesser degree than in the early decades of the twentieth century.

All Middle Eastern countries were underdeveloped and almost completely dependent on agriculture. They had low levels of technology, segmented markets, widespread barter trade, and low per capita incomes and purchasing power. All had very low rates of literacy. Several countries had unmarked boundaries, poorly defined political systems, and virtually no programs of economic development. Titles to land were often unsettled and landownership was highly concentrated, with widespread absentee ownership and tenancy. By necessity, external trade relations were common, since none of the countries was or could be self-sufficient in meeting basic needs. Domestic industry and the levels of technology in general were low, barely able to produce commodities that could compete on the international market.

On the positive side, Middle Eastern countries were relatively underpopulated, with highly favorable resource-to-population ratios. Beginnings of urbanization were evident, and a few capital cities had large concentrations of people. The following country profiles illustrate these points.[2]

■ North Africa

Northern Africa was still under colonial rule up to World War II. The French ruled Algeria, Tunisia, and part of Morocco. Spain ruled the rest of Morocco. Tripoli (Libya) was an Italian protectorate. Despite the different colonialists, the territories of North Africa developed similar economic structures.

The economies of the region exhibited considerable dualism during this period, with colonial expatriates holding virtually all the critical positions in the productive modern economy. They also controlled the trade relations, which consisted primarily of ties to the colonial center. In Algeria, for instance, the majority of the Arab workforce was employed in agriculture, whereas the French labor force was concentrated in urban manufacturing and trade. Most of the large farms and vineyards were in the hands of French farmers, whose properties were several times greater than the average Arab farm. Algeria was considered an integral part of France, and most of its trade was with that country. The economy functioned as a market system, although relations with France rendered it complementary to and dependent on the French economy. The other countries in the region were not as completely integrated into the colonial power's territory, although they had similar dependent economic relations.

All the territories in North Africa received development assistance in the 1920s. Transportation infrastructure was built, health and sanitation programs were promoted, some industrialization occurred, and irrigation and technology applications increased agricultural yields. However, development projects mostly benefited the colonial powers and their expatriates. Very little development occurred in the traditional economy, in which the Arab citizens lived and worked. Education policy favored the European expatriates. Few of the students enrolled in upper-level educational institutions were of Arab origin, thus precluding them from competing for lucrative opportunities in the modern sector.

The global economic depression of the 1930s harmed the economies of North Africa considerably. Unemployment increased, wages declined, and credit was difficult to secure. Banks extended loans on the security of land titles, but the benefits accrued mainly to expatriate farmers. The indigenous Arabs, largely uneducated in matters of banking and credit, depended mainly on the informal moneylenders, who often charged exorbitant rates of interest. By the end of this period, the region's economic structure had hardly changed. Although roads, electricity, and housing were improved, the indigenous economy stagnated. Some industrialization had occurred, but many enterprises failed during the Great Depression. Few were in the hands of indigenous owners and would not provide much of a base for development in the postcolonial era.

■ Egypt and Sudan

Egypt and Sudan had a different experience from their neighbors to the west, but the result was similar: both countries remained underdeveloped, highly dependent on agriculture, and heavily influenced by foreign interests. Britain was an imperial but not a colonizing power. Its impact was greatly enhanced when it acquired a big share in the Suez Canal, which gave it an excuse to land British troops in Egypt in 1882.

Then as now, Egypt and Sudan depended on the Nile, cotton, the Suez Canal, and tourism as sources of revenue and foreign exchange. Their populations were small. Egypt had 12.9 million people in 1918 and 16.3 million in 1938 (Mitchell, 1998). Sudan had 5–6 million inhabitants in 1930, but the qualifications of the labor force had changed little in both countries during this period. Following World War I, British expeditionary forces in Egypt gave the economy a push, providing a false impression of increased prosperity. Raw materials dominated exports, and processed goods dominated imports. An interesting feature of the early 1930s was the increasing frequency of barter transactions on the international level: cotton for machinery from Germany and for railway materials from Hungary and Sweden. (A similar trend prevailed in the second half of the twentieth century and continues today, although in some cases oil plays the role of cotton.) The Great Depression brought hardship to both countries, thus reinforcing the dualistic nature of their economies. By 1937, when the privileges granted to the European imperial powers were abolished, Egypt could feed but not clothe itself.

Sudan had less development in this period, with agriculture remaining its main resource. As in Egypt, Sudan's dependence on cotton made the economy vulnerable to fluctuations in cotton output and prices on the world market. As far as economic change was concerned, both countries had some exposure to Western development and lifestyle, but the benefits accrued only to foreigners and a few wealthy natives.

▦ The East

East of the Mediterranean, a different experience in development was under way. As detailed by Arthur Goldschmidt in Chapter 3, the Ottoman domains had been divided between Britain and France: Palestine, Transjordan (later Jordan), and Iraq had come under British control, and Syria and Lebanon under French administration. The British policy in Jordan, Iraq, and Palestine was roughly the same, except for the treatment of the Jewish population and economy in Palestine. These had privileged conditions, which permitted growth as in the developed countries. Early Jewish settlers came from Europe with high qualifications: education and skills as well as ideological commitment and determination. The population of Palestine in 1922 was about 757,000 people, rising to more than 852,000 in 1926. Of these, 628,000 were Muslim Arabs, 140,000 Jews, and 76,000 Christian Arabs. The rest were Druze Arabs (al-Amiri, 1974). Native-born Jews were few, mostly urban, but new Jewish settlement of the land was common, even as urban population centers were growing. For both political and economic reasons, the goal of the Jewish community was to maintain a standard of living for recent immigrants similar to what they had in their former home countries. To accomplish this, they developed modern agricultural techniques that in the moshav (cooperative settlement) and the kibbutz (collective settlement), were advanced enough to compete on the international market. Industrial development was a mix of private and public or semipublic ownership and management; it, too, was internationally competitive.

Assistance from the British government financed roads, bridges, railways, and other construction projects. Jewish agriculture expanded both by learning from the indigenous Arab cultivators and by applying techniques brought from Europe. Jewish farmers introduced new crops such as oilseeds, soybeans, fibers such as flax and hemp, and bananas. Factories were built, mostly but not exclusively in the Jewish sector: a silk factory in Tel Aviv, a match factory in Acre, a cement factory in Haifa. Power stations were created, irrigation systems were installed, and exploitation of the chemicals of the Dead Sea and hydropower of the Jordan River were under way. By the early 1930s the manufacturing sector was quite diverse, producing a variety of products from soap and artificial teeth to pharmaceuticals. Even so, agriculture continued to be the main source of employment and income in the country.

Jewish labor was organized early in this period in the General Federation of Trade Unions, or Histadrut. However, the unionization of Arab labor was slow, spotty, and ineffective. Joint organization of Arab and Jewish workers existed only in government employment and public enterprises. Jewish labor was better educated, better organized, and paid thirty to fifty times more than its Arab counterpart. By the end of the 1930s, despite political conflict between Arabs and Jews and between both of them and the mandatory government, the Jewish economic sector was solidly established, with a harbor in Haifa, extensive drainage of swamps in the Huleh district, an oil refinery, expanded irrigation, and a flourishing citrus industry for exports.

In contrast, with few exceptions, Arab agriculture continued to apply old methods of cultivation, had limited irrigation, and depended on traditional tenure systems. Except in selected urban centers, which were sometimes a mix of Arabs and Jews, the infrastructure in the Arab sector was poor, with few roads, no electricity, no running water, and limited facilities for credit, marketing, and education. Palestine was a small country with two virtually separate and unequal economies. The Arab economy had much in common with the economies of neighboring Arab states, whereas the Jewish economy more closely resembled those in Europe.

The same contrast was true of Jordan and Iraq. The population was scarce, mostly rural, nomadic, and tribal in social organization. The economy was based on agriculture and sheep and goat herding in Jordan, and grain, dates, and tobacco in Iraq. The methods of cultivation were traditional, land titles were mostly unsettled, and little industry existed, especially in Jordan.

Iraq by then was aware of its potential oil wealth and granted oil concessions to the British Iraq Petroleum Company (IPC) and the British Oil Development Company. The government of Iraq offered tax exemptions and loans to stimulate industry, but the results were limited. A few small factories produced cotton textiles, cigarettes, bricks, soap, canned fruit, and jute products, more like cottage industries in method, scale, and productivity. Land registration was introduced in 1932, but the lack of adequate documentation gave powerful tribal chiefs great advantages in appropriating large areas at the expense of the peasants and sharecroppers. In addition, the government took the initiative to build bridges, canals, and irrigation systems on the Tigris and the Euphrates Rivers. The port of Basra had already been built by the British army during World War I, as had railways for troop transportation. However, the maintenance of these facilities suffered during the Depression years. The country had some good roads, extensive river navigation, and a public airport that opened in 1933. The government did not have any plans for industrialization, but it built new roads and in 1926 decided to construct the Turko-Syrian railroad line.

Syria and Lebanon. After World War I and the exit of the Ottomans, Syria and Lebanon came under French mandate. The territory was segmented into districts or provinces: Beirut, Damascus, Aleppo, Latakia, and Jebel al-Druz. In addition to having internal ethnic conflicts, Syrian nationalists never accepted the domination of the French and political unrest was frequent. Economic activity responded to expenditures by the French army, but the economy depended mainly on agriculture, trade, and tourism, especially in Beirut and Aleppo. The French promoted road building and constructed a railway from Aleppo to Damascus. Imports consisted mostly of food and consumer items such as clothing, petroleum, motor fuels, and motorcars. The major exports were dried fruits, pistachio nuts, olive oil, and live animals, which were primarily re-exports from Turkey.

Interest in industry led to protectionism in Syria, the building of hotels in the cities, a free trade zone in Beirut, expansion of railways, and the building of roads. Air service was established to the French city of Marseilles in the west and the French colonial center of Saigon, Vietnam, to the east. Among the new industries were factories for perfume, blankets, hosiery, and cement tiles. Hemp, a widely used fiber-producing plant, was introduced in agriculture. The economies of Syria and Lebanon remained primarily agricultural, underdeveloped, and service-oriented. Opposition between urban and rural, rich and poor, literate and illiterate, and Western and traditional continued to be evident.

Iran. Iran, or Persia as it was known at the time, was not dominated by a colonial power, but strong foreign influence was always evident. Although rich in resources, Iran depended heavily on the outside world for basic needs. Its imports included sugar, cotton, tea, rice, animals, metal goods, machinery, and implements. Exports included petroleum products, textiles and carpets, opium, tobacco, pearls, and grains. A few new industries sprang up, but Iran had an underdeveloped structure. Most people traveled by pack animals and carts, although a few roads were good enough for motor cars. Mining was done by concession, mostly granted to foreigners, and a resident U.S. adviser guided economic decisions. Almost 25 percent of the budget went to the military in the mid-1920s, and government efforts to increase funds by securing foreign capital fell short. The economy was hardly monetized. The government resorted to unpaid forced labor (corveé) to build military and trade roads. Technical education was minimal, although the government established a technical school in the mid-1920s.

The second half of the decade witnessed increasing centralization, sometimes by ruthless means. Sugar and tea monopolies were created to generate revenues to subsidize railway building. Trade was limited by the poor infrastructure. The poor transportation system delayed delivery to such an extent that the Union of Soviet Socialist Republics (USSR) imposed a boycott on Persian goods for more than two years. To promote economic independence, in 1928 Iran abolished the Capitulations system, which had given significant rights to Europeans, and pursued nationalist economic policies. However, most contracts for railway building were awarded to foreigners, presumably because the local population lacked the skills and equipment needed for large building and engineering projects. In 1931 foreign trade monopolies were expanded and exporters were required to sell most of their foreign currency to the government. Nevertheless, industry remained underdeveloped and dependence on the outside world continued, with carpets the major export and manufactured goods the major import.

Finally, although protectionism was widespread, Iran concluded bilateral trade agreements (in 1935 with Syria and the USSR and in 1936 with Germany and Austria) as well as multilateral ones (in 1937 with Argentina, Mexico, and Turkey as well as with Iraq, Afghanistan, and Turkey). As the 1930s came to an end, Iran's economy remained underdeveloped, dualistic, and greatly influenced by foreign interests.

The Gulf region. Little development occurred in the Gulf countries prior to World War II. Kuwait, Bahrain, and Aden were transit centers and stations for pearling, fishing, and repairing ships. There was little agriculture and hardly any industry. Saudi Arabia, most of which is desert, had not yet begun exploiting its petroleum deposits, although signs of the potential oil wealth already existed. The most important source of revenue was spending by Muslim pilgrims coming to Mecca from all over the world. Agriculture was important on the east and west coasts of the region but not enough to satisfy the needs of the population. Population estimates for this period are imprecise, but there were probably less than 10 million people in the entire Gulf region.

Turkey. Turkey had been under foreign influence for a long time, first under the centuries-old system of Capitulations and then through heavy indebtedness to Western powers during the second half of the nineteenth century. The attempt to develop and industrialize the economy took the form of a mix between private and public enterprise. Between 1922 and 1934, development was promoted through investment banks created by the state. In addition to the Agricultural Bank already in existence, the state created the Ish Bank, a private company set up to organize and finance business enterprises. The Industrial and Mining Bank of Turkey, a state bank, had the charge of managing state-owned industrial enterprises. As a result, many new industrial projects were established, aided by the state. The number of workers in industry increased from 17,000 to 62,000 between 1927 and 1933. The output of cotton yarn, woolen textiles, sugar, leather, and cement increased rapidly. Agricultural output also expanded sufficiently to the extent that Turkey could feed itself.

*   *   *

To conclude, Middle Eastern countries were only beginning to change their economies during this phase. Consumption of manufactured products was more evident than production. Agriculture was the main sector in virtually all the countries. Dualism prevailed, with only a small portion of the population involved in efficient, profitable production. With the exception of the Jewish economy in Palestine under the British mandate, all countries had started on the road to industrialization and structural change, but only barely.

■ The War Years, 1939–1945

During World War II, Middle Eastern countries were allied, willingly or unwillingly, with one or another of the warring parties, and their economies were reorganized to serve that war machine. The Middle East Supply Center for the Allies, headquartered in Cairo, took charge of coordinating the distribution of supplies, allocating resources, maintaining infrastructure, and encouraging local production to substitute for imports and augment the war economy. Treating the whole region as a unit, the coordination was so successful that it was optimistically perceived as a prototype of regional planning and development, but little came out of it after the war's end (Wilmington, 1971).

During the war there was pressure to expand local production and reduce imports. In Egypt, for instance, the industrializing trend that had started before the war was encouraged, so that by the end of the war, Egyptian industry was able to satisfy 86 percent of its domestic needs for consumer nondurables, employ 8.4 percent of the labor force, and produce 12 percent of the GDP (Radwan, 1974:245). However, this level of industrial employment was the same as in 1937, which meant that little structural change had taken place in the meantime. Iran, in contrast, felt the negative shock of the war while experiencing few positive effects. There was more pressure on the infrastructure but no investment to maintain it. Foreign control directed all efforts toward war objectives in which Iran had no interest (Bharier, 1969:88).

More significant war effects were felt in Iraq's economy. Production of bricks, hand tools, oilseeds, tanned leather, and other traditional commodities expanded, but no modern factories were created. Railroads were expanded and maintained, as were roads and port facilities. Agriculture also benefited from the use of tractors, cultivators, and combines, in some places for the first time. In 1941 a college of agriculture was established (Longrig, 1968:320–323). Such improvements, however, were not common. Only Iran and Syria, like

Iraq, expanded their rail systems by more than 100 kilometers (60 miles) between 1940 and 1945. In contrast, Algeria lost some rail because broken tracks were not repaired.

Turkey, with ties closer to Europe, had a unique experience. At the end of World War I, it had just been reduced from a vast empire to a weak, poorly organized, underpopulated country. Turkey had a split identity, part European and part Asian. The revolution of the Young Turks and the advent of Mustafa Kemal Atatürk were perceived as the mechanisms to create a unified identity, with a republican constitution, an industrialized economy, and independence from foreign influence.

The thrust of Turkey's development during the first half of the century came between 1934 and 1947. This period witnessed the evolution of state socialism and economic planning. The five-year plan introduced in 1934 brought aid from the Soviet Union, both physical and managerial. Turkey chose to remain neutral during the war but still spent a great deal of money on armaments, presumably to protect its neutrality. The government emphasized industrialization, while agriculture seemed neglected. The mining sector responded to state efforts. Production and exports of coal increased. Electrical power generation increased from 2 stations in 1923 to 180 in 1945. Nevertheless, the movement to industrialize resulted in few changes in the structure of the economy. As late as 1946, imports included machinery and processed goods, whereas exports included tobacco, cereals and legumes, dried fruits, nuts, raw cotton, wool, and live animals (Thornburg, Spry, and Soule, 1968:chaps. 1–3, app.).

In sum, the war period brought the state into a more active role in managing the economies of the Middle East. Similar positive and negative effects of the war could be found in most countries. People had jobs and money to spend but suffered shortages of consumer and producer goods. Priorities were given to supplying the armies and the war industry, and coordination of economic and military activities, but even so, no positive or lasting impact on economic development and structural change was evident. Two side effects should be noted: a demonstration effect that introduced people to certain products and raised their expectations for the future, and a kind of indebtedness by the colonial powers that may have expedited political independence and the end of colonialism.

■ Post–World War II Expansion and the Oil Boom, 1945–1982

The end of the war signaled a new world order for the countries of the Middle East. Colonialism formally came to an end, although several regimes were replaced by military regimes posing as republics or monarchies supported by the former colonial powers. While peace prevailed in the West, the

Middle East witnessed wars in 1948, 1956, 1967, 1973, 1980, 1982, 1991, and 2003; coups in Egypt, Syria, Libya, Iraq, Iran, and Sudan; wars of independence in Algeria, Tunisia, and Palestine; and long periods of civil war in Algeria, Sudan, Yemen, Somalia, and Lebanon. New states came into being, including Israel, Djibouti, Somalia, and the Comoros.

Ambitious development programs were initiated throughout the region for agriculture and industry, education, technology transfer, and modernization. These programs complemented a strong tradition of government intervention: "Public policy in the Middle East and North Africa is driven by the belief that the state is the most effective agent for stimulating economic development. . . . Accordingly, nationalization and public ownership of the means of production figure prominently in public policy, and the state has sought to become the primary supplier of investment" (Anderson and Martinez, 1998:179).

Another feature of the period was the increase in consumerism, even in relatively poor countries that were dependent on aid and loans.

The oil price revolution of 1974 created a semblance of prosperity and growth for all the oil-exporting countries. In addition, the Cold War between East and West had its impact, as countries of the Middle East were pressured to line up with one camp or the other. Egypt, together with India and Yugoslavia, initiated the nonaligned movement to create a balance between the two superpower camps and promote neutrality for third world countries. Following World War II, Turkey tried to remain independent and neutral, but the advent of the Cold War and temptations of economic aid from the United States changed that policy. The promise of aid through the Marshall Plan, membership in the North Atlantic Treaty Organization (NATO) to provide protection against the giant USSR, and the power of the World Bank and the International Monetary Fund (IMF) redirected Turkey's economic policies toward the West. The impact was most strongly felt during what became known as the democratic decade (1950–1960), when a democratic government was in office. However, the role of government in the economy remained significant. After 1960 Turkey faced several military coups, which created a lasting role for the military in the economy.

During this period, the Middle Eastern countries varied in the extent to which they achieved economic development, industrialization, and structural change (see Tuma, 1987:chaps. 6–8, for an elaboration of the argument in this section; see also Wilson, 1995). On the whole, all countries except Israel remained underdeveloped and not much more industrialized than they were at the beginning of the period.

■ Agriculture

Agriculture continued to be a vital sector in most Middle Eastern economies as a source of employment and income for a large percentage of the steadily increasing population. Agriculture was also perceived as a stabilizing force within the economy because it could absorb surplus labor. As late as 1978, agriculture employed more than 40 percent of the economically active population in twelve countries and more than 50 percent in eleven others. Only three countries employed less than 25 percent of the active labor force in agriculture. Agricultural production increased in all countries of the region during the 1950s and 1960s, except Algeria. Taking 1952–1956 as the base period, Israel increased its agricultural output threefold by 1968. Lebanon, Libya, and Sudan almost doubled theirs. Iran and Iraq raised theirs by more than 50 percent; and the remaining countries raised theirs by a little less than 50 percent. Somalia and Mauritania increased agricultural output by more than 2 percent annually between 1960 and 1975 (IBRD, 1988; see also FAO, 1987).

After 1969, the advance in agricultural output slowed somewhat. Libya more than doubled its output between 1968 and 1978; Syria, Tunisia, and Israel all expanded production one and a half times in the same period. However, agriculture almost stagnated in Morocco, the Yemen Arab Republic, and to a certain extent, Egypt and Iraq. Even in countries with steadily increasing agricultural productivity, it was impossible to meet the demands of rapid population growth; indeed, a number of countries experienced a decline in per capita agricultural output. For instance, in Jordan, Morocco, Iraq, and the Yemen Arab Republic, food production per person decreased significantly. The most serious decline probably took place in Jordan, presumably because of the loss of the West Bank to Israel in the 1967 Six Day War (Tuma, 1987:tab. 1).

The overall increase in agricultural output between 1961 and the end of the 1970s was accompanied by expansion of the arable and permanent crop areas in all countries of the region (to various degrees) except in Syria. This was especially true in Algeria, Morocco, the People's Democratic Republic of Yemen (PDR Yemen), and Iraq. In spite of these gains in output and arable land, agriculture's relative contribution to GDP remained small or decreased in most countries. Labor productivity in agriculture was relatively low, and therefore the share of GDP produced by agriculture was less than the proportion of the population engaged in agricultural production (Tuma, 1987:109). Improvements in agriculture could also be seen in the changes in yield per unit of land. Most Middle Eastern countries experienced increases in yield between 1969 and 1979 in the production of cereals, roots and tubers, tomatoes, and tobacco leaves (Tuma, 1987:chap. 6).

The process of change and development was probably as significant as the actual effects. There were attempts to introduce major policies in agriculture to promote development and growth, equity, freedom, regime survival, and political stability. Policymakers sometimes had to trade economic efficiency for sociopolitical objectives. Agrarian reform was introduced in almost all countries of the region, but most dramatically in Egypt, Syria, Iran, Iraq, Algeria, and PDR Yemen. In these countries agrarian reform covered land tenure, tenancy, and patterns of production and farm organization. Ceilings on landownership were established, and most of the land above those ceilings was expropriated and redistributed to landless former tenants and to those who had less land than a specified minimum. Compensation was usually paid for expropriated land, and recipients of the land usually paid for it in long-term installments.

By contrast, agrarian reform in Tunisia, Morocco, and Libya primarily involved appropriating land held by foreigners and distributing it to local farmers. Jordan and Sudan concentrated their efforts on specific projects such as management of the Gezira scheme in Sudan and development of the East Ghor district in Jordan. Turkey's agrarian reform concentrated on distribution of public land, expansion of irrigation, use of fertilizers, and acquisition of tractors. In Lebanon, Saudi Arabia, and the Yemen Arab Republic, the policy focused on land consolidation and reclamation of new land.

Distributive reform was accompanied in virtually all cases by the creation of agricultural cooperatives whose functions varied from providing credit and marketing services to overseeing production and management. In most reforming countries, the government established state demonstration farms, large-scale production units on the socialist pattern, or agribusiness and farm corporate ventures, as in Iran and Saudi Arabia.

There were attempts to mechanize certain agricultural activities, increase irrigation, and increase consumption of fertilizers. Tractor use increased radically in Kuwait, the Yemen Arab Republic, Libya, Oman, Syria, and Iran. Turkey had a great opportunity to use tractors as part of the Marshall Plan, even though it lacked spare parts and facilities for maintenance. However, the distribution of tractors per unit of cultivated land varied widely from one country to another. Israel had one tractor for every 12 hectares in 1980, whereas Sudan had one tractor for every 1,124 hectares (Tuma, 1987:115).

An important feature of Middle Eastern agriculture in the post–World War II period was the building of large irrigation and hydroelectric projects. These projects had multiple objectives: to increase resources, enhance production, and show tangible results of government policy. The Aswan High Dam in Egypt, the Euphrates Dam in Syria, and the Hula-Negev project in Israel are only a few examples (Tuma, 1987:116).

Everywhere in the Middle East except in Israel's Jewish sector, agriculture continued to suffer from duality, with a large segment exhibiting low productivity, small scale, and archaic techniques. A much smaller segment enjoyed advanced technology with relatively large-scale operations and management. The rates of growth in agriculture in general were modest and the policies only partially successful.

Industrialization

Interest in agriculture was strong, but industrialization had a magic of its own. The three decades following World War II were remarkable in the history of industrialization in the Middle East. The rates of growth of industry

Drip irrigation makes agriculture possible even in the Egyptian Sinai.

and manufacturing rose, industry increased its contribution to GDP, and a higher percentage of the labor force worked in industry. By 1980, fully half of the countries of the region reported larger percentages of GDP originating in industry and manufacturing than previously.

Although industry and manufacturing increased their share of GDP, the average annual rates of growth varied widely, as Table 7.4 shows. The advance of industry was also demonstrated by increases in the consumption of industrial energy and rates of employment in industry and manufacturing. Energy consumption increased in all countries, dramatically in some, especially in the oil-rich countries. However, countries such as the Yemen Arab Republic and Sudan used very little energy due to their very low levels of industrialization.

The pattern and level of industrialization may also be explored by asking which country produced what and how much. A survey of twelve Arab countries (Shafii, 1978) in the late 1960s showed that the main industries were food processing, textiles, and light industries such as woodwork and printing. Machinery and basic metals were also produced in significant amounts in some countries. Specialization and concentration of production were also apparent in the survey. For instance, Egypt produced 23.2 percent of all machinery manufactured in the twelve countries, 76.8 percent of all basic metals, 39.5 percent of all textiles, and 43 percent of all paper, publishing, and printing products. Algeria produced 27.5 percent of all machinery, 23.8 per-

Table 7.4 Contribution of Agriculture and Industry to GDP (in percentage)

Country	1958 Agriculture	1958 Industry	1968 Agriculture	1968 Industry	1978 Agriculture	1978 Industry	1988 Agriculture	1988 Industry	2000 Agriculture	2000 Industry
Algeria	25	20	n/a	n/a	7	49	7	52	9	60
Egypt	33	24	25	24	24	27	16	31	17	34
Iran	32	30	22	34	9	46	21	20	19	22
Iraq	20	50	15	43	7	67	15	39	n/a	n/a
Israel	12	32	8	34	4	23	3	20	n/a	n/a
Jordan	18	14	15	21	6	21	6	22	2	25
Lebanon	n/a	n/a	11	21	9	21	9	21	12	22
Libya	n/a	n/a	4	65	2	68	5	49	22	n/a
Mauritania	n/a	n/a	n/a	n/a	25	24	21	26	22	31
Morocco	35	26	32	29	18	33	17	33	14	32
Saudi Arabia	n/a	n/a	6	62	1	79	2	73	7	48
Somalia	n/a	n/a	n/a	n/a	55	10	63	9	n/a	n/a
Sudan	59	12	39	15	36	14	29	15	37	18
Tunisia	n/a	n/a	18	21	16	27	13	28	12	29
Turkey	30	28	25	27	17	37	41	14	16	25

Sources: Mitchell, 1998, and World Bank, 2002b.
Note: n/a indicates data not available.

cent of all woodwork, and 16.9 percent of all nonmetallic industries. Lebanon produced 34.1 percent of all woodwork. Morocco produced 16.3 percent of all machinery, 28 percent of the processed foods, 24.3 percent of the paper, printing, and publishing materials, and 18.3 percent of all chemicals, petroleum, and coal products. Tunisia specialized in basic metals, providing 18.2 percent of the total produced by these twelve countries.

The specialization pattern within each country did not change much over the years. Major developments took place after 1975 in oil and petrochemicals, in car, truck and tractor assembly, and in the manufacture of arms (Deaver, 1996). The distribution of industrial projects within countries was concentrated in specific regions, either because of proximity to raw materials such as soil deposits or because of the development of infrastructure in and around the largest cities and near the coast. The few exceptions were Iran, which had the most dispersed industry among the large countries, followed by Egypt and Morocco, and by Israel, which had the widest dispersal of all in the region. In general, the pattern of industrialization within individual countries mirrored and reinforced the dualistic economic structures that had prevailed at the beginning of the period.

The development of industry and manufacturing was promoted by a combination of market control and planning activities. Until recently, three patterns of economic development could be observed in the Middle East. The first was the so-called Arab socialist pattern, as seen in Algeria, Libya, Syria, Iraq, and Egypt until the mid-1970s. The second was, and still is, the state capitalism pattern, as existed in Saudi Arabia and most other Gulf countries. In both of these patterns, the state owned or controlled most of the natural resources and carried the responsibility for large sectors of the economy. Thus, government and public forces in both groups of countries were conspicuously responsible for industrialization policy.

A third group of countries, including Bahrain, Iran before the 1979 revolution, Jordan, Lebanon, Morocco, Tunisia, and Yemen, minimized government involvement in the economy and depended more on market-oriented policies. The government intervened indirectly, however, through taxation, subsidies, and protectionism. Morocco and Lebanon also achieved a fair degree of advancement in light industry. Government policy in these countries was one of facilitating industrialization by improving infrastructure and raising incentives through higher wages, traditional benefits, and appeals to nationalistic sentiment. By the late 1970s, even some of the socialist countries had shifted toward the market economy. Egypt introduced its Infitah (open door policy), and Algeria began to open up to the private sector to combat the apparent retardation of the economy.

In spite of their differences, the three groups of countries had certain policies and measures in common. For instance, all countries had indicative economic plans, rather than command plans to be implemented by government.

Those plans specified the expected levels of expenditure in the main sectors of the economy, but the government had no way of enforcing the plans nor were the people indoctrinated enough or always willing to adopt them. Another common feature was a certain emphasis on large-scale turnkey industry. In such cases, contracts were concluded for establishing industries by foreign contractors, who took responsibility for all construction activities, leaving little room for the domestic labor force to learn by doing. Still another feature was the concentration of industrial production and manufacturing in commodities for the domestic market, thus ignoring international standards of quality and efficiency. Finally, it seems evident that when government did not interfere directly, industry remained small and often more traditional than otherwise. In conclusion, industry and manufacturing made some progress during the three decades following World War II, but they did not achieve competitiveness on the world market. Nor, with the exception of Israel, did they become major sectors in the various economies in terms of contribution to GDP, productive employment of labor, or changes in the patterns of trade, as will be seen below.

▪ International Trade

From 1945 to 1975, the Middle East experienced rapid expansion in international trade. Direction and volume varied according to endowment, alliances, and economic and political ideologies and objectives. The oil-exporting countries had relatively abundant purchasing power to spend on trade, while other countries had to depend on economic aid, loans, and military alliances to finance trade deficits. The socialist governments used some degree of planning and thus were able to regulate both the volume and composition of trade and avoid deficits more than the others. Yet in all cases, trade was expanded or curtailed largely according to political and military alliances (or semi-alliances), rather than according to economic and market conditions. Thus the socialist economies traded with the Soviet bloc and China, while the capitalist economies traded with the capitalist and Western-bloc countries with which they had concluded military or political alliances and treaties, regardless of economic or market efficiency or determination. (See Tuma, 1987:chap. 8, for a more detailed exploration.)

Although exports declined in the 1970s in most countries, imports generally continued to increase. During the 1970s, only Israel and Lebanon had declines in imports. Again, war was a major factor in both countries. The increase in imports by the non-oil-exporting countries caused large deficits in the balance of trade that had to be financed by foreign aid, loans, and foreign investments. Primary commodities, fuels, minerals, and metals dominated exports between 1960 and 1980. Some manufacturing exports came from Jordan, and industrial and manufactured products from Syria and Tunisia, but all other countries except Israel continued to export the same goods they had exported in the past. Some of the industrial and manufacturing exports were often re-exports by transit economies such as Lebanon, the UAE, and Jordan.

During this period, imports of machinery increased somewhat and imports of other manufactured goods decreased somewhat in Algeria, Egypt, Iran, Iraq, Morocco, Sudan, Syria, and Tunisia. Import substitution policies played a major role in that development. Israel, in contrast, reduced imports of machinery and transportation equipment and increased imports of other manufactures. It also increased the import and consumption of fuel, in the pattern of the industrialized countries. Turkey, however, increased its production and assembly of machinery and other manufactured goods and reduced imports of these items between 1962 and 1978.

The flow of trade within the region was not uniform. Intraregional trade concentrated within subregions was common. However, intraregional trade was relatively small compared with regional trade with other areas and countries. The reasons are clear. The countries of the Middle East duplicated each other's products and competed for markets and clients. The features of underdevelopment were as evident in the pattern of trade in the early 1980s as they were at the beginning of the period. The boom witnessed increased consumption, expanded infrastructures, and mounting debts. It also prompted modernization but little technology transfer, and expansion of trade but also dependency on foreign capital, technology, and markets (Roberts and Fowler, 1995). Therefore, when the developed countries suffered a recession in the mid-1980s and the price of oil declined in the 1990s, Middle Eastern countries began to suffer as well. In an extensive study of the effects of oil on the economies of the Gulf Cooperation Council, Hoosein Askari, Vahid Nowshirvani, and Mohamed Jaber ask, "Has oil been a blessing or a curse? If the rate of private sector growth is the basis for the answer, then oil seems to have been much more a curse than a blessing, especially for future generations of citizens. However, oil could be seen as a blessing because it affords the financial resources needed to support radical changes in policy" (1997:96).

The tendency to change policy and try to integrate national economies into the new global economy created new burdens for which these economies were scarcely prepared. The mechanism for such integration, under pressure of the World Bank, the IMF, and the U.S. State Department, was to introduce structural reform and privatization. Freer trade, less protectionism, and denationalization became the motto at the end of the period, even though these countries could hardly compete on the international market. Compliance, therefore, was found to be difficult and costly but still attempted (Barkey, 1992; Niblock and Murphy, 1993; el-Ghonemy, 1998).

■ Contemporary Middle Eastern Economies, 1982 to the Present

The economies of the Middle East have encountered several shocks during the past two decades. These shocks have directly and indirectly influenced the rates of economic growth, the level of employment and unemployment, poverty, income distribution, and the relationship with the global market. Another effect has been the decrease in capital, as in Iraq, Iran, Lebanon, and Palestine. The direct effects were primarily a response to the slowdown of the international economy and decline of the oil prices, which entailed major cuts in the revenue, and expenditure of the oil-exporting countries in the region.

Iraq fought Iran between 1980 and 1988, costing the two countries over 2 million people in casualties and waste of most of the oil revenues of the period to finance the war, in addition to the physical destruction of fixed capital. Iraq invaded Kuwait in 1990 and had to fight an international coalition, again costing the region about U.S.\$200 billion in destruction of capital and lost oil revenue. Since then Iraq has continued to suffer the impact of economic sanctions, which have limited the country's capacity to invest, trade, and grow. On the contrary, by 2002 the combined effects on Iraq reduced the economy almost to 60 percent of its pre–Gulf War level of production and income. Iraq's most recent tragedy of war is being played out now. The United States and British forces invaded the country in 2003, routed out the regime, and occupied the country. In the process, thousands of lives were lost and hundreds of buildings destroyed. Museums and other cultural institutions were looted and the economy was left in disarray. The full costs of this war and its aftermath are mounting and it will be a long time before a reliable estimate of the total damage can be calculated.

Libya has also faced economic sanctions and restriction of its commercial air service, which reduced its direct contact with the outside world as well as direct foreign investment. Israel invaded Lebanon in 1982 and stayed in the southern part of the country for eighteen years, wreaking havoc on Lebanon's economy, which was already suffering the effects of civil war since 1975. The destruction of capital in Beirut alone was sufficient to reduce the Lebanese economy significantly, as well as to divert the tourist industry away from the country. The civil war in Sudan has been another destructive force, dissipating the country's resources in addition to destroying physical and human capital. Even though Sudan recently discovered oil, much of the revenue from this resource has been used to finance the war. Somalia is yet another casualty of civil war.

The most destruction and economic disruption has occurred in Palestine (West Bank and Gaza). During the second intifada, the economy has been reduced to a level far below subsistence on the basis of domestic production. The infrastructure has been demolished and production has been disrupted because of curfews and restrictions on mobility, the closure of Israel's market to commuter employment, and loss of life and property in the process. The Palestinians have been reduced to survival on charity from other countries. Estimates of the Palestinian losses vary by source. As of mid-2003, the Palestine Red Crescent Society reported more than 2,400 lives lost and tens of thousands of people injured. Thousands of houses, office buildings, and small workshops and factories have been demolished. More than 52,000 dunams of land (13,000 acres) have been bulldozed and put out of commission for cultivation, and over 25,000 mature trees in orchards and olive groves have been uprooted (Institute for Palestine Studies, 2003:157–158). Furthermore, living conditions have deteriorated so much that, in 2000, more than 20 percent of the children under age five were malnourished (Mair, 2002). Conditions have since deteriorated immensely (Ajluni, 2003).

While the countries of the Middle East were reassessing their policies of the earlier periods, they had to cope with new crises, which have been reflected in slower growth, a decline of real per capita incomes, and widespread unemployment. For example, the gap between per capita income in the Arab countries and in the European Union has widened during the past two decades. The combined GDP of all the Arab countries is less than the GDP of Spain (UNDP, 2002). Table 7.5 shows the pattern of development and change between 1975 and 1999.

The economic growth rates since 1975 have been positive in all countries on which data are available, but the sustained growth of population has offset much of the growth of the economy, as can be seen in Table 7.5. However, the oil-exporting countries have experienced a decline because of the lower oil revenues, most conspicuously in Algeria, Kuwait, Saudi Arabia, and the UAE (Krimly, 1999). Since the 1990s, most countries have faced high rates of consumer price inflation, some reaching an annual inflation rate of over 80 percent, as in Sudan and Turkey. Virtually all countries have experienced high rates of unemployment, ranging from 30 percent in Algeria in 1995 to over 50 percent in Palestine in 2003. Even Jordan, Morocco, and Saudi Arabia, for which political stability has been evident, have suffered from unemployment.

Finally, the past two decades have witnessed little increase in labor productivity, especially in the Arab countries. For example, labor productivity in the Arab countries grew at an average rate of 4 percent between 1980 and 1997. However, total factor productivity in the Middle East and North Africa declined by 0.2 percent a year from 1960 to 1990 (UNDP, 2002:87). To their credit, the Middle East countries have avoided the extreme poverty suffered in other regions by offering subsidies and a social welfare program to mitigate poverty. Inequality also has remained at levels that compare favorably with most other regions, including many developed countries (UNDP, 2002:90).

Countries of the Middle East have faced another challenge in this period in the form of political and economic pressure to transform their economies

Table 7.5 Indicators of Development and Change

Country	Annual Population Growth Rate (%), 1975–1999	Annual Growth Rate Per Capita GDP (%)		Average Annual Change in Consumer Price Index (%), 1990–1999	Unemployment Rate (%)
		1975–1999	1990–1999		
Algeria	2.6	−0.4	−0.5	19.5	29.9 (1995) 26.4 (1997)
Bahrain	3.5	−0.5	0.8	1.2	26.5 (1997)
Comoros	3.2	−1.5	−3.1	n/a	n/a
Djibouti	4.5	n/a	−5.1	n/a	n/a
Egypt	2.3	2.9	2.4	9.6	8.7 (1996)
Iran	3.0	−0.9	1.9	27.1	16.0 (2002)
Israel	2.4	2.0	2.3	3.9	10.4 (2002)
Jordan	3.8	0.4	1.1	3.9	14.4 (1999)
Kuwait	2.5	−1.5	n/a	2.0	11.2 (1999)
Lebanon	0.9	n/a	5.7	n/a	8.5 (1997)
Libya	3.1	n/a	n/a	n/a	11.2 (1995)
Mauritania	2.6	−0.2	1.3	6.3	n/a
Morocco	2.2	1.4	0.4	4.2	17.8 (1997) 15.1 (1999)
Oman	4.3	2.8	0.3	0.2	17.2 (1996)
Qatar	4.9	n/a	n/a	n/a	5.1 (1997)
Saudi Arabia	4.2	−2.2	−3.1	1.2	15.0 (2001)
Sudan	2.5	n/a	n/a	81.1	17.0 (1996)
Syria	3.1	0.8	2.7	7.8	8.9 (1998) 6.5 (1999)
Tunisia	2.1	1.9	2.9	4.6	7.2 (1996) 15.6 (1999)
Turkey	2.1	2.1	2.2	81.5	10.8 (2002)
United Arab Emirates	6.8	−3.7	−1.6	n/a	2.6 (1995)
Yemen	3.9	n/a	0.4	33.6	8.2 (1998)

Sources: Data for columns 1–4 are from UNDP, 2001. Data for column 5 are from UNDP, 2002:tab. 4. Figures on Iran are from *The Economist,* special report, January 18, 2003; figures on Israel and Turkey are from www.tdctrade.com/mktprof/other/ and www/reference.guides.com/ (accessed September 8, 2003). All figures are rough estimates.

Note: n/a indicates data not available.

toward free enterprise, a market system, and political democracy. On one hand, the international institutions and the U.S. Agency for International Development (USAID) have put pressure on various countries to implement reform measures as demanded by the World Bank and the International Monetary Fund. These countries were pressured to remove restrictions on trade and price subsidies and to privatize the public sector. Measures of austerity and reduction of government spending were strongly recommended, regardless of the potential impact on the consumers. Some of the reactions were violent and disruptive, as in Algeria, Egypt, Jordan, and Tunisia. Four countries expedited their reform measures during the 1980s and 1990s, namely Egypt,

Jordan, Morocco, and Tunisia. Thus far, the effects appear to have been mixed. At first the economies showed positive growth, followed by a decline, with a high degree of fluctuation from one year to the next (Rivlin, 2001:chap. 5; for more on the impact and failure of globalization, see Stiglitz, 2002; and Dasgupta, Keller, and Srinivan, 2002).

The pressure for democracy has come in different ways, but the most economically relevant approach was the tendency to redirect foreign aid to non-governmental organizations (NGOs), which took over various functions previously administered by government. These organizations tended to undermine government authority, reduce its resources, and fragment the uses of available capital so that only small survival projects could be undertaken. The effects on democracy are hard to observe (Carapico, 2002).

Given their diverse patterns of historical evolution, it is not surprising that contemporary Middle Eastern economies vary widely in their economic outlook and philosophy. Although under pressure to reform their economic structures, privatize public enterprise, and liberalize trade, most countries still maintain some version of a mixed economy. The dominant form of mixed economic system is one in which public and private sectors interact, but the public sector has more power than the private sector. This pattern exists in Algeria, Tunisia, Egypt, Syria, Iraq, Mauritania, Somalia, Comoros, Yemen, and Turkey. Israel is similar, except that increasingly the private sector has more influence than the public sector. Another unique feature of Israel is that its economic institutions are sufficiently well developed to permit economic management through the use of monetary and fiscal policies, rather than by direct government intervention.

Workers lay cut stones in the *sa'ila* (drainage canal) in the old city in Sana'a, Yemen. The channel directs water outside of the city during the wet seasons and is used as a thoroughfare for cars and pedestrians during the rest of the year.

Among the Gulf oil-exporting countries, the mixed economy takes the form of state capitalism. Here the royal families control power and oil wealth and dole out benefits to their subjects, who then practice some form of market capitalism. However, little decisionmaking takes place through popular participation in the market. The same applies in Libya, which has no royal family; oil revenues go directly into the state coffers of the only remaining "Arab socialist" regime in the region.

Although traditional monarchies such as Jordan and Morocco lean toward a competitive market system, their economies are still too underdeveloped to allow the market to guide the economy. Hence government intervention, or management by the king, is not uncommon. The approach most closely resembling a free market probably exists in Lebanon and Bahrain. The Lebanese economy has been too chaotic since 1975 to be clearly defined, but signs of recovery are now evident. Bahrain depends heavily on offshore economic activities, to which domestic regulations do not apply, and therefore entertains free market practices in its domain (Edwards, 1996).

Finally, there is what has been called the Islamic economic system, which exists primarily in Iran and Sudan, although Saudi Arabia also claims to exercise this approach. The main rules in this system are twofold: there should be no interest charges on loans, and all investment capital must come from shareholders, either directly or through banks. The impact of Islamic economic institutions on economic development and growth has yet to be assessed. (Sudan has discovered oil, which is controlled by the government, but civil war still causes major distortions.) So far, the most operative economic model in the Middle East has been the mixed economy model, in which the weight of influence is concentrated in the public sector (Wilson, 1995).

Throughout most of the region, there is relatively low participation in paid labor in general and by women in particular. Although some countries, particularly Gulf states such as Kuwait, Qatar, and the UAE, can boast of relatively high rates of participation, at least of male labor, most of that labor is foreign. The exceptions to low workforce participation are the Comoros Islands, Israel, Turkey, and Mauritania. Active participation of female labor in the informal economy or within households, although presumably high, has not been adequately recorded or analyzed, an observation more fully developed by Valentine Moghadam in Chapter 9 and Lisa Taraki in Chapter 11. The combination of relatively low workforce participation with high population growth means that these economies face high rates of dependency on foreign labor and low capacity to generate earnings for investment.

A large percentage of the labor force is engaged in agriculture, although in many cases more than 50 percent of the potential workforce is engaged in the service industry or is unemployed or uncounted. The sectoral distribution of the labor force changed during the decade of the 1980s. A lower percentage of workers were engaged in agriculture and a higher percentage in indus-

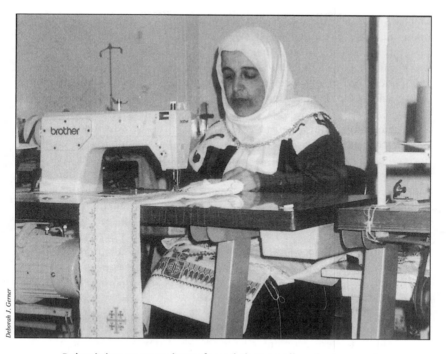

Deborah J. Gerner

Palestinian women have found that small-scale economic
activities such as sewing and embroidery allow them to earn
much-needed money while preserving a part of their culture.

try in 1990 than in 1980. In contrast, agriculture's contribution to GDP
increased in a few cases and declined in others. The same was true of the contribution of industry and manufacturing to GDP, which remained relatively
low, especially if the shares of extraction industries, such as potash, oil, and
rock quarries, are excluded. The late 1980s and early 1990s were not good
years for income earners in the Middle East.

Most countries of the Middle East do not report their patterns of income
distribution, but those providing such information do not show unusual
inequality compared with most other countries in the world, including the
United States. Nevertheless, there are differences within the region. For
example, Israel's income distribution was far more equal than that of Morocco
and Tunisia, which in turn was more equal than that of Jordan. Egypt had the
most equal distribution in the region, as measured by the shares of the two
income groups noted above and by the smaller gap between them (Eeghen,
1998).

The economic profile of the region may be understood more clearly by
exploring the composition of trade and the direction of trade of the individual

countries. The latest available data show a pattern of trade that is common among underdeveloped countries. Most exports are extractive products, raw materials including oil, gas, and potash, or agricultural commodities. The imports are mostly manufactured goods, processed chemicals, and appliances. This pattern has hardly changed over the past few decades, as is common among underdeveloped countries. This same pattern is illustrated in Tables 7.6 and 7.7.

Regional underdevelopment is also reflected in the direction of trade, a large percentage of which is conducted with industrial and developed countries since no country in the region has the quantitative and qualitative capacity to satisfy regional demand for manufactured products. Furthermore, intraregional trade is small relative to total trade, largely because all the countries produce similar goods and share a low level of industrialization. The fact that imports include industrial and investment capital may also be misleading because a large percentage of these imports consists of arms and military equipment, which do little to enhance development and growth (Edwards, 1996).

■ Conclusion

Over the past four decades, efforts have been expended to develop and bring Middle Eastern economies to the level of developed economies. Yet development has been elusive except in Israel. Sustained underdevelopment is reflected in the relatively low levels of technology and labor productivity and dependence on economic rent, foreign aid, and external borrowing. The countries of the region have received aid of various degrees from international agencies such as the United Nations, the Food and Agriculture Organization, and the World Bank. Bilateral agreements with developed countries brought easy credit, grants, trade agreements, and technology transfer to various states, especially during the Cold War. The oil price revolutions of 1973–1974 and 1979 generated large flows of capital into the region, primarily to the oil-exporting countries, but other countries benefited as well. Finally, new technologies were accessible upon request in most cases, at least for purposes of economic development.

Middle Eastern countries took advantage of these opportunities, but the results have been mixed. Most states applied some form of economic planning, subsidized private industry, created public enterprises, and regulated or sometimes liberalized their markets. Policymakers also tried to encourage technology transfer through subsidy, education, foreign investment, and import substitution policies. Moreover, the Arab countries explored possibilities of an Arab common market, though with little success. Even so, underdevelopment has persisted.

Table 7.6 Export Structure by Main Categories

Country	Year	Total Value	Food Items	Agricultural Raw Materials	Fuels	Ores and Metals	Processed Exports Total	Chemical Products	Manufactured Goods	Machinery, Transport	Unallocated
Algeria	1999	12,525	0.2	0.0	97.1	0.5	2.1	1.0	0.6	0.5	0.0
Bahrain	1995	4,104	2.0	0.0	61.0	21.9	15.0	5.1	8.9	1.0	0.0
Djibouti	1990	25	39.1	4.8	0.0	0.2	7.8	0.2	1.5	6.2	48.1
Egypt	1999	3,501	8.9	7.9	36.9	4.4	37.1	7.5	28.6	0.9	4.8
Iran	1999	19,726	4.2	0.6	85.4	0.9	8.4	1.2	6.8	0.4	0.5
Israel	1999	25,840	3.3	1.5	0.5	1.3	93.2	12.8	47.9	32.6	0.2
Jordan	1998	1,382	16.5	0.4	0.1	27.5	55.5	32.4	18.5	4.6	0.0
Kuwait	1999	12,140	0.5	0.1	90.6	0.3	8.5	5.8	1.5	1.3	0.1
Libya	1990	13,877	0.4	0.2	94.4	0.3	4.7	3.8	0.9	0.0	0.0
Mauritania	1995	483	55.8	0.1	0.5	40.4	0.2	0.0	0.0	0.2	3.0
Morocco	1999	7,503	20.9	1.7	2.7	9.3	65.3	12.9	41.8	10.6	0.0
Oman	1999	7,231	4.5	0.0	76.9	1.0	16.9	1.0	4.3	11.6	0.7
Qatar	1990	3,529	0.0	0.0	84.1	0.2	15.7	10.3	5.4	0.0	0.0
Saudi Arabia	1998	39,328	1.1	0.1	85.3	0.5	13.0	9.3	2.9	0.7	0.0
Sudan	1998	501	61.3	24.3	0.0	0.4	2.5	0.0	2.4	0.0	11.5
Syria	1999	3,389	14.8	4.7	68.4	1.1	7.4	0.4	7.0	0.0	3.6
Tunisia	1999	5,788	11.2	0.6	7.2	1.4	79.6	11.6	55.5	12.5	0.0
Turkey	1999	26,587	15.4	1.3	1.3	2.8	79.1	4.1	56.1	18.9	0.1
United Arab Emirates	1990	919	8.0	1.3	5.1	38.8	45.5	6.7	35.8	3.0	1.3
Yemen	1998	1,321	4.6	1.4	93.0	0.3	0.7	0.4	0.3	0.0	0.0

Source: UNCTAD, 2001.
Note: Total Value data are in U.S.$ millions; all other data are percentages.

Table 7.7 Import Structure by Main Categories

Country	Year	Total Value	Food Items	Agricultural Raw Materials	Fuels	Ores and Metals	Processed Imports				Unallocated
							Total	Chemical Products	Manufactured Goods	Machinery, Transport	
Algeria	1999	9,162	27.4	2.6	1.7	1.2	67.1	11.7	22.2	33.1	0.0
Bahrain	1995	3,716	12.1	1.0	37.3	4.6	44.3	5.3	22.3	16.7	0.7
Djibouti	1990	215	29.9	11.4	7.0	0.8	47.7	5.7	24.3	17.7	3.2
Egypt	1999	15,962	22.8	4.4	6.1	3.0	58.8	11.5	21.1	26.2	4.9
Iran	1999	12,622	20.4	2.8	1.7	2.3	72.5	14.8	19.4	38.3	0.2
Israel	1999	31,086	6.2	1.1	6.9	1.9	83.2	8.9	39.0	35.2	0.7
Jordan	1998	3,828	23.1	2.0	9.3	2.1	62.4	12.6	21.3	28.6	1.1
Kuwait	1999	7,617	16.8	0.9	0.6	1.9	78.2	8.4	30.0	39.7	1.5
Libya	1990	5,599	22.9	1.6	0.3	1.1	73.8	6.8	32.4	34.6	0.3
Mauritania	1995	455	23.6	0.6	22.0	0.3	53.3	4.3	15.8	33.3	0.0
Morocco	1999	10,788	13.3	3.4	12.3	2.3	68.7	9.1	29.8	29.8	0.0
Oman	1999	4,674	22.4	0.8	1.4	1.8	69.1	7.1	20.6	41.4	4.5
Qatar	1990	1,695	17.3	0.7	0.7	3.1	78.0	5.5	27.7	44.8	0.2
Saudi Arabia	1998	30,012	15.5	1.0	0.2	2.8	73.2	9.1	26.5	37.6	7.3
Sudan	1998	2,059	15.1	1.1	10.4	1.2	71.9	11.0	30.7	30.2	0.4
Syria	1999	3,611	21.6	2.9	2.5	1.3	58.8	9.9	29.2	19.7	13.0
Tunisia	1999	8,337	8.3	2.8	6.7	2.1	79.8	8.1	37.5	34.2	0.3
Turkey	1999	40,687	5.0	3.3	13.3	4.3	73.7	15.2	20.8	37.8	0.4
United Arab Emirates	1990	11,580	14.4	0.9	3.2	4.3	76.6	7.2	37.5	31.9	0.7
Yemen	1998	2,172	34.8	1.6	6.4	1.3	55.3	9.7	21.4	24.2	0.5

Source: UNCTAD, 2001.
Note: Total Value data are in U.S.$ millions; all other data are percentages.

Development efforts faced many obstacles, both external and internal. Among the external obstacles was the legacy of colonialism, which bred economic duality and left most economies so far behind in technology and development that it seemed virtually impossible to catch up. Wars of independence, civil wars, and intraregional wars were another obstacle that taxed most economies by wasting resources and detracting attention from economic development. The Cold War, although helpful in some cases, handicapped development because one or another of the dominant powers mandated some of the often-applied policies. Finally, intervention by international agencies and pressure to change policy, reform the economic structure, privatize public enterprises, liberalize trade, and let the market guide the economy were not always timely or helpful. On the contrary, such pressure has often interrupted the process of development and misdirected energies and resources away from development (Chossudovsky, 1997; Stiglitz, 2002).

However, the main obstacles were internal. First, most countries of the region are resource-poor, in both physical and human capital. Second, virtually all countries started at a relatively low level of development when the preconditions for development were totally lacking. But the most serious internal obstacle was the unfavorable behavioral structures and development contexts in the region (see Figure 7.1; Tuma, 1987:chap. 9, 1988). In all countries except Israel, these structures were not favorable to development. The philosophy that prevailed in these countries favored political, religious, and cultural values, as well as regime survival objectives over economic development and industrialization. The institutional framework was underdeveloped, as was the administrative machinery that would guide development. These handicaps were aggravated by equally discouraging factors such as uncontrolled population growth, which redirected resources away from economic development. Government stability and popular participation in decisionmaking remained below the minimum necessary for successful economic development and growth plans.

The infrastructure also remained underdeveloped. Transportation, communications, utilities, and marketing and financial facilities offered limited services relative to the needs of developing economies. This often caused segmentation of the market, raised the costs of production, and reduced the competitive power of these economies in the international market. Finally, most states failed to create a literate, highly skilled, and professional labor force that would meet the demands of development without depending on foreign experts and technologies. "Brain drain" and capital outflow were common whenever opportunities existed elsewhere, and technology transfer was minimal. Development efforts were handicapped, and underdevelopment remained the rule.

The only exception to this pattern was Israel, whose commitment to development resulted in the building of institutions and administrations that

Deborah J. Gerner

The influence of U.S.-based multinational corporations can
be seen throughout the Middle East. This McDonald's
fast food outlet is in the Tel Aviv Central Bus Station in Israel.

reflected the philosophy of development and allocated resources to promote it. As the population grew, especially through immigration, the Israelis made sure that resources would flow in as well. They built a democracy for the Jewish people and to a limited extent for the Arab citizens as well, which encouraged participation in governance and guaranteed political stability. They built the infrastructure fast enough and broadly enough to facilitate development and integrate Israel's economy into the international global economy. And most important, Israel exploited the high-quality human capital available in the form of immigrants. Israel also made sure to produce high-quality human capital in the domestic institutions of learning. These conditions, the combined favorable behavioral structure and development context, were conducive to development.

Furthermore, Israel had two unique advantages: access to large amounts of capital and a highly skilled labor force that could take advantage of scientific and rational approaches to development. However, other countries in the region, for example, Iraq, Iran, and other exporters of oil, also had large sums of capital available to them, but they did not have the commitment or the skills to develop their economies. These countries have adopted tradition, nonsecular religious values and conformity as their guiding principles. Their economies had no chance to develop to the aspired levels because they were unwilling to take the necessary steps.

■ Notes

This chapter was revised with the assistance of Jay Bhatt, to whom I am grateful.

1. Iran and Turkey were not ruled by other countries, but their economies were influenced by foreign powers through the Capitulations, a series of treaties granting residency and economic rights to Europeans (Tuma, 1989).

2. Unless explicitly stated, the rest of this section is based on Britain's Department of Overseas Trade Reports series and the U.S. Department of Commerce Reports series.

■ Bibliography

Ajluni, Salem. 2003. "The Palestinian Economy and the Second Intifida." *Journal of Palestine Studies* 32, no. 3:65–73.

al-Amiri, A. 1974. *Agricultural and Industrial Development in Palestine, 1900–1970.* In Arabic. Beirut: PLO Research Center.

Anderson, Robert E., and Albert Martinez. 1998. "Supporting Private Sector Development in the Middle East and North Africa." Pp. 178–193 in Nemat Shafik (ed.), *Prospects for Middle Eastern and North African Economies: From Boom to Bust and Back?* New York: St. Martin's Press.

Askari, Hoosein, Vahid Nowshirvani, and Mohamed Jaber. 1997. *Economic Development in the GCC: The Blessing and Curse of Oil.* Greenwich, Conn.: JAI Press.

Barkey, Henri J. 1992. *The Politics of Economic Reform in the Middle East.* New York: St. Martin's Press.

Bharier, J. 1969. "Capital Formation in Iran: 1900–65." Ph.D. Diss., University of London.

Carapico, Sheila. 2002. "Foreign Aid for Promoting Democracy in the Arab World." *Middle East Journal* 56, no. 3:379–395.

Chaudhry, Kiren Aziz. 1997. *The Price of Wealth: Economies and Institutions in the Middle East.* Ithaca: Cornell University Press.

Chossudovsky, Michel. 1997. *The Globalisation of Poverty: Impacts of IMF and World Bank Reforms.* Atlantic Highlands, N.J.: Zed Books.

Dasgupta, Dipak, Jennifer Keller, and T. A. Srinivan. 2002. *Reform and Elusive Growth in the Middle East: What Has Happened in the 1990s?* MENA Working Paper no. 25. Washington, D.C.: World Bank.

Deaver, Michael V. 1996. "Military Industrialization of Egypt: Development, Debt, and Dependence." Pp. 127–148 in Karen Pfeifer (ed.), *Research in Middle East Economics.* Greenwich, Conn.: JAI Press.

Department of Overseas Trade. 1921– . *Report on Trade, Industry, and Finance* (Middle East and North Africa by country). London: His Majesty's Stationary Office.

Edwards, Glenn M. (ed.). 1996. *Britannica Book of the Year: Events of 1995*. Chicago: Encyclopedia Britannica.

Eeghen, Willen van. 1998. "Poverty in the Middle East and North Africa." Pp. 226–261 in Nemat Shafik (ed.), *Prospects for Middle Eastern and North African Economies: From Boom to Bust and Back?* New York: St. Martin's Press.

FAO (Food and Agriculture Organization). 1987. *1948–1985 World Crop and Livestock Statistics*. Rome: FAO.

———. 2002. *Production Yearbook 2000*. Vol. 54. Rome: FAO.

———. 2003. http://apps.fao.org (accessed May 20, 2003).

el-Ghonemy, Riad. 1998. *Affluence and Poverty in the Middle East*. London: Routledge.

Hale, William. 1981. *The Political and Economic Development of Modern Turkey*. London: Croom Helm.

IBRD (International Bank for Reconstruction and Development). Various years. *Social Indicators of Development*. Washington, D.C.: IBRD.

———. 1988. *World Development Indicators*. Washington, D.C.: IBRD.

Institute for Palestine Studies. 2003. "Documents and Source Material." *Journal of Palestine Studies* 32, no. 126 (Winter):157–158.

Krimly, Rayed. 1999. "The Political Economy of Adjusted Priorities: Declining Oil Revenues and Saudi Fiscal Policies." *Middle East Journal* 53, no. 2:254–267.

Lavy, Victor, and Eliezer Sherrer (eds.). 1991. *Foreign Aid and Economic Development in the Middle East: Egypt, Syria, and Jordan*. New York: Praeger.

Longrig, Stephen Hemsley. 1968. *Iraq, 1900–1950: A Political, Social, and Economic History*. Oxford: Oxford University Press.

Mair, Lucy. 2002. "Survey Finds . . . Care International." Personal communication.

Mitchell, Brian R. (ed.). 1998. *International Historical Statistics: Africa, Asia, Oceania, 1750–1993*. 3rd ed. London: Macmillan Reference.

Niblock, Rim, and Emma Murphy (eds.). 1993. *Economic and Political Liberalization in the Middle East*. London: British Academic Press.

Palestine Red Crescent Society. 2003. http://palestinercs.org (accessed July 25, 2003).

Radwan, Samir. 1974. *Capital Formation in Egyptian Industry and Agriculture, 1882–1967*. London: Ithaca Press.

Ramsay, F. Jeffress (ed.). 1997. *Global Studies: Africa*. 7th ed. Guilford, Conn.: Dushkin/McGraw Hill.

Rivlin, Paul. 2001. *Economic Policy and Performance in the Arab World*. Boulder, Colo.: Lynne Rienner.

Roberts, Gwilym, and David Fowler. 1995. *Built by Oil*. Reading, England: Garnet.

Shafii, Irfan. 1978. "Processing Industry in the Arab World: Incentives and Objectives." In Arabic. *Journal of Social Sciences* 6, no. 1:7–28.

Spencer, William. 1998. *Global Studies: The Middle East*. 7th ed. Guilford, Conn.: Dushkin/McGraw Hill.

Stiglitz, Joseph. 2002. *Globalization and Its Discontents*. New York: W. W. Norton.

Thornburg, Max Weston, Graham Spry, and George Soule. 1968. *Turkey: An Economic Appraisal*. New York: Greenwood Press.

Tuma, Elias. 1987. *Economic and Political Change in the Middle East*. Palo Alto, Calif.: Pacific Books.

———. 1988. "Institutionalized Obstacles to Development. The Case of Egypt." *World Development* 16, no. 10:1185–1198.

———. 1989. "The Economic Impact of the Capitulations: The Middle East and Europe. A Reinterpretation." *Journal of European Economic History* 18, no. 3:663–682.

UN (United Nations). 2001. *Statistical Yearbook*. 45th issue. New York: UN.
UNCTAD (United Nations Conference on Trade and Development). 2001. *Handbook of Statistics, 2001*. New York: UN.
UNDP (United Nations Development Programme). 1998. *Human Development Report, 1997*. New York: Oxford University Press.
———. 2001. *Human Development Report, 2001*. New York: Oxford University Press.
———. 2002. *Arab Human Development Report*. www.undp.org/rbas/ahdr (accessed May 20, 2003).
U.S. Department of Commerce. 1940–1948. *International Reference Service*. Vols. 1–5. Washington, D.C.: Bureau of Foreign and Domestic Commerce.
World Bank. 2002a. *World Development Indicators, 2002*. Washington, D.C.: World Bank.
———. 2002b. *World Development Report, 2002*. New York: Oxford University Press.
Wilmington, Martin W. 1971. *The Middle East Supply Centre*. Ed. Laurence Evans. Albany: State University of New York Press.
Wilson, Rodney. 1995. *Economic Development in the Middle East*. London: Routledge.

8

The Political Economy of Middle Eastern Oil

Mary Ann Tétreault

The Middle East is the geographic "center of gravity" of the world oil industry. Oil is valuable both as a fuel and, if there is enough to export, as a source of foreign exchange. But to many oil-producing developing countries, the blessing has often turned out to be a curse. Oil has attracted major power intervention and, within these countries, has led to political corruption, militarization, and paradoxically, foreign debt. Oil wealth often distorts national economies and interferes with development strategies. This chapter examines the political economy of the Middle East's most lucrative resource.

The curse of oil often is linked to a colonial past, but, as Elias Tuma alludes to in Chapter 7, its social and economic impact differs from the impact of other forms of colonial exploitation. Oil production is geographically local-ized and its technology and capital intensity also isolate it from the rest of a national economy. In consequence, oil exploitation is less shattering to all but the most local life patterns than a shift from subsistence agriculture to cash crops (Munif, 1989). The relative ease with which foreigners could control oil exploitation in their own interests made it less necessary for them to replace local officials with client regimes than in places where imperial powers estab-lished plantation economies. Yet oil money did change the balance of power between state and society in oil-exporting countries, giving local rulers effec-tive tools for suppressing popular institutions and thwarting traditional checks on their authority (Gasiorowski, 1991). Thus, on the whole, oil decreased legitimate political participation in the Middle East (Crystal, 1990; Tétreault, 2000).

■ Industry Structure

The oil industry is inherently global because crude production and customers for products often are located in different countries (Penrose, 1968). As a result, almost ever since it was discovered, oil has been an engine of globalization (Sampson, 1975). Oil's importance in the evolution of the modern Middle East helps explain why this region is hyperglobalized. The complexity and global reach of the oil industry also present strategic opportunities, points of political and economic leverage where an actor such as a firm or a country can exert significant control. One obvious such "choke point" is oil production (Blair, 1976). Whoever controls the land controls the oil under it. In the nations of the Middle East, as in many other countries, mineral rights belong to the state. When oil was first developed there, oil companies had to negotiate with local governments to obtain exploration and production rights.

Before World War II, Middle Eastern countries competed for oil company investment in a market where the biggest companies were more afraid of a glut of oil than oil shortages. In the 1920s these companies agreed among themselves to limit production, fix prices, and reduce competition in product markets. In the Red Line Agreement of 1928, the three largest oil companies, Exxon, Shell, and British Petroleum (BP),[1] along with a few smaller partners, decided not to explore for oil or develop new production capacity anywhere in the old Ottoman Empire unless every partner consented. Countries inside the Red Line had difficulty attracting investment in oil exploration because the Red Line companies were so afraid of oversupply and falling prices. This problem was worst for Iraq because Red Line companies owned all the oil rights there (Anderson, 1981; Sampson, 1975).

Kuwaiti Petroleum Company/courtesy of World Oil

As in Iran, Iraq, Saudia Arabia, and most of the Gulf states, Kuwait's oil extraction and transport infrastructure are carefully maintained to enable the government to move petroleum products swiftly into the global market. This part of the installation is called a "Christmas tree."

Inexperience led most future Middle Eastern oil exporters to deal with only one company (e.g., Chisholm, 1975). Although many of these firms were joint ventures (partnerships of two or more oil companies), host countries still found themselves sitting across from a single operator on the other side of the bargaining table. When oil was first developed in Kuwait, the only operating company was the Kuwait Oil Company (KOC), a partnership between Gulf and BP. Even though both Gulf and BP invested the capital and took the profits from Kuwait's oil, all their business in Kuwait was conducted by a single entity, the KOC. Meanwhile, the big partners participated in several operating companies worldwide, enabling them to coordinate production based on what each learned about the others from their joint dealings. This structure also helped partners avoid competing for new contracts and provided a means to coordinate other global operations.

Kuwait's ability to choose which company it would sign with was limited by the British government, whose treaties with Kuwait gave Britain the final authority to determine who would exploit any oil found there. The British would not permit the Kuwaitis to contract with a non-British company, though the emir was able to hold out for a company that had at least one non-British partner (Chisholm, 1975). After the concession was granted, Kuwait's autonomy was even more limited. The terms of its contract with the KOC gave the company exclusive rights for ninety years to find and produce oil over Kuwait's entire land area. If the government were to try to seek better terms elsewhere during the period of the KOC concession, that firm would face legal challenges from BP and Gulf. An even bigger threat was the possibility of intervention by a home government—in Kuwait's case, Britain and the United States should Kuwait try to remove the KOC from its privileged position.

The powerful home governments of oil company operators also exerted pressure on the governments of exporting countries. In 1951 the Iranian government, under Prime Minister Mohammad Mossadeq, nationalized Iran's oil. Iran's operating company was unusual in the Middle East because a single company, BP, owned it. When its holdings were nationalized, BP obtained court orders enjoining other companies from buying oil from the Iranian government. Afraid of the example that a successful nationalization might set for other Middle Eastern oil-exporting states, the British and U.S. governments worked to destabilize and eventually to overthrow the Mossadeq regime (Gasiorowski, 1998). The restoration of the Shah of Iran in 1953 following a brief period of ouster also reinstated foreign oil companies as managers of the nationalized Iranian oil company. However, instead of restoring BP to its former position as sole owner, the Iranian government sought a "Kuwait solution." The shah invited non-British participation in the National Iranian Oil Company (NIOC). When the NIOC was reorganized, U.S. companies and the French National Oil Company (CFP), were given 60 percent of the shares, and BP was left with only 40 percent (Sampson, 1975).

The one company–one country pattern of concessions throughout much of the Middle East helped to make the region the marginal supplier of oil to the international market, that is, the source of however much oil was needed to balance global supply and demand. This balancing act was made possible by the participation of the largest companies, whose production holdings stretched across the globe, in one or another Middle Eastern concession. Once they had decided what total supply should be, the companies could regulate production by increasing or decreasing offtake in countries whose governments could not easily retaliate against them. The one company–one country pattern did not hold in Libya, whose oil was discovered and developed much later than that of most of the Gulf countries (Rand, 1975). But as long as most exporting countries had little leverage over their operators, the companies' cartel was difficult to overthrow.

The company-managed oil cartel was able to suppress production and reduce competition some of the time in some markets even during the 1930s, when world demand for oil dropped to very low levels because of the Great Depression, which also eliminated whole companies and thereby made the management task of the survivors much easier. Another boost to the cartel resulted from declining exports from two major oil-producing countries. Geological problems caused Mexico's production to drop from its high levels in the early 1920s, and an international boycott imposed when Mexico nationalized its oil industry in 1938 caused it to drop even further. Also, after Joseph Stalin assumed leadership of the Soviet Union, he reduced oil production there because he preferred to emphasize other fuels (Tétreault, 1985).

At the same time, governments and corporations in developed countries tried to regulate production to protect domestic industries and foreign investments. Regulations were even applied in the United States, where the antitrust tradition was strong but not so strong as to counter either the threat of business failure in the 1930s or the Cold War politics of the period following World War II. Indeed, oil policy during the Cold War found the biggest oil companies and their home governments continuing to cooperate for their mutual benefit. The companies developed an ethic of oil statesmanship to justify their interference in politics and markets and to explain why they were entitled to their home governments' assistance. The governments, in turn, expanded their use of oil companies as foreign policy surrogates in relations with host governments. By the end of World War II, foreign oil was widely regarded as an important ingredient of national power and one of the most lucrative businesses in the world (Penrose, 1968).

■ The System Unravels

Economic theory tells us that an industry where firms make huge profits soon attracts new firms whose competitive behavior reduces profits for all.

This is exactly what happened in the international oil industry. The success of even imperfect cartel arrangements made oil vastly profitable and oil companies among the world's largest and richest firms. Competition came from new oil companies, companies that formerly operated only in their own home countries, and from state-owned firms. These new competitors offered potential oil-exporting countries more money and better terms, and also offered attractive terms for offshore rights in countries whose onshore operators had not thought to acquire these rights in their original contracts. This willingness to write contracts highly favorable to host countries encouraged Middle Eastern governments to ask all their operating companies to liberalize contract terms.

Even the largest companies found themselves having to compete for new contracts. Some decided to sweeten the terms of ongoing contracts to maintain good relations with their hosts. Others were asked to relinquish territory they were not developing so that the host governments could sell the rights to those lands to someone else. All of this increased the costs of doing business and reduced company profits. Competition in other segments of the market also squeezed profits. Shortly after the end of World War II, the Venezuelan government threatened to nationalize foreign oil operations unless the companies agreed to split their profits on Venezuelan oil 50–50 with the government. Mindful of Mexico's nationalization in 1938, companies operating in Venezuela agreed. Soon after, Middle Eastern governments began demanding the same terms. This was the trigger of the conflict between Mossadeq's Iran and BP in the early 1950s.

A requested reinterpretation of a 1926 U.S. tax law allowing companies to deduct taxes paid to foreign governments from their U.S. tax liabilities helped the four U.S. companies that were partners in Saudi Arabia's Arabian American Oil Company (ARAMCO). This favorable treatment was available to every U.S. firm operating abroad, but BP was not able to pass on all of its foreign taxes to taxpayers in Britain. This caused the community of interests among the largest oil companies to diverge. Another unexpected source of competitive pressure on the oil companies came from the Soviet Union, which found its trade with the West constricted by U.S. Cold War policies. As a result, it had to rely increasingly on oil and gold sales to earn foreign exchange. Under Nikita Khrushchev, the Stalinist policy was reversed and total Soviet oil production doubled in the five years following Stalin's death in 1953.

Perhaps the last straw for the international oil companies was the 1959 decision of the U.S. government to impose a limit—a quota—on the amount of oil that they could import into the United States. The U.S. market was the biggest in the world and doubly lucrative because the high cost of domestically produced oil gave sellers of lower-cost foreign oil the potential to reap greater than normal profits. But U.S. oil companies that operated entirely at home were politically strong in the postwar era and the quota allowed them to defend themselves against competition from companies with cheap oil supplies from abroad. These domestic producers, citing national security and the risk of becoming dependent on foreign oil imports, demanded protection against cheap imported oil and, in 1959, what had started as a voluntary program in 1954 became law (Vietor, 1984).

The multinational firms could see which way the wind was blowing in their markets and shifted their strategy for propping up declining profits. In the early 1950s they had developed the "posted price" system to help host governments estimate their anticipated oil revenues more easily. The companies "posted," or published, these prices, and host governments used them to calculate the amount of taxes the companies would have to pay, even though little oil actually traded at these prices. When posted prices were first introduced, company profits on foreign operations were very high and small deviations in the real prices at which crude oil traded did not worry them. Stable posted prices soon became an accepted industry norm. Host country governments also did not pay much attention to posted prices, lobbying instead for profit sharing and improved concession terms to increase their shares of oil profits (Penrose, 1968).

But as costs and competition increased, the operators began to look at posted prices as a tactic for boosting profits. In February 1959, after consulting one another (but not their hosts), the companies lowered posted prices—and thereby the taxes they owed their host governments. An immediate outcry arose from the host governments, which were prompted to consider coordinating their own actions to protect their interests. Coordination was difficult. These countries were competitors for investment and production, and their industries, organized at different times by different firms, were highly varied. The Venezuelan industry was organized in many independent segments instead of the one company–one country pattern common in the Middle East. The age of its industry also meant that it was more expensive to produce oil there than in the Middle East. Yet when the oil companies, still enmeshed in their own desires and conflicts, lowered posted prices again in August 1960, five oil governments tried once more to set aside their political differences in order to salvage their economic interests. These five, Venezuela, Saudi Arabia, Iran, Iraq, and Kuwait, formed the Organization of Petroleum Exporting Countries (OPEC) in September 1960 (Mikdashi, 1972).

OPEC's aims from the very beginning included helping host governments gain autonomy and greater control over their oil, but progress was incremental during its first ten years. As OPEC became stronger, other countries, some from Africa and East Asia, also joined. Competition among members remained a constant problem, one that was aggravated by political divisions between conservative, monarchical states like Saudi Arabia and postrevolutionary radical states like Iraq (Dawisha, 2003). There also were political differences between Arab and non-Arab states. One important political conflict centered on the "oil weapon," production cuts by Arab oil producers intended to force political concessions from countries supporting Israel.

The oil weapon was used in conjunction with the Arab-Israeli wars of 1948, 1956, and 1967, but was mostly ineffective in influencing importing-country policy. Arab production cuts were offset by higher production from other producers—including other members of OPEC—and by the ability of the oil companies to redistribute supplies internationally. Dependence on oil revenues limited the length of time the embargoing countries could manage financially. Until 1967, short and unevenly administered attempts to use the oil weapon had little impact on policy toward Israel. The 1967 oil embargo succeeded in moving France away from Israel toward closer relations with Arab governments because, following the loss of Algeria, it had fewer assured sources of petroleum. France also distrusted U.S. leadership of the Western alliance, which made it wary of sacrificing good relations with Arab oil suppliers for the benefit of a U.S. client with no oil.

Perceiving the 1967 Arab oil embargo as a nonevent, oil companies became complacent. They continued to be more preoccupied by fears of over-supply than the structural changes in the world oil market brought about by war and a booming world economy. The 1967 war closed the Suez Canal. This created an effective tanker shortage for oil shipments to Europe from the Gulf because tankers had to travel the far longer distance around Africa to reach the Mediterranean. In spite of this, the companies did not think it was prudent to take precautions against a possible supply cut by exporters on the Mediterranean. Indeed, most looked at the narrowing supply-demand gap as beneficial to their interests. They were skeptical that the global oil market could be disrupted by political pressure since so little disruption had resulted during attempts to apply such pressure in the past (Vernon, 1976).

The companies also were unconcerned by rising demand for oil world-wide, and by falling oil production in the United States. U.S. oil production peaked in 1970 even as demand continued to rise and increasing amounts for ever-growing U.S. consumption had to come from foreign sources. Another effect of the shift in the U.S. energy balance was that as actual U.S. production approached total production capacity, excess capacity under direct U.S. control shrank. Should the oil weapon be used again, there would be no way to increase production from the United States, a tactic that had minimized the oil crises of 1956 and 1967.

■ Rumblings of Change

In September 1969 a revolution in Libya replaced a pro-Western king with a militantly anti-U.S. colonel determined to increase Libya's oil income. Muammar Qaddafi isolated two of Libya's more than forty operators, demanding that they increase payments to the Libyan government or else be shut down. One operator had no other sources of oil in the Eastern Hemisphere, while it did have contracts with European buyers that included financial penalties should it fail to deliver. That company soon gave in, leading Qaddafi to apply the same technique to other operators until they all agreed to the higher price. Qaddafi's success made the Shah of Iran jealous, and in 1971 he demanded higher prices for Gulf producers too.

The oil companies wanted to negotiate simultaneously with Libya and the Gulf producers to prevent their being picked off one at a time in Teheran as they had been in Tripoli. However, the U.S. companies could not get the government support they needed to make this happen because of the cliency relationship between the United States and Iran. The United States could not apply pressure on Iran without making major concessions to the shah or risking his strategic cooperation in the future. As the oil companies feared, alternating demands between Teheran and Tripoli led to a short volley of negotiations between Libya and the Gulf. The oil revolution was under way: oil-exporting countries were commanding higher prices for their oil in spite of the existence of long-term contracts specifying much lower prices. The speed with which the negotiations were conducted was heightened by deterioration in the U.S. economy, which caused the U.S. government to devalue the dollar in 1971 and again in 1973. Devaluations reduced the value of the dollars received by oil exporters, leading to demands for more dollars to compensate for the purchasing power lost after each devaluation. Negotiations after the second devaluation were still in progress in the fall of 1973, when other events snowballed the price issue into the larger question of who would control OPEC oil (Tétreault, 1985).

Oil company authority had deteriorated long before the oil revolution. The Tehran-Tripoli negotiations and agreements set procedural and substan-

Libyan leader Muammar Qaddafi was the first Arab leader to successfully challenge Western oil companies by demanding they increase payments for petroleum. His actions set the stage for the 1973 OAPEC oil embargo.

Thomas Hartwell

tive precedents that reduced it even further. U.S. companies also were in trouble at home. Domestic oil supplies in the highly regulated U.S. market increasingly fell behind demand, while restrictions on oil imports triggered spot shortages and price increases. These, in turn, prompted congressional hearings and widespread public criticism of the oil companies. The supply situation became so dire that oil import quotas were ended in April 1973. The energy crisis, which is remembered as the result of the use of the oil weapon in the October 1973 war, had in reality begun months—if not years—before.

The October 1973 decision by Arab oil exporters to try the oil weapon once again could have been predicted by an effective political "early warning" system. Throughout 1972–1973, Arab governments promised openly and repeatedly to use the oil weapon against the United States if a Middle East settlement conforming to United Nations (UN) Resolution 242, which required Israeli withdrawal from the Occupied Territories, was not achieved. Saudi Arabian officials went so far as to call in representatives of all four of their operating company partners to deliver a message. They said that another war between Israel and Arab governments was imminent and that, when it came, Arab oil would be cut off to supporters of Israel. One partner, Mobil, regarded this warning as so serious that it took out an ad in the *New York Times* to urge a settlement of the Arab-Israeli conflict. The other partners relied on private channels to communicate their message (Tétreault, 1985).

By the summer of 1973, the exposure of criminal behavior in what has come to be known as the "Watergate affair" had reached a critical stage in congressional hearings. But Richard Nixon's political problems were not alone in inhibiting direct U.S. involvement in a Middle Eastern settlement. The new Nixon Doctrine had inaugurated a strategy based on U.S. reliance on a few chosen client regimes, built up by foreign aid and arms transfers, that would pursue U.S. interests throughout the world without requiring direct intervention by the United States. This was the philosophy behind the "Vietnamization" of the Vietnam War, and the arming of Israel and Iran in the Middle East. U.S. dependence on its two Middle East clients meant that the United States could not force Israel to accept UN Resolution 242 in 1972 and 1973 any more than it could force the Shah of Iran to accept joint negotiations with the oil companies in 1971 (Tétreault, 1985).

When war came in October 1973, the Arab governments waited for some sign that the United States would respond to their concerns. Finally, on October 17, at the request of the Arab League, the Organization of Arab Petroleum-Exporting Countries (OAPEC), a group that included the Arab members of OPEC along with Bahrain, Egypt, and Syria—imposed an oil embargo against Israel's allies (Tétreault, 1981). Intended to be effective rather than mostly performative, as the embargoes of 1956 and 1967 had been, the 1973–1974 embargo was designed to be both more extensive and more discriminating.

OAPEC aimed to keep Arab oil from enemies of the Arab states while at the same time allowing Arab oil to flow to friendly nations.

Some aspects were very successful. Total supplies of oil to the world market were cut, creating local shortages and higher prices in most oil-importing countries. Another success was to alter the general perception of the Arab governments as weak and ineffective. But despite the care with which embargo provisions had been drawn up, and the nominal compliance of even U.S. oil companies in implementing them, the spirit of the embargo was systematically violated in ways that prevented the targeting plan from working. As in earlier applications of the oil weapon, oil supplies were exchanged between and within companies so that Arab oil that could not be sent to the United States or Holland was swapped for unrestricted supplies from non-Arab sources. All importing countries experienced about the same degree of shortfall whether they supported the Arab states or Israel. The failure of targeting meant that although the embargo did succeed in inflicting hardship on the friends of Israel, it also inflicted hardship on the friends of the Arabs.

The most important effect of the embargo was to consolidate the oil price revolution. Bids for "spot" or individual cargoes of crude oil reached very high levels. The "price hawks" in OPEC, countries like Libya, Iraq, and Iran, insisted that OPEC members stop negotiating with the companies and simply set their own prices—very high. Others, like Saudi Arabia, supported setting an OPEC price but opposed the size of the price increase advocated by the price hawks. The two groups fought during OPEC's December 1973 meeting and eventually compromised on a price between the two extremes. This price, $11.65 per barrel, was four times higher than the average price of OPEC crude just a year earlier.

■ The Oil Revolution

The oil revolution was not simply a price revolution, although that was an important component of it. It also involved a change in the ownership of oil. Prior to 1973, multinational oil companies controlled the oil of most OPEC members. These companies decided how much oil to produce and how much money to invest in the host's national industry. Although companies and host governments bargained over prices and production levels, the companies had the last word.

Several oil-exporting countries had nationalized their oil industries prior to the oil revolution, but this did not always mean that control of nationalized oil had passed from the companies to the host government. Although Iran nationalized its industry in 1951, the restoration of the shah also restored foreign control over Iran's oil. Nationalizations by Iraq and Libya were more effective in transferring control of domestic industries to host governments. As other countries nationalized their industries or assumed equity control more gradually through a process known as "participation," decisionmaking power passed from the multinationals to the oil ministries of the host governments. This transfer of authority also took place in Iran.

The oil companies were criticized for being nothing more than "tax collectors for OPEC" rather than independent actors in the international oil market (Adelman, 1972–1973). Few companies cared and most probably were rooting for the host governments to succeed in keeping prices high. High prices made for vastly higher profits while the nationalizations neither cut off nor reduced the revenues of most oil companies operating in the Middle East (Nitzan and Bichler, 2002). Many made so much money that they invested in high-cost exploration and development outside of OPEC, much of it in the very expensive United States. They bought other oil companies and invested in companies producing coal and nuclear energy. Some bought firms in industries totally unrelated to energy. One even tried to buy a circus.

State-owned national oil companies took over their old operations. Some host governments already had state firms and others created them expressly to take charge of newly nationalized industries. This shift in corporate ownership led to a restructuring of the industry as a whole. Now that OPEC set crude oil prices, the former owners ceased using oil production to subsidize other operations. In the past, they would set the "transfer prices" at which oil was sold between subsidiaries of the same company to show high profits on crude sales and low profits on refining and marketing. Because tax rates were lower in producing countries than in consuming countries, they could save money on taxes if it looked as though they were earning most of their profits from producing oil overseas rather than from refining and marketing oil in the United States, Europe, or Japan.

After the oil revolution, the price of crude oil became a real cost, not a fiction enabling oil companies to evade taxes. Losing production from now-nationalized holdings meant that the multinationals' other operations had to earn real—and not paper—profits. Obsolescent equipment was replaced and the "downstream" phases of the industry—refining and marketing—were rationalized wherever possible. Where these operations could not be made profitable for their owners, they were sold off. Gasoline stations were snapped up by national oil companies of OPEC countries that were eager to have marketing outlets in oil-importing countries. Some had to take less attractive operations, like obsolete refineries, as part of these packages (Tétreault, 1995).

Another effect of the new OPEC price structure was that production anywhere in the world earned its owners "windfall profits," the difference between the marginal cost of what they produced and the much higher OPEC prices at which oil now was sold. Increasing production in the United States and elsewhere outside OPEC became a company priority, even though U.S. regulations limited the amount of windfall profits companies could reap and other governments began to charge higher royalties and fees for oil produced in their countries (Tétreault, 1985).

But higher oil prices also depressed demand. By 1978, inflation had eaten away most of the value of the 1973–1974 price increases. Even so, consumers still felt that they were paying more for oil because the nominal prices of products like gasoline and heating oil stayed about the same. But because real prices had actually fallen, consumption, which had dropped in 1974 and 1975, soon began to rise again. By the time of the second round of huge price increases during the Iranian revolution, consumer demand had reached about the same level that it was in 1973, before the oil embargo.

■ Oil Politics in the OPEC Middle East

Higher oil prices and the increase in national autonomy and control over oil did not take oil out of Middle Eastern politics. On the contrary, OPEC's new power in the international industry increased its appeal as an arena for pursuing political goals. Ongoing ethnic, religious, and territorial disagreements between Iran and Arab Gulf nations often were expressed as conflicts over oil prices. Yet no single cause motivated any of the conflicts within OPEC. For example, Arab states, chiefly Libya, Algeria, and even Iraq, occasionally joined Iran in pressing for oil price increases, and Saudi Arabia and its allies among the smaller Gulf states opposed all of them. Thus the Arab-Iranian conflict often cut across other ongoing regional conflicts, such as the "Arab civil war" between traditional and revolutionary regimes (Skeet, 1988).

Disagreements over oil prices are usually thought to arise from fundamental differences in economic interests. Price hawks like Iran and Algeria have relatively large populations needing oil revenues, but their oil reserves are limited. If they could force prices higher they still would be able to sell nearly all of their oil before less expensive substitutes could be found to replace it (Mitchell et al., 2001). Price moderates like Saudi Arabia have small populations and too much oil to be able to sell it all before high prices could bring substitutes into the market. Therefore the Saudis support smaller price increases. Yet even this is much too simple a rule of thumb. Libya, and sometimes Kuwait, are price hawks too. Neither has a large population and Kuwait can expect to produce oil for 200 years at current rates of production. Another illustration of the inadequacy of simple economic explanations was the defection of the Shah of Iran from the price hawk coalition in December 1978. Weakened and beset by illness and domestic unrest, he joined the Saudis in a coalition to freeze prices as part of a bid to attract regional allies. Politics is as important as economics in OPEC price conflicts, and goals change with changing circumstances.

The Iranian revolution aggravated conflicts within OPEC over oil prices and organization leadership. The government of the Ayatollah Khomeini saw raising oil prices as a way to attack the United States while increasing Iran's national income and foreign exchange reserves. Iranian price militancy was effective in raising oil prices as long as the panic set off by Iran's revolution continued. Throughout 1979, Iran and other price hawks imposed extravagant price increases that pulled the prices of more moderate OPEC members up in defensive emulation. But when prices weakened in 1980, Iran also proved to be an aggressive price cutter, despite government denials.

Iran's aggressive nationalism in oil marketing was matched by its aggressive nationalism in regional politics. Iran hoped to export its revolution to other Islamic states, and OPEC meetings soon became places for revolutionary exhortation and guerrilla tactics. Iraq was a favorite target because of its large Shi'i population, its convenient location on the western border of Iran, and a history of enmity between the two countries. As detailed in Chapter 5, rivalries over oil and oil revenues added to other axes of conflict between these two oil powers.

Iraq's oil power, long obscured by oil company limits on expansion of supply capacity in selected parts of the Middle East, promised to overtake Iran's. Iraq was more successful in its economic development policies than Iran, and its growing economic and political strength made it confident that it could force a revision in its favor of the 1975 settlement with Iran of the long-running border dispute between them. In September 1980, Iraq attacked Iran, setting off a long war marked by extreme brutality to civilians and soldiers alike on both sides.

The effect of the war on OPEC also was devastating. Meetings turned into acrimonious shouting matches. With OPEC facing competition from new production in Britain and Norway, and the Soviet Union dumping large quantities of crude oil into Western European markets, the Iran-Iraq War impeded efforts to coordinate production and maintain a united OPEC front. Even the day-to-day operations of OPEC were affected when neither Iran nor Iraq would accept a secretary-general from the other country, and the organization had to be run for several years by the assistant secretary-general, Fadhel al-Chalabi—an Iraqi.

■ The Price Bust

The most serious effect of the Iran-Iraq War for Middle Eastern oil exporters was that it prevented accommodation within OPEC that might have enabled it to withstand outside assaults on its price structure. At that time there were three main threats to oil prices in addition to price cutting by OPEC members themselves. Two were direct responses to the huge price increases of 1979–1980. First, just as in 1973–1974, higher prices depressed consumer demand; second, the same high prices attracted oil companies to expand supplies, especially supplies originating outside of OPEC; third, the Soviet Union became an aggressive crude seller in dollar-denominated markets. These and related market developments marginalized OPEC as the dominant world supplier of crude oil and slashed OPEC government revenues.[2]

When oil companies looked more carefully at supplies, they found that oil exploration and development begun in response to the oil price increases of the early 1970s started paying off within a few years. New oil came to the market from the North Sea, non-OPEC developing countries, and even the United States. The Soviet Union was so attracted by high prices that it reneged on contracts to sell oil to its clients in Eastern Europe. The oil so diverted was sold at or close to OPEC prices in Western markets. Refiners bought crude oil first from these sources and only afterward from OPEC. In 1979, OPEC production had recovered to about the same level it had been in 1973, 31 million barrels per day. In 1980 this dropped to 27 million barrels per day and by 1983 it plummeted to 17.6 million barrels per day.

Extra crude supplies also came from unexpected sources. One of them was inventories. After the 1973–1974 oil embargo, most of the developed countries belonging to the Organization for Economic Cooperation and Development (OECD) came together to form a kind of counter-cartel, the International Energy Agency (IEA). The IEA required each member to maintain a ninety-day supply of oil in a strategic reserve to be used in case of oil supply interruptions. If the amount of oil available to any member were to fall below 7 percent of requirements, it could apply to the IEA and draw supplies from its own and other members' strategic stocks. These stocks were too low to be useful during the 1979 crisis. In fact, the crisis encouraged importers and companies to buy more stocks, contributing to the upward pressure on prices. Afterward, many found that the combination of falling consumer demand and the massive buildup of stocks resulting from their frantic purchases in 1979 and 1980 meant that they had much more oil than they needed to meet IEA requirements.

In 1983 and again in 1985, large quantities of excess stocks were dumped onto the market, pushing prices downward. In 1983, OPEC so feared the loss of customers, revenues, and control over the market that it lowered the price of its marker crude, the reference crude against which the prices of crudes of different quality were set, by U.S.$5.00 per barrel. It also decided to make mandatory a production regulation scheme it had adopted as a voluntary measure to restrict production the year before. The intention was to punish price cutters inside and outside OPEC by reducing their oil incomes, and to halt or reverse the drop in oil demand by reducing prices. Neither plan succeeded, in part because of the independent effect of exchange rate fluctuations.

U.S. monetary policy from 1981 through most of 1985 affected exchange rates by keeping the value of the dollar, the currency for which virtually all crude oil was sold, very high. Dollars acquired through oil sales could be traded for pounds, yen, marks, francs, and other hard currencies, maintaining the purchasing power of oil sellers even after prices were cut. Although both price cutters and price defenders in OPEC complained about the oil price reduction, few actually suffered from it unless they also had to pay off loans or make purchases in dollars.

Consumers outside the United States experienced the reverse. Higher and higher prices for the dollars needed to buy oil meant that oil prices in local currencies at best remained constant and at worst actually rose, even after the OPEC price cut. These higher real prices erased any incentive that nondollar consumers might have had to buy more oil. Although U.S. consumers, whose dollar economy enjoyed the full effects of the price reduction, did react as OPEC had hoped, their contribution to world demand for crude oil was not enough to solve OPEC's problems because of the ineffectiveness of its production controls.

OPEC's inability to control production contributed to global oversupply. The production control regulations it adopted for its members were complicated and full of loopholes. For example, very heavy crudes and condensates—liquids precipitated from natural gas—were not counted as oil production. During the Iran-Iraq War, the cutoff of Iraq's pipelines by Iranian bombing led to extra production by Kuwait and Saudi Arabia "on Iraq's account," but the amounts produced tended to be more than Iraq's share and they were not cut back when Iraqi exports resumed. Poor global economic conditions encouraged barter and other countertrade arrangements outside normal oil sales channels, making it hard for OPEC accountants to find out which country was exporting how much oil and to whom. Several OPEC members cheated outright, producing oil over their allotted quotas, while non-OPEC members continued to enjoy a free ride on the OPEC price structure.

The main responsibility for holding OPEC production to the ceiling set by the group as a whole belonged to Saudi Arabia, the "swing producer." Saudi Arabia also was a primary target of Iranian political pressure, and the combination of declining oil production and continuing threats from Iran pushed the Saudis to push back. After months of warning, the Saudis "turned up the faucet" on their oil production in October 1985. A price that was wobbly but holding at about U.S.$25.00 per barrel at the end of 1985 became U.S.$12.00 per barrel and not holding six months later. The consequent drop in oil income was painful for all oil producers. In January 1986, officials of the Mexican government visited other oil-exporting countries to coordinate efforts to try to stem the fall in oil prices, but it was as though a plug had been pulled out of a full bathtub and the whole OPEC price structure just slid down the drain.[3]

Prices rose a little over the next few years but seldom reached OPEC's new target level of U.S.$18.00 per barrel while they continued to be exquisitely vulnerable to destabilizing events and rumors of events. Persistent depressed demand coupled with very low per-barrel prices affected every member country. Budgets contracted and even "low absorbers," those countries whose populations were small compared to their incomes, had to make painful financial adjustments, including foreign borrowing. Adjustment coincided with fiscal strains on Arab Gulf exporters from war loans and payments to Iraq during the Iran-Iraq War, and further reductions in income when Gulf shipping became a target during the "tanker war" phase of that conflict (al-Assiri, 1990).

Yet the end of the war in 1988 did not bring relief to economies and civil societies anywhere in OPEC. Oil demand and prices remained depressed while domestic populations grew restive, even in relatively wealthy Kuwait. There, citizen protests against the continued suspension of the parliament and constitutionally protected civil liberties, imposed in July 1986 ostensibly because of external threats arising from the war, became widespread in 1989. High prices and a depressed local economy contributed to criticism of the regime's economic policies and to charges of corruption. The government felt pressed to satisfy the population's economic demands so as to mute the political demands it was even less happy to deal with. That year, Kuwait's oil production consistently exceeded its OPEC quota. And Kuwait was not alone. Other Gulf exporters, most notably the United Arab Emirates (UAE) but also Saudi Arabia, also produced over their quotas.

A traditional *dhow* (boat) passes an oil tanker in the Bahraini port.

Overproduction by OPEC members contributed to the market factors that depressed world oil prices. But Kuwait suffered from a special disability in taking this route. Its boundary with Iraq had been contested since the 1930s, and years of diplomatic efforts and billions of dollars in loans and grants had not been enough to persuade Iraq to drop its claims to Kuwait. Continuing to produce at levels above its OPEC quota made Kuwait vulnerable to Iraqi retaliation.

Iraq's economic problems, which included huge war debts to foreign banks as well as to Kuwait and other governments, also were pressing. It was convenient for Iraqi president Saddam Hussein to blame Kuwait as the source of Iraq's problems. He clothed his invasion of Kuwait as an "oil war," a war to remove Kuwait's oil weapons, which he said were overproduction and theft of Iraqi oil produced along the disputed boundary. But just as many other conflicts in the Middle East concern much more than oil, so did this one. Saddam's problems required a quick infusion of cash. His diplomatic probes during the six months prior to the invasion convinced him that no power capable of stopping him would intervene if he were to invade Kuwait and take what he needed. He expected that some Kuwaitis would welcome his actions, and that a victory in Kuwait would be quick and easy rather than the disaster that his attack on Iran a decade earlier had turned into. But Saddam was wrong in his assumptions; his 1990 invasion of Kuwait was reversed seven months later by a multilateral force led by the United States (Freedman and Karsh, 1993; Sciolino, 1991; Smith, 1992; Tétreault, 1993).

The Iraqi invasion began the Gulf War (1990–1991) and introduced two new oil weapons into world politics. The first was the one cited by U.S. president George H. W. Bush when he said that the United States had to fight to keep Middle Eastern oil from being controlled by Saddam Hussain. From Bush's perspective, the Gulf War was intended to preserve an oil market where major oil-exporting countries participate individually rather than under the hegemony of a regional military power. For Saddam, one objective of the war was to create just such hegemony under his leadership.

The other oil weapon was ecological. Saddam promised to release Kuwaiti oil into the Gulf and to destroy Kuwait's production, processing, and export facilities if Iraq were attacked either at home or in Kuwait. In the end, these threats became real when the allies drove Iraq out of Kuwait and departing Iraqi soldiers set fire to Kuwait's oil fields. This demonstrates once again the strategic inferiority of oil weapons to deter undesired behavior when the stakes include the survival of a nation or its current regime.

■ A New Gulf War—A New Oil Regime?

The end of the Gulf War left world oil markets in a state of uncertainty. Iraq was kept out of the market by a boycott until 1996, when the UN's Oil for Food program finally went into effect. This gave the United Nations authority to sell Iraqi oil and spend the proceeds on humanitarian assistance to the Iraqi population. It also allowed the UN to sequester 30 percent of these proceeds to pay reparations to those making claims against Iraq for the war damages it had inflicted. Both before and after the Oil for Food program went into effect, however, illicit Iraqi oil seeped into neighboring countries and was smuggled by ship to buyers farther away. The money earned on this illegal trade sustained the Iraqi regime through the long years of economic sanctions imposed by the victors of the Gulf War. Their primary burden fell on the population.

In 2002 the United States and Britain spearheaded a new attack on Iraq, first in the United Nations, where an arms inspection regime, imposed after the Gulf War, was reinstated and strengthened. In March 2003, the United States, Britain, and Australia launched a military invasion attacking Iraq. This war differed from both of its predecessors. Rather than a conflict initiated by Iraqi aggression, this war was the first implementation of a new U.S. strategic doctrine. First published in September 2002, this doctrine asserted a U.S. right to mount preemptive attacks against countries accused by the U.S. government of aiding or harboring terrorists and governments with "weapons of mass destruction"—nuclear, chemical, and biological. It included as a goal the acquisition of "bases and stations within and beyond Western Europe and northeast Asia" for future U.S. force projections (U.S. Government, 2002:6, 15, 29). The outcome of this new gulf war is still unfolding and, for oil markets, bears close watching. Its effects on Middle East oil, in particular, could be massive.

Ratification of the U.S. conquest of Iraq by the United Nations could produce a flood of Iraqi oil onto the market fairly quickly in spite of the poor condition of Iraq's oil infrastructure. Reconstructing Kuwait's oil industry, including extinguishing 732 oil well fires, took far less time than most had anticipated. The fires were put out in a little under nine months. Current production is about 2 million barrels per day; production capacity exceeds that amount and continues to expand. Iraqi production capacity could reach 4 million barrels per day within two years of the end of the fighting, and most oil experts believe that the size of its reserves could support a much larger rate of production.

Excess capacity is another oil weapon, most useful when deployed against other producers. This could be done for a variety of reasons—economic and political. If control over Iraq's oil industry is transferred to a large private oil company, production might be constrained to stabilize prices or raised to capacity to undercut other companies and make their assets easier to acquire—a Wal-Mart strategy. If Iraqi oil is transferred to an agent of an occupying government, production could be ratcheted up to undercut the stability of other Middle Eastern oil exporters like Iran and Saudi Arabia. This would indirectly act to bring down these governments and to support the accession of new governments willing to reprivatize their oil. If Iraqi oil remains in the hands of an Iraqi regime (however constituted), OPEC would be forced to accommodate Iraq's legitimate needs for income to reconstruct its country and rehabilitate its people. This means that other OPEC members would have to accept cuts in their own quota allocations to allow Iraq the opportunity to earn the money it needs to rebuild. Any of these outcomes requires a high degree of collective discipline over production by OPEC members.

Consumers also face consequences from conflicts in this region. Wars and rumors of wars tend to make consumers nervous, and military actions such as Iranian attacks on oil tankers during the 1980s, the torching of Kuwait's oil wells in 1991, and internal unrest in regions where oil is produced, a consequence of the 2003 war in Iraq, all raise costs and push prices up. The best example occurred following the Iraqi invasion of Kuwait, which touched off a rapid increase in oil prices that persisted for months. Political paralysis prevented the IEA from releasing oil stocks, so the entire burden of price stabilization fell on OPEC members. In January 1991, in conjunction with the allied counterattack, the IEA did initiate a planned release of stocks to keep the market from skyrocketing upward again. But IEA action was so heavy-handed that prices nearly collapsed. Oil prices also fluctuated wildly during the 2003 war in Iraq, when oil markets also had to contend with a strike in Venezuela and production shutdowns in Nigeria. In all three cases, uncertainty was as much or more responsible for sharp price movements than actual shortages, although technical problems in refining and transport also contributed to the sharp rise in gasoline prices in 2003. War itself is the primary destabilizer of oil markets.

But war is not the only threat to the economic security of Middle Eastern oil exporters. Another comes from the breakup of the Soviet Union and the desperation of the impoverished governments of the successor states, which hope for a new "oil rush" by even larger and more powerful oil companies than existed just a few years ago. Despite high costs for oil and gas exploration and development worldwide, the proliferation of nations seeking investments and giant energy companies with piles of money to invest promise to keep everyone's profit margins down as producers struggle to capture and hold customers. At the same time, concerns about global warming and other effects of oil pollution are pushing consumers to find alternative sources of energy. These pressures will limit the degree to which oil prices can rise in the absence of a general worldwide economic recovery.

■ Oil and Money in the Middle East

I began this chapter with the statement that oil is a blessing for countries that have it. One of the chief blessings of oil comes from its easy convertibility into foreign exchange. The higher oil prices that resulted first from the oil revolution and then from the revolution in Iran raised the earnings streaming into oil-exporting countries to flood levels. Yet as we all know, floods, whatever their other qualities, are also disasters. This flood was no exception; it too brought good news and bad news.

The good news was that a huge amount of money was suddenly available to oil-exporting countries to use for economic development and national defense, and to provide for the economic and social welfare of their people. The bad news was that the biggest increase came too fast and income over the medium and long term was neither steady nor predictable. In 1973, economists worried that rising oil prices would cause an economic depression in oil-importing countries. They also predicted that higher oil incomes would be virtually unusable by most oil-exporting countries, especially the Arab states along the Gulf with their small populations and very large revenues. Both worries were overstated. The "unusable" dollars that so concerned these economists turned out to be a chimera. Nicknamed "petrodollars," the cash balances of oil-exporting countries went into the international banking system, where they were recycled as loans and investments.

But all this money was a mixed blessing to the domestic economies of oil-exporting states. Rising imports and the flood of new money aggravated domestic inflation rates and demand for imports—the so-called Dutch disease. Oil exporters quickly learned to spend their money as fast as it came in so that, by the time of the second round of price increases in 1979–1980, many had started to amass their own foreign debt. Much of it went for investment and to pay for an explosion of arms purchases. As discussed in Chapter 4, arms purchases were an especially perverse outcome of the oil price increases of the 1970s (Nitzan and Bichler, 2002). The diversion of excessive amounts of oil revenue to buy weapons took resources from the domestic economies of states like Iran and Iraq, whose rural populations suffered

Courtesy of World Oil

Local workers at an oil production site take a break to brew Ceylon tea, which is served very sweet and sometimes with fresh mint or sage.

extreme deprivation. Oil money aggravated the conflict in Israel/Palestine and financed all three Gulf wars. It made Saddam Hussein a greater power in his region than he would have been otherwise by allowing him to buy more weapons and build a larger army than he could have produced on his own.

Some states, like Kuwait, the UAE, and Bahrain, made extensive efforts to redistribute oil revenues across their populations. They did this through direct transfers and by subsidizing housing, utilities, education, and medical care. Some capital redistribution was effected through real estate transfers. In Kuwait, the state purchased land from citizens at highly inflated prices, while in Bahrain the government sold housing to citizens at very low prices. Both put wealth in the hands of the lucky recipients. Oil money also supported conspicuous consumption, corruption, and gross waste. Kuwait's "underground" stock exchange, the Suq al-Manakh, was little more than a casino. Its collapse in 1982 resulted not only in a huge loss of capital but also in a loss of confidence in the government, which was slow to intervene because of involvement by high officials and members of the ruling family. Subsidized and pampered native populations in many Gulf states lost interest in low-status jobs, requiring the importation of guest workers to make local economies function. The economy and ecology of Saudi Arabia was damaged by government assistance, which included providing unlimited fossil water to support wheat production. Countries exporting labor to the rich oil exporters found their domestic economies and societies as radically altered as those of their richer neighbors by the roller-coaster economy they suddenly were subjected to, if only "secondhand" (Chaudhry, 1997).

Oil money also increased the foreign policy autonomy of oil-exporting countries. They found it less necessary than before to bind themselves as clients to an extraregional patron state in exchange for economic or military assistance. The oil-rich states of the Middle East are often criticized for "wasteful" development projects, yet most have done no worse than their oil-poor peers whose economic decisions are overseen by foreign bankers and officials of patron governments. Significantly, the influx of oil money into the Middle East allowed countries such as Egypt to discard its client relationship to the Soviet Union in favor of more egalitarian relationships with Arab oil-exporting countries. Oil money also enabled Saudi Arabia to loosen its Israeli-mediated military dependency on the United States. Thus, oil money hastened the breakdown of the kind of great power primacy in the Middle East that had shaped the region's politics for so long.

■ Conclusion

Oil gave a number of Middle Eastern countries the economic independence to try development strategies and form political bonds foreclosed to poorer states. It also offered a substitute for conventional—that is, military—attributes of power, forcing other nations to reexamine their own foreign policies in the light of long-term economic interests. Thus it helped to erode the post–World War II dominance of the superpowers by providing incentives and resources for their Middle Eastern alliance partners, clients, and dependencies to act more autonomously.

But oil also instilled a false sense of power and economic security in the minds of policymakers in oil-exporting states. Few used the fat years following the two enormous oil price hikes to prepare for the lean years that came after. In 1978, financial analyst Walter J. Levy (1978–1979) mourned "the years that the locust hath eaten," the years when money was spent, borrowed, and lent as though the golden faucet would never fail. Now the ravages of rapid changes in income, both up and down, are visible everywhere in the Middle East.

The most unfortunate result of the oil revolution was its role in providing oil revenues to finance regional wars and to arm and train forces committed to Islamist revolution from North Africa to Southeast Asia. Yet even here, the results are ambiguous. Among the casualties of the 1990–1991 Gulf War is an Arab nationalism that had impeded the development of independent foreign policies with partners outside the region and also with Israel. Although the 2003 war in Iraq could restore Arab nationalism as a counterweight to the reassertion of great power authority by the United States, the inevitability of any particular scenario no longer seems assured. Arab countries are likely to continue to exercise significant foreign policy autonomy individually, regionally, and in their immediate neighborhoods.

Despite oil's opportunities, its exploitation has exacted high social, political, and economic costs. Uncertain as to the shape of the new regional order that will rise on the debris generated by the most recent crisis, coming as it does in the company of other rapid political changes in the Middle East, we can only speculate whether oil has been a blessing or a curse to its nations and their peoples. A similar analysis of the energy politics of other regions is likely to reveal equally ambiguous effects and equally uncertain prognoses for the futures of oil exporters and importers alike.

■ Notes

1. To reduce the confusion that might arise from the frequent name changes of the various oil companies operating in the Middle East, these companies will be referred to by their contemporary names rather than by whatever names they might have been called at the time of the particular events discussed.

2. Except where noted, material in this section comes from Tétreault, 1985.

3. I have written elsewhere (1993) about the effect of the price collapse on the two combatants in the Gulf War (1990–1991). Low oil prices were felt disproportionately

by Iran, which did not have neighbors sending it financial and military assistance. In an interesting way, the price collapse of the mid-1980s acted as another kind of oil weapon.

■ Bibliography

Adelman, M. A. 1972–1973. "Is the Oil Shortage Real? Oil Companies as OPEC Tax Collectors." *Foreign Policy* 9 (Winter):69–107.

al-Assiri, Abdul-Reda. 1990. *Kuwait's Foreign Policy: City-State in World Politics.* Boulder, Colo.: Westview.

Anderson, Irvine H. 1981. *Aramco, the United States, and Saudi Arabia: A Study of the Dynamics of Foreign Oil Policy, 1933–1950.* Princeton: Princeton University Press.

Blair, John. 1976. *The Control of Oil.* New York: Pantheon.

Chaudhry, Kirin Aziz. 1997. *The Price of Wealth: Economies and Institutions in the Middle East.* Ithaca: Cornell University Press.

Chisholm, Archibald H. T. 1975. *The First Kuwait Oil Concession Agreement: A Record of the Negotiations, 1911–1934.* London: Frank Cass.

Crystal, Jill. 1990. *Oil and Politics in the Gulf: Rulers and Merchants in Kuwait and Qatar.* Cambridge: Cambridge University Press.

Dawisha, Adeed. 2003. *Arab Nationalism in the Twentieth Century: From Triumph to Despair.* Princeton: Princeton University Press.

Freedman, Lawrence, and Efraim Karsh. 1993. *The Gulf Conflict, 1990–1991: Diplomacy and War in the New World Order.* Princeton: Princeton University Press.

Gasiorowski, Mark J. 1991. *U.S. Foreign Policy and the Shah: Building a Client State in Iran.* Ithaca: Cornell University Press.

———. 1998. "The 1953 Coup d'État in Iran." www.payk.net/politics/1953 mossadeqcoup/markgasiorowski_1998/main.pdf (accessed April 6, 2003).

Levy, Walter J. 1978–1979. "The Years That the Locust Hath Eaten: Oil Policy and OPEC Development Prospects." *Foreign Affairs* 57 (Winter):287–308.

Mikdashi, Zuhayr. 1972. *The Community of Oil Exporting Countries.* Ithaca: Cornell University Press.

Mitchell, John, Koji Morita, Norman Selley, and Jonathan Stern. 2001. *The New Economy of Oil: Impacts on Business, Geopolitics, and Society.* London: Royal Institute of International Affairs.

Munif, Abdulrahman. 1989. *Cities of Salt.* New York: Vintage International.

Nitzan, Jonathan, and Shimshon Bichler. 2002. *The Global Political Economy of Israel.* London: Pluto Press.

Penrose, Edith. 1968. *The Large International Firm in Developing Countries: The International Petroleum Industry.* Cambridge: MIT Press.

Rand, Christopher T. 1975. *Making Democracy Safe for Oil.* Boston: Little, Brown.

Sampson, Anthony. 1975. *The Seven Sisters: The Great Oil Companies and the World They Shaped.* New York: Viking.

Sciolino, Elaine. 1991. *The Outlaw State: Saddam Hussein's Quest for Power and the Gulf Crisis.* New York: John Wiley.

Skeet, Ian. 1988. *OPEC: Twenty-five Years of Prices and Politics.* New York: Cambridge University Press.

Smith, Jean Edward. 1992. *George Bush's War.* New York: Henry Holt.

Tétreault, Mary Ann. 1981. *The Organization of Arab Petroleum Exporting Countries: History, Policies, and Prospects*. Westport, Conn.: Greenwood Press.
———. 1985. *Revolution in the World Petroleum Market*. Westport, Conn.: Quorum Books.
———. 1993. "Independence, Sovereignty, and Vested Glory: Oil and Politics in the Second Gulf War." *Orient* 34, no. 1 (March):87–103.
———. 1995. *The Kuwait Petroleum Corporation and the Economics of the New World Order*. Westport, Conn.: Quorum Books.
———. 2000. *Stories of Democracy: Politics and Society in Contemporary Kuwait*. New York: Columbia University Press.
U.S. Government. 2002. "The National Security Strategy of the United States of America." www.whitehouse.gov/nsc/nss.pdf (accessed March 15, 2003).
Vernon, Raymond (ed.). 1976. *The Oil Crisis*. New York: Norton.
Vietor, Richard H. K. 1984. *Energy Policy in America Since 1945: A Study of Business-Government Relations*. New York: Cambridge University Press.

9

Population Growth, Urbanization, and the Challenges of Unemployment

Valentine M. Moghadam

The Middle East has been experiencing rapid rates of urbanization and population growth over the past several decades. Although countries are at different levels of urbanization, the region as a whole has a majority of its population living in urban areas. At the same time, population growth rates in the Middle East–North Africa (MENA) region have been among the highest in the world, second only to those in sub-Saharan Africa, although fertility rates have been falling, especially among young, educated women in urban areas. The population is expected to swell to 576 million by 2025—more than double the current size. Given the aridity of much of the region, these growing numbers will place increasing demands on water and agricultural land, and urban services, currently strained, will need to be vastly expanded and improved.

Rapid urbanization and rapid population growth have transformed the structure of the labor force. In many countries, the population has shifted from one engaged predominantly in rural and agrarian production systems to one involved in various types of urban industrial and service-oriented economic activities. Moreover, because of previously high fertility rates, the age structure of the labor force is skewed toward the under-twenty-five group. Meanwhile, due to both economic and demographic factors, urban labor markets have been unable to absorb the growing labor force. This has resulted in the expansion of the urban informal sector, income inequalities, urban poverty, and rates of unemployment that are among the highest in the world. In particular, women's unemployment rates are exceedingly high.

This chapter examines the interrelated processes of urbanization, population growth, employment challenges, and poverty in the Middle East and

North Africa. For ease of exposition, I examine each separately, even though the issues are linked. Furthermore, to reflect differences in population and labor force size as well as income levels, I frequently refer to the region in terms of two sets of countries: the small, oil-rich states that belong to the Gulf Cooperation Council (GCC), including Bahrain, Kuwait, Oman, Qatar, Saudi Arabia, and the United Arab Emirates (UAE); and the larger and more diversified countries (Algeria, Egypt, Iran, Iraq, Israel, Jordan, Lebanon, Libya, Morocco, Syria, Tunisia, Turkey, and Yemen). To the extent possible, I shall also include the West Bank and Gaza Strip in the analysis.

■ Urbanization

The urban population of the region has been growing rapidly since 1950. Its share of the total population grew from 24 percent in 1950 to 57 percent in 1990 (Omran and Roudi, 1993:21). The most rapid growth in urbanization occurred in the oil-exporting countries; the population doubled between 1960 and 1980 in Saudi Arabia, Oman, Libya, and the UAE, and between 1950 and 1985 in Iran and Iraq (Assaad, 1995:21). Among countries that are not already highly urbanized, the slowest rate of urbanization was in Egypt, whose urban share increased from 32 percent in 1950 to 43 percent in 2001. The three largest countries in the region—Iran, Turkey, and Egypt—also have extensive

More than half the population of heavily
urbanized Lebanon lives in the capital city of Beirut.

land with relatively large rural populations that constitute a pool of future rural-to-urban migrants. Yemen is the least-urbanized country in the region, whereas Kuwait, Qatar, and Bahrain are virtually city-states. Table 9.1 illustrates the varying levels of urbanization across the region. It should be noted that after Latin America, which is about 71 percent urbanized, the MENA region has the highest level of urbanization in the developing world.

Urbanization is a key aspect of social change and of economic development. It entails the implementation of policies leading to the growth of cities and rural-to-urban migration. The latter is typically fueled by both push and pull factors: the push of population pressure on natural resources and the lack of economic opportunity in the rural areas, and the pull of perceived economic opportunity and a better lifestyle in the big cities (Omran and Roudi, 1993:21). The continuing growth of cities and of rural-to-urban migration is often exacerbated by the "urban bias" of government policies and development strategies, which leads to underdevelopment of rural areas, greater investment in urban infrastructure, and income gaps between rural and urban workers.

International migration can also play a part in urbanization. For example, in the case of Israel, immigration by Jews from other countries has con-

Table 9.1 Population and Urbanization in MENA

Country	Population, 2000 (in millions)	Projected Population, 2015 (in millions)	% Urban in 2001	% Urban in 1950
Algeria	30.4	39.8	57.7	22
Bahrain	0.7	n/a	n/a	64
Egypt	64.0	78.7	42.7	32
Iran	63.7	82.1	64.7	27
Iraq	23.3	31.3	67.4	34
Israel	6.2	7.6	91.8	65
Jordan	4.9	6.7	78.7	35
Kuwait	2.0	2.9	96.1	59
Lebanon	4.3	5.2	90.1	23
Libya	5.3	7.4	88.0	19
Mauritania	2.7	3.7	59.1	2
Morocco	28.7	35.3	56.1	26
Oman	2.4	3.3	76.5	2
Saudi Arabia	20.7	33.7	86.7	16
Syria	16.2	21.8	51.8	31
Tunisia	9.6	11.5	66.2	31
Turkey	65.3	77.9	66.2	21
United Arab Emirates	2.9	3.7	87.2	25
West Bank and Gaza	3.0	5.0	n/a	n/a
Yemen	17.5	26.6	25.0	6

Source: UN (2002:29); www.worldbank.org/data/wdi2002 (tab. 2-1).
Notes: Djibouti and Qatar have populations of under 600,000; Comoros is 820,000.
n/a indicates data not available.

tributed to the growth of Tel Aviv and West Jerusalem, and in the case of the small, oil-rich GCC countries, labor migration from other Arab countries contributed to the rapid rates of urbanization, especially during the 1970s and 1980s.

Between 1950 and 1980, there was tremendous growth of the large cities in the region, including Tehran, Cairo, Istanbul, and Baghdad, as a result of both high fertility rates and rural-to-urban migration. In 1950 only four cities had populations exceeding 1 million; by 1970 there were nine (Assaad, 1995:22). By 1990 the number of such cities had exceeded twenty, and ten years later, some twenty-five cities had populations of over 1 million. Megacities such as Cairo, Istanbul, and Tehran saw the growth of their populations during the 1980s, but so did a second tier of cities, such as Alexandria, Isfahan, Mashhad, Riyadh, Ankara, and Adana (see Table 9.2). Some of the megacities, and especially Cairo, have extremely high population densities, severe shortages of housing and services, and lack of regulation of construction and urban development. Indeed, the economies of the cities cannot absorb their large urban populations, leading to unemployment, underemployment, and poverty among urban

Table 9.2   MENA Cities with Populations over 1 Million, 2001

Country	City	Population (in millions)
Algeria	Algiers	2.761
Egypt	Cairo	9.462
	Alexandria	3.506
Iran	Tehran	6.979
	Isfahan	1.381
	Mashhad	1.990
	Shiraz	1.124
	Tabriz	1.274
Iraq	Baghdad	4.865
Israel	Tel Aviv	2.001
Jordan	Amman	1.148
Lebanon	Beirut	2.070
Libya	Tripoli	1.733
Morocco	Casablanca	3.357
	Rabat	1.616
Saudi Arabia	Jeddah	3.192
	Riyadh	4.549
Syria	Aleppo	2.229
	Damascus	2.144
Tunisia	Tunis	1.892
Turkey	Adana	1.091
	Ankara	3.155
	Bursa	1.166
	Istanbul	8.953
	Izmir	2.214

Source: UN, 2002:128.

populations. Other problems include a shortage of clean drinking water, the growth of slums or shantytowns, polluted air, and inadequate waste disposal systems (Omran and Roudi, 1993:30).

■ Population Growth

According to theories of epidemiological and demographic transitions, a population's fertility and mortality will decline from high to low levels as a result of economic and social development. The decline in mortality usually precedes the decline in fertility. This transition occurred in European countries during the nineteenth century and in the developing world during the twentieth century. Currently, the countries of the Middle East and North Africa are differentially situated along the transition continuum and are characterized by varying levels and combinations of mortality and fertility.

In the 1950s there was a population explosion in the Middle East and North Africa, a result of high fertility and declines in the crude death rate, although infant mortality rates were still very high. In the 1960s the region had the world's highest fertility rate among developing regions, but since about 1970 fertility has been falling, and fertility rates in sub-Saharan Africa have now surpassed those in the Middle East. MENA's annual population growth reached a peak of 3 percent around 1980, while the growth rate for the world as a whole reached its peak of 2 percent annually more than a decade earlier (Roudi, 2001).

For the region as a whole, the total fertility rate (average number of births per woman) went from 7 children per woman in the 1950s to 4.8 in 1990 and declined further to about 3.6 in 2001. Today, the total fertility rate is less than 3 in Bahrain, Iran, Lebanon, Tunisia, and Turkey, and is more than 5 in Iraq, Oman, Palestine, and Saudi Arabia. There have been impressive fertility declines in Morocco and Egypt since the 1980s, but only a slight decline in Saudi Arabia and none at all in Yemen, where the average number of births per woman is more than 7. The fertility decline in the region is associated with effective family planning campaigns and increases in women's education and employment (see Table 9.3).

The infant mortality rate, which was as high as 200 per 1,000 live births in 1955, began to decline in 1960, and by 1990 it had reached about 70 per 1,000 live births (Assaad, 1995). Eight years later it was down to 45—still higher than Latin America, the Caribbean, eastern Asia, and Europe and Central Asia, but lower than southern Asia and sub-Saharan Africa (see World Bank, 2000:tab. 2.18, p. 108). For some countries, the changes in infant, child, and maternal mortality occurred rapidly and dramatically. For example, in 1960 Tunisia had an infant mortality rate of 159, and its under-five child mortality rate was 255. In the 1980s these declined to 58 and 83 respectively. By

Table 9.3   Sociodemographic Features in MENA, Late 1990s

Country	% Females Literate, Ages 15 and Over, 2000	Female Enrollments in Secondary School (%), 1993–1997	Female Share of Tertiary Enrollment (%), Mid-1990s	Singulate Age at First Marriage (women) 1990s	% Married Women Using Contraception (total)	Total Fertility Rate
Algeria	57	62	n/a	24	52	3.1
Bahrain	83	97	58	23	62	2.8
Egypt	44	73	n/a	22	56	3.5
Iran	70	73	36[a]	21	73	2.6
Iraq	46	32	n/a	22	n/a	5.3
Israel	94	87	n/a	24	n/a	3.0
Jordan	84	n/a	47	25	56	3.6
Kuwait	80	66	62	25	50	4.2
Lebanon	80	84	49	n/a	61	2.5
Libya	68	n/a	17	n/a	49	3.9
Morocco	36	34	41[b]	22	58	3.4
Oman	62	66	46	19	24	6.1
Palestine	n/a	n/a	44	n/a	n/a	n/a
Qatar	83	79	73	23	43	3.9
Saudi Arabia	67	57	47	22	32	5.7
Sudan	46	20	n/a	26	10	4.9
Syria	61	40	41	n/a	49	4.1
Tunisia	61	63	45	25	60	2.3
Turkey	77	48	38	22	64	2.5
United Arab Emirates	79	82	n/a	23	28	3.5
Yemen	25	14	13	n/a	21	7.2

Sources: Population Reference Bureau, *Women of the World 2002* [poster], except female share of tertiary enrollment from CAWTAR, 2001:tab. A/33, p. 229, and UN, 2000:tab. 4.A; and singulate age at marriage from UN, 2000.

Notes: a. The figure for Iran does not include private universities. In 2002 the female share of university enrollments rose to over 50 percent.

b. The CAWTAR report cites a figure of 21 percent female share of university enrollment in Morocco.

n/a indicates data not available.

2000 the rate of infant mortality had dropped to just 30. Iran similarly saw impressive achievements in the health of children as well as of mothers during the 1990s. Indeed, maternal mortality rates have dropped throughout the region, though they remain highest in Yemen and Sudan, the poorest and most rural countries. Life expectancy varies; it is highest in the oil-rich Gulf states (72 years) and Israel (80 years), lowest in Sudan (55 years) and Yemen (56 years).

Following the analysis by Abdel R. Omran and Farzaneh Roudi (1993) but with some modifications, we may divide the countries of the Middle East and North Africa into four groups based on the trends in birth and death rates and their socioeconomic settings. Group 1 is characterized by persistent high fertility and declining mortality among middle-income and poor countries in an intermediate-to-low socioeconomic setting and includes Jordan, Iraq, Syria,

Yemen, and the West Bank and Gaza Strip. Group 2 is characterized by declining fertility and mortality among middle-income countries in an intermediate level of socioeconomic development and includes Egypt, Lebanon, Turkey, Iran, Morocco, and Tunisia. A third group, made up of the rich GCC countries, is characterized by high fertility amid rapidly declining mortality in a high socioeconomic setting. Finally, Israel is the only country in the region that follows the European-style transition of low fertility and mortality in an upper-middle-income and above-average socioeconomic setting.

Iran and Turkey have had some volatility in their demographic transitions. Turkey began its transition earliest, in the 1950s, only to experience a kind of baby boom in the early 1970s. Iran's total fertility rate declined during the 1970s but increased during the 1980s following the Iranian revolution. The dramatic population growth rate of the 1980s is attributed to the pronatalist policies of the new Islamic regime, which banned contraceptives and encouraged marriage and family formation (Moghadam, 2003:chap. 6), but it may also be a result of rural fertility behavior, which was slow to decline during the 1970s. Since the reversal of the pronatalist policy following the results of the 1986 census and the introduction of an aggressive family planning campaign after 1988, there has been a change from the fertility and population growth trends of the 1980s. In the mid-1990s, fertility declined again.

In some countries, fertility rates are considerably higher in rural areas than urban areas, as confirmed by recent Demographic and Health Surveys (DHS).[1] For example, in Egypt, fertility rates remain very high in the rural areas of Upper Egypt, where infant and under-five mortality rates also are high. A 1992 DHS measured a total fertility rate of 2.9 children per woman in urban Egypt, compared with 4.9 children in rural areas. A 1990 DHS in Jordan found that women in the largest cities had 4.8 children on average, those in smaller urban areas had 5.6 children, and women in rural areas had 6.9 children. In Yemen a 1991–1992 DHS measured a total fertility rate of 5.6 among urban women, compared with 8.1 among rural women (Omran and Roudi, 1993:13).

Like the World Fertility Surveys of the late 1970s and early 1980s, the more recent Demographic and Health Surveys research confirmed the link between mother's education and total fertility rate: the higher the educational attainment, the smaller the number of children. In Jordan, for example, women with no formal education had an average fertility rate of 6.9, whereas the figure for those with a secondary or higher education was 4.1 per woman. Still, Jordan is unique in its relatively high fertility rate among educated women; this may be a function of the very low labor force participation of women.

In Morocco, Tunisia, and Turkey, fertility has declined faster in urban than in rural areas, suggesting the effect that urbanization and its correlates— mainly female education, employment opportunities, delayed marriage, and access to contraceptives and family planning information—have had in those countries. But in Turkey and Tunisia and to a lesser degree in Morocco and Iran, fertility declines are being registered in rural areas as well, partly due to the availability of contraception.

MENA countries have exhibited a variety of population policies and concerns. "Population policy" is understood to be an intention to improve the overall well-being of the nation's citizens. Definitions of "well-being" vary and are certainly debatable, as are prescriptions of how to reach objectives. In the 1990s, countries that were concerned about the rate of population growth (e.g., Iran and Egypt) faced the dual goal of improving health facilities on the one hand, thus reducing natal and infant mortality, and of decreasing the birthrate on the other hand. Other countries seek to reduce mortality rates and improve the population's health but do not actively seek to reduce birthrates (e.g., Israel, Saudi Arabia). At the level of state policymaking, the approach to population growth ranges from pronatalist to laissez-faire to pro–family planning. In several of the countries—notably Iran, Lebanon, Tunisia, and Turkey—the combined effects of socioeconomic development, women's educational attainment, and state-sponsored family planning programs have produced the lowest fertility rates of the region. Indeed, the average of about 2.5 children per woman in these MENA countries today is even lower than the fertility rate of many Latin American countries.

Still, decades of high birthrates have helped to keep the population of Middle Eastern countries young. More than 40 percent of the region's population is under fifteen years of age, whereas only 4 percent is over age sixty-five. These percentages are similar to the average for all developing countries but very different from the pattern in industrial countries. There are also variations across the region. In 2000 the share of the population under age fifteen ranged from 26.7 percent in Qatar to over 50 percent in Yemen and the West Bank and Gaza. The share of the population aged sixty-five or older ranged from 9.9 percent in Israel to 2 percent or less in Yemen, Kuwait, and Qatar (UNDP, 2002a:tab. 5). These differences in age structure are tied to the different birth rates across the region.

Countries with young populations exhibit a high dependency ratio and small tax base, a situation exacerbated by the low labor force participation of women in nonagricultural and modern occupations.

■ Labor Force Growth and Employment Challenges

Despite growing urbanization in the Middle East and North Africa, roughly one-third of the total population still depends on agriculture for its livelihood. The proportion of the labor force in agriculture varies from around 50 percent in Turkey, Yemen, and Syria to less than 5 percent in Israel and the small Gulf states. Economic modernization, however, has resulted in changes in the sectoral distribution of the labor force, with a growing proportion of workers involved in services and, to a lesser degree, in industry. The emergence of the services sector has been especially evident in Jordan, where the share of agriculture in total employment declined from 42 percent in the 1960s to less than 7 percent in the early 1990s (Shaban, Assaad, and al-Qudsi, 1995:71). Although the services sector has been expanding and thriving throughout the region, the manufacturing sector has not fared as well, partly due to the reliance on wealth generated from oil exports. Still, in a number of countries, the economic development strategy of the 1960s–1980s, which included protection and promotion of the manufacturing sector, did lead to increases in (mostly male) employment in industry. Throughout the region, the structural transformation of the regional economy was accompanied by the emergence of a female labor force, but it has remained a relatively small percentage of the total salaried workforce. Labor force statistics in the region are not always exact, and women's economic activity outside the formal and modern sector has tended to be underestimated, but the available evidence suggests that a large part of the female economically active population in many of the countries, such as Egypt, Iran, Iraq, Syria, and Turkey, remains rooted in agriculture.

In the highly urbanized GCC countries of Bahrain, Kuwait, Qatar, and the UAE, the agricultural workforce is quite small. There is greater involvement in agriculture in Oman and Saudi Arabia, but more so on the part of men than of women, which raises the question of whether women's agricultural activity is properly measured. In the GCC countries, with the exception of Oman, the vast majority of the female workforce (nationals) is engaged in service-sector work. Less prestigious service work is performed by imported female labor. The involvement of women in industry is negligible, except in Oman.

Among the larger and more diversified countries of the region, Turkey remains anomalous, in that it is the most modernized of the countries and yet the one where women are most likely to be found in agriculture. In Algeria, Egypt, Jordan, Lebanon, and Libya, the majority of the measured female workforce is concentrated in the service sector. Only in Morocco and Tunisia are large percentages of the female workforce involved in the industrial (manufacturing) sector. In all countries, the male workforce is more evenly distributed across the sectors and more likely to be found in modern occupations. Moreover, the female share of the total salaried workforce is very small, under 20 percent. Clearly, salaried work is a male domain in the region (Moghadam, 2003:chap. 2).

The height of the region's oil-based economic development during the 1970s saw considerable intraregional labor migration, characterized by a massive outflow of surplus labor from countries such as Egypt, Jordan, the West Bank, Tunisia, Yemen, and Lebanon to capital-rich and labor-poor GCC countries, as well as to Libya and Iraq. These countries also imported non-Arab workers, including Koreans, Filipinos, Sri Lankans, and Yugoslavs, who were attracted by the high wages offered in the capital-rich Arab countries. In 1975, foreign labor constituted 47 percent of the labor force in the Gulf countries, and by 1990 the figure had increased to 68 percent. In Kuwait in 1990, fully 86 percent of the workforce was foreign (ESCWA, 1993). Remittances from nationals working abroad became especially important to the economies of Egypt, Jordan, and Yemen.

Jordan was unique among Arab countries in being a labor-exporting country that also imported labor. It exported skilled workers and educated professionals to the rich Gulf states, but it also imported unskilled and low-wage workers for construction, domestic services, and some public services that Jordanian nationals would not perform, such as waiting tables, cleaning buildings, and cleaning streets. Most of the imported Arab labor was (and remains) Egyptian. Almost all domestic workers are from the Philippines. A rather peculiar result has been the underutilization of Jordanian women, who in the absence of labor force attachment tend to have nearly four children on average, as discussed above (see also Moghadam, 1998).

The labor migration patterns of North Africans and Turks have been different. Their preferred destination has been Europe, notably Germany for Turks and France for Algerians, Moroccans, and Tunisians (although Tunisians also went to Libya, as mentioned above). Furthermore, labor migration began earlier, during the 1950s and 1960s, in response to European guest worker programs. In the 1970s, European countries began to reduce the influx of guest workers, although the number of Turks in Germany has continued to grow through a combination of natural increase, family reunification, and illegal immigration (OECD, 1992; Omran and Roudi, 1993:24). Tunisian emigrants continued to head to Europe in the 1980s, and, in a new development, the migration streams have started to include women on their own.

In Arab countries, political and economic instabilities have resulted in a reduction of intraregional labor flows, affecting mainly Jordanian, Palestinian, and Yemeni workers laboring in Kuwait and Saudi Arabia. The expulsion of the expatriate workers was a punishment for their countries' stance on the 1991 Gulf War, revealing once again the facade of Arab unity. At the same time, Kuwait and Saudi Arabia rewarded Egypt for its position against Iraq and in favor of the war by replacing expelled Jordanians, Palestinians, and Yemenis with Egyptian workers. Still, a large number of Egyptians left the Gulf and returned to Egypt as a result of the Gulf War. The UN's Economic and Social Commission for West Asia (ESCWA) estimated the total number of returnees at 2 million people. Most returnees were nationals of Yemen (732,000), Egypt (700,000), and Jordan (300,000, including Palestinians). The return of expatriates has been a mixed experience; in some cases returnees contributed to a boom in the construction industry and in small businesses (especially in Jordan), but in other cases returnees have experienced unemployment, slow absorption into the local labor market, or poverty. Poverty has been especially acute for Yemenis, who were largely unskilled workers unable to find employment at home.

■ Rising Unemployment

Thus, by the mid-1990s, the demographic transition characterized by high fertility, rural-to-urban migration, and changes in the pattern of intraregional labor migration had led to rapid growth of the labor force. In a situation of economic stagnation, this resulted in high rates of unemployment, especially in urban areas.

The unemployment situation was a shock to the educated population in particular, who had come to expect guaranteed jobs in the public sector. During the 1960s and 1970s, state-sponsored economic development resulted in an expansion of public-sector employment. For example, Egypt had a policy of guaranteeing public-sector jobs to graduates of vocational secondary schools and universities. Morocco had a similar scheme, albeit one that provided "temporary employment" to graduates. As a result of these policies, some countries, such as Egypt, Jordan, and Algeria, employed more than 50 percent of the labor force in the public sector. A majority of the workforce in the GCC countries was also employed in the public sector.

As a result of the recessionary conditions experienced in the region since the mid-1980s and structural adjustment policy prescriptions to contract the public-sector wage bill, public sectors are no longer hiring as expansively as before, although they are not yet laying off large numbers of workers (as occurred in Latin America and sub-Saharan Africa, where structural adjustments were implemented earlier). Indeed, due to political and social concerns, MENA governments have preferred the strategy of wage deterioration or encouragement of early retirement rather than outright layoffs. Of course, economic restructuring in the private sector did result in worker layoffs in Tunisia, Morocco, and Turkey. But for the most part, the unemployed population has consisted of first-time job seekers, mainly but not exclusively secondary school graduates, male and female alike, who are seeking jobs out of economic need.

The contraction of public-sector employment and declines in government social spending led to the deterioration of real wages, which in turn made household incomes fall substantially in many countries (Karshenas, 1994). For example, the real wage rate in Jordan increased by 45 percent over the period 1975–1987, but by 1990 it had declined to roughly its value in 1975 (Shaban, Assaad, and al-Qudsi, 1995:74). The drop in real wages was not, however, accompanied by an increase in job creation or the demand for labor or by a decrease in the unemployment rates. This suggests that the problem in the labor market was not high wages (as in the past) but a lack of competitiveness and productivity and inefficient utilization of human resources. It also suggests the underdevelopment of the private sector in the region and its inability to absorb the growing labor force.

Compared to other regions in the world economy, unemployment rates are very high in the Middle East and North Africa, and they are exceptionally high for women. Even the GCC countries, which historically had very low rates of unemployment and in fact imported labor to meet demand, now came to face increasing joblessness among their native populations. Unemployment is often difficult to measure in developing countries. Most of the countries in the Middle East have only recently started to count those who are either unsuccessfully seeking jobs for the first time (as with high school and college graduates) or who have lost jobs due to enterprise restructuring (a far smaller proportion). Measured unemployment is usually urban, although countries are now increasingly including the rural areas in their enumeration; thus some countries now disaggregate unemployment by urban or rural area as well as by gender.

Urban unemployment rates began increasing in the 1980s and reached highs of 10–18 percent in Algeria, Tunisia, Egypt, Jordan, Iran, Turkey, and Yemen. According to the ESCWA, the rates were as high as 30 percent in Yemen, the West Bank, and Gaza. As mentioned previously, unemployment is age-specific, with much of it consisting of new entrants to the workforce in the age groups fifteen to nineteen and twenty to twenty-four. Joblessness varies by educational attainment, but in some countries college graduates experience high rates of unemployment. In the early 1990s, unemployment rates among high school graduates were between 17 percent and 29 percent in Algeria, Egypt, Jordan, Morocco, and Tunisia; college graduates showed unemployment rates of 15 percent and 23 percent in Egypt and Morocco respectively; and among workers with primary education or less, unemployment rates were 17–27 percent in Algeria, Morocco, and Tunisia (ILO, 1999).

In the 1990s, female unemployment rates soared to highs of 25 percent, indicating a growing supply of job-seeking women, in contrast to an earlier pattern of "housewife-ization." Table 9.4 shows that in almost all countries, female unemployment rates were considerably higher than male rates. In Algeria, unemployment rates were high for both women and men (24 percent and 26.9 percent respectively in 1997), but women's unemployment was disproportionately high, given that they constituted a mere 10 percent of the labor force. This holds true also for Lebanon. Table 9.5 illustrates the prevalence of joblessness among young women, especially in Bahrain, Egypt, Jordan, Oman, Palestine, Syria, and Tunisia. Women's high unemployment rates appear to be a function of both women's preferences for public-sector jobs, which are not available, and the private sector's discrimination against women, typically due to maternity leave requirements in labor law. Iranian

Deborah J. Gerner

This proud high school graduate of the Friends Boys School in Ramallah, West Bank, hopes that attending college in the United States will improve his chances for future employment.

women's very high rate of unemployment in 1991 was almost halved by 1996, and this may be because more women have been starting their own businesses and nongovernmental organizations (NGOs) and entering university. Yemen seems to depart from the regional norm of very high rates of female unemployment, and this may reflect the effects of returning male migrant workers as well as very low rates of female labor force participation (Yemen Ministry of Planning and Development, 1998). Still, the available evidence suggests that the feminization of unemployment is a defining feature of the urban labor markets of the Middle East and North Africa.

How do the unemployed—those who expect jobs in the formal sector but do not find them—fare in countries where unemployment insurance is not in place or is not available to new entrants? Some of the job seekers—and especially the men—appear to have gravitated to the urban informal sector, which by all accounts has grown tremendously in the region. Informal-sector workers may include taxi drivers, construction workers, domestic workers, people who work in souks and bazaars (the traditional markets in the Middle East), hairdressers, barbers, seamstresses, tailors, workers in or owners of small industrial or artisan workshops, hawkers of sundry goods, repairmen, and so on. It also includes home-based female pieceworkers, such as women in Turkey, Syria, and Jordan who are engaged in sewing and embroidery for a contractor or subcontractor. The nature and function of the informal sector has

Table 9.4   Unemployment Rates, Selected MENA Countries, 1990s

Country	Year	Male (%)	Female (%)	Total (%)
Algeria[a]	1992	24.2	20.3	23.8
	1997	26.9	24.0	26.4
Bahrain[b]	1991	5.5	13.4	6.8
Egypt	1995	7.0	22.1	10.4
Iraq	1987	4.3	7.4	5.1
Jordan	1991	14.4	34.1	17.1
	1994	12.9	28.3	15.0
	1997	11.7	28.5	14.4
	2000	12.6	19.8	13.7
Lebanon	1996	8.6	7.2	7.0[c]
Morocco (urban)	1992	13.0	25.3	16.0
	1998	17.4	22.9	18.7
Oman	1993	4.7	8.7	5.1
Palestine	1997			
West Bank		17.2	17.7	15.5
Gaza		26.5	29.8	26.2
Sudan	1993	8.6	9.6	n/a
Syria	1981	3.2	2.0	3.0
	1991	5.2	14.0	6.8
	1995	5.1	11.6	6.5
Tunisia	1993	14.7	21.9	16.1
Yemen	1991	14.0	6.0	12.3
	1994	10.1	5.4	18.1

Sources: World Bank, 1995b:5; ERF, 1996:103, 1998:128; ESCWA, 2000:37; ILO, 1999: tab. 3A; Moghadam, 1998; Yemen Ministry of Planning and Development, 1998; Jordan Department of Statistics, *Employment and Unemployment Survey* (various issues).

Notes: a. 1997 data on Algeria from Republique Algerienne, 2000, and World Bank, *Genderstats,* http://genderstats.worldbank.org/.

b. 24.8 percent female unemployment in 1991, compared to 12.3 percent for men (UNDP, 1998).

c. Lebanon's total unemployment rate for new entrants is 22 percent.

n/a indicates data not available.

been much debated; although it is agreed that it serves to absorb the labor force and to provide goods and services at relatively low cost, it is also unregulated and untaxed, leading to poor labor standards and income (such as the wealth of many merchants) that is not distributed. The informal sector both contributes to, and is a reflection of, income inequality in the society.

■ Poverty and Inequality

Poverty and inequality are measured by household income and consumption and by quality-of-life indicators. Conventional studies distinguish between "absolute poverty" and "relative poverty," and they establish an income-based "poverty line" against which households are measured. In an

Table 9.5 Youth Unemployment by Sex, Selected MENA Countries, Latest Available Years

Country	Year	Female (%)	Male (%)	Total (%)
Egypt	1995	41.1	24.5	n/a
Iraq	1987	18.5	6.3	7.7
Jordan	1983	25.9	7.9	10.7
	1994	63.9	28.5	35.2
Lebanon	1997	12.6	23.8	21.3
Palestine	1997	31.6	27.7	n/a
Sudan	1993	17.1	16.6	n/a
Syria	1983	3.8	6.9	6.2
	1995	19.7	11.3	13.6
Tunisia	1984	17.2	30.5	n/a
	1994	24.7	28.4	n/a
Yemen	1986	1.8	8.6	6.5
	1994	9.8	20.2	17.9
Gulf Cooperation Council				
Bahrain	1981	42.8	8.4	17.1
	1991	33.9	22.4	25.4
Kuwait	1985	6.3	6.3	6.3
Oman	1993	25.8	16.2	17.6
Qatar	1986	8.0	2.9	3.2
United Arab Emirates	1985	3.5	3.7	3.7

Source: ESCWA, 2000:annexes 13–14.
Note: n/a indicates data not available.

alternative conceptualization, the definition of poverty is broadened to include measures of "capabilities" or "human development" such as literacy, life expectancy, access to clean water, and so on. This better captures gender differences while also recognizing the multidimensionality of poverty. Studies show that there has been considerable improvement over time in standards of living in the Middle East and North Africa, as measured by such social indicators as life expectancy, infant mortality, maternal mortality, access to safe water, adequate sanitation facilities, rising age of first marriage, fertility rates, literacy, and school enrollments, as well as by wage rates and household incomes. However, gender gaps exist, and given the income levels of many countries in the region, the social indicators should be better. Moreover, it appears that although levels of absolute poverty have been decreasing in some parts of the region, poverty has actually been increasing in other parts. This is mainly a function of high population growth, but it is also due to the creation of new poverty groups in urban areas caused by economic recession, rising prices, deteriorating wages, and unemployment. This shift has been occurring since the mid-1980s, when the price of oil and hence gross national product (GNP) declined, the external debt rose, and government spending was reduced.

According to the World Bank and ESCWA, the number of poor people in the Middle East and North Africa increased from an estimated 60 million in 1985 to 73 million in 1990, or from 30.6 percent to 33.1 percent of the total population (World Bank, 1993:5; ESCWA, 1993:121; see also ESCWA, 1995b, 1995c). Poverty assessments prepared by the World Bank, which were derived from surveys of living standards undertaken within various countries, revealed growing poverty in Egypt and Jordan and the emergence of urban "working poor" in Tunisia and Morocco. According to official statistics, 23 percent of the population in Egypt in 1991 and 18 percent of the population in Jordan in 1993 were considered to be living under the poverty line. Most believed that the poverty incidence could be as high as 30 percent in both countries (Moghadam, 1997, 1998). In both countries poverty was largely rural, and the rural poor were small landholders and tenants, landless agricultural workers, and pastoralists (ESCWA, 1993:6). In Egypt the urban poor included the unemployed and female-headed households. In all countries, because of gender differences in literacy, educational attainment, employment, and income, women are especially vulnerable to poverty during periods of economic difficulty or in the event of divorce, abandonment, or widowhood.

Even though poverty is not as severe in the Middle East as in some other regions (UNDP, 2002b), it has been increasing, and according to some observers, income inequalities have been widening (el-Ghonemy, 1998; Richards and Waterbury, 1996). This is said to be the result of the new eco-

Children sift through a garbage dump in a poor part of Cairo, looking for clothing and other salvageable items.

nomic policies of structural adjustment and trade and price liberalization, as well as the old policies of high military spending and inadequate taxation.

In Lebanon, the main factors behind the alarming increase in the incidence of poverty have been the civil war and misguided economic policies, including tax write-offs for large firms engaged in the country's reconstruction and the absence of any property taxes. According to ESCWA, in 1996 about 1 million Lebanese (28 percent of the population) were living below the poverty line, and some 75 percent of the poor were urban dwellers. The country's unemployment rate reached 15 percent in 1996, compared with 8.1 percent of the workforce in 1975, before the country's long civil war began. The ESCWA report singled out the absence of government social spending and "unjust wealth distribution" as the factors behind the rise in nutritional deficiencies, lack of sanitation in poor areas, and the lowering of teaching and health standards (*Middle East Times*, 1996:19).

For some countries, poverty and lack of progress in human development have resulted from very high military expenditures. In Iraq, Oman, Saudi Arabia, Syria, and Yemen, military expenditures in 1990 far exceeded expenditures on education and health care (see UNDP, 1996:tab. 19). As recently as 2000, military expenditures in Saudi Arabia amounted to 11.6 percent of gross domestic product (GDP); in Jordan, the figure was 9.5 percent. Even Turkey committed nearly 5 percent of GDP toward military expenditure, compared with 2.2 percent of GDP for education and 3.3 percent for health care (UNDP, 2002a:tab. 17). In the case of Iraq, of course, war and economic sanctions have exacerbated the situation of the poor and created new poverty-stricken groups. The destruction of Iraq's infrastructure by U.S.-led coalition bombings in January 1991 (see Drèze and Gazdar, 1992) and again in March–April 2003, the shortage of medical supplies and foodstuffs caused by the long sanctions regime, and the collapse of public services following the 2003 invasion have completely transformed a country that was once urbanized, mechanized, and prosperous.

The available evidence suggests that in the large and diversified economies—such as Turkey, Lebanon, and Iran—inequalities or relative poverty are quite pronounced and have been growing. The persistence of destitution, or absolute poverty, mainly in rural areas, is a problem in such low-income countries as Egypt, Yemen, and Morocco, and perhaps also in the Gaza Strip. Social indicators on health, safe water, and sanitation reflect the quality of life of citizens as well as urban-rural disparities. Although urbanization has brought about access to health, safe water, and sanitation for residents in most of the countries, some countries—including Algeria, Syria, and Yemen—continue to have difficulties in the provision of such urban services, as noted earlier in this chapter. In other countries there are distinct rural-urban disparities. Table 9.6 shows the population without access to health care, safe water, and sanitation, most of whom would be rural dwellers. (The high rates of access to health care, water, and sanitation as reported by several of the

Table 9.6 Percentage of Population Without Access to Services, Selected MENA Countries

Country	Health Care, 1981–1993	Safe Water, 1990–1998	Sanitation, 1990–1998
Algeria	n/a	10	9
Egypt	1	13	12
Iran	27	5	36
Iraq	2	19	25
Jordan	10	3	1
Kuwait	0	n/a	n/a
Lebanon	5	6	37
Morocco	38	35	42
Oman	11	15	22
Saudi Arabia	2	5	14
Syria	1	14	33
Tunisia	10	2	20
Turkey	0	51	20
United Arab Emirates	10	3	8
Yemen	84	39	34

Source: UNDP, 2000:tab. 4, pp. 169–171.
Note: n/a indicates data not available.

countries should be viewed with some skepticism.) In terms of access to services, urban living is certainly superior to rural living, but population growth and reductions in government social spending are straining the quality and quantity of urban services. These pressures are not conveyed by the statistics but are best discerned by visits to and stays in the nonelite sections of the cities of the Middle East and North Africa, where overcrowding, rundown and inadequate public transportation, streets in disrepair, polluted air, high noise levels, and lack of building codes are only some of the many problems that low-income urban dwellers endure.

I end this section with profiles of poverty and inequality in Morocco, Tunisia, Egypt, and the Palestinian Authority/Occupied Territories, based on World Bank poverty assessments and other sources. The profiles show that in addition to external factors such as occupation, war, or unfair terms of trade, crucial internal factors in the creation or perpetuation of poverty and inequality are state policies, class structure, and the status of women.

Morocco

Morocco's 1991 living standards measurement survey counted 2.5 million poor, of whom 72 percent lived in rural areas and more than half were extremely poor. The highest poverty levels were (and remain) among rural wage earners, and women are the most disadvantaged. The survey found that in urban areas, the poor were mainly self-employed. The typical poor worker earned one-third the average wage or one-half the legislated minimum wage; poor women received as little as half the wage rate per hour earned by poor males (World Bank, 1994). During the 1980s, as Moroccan exports expanded, women's employment grew, especially in the most competitive sectors of clothing, food, leather, and shoes. But these sectors offered very low wages. Unemployment remains high in Morocco, especially among the poor and among women. Some 30 percent of the urban poor are unemployed, and women in the poorest households experience the highest rates of unemployment in urban areas. In the mid-1990s, Morocco did not have a system of social protection in place to address poverty or unemployment.

The new economic policies of the 1980s, although promoting growth through increased production and exports, also brought about rising prices, a deterioration of wages, and cuts in social spending by the government. Not enough of the national income was channeled into public spending on basic health care, schooling, and essential infrastructure services, which would have improved the well-being of the poor. In the 1980s, poor parents were forced to withdraw their children from school. Indeed, enrollments in primary education actually declined after 1982, recovering only in 1990. But as late as 2000, Morocco still did not have universal primary and secondary school enrollments, and the gender gaps in school enrollments continued to be very wide (see UNDP, 2002a:tab. 24). Such gender inequalities make Moroccan women especially vulnerable to poverty.

The World Bank's 1991 study found that rural women in Morocco were largely unpaid family workers, whereas men tended to work as independent, small-scale farmers or in commerce, and about 25 percent of them were wage earners. The structure of rural social relations and its gender dimension in Morocco was captured in the following observation: "While women rarely obtain a job of their own for a wage, they often share in their husband's work outside the household farm. And having command over family labor, women and often children, gives a laborer a competitive edge in the labor market" (World Bank, 1994:vol. 1, p. 48). Clearly what Morocco needs is more social investment by the government to create a skilled, educated, and better-paid labor force, to raise female literacy and educational attainments, and to reduce rural-urban gaps. In fact, these objectives were inscribed in the proposed Action Plan for the Integration of Women in Development, which was promoted by the Moroccan government and women's organizations in the late 1990s. However, the plan was met by an Islamist backlash and shelved in 2002.

▣ Tunisia

In Tunisia, poverty is predominantly rural, but a growing percentage of poor households are in urban areas. The 1990 Household Consumption Survey found that about 600,000 people, or 7 percent of the population, had annual expenditures below the poverty line, and another 7 percent were "near poor." Most of the urban poor were wage earners in the construction sector with little or no formal education. Others were involved in temporary, low-wage, and low-skill employment in the expanding sectors of tourism and textiles (World Bank, 1995a). Still others were unemployed. As mentioned earlier in this chapter, unemployment is high in Tunisia; as in Morocco, it is especially high among the poor, youth, and women. And because of the sluggish growth of the private sector, there is also a high incidence of unemployment among skilled workers.

In contrast to Morocco, however, Tunisia has demonstrated a commitment to social spending and has been expanding its social insurance program. The Tunisian government cut social expenditures less than other expenditure categories during its period of fiscal restraint. The social security system covers wage earners in both the public and private sectors, including self-employed workers and government employees. Furthermore, there are two types of social assistance programs to alleviate poverty—direct transfers and consumer subsidies. Free health care and schooling are available to all, and Tunisia spends far less on the military than do other countries. Among countries of the Middle East and North Africa, only Tunisia has established effective social programs to tackle poverty, increase employment through public works, and encourage employment among women. According to one report, Tunisian labor unions, though not large, were instrumental in maintaining food subsidies for the poor (see UNDP, 1999:90).

Egypt

In Egypt, poor households constitute 20–25 percent of the total, most of which are concentrated in Upper Egypt, where women and children are the most vulnerable. Female-headed households are poorer than male-headed households in both rural and urban areas. Labor among children under twelve years of age is very high, especially in rural areas, and there is a high prevalence of anemia among women and small children. The poor are agricultural laborers or farmers with little or no land. A World Bank study found that in urban areas, the poor were construction workers or service workers and included "a significant number of government employees" (World Bank, 1991:35), partly because of the drastic deterioration in real wages that the government has allowed in the public sector. Wages continued to fall in sectors where women predominate. Although most poor males in both the urban and rural sectors are engaged in casual labor, such is not the case for women. A higher proportion of poor women are employed as salaried workers, and more poor females are found working in community services and in trade and services than is the case for men, which indicates the very low wages that working women must accept. What is more, unemployment rates are strikingly higher for females than for males, as shown earlier. Poor women are also less literate and educated than poor men. Whereas poor men average 5.8 years of schooling, poor women have only 3.1 years; 63 percent of poor men can read and write, compared to only 33 percent of poor women (Jolliffe, 1997). For the country as a whole in 2000, only 63 percent of young women aged 15–24 were literate, and the figure for all adult women was just 44 percent.

Unsurprisingly, given the gender gaps in Egypt, widows and members of multiple-person female-headed households constitute two of the most economically vulnerable groups of people. According to one account:

> Even the youngest widows have no realistic prospect of making anything but the most casual and intermittent earnings, and the more elderly none whatsoever. Despite the traditional custom of support for widows through transfers from family members, even if they do not live in the same household, many widows in practice are not adequately supported by members of their family. They are destitute and depend on casual charity from neighbors to survive. Field reports from charity organizations operating in Cairo reveal that elderly widows form the single most important client group. Nongovernmental organizations recognize them as a group prone to poverty and in need of special assistance. (World Bank, 1991:11)

According to official statistics, about 12 percent of households in Cairo had a female head in 1988, although this figure now may be as high as 18 percent. Egyptian sociologist Iman Bibars studied the growing phenomenon of female-headed households. This category "is not exclusive to widows, divorcees and the deserted but to a new rising category of wives of 'useless' husbands" (1996:13), including men who are imprisoned, terminally ill, disabled, or unemployed. In one study of a poor urban quarter in Cairo, women headed 29 percent of the sampled households. The majority of those women were illiterate and either widowed or divorced. They tended to have half the disposable income of poor male-headed households, lived in poorer housing units, and owned very few consumer durables (Fergany, 1994). Egypt has an inadequate system of social protection, and many poor women have difficulties dealing with the bureaucracy. Thus they often turn to charitable foundations—many of which are now run by Islamist organizations.

▪ The Occupied Territories

In the Palestinian Authority/Occupied Territories, Gaza has been the region worst off, which is closely related to its high share of economically deprived refugees. The most important type of household income—earnings from labor activity—has been rendered unstable by curfews, strikes, and restrictions on employment in Israel since the second intifada. But even accounting for the injustices and hardships suffered by all Palestinians, women's lot is especially dire. Gender discrimination and social controls on women make them especially vulnerable to poverty. Early marriage, incomplete education, and high fertility have kept women tied to the home and have increased pressures on household budgets (Heiberg et al., 1994; Olmsted, 1999).

In 1992, a survey by the Fafo Institute for Applied Social Science in Oslo, Norway, estimated the total fertility at 6.84 births per woman (Heiberg et al., 1994:65). In Gaza, more than a third (37 percent) of the entire female population married under the age of seventeen—the legal minimum age for women. The Fafo survey found a female labor force participation ratio of only 14 percent, indicating that most Palestinian women worked in household production and in the domestic sphere rather than in paid employment outside the home. Examples of work in the family sphere done by housewives were contract/piecework, involvement in a family business or shop, and work on the family farm. Employment outside the family sphere requiring education and training or involvement in unskilled paid labor was relatively limited. Female labor force participation was especially low in Gaza and in the refugee camps, although these areas offered very weak employment possibilities for men as well. Divorced and separated women and wealthy and educated women had the highest labor force participation rates. Many women accepted low-paid piecework at home rather than participation in the Israeli labor market.

In a social context in which so few women directly participate in the labor force, individual women get access to economic resources and thus try to avoid poverty through other means. One source is the dowery. The Fafo study found that although jewelry constituted the major form of women's independent property ownership in the West Bank, Gaza Strip, and Arab Jerusalem, women did own other forms of property, such as land, although to a much lesser degree. Most women sampled claimed they had nothing to sell or mortgage in case they needed money badly. Over time, women's jewelry acquired at marriage gradually dissipated to pay for various investments for the family, husband, or children (Heiberg et al., 1994:295–300).

■ Conclusion

This chapter has surveyed trends in population growth, urbanization, labor force growth, rising unemployment, and poverty. These social and demographic trends have implications for household well-being, individual capabilities, and political stability. Although urbanization holds many promises for people, including a wider range of options, activities, and services, unchecked population growth has created enormous pressures on urban services. At a time of reduced government spending, these demographic pressures on health care, education, and utilities are likely to increase inequalities and deprivation. High fertility rates have resulted in the emergence of a large population of young people who are seeking but not finding jobs. In a context of reduced government spending and rising unemployment, poverty increases rather than diminishes. Although poverty and inequality are social phenomena, reflecting a class structure and skewed distribution of income, wealth, and opportunities, gender inequality clearly renders women more vulnerable than men to poverty.

The countries of the Middle East and North Africa, therefore, are faced with a number of social and demographic challenges that require concerted action involving governments, nongovernmental organizations, citizen groups, and international organizations. Identifying problems and solutions will require short-term, medium-term, and long-term perspectives informed by both developmental imperatives and the social entitlements of citizens. These include policies and measures to enhance women's access to education and jobs as a way of stabilizing population growth and reducing fertility rates as well as expanding women's capabilities and raising household incomes; investments in the physical and social infrastructure to upgrade urban services as well as create employment; enhancement of the legal and regulatory framework to improve labor and environmental standards as well as to improve the system of taxation; and community development programs that involve high school and college graduates, as a way of mitigating youth unemployment, alleviating urban poverty, and instilling solidarity.

■ Note

1. The Demographic and Health Surveys (conducted during the 1990s) and the earlier World Fertility Surveys (conducted during the late 1970s and early 1980s) are international surveys undertaken by governments but coordinated by a central body elsewhere, which also undertakes the cross-national analyses and global assessments. The Demographic and Health Surveys are coordinated by Macro International, Inc., in Maryland, in the United States, and the World Fertility Surveys were coordinated by the International Statistical Institute in the Netherlands. The World Fertility Surveys sought to examine trends in fertility and its correlates (contraceptive use, mother's education, child health, mother's health); the Demographic and Health Surveys similarly have been designed to collect data on fertility, family planning, and maternal and child health.

■ Bibliography

Assaad, Ragui. 1995. "Urbanization and Demographic Structure in the Middle East and North Africa with a Focus on Women and Children." New York: Population Council, Regional Papers no. 40 (January).

Bibars, Iman. 1996. "Women: Reconciling Contradictory Roles." *Civil Society* 5, no. 56 (August):13.

CAWTAR. 2001. *Globalization and Gender: Economic Participation of Arab Women.* Tunis, Tunisia: Center for Arab Women's Research and Training.

Drèze, Jean, and Haris Gazdar. 1992. "Hunger and Poverty in Iraq." *World Development* 20, no. 7.

ERF (Economic Research Forum). 1996. *Economic Trends in the MENA Region.* The Economic Research Forum for the Arab Countries, Iran and Turkey. Cairo: ERF.

———. 1998. *Economic Trends in the MENA Region.* The Economic Research Forum for the Arab Countries, Iran and Turkey. Cairo: ERF.

el-Ghonemy, M. Riad. 1998. *Affluence and Poverty in the Middle East.* London: Routledge.

ESCWA (Economic and Social Commission for West Asia). 1993. *A Conceptual and Methodological Framework for Poverty Alleviation in the ESCWA Region.* New York: United Nations, January 19.

———. 1995a. *Statistical Abstract of the ESCWA Region, 1984–1993.* 15th issue. New York: United Nations.

———. 1995b. *Survey of Economic and Social Developments in the ESCWA Region, 1994.* New York: United Nations.

———. 1995c. *Women and Poverty in the ESCWA Region: Issues and Concerns.* Series of Studies on Arab Women and Development no. 22. New York: United Nations.

———. 2000. *Women and Men in the Arab Region: A Statistical Portrait, 2000.* Amman, Jordan: United Nations.

Fergany, Nader. 1994. *Urban Women, Work and Poverty Alleviation in Egypt.* Pilot study sponsored by the International Labour Organization and the United Nations Development Programme. Cairo: Al-Mishkat Research Institute.

Heiberg, Marianne, et al. 1994. *Palestinian Society in Gaza, West Bank, and Arab Jerusalem: A Survey of Living Conditions.* Oslo: Fafo Institute for Applied Social Science.

ILO (International Labour Organization). 1999. *World Labour Report, 1999.* Geneva: ILO.

IRI (Islamic Republic of Iran). 1993. *Amargeeriye Jariye Jamiat 1370, Natayeje Omoumi, Kole Keshvar* [Population Census, 1991, National Summary]. Tehran: Statistical Centre of Iran.

———. 1997. *Salnameh Amari Keshvar 1375* [Iran Statistical Yearbook 1997]. Tehran: Statistical Centre of Iran.

Jolliffe, Dean. 1997. "What Do We Know About Poverty in Egypt? An Analysis of Household Survey Data for 1997." Paper presented at the annual meeting of the Middle East Studies Association, San Francisco, November 22–24.

Karshenas, Massoud. 1994. *Structural Adjustment, Wages, and Employment in the Middle East.* World Employment Program Working Paper. Geneva: International Labour Organization.

Middle East Times. 1996. November 3–9.

Moghadam, Valentine M. 1997. *The Feminization of Poverty? Notes on a Concept and Trends.* Occasional Paper no. 3. Normal: Women's Studies Program, Illinois State University, August.

———. 1998. *Women, Work, and Economic Reform in the Middle East and North Africa.* Boulder, Colo.: Lynne Rienner.

———. 2003. *Modernizing Women: Gender and Social Change in the Middle East.* 2nd ed. Boulder, Colo.: Lynne Rienner.

OECD (Organization for Economic Cooperation and Development). 1992. *Trends in International Migration.* Paris: OECD.

Olmsted, Jennifer. 1999. "Linking Fertility, Economic Policies and Gender in the Middle East and North Africa: A Case Study of Fertility Patterns Among Bethlehem Area Palestinians." Paper prepared for the sixth annual Economic Research Forum for the Arab Countries, Iran, and Turkey Conference, Cairo, October.

Omran, Abdel R., and Farzaneh Roudi. 1993. "The Middle East Population Puzzle." *Population Bulletin* 48, no. 1 (July).

Republique Algerienne. 1999. *Données Statistiques* [Statistical Data], no. 263. Alger: Office National des Statistiques.

Richards, Alan, and John Waterbury. 1996. *A Political Economy of the Middle East.* 2nd ed. Boulder, Colo.: Westview.

Roudi, Farzaneh. 2001. "Population Trends and Challenges in the Middle East and North Africa." Population Reference Bureau policy brief, October.

Shaban, Radwan A., Ragui Assaad, and Sulayman S. al-Qudsi. 1995. "The Challenge of Unemployment in the Arab Region." *International Labour Review* 134, no. 1:65–81.

UN (United Nations). 1993a. *The Sex and Age Distribution of the World's Populations: The 1992 Revision.* New York: UN.

———. 1993b. *World Urbanization Prospects: The 1992 Revision.* New York: UN.

———. 1995. *World Urbanization Prospects: The 1994 Revision.* New York: UN.

———. 2000. *The World's Women, 2000: Trends and Statistics.* New York: UN.

———. 2002. *World Urbanization Prospects: 2001 Revision.* New York: UN.

UNDP (United Nations Development Programme). 1995, 1996, 1997, 1998, 1999, 2000, 2002a. *Human Development Report.* New York: Oxford University Press.

———. 2002b. *Arab Human Development Report.* New York: UNDP.

UNESCO (United Nations Educational, Scientific, and Cultural Organization). 1995. *World Education Report.* Paris: UNESCO.

World Bank. 1991. *Egypt: Alleviating Poverty During Structural Adjustment.* Washington, D.C.: World Bank.

———. 1993. *Implementing the World Bank's Strategy to Reduce Poverty: Progress and Challenges.* Washington, D.C.: World Bank.

———. 1994. *Morocco: Poverty, Adjustment, and Growth.* Vols. 1–2. Washington, D.C.: World Bank.

———. 1995a. *Republic of Tunisia: Poverty Alleviation: Preserving Progress While Preparing for the Future.* Washington, D.C.: World Bank, August.

———. 1995b. *World Development Report: Workers in an Integrating World.* New York: Oxford University Press.

———. 2000. *World Development Indicators.* Washington, D.C.: World Bank.

Yemen Ministry of Planning and Development. 1998. *Yemen Human Development Report 1998.* Sana'a: Yemen Ministry of Planning and Development.

Kinship, Class, and Ethnicity

Laurie King-Irani

"**S**o, Khalid," said my husband, George, accepting a demitasse of strong, black, Turkish coffee from Hussein, our waiter, "I guess Adnan told you all about his adventures in Lebanon during his first visit in fifteen years. He sure was received like royalty—I don't think that he paid for a single meal the entire month he was there!" Khalid smiled broadly at George and replied, "Oh, I think that there was at least *one* meal that he definitely paid for! Has Adnan told you that he will soon be going back to Beirut?" All eyes turned to Adnan for clarification of this surprising piece of news. With the San Francisco Bay forming a backdrop to his happy face that September day in 1996, Adnan leaned back in his chair and tried unsuccessfully to repress a grin. "Well, you might as well hear it from the source: I am going to get married in Lebanon next month!" Adnan announced with evident satisfaction.

"Mabruk!" (congratulations), my husband and I answered as one. "Who is the lucky bride?" I asked, wondering to myself what had happened to Adnan's American girlfriend, Lisa, a rising young graphic designer. "Laila Karam," he answered. "She's the sister-in-law of my cousin Rima, *bint 'ammi* [daughter of my father's brother]. I met her at a family picnic up in the Shuf [a mountainous area in south-central Lebanon], near the village where her family used to live before the war and the massacres [between Maronite and Druze militias in 1983], and then I went to see her with some other cousins a few more times after that. She's twenty-six, really pretty and clever, and a terrific cook as well!

"During my last week in Beirut, *'amm Waseem* accompanied me to her father's house. We made the formal request for her hand in marriage, and after we had worked out all of the logistical details and decided on the *mahr* [the dowry paid by the groom's family to the bride's family], we celebrated our *khitbe* [formal announcement and celebration of an engagement] with a big dinner—the one I paid for!

"So it's official: We will be married at the end of October in my family's church, the big Melkite [Greek Catholic] cathedral above the city of Jounieh. You are, of course, going to receive a formal invitation from Laila's family. They are Maronite Christians, like my mom's family. I hope that will be a good basis for Laila and my mother to start their relationship, because after the honeymoon, I will be bringing her back here to live with me and my mom in a house I just bought near Palo Alto."

"Will Laila work here?" George asked. "No," said Adnan. "First, she'll have to learn English; she's French-educated. Maybe she can help me and Khalid at the office, since she has an associate's degree in accounting, but I think we are going to be focusing on starting a family in the very near future."

"The guy's in a hurry!" said Khalid with a wink to me and George, before saying, half-jokingly, "Hey, Adnan, I just thought of a potential problem: Laila's a Maronite—does she know that I, your best friend and business partner, am a Palestinian Muslim from Jerusalem? Maybe she won't be so happy about that!" Adnan dismissed his question with a smile and a wave of his hand, answering, "Look, as long as you're not a Druze [a religious sect that broke away from Islam in the eleventh century, and whose members have had a history of conflict and competition with Maronite Christians in the Mount Lebanon area of contemporary Lebanon, a region they have shared for the past three centuries], I don't think she'll mind!"

After the waiter had brought us baklava (sweet pastry), I turned to Adnan and said, "I am really happy for you, but I have to admit that this is a big surprise. Forgive me for prying, but what happened to Lisa?"

Adnan took a deep breath, pushed his empty dessert plate aside, and lit a cigarette. "A lot of people are surprised, and many have asked me the same question. It is a complicated story; I guess it all began back in April of this year. One morning I woke up, and realized that it was twenty years to the day since a sniper shot and killed my dad in Beirut during the second year of the war. Then I realized that I am the same age now as he was then: thirty-six. When he was my age, he had already been married for sixteen years and had a fifteen-year-old son and two small daughters; it made me realize how fast time passes, and I started to wonder what I was doing with my life. Okay, I have an M.A. in computer programming, and *nishkur'allah* [thank God], I have a very successful business, but if I knew I was going to die tomorrow, I would have one very big regret: I don't yet have any kids.

"Later that same day, I turned on the news, and heard that Beirut had been attacked for the first time in fourteen years by the Israeli Air Force. Lisa and I were having a dinner party that evening, and I was in a bad mood from remembering my father's death and hearing the news from Beirut. Our guests noticed I wasn't my usual happy and hospitable self. When I tried to explain why the news reports had upset me, they didn't seem very sympathetic. One of Lisa's colleagues—who, as I later discovered, thought I was Mexican!—said, 'Well, that's the Middle East; what do you expect? All those people over there are just a bunch of warring tribes who have been fighting for thousands of years!'

"After the guests had gone, Lisa and I were cleaning up and I told her that her colleague's comment had really bothered me; she said I was being too sensitive. I also told her that I felt it was about time I got married and had children, since the family name and line will die out if I don't continue it. My dad is gone, his two male cousins died during the war, I am the only son, and all my father's brothers had only daughters. After I explained all of this, Lisa just looked at me like I was crazy, and said, 'I hope you have a candidate besides me for childbearing, because I don't plan on sacrificing my art career for motherhood—not now or ever!' That was the beginning of the end of our relationship. Three weeks later, after the hostilities in Lebanon had ended, I called my uncles in Beirut and told them to expect me for a long visit in July."

Khalid, who had been listening sympathetically, remarked, "I don't know how it is for other immigrants to the U.S., but if you're an Arab in America, you can never forget where you come from. Every day, something on the news, or someone's question about your accent, or some remark on television or in a movie about Arabs being terrorists, will always remind you of who you are, the world you left behind, and all of its problems. Adnan and I have been American citizens for more than a decade, and this is a great country which has given us so many opportunities, for which we are grateful, but his heart will always be in Beirut, and mine in Jerusalem. You can never forget your people; their joys are your joys, and when they suffer, you suffer. Any time you can do something for them, whether here or back home, you don't hesitate. Adnan has now realized this, as I did during the *intifada*.

"You should hear the waiter, Hussein's, story of how he felt during the 1991 Gulf War. He's a Shi'a from southern Iraq, and even though he hates Saddam Hussein, he was outraged to see the U.S. and its allies attacking Iraq so forcefully; he took it personally, like his whole self and heritage were being attacked. Once, he was almost beaten up by some American teenagers who started a fight with him on the bus during the war. The poor kid went through a real identity crisis that year!"

Silence enveloped our table as Adnan stared pensively at his empty coffee cup. Dispelling the somber mood, Khalid informed us in a cheerful voice, "Okay, now we are going to tell you how, with the help of Laila's family in Syria and my relatives in Israel, our company is going to corner the computer games market in the new Middle East!" Adnan chuckled and looked at George, who was raising his eyebrows in surprise and curiosity. "If they ever work out a peace agreement in the Middle East," said Adnan, "Khalid and I will have all our networks in place. Some of his cousins are Palestinian citizens of Israel living in Nazareth, one of whom is a computer programmer who is thinking of opening a computer supplies store and training center. Laila's mother is Armenian, and most of her family lives in Syria, especially in Aleppo and Damascus, where they manage a number of bookstores, and from what I hear, business has been very slow there the last couple of years. So, what could be more natural than forming a regional marketing and distribution network with *ibn khal* [male maternal cousin] Khalid in Nazareth and *ibn khal* Laila in Syria? If all goes well, we could make millions!" exclaimed Adnan. "And then we'll make another couple of millions by selling our company to one of the big multinationals that will be eager to get into the Middle East market after a peace agreement!" added Khalid. "If we're lucky, we can both retire before we're fifty, go back to Jerusalem and Beirut, build nice houses, and raise our kids in a cultural environment that has stronger family values than they have here in the U.S.!"

"*Insha'allah!*" (if God wills it), said George with a smile. "Yes, *insha'allah!*" echoed Adnan and Khalid.

Although this conversation among friends took place half a world away from the Middle East, it provides insights into some prevailing social, cultural, political, and economic realities of an important but troubled region of the contemporary world while revealing the extent to which the Middle East is enmeshed in complex and long-standing political and economic relationships with the West. Adnan's story and Khalid's comments illustrate the salient role of kinship and marriage in Middle Eastern societies and also highlight the political and psychological dynamics of ethnicity while hinting at the existence of conflicts within and between countries of the region. Their future business plans reveal mercantile economic patterns and social class structures characteristic of the Middle East, and Khalid's observation about the interests of multinational corporations indicates the extent to which the Middle East is, or soon may be, firmly incorporated into complex global markets that could have a profound impact on the way the peoples of this region, be they Arabs, Turks, or Iranians, Jews, Christians, or Muslims, live their lives in the twenty-first century.

Khalid and Adnan's tracing of kinship connections across state borders hints at the recent imposition of national boundaries that do not coincide with ethnic, religious, or linguistic boundaries (Chapter 2; Zubaida, 1994) and alerts us to the important role of informal, open-ended personal networks in economic and social matters. Last but not least, Khalid and Adnan's lives and careers in the United States reflect prevailing patterns of labor migration while also illustrating the deterritorialization of culture and identity in an era of globalized markets and media (Mitchell, 1989; McMurray, 2002).

This chapter employs an anthropological perspective on kinship, ethnicity, and social class in the contemporary Middle East in order to illustrate the contexts and processes of daily interaction for peoples of the region. Kinship and ethnicity are examined here not as monolithic, unchanging facts, nor as independent variables, but rather as social constructs, adaptive strategies, political resources, and emotionally charged symbolic expressions of belonging. An anthropological approach to any society views human social behavior through the twin lenses of modes of organization (social, economic, and political) and frames of meaning (values, beliefs, ideologies, affect, and worldviews). Kinship and ethnicity are simultaneously modes of organization *and* frames of meaning.

Although the concept of social class seems, at first glance, to be related to economic phenomena, ethnographic field research quickly reveals that collective political goals, the maintenance of key social relationships, and strategic invocations of identity and morality shape individuals' class status and life chances in ways that purely statistical data could never reveal. The sociocultural dimensions of class in the Middle East become particularly clear when we examine informal social networks and an associated, recurrent type of relationship of unequal interdependence found throughout the region: the patron-client tie (Denoeux, 1993; Roniger and Ayata, 1994; Singerman, 1995; Gilsenan, 1996).

Since Middle Eastern societies are hierarchically organized, culturally and ethnically plural, and rooted in highly literate and ancient urban cultures, we cannot examine kinship, ethnicity, and social class as isolates or as phenomena in a vacuum. In the simpler, smaller-scale societies that anthropologists commonly studied in the early twentieth century, kinship was often the primary mode of organization structuring the domains of politics, economics, law, morality, and religion. Kinship, like ethnicity and religion, intertwines and interacts dynamically with many other, often competing modes of organization and frames of meaning in the large-scale, centrally administered, and rapidly urbanizing societies of the region. Formal institutions and legal codes transcending family, faith, and tribe sometimes harmonize with, and sometimes contradict, the frames of meaning and modes of belonging provided by primary identity categories. New organizational and expressive forms, ranging from politicized Islam to hip hop youth culture, are emerging in the cities of the Middle East (and among the Middle Eastern diaspora in European and North American cities) in response to globalized markets and media (McMurray, 2002).

Yet even in the rapidly changing nation-states and burgeoning cities of the contemporary Middle East, kinship as a symbolically rich and morally compelling system of meanings and values retains considerable power to galvanize ideologies, shape perceptions, and guide actions in the realm of politics, commerce, and administration. Symbols of shared blood and belonging help to structure the social and legal classifications that are so crucial for the establishment of large-scale state institutions and organizations (Herzfeld, 1997). Kinship imagery and symbolism have been instrumental in the construction of conceptions of citizenship and national identity in newly formed and externally imposed nation-states lacking broad-based legitimacy (Shryock, 1997; Wedeen, 1999; Joseph, 2000).

Symbols associated with family and blood ties are often used to express issues of rights and power on the local and global stage. In my own research in Nazareth, the largest Arab Palestinian city in Israel, I noted that the sentiments and values associated with close family relations, particularly the nurturing mother-child bond and the egalitarian brother-sister tie, served as models of proper political behavior for the city's Communist-dominated political coalition. Similarly, the community's conception of its relation to the state as a nonassimilating minority group (i.e., non-Jews in a Jewish state) frequently employed metaphors of foster-parenting and stepparent/stepchild relationships to emphasize an unnatural and stilted relationship devoid of strong affective ties of nurturance and belonging. The importance of kinship as a cultural system of meanings was also implicit in another term Communist Party members frequently used to describe Palestinian citizens in Israel: *aytaam* (orphans), particularly following the collapse of the Soviet Union (King-Irani, 2001).

One of the goals of anthropology is to make the strange familiar and the familiar strange. An anthropological approach to the prevailing modes of organization and frames of meaning structuring everyday life in the Middle East may lead us to ask critical questions about Western assumptions, rooted in liberal political traditions, concerning the dividing lines between the individual and the group, the formal and the informal, and the public and the private. Anthropologically informed inquiries go to the very heart of contentious issues of identity, rights, and power that now occupy center stage in Western political and media discussions about the Middle East, and can even illuminate the interactions and connections between the Middle East and the West in ways that may surprise us (Pitcher, 1998; Jean-Klein, 2000; Antoun, 2000; Mamdani, 2002; McMurray, 2002).

To understand the modes of organization and frames of meaning that impact most people's daily lives in the contemporary Middle East, we must first grasp some of the historical, ecological, and administrative contexts of kinship, ethnicity, and social class in the region before discussing how individuals and groups can employ kinship and ethnic identity to access networks of affiliation and assistance not only to make a living, but just as important, to make a meaning, in the face of the rapid changes, conflicting cultural values, and pervasive uncertainties characteristic of the early twenty-first century. Although economic pressures and political instability are certainly not unique to the Middle East, the strategies that the peoples of this region have developed in responding to contemporary challenges draw upon a particular constellation of historical experiences, cultural traditions, religious values, symbolic systems, and modes of socioeconomic organization, all of which distinguish the Middle East from European, Asian, or African sociocultural systems.

■ Persistent Challenges and Adaptive Strategies: The Environmental and Historical Context

Kinship and ethnicity are employed as adaptive strategies to environmental challenges. As modes of organization and identification, they help to define individual and collective rights and duties and allocate resources necessary for survival, whether in rural or urban contexts. For centuries, the most common modes of subsistence in the Middle East were agriculture and horticulture, pastoral nomadism, commerce, and small-scale industry and resource extraction. Although popular stereotypes of the landscapes and peoples of the region usually feature the camels, tents, and caravans distinctive of a nomadic lifestyle, it has been the region's urban settings and institutions that have played a decisive role in shaping the cultures, traditions, and values of the Middle East. After all, it was in the fertile river valleys of the Nile and the Tigris and Euphrates that some of the earliest cities and urban civilizations first emerged, thanks to irrigation and intensive agricultural practices.

Whether living in nomadic, agricultural, or urban settings, however, the peoples of the Middle East have not been strangers to harsh and uncertain environments, whether natural, economic, or political. Inhabiting an ecological zone characterized primarily by semiaridity, steep valleys, rugged mountains, widely separated riparian systems, unpredictable rainfall, and poor soils — as detailed by Ian Manners and Barbara Parmenter in Chapter 2 — Middle Eastern communities were often compelled to combine a variety of modes of subsistence, such as pastoral nomadism, small-scale agriculture, commerce, hunting, and fishing in order to make a living. The resulting mixed economies linked urban, nomadic, and agricultural communities in interdependent (and at times unequal) relationships of reciprocity, redistribution, and market exchange. The lack of large-scale, widespread, and permanent agricultural modes of subsistence rendered the formation of large-scale, enduring, and clearly defined corporate institutions difficult. Social, economic, and administrative structures tended to have shifting borders and negotiable boundaries. Up until the nineteenth century, the region saw a lack of large-scale, long-term, economic integration and the corresponding lack of an enduring, centralized administrative integration of large areas into clearly bounded corporate structures. As a result, local and regional coalitions centering on cities, sects, and families were common modes of organizing political and economic life.

Groups dwelling in this arid and semiarid region elaborated distinctive cultural patterns and sociopolitical institutions that served to minimize the hardships and uncertainties arising from the conditions of their natural environment. Today, as in the past, the peoples of the Middle East remain justly famous for their loyal attachment to their families, distinctive rituals of hospitality and conflict mediation, and effective and flexible kin-based collectivities, such as the lineage and the tribe, which until quite recently performed most of the social, economic, and political functions of rural communities in the absence of centralized state governments (Khoury and Kostiner, 1990; Tapper, 1990).

Although far-flung empires and tribal confederations in the Middle East were replaced by clearly bounded nation-states in the nineteenth and twentieth centuries, and even though the vast majority of nomadic peoples have been sedentarized—settled into villages and cities where they earn a modest living as farmers, skilled and unskilled laborers, or professionals—everyday life in the modern Middle East continues to revolve around family membership to an extent that North Americans usually find surprising. The contemporary Middle East is a region of rich and ancient civilizational heritage and immense human potential. Yet it is also a region beset by political volatility, economic disparities, and ecological vulnerability. Despite the fact that the state bureaucracies of most countries in the region are well entrenched and heavily subsidized, few states have succeeded in distributing resources equitably, administering justice fairly, protecting and advancing the interests of the majority of the people, and thereby winning public support and popular participation through legitimate means. National integration remains a contentious issue throughout much of the region. Most states in the Middle East serve narrow elite interests rather than the common good (Sharabi, 1990; Tibi, 1990; Barakat, 1993; al-Khafaji, 1995).

The overwhelming majority of the region's population does not participate in the economic and political decisionmaking processes that will greatly influence their lives and their children's lives. Middle Eastern states usually rule rather than govern their populaces, employing various degrees of coercion, manipulation, and co-optation to achieve control and compliance. Consequently, the peoples of the Middle East have learned to place their trust in those whom they know well and with whom they share similar interests, goals, and characteristics: their relatives, neighbors, friends, and members of their own ethnic, religious, and linguistic groups (Sayigh, 1981; Singerman, 1995).

The Middle Eastern nation-state, an externally imposed system of sociopolitical organization, still cannot claim the same kind or degree of support, loyalty, and legitimacy that Middle Eastern kin and patron-client networks have always claimed (Zubaida, 1994; Denoeux, 1993; Ayubi, 2001; Joseph, 2000). Even a half century after the nation-state's advent in the region, kinship relations (or relations modeled on a kinship pattern) mediate individuals' personal, economic, and political lives to an extent almost unimaginable to anyone who has grown up in Western Europe or North America.

For example, individuals' interactions with state bodies and governmental bureaucracies take place primarily through patron-client relationships (interdependent but unequal relationships based on an ideology of mutual benefit that reaffirm and reproduce institutionalized hierarchies) mediated by ties of kinship (actual or fictive), political party membership, or ethnic and sectarian affiliation (Cunningham and Sarayrah, 1993). In most Middle Eastern societies, governmental ministries primarily serve those who have connections and contacts (*wasta* in Arabic, *protektzia* in Hebrew). Those who participate in informal networks of interlocking patron-client relationships can traverse physical and social space through their links to individuals and groups on the other side of class, political, and ethnic dividing lines in order to pursue their interests and goals (Denoeux, 1993; Singerman, 1995). Citizenship, an identity category that derives its significance from the jural, formalized relationship of each individual to the nation-state, carries much less emotional, moral, legal, and political weight in the Middle East than do identity categories rooted in ideologies of mutual assistance, moral duty, and group solidarity—that is, kinship, ethnicity, and religion.

Understanding why citizens of Middle Eastern nation-states cling to prestate and subnational primary affiliations (i.e., family, ethnicity and religion) will help us understand the causes of intrastate turmoil and interstate hostilities in a more objective manner than did Adnan's insensitive dinner guest. Discovering how Middle Eastern peoples strategically invoke and manipulate kin ties, ethnic affiliations, and patron-client relationships will give us a new appreciation of the creative and effective means through which individuals and groups survive and thrive in a challenging socioeconomic environment while preparing for future contingencies. To analyze the interrelationship of kinship, ethnicity, and social class formation in the context of the contemporary Middle East, let us first review some key anthropological viewpoints on these important modes of organization and frames of meaning.

■ Kinship

At first glance, it would seem self-evident that kinship is a naturally occurring phenomenon rather than a cultural construct. After all, every living person has or has had kin (relatives), linked to him or her through blood and probably through marriage too. Common sense tells us that biological relationships are a human universal; even "test tube" babies have biological parents, regardless of whether or not they have ever met them. Anthropologists, however, are forever questioning the easy assumptions underlying "common sense." Instead of appraising human phenomena according to its obvious surface characteristics, anthropologists look at human social interaction holistically and relativistically—that is, from every possible angle and in every relevant context, in an effort to understand the totality of human experience and behavior.

The anthropologist's goal is interpretive rather than explanatory. He or she aims to decipher the meanings of the underlying concepts, attitudes, and values that guide people's choices and interactions. These meanings are not visible; they must be inferred from carefully observed behavior over time. Whereas a geneticist would examine DNA (deoxyribonucleic acid) to determine kinship, an anthropologist attends simultaneously to the biological as well as to the cultural, economic, moral, and political dimensions of kin ties. Indeed, one anthropological definition of kinship is that it concerns "biological relationships, culturally defined" (Keesing, 1975). Hence, an anthropologist investigating the kinship system of a particular community will be less concerned with discovering the actual, empirically verifiable genetic links between individuals than with ascertaining how individuals in this community conceive of kinship connections and the extent to which these cultural conceptions influence behaviors among individuals who consider themselves kin.

Although the act of sexual procreation and the phenomenon of birth are human universals, not all human societies interpret and value biological connections in precisely the same way. In societies characterized by bilateral kinship systems, such as found in North America, individuals recognize and value their links to relatives on both their mother's and father's sides of the family equally. In other societies, classified as matriarchies, only an individual's maternal relatives will be recognized for economic, social, and political purposes.

In North American society, individuals consider children of their mother's siblings (maternal cousins) to occupy the same social category and moral status as children of their father's siblings (paternal cousins). A particular set of cultural expectations and values guide interactions between cousins in North America (Schneider, 1968). Cousins are people you enjoy seeing; you feel a connection to them that is stronger than friendship but not as complicated or demanding as the tie between siblings. Very few people in North America would contemplate marrying a first cousin. In fact, such a marriage would be illegal in some U.S. states.

In the Middle East, however, people can and do marry their first cousins; in some communities, the union of a man and his father's brother's daughter is still considered to be the preferred marriage choice (Murphy and Kasdan, 1959; Abu-Lughod, 1986). Maternal and paternal cousins are distinctly different categories in the Middle East. An individual will behave differently toward his female paternal cousin than he does toward his female maternal cousin, and the tone of his relationship to a male paternal cousin is likely to be more formal, reserved, and subdued, whereas mutual affection and joking usually characterize his relationship with a male maternal cousin. To understand the reasons for differential treatment of maternal and paternal kin and marriage preferences in the Middle East, we must examine the observed patterns of kinship relations as a system, in this case one that is patrilineal.

Anthropologists researching Middle Eastern societies as widely separated as Morocco and Iran have identified several key characteristics of kinship in the region. Middle Eastern kinship systems are patrilineal (determining membership, defining rights, and allocating resources based on blood ties through fathers, sons, brothers, and uncles), extended, patriarchal, hierarchical, and often endogamous (Murphy and Kasdan, 1959; H. Geertz, 1979; Abu-Lughod, 1986; Barakat, 1993; Joseph, 1994). The extended family plays a crucial economic, political, and socializing role in Middle Eastern societies. Within the family, authority and respect are accorded to men and elderly family members of both sexes, who, occupying the top positions in the family hierarchy, wield more power, prestige, and rights than female family members and children of either sex.

The Middle Eastern family is not an egalitarian structure. Men's and women's roles are considered to be complementary and integrative, not equal. Men are the primary decisionmakers and breadwinners, and they usually control material resources, although women have always exercised more power within the family "behind the scenes" than is immediately apparent (Abu-Lughod, 1986; H. Geertz, 1979; Friedl, 1991; Bahloul, 1992; Peteet, 1991; Sayigh, 1994; Mundy, 1995; Singerman, 1995; Kapchan, 1996; Jean-Klein, 2000; Joseph, 2000). Traditionally, a man's overarching responsibility has been to lead, protect, and provide for his family completely. A woman's primary role has been to make a comfortable home, oversee all aspects of the private, domestic sphere, and bear and nurture children.

As Lisa Taraki discusses in Chapter 11, however, gender roles in the Middle East, as in the rest of the world, are undergoing rapid changes as a result of increased education, rapid urbanization, new economic configurations, and the employment of women. Nonetheless, Middle Eastern men and women continue to place a high value not on their own personal achievements, but rather on their family affiliations in general and on their roles as generators of new families in particular. In other words, men's and women's roles as parents are more important and valued than virtually any other role they can fulfill. Young people in most Middle Eastern societies are not considered to be truly adult until they have completed the important rites of passage of marriage and parenthood. Westerners visiting Middle Eastern societies are invariably asked about their marital status, and women who are still unmarried or married and not yet mothers after the age of twenty-five will find themselves repeatedly explaining their unusual single or childless state to their concerned Middle Eastern hosts (Fernea, 1969; Singerman, 1995).

An oft-noted characteristic of Middle Eastern kinship systems is the practice of endogamous marriage, or marriage between men and women belonging to the same kinship group. As previously mentioned, a preferred form of marriage in the Middle East has traditionally been that between a man and his father's brother's daughter (*bint 'amm* in Arabic), henceforth abbreviated as the "FBD marriage preference." Because Middle Eastern kinship systems are patrilineal, that is, based on ties of agnation and descent traced through paternal relatives, a man and his FBD are always members of the same lineage. In anthropological terminology, cousins in this category of relationship to each other are known as parallel cousins. The daughters of a man's mother's brother usually do not belong to his patrilineage; anthropologists refer to this category of cousins as cross cousins.

Marriages can and do take place between both categories of cousins in the Middle East, and many scholars have noted that endogamy refers more to an ideological preference than an actual practice. For instance, the Lebanese anthropologist Fuad Khuri (1970), conducting research among Muslim residents of Beirut in the late 1960s, discovered that only 11 percent of marriages in his sample were endogamous (FBD) marriages. My research among Palestinian citizens of Israel in Nazareth in 1992–1993 indicated that less than 10 percent of a sample of 341 households consisted of spouses who were parallel cousins (King-Irani, 2001).

Given the prevalence of labor migration and rapidly increasing urbanization in the region (see Chapter 9), extended families of grandparents, parents, brothers, sisters, cousins, aunts, and uncles living under the same roof and sharing the same resources are less and less common. In the major cities of the Middle East, where the bulk of the region's population now lives, anthropologists have discovered that unions between members of the same neighborhood, sect, ethnic group, and social class compose the overwhelming majority of marriages. Hence, a form of sociocultural, if not familial, endogamy still persists in the region because families prefer that their sons and daughters marry individuals whose social backgrounds and kinship networks are well known to them (al-Akhras, 1976; Singerman, 1995). Adnan's fiancée's family, for instance, readily accepted his proposal of marriage, despite the short period of time that Adnan and Laila had known one another. Such acceptance would have been less forthcoming if Adnan had not been a part of Laila's larger kinship network.

Endogamous marriage patterns, which are practiced by very few cultures outside the Middle East, stem not from exotic cultural beliefs, a peculiar mentality, or unquestioned obedience to ancient traditions, but rather from a desire to enhance and strengthen the group's internal solidarity and external boundaries. Endogamy is a strategy for retaining individuals' loyalty and commitment, as well as their wealth (whether in the form of bridewealth, productive property, or inheritances), within the family circle, widely defined. Such desires and strategies are indices of a long historical experience of economic scarcity, harsh environmental conditions, political uncertainty, and pronounced competition for limited resources in this vast, semiarid zone. The interplay of these ecological, political, and economic factors has at times engendered an atmosphere of unpredictability and mistrust in Middle Eastern societies (Schneider, 1971; Meeker, 1979).

In examining the patrilineal nature of Middle Eastern kinship systems, we must look beyond the domain of the nuclear family's domestic concerns to the public realm of the community's political and economic interests, which are greatly affected and conditioned by the natural and human environments. As one anthropologist notes, "kinship is the dominant mode of forming the larger groupings central to social and political life in pre-industrial societies. Kinship provides solutions to ecological and organizational challenges in space and time" (Keesing, 1975:8).

The choice of the patrilineage as the key sociopolitical mode of organization in the Middle East was not arbitrary, since "unilineal descent groups [whether matrilineal or patrilineal] were a crucial development in the evolution of tribal societies. They provided an adaptive solution in different ecological settings to the problem of maintaining political order and defining rights to land and other resources across the generations" (Keesing, 1975:24). Nomadic, agricultural, and urban communities all evidenced patrilineal modes of organization and frames of meaning. Kinship was an idiom, a language, for expressing and negotiating economic and political relationships and assigning groups their roles within regional administrative arrangements. The lives of nomads, farmers, and city-dwellers were always in actual or potential contact, and their respective interests were occasionally in conflict (Ibn Khaldun, 1967; Nelson, 1973; Khoury and Kostiner, 1990).

In the absence of a strong, centralized governmental administration, well-armed, roving bedouin tribes (i.e., coalitions of patrilineages claiming descent from a common, distant ancestor) could easily sweep into poorly defended agricultural settlements mounted on their formidable camels and take goods, crops, livestock, and other forms of wealth by force. Some nomadic tribes coalesced into powerful federations capable of extracting payments of tribute (in effect, protection money) from sedentary villagers over a very wide area. In some cases, wealthy urban elites formed alliances with leaders of bedouin tribal federations in an effort to extract maximum economic resources from the land and people in the countryside, thus controlling the political dynamics of an entire region (Khoury and Kostiner, 1990; Barakat, 1993).

Pastoral nomadism as a primary mode of subsistence is now rare in the Middle East. A lifestyle that requires constant movement does not mesh with the needs and requirements of nation-states demarcated by well-defended, often impassable borders. Pastoral modes of subsistence continue, but the rapid and dramatic urbanization and proletarianization of the region's population eclipse them. Yet the traditional values and practices of tribally based groupings have left a deep imprint on Middle Eastern culture, society, and politics, as evidenced by oral and written literature, everyday morality, and the phenomenon of "fictive kinship" ties that link friends, colleagues, neighbors, and business partners through relationships that have the emotional closeness and moral implications of actual blood relations.

The patrilineal descent groups found throughout Middle Eastern society had their genesis thousands of years ago as an adaptive response to the interrelated ecological and political conditions of the region (Schneider, 1971; Meeker, 1979). Pastoral nomadism, previously a key component of the region's mixed economy, is a strenuous mode of subsistence that both demands and frustrates cooperative, interdependent social relations. Pastoral nomadism requires the careful and timely coordination of different activities by different people. If the needs of the herds and flocks are not met, they and the human community dependent upon them for its livelihood can easily perish. Members of nomadic groups are thus willing to pitch in for the common good and extend themselves magnanimously if the situation demands brave and generous behavior. But in this arid and unpredictable ecological zone, people also had to be selfish and calculating at times in order to survive. This fact "places heavy burdens on interpersonal relations, for everyone must think first of his immediate household's interests and needs and resist undue claims for assistance from kinsmen and friends" (Schneider, 1971:5). Among pastoral nomads, the immediate need for water may well outweigh compelling claims of blood ties.

The natural environment in which pastoral nomads live is clearly harsh and uncertain. The social environment is also threatening since it is highly competitive. It is thus imperative for all pastoral nomadic peoples to institute

> organizational solutions to the compelling ecological problem of regulating access of humans and animals to natural resources. . . . Migratory groups cannot establish rights to land on a permanent basis, or fence it off against incursions. Raiding and animal theft are therefore endemic. . . . The determination of boundary lines is subject to continual human intervention; the definition of the group is problematic as well: social boundaries are difficult to maintain, and internal loyalties are questionable. . . . Individuals and groups are at once . . . vulnerable and opportunistic. (Schneider, 1971:24)

The organizational solution instituted by peoples of the Middle East to the challenges presented to them by their difficult environment consisted of adopting a social, political, and moral idiom (i.e., symbol system and rhetorical discourse) of paternal blood relationship: the patrilineage. Members of a patrilineage could invoke their blood connections to other individuals and groups in order to obtain mutual support, defense, assistance, and protection in their unending struggle to eke a living out of the harsh environment. Patrilineal principles also facilitated the equitable division of wealth in inheritances, thus limiting the likelihood of contention and destructive conflict among surviving heirs, whose continuing cooperation was imperative for their own and their families' survival.

Depending on the need or the task at hand, nomadic peoples could employ patrilineal ideologies and rhetoric in order to mobilize groups ranging from a person's immediate male kin (brothers, father, grandfather, sons, uncles, and cousins) to a huge tribal federation numbering thousands of individuals representing many different patrilineages related through a distant founding (or "apical") ancestor. Yet since the natural environment could not support a large number of nomads and their animals living at the same place for any significant length of time, Middle Eastern patrilineages never developed into the sustained, enduring, clearly bounded unilineal descent groups found in more temperate and fertile ecological zones. Rather than becoming corporations, Middle Eastern kin groups were shifting coalitions that could be forged and broken, quickly and repeatedly, according to the relevant context and prevailing interests. Anthropologists term this process *segmentation,* and many social scientists characterize Middle Eastern societies as segmentary because of the prevalence of many similar yet differentiated components (e.g., families, lineages, guilds, ethnic groups, or sects) that can coalesce to cooperate or fragment to fight in the unending struggle for scarce and valuable resources.

Kinship, as an idiom of identity and social organization no less than as a basis of affiliation, protection, and cooperative action, is just as important in the Middle East today as it was hundreds of years ago. A person's identity as a member of a kin group entitles him or her to rights and services, just as it entails making considerable sacrifices for the sake of the group. In spite of the establishment of nation-states in the postcolonial period, often the primary identification of the peoples of the Middle East is not civil, religious, or even ethnic, but familial. For instance, the kingdom of Saudi Arabia is often called "the house of Saud" in recognition of its roots in a particular kinship grouping. Syria is and Iraq was run by tightly knit, patrilineal coalitions of brothers and cousins; indeed, the Iraqi government under Saddam Hussein was known, in diplomatic circles, as "the Tikriti regime" after the name of the Sunni Muslim village in north-central Iraq from which Saddam Hussein and his family hailed. It is instructive to note that both Syria's Bashar al-Assad and Iraq's Hussein are members of religious minority groups in their own countries. Sunni Muslims are the majority community in Syria, where al-Assad's Alawite community holds the decisive reins of power; in Iraq, a majority population of Shi'a lived under the rule of Hussein, a Sunni, for more than two decades. These two leaders' rise to the top posts in their countries in spite of their minority status speaks volumes about the strength and efficacy of kin ties and networks in Middle Eastern societies and polities.

As a strategy for survival, the patrilineal kinship system has certainly proved flexible and effective over many centuries under a variety of social, economic, and political conditions in the Middle East. What began as an adaptive response to ecological and social limitations gradually became a valued institution embodying a rich cultural complex of expectations, attitudes, val-

ues, beliefs, rituals, and behaviors. The distinctive kinship systems and practices of the Middle East are a valued part of the region's civilizational heritage. Kinship is implicated in nearly every aspect of life and most social institutions, including religion and morality. Michael Meeker speculates that "the
cultural uniformity which we now find in the arid zone does not reflect the traditions of a people bent on violence. On the contrary, it reflects . . . a moral
response to the threat of political turmoil" (1979:19).

Despite the changes in urbanization, modernization, and emigration
detailed by Valentine Moghadam in Chapter 9, individuals are still judged primarily by how they perform their family duties. An individual's identity, decisions, and social reputation are profoundly influenced by his or her kin group.
Adnan, for instance, decided to marry not for love but to discharge his responsibilities to his family, since he was the sole surviving male capable of carrying on his patrilineage's name, a decision that his U.S. girlfriend found
strange.

Not all anthropological studies of kinship in the Middle East center on the
politics of patrilineal competition, however. Since the late 1970s, a growing
number of ethnographies of Middle Eastern communities have taken women's
lives, domesticity, reproduction, and sexuality as their point of departure (H.
Geertz, 1979; Abu-Lughod, 1986; Inhorn, 2003; Mundy, 1995; Joseph, 1994;
Peteet, 1991; Singerman, 1995; Kahn, 2000; Kanaaneh, 2002). The majority of
these ethnographies have been written by women, and most are influenced by
feminist and postmodern theories emphasizing the contentiousness of power
relations, the mutability of identity, and the social construction of gender (i.e.,
sexual differences, culturally defined). By including the perspectives and
voices of women in ethnographic depictions of daily life in Middle Eastern
societies, these ethnographers have highlighted important questions about how
power is conceptualized and deployed in the most intimate spaces of everyday
life. A recurring theme in these works centers on strategies of resistance to hierarchical power arrangements and the elaboration of counternarratives that
challenge and occasionally subvert dominant narratives that legitimate the
patriarchal status quo (Abu-Lughod, 1986; Layoun, 1999).

Gender-oriented kinship studies have enriched our understanding of the
symbolic and interactive processes that produce and reproduce the structures
and categories of everyday life, while showing how and where changes and
contradictions emerge by tracing these developments through the experience,
choices, and negotiations of individuals' interactions. Gendered studies of
kinship and family also highlight the affective and moral frames of meaning,
in addition to the economic and political modes of organization, associated
with kinship. As such, these studies show the interrelationship of men's and
women's worlds and lives, no less than the connections and interrelationships
between the intimate domain of the household and the public domain of governance and resource distribution (Singerman, 1995).

Let us now examine another adaptive strategy of contemporary Middle Eastern societies, which like kinship centers on the individual's identification and affiliation with extensive and potentially far-reaching networks. Through these connections, one can construct meaningful moral boundaries while obtaining access to power, protection, and resources in a highly competitive socioeconomic and political environment.

■ Ethnicity

It is easy to assume that ethnic differences are essentially racial differences and thus to conclude that ethnic groups are determined and delimited largely by biological criteria such as hair, skin and eye color, height, and physique, and only further distinguished by such characteristics as language, cultural patterns, and religious faith. Scholars examining the phenomenon of ethnicity, however, note that it is a strategic, more so than a genetic, phenomenon (Cohen, 1978; Royce, 1982; Anderson, 1993; Eller and Coughlan, 1993). Ethnic identity, whether referring to subjective criteria (an individual's awareness of and feelings about his or her membership in a particular ethnic category) or objective criteria (others' categorization of an individual on the basis of physical or cultural characteristics), cannot exist in a homogeneous society in which everyone shares the same cultural, religious, class, and linguistic background. Ethnicity and ethnic identity are oppositional and relational phenomena par excellence; they emerge only in societies comprising different types of peoples from a wide variety of backgrounds. Ethnicity is a product of plural societies characterized by cultural, economic, linguistic, or religious heterogeneity. Due to migration from rural to urban areas and the impact of enhanced communications and transportation systems, individuals and groups from a wide variety of cultural, linguistic, socioeconomic, and religious backgrounds are suddenly brought into contact.

Ethnicity, with its affective, symbolic, and political dimensions, has been a key topic of anthropological inquiry for decades. Urban anthropologists have tended to approach ethnic groups as "subcultures" (Hannerz, 1980), and the past thirty-five years have witnessed a gradual shift from primordialist theories of ethnicity, which view ethnic identity as somehow inborn, innate, and ascribed (Geertz, 1969; Fishman, 1980), to constructivist, utilitarian, and circumstantialist theories (Barth, 1969; Cohen, 1974; Royce, 1982), which view ethnicity as rooted in political processes and as constructed, strategic, and even achieved identity categories. The latter theoretical approach holds that ethnic identity is not a state of being, nor a "noun," but rather a verb (identifying with an ethnic group) that can be viewed from the bottom up or the top down. Bottom-up identification processes are evident in resistance movements and coalition building. Top-down identification processes are visible in state policies and legislation defining the boundaries between, and hierarchies among, groups characterized by particular cultural, linguistic, and religious characteristics. Both of these perspectives on identification processes depict ethnicity as a political phenomenon found in complex societies having centralized systems of political and economic administration.

In the rapidly growing cities of the Middle East, various ethnic groups interact and compete with one another in new and often alienating sociopolitical contexts characterized by economic scarcity and uneven development. The recognition of ethnic differences thus implies the recognition of economic and political differences as well. Depending on administrative frameworks of governance and the economic status of the groups involved, individuals' growing awareness of relative and absolute economic differences can easily lead to conflict, competition, and opposition organized along ethnic lines. As anthropologist Ronald Cohen notes, "Ethnicity is . . . one of the many outcomes of group interaction in which there is differential power between dominant and minority groups. From this perspective, ethnicity is an aspect of stratification, rather than a problem on its own" (1978:386).

The categorization of individuals or groups according to their ethnic identity and membership is a salient feature of most contemporary complex societies. What is crucial are not cultural, religious, or linguistic differences per se, but rather the structured arrangement of relationships between the different groups, and most notably, the administrative and economic frameworks in which these various groups are encapsulated. The vertical integration of ethnic groups in the context of new nation-states may be complementary or conflictual (Denoeux, 1993), but either way, what creates tension or harmony is not the supposedly essential cultural attributes or traditional customs of various groups, but rather the institutionalized structure of relationships between them. Are they egalitarian or hierarchical? Symmetrical or asymmetrical? Are differences codified in law such that identity becomes ineluctable and determinative of one's rights, duties, and life chances, as is the situation for many ethnic and religious minority groups in the new nation-states of the Middle East? If so, conflicts are likely to result.

One of the greatest analytical and methodological challenges facing sociologists and anthropologists conducting research on societies of the non-Western developing world lies in determining the dividing lines (if any) between ethnic groups, kinship groups, and socioeconomic classes (Barakat, 1993). Ethnicity in the Middle East presents many definitional and methodological challenges for researchers since ethnic groups often behave like kin-based tribal groupings, especially in the way they mobilize their members by invoking a shared identity in some contexts, while segmenting into competing groups in other contexts. At the same time, ethnic differences seem to correspond closely to socioeconomic distinctions.

For instance, in Israeli society, Western-oriented Ashkenazi Jews, although numerically the minority community, are the dominant class in terms of wealth and control of the state's decisionmaking bodies in comparison with the more numerous Sephardic (or Mizrachi) Jews, who come from Arab countries and whose cultural attitudes and practices have long been looked down upon by Ashkenazi Jews. Prior to the convulsions of the Lebanese civil war (1975–1990), the wealthy power brokers and owners of factories, banks, and businesses in Lebanon were usually Maronite Christians, whereas the poorer, less powerful, agricultural communities in Lebanon tended to be populated by Shiʻa Muslims.

There are, of course, exceptions to these correlations between class, ethnicity, and kinship. Only sustained and fine-grained research can elucidate the dynamic interrelationships of kinship, class, and ethnicity in the contemporary Middle East. Most social scientists consider ethnic political organizations and activities key phenomena of the modern world. Some scholars forecast the further solidification and entrenchment of ethnic and cultural identities as competition and conflict over limited goods increase throughout the world (Huntington, 1996). These recent predictions of social unrest and political violence between different cultural groups stand in stark contrast to the expectations of an earlier generation of academics and policymakers who, in the post–World War II era, expressed confidence that the universal adoption of a modernizing, liberal, secular, and technologically advanced culture and social system would facilitate homogenization and harmonization between different peoples within and between states. What these optimistic observers left out of their social equations were cultural dissonance, alienation, relative and absolute economic deprivation, the unequal distribution of resources, and differences in the types and amounts of power available to various ethnic groups in any given society. It is not the differences in cultural practices, religious beliefs, or linguistic characteristics that cause friction between members of opposing ethnic communities. Rather, "inequality, not ethnicity, is the basis of social stratification" and thus conflict (Cohen, 1978:400).

If Middle Eastern kin-based institutions like patrilineages and the tribe were the primary adaptive responses to the ecological challenges and socioeconomic problems of intense competition over scarce resources in a harsh natural environment, then the ethnic group is the chief survival strategy of the politically marginalized individual in the harsh social and economic environments of the contemporary Middle East. Torn loose from the familiar moorings of village, home, and family as a result of poverty or war, struggling to make a decent living in crowded, impoverished, and poorly serviced cities, and underrepresented by or provided for by a concerned government, the average individual in the contemporary Middle East is likely to feel lost, lonely, alienated, and powerless. If he or she cannot find kin or people from his or her region to provide guidance, mutual assistance, and support, an uprooted individual will most likely turn to other individuals and groups with whom he or she shares some common background characteristics, values, orientations, and goals. Hence we see the development of the ethnoreligious

A fraction of the ethnic diversity that is in the Middle East

Egypt

Yemen

Syria

Israel

Lebanon

West Bank

Kuwait

group, which performs some of the same functions as the tribe but is neither based entirely on blood relationships nor as clearly bounded in terms of its membership as is the tribe. An organized and mobilized ethnic group or religious sect may serve the economic, social, and political needs of its members far better than the state apparatus of many Middle Eastern countries.

At the beginning of the twentieth century, city-dwellers accounted for less than 10 percent of the total population of the Middle East. As Moghadam describes in Chapter 9, urbanization has increased dramatically in recent decades, and studies by the UN predict that urban populations will reach 80 percent of the total for the Middle East within the next decade. Thus the current trend of relying on family and ethnoreligious ties to survive in Middle Eastern cities is likely to continue. Cohen succinctly describes how comforting and empowering an ethnic reference group and support network can be to such displaced young people:

> If alienation is a malfunction of modern society, then ethnicity is an antidote. ... Ethnicity provides a fundamental and multifaceted link to a category of others that very little else can do in modern society. ... In a multiethnic society in which a plurality of groups, ethnic and non-ethnic, vie for scarce rewards, stressing individual human rights leads ultimately to unequal treatment. ... Individuals are fated to obtain more rewards because of their group identities. Organized ethnic groups can fight for equal rights. (1978: 401–402)

In other words, an ethnic group is not simply a racial unit or a cultural unit but also a political unit. Ethnic groups are interest groups; they are structured to serve the various needs of affiliated members while competing with other interest groups for the limited resources to be obtained within the framework of the modern state. The group that can mobilize the greatest numbers of supporters and patrons, deliver the highest number of voters during elections, forge the strongest links with powerful groups within or without the society, and devise the most compelling and convincing arguments to advance its rights to resources, political posts, or economic redress will take the lion's share of the services, governmental posts, protection, and wealth that can be extracted from the state. Indeed, in the Middle East, a well-organized and ambitious ethnic or religious group can even take complete control of the entire state apparatus, as did the Alawites of Syria and the Sunnis of Iraq in the early 1970s.

■ The Historical Context of Ethnicity

In the Middle East, ethnic groups and officially recognized ethnoreligious identity categories predate the creation of the region's nation-states. Prior to the advent of the nation-state system in the Middle East and even before the colonial era, most of the peoples of the region (with the exception of those living in Morocco and Iran) lived under Ottoman rule in the sociopolitical framework of a vast, decentralized empire. Day-to-day matters of administration and basic governance were in the hands of local political elites chosen by the Ottoman leadership, as well as the local clergy. As an empire, the Ottoman system was organized not according to ethnic or national principles and categories but according to religious distinctions. Individuals living in the Ottoman Empire did not identify themselves as Ottomans, Turks, Arabs, or Kurds, but rather as Muslims, Christians, Jews, or Druze. Within this system of organization, Muslims were in the majority, both in terms of absolute numbers and in terms of privilege, rank, status, and opportunities. Christians and Jews were formally recognized as religious minorities.

Considered "Peoples of the Book" and categorized as *dhimmi* communities (literally meaning "on the conscience" of the larger and more powerful Muslim community), Christians and Jews were supposed to be protected from harm or persecution by the majority Muslim community in return for their acceptance of a subordinate status, payment of a special tax *(jizyah),* and abstention from any public display of their religious practices such as processions and liturgical ceremonies. As long as the non-Muslim communities obeyed Ottoman laws and paid their taxes, they were supposed to be left unmolested to conduct their lives alongside the Muslim community. *Dhimmi* communities were under the jurisdiction of Islamic courts in criminal cases and some property disputes but obeyed the jurisdiction of their own communities' religious laws and precepts concerning any issues related to religious and family matters. As non-Muslims, Christians, Druze, and Jews were not subject to the rulings of *sharia* in matters of personal status such as marriage, divorce, inheritance, and other family issues. Instead, Christian sects and Druze and Jewish communities sought guidance, mediation, and rulings from their own religious hierarchy, the leaders of which had the power to make binding judicial decisions in the domain of family law and to represent their religious communities in official dealings with the Ottoman authorities. As detailed by Arthur Goldschmidt in Chapter 3, this system of legally recognized non-Muslim communal autonomy was known as the *millet* system (meaning "people" or "community" in Turkish).

As this brief historical overview indicates, the Middle East has always been culturally heterogeneous. During the Ottoman era, the rugged mountainous areas of the eastern Mediterranean became a refuge for a variety of Christian and Islamic religious sects and splinter groups seeking to escape persecution by orthodox religious authorities. Dwelling high atop these mountains, minority groups such as the Maronites, Druze, Shi'a, and Alawites could pursue their religious traditions free of interference from either Christian or Muslim authorities. The plural nature of Middle Eastern urban areas is inscribed in the very towers, walls, and gates that marked off the various named quarters of traditional urban settlements, such as the "Muslim Quarter," "Armenian Quarter," "Jewish Quarter," "Orthodox Quarter," and so on, as we find in such ancient cities as Jerusalem, Cairo, Damascus, Istanbul, and Baghdad. A division of labor among these distinct communities paralleled the spatial separation of different religious and ethnic groups in the traditional Middle Eastern city.

Christians, Muslims, and Jews occupied different professional categories in the Ottoman social and economic structure. The traditional city's division of labor was usually characterized by accommodation, complementarity, and integration rather than by competition and conflict. Muslims held positions in religious courts and schools as well as in the military and in local governmental administration, and non-Muslims served primarily as doctors, merchants, advisers, artisans, and religious and legal specialists for their own sectarian communities. The Ottoman division of labor is recorded to this day in the names of many Christian families from Lebanon, Palestine, and Syria, which designate the professional and artisan roles that their ancestors played in Ottoman society: *sabbagh* (dyer), *hakim* (doctor), *khabbaz* (baker), *banna* (builder), *sayigh* (goldsmith), *hayek* (weaver), *najjar* (carpenter), *khoury* (priest), and *shammas* (sexton).

The cultural and religious heterogeneity of the Middle East did not result from rapid urbanization or the establishment of nation-states in the twentieth century, nor is it a byproduct of colonialism (although colonial powers certainly employed tactics based on a policy of "divide and rule" to consolidate their control of local political systems). Different ethnic and religious groups have been living side by side in the great cities of the Middle East for centuries, sometimes in conflict but more often than not in harmony. What *is* new in the ethnic and religious configuration of the contemporary Middle East is the encapsulating social, political, and economic framework in which different groups live, work, and struggle. The relatively recent political processes that led to the region's incorporation into the global economy and then to the establishment of nation-states have altered the traditional balance of power and the system of accommodation that had prevailed during the Ottoman era (Makdisi, 2000). Although the Ottoman Empire was hardly a model of economic efficiency or social justice, it nonetheless encouraged a relatively stable and viable form of accommodation and cooperation among the region's diverse ethnic and religious groupings.

To understand how the various ethnic and religious communities of the Middle East became embroiled in conflicts that are still continuing, we must now examine the historical processes of social class formation, which exacerbated competition and thus engendered conflicts between the different ethnic communities of the region.

■ Social Class

Unlike the identity categories of kinship and ethnicity, social class is not based on biological or cultural criteria, but rather on economic and political differences. Like ethnic groups, social classes are oppositional phenomena: a social class cannot exist except in relation to other social classes, since the idea of a class entails a hierarchical arrangement of groups based on differences of wealth, power, and control over resources. A society whose members all share the same resources equally, own wealth in common, participate fully in all decisionmaking, and have equal rights and duties in relation to one another would be a classless society. The distinguishing criteria of any social class structure are inequalities of wealth and differential access to resources and means of economic production. Thus, class distinctions entail relationships of dominance and subordination between different competing groups, each of which continually strives to improve its relative position, or having attained a position of relative advantage, struggles to retain it.

According to social historian Philip Khoury, the social class structure of the Middle East was relatively simple and stable until the middle of the nineteenth century. Just 150 years ago, the Middle East began to be integrated into the capitalist world system. Consequently, new social classes gradually emerged as a result of changing modes of economic production and new forms of ownership and control of resources (Khoury, 1983). The most significant economic change during the nineteenth century was the advent of new forms of landownership. Following a series of military and economic defeats at the hands of rising European powers, the Ottoman leadership decided to institute a number of administrative reforms in an effort to improve and strengthen the Ottoman system by imitating European societies and governments.

Chief among these reforms were new land laws that encouraged private rather than communal ownership of productive property. Muslim and non-Muslim elites favored by the Ottoman rulers benefited from these reforms by taking control of formerly communal properties, on which they planted cash crops such as tobacco in place of subsistence crops. This agricultural regime served the interests of international markets rather than the needs of the local populace. At the same time, merchants (often Christians and Jews) in cities such as Beirut, Damascus, Acre, Cairo, Alexandria, and Ladhakia began to earn a considerable profit as middlemen overseeing trade between European producers of goods and newly wealthy Middle Eastern consumers of fine furnishings, clothing, household equipment, and medicines. This shift from local to foreign markets for consumer goods had a debilitating effect on local artisans and manufacturers, who, along with peasants displaced from agricultural lands by private landownership, high taxation, and wars, became members of a new social class formation: the urban proletariat. This period marked the advent of a sharply pyramidal class structure characterized by the political and economic domination of a large mass of impoverished people by a handful of extremely wealthy landowning families.

Although markets and modes of production have changed dramatically since the mid–nineteenth century, the social and economic class structure of the Middle East is still profoundly pyramidal. Despite the omnipresent stereotype of the super-rich Arab oil shaikh, the vast majority of people in the region live at or below the poverty line, and only a handful of people own and control considerable wealth derived from the oil industry, its subsidiaries, and the consumption habits of the oil-producing elite. Economic activity in the region as a whole consists of consumption more than production, and the exchange of goods and services between countries of the region is limited, resulting in poor regional economic integration and heightened dependency on Western goods and services (World Bank, 1996).

A close examination of the economies of the region quickly reveals a glaring absence of industry and manufacturing in most countries, with the exception of oil-related industries in the Gulf region, computer and military industries in Israel, and a variety of industrial activities in Turkey. By and large, the countries of the region consume much more than they produce. Agriculture is underdeveloped in Lebanon and Syria, countries that could technically produce significant amounts of agricultural goods; hence, most foodstuffs are imported and therefore too expensive for the average family to afford on a daily basis (World Bank, 1996).

Investments of oil revenues within the region have traditionally been limited. Until recently, well-to-do oil-producing countries preferred to invest their money in Europe and North America (Makdisi, 1991), thus limiting economic diversification and the expansion of bases of production in the region. Commercial revenue from tourism has been limited due to a series of wars and continuing political tensions, and particularly after the advent of the al-Aqsa intifada in 2000 and the Al-Qaida attacks on the United States in 2001. The pronounced reliance on oil revenue has increased the region's economic vulnerability to external developments and decisions. Indeed, the countries of the Middle East are very dependent on economic and political decisions emanating from outside the region. Hence, "their economic autonomy, defined as their ability to develop independently and/or to take policy actions without regard to developments and reactions elsewhere, is greatly constrained. . . . This economic dependence implies political dependence" (Makdisi, 1991: 133).

As a result of the poor performance of the oil sector since the mid-1980s, countries throughout the region have felt the effects of falling oil prices in the form of decreasing remittance payments sent back to countries such as Syria, Lebanon, Egypt, and Jordan by migrant workers in the Gulf, particularly after the Gulf War of 1991. Even before the fall in oil prices, poverty in the region was already pronounced: in 1980, approximately 44 percent of the population in Morocco and Egypt were living below the poverty line (Barakat, 1993); the situation has improved little since then. During the past two decades, the Arab world has seen a

> progressive decline, or perhaps near elimination, of subsistence production, massive occupational shifts from agrarian to service . . . activities; a massive exodus of surplus rural labor to urban conglomerations [while at the same time witnessing] the rise of a new Arab bourgeoisie, a class of contractors, middlemen, brokers, agents of foreign corporations, and wheeler-dealers . . . typically engaged in nonproductive work. (Farsoun and Zacharia, 1995:273)

In the narrow space between the upper class (those few who possess and control great wealth) and the lower class (the millions of impoverished former peasants who are constantly streaming into the crowded urban areas of the region), we find the only productive sector of Middle Eastern society: a relatively small middle class composed primarily of small-scale commercial enterprises, self-employed merchants, repairmen, artisans, teachers, some white-collar professionals, and government employees. The members of this weak and vulnerable socioeconomic formation have discovered that remaining middle class requires a concerted family effort. Hence the patrilineal kinship group that emerged as a strategic adaptation to desert conditions so long ago is once again the basic productive unit among the urban middle classes in the modern Middle East. As Samih Farsoun notes, "[R]ent income, small business income, and income from wages and other labor have emerged as key sources for an increasing number of multiple income families. . . . Most of these petty economic activities are traditional in style of organization and in the social relations of work, i.e., patriarchal and patronage" (1988:224).

■ Kinship, Ethnicity, and Class in Context: Strategies or Straitjackets?

Negatively affected by social and political transformations and economic restructuring at the local, regional, and international levels, particularly in the post–Cold War era, individuals in the Middle East have turned to their nuclear and extended families for support and mutual assistance. They have reactivated and emphasized traditional family structures, kinship networks, affiliations to ethnoreligious groups, and ties of patronage even as they have embraced the latest developments of modern technology, such as cellular telephones and the Internet. Consequently, the contemporary Middle East is a world of startling contradictions and ironic juxtapositions.

Halim Barakat reflects that it is very difficult for observers to interpret socioeconomic developments in the region because "the contemporary Arab economic order is a peculiar cluster of different modes of production, all operating at once, which renders it simultaneously semi-feudal, semi-socialist, and semi-capitalist" (1993:77). The existence, side-by-side, of patrilineages and multinational corporations, rationalized bureaucracies and religious brotherhoods, modern nation-states and tribal federations, and traditional practices and cosmopolitan attitudes, which political scientist Bassam Tibi refers to as "the simultaneity of the unsimultaneous" (1990:127), illuminates the challenges of nation-state formation and national integration in the contemporary Middle East. It also reveals the degree to which the peoples of the region have compensated for nation-states' weaknesses by adapting and revitalizing traditional sociocultural modes of survival:

> Unlike the imperial and the territorial dynastic states that were familiar in Middle Eastern history, the externally imposed new pattern of the nation state is defined as a national, not as a communal, polity. Its underlying concept is sovereignty, which not only presupposes the capability of the central power to establish itself over the entire territory, but also requires established citizenship and a corresponding national identity and loyalty. In varying degrees, all states of the Middle East lack this infrastructure. . . . In most of the states of the Middle East, sovereignty is nominal. The tribal ethnic and sectarian conflicts that the colonial powers exacerbated did not end with the attainment of independence. The newly established nation states have failed to cope with the social and economic problems created by rapid development because they cannot provide the proper institutions to alleviate these problems. Because the nominal nation state has not met the challenge, society has resorted to its pre-national ties as a solution, thereby preserving the framework of the patron-client relationship. (Tibi, 1990:147–149)

Perhaps it is not too far-fetched to argue that extensive networks of overlapping kin- and ethnic-based patron-client relationships linking those in the government with those outside of it constitute the actual "glue" that holds the Middle Eastern nation-state together. Although patron-client relations "play an important role in facilitating the distribution of goods and services among the population and harnessing popular support behind leaders" (Khoury and Kostiner, 1990:18), ties of patronage are essentially asymmetrical: perpetuating these relationships also perpetuates and reinforces unequal power structures in the starkly stratified societies of the contemporary Middle East. Patron-client ties ensure that people are kept "in their place": the rich and powerful maintain their dominant positions, from which they have the advantage of becoming even more rich and powerful, and the less fortunate are kept in their subordinate position of dependency, remaining powerless over the decisionmaking processes and larger forces that shape their lives.

Taking a broader view of the Middle East in a global context, and examining the structures and processes through which the region is encapsulated at the international level, it appears that the vertical integration of society, polity, and economies through patron-client relations at the local and national levels have clear echoes and similarities in the asymmetrical patterns of integration between the Middle East and the global economy. Many countries in this region are clients of the world's current superpower: the United States. A holistic and contextualized anthropological approach demands that we view kinship, ethnicity, social class, and nation-states in the Middle East within all relevant contexts, including that of the global political economy. In so doing, we may discover that not all of the Middle East's problems are internally generated or self-inflicted. Critiquing the 2002 United Nations Development Programme report on the social and economic state of the Middle East and North Africa, historian Mark Levine noted the absence of a contextualized, culturally sensitive analysis in the report's findings:

> [The r]eport [does not] consider the strategic yet marginalized (or better, strategically marginalized) position of the Middle East and North Africa in the larger world political economy. Such lacunae allow the authors to avoid grappling with the cycle of Arab petrodollars for Western arms, the disproportionate and generally increasing military budgets of Arab governments, or the disastrous impact of US and European agricultural subsidies (which flood markets with under-priced Western products that force local farmers out of business) that are crucial to the region's perpetual economic dependence on the West. (2002)

The foreign aid policies of powerful states, no less than the decisions and dictates of the World Bank and the International Monetary Fund, serve to replicate relations of dependence between the most populous states of the Middle East and the West while consolidating mutually supportive ties between the regimes of the region and Western suppliers of military and economic aid packages (Pfeifer, 1999). This is not a recipe for national and regional integration, nor does it strengthen the institutions of civil society and civic participation at the grassroots level.

Although relying on subnational, primary identities and traditional relationships in order to survive in a challenging world can be interpreted as logical and strategic, it also entails costs and consequences that can have negative repercussions on individuals and collectivities in the region. Relying on kin rather than the state, affiliating with narrowly defined ethnoreligious groups rather than forming broad-based coalitions and solidarities, and participating in patron-client exchanges of goods and services that perpetuate socioeconomic inequalities while consolidating age-old forms of political domination, impede economic, cultural, and political integration on the national and regional levels and discourage processes of empowerment, the attainment of social justice, and the implementation of democratic reforms.

Turning inward to family, clan, or confessional sect is a valuable method of coping with a variety of daily challenges, but in so doing, the peoples of the region may lose sight of the common interests and goals that could unite them on bases of affiliation and organization that are much wider and potentially more effective than the narrow foundations provided by primary identities of blood and faith. Hence, Middle Eastern peoples may remain unaware of opportunities for large-scale cooperation and coordination to improve some of the difficult circumstances of their lives, particularly in areas such as environmental conservation and economic integration. Also, a public that has fragmented into separate, segmentary groups of kinsmen and co-religionists is facilitating its own control, exploitation, co-optation, and manipulation by repressive state governments. A divided population is much easier to rule, as the colonial powers so deftly proved.

The institutionalization—and essentialization—of ethnic and religious identities for legal and administrative purposes, seen most clearly in states such as Lebanon and Israel, is a double-edged sword. Although official recognition of cultural heritage and religious laws may provide answers to individuals' psychological needs and communal organizational problems, institutionalized identities can also trap individuals in the vise of inflexible collective categories not of their own choice or making, thus limiting their personal options and opportunities while preventing the development of a more inclusive sense of overarching national loyalty and identity. The most extreme example of the triumph of the ethnic group over both the individual citizen and the overarching state is that of Lebanon, a state composed entirely of seventeen officially recognized ethnoconfessional groups, membership in which defines Lebanese individuals' rights and duties in the context of the state. Reflecting on the tragedy of Lebanon, Lebanese sociologist Samir Khalaf notes that

> [t]he very factors that account for much of the viability, resourcefulness, and integration of the Lebanese are also the factors that are responsible for the erosion of civic ties and national loyalties. . . . In short, the factors that enable at the micro and communal level disable at the macro and national level. This is, indeed, Lebanon's predicament. (1986:14)

Or, in the words of Ziad Rahbani, the bard of the Lebanese civil war whose captivating music and ironic lyrics allowed the Lebanese to look at themselves with jaundiced but compassionate eyes: *yaa zaman at-ta'ifiyya! ta'ifiyya, ta'ifiyya / kheli eidek 'alal-howia; shidd 'alaiha qad ma fiik!* ["Oh, these are confessional times, such confessional times! / So best keep your hand on your identity [card]; and grasp it for all that you are worth!"]. The song refers both to the wartime retreat into primary identities and the horrifying practice of political murders perpetrated by militiamen who routinely killed civilians on the basis of their religious confession, which is recorded on every Lebanese citizen's identity card.

Another danger posed by the inward-looking tendencies and the resultant social and political fragmentation of Middle Eastern societies is that individuals and groups in this region may be less prepared to deal with the multifaceted challenges posed by media and market globalization and the coming ecological crises. As detailed by Elias Tuma in Chapter 7, the Middle East is already economically marginalized and dependent in the current world economic system. As a result, the region may be at risk of being even further sidelined by the coming global restructuring of economic and political relationships. To succeed in the new global markets, Middle Eastern countries should be integrated into a regional economic framework, rather than being more closely linked to the West and its markets than they are to one another. In our opening story, Adnan and Khalid were clearly looking forward to increasing regional economic integration as the condition of their own hoped-for personal success and familial happiness. But so long as asymmetrical vertical integration between the region and the West at the global level, economic inequalities and political conflicts at the regional and national levels, and mistrust, uncertainty, scarcity, and poverty at the local levels drive Middle Eastern peoples further into the traditional refuge of kinship, ethnicity, and patron-client ties, the peoples of the region will be unlikely to achieve national and regional integration and the resulting levels of cooperation and coordination needed to meet so many of their interrelated economic, ecological, and political challenges.

The problems of the contemporary Middle East are not cultural ones centered on the resilience of traditional practices and primary identity categories in a modern world. Rather, the region's political and economic problems stem primarily from the weaknesses and deficiencies of an imposed nation-state system that is not meeting people's basic needs, and from regional hostilities rooted in historical injustices and shortsighted policies initiated by Western powers during the colonial period and replicated in today's globalized, "neo-colonial" era, characterized by a form of economic integration that is neither egalitarian nor sustainable.

The Middle East remains a region in which citizenship and its accompanying rights and duties have little meaning, but where

> membership in kin-based groups is the individual's chief guarantee of security and access to resources—hence the necessity for strong group maintenance mechanisms. Arab familism (or tribalism) must be viewed, not as a cultural trait, but as a very ancient adaptive response to insecurity; group cohesion is as important for survival under state oppression as it is for survival in the absence of the state. (Sayigh, 1981:267)

■ Conclusion

This chapter began with a lively conversation among American, Lebanese, and Palestinian friends in an Arabic restaurant in California and ended with an abstract observation about the deficiencies of the nation-state in its Middle Eastern incarnation. My goal has been to analyze and interpret kinship, ethnicity, and social class in the contemporary Middle East by showing how these sociocultural phenomena are related to ecological, economical, psychological, administrative, and political realities and how they interact with and shape one another. We have learned that social, political, and cultural behaviors in the Middle East have historically been greatly affected by the limitations of a harsh natural environment in which economic scarcity and pronounced political competition were constants, whereas sustained relationships of mutual trust and permanent, broad-based, sociopolitical formations were not. Furthermore, we have seen that the region underwent rapid economic and political changes in the nineteenth century, encapsulating the Middle East in a Western-dominated political and economic order that permanently altered traditional class structures and produced sharp socioeconomic inequalities, which were then exacerbated by colonialism and the imposition of arbitrarily defined nation-states. The resulting conundrums and inequalities remain unresolved to this day.

Lacking meaningful representation by or assistance from most nation-states of the region, many Middle Eastern peoples have turned to localized identity categories and traditional organizational structures in an effort to make a living—and to make a meaning—in the challenging world that confronts them. Although they have succeeded in this effort, it has not been without costs and consequences. In the long run, resorting to kinship, ethnicity, and patron-client ties could have a negative effect on societies that may soon be forced to reconcile their segmented and fragmentary nature with increasing political and economic pressures for integration, coordination, and cooperation in the globalizing economy.

There is much room for optimism, however. The scholars cited here, no less than Adnan and Khalid's conversation, demonstrate that the peoples of the Middle East are talented survivors possessing an exceptionally rich and resilient cultural heritage that can be adapted to serve them in all political, economic, and temporal environments.

■ Bibliography

Abu-Lughod, Lila. 1986. *Veiled Sentiments*. Berkeley: University of California Press.
——. 1990. "Anthropology's Orient." Pp. 81–131 in Hisham Sharabi (ed.), *Theory, Politics, and the Arab World: Critical Responses*. London: Routledge.

Ahmed, Akbar. 1995. "Islam in the Age of Post-Modernity." Pp. 1–22 in Akbar Ahmed and Hastings Donnan (eds.), *Islam, Globalization, and Postmodernity.* London: Routledge.

al-Akhras, Muhammad Safouh. 1976. *The Structure of the Arab Family.* Damascus: Ministry of Culture.

Anderson, Benedict. 1993. *Imagined Communities.* London: Verso.

Antoun, Richard. 2000. "Civil Society, Tribal Process, and Change in Jordan: An Anthropological View." *International Journal of Middle East Studies* 32:441–463.

Ayubi, Nazih. 2001. *Overstating the Arab State.* London: I. B. Tauris.

Bahloul, Joelle. 1992. *The Architecture of Memory: A Jewish-Muslim Household in Colonial Algeria, 1937–1962.* Cambridge: Cambridge University Press.

Barakat, Halim. 1993. *The Arab World: Society, Culture, and State.* Berkeley: University of California Press.

Barth, Frederik. 1969. *Ethnic Groups and Boundaries.* Boston: Little, Brown.

Bosworth, C. E. 1982. "The Concept of Dhimma in Early Islam." Pp. 37–54 in Benjamin Braude and Bernard Lewis (eds.), *Christians and Jews in the Ottoman Empire,* vol. 2: *The Arabic Speaking Lands.* New York: Holmes and Meier.

Cohen, Abner. 1974. *Two-Dimensional Man: An Essay on the Anthropology of Symbolism and Power in Complex Societies.* Berkeley: University of California Press.

Cohen, Ronald. 1978. "Ethnicity: Problem and Focus in Anthropology." *Annual Review of Anthropology* 7:379–403.

Cunningham, Robert B., and Yasin K. Sarayrah. 1993. *Wasta: The Hidden Force in Middle Eastern Society.* Westport, Conn.: Praeger.

Denoeux, Guilain. 1993. *Urban Unrest in the Middle East: A Comparative Study of Informal Networks in Egypt, Iran, and Lebanon.* Albany: State University of New York Press.

Eller, Jack, and Reed Coughlan. 1993. "The Poverty of Primordialism: The Demystification of Ethnic Attachments." *Ethnic and Racial Studies* 16, no. 2:183–202.

Farsoun, Samih K. 1988. "Class Structure and Social Change in the Arab World." Pp. 221–238 in Hisham Sharabi (ed.), *The Next Arab Decade: Alternative Futures.* Boulder, Colo.: Westview Press.

Farsoun, Samih K., and Christina Zacharia. 1995. "Class, Economic Change, and Political Liberalization in the Arab World." Pp. 261–282 in Rex Brynen, Bahgat Korany, and Paul Noble (eds.), *Political Liberalization and Democratization in the Arab World,* vol. 1: *Theoretical Perspectives.* Boulder, Colo.: Lynne Rienner.

Fernea, Elizabeth Warnock. 1969. *Guests of the Sheikh.* New York: Doubleday.

Fishman, Joshua. 1980. "Social Theory and Ethnography." Pp. 84–97 in Peter Sugar (ed.), *Ethnic Diversity and Conflict in Eastern Europe.* Santa Barbara: ABC-Clio.

Friedl, Erik. 1991. *Women of Deh Koh.* New York: Penguin Paperback.

Geertz, Clifford. 1969 [1973]. *The Interpretation of Cultures.* New York: Basic Books.

Geertz, Clifford, Hildred Geertz, and Laurence Rosen. 1979. *Meaning and Order in Moroccan Society.* New York: Cambridge University Press.

Geertz, Hildred. 1979. "The Meaning of Family Ties." Pp. 315–391 in Clifford Geertz, Hildred Geertz, and Lawrence Rosen (eds.), *Meaning and Order in Moroccan Society.* New York: Cambridge University Press.

Gilsenan, Michael. 1996. *Lords of the Lebanese Marshes: Violence and Narrative in an Arab Society.* Berkeley: University of California Press.

Harik, Iliya. 1972. "The Ethnic Revolution and Political Integration in the Middle East." *International Journal of Middle Eastern Studies* 3:303–323.

Halliday, Fred. 1999. "The Middle East at the Millennial Turn." *Middle East Report* 213:4–7.

Hannerz, Ulf. 1980. *Exploring the City: Inquiries Towards an Urban Anthropology.* New York: Columbia University Press.

Herzfeld, Michael. 1997. "The Dangers of Metaphor: From Troubled Waters to Boiling Blood in Europe." Pp. 74–88 in Michael Herzfeld, *Cultural Intimacy: Social Poetics in the Nation State.* London: Routledge.

Huntington, Samuel. 1996. *The Clash of Civilizations and the Remaking of World Order.* New York: Simon and Schuster.

Ibn Khaldun. 1967. *The Muqaddimah: An Introduction to History.* Trans. Franz Rosenthal. Bollingen Series. Princeton: Princeton University Press.

Inhorn, Marcia. 2003. *Local Babies, Global Science: Gender, Religion, and In Vitro Fertilization in Egypt.* London: Routledge.

Jean-Klein, Iris. 2000. "Mothercraft, Statecraft, and Subjectivity in the Palestinian Intifada." *American Ethnologist* 27:100–127.

Joseph, Su'ad. 1994. "Brother-Sister Relationships: Connectivity, Love, and Power in the Reproduction of Patriarchy in Lebanon." *American Ethnologist* 21, no. 1:31–54.

———. 2000. *Intimate Selving in Arab Families: Gender, Self, and Identity.* Syracuse, N.Y.: Syracuse University Press.

Kahn, Susan Martha. 2000. *Reproducing Jews: A Cultural Account of Assisted Conception in Israel.* Durham, N.C.: Duke University Press.

Kanaaneh, Rhoda Ann. 2002. *Birthing the Nation: Strategies of Palestinian Women in Israel.* Berkeley: University of California Press.

Kapchan, Deborah. 1996. *Gender on the Market: Moroccan Women and the Revoicing of Tradition.* Philadelphia: University of Pennsylvania Press.

Karpat, Kamal. 1982. "Millets and Nationality: The Roots of the Incongruity of Nation and State in the Post-Ottoman Era." Pp. 141–170 in Benjamin Braude and Bernard Lewis (eds.), *Christians and Jews in the Ottoman Empire,* vol. 2: *The Arabic Speaking Lands.* New York: Holmes and Meier.

Keesing, Roger. 1975. *Kin Groups and Social Structure.* New York: Holt, Rinehart, and Winston.

al-Khafaji, Isam. 1995. "Beyond the Ultranationalist State." *Middle East Report* 187–188:34–39.

Khalaf, Samir. 1986. *Lebanon's Predicament.* New York: Columbia University Press.

Khoury, Philip. 1983. *Urban Notables and Arab Nationalism: The Politics of Damascus, 1860–1920.* Cambridge: Cambridge University Press.

Khoury, Philip, and Joseph Kostiner (eds.). 1990. *Tribes and State Formation in the Middle East.* Berkeley: University of California Press.

Khuri, Fuad. 1970. "Parallel Cousin Marriage Reconsidered: A Middle Eastern Practice That Nullifies the Effects of Marriage on the Intensity of Family Relationships." *Man* 5:596–618.

King-Irani, Laurie. 2001. "Maneuvering in Narrow Spaces: An Analysis of Emergent Identity, Subjectivity, and Political Institutions Among Palestinian Citizens of Israel." Unpublished Ph.D. diss., Bloomington, Indiana University.

Layoun, Mary. 1999. "A Guest at the Wedding: Honor, Memory, and (National) Desire in Michel Khleife's Wedding in Galilee." Pp. 92–110 in Caren Kaplan, Normal Alarcon, and Minoo Moallem (eds.), *Between Woman and Nation: Nationalisms, Translational Feminisms, and the State.* Durham, N.C.: Duke University Press.

Levine, Mark. 2002. "The UN Arab Human Development Report: A Critique." *Middle East Report Online*, www.merip.org/mero/mero072602.html (accessed May 25, 2003).

Makdisi, Samir. 1991. "The Arab World and the World Economy: An Overview." Pp. 123–146 in Hala Esfandiari and A. L. Udovitch (eds.), *The Economic Dimensions of Middle Eastern History: Essays in Honor of Charles Issawi*. Princeton: Darwin Press.

Makdisi, Ussama. 2000. *The Culture of Sectarianism: Community, History, and Violence in Nineteenth-Century Ottoman Lebanon*. Berkeley: University of California Press.

Mamdani, Mahmood. 2002. "Good Muslim, Bad Muslim: A Political Perspective on Culture and Terrorism." *American Anthropologist* 104:766–775.

McMurray, David. 2002. *In and Out of Morocco*. Minneapolis: University of Minnesota Press.

Meeker, Michael. 1979. *Literature and Violence in North Arabia*. Cambridge: Cambridge University Press.

Mitchell, Timothy. 1989. "Culture Across Borders." *Middle East Report* 30, no. 3:4–6.

Mundy, Martha. 1995. *Domestic Government: Kinship, Community, and Polity in North Yemen*. London: I. B. Tauris.

Murphy, Robert, and Leonard Kasdan. 1959. "The Structure of Parallel Cousin Marriage." *American Anthropologist* 61:17–29.

Nelson, Cynthia (ed.). 1973. *The Desert and the Sown: Nomads in the Wider Society*. Berkeley: Institute for International Studies, University of California.

Peteet, Julie M. 1991. *Gender in Crisis: Women and the Palestinian Resistance Movement*. New York: Columbia University Press.

Pfeifer, Karen. 1999. "How Tunisia, Morocco, Jordan, and Even Egypt Became IMF 'Success Stories' in the 1990s." *Middle East Report* 210:24–30.

Pitcher, Linda. 1998. "'The Divine Impatience': Ritual, Narrative, and Symbolization in the Practice of Martyrdom in Palestine." *Medical Anthropology Quarterly* 12, no. 1:8–30.

Roniger, Luis, and Ayse Gunes Ayata (eds.). 1994. *Democracy, Clientelism, and Civil Society*. Boulder, Colo.: Lynne Rienner.

Royce, Anya Peterson. 1982. *Ethnicity: Strategies of Diversity*. Bloomington: Indiana University Press.

Sayigh, Rosemary. 1981. "Roles and Functions of Arab Women: A Reappraisal." *Arab Studies Quarterly* 3:258–274.

———. 1994. *Too Many Enemies: The Palestinian Experience in Lebanon*. London: Zed Books.

Schneider, David M. 1968. *American Kinship: A Cultural Account*. Englewood Cliffs, N.J.: Prentice-Hall.

Schneider, Jane. 1971. "Of Vigilance and Virgins: Honor, Shame, and Access to Resources in Mediterranean Societies." *Ethnology* 10:1–24.

Sharabi, Hisham (ed.). 1990. *Theory, Politics, and the Arab World: Critical Responses*. London: Routledge.

Shryock, Andrew. 1997. *Nationalism and the Genealogical Imagination: Oral History and Textual Authority in Jordan*. Berkeley: University of California Press.

Singerman, Diane. 1995. *Avenues of Participation: Family, Politics, and Networks in Urban Quarters of Cairo*. Princeton: Princeton University Press.

Tapper, Richard. 1990. "Anthropologists, Historians, and Tribespeople on Tribe and State Formation in the Middle East." Pp. 48–73 in Philip Khoury and Joseph

Kostiner (eds.), *Tribes and State Formation in the Middle East*. Berkeley: University of California Press.

Tibi, Bassam. 1990. "The Simultaneity of the Unsimultaneous: Old Tribes and Imposed Nation-States in the Modern Middle East." Pp. 127–152 in Philip S. Khoury and Joseph Kostiner (eds.), *Tribes and State Formation in the Middle East*. Berkeley: University of California Press.

Wedeen, Lisa. 1999. *Ambiguities of Domination: Politics, Rhetoric, and Symbols in Contemporary Syria*. Chicago: University of Chicago Press.

World Bank. 1996. *Middle East and North Africa*. Washington, D.C.: World Bank.

Zubaida, Sami. 1994. "National, Communal and Global Dimensions in Middle Eastern Food Cultures." Pp. 33–48 in S. Zubaida and R. Tapper (eds.), *Culinary Cultures of the Middle East*. Berkeley: University of California Press.

The Role of Women

Lisa Taraki

Approaching the study of women in the contemporary Middle East is a difficult and challenging task. Decades of orientalist scholarship and popular and journalistic writing have left their indelible mark on the representation of the women of the Middle East. A priori assumptions, preconceptions, and stereotypes regarding Middle Eastern women abound, and generalizations about women in a region as internally diverse as the Middle East continue to predominate in current discourse. Scholars and others attempting an objective study of Middle Eastern women thus have a heavy intellectual legacy to contend with, and it is not surprising that much of the energy of scholars today is directed at challenging long-standing preconceptions and stereotypes concerning Middle Eastern women.

The more intractable of the impediments to understanding the reality of women living in the Middle East are lodged at the level of culture. What may be termed a "culturalist" bias presents a major challenge to those interested in the objective study of women's lives in the Middle East. Culturalists have approached issues such as women's labor force participation, status within the family, marriage patterns, fertility behavior, educational attainment, and political participation from within the broad framework of an unchanging and essential "Islamic" value system in the Middle East, which is assumed to hold a firm grip not only in matters of belief and attitude but also in practice and in the conduct of everyday life.

This chapter is based on the premise that, as in all societies, a multiplicity of social, economic, political, and cultural forces and factors have shaped the statuses, experiences, and living conditions of Middle Eastern women. I also stress the fact that just as an ahistorical conception of Islamic values as determinants of practice does not advance our understanding of complex historical processes, so too does the use of the unitary concept of the "Middle Eastern woman" obscure the rich diversity in women's lives across the Middle East. Important regional differences exist within the broad area covered in this book. In addition, within regions and countries, women's life chances, experiences, and statuses diverge and are shaped by a number of important factors, the most significant of which are class and place of residence (primarily urban or rural); ethnicity, refugee or nonrefugee status, and religious affiliation also have important effects. Attributes pertaining to women as individuals, such as age, marital status, and number of children, also influence women's differential status, power, and access to opportunities within households, kinship groups, communities, and even the labor force.

■ The Modern Nation-State

We begin our discussion of the realities of women's lives with an examination of the relationship between women and the state in the modern Middle East. A number of authors have stressed the importance of understanding the relationship between women's status, rights, and position within society and state-building projects in the region (Joseph, 1991; Kandiyoti, 1991c; Moghadam, 1995, 2003; Molyneux, 1991). Whether states adopt positive strategies that effect changes in women's status or choose not to upset what is perceived to be the status quo has important implications for society in general and women in particular. The postcolonial state in the Middle East has had to face choices not only on the economic and political-strategic levels but also in relation to the kind of society it envisions for its citizens, both female and male.

As discussed by Arthur Goldschmidt in Chapter 3 and Deborah Gerner in Chapter 4, the emergence of the modern nation-state in the Middle East in the twentieth century was accompanied in most instances by a modernizing agenda by which state elites attempted to transform or modify basic relations in society, including prevailing gender relations. A variety of legal-administrative measures, social policies, and a modernizing nationalist ideology were deployed to weaken the grip of primordial loyalties and affiliations, build the construct of *citizen* in the modern sense, and launch programs of social and economic development.

Education is perhaps the one domain where almost all Middle Eastern countries have achieved remarkable successes as a result of direct state policy. Although reforms in areas pertaining to personal status and political rights for women have been very uneven, the trend toward increasing educational levels for both women and men has been nearly universal. One measure of this success is that Arab states made some of the greatest gains in women's education anywhere in the world in the period from 1970 to 1990, more than doubling women's literacy rate in these two decades. They also nearly doubled female primary and secondary enrollment, from 32 percent in 1970 to 60 percent in 1992 (UNDP, 1995:29). There are indications, however, that Arab states' commitment to expanding education may be eroding; the widely acclaimed *Arab Human Development Report, 2002* notes that the overall rate of increase in enrollment in the three levels of education for both males and females slowed during the 1990s, with the rising expenditure on education tapering off after 1985. The report suggests that this slowing rate of growth in educational spending is related to economic difficulties and structural adjustment programs adopted by Arab states (UNDP, 2002a:52–54).

Reforms of legislation and policies pertaining to women's rights within the family have been the subject of great debate and controversy all over the Middle East. Primarily because family legislation has historically been grounded in Islamic law *(sharia)*, most state elites (with the exception of Turkey) have been very hesitant to introduce significant changes that would challenge prevailing gender hierarchies and the sexual division of labor that these laws took for granted.

Turkey was the first state in the Middle East to introduce legal and administrative reforms aimed at developing the economy and altering prevailing social relationships. The replacement of Islamic law with the Civil Code of 1926 and the enfranchisement of women in the early 1930s were measures undertaken by the new republic under Mustafa Kemal Atatürk (Father of the Turks) to change gender relations. Women became citizens of the republic, and the new laws banned polygamy and gave divorced women more rights. National ideologues and feminist writers and activists promoted a modernizing nationalist ideology stressing women's equality with men. This

Thomas Hartwell

Girls of diverse social and economic backgrounds attend a range of public and private schools as in this Cairo classroom.

ideology has been viewed by some scholars as part of the arsenal of the new secular republic against the caliphate as an institution and as proof that Turkey was a democratic country, unlike the dictatorships in Germany and Italy with which it was allied (Kandiyoti, 1989:127).

In the decades that followed, Turkey continued on its trajectory as a modernizing and secular state, expanding civil and social liberties in the Constitutions of 1961 and 1982. However, the civil code, although more progressive than those in surrounding countries, still grants privileges to men in the areas of child custody, determination of place of residence, and personal freedom (Arat, 1996:29). Turkey is often singled out as the Muslim Middle Eastern country to have achieved the greatest levels of "modernization" and "Westernization." If progress is measured by basic indicators, however, we find that this leadership position is not warranted. Adult female illiteracy is still high (23.5 percent of women fifteen years of age and older are illiterate, compared to only 6.5 percent of men) and reflects a significant gap between urban and rural areas (UNDP 2002b:223). Women's labor force participation rates and school enrollment figures are also modest (Arat, 1996:30).

It is important to note that recent years have witnessed the unraveling of the secularists' historical hegemony in Turkish society. As with other confrontations between Islamist and secular forces throughout the Muslim world, women have been at the center of some of the most flammable debates and conflicts. The "headscarf" issue in 1999, for instance, brought Islamists and secularists to a confrontation, with implications beyond the Turkish parliament, where the issue initially exploded in 1999 (Arat, 2000).

The case of Israel is unique in the Middle East and presents some contradictions. The secular political elites of the immediate poststate period were in a most favorable position to build a modern nation-state in line with the democratic and secular principles they claimed formed the basis of the new society and polity. In addition to being culturally and politically hegemonic in the new state, they were not saddled by the heavy weight of entrenched institutions (such as a powerful religious authority) and did not have to face traditional and conservative groups with a vested interest in maintaining the status quo. An examination of legislation affecting women, however, reveals that not all the opportunities were seized. The Women's Equal Rights Law of 1951, although abolishing blatant discrimination against women embodied in Ottoman law, was intended to protect the rights of women as mothers and wives, not as citizens; thus a whole range of rights outside the domestic domain—such as in employment—were left out of the law (Berkovitch, 1996:20–21).

In the area of family status, Israel is much more in line with its neighbors in the region. It has not adopted secular laws, and the religious establishment exercises considerable influence. For instance, marriages can be contracted and dissolved only in religious courts. Women are not allowed to become judges in the orthodox rabbinical state courts, and as a rule, their evidence is not accepted, especially if there are male witnesses (Yuval-Davis, 1989:105). The army is another institution in which women do not enjoy equal opportunities with men. At least 70 percent of women in the military are trained to occupy traditional women's roles; furthermore, despite the mandatory recruitment law, only 65 percent of Jewish Israeli women serve in the army. The rest either opt out on religious grounds or fall under various categories of women exempted from military service (Sharoni, 1995:45–47; see also Swirski and Safir, 1991; Yuval-Davis, 1982).

Iran under Mohammad Reza Shah was also among the first of the Middle Eastern states to articulate a modernizing agenda including the emancipation of women. However, unlike the Turkish republic, which was avowedly secular, the Iranian state in the early decades of the twentieth century was more mindful of powerful religious institutions, and thus the pace and nature of the changes were more modest. The major reforms and developments affecting women were introduced in the 1960s. Women were enfranchised in 1962, and significant gains in women's education were made during the 1960s and 1970s. In 1967, the new Family Protection Act gave women expanded rights within marriage and the family. In the early years of the Islamic Republic, however, several of these reforms were revoked, and an ideology stressing women's domesticity was articulated and encouraged.

Iran's situation calls into question some of the prevailing assumptions about the relationship between Islam and women's status. While remaining "Islamic," contemporary Iran has reconsidered certain postrevolutionary policies concerning women's rights within the family and the public domain. For example, although the Family Protection Act of 1967 was revoked after the revolution and replaced by legislation dating back to the 1930s, eventually the government responded to the agitation of Islamist women activists and revised the law to grant women more rights. Under legislation passed in 1992, for instance, divorced women are granted half of the wealth accumulated during the marital union, as well as wages for housework performed during the marriage (Hoodfar, 1995:124). Postrevolutionary population policy is another example. After dismantling family planning centers after the revolution, within a few years the state was actively reconsidering its pronatalist approach. In 1989 the state ratified a new birth control policy and launched a national campaign to convince the population to accept and practice family planning (Hoodfar, 1995:108–109). Policies in education provide a further illustration. After initially setting a maximum limit for female university applicants in a wide range of scientific and professional fields, most of the quotas were removed in 1989 (Moghadam, 2003:208).

Most of the Arab states began to articulate and implement their social agendas during the second part of the twentieth century, in the aftermath of achieving national independence and following the consolidation of a new state elite. As in Turkey and Iran, state elites introduced reforms in family law, encouraged women's education, and in some cases sought an increased female presence in the state bureaucracy and the labor force. Egypt, Iraq, Tunisia, and the People's Democratic Republic of Yemen (South Yemen) stand out as the pioneers, with the last instituting the most far-reaching revisions. Exceptions to this trend include Saudi Arabia and some of the Gulf states, where the pace of reforms has been very slow.

Of the three countries of the Arab Maghreb Union emerging as independent states following colonial rule (Tunisia, Algeria, and Morocco), Tunisia was the leader in introducing significant changes. The Personal Status Code of 1956, amended in 1964, 1966, and 1981, is the most progressive in the Arab world, outlawing polygamy and granting expanded rights to divorced women; labor legislation enacted in 1966 provides some protection for working mothers (Galal, 1995:63–64). In Algeria, however, reform came much later and was more modest in its content. Although the state abolished all colonial legislation pertaining to family matters in 1975, it was not until 1984, after considerable agitation by Algerian women, that a new family code was finally enacted. This code, like those in all Arab countries, was enacted within the framework of *sharia* and offered only limited modifications in marriage, divorce, and custody laws (Hijab, 1988:26–29; Lazreg, 1994:150–157). Morocco has perhaps been the slowest country in the Arab Maghreb Union to respond to pressures for change in matters of family law. New legislation was enacted in 1957–1958 that granted women some rights in the matter of divorce, but it was not far-reaching and has remained virtually unchanged during more than four decades (Mir-Hosseini, 1991).

Recent research on the integration of women into the nation-state in the Middle East through reforms at the state level recognizes the limits of state-sponsored policies and legislation in bringing about significant changes in social relations in general and gender relations in particular (Joseph and Slyomovics, 2000; Joseph and Kandiyoti, 2000). Despite the adoption of policies drawing women into the labor force and increasing women's education in several countries, wide gaps continue to exist between men and women in terms of labor force participation, educational attainment, and access to resources and opportunities.

This brings us to the crucial issue of the uneven manner in which state policies and reforms affect women. If we examine women's education and employment, we find that rising educational levels for women have generally been accompanied by an increase in the participation of women in the non-agricultural labor force, primarily in the service sector. Because most service jobs are concentrated in urban areas, women's increased participation in such work indicates that educational gains for women have been greater in urban areas and have prepared women to join occupations unrelated to the agrarian economy. These observations underline the fact that recent decades have wit-

In depressed or weak economies, well-educated, urban women like this Palestinian often find their best opportunities for employment are with international nongovernmental organizations.

Deborah J. Gerner

nessed a tremendous expansion of urban centers and an increasing differentiation between the city and the countryside. The consolidation of an urban middle class throughout the Middle East has had as an important component the increased visibility of women in the educational system, the labor force, and the public domain in general. It is these women who have been the main beneficiaries of state policies in education, labor, and other public services, which points to the fact that urban middle-class (and upper-class) women have been most positively affected by state policies. Women marginalized in the state modernization project, mainly peasant and poor urban women, live different realities and have not been able to benefit from state reforms on a wide scale.

■ Economic Activity

As Valentine Moghadam points out in Chapter 9, measuring the economic activity of the population in the Middle East, as in many other third world countries, is fraught with difficulties. Women's economic activity is particularly elusive, and it is widely acknowledged that national labor force figures and other statistics do not represent the true magnitude of women's role in the economy. The reasons for this situation are many. First, women's unpaid domestic labor is unregistered and unquantified; the long hours and hard work that women expend in raising children and in household management are not reflected in national statistics. Second, the contribution of women to the household economy in the form of provision of home-use items is also largely unrecorded. This is due both to biases in data collection systems and also to the perceptions of respondents in national surveys concerning economic activity.

(For instance, a woman who produces food and sews clothing for her family as an economizing measure will not likely be perceived by herself or a male household member to be economically active.) Third, and most important, women's economic activity in the informal sector is largely unmeasured in standard labor force statistics. This sector is an important component of the economy throughout the Middle East and includes a wide array of activities, many of them carried out by women, either within the household or on the streets and in workplaces in the public sphere.

Due to the inadequacy of data on economic activity in the Middle East, it is indeed difficult to gain an accurate understanding of the magnitude of women's participation in the national economies of the region. Although small-scale studies of women's informal-sector activities in several countries have enriched our knowledge of the various strategies that households and women within them deploy to deal with economic hardship, we still have only formal labor force statistics—with all their weaknesses—as the most reliable cross-national indicators of women's economic activity.

Even though the participation of women in the formal labor force in the Middle East is still small compared to that in other world regions, it has been steadily increasing since the 1960s (Moghadam, 2003:chap. 2). Factors such as the tremendous expansion of the state bureaucracy and related services (especially in education, health, and social services), economic development, falling fertility levels, the rising age at first marriage, rapid urbanization, increased educational levels for women, and male labor migration from the poor to the oil-rich countries of the Gulf all played a part in encouraging the increase in rates of female employment. How these dimensions have come together in a given national setting has varied, however, and the outcomes in terms of participation levels have also been very different. Economic activity rates for women age fifteen and older in the Middle East for the years 1995–2001 ranged from rates below 30 percent in Oman, Libya, Saudi Arabia, Lebanon, Iran, Syria, and Jordan to 50 percent in Turkey, 48 percent in Israel, 41 percent in Qatar, 37 percent in Kuwait and Tunisia, and 35 percent in Sudan and Egypt (UNDP, 2002b:234–236).

In terms of the distribution of the female labor force by occupation, the highest percentages are found in the service sector (ranging from a high of 86 percent in Israel to 56 percent in Egypt and 54 percent in Morocco), a pattern found the world over, with high percentages in agriculture recorded only in Egypt (35 percent) and Turkey (72 percent) (UNDP 2002b:234–236). As Moghadam has pointed out (2003:45), however, in some countries women in agriculture are not counted as part of the labor force, which explains the low figures for this sector of economic activity.

What do these figures tell us about working women in the Middle East? First, the high concentration of women in public services (occupations such as teaching) reinforces stereotyping that identifies certain occupations as

Deborah J. Gerner

It is unusual to find female shopkeepers in the Middle East except in African Arab countries such as Mauritania.

women's occupations. Women from well-off families are most likely to be formally employed, especially in the Gulf states. Other relevant conditions include the compatibility of some occupations (particularly teaching) with women's reproductive roles as mothers and domestic caregivers and the fact that most women in these occupations work in the public sector, where working women's rights (such as paid maternity leave) are generally better protected than in the private sector (Moghadam, 2003:48–55). At the same time, women have been underrepresented in administrative and managerial fields and "have been conspicuously absent from . . . private sales and services and in the sector of hotels, restaurants, and . . . trade" (Moghadam, 2003:51).

The concentration of younger women in the formal labor force is another reflection of the organic link between women's reproductive and productive activities. We can assume that most women in this age group are either single or newly married with few children and are therefore freer to take on employment outside the home. Furthermore, based on educational data for the region, these women also have the highest rates of educational achievement. Indeed, in the Middle East, employment in the formal nonagricultural labor force is positively linked to education (Moghadam, 2003:51).

An important determinant of women's formal labor force participation is the degree of public investment in working women with children, both in the provision of child-care services and in the enactment and enforcement of labor laws protecting these women's rights. Three demographic characteristics of the region are relevant in this regard: first, a substantial proportion of the female population is in the reproductive age group; second, the great majority of women are married; and third, fertility rates are high (Zurayk and Saadeh, 1995:38). These attributes, which Huda Zurayk and Fadia Saadeh cite with respect to the Arab world, apply to Iran and Turkey as well; however, the demographic profile is different in Israel.

The implication of these demographic attributes is that some of the impediments to women's labor force participation could be attenuated by increased public and private investment in child-care facilities for working women and, more important, by the enactment and enforcement of labor laws favorable to working women with children. As long as women's reproductive tasks are not socially supported and are considered private burdens, many women will not be encouraged to join the paid labor force. A further factor inhibiting women's employment is the relatively high cost of those child-care facilities that do exist (whether public or private) as compared with the low wages that women command in the market, thus making the option of employment outside the home unattractive to women and their families.

Another consideration that influences women's formal labor force participation is located at the level of the family and household. Seteney Shami (1990) has proposed that women's work should be viewed as part of the strategies deployed by families and households for adapting to the circumstances of their class. In this view, families of modest means diffuse economic risk by diversifying the employment of family members: men and boys enter the more remunerative activities due to their higher education levels, whereas women tend to enter the informal sector or become the mainstay of subsistence agriculture. Thus women perform activities related to family survival while men enter areas of the economy leading to family mobility. In those cases where women seem to be offered the opportunity for mobility, women do participate in the formal labor force and become a further economic asset to the family (Shami, 1990:xiv–xv).

It has become clear that a number of factors come together to condition and determine the extent and nature of women's economic activity in the Middle East. The lack of public support for women's employment, demographic factors such as those cited above, and issues having to do with the structure of the labor market and the household together explain to a large extent the low labor force participation of women.

What becomes of the widely held view that conservative attitudes deriving from an Islamic worldview constitute the major impediment to women's work in the public domain? Although it would be incorrect to dismiss the relevance of conservative attitudes—whether derived from a religious ethos or not—it is more reasonable to assume that a host of factors having to do with the structure of the economy, the educational system, population characteristics, and state policies are equally, if not more, influential in determining the magnitude and distribution of women in the labor force. It is true that rationales and justifications for women's exclusion from employment are often part of popular idiom and are couched in religious terms, but it is important to recognize how widely they are overlooked or disregarded in practice in the Middle East. Any person familiar with urban life in the Middle East will be struck by the numbers of women engaged in some kind of employment outside the home, whether they are women bosses *(mu'allimat)* on Cairo's streets, or female vegetable peddlers in the markets of Arab Jerusalem, or the armies of young women coming out of sewing workshops at the end of a day's work in Istanbul. It also goes without saying that the increasing numbers of women students enrolled in postsecondary educational institutions all over the Middle East would not be making the considerable investment in education if they did not hope to join the labor force.

■ Family and Kinship

The preceding discussion has highlighted some features of Middle Eastern society relevant not only to the economic activity of women but also to dynamics within the family. We now examine some of the major features of familial gender relations, an issue also addressed by Laurie King-Irani in Chapter 10. It may be useful to begin our examination of the family with the concept of patriarchy, which in broad terms refers to a system that privileges males and elders and justifies this privilege in kinship terms (Joseph, 1994:2). The anthropologist Deniz Kandiyoti finds the clearest instances of "classic patriarchy" in North Africa, the Muslim Middle East, and southern and eastern Asia. Under this system, girls marry young into households headed by their husbands' fathers and are subordinate there to all men and to the more senior women, especially their mothers-in-law. Women frequently do not inherit from their fathers, although their access to resources and control over the *mahr* (bride price) and property can be highly variable (Kandiyoti, 1991b:31–32).

Patriarchy, representing a gender and age hierarchy based on the household as a productive unit, has been seriously challenged in recent decades by social transformations sweeping the regions in which it prevails. Wage labor opportunities outside the household (mostly for young men but also for a growing segment of urban women), the breakup of the extended family, the increasing age of marriage for both women and men, the rise in educational levels, and rural-to-urban migration, among other factors, have begun to erode some of the foundations of this system.

Households headed by women due to divorce or death of the husband, those in which men are away for extended periods for work, or situations in which women earn wages outside the home all present problems for patriarchy. The economic independence of sons and their move away from the natal household after marriage also challenge gender and age hierarchies, both in the case of the sons vis-à-vis their fathers and in the case of the sons' wives in relation to their mothers-in-law.

However, certain circumstances can mitigate against the breakdown of patriarchy and in some cases may actually strengthen it. Let us take the example of the persistence in functional terms of the extended family household, despite the setting up of nuclear family households by married sons. Although this arrangement, which is an adaptation to the absence of social security and other state assistance to the elderly, may give sons authority over their fathers, it may also solidify the position of elder working sons vis-à-vis their sisters and brothers still at home, thus preserving gender and age hierarchies in another form. In the same vein, although the sons' wives may be liberated from the direct and daily control of domineering mothers-in-law, they may be dependent upon them if they go out to work. In the absence of adequate public facilities, women often rely on their mothers-in-law for child care, and may have to put up with the burdens—and interference in their children's upbringing—that this arrangement entails.

The preceding discussion has touched upon the issue of women's position within the household, and it is to this that we now turn. As with labor force participation, a number of factors help determine a woman's position—and particularly her authority—within the household. Age and marital status are two important determinants: a young wife is decidedly at a disadvantage compared to an older one, especially with a mother-in-law, and unmarried women generally have less authority than married ones. However, unmarried women with access to financial resources such as income from property or employment may wield considerable authority over members of the household, including their parents and younger siblings. Divorced women, unless they have adequate resources, are among the more vulnerable, and may be almost totally dependent on their fathers and brothers in financial terms, even if they do not live with them in the same household.

The number of children—especially sons—a woman bears is another factor influencing her status in the household. This feature of Middle Eastern family life has often been highlighted in accounts of the region and requires an explanation. Rather than understanding the preference for male children as a timeless cultural value derived from some primordial valuation of male offspring by Middle Easterners, it is more useful to view it as essential to the survival of the informal system of social security in Middle Eastern societies. In most societies in the Middle East, male children not only contribute their labor or income for the welfare of the household but also are a source of old-age security for their parents and any unmarried sisters in the absence of state-supported pensions and other compensations for the elderly and retired. For women, who are likely to be widowed earlier than men, the presence of sons is not so much a source of status—although it is expressed as such in the cultural idiom—but a form of security for which no real alternatives yet exist in the public sector.

Yet another important determinant of status is access to or control over economic resources. Literature on the Middle East often mentions that women, although entitled by law to a share of their fathers' estates (albeit unequal to that of their brothers), are routinely deprived of the right to inherit this property. Although it is undoubtedly true that Middle Eastern women continue to be disinherited in this sense—often with their own "consent"—it is important to understand the social and cultural logic behind what appears to be a flagrant violation of basic rights.

The material foundation of classic patriarchy, as discussed earlier, is the patrilocally extended household (Kandiyoti, 1991b:31). Within it, older males are regarded as having responsibility for the economic welfare of all members of the family, including women marrying into the household. Daughters marrying out become members of their husbands' households and are considered part of their responsibility. However, married women maintain a special relationship with their brothers, upon whose support they can count when facing marital problems, financial distress, or in the extreme case, divorce or abandonment. Clearly, this system rests on the assumption of female dependence on men, whether these men are husbands or brothers. Denial of inheritance to women is affirmation of this fact and is based on the widely acknowledged belief that men require the inherited property to meet the family obligations women are not expected to shoulder.

As patriarchy erodes due to the social transformations mentioned earlier, challenges also begin to face the inheritance system. Working women who contribute their incomes to family welfare or self-supporting single women are realities with which this system increasingly has to deal. However, even within the sexual division of labor assumed by the inheritance system, it has not always been the case that women have without exception been denied their inheritance.

Research findings from Palestine may be indicative of wider patterns. Anthropologist Annelies Moors has shown, for instance, that the crucial factors determining whether Palestinian women in the Nablus region receive or claim their share of inheritance are marital status, social class, and position in the family. Brotherless daughters and their widowed mothers show the most interest in claiming their shares; daughters from wealthy families are also in a better position to inherit some of the family property. In the case of the majority, that is, married women from families of modest means who do have brothers, the situation is different. Here, sisters refrain from claiming their share in favor of their brothers as part of an optimizing strategy: being ulti-mately dependent on their kin for their socioeconomic security, it makes sense for women to relinquish their inheritance in order to highlight their kin's obli-gations toward them (Moors, 1996:69–84).

The preceding discussion has shown that within the patriarchal family structure, denial of inheritance to women is not tantamount to a denial of all their rights to family resources. However, it must be realized, as Moors (1996:83) has pointed out, that women's dependence on men, which is the basis of this system, may become increasingly shaky; as the conjugal (hus-band-wife) tie becomes more important and as the extended family becomes more fragmented, women will be left without the "protections" that the inher-itance system entailed for them, and their vulnerability may increase.

■ Values and Norms

The idea that traditional norms and values surrounding women and the family dictate current social practices and serve to limit women's freedom and opportunities has become part of the commonsense understanding of gender relations in the Middle East. Many scholarly and popular works by Western-ers and Middle Easterners alike routinely attribute women's low labor force participation or educational achievement, for example, to the hold of tradi-tional conceptions of family honor and conduct appropriate to women.

It may be useful to take note of two features of explanations of social practices and behavior that refer to "tradition." First, such explanations deal almost exclusively with non-Western societies. The assumption appears to be that non-Western and particularly Islamic Middle Eastern societies are still under the grip of immutable traditional value systems. The almost mandatory prefacing of many examinations of women's current realities by a discussion of the traditional context is an outstanding example of this approach. It would indeed be very strange to see a discussion of French, Swedish, or North Amer-ican women's lives framed similarly, implying that we could not hope to understand their current realities before first setting out the *traditional* context of gender relations. Second, the reference to traditional norms and values is almost invariably produced when matters concerning gender relations, roles, and identities are at issue.

How can we understand social practices and behavioral patterns that appear on the face of it to be dictated by traditional values and norms? To address this question, we must first recognize that norms and values are his-torical constructs above all; in no society are they "handed down" from gen-eration to generation without undergoing redefinition and reformulation. This process of transformation is conditioned by changing realities and reflects the struggle between different social groups and collectivities in pursuit of their particular and common interests.

A prime example is the presumably timeless "honor code" believed to regulate women's conduct in Muslim Middle Eastern societies. An examination of social practices and values in these societies reveals that the meaning of *honor* has changed considerably over the past decades, as has what constitutes the violation of the honor code. Practices and conduct that may have been viewed as a grave breach of the honor code decades ago do not produce similar reactions today. Segregation of men and women, which is often regarded as an underpinning of the system of honor, is one example of a practice that has been seriously undermined, if not swept away, by the major social transformations taking place in the region. Although it is still a subject of debate among contending social forces, hundreds of thousands of Middle Eastern women today work and study in mixed-sex institutions without social censure or opprobrium. Even Islamists, interestingly, have reinterpreted supposedly fixed honor codes such as those forbidding the mixing of men and women by adjusting them to the exigencies of modern life, as in women's participation in the labor force or study at universities. Such accommodation to modern society by Islamists is the norm rather than the exception today, as I have tried to show in the discussion of Iran above.[1]

As noted earlier, and as in any society, contending social and political forces as well as individuals are constantly negotiating the definition and boundaries of honor. The great diversity in women's dress in the Middle East today can be regarded as a reflection of this silent struggle. Large numbers of urban women have adopted various versions or degrees of "Islamic" dress; there are equal numbers dressing in variations of international styles. All of these women are mindful of proper and improper ways of dressing but are by their choices defining the different—and differing—codes of modesty and decorum. We thus witness the almost daily setting of new standards and norms by which women are continually negotiating and stretching the boundaries of the supposedly immutable codes of honor.

We must also consider the possibility that certain values and norms are group- or class-specific and can not be generalized at the level of whole societies, let alone the region. How the process of generalization takes place is itself a subject for investigation, since a host of factors come into play in the designation of values and norms as universal. For instance—and contrary to the impression given in much of the Western popular press—women's seclusion in the domestic sphere has not been the practice for the majority of women in Middle Eastern societies, whether in rural or urban areas. One of the main requirements for seclusion is the freedom from labor in the field, the neighborhood, or other public spaces; this is not an option for many women, even if it is viewed as preferable.

Judith Tucker's historical research in Egypt and Palestine, for example, has shown that in the nineteenth century in Cairo and Nablus, adherence to the modesty code was tempered by class: among the upper class, notions of women's honor were important and women were confined to the harem, but for the poor, women were very much part of a public work life that precluded all but the most formal adherence to the ideal of female seclusion (Tucker, 1993:205). Agricultural communities could afford the seclusion of women even less. The pioneering research of Richard Antoun in a Jordanian village in the 1960s showed that peasant women's labor was crucial to the survival of dry-cereal farming in the village. This entailed women's presence in public space alongside men of their own families as well as unrelated men. Thus the agricultural regime and the sexual division of labor whereby women played an important part in agriculture were among the major factors that undermined adherence to the modesty code, even though it was upheld as an ideal in local discourse (Antoun, 1968:681–682).

■ Politics

Middle Eastern women's organized participation in the political process dates to the early years of the twentieth century and was linked from the start with two major overlapping currents sweeping the region: the drive for modernization and social reform and the nationalist struggle for independence from colonial domination.

The "woman question" has been an important component of the ideologies of reformist and nationalist currents throughout the Middle East. The first organized women's movements with a feminist agenda took shape in Turkey, Iran, and Egypt in the first decade of the twentieth century. Their agenda included demands for education and work opportunities and for reform of legislation governing matters such as marriage, divorce, child custody, and inheritance (Graham-Brown, 1993:2). The first women's organizations were established in Turkey and Iran in the first decade of the twentieth century (Afary, 1989:66; Kandiyoti, 1991a:29), followed by the rapid expansion of women's organizations all over the Middle East.

It is important to note that the founders and, to a large extent, the members of the earlier women's organizations were drawn from the upper and middle classes; frequently they were wives, daughters, and sisters of men prominent in public life. Many of these women were also engaged in charitable work in their societies, a pursuit consistent with their status and privilege and part of a pattern found the world over. Despite these commonalities, women's participation in politics in the Middle East has not been restricted to activism within the framework of women's organizations agitating on women's issues.

Women campaign outside a women's polling site in 1997 in the Baqa'a refugee camp northwest of Amman, Jordan. Many Middle Eastern countries maintain separate polling sites for men and women.

A rich diversity of forms and modes of women's participation in politics can be identified in the Middle East. The first is women's participation as fighters and support staff in national liberation struggles or revolutionary movements, notably in the Algerian war of independence, the Palestinian resistance, and the Iranian revolution. The second mode of women's political activism is that of women's "arms" or "branches" of political parties and fronts. Third, women participate as members of political parties and groups. Fourth, women also have been active in women's organizations created or sponsored by ruling parties and states, such as women's federations in many Arab countries and Iran.

The fifth mode of women's political activism is in independent (but not necessarily apolitical) organizations whose agendas greatly vary in terms of the nature and content of their activism on gender issues and causes. Although organizations such as these, in the form of charitable societies and the like, have existed in the Middle East for a number of decades, we focus on the new, more gender-conscious organizations that have been proliferating since the late 1980s, many of which are funded by international governmental and non-governmental organizations (NGOs). Finally, the sixth mode of women's participation in politics is involvement in the electoral process as voters and candidates and in responsible positions in governments.

This typology of modes of women's participation in politics must be treated with caution, however, since the categories are not exclusive, and considerable overlap between them may be found. For example, many Palestinian women participated in military and paramilitary activity within the framework of the Palestinian resistance in the 1970s, while at the same time being members of political parties *and* affiliated with the women's organizations of those parties.

■ National Liberation and Revolutionary Movements

The best-documented cases of women's participation in national liberation struggles and popular revolutions are those of Algeria, Iran, and Palestine.[2] Despite many similarities in these and other cases, it is very difficult to generalize about the role and status of women in such struggles. Algeria's and Iran's struggles were carried out on national soil, but Algeria's was an armed struggle, whereas the revolution in Iran—and women's participation in it—was not of a military nature. (It must be noted, as Hammed Shahidian [1997] points out, that Iranian women *were* active in guerrilla organizations—primarily the People's Mujahidin Organization of Iran and the Organization of People's Fida'i Guerrillas—under the shah's rule in the 1970s, and also after the revolution and until the mid-1980s.)

In Palestine, most of the guerrilla activity was based outside Palestine in the 1970s, whereas inside, in the Occupied Territories, military struggle was crushed and did not have a popular mass base as in Algeria. While the Palestinian struggle in the Occupied Territories during the first uprising of the late 1980s and early 1990s was largely nonmilitary, the second uprising since late 2000 has witnessed a significant increase in armed actions. Women, however, have been largely absent from the armed resistance, notwithstanding the few and highly publicized cases of women involved in bombings.

What is common to each of these examples is that women of all social classes, both urban and rural, participated in the struggles, although the balance was always in favor of women of more modest means. In addition, women did not have decisionmaking or frontline military positions in any of these revolutionary movements. Most of the tasks assigned to women were of a support nature. Even in Algeria, where women played an important and crucial role in the liberation war, including in the military arm of the National Liberation Front (FLN), paramilitary acts of destruction of civilian targets involved barely 2 percent of the women who joined the movement (Lazreg, 1994:124).

■ Women's Front Organizations

The creation of women's "front" organizations or branches by parties and movements in order to mobilize women for the larger national cause is a well-known pattern in the Middle East. The relationship between the Sudanese Communist Party and the Sudanese Women's Union is one example (see Hale, 1996:151–183); in the Palestinian case, the women's organizations attached to the various political parties and fronts in the Occupied Territories and the diaspora are another. From Iran comes another example of women's organizations affiliated to political movements before and during the revolution.

In general, women's organizations affiliated with political parties have had little autonomy; this has meant in the majority of cases that feminist concerns have been subordinated to larger national ones and that women's energies have not been primarily concentrated upon representing and fighting for the interests of women as women. This situation is not surprising, however, especially in the case of parties engaged in popular struggles for independence, such as in the Palestinian case.

The demise of mass nationalist politics in the Middle East as a whole could very well mean that women's front organizations are becoming a thing of the past. The decline of radical nationalist parties and movements, the increasing globalization of the women's movement, and the hegemony of discourses of democratization and "civil society" among intellectuals and other elites all point to the fact that women's front organizations are becoming anachronistic vestiges of old-style politics in the region. While women's front organizations continue to exist in authoritarian states, their ability to mobilize and capture the imagination of wide sections of women in their societies may be becoming increasingly compromised.

The Palestinian case may be instructive if not entirely representative of the Middle East as a whole. With the demise of nationalist mass politics and the installation of the Palestinian Authority in the early 1990s, women's front organizations underwent a dramatic transformation. Many remodeled themselves along the NGO model, eschewing direct association with the political parties and movements within whose frameworks they had incubated and grown. Partly through pressure from international donors but also in recognition of the fact that women's interests had been marginalized in the nationalist movement and its parties, these women's organizations began to articulate gender agendas and projects at odds with their previous discourse. Paradoxically, however, the expansion of Islamist politics and activism may be giving rise to new incarnations of women's front organizations. How successful these organizations may be in articulating women's agendas within the overall project of Islamization of the society and polity remains to be seen.

▨ Political Parties

There is not a lot of research that exists on women's participation in political parties. A general familiarity with the major political parties in the region shows, however, that women have not achieved leadership positions in either ruling or opposition parties across the Middle East. The lone exceptions are Israel and Turkey, where Golda Meir in the early 1970s and Tansu Çiller in the 1990s led political parties and headed their countries' governments. As is true in much of the world, political parties have thus been true bastions of male privilege and exclusivity in the Middle East, with little difference between liberal or leftist and more conservative right-wing parties.

One factor that accounts for the paucity of information on women's—or men's—participation in political parties is that the democratic process, whereby contending parties compete for constituencies, is still not the norm in many countries of the Middle East. In the Arab world in particular, political participation is weak at best (UNDP, 2002a:9). Political parties are thus quite restricted in size, since they are robbed of their raison d'être, which is to represent their constituencies' interests in a political contest for power.

It is therefore difficult to speak about women's participation in political parties in a climate where the ability of those parties to mobilize large masses of people seems to be at an all-time low. Paradoxically, however, women organizing *outside* political parties and frameworks seems to be growing. An understanding of this state of affairs, which on the face of it may appear to indicate a depoliticization of women's activism, requires a careful examination of the global, regional, and local factors leading to the weakening of formal political groupings and the strengthening of NGO-style activism. This new style of politics is not restricted to women's work; it has permeated many other forms of organizing previously subsumed under parties, such as youth and labor organizing.

▨ "Establishment" Women's Organizations

Many feminists have argued that women's organizations in the Middle East have not developed autonomously, that is, their agendas and activism have been dictated either by political parties or, more important, by the state. A review of the major women's organizations in the various countries of the Middle East bears out this observation. Historically, we have seen how the first women's organizations arose out of the nationalist and reformist movements of the early twentieth century and articulated demands and goals consistent with the agendas of the modernizing elements within these movements.

In the decades following the establishment of the first women's organizations, women's organizing energies were, with few exceptions, harnessed by the state and in some cases made part of its state-building project. In Iraq, for example, the ruling Ba'th Party created the General Federation of Iraqi Women in 1968 as a female arm of the party, with the aim of drawing women into the state and as part of its drive toward the resocialization and mobilization of women. The federation was funded by the state, and leadership positions were held by party members (Joseph, 1991:182). Iran is another case of a centralizing state attempting to contain and control women's organizing energies. In the 1960s, under Mohammad Reza Shah, the state began to solidify its control over women's organizations, ending in the establishment of the influential Women's Organization of Iran, with significant power and resources at its disposal (Najmabadi, 1991:60–61). Algeria is another example. After independence, the ruling National Liberation Front set up the National Union of Algerian Women to represent the country's female population.

The drive to set up national women's organizations was given a great boost by the UN Decade for Women, launched in 1975. Governments were thereafter required to send delegates to the successive world conferences on women and the growing number of international and regional conferences organized to discuss women's issues. The question, therefore, of how the country and its progress in achieving women's rights was to be represented acquired great importance. Many Middle Eastern countries were represented at the official level by their women's federations, which were by and large state-controlled. Forums for nongovernmental organizations were made available at the world conferences, however, and provided an opportunity for women in independent organizations to voice their concerns, which at times conflicted with the official line presented by the official delegations.

▦ Independent Women's Organizations

The years since the late 1980s have witnessed the emergence of a new and diverse body of independent and semi-independent women's organizations (more commonly termed "women's NGOs") in the Middle East. Although many are not overtly political in the conventional sense of the term and most do not have a grassroots constituency, all may be viewed as engaged in gender politics of one kind or another. The growth of these organizations (particularly in Egypt, Turkey, Tunisia, Morocco, Jordan, Palestine, and Lebanon) is part of a wider development at the level of civil society in the Middle East, represented by the proliferation of nongovernmental organizations of various sorts. Human rights groups, development and social policy institutes, research centers, and legal assistance services are just some examples.

The new women's organizations can be distinguished from the more politicized women's "front" organizations, state-controlled women's federations, and traditional charitable organizations by their membership profile, their social and political agenda, and the range of their contacts within and outside the region. Founded and staffed mainly by urban middle-class professional women (such as lawyers, physicians, and academics), these organizations are engaged in formulating a feminist agenda around such issues as political and legal reform, social policy, reproductive health and population policy, domestic violence, and other issues of concern to women. They have become increasingly visible in international and regional forums, and have linked up with women's organizations around the world in networks of trainers, lobbyists, legal experts, policy analysts, and activists. Women's organizations have thus been vying with the official women's federations of their countries for attention in the national and international arenas and have been successful due to their familiarity with the global women's discourse and their considerable professional skills.[3] The social impact of these organizations at home, however, remains limited, since many do not have access to the sources of power in society and are largely removed from the mass of women in their own societies.

▦ Women in the Electoral Process and in Government

Accurate data on women's participation in the electoral process are patchy. We do know that in most countries, women's participation as voters in national and local elections is moderate to substantial (with the exception, of course, of those countries that do not have electoral processes, or in Kuwait, the one Middle Eastern country in which women are not enfranchised but men are).

Women's representation in state structures, primarily parliaments and governments, however, is quite limited. Among parliaments in the Arab states, the highest percentages of female representation are found in Tunisia (11.5 percent), Syria (10 percent), and Sudan (10 percent). In Iran and Algeria about 3 percent of representatives are women, but the numbers are still lower in Egypt (2.4 percent) and Lebanon (2.3 percent). Turkey does not fare much better, with slightly over 4 percent. Israel has the highest percentage of women in parliament at 13 percent. Women's presence at the ministerial level is even less significant. Figures for 2000 show no women at the ministerial level in the Gulf states of Algeria, Jordan, Turkey, and Lebanon; Syria has the highest percentage (11 percent), followed by Tunisia at 10 percent, Iran at 9 percent, and Israel and Egypt at 6 percent (UNDP, 2002b:239–241).

These figures must be viewed in context, however. In the United States, less than one-sixth of congressional representatives are women (14 and 13 percent in each of the houses); in Japan, the percentage of women in each of the two houses is 7 and 15 percent. This is in sharp contrast to world pioneers in women's representation in parliament: Sweden (42.7 percent), Denmark (38 percent), and Finland and Norway (36 percent) (UNDP, 2002b:239).

Deborah J. Gerner

Palestinian Samiha Khalil, head of the charitable society In'ash al-Usra, ran against Yasser Arafat in the 1996 presidential election.

Islamist Women's Activism

Feminist activism in the Middle East has had an uneasy relationship with Islam since the beginning of the twentieth century. The engagement with Islam could not be avoided in societies where many of the laws affecting women's personal status were based upon *sharia* and where state elites were not keen on antagonizing the religious establishment or adopting positions that might offend what were perceived to be prevailing religious sensibilities. Thus, from the very beginning, feminists—as well as state institutions— sought to show that Islam was not opposed to women's education, enfranchisement, participation in the public domain, and work outside the home. However, even though Islam may have been invoked to justify women's emancipation, most feminists have been secular in their pursuits, lifestyles, and political convictions.

The growth of Islamist forces throughout the Middle East has posed a challenge to secular feminism and, more important, has led to the emergence of what may be called Islamist feminist currents. These currents receive state sanction in Iran, Sudan, and some Gulf states, and in the rest of the Middle

East they are emerging as significant social and ideological forces in the political arena, competing with secular feminism for women's sympathies and support.

Islamist women do indeed attempt to create an alternative to secular feminism. Because Islamist women activists are by and large educated and professional women and not obscurantist male theologians or ideologues, they cannot be dismissed as archaic or irrelevant by secular feminists. Moreover, in countries all over the Middle East, ranging from Iran to Kuwait, they are gaining visibility and entering the public political arena. Although on the whole Islamist women have not publicly challenged the Islamist construct of the ideal Muslim woman or the prevailing sexual division of labor, they are, by their own lifestyles and professional and political pursuits, departing in many ways from the ideal (Clark and Schwedler, 2003). Some Islamist women have even won seats on party councils, an opportunity not available to women in most secular parties, where internal elections are seldom held. Now, at the beginning of the twenty-first century, a new model is being offered to young women, the model of an educated, professional, "Muslim" woman.[4]

One indicator of the serious challenge posed by Islamists to secular feminists is the increasing visibility and presence of Islamist women in magazines, in newspapers, and on airwaves and television channels directed at millions of Arab women. Once the preserve of secular, middle-class women activists, these media (and particularly the satellite television channels) are providing forums where Islamist women are challenging the once-hegemonic discourses of secular feminism. The popular al-Jazeera television channel, broadcasting from Qatar and reaching wide audiences all over the Arab world (and beyond), is a prime example; from the time it began to air a women's program in January 2002, it has consistently provided a platform for debates between secular and "Islamist" (or conservative) feminists around women's issues ranging from polygamy to the rights of foreign domestic workers in the Gulf.[5]

In Iran, the role of Islamist women in challenging postrevolutionary state policies that restricted women's rights has been unique and noteworthy. After the revolution, the state encouraged the development of an Islamic women's movement to counter the threat from secular feminism; very soon, however, Islamist women began to voice their criticism of some Islamization policies, such as Islamist dress codes, leading in the late 1980s to the emergence of an Islamist feminist opposition. Islamist feminists have campaigned for issues relating to rights within the family, dress codes, employment, political participation, and education (Paidar, 1996:59–62).[6] It must be noted here that the concept of Islamist feminism has not been unproblematic; indeed, a heated debate around the independence and emancipatory potential of Iranian Islamist feminism has been raging among Iranian feminists.[7]

■ Conclusion

This chapter has attempted to highlight the diversity of women's status and realities in the Middle East while at the same time underlining the broad similarities in the social, economic, and political circumstances under which women live their lives. As we have seen, state-building projects have had important consequences for women's status in society and for the rights of which they are deprived or enjoy.

We have also seen that Middle Eastern women have been active in the political arena, a role not consistent with commonsense representations of Middle Eastern women as passive political subjects locked into the domestic arena. The massive participation of Iranian women in the revolution, for instance, flies in the face of such conceptualizations of Middle Eastern women as being outside the domain of politics. Women's lives in the Middle East, as elsewhere in the world, are shaped by a multiplicity of influences and factors. Concrete material factors related to socioeconomic realities and state policies explain social practices and institutions better than do monolithic belief systems. These belief systems, although important in the overall scheme of things, are variable, flexible, and dynamic.

■ Notes

1. My research in Jordan (Taraki, 1996) supports these conclusions about Islamists' accommodation to the requirements of life in a rapidly changing society. For further discussion and analysis of Jordanian and other Islamists' preoccupation with women's conduct in modern society, see Taraki, 1995.

2. Useful sources for the study of women's participation in revolutionary movements are, for Palestine, Peteet, 1991; Sayigh, 1993; and Jad, 1990; for Algeria, Lazreg, 1994; and for Iran, Nashat, 1983; Ferdows, 1983; and Shahidian, 1997.

3. For an overview of Arab women organizing around feminist issues, see the special website launched by the Arab States Regional Office of the United Nations Development Fund for Women (UNIFEM) under the framework of the Arab Women Connect project: www.arabwomenconnect.org/english/main_links.html (accessed May 11, 2003). Of particular interest is UNIFEM, 2000.

4. An interesting volume including articles on women and Islamist movements in Sudan, Tunisia, Algeria, Egypt, Turkey, and Iran is Moghadam, 1994.

5. Full transcripts (in Arabic) of the women's program "For Women Only" can be found at www.aljazeera.net (accessed May 28, 2003).

6. It is important to caution against viewing Islamist women in Iran as a monolithic group, however. See Moghissi, 1996, for a discussion that distinguishes between "conservative" and "reformist" Muslim elite women. The conservatives, apologists for the clerical state, occupy prominent public posts, are almost all related to powerful male elites, and are the main beneficiaries of financial and ideological support from the state. The reformists represent a growing disenchantment with the legal system and

government policies in education and employment, although it appears that they are of the same social class and background as the conservative group.

7. The journal *Iran Bulletin* (www.iran-bulletin.org [accessed May 28, 2003]) has published articles by Iranian feminists debating these issues. As examples, see Moghadam, 2000, and Moghissi, 2000.

■ Bibliography

Afary, Janet. 1989. "On the Origins of Feminism in Early Twentieth Century Iran." *Journal of Women's History* 1, no. 2:65–87.

Antoun, Richard. 1968. "On the Modesty of Women in Arab Muslim Villages: A Study in the Accommodation of Traditions." *American Anthropologist* 70:671–698.

Arat, Yesim. 1996. "On Gender and Citizenship in Turkey." *Middle East Report* 198 (January–March):28–31.

———. 2000. "Islamist Women, Their Headscarves, and Democracy in Turkey." Paper presented at Ben Gurion University. www.bgu.ac.il/humphrey/seminar/yasim.htm (accessed May 11, 2003).

Berkovitch, Nitza. 1996. "Women and the Women's Equal Rights Law in Israel." *Middle East Report* 198 (January–March):19–21.

Clark, Janine Astrid, and Jillian Schwedler. 2003. "Who Opened The Window? Women's Activism in Islamist Parties." *Comparative Politics* 35, no. 3 (April): 293–312.

Ferdows, Adele. 1983. "Women and the Islamic Revolution." *International Journal of Middle East Studies* 15:283–298.

Galal, Salma. 1995. "Women and Development in the Maghreb Countries." Pp. 49–70 in Nabil Khoury and Valentine Moghadam (eds.), *Gender and Development in the Arab World*. London: Zed Books.

Graham-Brown, Sarah. 1993. *Women and Politics in the Middle East*. Special MERIP Publication no. 2. Washington, D.C.: Middle East Research and Information Project.

Hale, Sondra. 1996. *Gender Politics in Sudan: Islamism, Socialism, and the State*. Boulder, Colo.: Westview Press.

Hijab, Nadia. 1988. *Womanpower: The Arab Debate on Women at Work*. Cambridge: Cambridge University Press.

Hoodfar, Homa. 1995. "Population Policy and Gender Equity in Post-Revolutionary Iran." Pp. 105–135 in Carla M. Obermeyer (ed.), *Family, Gender, and Population in the Middle East*. Cairo: American University in Cairo Press.

Jad, Islah. 1990. "From Salons to the Popular Committees: Palestinian Women, 1919–1989." Pp. 125–142 in Jamal Nassar and Roger Heacock (eds.), *Intifada: Palestine at the Crossroads*. New York: Praeger.

Joseph, Suad. 1991. "Elite Strategies for State-Building: Women, Family, Religion, and State in Iraq and Lebanon." Pp. 176–200 in Deniz Kandiyoti (ed.), *Women, Islam, and the State*. London: Macmillan.

———. 1994. *Gender and Family in the Arab World*. Special MERIP Publication no. 4. Washington, D.C.: Middle East Research and Information Project.

Joseph, Suad, and Deniz Kandiyoti. 2000. *Gender and Citizenship in the Middle East*. Syracuse, N.Y.: Syracuse University Press.

Joseph, Suad, and Susan Slyomovics. 2000. *Women and Power in the Middle East*. Philadelphia: University of Pennsylvania Press.

Kandiyoti, Deniz. 1989. "Women and the Turkish State: Political Actors or Symbolic Pawns?" Pp. 126–149 in Nira Yuval-Davis and Floya Anthias (eds.), *Woman-Nation-State*. London: Macmillan.

———. 1991a. "End of Empire: Islam, Nationalism, and Women in Turkey." Pp. 22–47 in Deniz Kandiyoti (ed.), *Women, Islam, and the State*. London: Macmillan.

———. 1991b. "Islam and Patriarchy: A Comparative Perspective." Pp. 23–42 in Nikki Keddie and Beth Baron (eds.), *Women in Middle Eastern History: Shifting Boundaries in Sex and Gender*. New Haven, Conn.: Yale University Press.

———. 1991c. "Women, Islam, and the State." *Middle East Report* 173 (November–December):9–14.

Lazreg, Marnia. 1994. *The Eloquence of Silence: Algerian Women in Question*. New York: Routledge.

Mir-Hosseini, Ziba. 1991. "Contrast Between Law and Practice for the Moroccan Family: Patriarchy and Matrifocality." *Moroccan Studies* 1:39–52.

Moghadam, Valentine (ed.). 1994. *Identity Politics and Women*. Boulder, Colo.: Westview Press.

———. 1995. "The Political Economy of Female Employment in the Arab Region." Pp. 6–34 in Nabil Khoury and Valentine Moghadam (eds.), *Gender and Development in the Arab World*. London: Zed Books.

———. 2000. "Islamic Feminism and Its Discontents: Notes on a Debate." *Iran Bulletin* 25–26:1–20. www.iran-bulletin.org/islamic_feminism.htm (accessed May 11, 2003).

——— (ed.). 2003. *Modernizing Women: Gender and Social Change in the Middle East*. 2nd ed. Boulder, Colo.: Lynne Rienner.

Moghissi, Haideh. 1996. "Public Life and Women's Resistance." Pp. 251–270 in Saeed Rahnema and Sohrab Behdad (eds.), *Iran After the Revolution: Crisis of an Islamic State*. New York: I. B. Tauris.

———. 2000. "Women, Modernity and Political Islam." *Iran Bulletin*. www.iran-bulletin.org/women (accessed May 11, 2003).

Molyneux, Maxine. 1991. "The Law, the State, and Socialist Policies with Regard to Women: The Case of the People's Democratic Republic of Yemen 1967–1990." Pp. 237–271 in Deniz Kandiyoti (ed.), *Women, Islam, and the State*. London: Macmillan.

Moors, Annelies. 1996. "Gender Relations and Inheritance: Person, Power, and Property in Palestine." Pp. 69–84 in Deniz Kandiyoti (ed.), *Gendering the Middle East: Emerging Perspectives*. London: I. B. Tauris.

Najmabadi, Afsaneh. 1991. "Hazards of Modernity and Morality: Women, State, and Ideology in Contemporary Iran." Pp. 48–76 in Deniz Kandiyoti (ed.), *Women, Islam, and the State*. London: Macmillan.

Nashat, Guity (ed.). 1983. *Women and Revolution in Iran*. Boulder, Colo.: Westview Press.

Paidar, Parvin. 1996. "Feminism in Islam in Iran." Pp. 51–67 in Deniz Kandiyoti (ed.), *Gendering the Middle East: Emerging Perspectives*. London: I. B. Tauris.

Peteet, Julie. 1991. *Gender in Crisis: Women and the Palestinian Resistance Movement*. New York: Columbia University Press.

Sayigh, Rosemary. 1993. "Palestinian Women and Politics in Lebanon." Pp. 175–192 in Judith Tucker (ed.), *Arab Women: Old Boundaries, New Frontiers*. Bloomington: Indiana University Press.

Shahidian, Hammed. 1997. "Women and Clandestine Politics in Iran, 1970–1985." *Feminist Studies* 23, no. 1:7–43.

Shami, Seteney. 1990. "Introduction." Pp. xiii–xix in Seteney Shami, Lucine Taminian, Soheir A. Morsy, Zeinab B. El Bakri, and El-Wathig M. Kameir, *Women in*

Arab Society: Work Patterns and Gender Relations in Egypt, Jordan, and Sudan. Paris: Berg/UNESCO.

Sharoni, Simona. 1995. *Gender and the Israeli-Palestinian Conflict: The Politics of Women's Resistance.* Syracuse, N.Y.: Syracuse University Press.

Swirski, Barbara, and Marilyn Safir (eds.). 1991. *Calling the Equality Bluff: Women in Israel.* New York: Teachers College Press.

Taraki, Lisa. 1995. "Islam Is the Solution: Jordanian Islamists and the Dilemma of the 'Modern Woman.'" *British Journal of Sociology* 46, no. 4:643–661.

———. 1996. "Jordanian Islamists and the Agenda for Women: Between Discourse and Practice." *Middle Eastern Studies* 32, no. 1:140–158.

Tucker, Judith. 1993. "The Arab Family in History: 'Otherness' and the Study of the Family." Pp. 195–207 in Judith Tucker (ed.), *Arab Women: Old Boundaries, New Frontiers.* Bloomington: Indiana University Press.

UNDP (United Nations Development Programme). 1995. *Human Development Report, 1995.* New York: Oxford University Press.

———. 2002a. *The Arab Human Development Report, 2002.* New York: UNDP and Arab Fund for Economic and Social Development.

———. 2002b. *Human Development Report, 2002.* New York: Oxford University Press.

UNIFEM (United Nations Development Fund for Women). 2000. *Arab Regional Alternative Report: Five Years After Beijing.* www.arabwomenconnect.org/docs/asro_gov_arabregional.doc (accessed May 11, 2003).

Yuval-Davis, Nira. 1982. *Israeli Women and Men: Divisions Behind the Unity.* London: Change.

———. 1989. "National Reproduction and the 'Demographic Race' in Israel." Pp. 92–109 in Nira Yuval-Davis and Floya Anthias (eds.), *Woman-Nation-State.* London: Macmillan.

Zurayk, Huda, and Fadia Saadeh. 1995. "Women as Mobilizers of Human Resources in Arab Countries." Pp. 35–48 in Nabil Khoury and Valentine Moghadam (eds.), *Gender and Development in the Arab World.* London: Zed Books.

12

Religion and Politics in the Middle East

John L. Esposito, Mohammed A. Muqtedar Khan, and Jillian Schwedler

Religion and politics enjoy a special place in the history and politics of the Middle East. The homeland for three of the world's great religions, the region is strategically located between the West and East and oversees important trade routes on land and sea. Today, the global resurgence of religion, with its influence on politics, has been particularly visible in the Middle East.

Religion, tribalism, and other "traditional" forms of governance were never as discredited in the Middle East as in Europe; they were merely marginalized. In Europe, the experiences of the Renaissance, Enlightenment, and Protestant Reformation were indigenous and precipitated the secularization of politics in the West. Secularism, the separation of religion and politics, came to be accepted as the norm in political development by many governments, policymakers, experts, and the media.

In contrast, secular values came to the Middle East through European colonization. Religion, however, continued to play a major role in society and politics. There was no mass intellectual and political movement that explicitly sought to secularize the Middle East. European colonial governments attempted to impose secular political institutions in the region, and in response, some wars of independence were waged as jihad (divine struggle) against European secularism, as in Algeria and Sudan.

After World War II, when much of the Middle East became independent, religion was often marginalized in state formation. This pattern was set in the 1920s when Turkey, under Mustafa Kemal (later called Atatürk, "Father of the Turks"), became secular. Then in the post–World War II era, many other states such as Tunisia, Egypt, Iran, Syria, and Iraq limited religion's status and role in politics and society while continuing to recognize Islam as a state religion.

363

In contrast, Saudi Arabia was established as a self-proclaimed Islamic state, and Pakistan, created in the name of Muslim nationalism, took the title Islamic Republic of Pakistan. At the same time (1948) the modern nation of Israel was established as a Jewish state.

This chapter plots this fascinating relationship between religion and politics across space and time and across faiths from its historical origins to its contemporary resurgence. Just as power and knowledge are inextricably intertwined in the modern world, in the Middle East power and religion often seem to be similarly inseparable.

■ The Historical Role of Religion in the Middle East

The history of the Middle East shares much with the history of monotheism, the belief in a single, supreme God. First Judaism, then Christianity, and later Islam have been a defining presence in the region. Islam spread throughout the Middle East, culturally expanding the territorial frontiers of the ancient Middle East to include North Africa, Iran, Turkey, Pakistan, and central Asian regions such as Uzbekistan, Turkmenistan, and Tajikistan. At present, a majority of the Middle Eastern population is Muslim (although they compose a minority of the world's 1.2 billion Muslims). Jews are concentrated in Israel, with tiny minorities in Iran, Tunisia, Syria, Morocco, Egypt, and Yemen. The most significant presence of Christian minorities in the Arab world is in Lebanon, Syria, Egypt, and Iraq.

Judaism

Judaism is a 4,000-year-old faith. The origins of the Jewish community can be traced back to Moses, who according to Hebrew traditions rescued the Jewish people from slavery in Egypt and brought them to the Holy Land to establish a kingdom of God (about 1450–1250 B.C.E.). The Torah, which includes the first five books of the Hebrew Bible, was revealed to Moses as a guide for the Jewish people. The Jewish people derive their religious principles from the Torah and the Talmud (a secondary text that compiles interpretation of the Torah and Jewish law, the halakah). Jews have always believed themselves to be a "chosen people" who would eventually establish God's domain on Earth, and this belief has informed their modern national self-consciousness. They represent a religious-racial community that values and guards its communal identity (Cavendish, 1980:133–170).

Just as in early biblical conflicts, when Jewish religious identity and political aspirations intertwined with war and peace, so too religion and politics in the late nineteenth and twentieth centuries merged to create a unique form of nationalism—Zionism—that is often simultaneously religious and secular. As detailed by Simona Sharoni and Mohammed Abu-Nimer in Chapter 6, this convergence of religion and politics was finally manifested in the creation of the State of Israel. For those Israelis on the religious right, the Jewish nature of the State of Israel refers primarily to its faith; for those on the left, the Jewish nature of the state is the glue that cements a community. In either case, Judaism is a source of identity. An understanding of these religious beliefs and their appeal cannot be divorced from any contemporary understanding of the region's politics or society.

Historically, all three Abrahamic faiths—Judaism, Christianity, and Islam—have used religion to justify and legitimate expansion and warfare. Although much has been written and continues to be written about the significance of holy wars to Islam (jihad) and Christianity (Crusades), the importance of holy war in Judaism has received less attention. Yet it has influenced political affairs in the past and present. The idea of holy war occurs early in Jewish belief and history. Like Christianity and Islam, Jews associated holy war with divine guidance and mission. Thus, in the Hebrew Bible, whenever they fought against the enemies of Zion, God (Yahweh) fought on their side (Esposito, 1998). In the first two centuries of the second millennium B.C.E., Jews waged wars against the Canaanites who lived on the land Jews believed God had intended for them, gradually capturing enough territory to establish the first kingdom of Israel. These early holy wars are, in the eyes of many believers, likened to the 1947 and 1948 Zionist capture of territory from Arabs to build the new Israel (Armstrong, 1991:7–12).

After their dispersal from Jerusalem and Judea, Jews preserved and sustained their identity by belief in their divine election and distinctiveness and adherence to religious law and ritual practices. For more than 2,000 years the Jewish people lived in a diaspora—exiles from the land of Israel—and were marginalized and often persecuted in the Christian West. In contrast, during the Islamic age in Spain and in other parts of the Muslim world, Jews enjoyed some degree of tolerance and flourished there as a religious community as well as a cultural entity (Cavendish, 1980:165). In the late nineteenth century, a new wave of violence and discrimination against Jews in Europe compelled some Jewish leaders to once again search for a national solution. A Jewish activist, Theodor Herzl (1860–1904), renewed the call for the establishment of a Jewish state, giving the Zionist movement great momentum in the realization of the national aspirations of world Jewry (Cleveland, 1994:223–225).

The first Zionist congress met in 1897. It was after this meeting that the idea of a Jewish state captured the imagination of Jews in eastern as well as western Europe. The end of World War I saw the defeat of the Ottoman Empire and its subsequent dismemberment by Britain and France, which placed most of Palestine under British control. The leaders of the Zionist movement convinced the British to draw up the Balfour Declaration in 1917, which essentially approved the establishment of a Jewish state in Palestine. The League of Nations accepted the Balfour Declaration, and hundreds of thousands of Jews migrated to Palestine. In 1947, the United Nations (UN) passed a resolution for the division of Palestine and the creation of the State of Israel. Between that date and May 15, 1948, when the British mandate over Palestine was scheduled to come to an end, the Zionists and the Arabs in Palestine fought a civil war that drove many Palestinians into exile by the time Israel's independence was declared on May 15.

The establishment of the State of Israel marked a watershed in modern Middle Eastern politics. Israel was not only a reminder that religious identity could mold and motivate a modern nation-state but also a challenge to the predominantly Muslim states of the region. The conflicts between Israel and its neighbors, as well as with Palestinian Arabs displaced by these conflicts, would dominate much of the politics of the region into the twenty-first century.

Christianity

Christianity is the largest religion in the world, with more than 1.5 billion adherents. The origins of Christianity can be traced to the teachings of Jesus of Nazareth. Born in Bethlehem, Jesus was crucified by the Romans in Jerusalem and was declared as Messiah and as a son of God by his followers. From its Jewish roots, Christianity spread first throughout the Mediterranean and subsequently has attracted followers on every continent. Christianity has had a major impact on the social and political development of the West and a significant, although somewhat lesser, impact on the rest of the world.

The expulsion of Jews from Jerusalem in 70 C.E. had put the city in Roman hands. Even though Christian Scriptures espoused the separation of church and state—"Render to Caesar the things that are Caesar's and to God the things that are God's" (Mark 12:17, Bible, King James Version)—religion was viewed as a threat to the unity of the Roman Empire. For more than 300 years Christians suffered repression at the hands of Roman authorities. The faith, however, acquired followers rapidly, and within a hundred years (313 C.E.) Christianity was declared an officially tolerated religion by Constantine I. By 380 C.E., through the edict of Theodosius I, it became the official religion of the Roman Empire, inaugurating a new phase in the history of Christianity that reflected the confluence of religion and politics. From that point until the advent of Islam, Christianity thrived in what is the contemporary Middle East.

With the conquest of the Middle East by Islamic forces in the seventh century, the focus of Christianity shifted to Europe. By the twelfth century under Pope Innocent III (pope from 1198 to 1216), Christianity, as epitomized in the papacy, reached the zenith of its political power, deeply involved in politics through its control of vast territorial resources, its near-monopoly on education, and its influence on the appointment and legitimacy of many political positions. In this golden age of the papacy, Europe came closest to being a Christian empire. This was the period when the papacy, kings, and emperors struggled for sovereignty over land and people, a struggle that eventually precipitated the Protestant Reformation (1500–1650).

The Crusades

The increase in the influence of the church in European politics led to the launch of the Crusades. In 1096, responding to the summons of Pope Urban II, Christian armies from Europe began a series of holy wars against Muslims to gain control of the Holy Land and once again establish the kingdom of God in Jerusalem.

The Crusaders enjoyed successes but failed either to regain the Holy Land permanently or to drive Islam out of it. The power of Islam continued unabated until the fifteenth century. The Crusades, however, remain a landmark event in Christian politics in the Middle East. They are the beginning of external Christian influence on politics in that region.

In 1099, the Crusaders captured Jerusalem and established a Christian kingdom in the Holy Land. The Crusaders accepted the Muslims' surrender and then proceeded to massacre all Muslim survivors, including women and children.[1] They desecrated Muslim religious sites, including the Dome of the Rock, which was converted into a church, and they made the al-Aqsa Mosque the residence for the Christian ruler after renaming it the Temple of Solomon.

But Christian control was relatively short-lived. In 1187, Saladin recaptured Jerusalem but, unlike the Crusaders, spared all Christian civilians and left churches and shrines untouched.[2] The Third Crusade, under Richard the Lion-Hearted of England, attempted to regain control of Jerusalem but failed even to reach the walls of the city. By 1291, the last Crusader stronghold at Acre was captured by Muslim forces, and this era of Christian political influence ended.

The Crusades expanded and strengthened the Islamic world. Muslim armies not only defeated the Crusaders, but the Crusades themselves actually weakened Christian influence in the region. In 1204, Crusaders captured and sacked Constantinople, capital of the Christian (Greek Orthodox) Byzantine Empire, further weakening this outpost of Christian influence in the region. In 1453 Constantinople fell to Muslim armies and was renamed Istanbul. Memories of the Crusades, both real and mythical, would continue to influence relations between Islam and Christianity, the Muslim world and the West, down through the centuries.

Qabat al-Bahr (the Sea Castle), in Sidon, Lebanon, is a thirteenth-century Crusader fortress built on the site of an older temple dedicated to Baal.

■ European Colonialism

Since the eighteenth century, first the British and the French and later the United States have politically dominated the Middle East. The British, and to a lesser extent the French, reorganized the Middle East into a number of nations and kingdoms. Along with the United States, they also supported the creation of the Jewish State of Israel in 1947. In addition, Christianity remains a force with certain interests in the Middle East, including Israel, Jerusalem, and the survival and welfare of Christian minorities.

European colonization of the area, many scholars believe, was inspired more by secular motives of national pride and trade than by any religious impulse. However, Christian missionaries benefited from the patronage of European imperial powers in their efforts to proselytize Muslims and spread European Christianity.[3] The collaboration between the cross and the crown was a subtheme of the colonial experience that led many Muslims to view the colonial conquests as a continuation of Christianity's Crusades against Islam. It is not coincidental that many of the wars of independence against colonial rule were fought in the name of religion (Esposito, 1999).

Christian missionaries accompanied the European soldiers and bureaucrats. The relationship between government officials and missionaries was celebrated by France's marshal Thomas-Robert Bugeaud de la Piconnerie as a *"grand rapport,"* and he commented that the clergy "gain for us the hearts of the Arabs whom we have subjected to force of arms." The missionaries opened schools, hospitals, and publishing houses. They sought to supplant not only local religion but also Arabs' historical understanding of themselves, their culture, and their language (Esposito, 1999).

European successes were interpreted as the result of Christianity's superiority, and Muslim defeats were seen as a result of the inferiority of Islam by colonial powers. With the seizure of the Grand Mosque of Algiers and its conversion into the Cathedral of Saint-Phillippe, the French flag and the cross on its minaret symbolized the close relationship between the crown and the cross under colonialism. Thus in the short term, Christianity gained from the colonial conquests even though much of the rationale for European imperialism was political and economic.

Contemporary historians and social scientists, who often share a secular worldview, sometimes de-emphasize the role and activities of missionaries in the former colonies. But in the Muslim mind, the threat of Christianity was foremost. Thus it was fear of losing their faith—in addition to well-justified skepticism about European motives—that led to a policy of withdrawal and noncooperation with European efforts at development and modernization.

▨ Islam

In the early seventh century, Muhammad of Mecca (570–632 C.E.) declared himself the prophet of God (610 C.E.) and united the tribes of Arabia under the banner of Islam. Muhammad claimed to be a prophet like the biblical prophets Abraham, Moses, and Jesus. He maintained that his message was the same as that revealed to Abraham and the rest of the prophets: that there

Mosque at Job's Tomb near Salalah, Oman, which serves as a memorial for a man important to Jews, Christians, and Muslims.

Deborah J. Gerner

is only one God, and no other god is worthy of worship. The simplicity of Muhammad's message and the fervor of his followers made Islam a major force in the region and globally.

Within seventy-five years of Muhammad declaring himself the prophet of God, the followers of Islam had extended their control from Arabia to Morocco. It was as early as 637 C.E. that the entire Holy Land, including Jerusalem, came under Islam. Many of the Jews and Christians who lived under Muslim rule eventually adopted the new faith or prospered in its relatively more tolerant environment in which, in sharp contrast to Europe, followers of other monotheistic religions did not suffer systematic repression.

Islam expanded beyond Arabia and soon Islamized as well as Arabized most of the Middle East. (Iran was a major exception, accepting Islam but retaining Persian language and culture.) The advent of Islam had a profound cultural and political impact on the Middle East, giving the varied peoples and societies of the region a common heritage. By the sixteenth century, Islam consisted of three great empires: the Ottoman, the Safavid in Iran, and the Mogul on the Indian subcontinent.

In the early centuries of Islam, Muslims created great centers of higher learning. They acquired and revived the lost wisdom of the classical period of Greek and Roman civilization (Lindholm, 1996). Poetry, literature, art and architecture, medicine, mathematics, chemistry, and philosophy all thrived and contributed to the cultural enrichment of the region from the seventh to the fifteenth centuries. The creation of universities spread Islam and brought the learning of other societies to the Islamic world. A rich synthesis of peoples, cultures, and knowledge took place under the umbrella of Islam. To a great extent, Islamic civilization and Middle Eastern political power reached their peak at the same time. In the following centuries, the decline and fragmentation of Islamic empires led to the gradual decline in the region's power and culture.

■ Islam and Public Life

For many Muslims, Islam is a complete way of life that provides guiding principles for the personal and the public, for the individual and the community, for state as well as society (Hamidullah, 1979; Zubaida, 1993; el-Awa, 1980; Esposito, 1991). Muslim tradition teaches that the purpose of Islamic law *(sharia)* is to establish peace and justice, forbid evil, and enjoin the good. The purpose of politics in Islam is for governments to provide ethical governance in consultation with their citizens. Although Islam is not particular about the *form of government,* it is clear about the *purpose as well as ethics of governance* (Osman, 1994; Ahmad, 1986; Adams, 1983; Turabi, 1983). For many Muslims, this quality makes quranic injunction relevant to politics and society regardless of time and space. Thus politics and power have always been central to Islam, in contrast to early Christianity. The impact of European colonialism and the influence of a post-Enlightenment understanding of the nature of religion increasingly limited Islam to the private domain, but the continued political dimensions of Islam can be seen in a variety of events (Haynes, 1994:1–21).

Long before the Islamic Republic of Iran made a traumatic entry into world politics, Saudi Arabia had been created by the House of Saud as an Islamic state (Esposito, 1998:96–157). The Khilafat (caliphate) movement in India, the creation of a Muslim Pakistan, and the use of Islamic symbolism that accompanied the struggles for freedom from European colonialism (Libya, Algeria, Morocco, Sudan, and Pakistan) are all indications of how Islam played a major role in mass mobilization in moments of political crisis. Similarly, the use of *Allah-u-Akbar* (Allah Is Great) as the slogan of the Egyptian military in the Egyptian-Israeli war of 1973 and then by the secular Iraqi leader Saddam Hussein (in 1990, the slogan was hastily added to the Iraqi flag when it became evident that the U.S.-organized coalition would strike) underscores the importance of religion in popular politics in the Middle East.

This fusion of religion and politics is a characteristic feature of the contemporary resurgence of Islam. Islamic activists believe that once Islam is restored to its rightful place, at the center of all human affairs, the Muslim world will in turn regain its rightful place in international politics.

The Ommayad Mosque in Damascus, Syria, was originally constructed in 705 c.e. on the site of an ancient temple to the Roman goddess Jupiter.

■ Jerusalem: The Convergence of Power and Religious Symbolism

The present struggle for sovereignty over Jerusalem is symbolic of the convergence of the spiritual and the physical, the religious and the political in the Middle East. This "holy" city is historically as well as scripturally claimed by Jews, Muslims, and Christians. For the Jews, Jerusalem is the "mountain of the Lord." The Mishnah (second-century compendium of Jewish laws) asserts that the divine presence (*scechina*) has never left the Western Wall (Breger, 1996:91–118). Jerusalem has become the symbol and source of Jewish religious as well as nationalist identity.

In 70 C.E. the Romans destroyed the Second Temple in Jerusalem and expelled its Jewish population. Jews scattered throughout the world. Although many assimilated into the countries of their diaspora, they retained their faith and Jewish identity. Each year, Jews across the world conclude the Passover ceremonies with the determined wish, "Next Year in Jerusalem." The prophetic idea of an eventual gathering of all Jewish exiles into the land of their origin has influenced the attitudes of Westerners, Jewish as well as Christian, toward Jerusalem. The repeated assertion by Israeli leaders that a united Jerusalem is the eternal capital of Israel is an articulation of this biblical belief translated into a political vision. For 2,000 years, Jews have nursed the idea of returning to reclaim Jerusalem.

For Christians, Jerusalem is the site of their faith's origins and early history, where Jesus preached his message, was crucified, died, and was buried. It was there that in Christian belief Jesus was miraculously resurrected from the grave and ascended into heaven. The religious significance of Jerusalem was translated into the political when Pope Urban II summoned the First Crusade to recover Jerusalem and establish a Christian kingdom there (Runciman, 1992).

Christian political interest in Jerusalem was manifest more recently in the British mandate over Palestine and in continuing U.S. support for Israel. Christian groups and institutions such as the World Council of Churches and the Vatican have also maintained keen interest in the status of Jerusalem. Most important, Jerusalem and Palestine continue to be the home of Arab Christians, who have lived there for centuries. It is also significant to the many Christians who make pilgrimages to the historical Christian churches and sites in Jerusalem.

Jerusalem is one of the three most sacred places of Islam. It was the first city to which Muslims turned in prayer (subsequently changed to Mecca), and in Muslim belief, it is the place from which the Prophet Muhammad ascended to the heavens (*miraj haqq*) on a winged horse. According to Muslim eschatology (an aspect of theology that addresses the final events of human history), Jerusalem is the place where the end of time commences. Today, the loss of control of Jerusalem indicates to Muslims their ultimate defeat in what many regard as the unending Crusades launched by Christians against Islam. Failure to regain sovereignty over Jerusalem, they believe, is indicative of the decline of Islamic civilization and the failure of Palestinian aspirations to decolonize their land.

Jerusalem has also become a symbol of Western imperialism for many Muslims who see the continued expansion of Israel as a Western plot to dominate their lands and destroy Islam. They fear that under Israeli rule, Islam's third most important mosque (al-Aqsa/Bait-ul-Maqdis) will eventually be destroyed. Indeed some Jewish religious leaders and groups have expressed plans to rebuild the temple of King Solomon on that very site (Sprinzak, 1991:3–7; see also Mergui and Simonnot, 1987; Lustick, 1988; Friedman, 1990).

The continued settlement of Jews in Arab East Jerusalem and the forced evacuation of Palestinians, both Christian and Muslim, have only reinforced Muslim fears. Muslims see themselves as the inheritors of Judaism and Christianity. For them Islam bears the same message as Judaism and Christianity. They believe that Islam is a continuation and completion of Abraham's faith and that the Quran is the final revelation sent by the same God who sent his revelations through Moses and Jesus. In that same vein, many believe that they are the true inheritors of the Holy Land, symbolized by the conquest of Jerusalem by Umar ibn al-Khattab, the second of the "Rightly Guided Caliphs," in 637 C.E.

The struggle for Jerusalem is indeed representative of the intersection of religion and politics in the Middle East. It is in Jerusalem that the temporal, spiritual, political, cultural, and territorial converge. Jerusalem is both modern and traditional. It is modern in its status as the aspiration of Jewish and Palestinian nationalism, and it is traditional in its sacred significance to three religions. For many there can be no political solution for Jerusalem without a religious solution (Friedland and Hecht, 1995; Esposito, 1998:99–157). In Israel, where Zionism fuses religion and nationalism, the modern and the traditional are not distinguishable; neither are the religious and the political (Liebman, 1990; Liebman and Don-Yehiya, 1983). Thus Jerusalem symbolizes the significance of religion in the politics of the Middle East.

■ The Contemporary Role of Religion in Middle Eastern Politics

Religion continues to play a significant role in contemporary Middle Eastern politics. In Lebanon, Egypt, and Sudan, Christian minorities face issues regarding their status and role within Muslim majority societies. Jewish fundamentalism is altering the political equations in Israel and influencing the direction of the Arab-Israeli peace process. In terms of breadth of political impact, Islamic movements have often occupied center stage in attempts to transform the political and religious landscape of the Middle East.

◼ Christianity and Contemporary Politics

Christians in the Middle East constitute a diverse group spread widely across the Muslim world (Cragg, 1991). Because of their minority status in the states of the region, Christians have often espoused sharing power either through a quota system of proportional representation (Lebanon) or through secularization (Sudan), since it is only in secular or pluralistic societies that Middle Eastern Christians can hope to share power. Christians have made their presence felt politically in Egypt, where Egyptian Copts are often the standard for measuring the tolerance and pluralism of Egyptian society. The issue of Christians in Egypt has often been synonymous with the status of religious minorities within Islam (Haddad, 1995). Copts, whose presence in Egypt predates the advent of Islam, make up about 10 percent of the Egyptian population. They have heightened concerns about freedom of religious practice and protection from religious extremists such as the Gamaa Islamiyyah (Islamic Group) who target Copts and their businesses.

In Lebanon, the political system until recently favored Christian dominance. Today Muslims and Christians struggle to redefine their situation politically and socioeconomically. Lebanese Christians are significant in numbers, are politically very active, and share power with Sunni and Shi'a Muslims. Lebanon is a pluralist, multiethnic, and multireligious society that has experienced a fifteen-year civil war. Today the propensity for religious communities and political leaders to have their own armed militias is further compounded by the actions of Syria and Israel, which have occupied parts of the country in order to extend their influence and interests. Indeed, the term *Lebanization* has come to equal the older term *balkanization* as symbolic of widespread violence, political fragmentation, identity conflicts, and chaos (Salibi, 1981; Entelis, 1981).

In Sudan, resistance to the Islamization and Arabization policies pursued by the fundamentalist Sudanese government has produced an uneasy (and internally divided) alliance among Christians, moderate Muslims, and followers of traditional religions. Factions of this alliance have pursued both political resistance and civil war since then-president Jaafar Nimeiri's declaration of Islamic law in 1983 (Voll, 1991). In Sudan as well as Lebanon, Christian politics are also the simultaneous manifestation of sectarian, ethnic, and ideological cleavages.

Christian intervention in Middle Eastern politics today occurs on two levels. First, domestic Christian lobbies in the West pressure governments to accommodate religious considerations in their foreign policy (Spiegel,

1982–1983; Haynes, 1994; Thomas, 1995). Second, international actors such as the World Council of Churches and the Vatican have direct contact and influence with foreign governments and their constituencies to advance Christian interests. The contemporary concerns of Christian politics in the Middle East include (1) protecting the interests of the Christian minorities in Muslim states, (2) moderating Zionist and Israeli extremism in the Holy Land, and (3) preaching and proselytizing wherever and whenever possible (Breger, 1996:113).

■ Jewish Fundamentalism in Israel

Judaism, like Islam, has a religious-political tradition. Just as Islamic law *(sharia)* has been preeminent within Islamic traditions, so has Jewish law (halakah) been very important in the practice of the Jewish faith (Sivan, 1990a:3). Jewish politics today is a complex convergence of ethnicity, nationalism, and religious communalism.

In Israel, there is the presence of both Jewish nationalism and Jewish communalism. Israel's dominant ideology has been Zionism, a form of socialism that has provided a common nationalist identity to religious as well as secular Jews from various ethnic backgrounds such as Africa, the Middle East, Russia, Eastern and Western Europe, Palestine, and North America. It is an ideology driven by existential concerns to create a religious polity, Israel, that would guarantee the survival and future of the Jewish people (Vogel, 1986).

In recent years there has been a perceptible growth in Jewish radicalism and fundamentalist movements (Sprinzak, 1991). Religion and politics were fused in the conception of a Jewish/Zionist state, its secular and socialist ideology notwithstanding. The contemporary resurgence of hyper-Judaism in the Jewish right goes beyond the preexisting fusion of religion and politics. Fear that the territorial gains made in 1967 to realize the biblical or greater Israel of Judea and Samaria will be squandered and a growing disenchantment with the failure to institutionalize more fully the Jewish religious identity of Israel are two of the driving forces behind the contemporary resurgence of the Jewish right. The combination of this group's religious beliefs with their political interpretations are today a significant force affecting the Middle Eastern crisis (R. Friedman, 1992; M. Friedman, 1992; Hertzberg, 1992; Damant, 1995).

The various meanings of the diverse, sometimes contradictory beliefs incorporated in Jewish fundamentalism provide an important guide to understanding the changing political climate in Israel. Although Jewish fundamentalists may disagree on important matters, all agree on their people's right to their homeland. The cleavages in Jewish society have been identified by Ian Lustick (1988:1–17) as separating Jews into three groups: secular Zionists, Orthodox Jews, and Jewish fundamentalists.

An Orthodox Jewish youth praying at the Western Wall in Jerusalem.

Traditional Zionists, as discussed earlier, are basically secular Jews who connect the future of Jewish identity to the existence of a strong and independent Jewish nation-state. Their Jewish identity is a source of Jewish nationalism, which was harnessed for generating the political momentum necessary for the creation and sustenance of a Jewish state (Lustick, 1988). Historically, these individuals have tended to associate with the Labor Party in Israel.

The Haredim (literally meaning "the fearful" or "the God-fearing") constitute Orthodox Jewry.[4] They do not actively engage in politics in order to achieve rapid and comprehensive change in Israel. Their primary focus is that of religious observance, fulfilling the many and detailed rules and rituals that constitute Jewish law, the halakah. Wearing distinctive garb, they live in segregated neighborhoods and either isolate themselves from or oppose Zionism. However, their strong support for right-wing religious parties, their frequent confrontations with more secular Jews over issues of public religious observance, and their substantial financial support from the United States make them a significant force that can radicalize and desecularize Israeli politics (Ravitsky, 1993; see also Lustick, 1988; and Sprinzak, 1991).

Jewish fundamentalism is epitomized in Gush Emunim ("the bloc of the faithful"). The Gush Emunim believe that Jews are special and different because they are the "chosen people" selected by God to lead humanity in religious redemption. They do not consider Israel to be an ordinary nation-state. For them it is the divinely mandated state intended by God for a chosen people according to the Torah (Silberstein, 1993). Thus, they believe, Jews need to possess the land of Israel without remorse and self-doubt as they did more than 2,000 years ago through holy wars against the Canaanites. Indeed, many prominent leaders of Gush Emunim publicly refer to present-day Palestinians as Canaanites. They believe that Palestinian nationalism must be destroyed and view Arabs as the present manifestation of evil that must be conquered in order to establish the will of God and assert Jewish sovereignty over Israel (Lustick, 1988:72–91).

For the Gush Emunim, commitment to the realization of biblical political and territorial goals is a greater measure of faith than the Haredim's pursuit of ritualistic perfection. The Gush Emunim have strong symbiotic relations with the conservative Likud Party in Israel. They reinforce each other's political aspirations and in the process strengthen each other (Ravitsky, 1993).

From the early 1980s, a series of events pointed to the existence and growth of the Jewish right. On April 27, 1984, a plot to blow up five buses full of Arab passengers was discovered. This was followed by the discovery of a plan to destroy the Dome of the Rock using twenty-eight precision bombs. In both cases the would-be terrorists were members of Gush Emunim. These events were followed by the election to the Knesset of the late rabbi Meir Kahane, founder and leader of the aggressive and violent fundamentalist Jewish movement Kach (Thus), who advocated the violent expulsion of all Arabs from his vision of "Greater Israel" (Sprinzak, 1991:3–7).[5] In 1995, the assassination of Israeli prime minister Yitzhak Rabin by a rightwing Jewish extremist, who cited Jewish religious law to justify his actions (*New York Times,* November 19, 1995:1), stunned Israelis and the international community.

The Jewish right is primarily a domestic force within Israel. However, its opposition to any reconciliation with the Palestinians or the Arabs made it a regional player in Middle Eastern politics. The unwillingness of the religious right to support negotiations on the status of Jerusalem proved to be a major hurdle to a peaceful solution of the Arab-Israeli conflict. For the religious right to renegotiate what they believe is a religious mandate is to compromise religion for politics. Religion, they say, should dictate politics, not vice versa.

■ The Resurgence of Political Islam

The contemporary resurgence of Islam and its impact on regional and world politics has generally overshadowed Christian and Jewish religious politics in the Middle East. It has transformed the basic character of two prominent states—Iran and Sudan—and significantly influenced many others. Political Islam has seriously challenged the seventy-year-old secular trajectory of Turkey (Khan, 1996), and in December 1991 and January 1992 the Islamic

Salvation Front (FIS) would have won parliamentary elections in Algeria if not for the intervention of the secular military elite. Islamic nationalist movements such as Hamas and Hezbollah, using Katyusha rockets and suicide bombings, have compromised Israeli security in Lebanon and Israel/Palestine. Egypt, Saudi Arabia, Tunisia, Bahrain, and Jordan have experienced Islamic resurgence and, at times, its challenge to the legitimacy of their political regimes (Esposito, 1999; Ayubi, 1991; Keppel, 1985; Abu-Amr, 1994).

The Islamic resurgence is a response to an amalgam of crises in the Middle East. Because of a crisis of identity, Muslim societies are caught between traditional loyalties, secular nationalism, and modern Islamic thrusts toward Islamic nationalism (Esposito, 1999; Choueiri, 1990; Husain, 1995). In the crisis of modernization, top-down attempts at modernization have led to urbanization but limited economic development, resulting in a large, educated, urban class disaffected by high unemployment, a growing gap between rich and poor, and widespread corruption. A crisis of change has occurred because decolonization from the West, although successful, resulted in regime change but very little system change (Rahnema, 1994; Sidahmed and Ehteshami, 1996). People found themselves under authoritarian and military rule, in states where the ruling elites equated modernization with Westernization. Critics dismissed secular Westernized elites as "Westoxicated" or the product of "Westruckness." Finally, a crisis of power was engendered by conflict with Israel. The failure to recover territories from Israel and its continued expansion, including its control over Jerusalem, has merely underscored for many the inability of Muslims to protect their lands and their religion from the repeated assaults of an imperial West (Esposito 1983, 1998:11–24).

Thus the current Islamic resurgence is a broad-based grassroots response to multiple crises. It is a struggle for both cultural authenticity and self-determination (Ayubi, 1991:214–220; Esposito, 1998; Haynes, 1994:66–94). Some have described it as "civil society striking back" at incompetent and inefficient yet authoritarian and dictatorial states (Sivan, 1990b; Fuller, 1995). In many places it plays role similar to that of a state by providing health care, education, and economic assistance. Some see moderate Islamic movements as not just an institution of civil society but as the authentic impulse of the masses to democratize Muslim polities. Others in the West as well as in the Muslim world fear that democratization will facilitate Islamization in the Middle East, destroying regimes, threatening access to oil, and undermining the Arab-Israeli peace process (Pipes, 1995:57; Miller, 1993; also see Rodman, 1994).

Islamic movements and organizations, both moderate and extremist, have become major actors and agents of change. They have established modern political and social organizations and embrace modern means to disseminate their messages in the media, in audio- and videotapes, through faxes, and over the Internet. The majority of them function within civil society as social and political activists. The Muslim Brotherhoods of Egypt and Jordan, Pakistan's Jamaat-i-Islami, Turkey's Refah Party, Tunisia's Al-Nahda, and Algeria's Islamic Salvation Front, to name a few, eschew violence and participate in electoral politics. They build schools, hospitals, clinics, and banks; offer inexpensive legal and social services; and are leaders in politics and in professional associations of doctors, lawyers, engineers, and teachers.

At the same time, a minority of extremists seek to overthrow regimes and impose their own brand of Islam. Egypt's Gamaa Islamiyyah, Algeria's Armed Islamic Group, and jihad organizations in many countries have engaged in violence and terrorism that have threatened the stability and security of many regimes and extended its reach to Europe (bombings in Paris) and the United States (attacks of September 11, 2001).

Islamic movements aim to liberate Muslim societies from Western (European, Soviet, and U.S.) colonial domination as well as from cultural imperialism (Esposito, 1999). Some seek to revive Islamic values in order to establish Islamic states as first steps toward the higher end of establishing a global Islamic *umma* (community) (Abu-Rabi, 1994). Political Islam has not opposed modernization, but it does oppose the Westernization and secularization of society. It embraces modern technology and science but rejects Western secular and cultural values. Islamists see no necessary linkage between technological advancement and economic development on the one hand, and Western secular modernization on the other (Voll, 1994; Esposito, 1998).

In Algiers, Algeria, women march to protest
the policies of Islamic militants.

They believe that the primary interest of the West in the Middle East lies in exploiting the natural resources of the Muslim world, notably oil. They see the threat from the West as one of political domination and cultural penetration (Abu-Rabi, 1996; Esposito, 1999).

The role of Islam in contemporary Middle Eastern politics is unlikely to wane in the near future. It is gaining strength across social and economic strata in many Muslim societies. Many governments are plagued by issues of legitimacy, authoritarianism, failing economies, maldistribution of wealth, corruption, and human rights abuses. Although the impact of change is felt by almost all, the benefits of modernization have been shared by very few. Many of the younger generation resent existing regimes and their failure to deliver on their promises and are more critical of political, economic, and cultural dependence on the West. Secular elites, a minority often blamed for the failures of their societies, are increasingly challenged by the emergence of an alternative elite, more educated, more Islamically oriented, and more critical of the failures and excesses of modernity.

■ Understanding the Role of Religion in Middle Eastern Politics

The study of religion has once again become important in the early twenty-first century, especially with the end of the Cold War (1945–1989), during which the study of developing societies by most social scientists and other experts proceeded from a Eurocentric assumption that sooner or later the Middle East, like the rest of the third world, would resemble the West in its modern and secular outlook. This precluded any systematic study of religion and its political potency (Appleby, 1994:chap. 1).

The study of religion and politics was left to sociologists and historians of religion (Mottahedeh, 1985; Voll, 1994). The failure of most political analysis to take religion seriously was exposed when the Iranian revolution exploded on the scene of world politics in 1979 (Esposito, 1990). Since then the religious resurgence of Islam in the Middle East has provided the necessary impetus for political scientists to study the contemporary ascendance of religion in the political sphere (e.g., Ayubi, 1991; Zubaida, 1993; Burgat and Dowell, 1993; Fuller and Lesser, 1995; Esposito, 1998; Sivan, 1985; Munson, 1988; Choueiri, 1990).

The global resurgence of religion shattered the expectations of most experts, who had assumed that the rest of the world would duplicate the Western experience of political development (Thomas, 1995:289). None had anticipated the force with which religion would once again enter the realm of politics. William Swatos, a sociologist, expressed the sentiments of the academic community: "There is no weapon in the theoretical arsenal of the social scientific study of religion or of political science that can attack the problem of worldwide religious resurgence. The two primary theories of "moderniza-tion"—development or exploitation—both proceed from the assumption that religious "prejudices" hamper "progress" and are disappearing throughout the world" (1989a:1).

Scholars had allowed their bias for secularism to incapacitate their disci-plines when it came to the study of religion, transforming a theory into a dogma. Jeffery Hadden, in his 1986 presidential address to the Southern Soci-ological Society, noted that "in form and its genesis" secularization consti-tuted a "*doctrine* more than a theory," based upon presuppositions that repre-sent a "taken-for-granted *ideology*" of social science "rather than a systematic set of interrelated propositions." He further argued that over time, "*the idea of secularization became sacralized*," that is, it became a belief system accepted "on faith" (quoted in Swatos, 1989b:146).

In a powerful indictment of social scientists' antipathy for religion, Fred Von Der Mehden (1986:13–19) argues that not only are these scholars alien-ated from religion but they are also hostile toward it. He also points out that theoretical conclusions about the relations of tradition and religion to mod-ernization, particularly in the third world, were often drawn without any first-hand experience of or familiarity with the regions, religions, or traditions.

This blind faith in secularization has had two negative impacts on the study of religion and politics. First, religion was either excluded or boxed in the amorphous category of "culture," along with ethnicity, tradition, and trib-alism, only to be taken seriously after unexpected events such as the Islamic revolution in Iran. Second, this ideology has led to an a priori delegitimiza-tion of ideas such as the Islamic state or Islamic governance because they challenge the dominant faith in secularization. Some scholars of international relations, who faced a similar crisis at the failure of their theories to anticipate the Cold War, mused: "Theory is supposed to free scholars from their politi-cal, generational, and cultural biases. But social theory inevitably reflects these biases. It does a disservice when it confers an aura of scientific legiti-macy on subjective political beliefs and assumptions" (Lebow and Risse-Kappen, 1995:5). Thus a belief in secularism, or what some have called "sec-ular fundamentalism," as a necessity for development prevented many analysts from appreciating the significant role that religion plays in Middle Eastern politics.

■ Conclusion

Religion has once again become a major theme in the study of world pol-itics, particularly in the context of the Middle East. Rather than receding, reli-gion has returned to the center stage. History is not progressing according to the script that modernity had envisaged for the region, which is developing both in political and economic terms, but also not along the lines that Western social sciences had predicted. The long history of the nexus between power and religion and current conditions in the Middle East suggests that Western-style secularism will continue to be challenged by the contemporary religious resurgence.

A particular reading of postcolonial history created the false expectation that the Middle East was well on the way toward secularization. In recent years, new Islamic republics have been declared in Iran, Sudan, and Afghanistan. In Morocco, as in Saudi Arabia, the monarchy is strongly legitimized by its close association with Islam. In Jordan, King Hussein never forgot to mention his lineage, which he traced back to the Prophet Muhammad. Muslim rulers remain acutely sensitive to the power of religion, and opposition movements also appeal to Islam for legitimacy and popular support.

Similarly, Israel's very existence and identity remain tied to Judaism. Many believers base their political agenda on issues and sites that their faith holds sacred. Whether to defend the status quo or to condemn it, politicians in the Middle East, Jews as well as Muslims, invoke religious categories. The difference between the role of religion in contemporary politics, in politics in the precolonial past, and in politics in the postcolonial secular era has been one of degree, not of kind.

In the twenty-first century, religion will continue to be a major driving force in global politics. It performs many political functions, just as politics serves many religious functions in the traditional land of God, the Middle East. Religion is a source of identity as well as signification, providing symbols of authentication and meaning for social and political existence. It is the basis for states as well as a source of civil society. It is invoked to give legitimacy to systems and regimes and to provide revolutionary fodder to challenge the legitimacy of states, systems, and regimes. Jerusalem represents the locus where all three Abrahamic faiths have come together in the past and remains the subject of common and at times competing claims. The challenge for the religious politics of the Middle East in coming years, as with the issue of Jerusalem, will be developing a pluralistic mode of existence based on the recognition of shared principles, values, and interests amid acknowledged religious and political differences.

■ **Notes**

This chapter was written by John L. Esposito and Mohammed A. Muqtedor Khan for the first edtion of the book; it was updated and revised by Jillian Schwedler for this edition.

1. For a graphic description of the massacre in Jerusalem, see Runciman, 1992:187–188, and Mayer, 1988.

2. Islamic traditions refer to Jews and Christians as "People of the Book" and recognize the common origins of the Torah, the New Testament, and the Quran.

3. Ironically, considerable missionary efforts were expended in Arab communities who had been Christian for centuries but who followed ancient branches of Christianity not fully understood by nineteenth-century Western churches.

4. The Islamic equivalent of this term is Mutaqqi, also meaning "the God-fearing."

5. In March 1994, following the massacre of twenty-nine Muslim worshipers in Hebron by a Kach follower, Kach and another Kahane-inspired organization were banned by the Israeli government under its antiterrorist laws.

■ Bibliography

Abu-Amr, Ziad. 1994. *Islamic Fundamentalism in the West Bank and Gaza: Muslim Brotherhood and Islamic Jihad*. Bloomington: Indiana University Press.

Abu-Rabi, Ibrahim (ed.). 1994. *Islamic Resurgence: Challenges, Directions, and Future Perspectives*. Tampa, Fla.: World and Islam Studies Enterprise.

———. 1996. *Intellectual Origins of Islamic Resurgence in the Modern Arab World*. New York: State University of New York Press.

Adams, Charles. 1983. "Maududi and the Islamic State." Pp. 99–133 in John Esposito (ed.), *Voices of Resurgent Islam*. Oxford: Oxford University Press.

Ahmad, Mumtaz (ed.). 1986. *State Politics and Islam*. Indianapolis, Ind.: American Trust.

Appleby, Scott R. 1994. *Religious Fundamentalisms and Global Conflict*. New York: Foreign Policy Association.

Armstrong, Karen. 1991. *Holy War: The Crusades and Their Impact on Today's World*. New York: Doubleday.

Ayubi, Nazih. 1991. *Political Islam: Religion and Politics in the Arab World*. London: Routledge.

Breger, Marshall. 1996. "Religion and Politics in Jerusalem." *Journal of International Affairs,* 50, no. 1:91–118.

Burgat, François, and William Dowell. 1993. *The Islamic Movement in North Africa*. Austin: University of Texas Press.

Cavendish, Richard. 1980. *The Great Religions*. New York: Arco Press.

Choueiri, Youssef. 1990. *Islamic Fundamentalism*. Boston: Twayne.

Cleveland, William L. 1994. *A History of the Modern Middle East*. Boulder, Colo.: Westview Press.

Cragg, Kenneth. 1991. *The Arab Christian: A History in the Middle East*. Louisville, Ken.: Westminster/John Knox Press.

Damant, Peter. 1995. *Jewish Fundamentalism in Israel: Implications for the Mideast Conflict*. Jerusalem: Israel/Palestine Center for Research and Information.

el-Awa, Muhammad. 1980. *On the Political System of the Islamic State*. Indianapolis, Ind.: American Trust.

Entelis, John. 1981. "Ethnic Conflict and the Reemergence of Radical Christian Nationalism in Lebanon." Pp. 227–246 in Michael Curtis (ed.), *Religion and Politics in the Middle East*. Boulder, Colo.: Westview Press.

Esposito, John L. (ed.). 1983. *Voices of Resurgent Islam*. Oxford: Oxford University Press.

——— (ed.). 1990. *The Iranian Revolution: Its Global Impact*. Miami: Florida International University Press.

——. 1991. *Islam: The Straight Path*. 2nd ed. New York: Oxford University Press.

——. 1998. *Islam and Politics*. 4th ed. Syracuse, N.Y.: Syracuse University Press.

——. 1999. *The Islamic Threat: Myth or Reality?* 3rd ed. New York: Oxford University Press.

Esposito, John L., and John Voll. 1996. *Islam and Democracy*. London: Oxford University Press.

Friedland, Roger, and Richard D. Hecht. 1995. "The Politics of Time and Space in Jerusalem: Interest, Symbol, and Power." Pp. 373–424 in Sabrina P. Ramet and Donald W. Treadgold (eds.), *Render unto Caesar: The Religious Sphere in World Politics*. Boston: American University Press.

Friedman, Menachem. 1992. "Jewish Zealots: Conservative Versus Innovative." Pp. 159–176 in Lawrence Kaplan (ed.), *Fundamentalism in Comparative Perspective*. Amherst: University of Massachusetts Press.

Friedman, Robert. 1990. *The False Prophet: Rabbi Meir Kahane from FBI Informant to Knesset Member*. Chicago: Lawrence Hill Books.

——. 1992. *Zealots for Zion: Inside Israel's West Bank Settlement Movement*. New York: Random House.

Fuller, Graham. 1995. "Has Political Islam Failed?" *Middle East Insight* (January–February):8–11.

Fuller, Graham, and Ian Lesser. 1995. *A Sense of Siege: The Geopolitics of Islam and the West*. Boulder, Colo.: Westview Press.

Gellner, Ernest. 1992. *Postmodernism, Reason and Religion*. London: Routledge.

Haddad, Yvonne. 1995. "Christians in a Muslim State: The Recent Egyptian Debate." Pp. 381–398 in Yvonne Haddad and Wadi Haddad (eds.), *Christian-Muslim Encounters*. Miami: University of Florida Press.

Hamidullah, Muhammad. 1979. *Introduction to Islam*. London: MWH London.

Haynes, Jeffrey. 1994. *Religion in Third World Politics*. Boulder, Colo.: Lynne Rienner.

Hertzberg, Arthur. 1992. "Jewish Fundamentalism." Pp. 152–159 in Lawrence Kaplan (ed.), *Fundamentalism in Comparative Perspective*. Amherst: University of Massachusetts Press.

Huntington, Samuel. 1968. *Political Order in Changing Societies*. New Haven, Conn.: Yale University Press.

Husain, Mir Zohair. 1995. *Global Islamic Politics*. New York: HarperCollins College.

Keppel, Gilles. 1985. *Muslim Extremism in Egypt: The Prophet and Pharaoh*. Los Angeles: University of California Press.

Khan, Mohammed A. Muqtedar. 1996. "Turkey Returns." *The Message,* August, pp. 15–17.

Lamb, Harold. 1930. *The Crusades*. New York: International Collectors Library.

Lebow, Richard Ned, and Thomas Risse-Kappen (eds.). 1995. *International Relations Theory and the End of the Cold War*. New York: Columbia University Press.

Lewis, Bernard. 1968. *The Emergence of Modern Turkey*. London: Oxford University Press.

——. 1993. *Islam and the West*. New York: Oxford University Press.

Liebman, Charles. 1990. "The Jewish Religion and Contemporary Israeli Nationalism." Pp. 77–94 in Emmanuel Sivan and Menachem Friedman (eds.), *Religious Radicalism and Politics in the Middle East*. New York: State University of New York Press.

Liebman, Charles, and Eliezer Don-Yehiya. 1983. *Civil Religion in Israel*. Los Angeles: University of California Press.

Lindholm, Charles. 1996. *The Islamic Middle East: An Historical Anthropology*. Oxford: Blackwell.

Lustick, Ian S. 1988. *For the Land and the Lord: Jewish Fundamentalism in Israel*. New York: Council on Foreign Relations.

Mahallati, Mohammad. 1996. "The Middle East: In Search of an Equilibrium Between Transcendental Idealism and Practicality." *Journal of International Affairs* 50, no. 1:119–141.

Marcus, Abraham. 1989. *The Middle East on the Eve of Modernity*. New York: Columbia University Press.

Mayer, H. E. 1988. *The Crusades*. New York: Oxford University Press.

Mergui, Raphael, and Philippe Simonnot. 1987. *Israel's Ayatollahs: Meir Kahane and the Far Right in Israel*. London: Saqi Books.

Miller, Judith. 1993. "The Challenge of Radical Islam." *Foreign Affairs* 72, no. 2:43–56.

Minault, Gail. 1974. "Islam and Mass Politics: The Indian Ulama and the Khilafat Movement." Pp. 168–182 in Donald E. Smith (ed.), *Religion and Political Modernization*. New Haven, Conn.: Yale University Press.

Mottahedeh, Roy. 1985. *The Mantle of the Prophet: Religion and Politics in Iran*. New York: Pantheon Books.

Munson, Henry, Jr. 1988. *Islam and Revolution in the Middle East*. New Haven, Conn.: Yale University Press.

Osman, Fathi. 1994. *Sharia in Contemporary Society: The Dynamics of Change in Islamic Law*. Los Angeles: M. V. International.

Pipes, Daniel. 1995. "There Are No Moderates: Dealing with Fundamentalist Islam." *National Interest* 41:57.

Rahnema, Ali (ed.). 1994. *Pioneers of Islamic Revival*. London: Zed Books.

Ravitsky, Aviezer. 1993. *Messianism, Zionism, and Jewish Religious Radicalism*. Chicago: Chicago University Press.

Rodman, Peter. 1994. "Co-opt or Confront Fundamentalist Islam?" *Middle East Quarterly* 1, no. 4:61–64.

Runciman, Steven. 1992. *The First Crusade*. Abridged ed. New York: Cambridge University Press.

Salibi, Kamal. 1981. "The Lebanese Identity." Pp. 217–226 in Michael Curtis (ed.), *Religion and Politics in the Middle East*. Boulder, Colo.: Westview Press.

Shahin, Emad Eldin. 1995. "Under the Shadow of the Imam." *Middle East Insight* 11:40–45.

Sidahmed, A. Salam, and A. Ehteshami (eds.). 1996. *Islamic Fundamentalism*. Boulder, Colo.: Westview Press.

Silberstein, Lawrence (ed.). 1993. *Jewish Fundamentalism in Comparative Perspective: Religion, Ideology, and the Crisis of Modernity*. New York: New York University Press.

Sivan, Emmanuel. 1985. *Radical Islam: Medieval Theology and Modern Politics*. New Haven, Conn.: Yale University Press.

———. 1990a. "Introduction." Pp. 1–9 in Emmanuel Sivan and Menachem Friedman (eds.), *Religious Radicalism and Politics in the Middle East*. New York: State University of New York Press.

———. 1990b. "The Islamic Resurgence: Civil Society Strikes Back." Pp. 96–108 in Lawrence Kaplan (ed.), *Fundamentalism in Comparative Perspective*. Amherst: University of Massachusetts Press.

Spiegel, Steven. 1982–1983. "Religious Components of U.S. Middle East Policy." *Journal of International Affairs* 36, no. 2:235–246.

Sprinzak, Ehud. 1991. *The Ascendance of Israel's Radical Right*. New York: Oxford University Press.

Swatos, William, Jr. 1989a. "The Kingdom of God and the World of Man: The Problem of Religious Politics." Pp. 1–10 in William Swatos Jr. (ed.), *Religious Politics in Global and Comparative Perspective*. New York: Greenwood Press.

——. 1989b. "Losing Faith in the 'Religion' of Secularization: Worldwide Religious Resurgence and the Definition of Religion." Pp. 147–154 in William Swatos Jr. (ed.), *Religious Politics in Global and Comparative Perspective*. New York: Greenwood Press.

Thomas, Scott. 1995. "The Global Resurgence of Religion and the Study of World Politics." *Millennium: Journal of International Studies* 24, no. 2:289–299.

Turabi, Hassan. 1983. "The Islamic State." Pp. 241–251 in John Esposito (ed.), *Voices of Resurgent Islam*. Oxford: Oxford University Press.

Usher, Graham. 1996. "Picture of War." *Middle East International* 535:3–5.

Vogel, Manfred. 1986. "The State as Essential Expression of the Faith of Judaism." Pp. 11–20 in Nigel Biggar, Jamies S. Scott, and William Schwieker (eds.), *Cities of God: Faith, Politics, and Pluralism in Judaism, Christianity, and Islam*. Westport, Conn.: Greenwood Press.

Voll, John (ed.). 1991. *Sudan: State and Society in Crisis*. Bloomington: Indiana University Press.

——. 1994. *Islam: Continuity and Change in the Modern World*. Syracuse, N.Y.: Syracuse University Press.

Von Der Mehden, Fred. 1986. *Religion and Modernization in Southeast Asia*. Syracuse, N.Y.: Syracuse University Press.

Zubaida, Sami. 1993. *Islam, the People, and the State: Political Ideas and Movements in the Middle East*. London: I. B. Taurus.

Middle Eastern Literature

miriam cooke

In this chapter I discuss the emergence of literature in the Middle East as a new art form. European modernity hit the countries of the Middle East hard. Everything formerly accepted as normative came under question, nothing more so than literature. Traditional notions of what literature was and what function it should fulfill in the life of the individual and society changed. No longer the repository for all knowledge, *adab* (literature) branched out into the various genres of drama, short story, novel, and a radically new conception of poetry.

It is not possible to understand the role of literature in the Middle East without first glancing at its history and, above all, its evolution during the first half of the twentieth century. Although Middle Eastern literatures have become privileged sites for recording and engaging with sociopolitical tensions and conflicts, this was not always the case. In the medieval and early modern periods, Middle Eastern literatures had been the preserve of the elite, providing them with literary frames in which they might elaborate an already familiar tradition and demonstrate formal skills and erudition. Popular literature such as *A Thousand and One Nights* also relied on the already known. The roles of the imagination and of social commentary were generally downplayed in the Middle Eastern context.

■ European Colonialism and Its Discontents

The arrival in the late eighteenth and nineteenth centuries of the French and British colonial expeditions, with their technological, cultural, and intellectual institutions, forced a new look at society and culture. Contact with

European modernity cast Islamic cultures in a poor contrastive light. Egyptians in particular, because they were the first to experience French colonialism, became concerned to learn about Western culture and science.

Under such Ottoman rulers as Muhammad Ali Pasha and his son Ibrahim Pasha, groups of male scholars traveled to Western Europe, and particularly to France, to study scientific texts and to translate them into Arabic. Because of the enormity of the task, these scientific missions might stay in Europe for months on end. When they were not squirreled away in the libraries or archives, they were in the theaters watching plays by French playwrights like Jean-Baptiste Molière or in their rooms reading short stories in French by such writers as Guy de Maupassant or the Russian Anton Chekhov in French translation. The genre that was the newest and the most intriguing was the novel, and these men returned with translations of European masterpieces by Honoré de Balzac, Gustave Flaubert, Leo Tolstoy, and Ivan Turgenev, to mention only a few.

Some of these intellectuals understood that the writing and function of literature in the Middle East had to change to accommodate the new realities in their lives. They knew, however, that those who were unfamiliar with the new genres of short story, novel and play, and modern poetry might resist their introduction. The apparent focus of European fiction writers on entertainment at the expense of traditional education, on communication of sociopolitical messages of current concern and not so much on literary artifice and excellence was greeted by some with the skepticism reserved for the introduction of anything new anywhere. Like the reactionary defenders of the Western canon, who in the 1980s announced the end of civilization as we know it if subaltern, marginalized literatures were to replace some of the time-tested writings of dead white Western men, the conservative elites of the region warned of civilizational decline, even extinction. Some feared that the great classical literatures of the Arabs, Persians, and Turks might not survive the invasion into literature of the trivia of the modern world. Literary practitioners would surely lose their storehouse of classical knowledge if they did not continually tap into it and thus renew it. They would lose their verbal agility if they turned from the eloquent description of great events in history to the banality of the world around them. Others saw in the dialogue between their own cultural traditions and those of the Europeans the possibility of reimagining national identity within a common modernity.

Whether they were closed or open to the outside world, Middle Eastern intellectuals became engaged in the question of language as central to the process of modernization. They questioned, first of all, the boundary between the high-culture languages and the vernaculars of importing foreign words. In Iran, historian Mohamad Tavakoli-Targhi explains, the key was to disassociate from the Islamic past and to project a "pure" national origin. Arabic words that had been part of the language for half a millennium were purged, and "authentic" Persian terms were forged, and neologisms and lexicography were constituted as endeavors for "national reawakening." . . . The invention of an idealized past was contemporaneous with the restyling of language, which was achieved in a dialogic relationship with Iran's Arab-, European-, and (the often ignored) Indian-Other. . . . The Persian language was reconstituted as the essential component of Iranian national identity. (Tavakoli-Targhi, 1990:77, 86)

Language reform "was not an aftereffect of the constitutional revolutions in Iran and the Ottoman Empire but a prelude to them. Purists constituted language as the essential component of the national identity" (Tavakoli-Targhi, 1990:91). History could not be reconceived without a radical transformation of the language and its grammar.

In the case of Turkish and Arabic, the linguistic situation was more extreme because of the distance between the classical and the colloquial languages. Indeed, in both cases there had emerged a kind of bilingualism. The written language of the Turks was so different from the spoken that it was even named differently: it was called Ottoman Turkish. Written in the Arabic script and filled with Persian and Arabic vocabulary—as much as 75 percent—this Ottoman Turkish had to be learned as an entirely distinct language with its own rules of grammar (Halman, 1982:36). Paradoxically, the poetry of the mystic Yunus Emre (d. ca. 1321), written before the Turks' importation of a foreign lexicon (partly as a result of their embracing Islam), is more accessible to Turks schooled in the post-Atatürk era than the literature they learned from their grandparents. Mustafa Kemal Atatürk's Westernization campaign in the 1920s, which entailed the eradication of Islamic elements in the language, put an end to the "bilingual" situation that had pertained in Turkey for centuries.

There has been no comparable revolution in the Arab world, and so the split between the classical and colloquial Arabic languages persists until today. The codification of the spoken language is still tentative because the Arabic of the Quran retains its place of honor as the literary medium of expression. Conservative Arab intellectuals feared that the use of colloquial expressions in literature, particularly since there was no consensus over the way in which the colloquial should be codified, might herald the demise of the scriptural language; it might put an end to a pan-Arab literature, because these vulgar languages would create a tower of Babel in which multiple, mutually incomprehensible local literatures would vie for a small spot on the grand stage of what had once been a great and unified literary tradition.

Such anxieties notwithstanding, some Middle Eastern intellectuals, particularly those who had traveled to Europe with the scientific missions, turned their attention to the great French, English, and Russian writers of the day. Indeed, French had become the lingua franca in many Middle Eastern countries, even in those like Turkey that had not experienced the *mission civil-*

isatrice (civilizing mission). Flaubert and Maupassant, Charles Dickens and Percy Bysshe Shelley, as well as Chekhov and Tolstoy in French translation, all provided models of how the crises and concerns of the modern world could be turned into works of literary merit. During the earliest periods, these modernist intellectuals translated nineteenth-century European literature into their own languages. By the 1880s, however, some were experimenting with this new kind of writing. The Syrian-Lebanese Jurji Zaydan (1861–1914), for instance, wrote a series of historical novels and even a short autobiographical piece. Despite the general disapproval of writing one's own life, Zaydan published the story of his education during a time of major upheaval, having recognized in his experiences those of others.

■ Cultural Ferment at the Turn of the Twentieth Century

Early-twentieth-century Egypt provided the regional context for literary experimentation and excitement. Middle Eastern intellectuals who did not go to Paris might move to Cairo to participate in the excitement of cultural innovations and transformations. Literary salons convened men and sometimes even women to discuss the new trends in politics and literature. At a time when most middle- and upper-class women were confined to their homes, these gatherings of intellectuals were almost the only places where women could appear with men. Literary schools in Egypt, such as the Diwan School, the New School, and the Apollo School (none of which included women among their numbers), encouraged the production of new kinds of writing that were then often published in their own journals and newspapers. These debates and their publication produced a new space, that of the public sphere. Discussions about national identity and the new roles women and men were expected to play in the nation of the future became matters concerning everyone and not merely a restricted community of scholars, often religious scholars. In the process, new conceptions of literary criticism appeared.

The new critics' insistence on the centrality of the imagination in works of art and the need for the work to interact with and hopefully to change society influenced a new generation of critics and writers. The notion that criticism should be neither descriptive nor evaluative but rather investigative led to some radical critical writing. Taha Husayn (1889–1973), the Egyptian author of dozens of books, including novels, works of philosophy, and his own autobiography, titled *The Days* (1929), published in 1926 his book *On Pre-Islamic Poetry,* which calls into question the dating of some of this poetry. There was an uproar because this poetry, composed before the time of the prophet Muhammad, was considered to be the paragon of literary expression, and with the Quran, it was cherished as the perfect classical Arabic language that the prophet spoke. To cast doubt on its authenticity was to throw into turmoil other certainties connected to the founding moment of Islam. New literary critical tools were opening up new ways of approaching old texts, and above all they were revolutionizing literary production.

Simultaneous with this literary activity in Egypt, two revolutions broke out in Turkey and Iran. Young Turks and Iranians brought up on Enlightenment ideals rebelled against autocratic, self-indulgent rule by the last rulers of the Ottoman and the Qajar Empires. Between 1919 and 1922 Mustafa Kemal (1881–1938, known as Atatürk after 1933), waged his war of independence against the British, French, Italians, and Greeks. The expulsion of these foreigners was followed by a series of revolutions that continued beyond the 1923 founding of the Turkish republic. Upon assuming national leadership, Atatürk abolished the Ottoman caliphate in 1924 and then implemented his secularization program. He introduced a new Europeanized dress code and declared illegal the wearing of Islamic dress, such as the veil. Most traumatic for traditional litterateurs, in 1928 he replaced the Arabic-based Ottoman script with the Latin alphabet. Yakup Kadri Karaosmanoglu (1889–1974) is the writer who best encapsulates the mood of the times, which Talat Halman describes as being marked by "the disintegration of Ottoman society, ferocious political enmities, and the immoral lives of religious sects, as well as the conflicts between urban intellectuals and poverty-stricken peasants" (1982:29). Karaosmanoglu saw himself as a representative of the new cultural revolution that had to be spread throughout the country. His book *The Outsider* tells a typical story of the alienation of the Middle Eastern government official when confronting rural peoples to whom he has been sent. But in this case, Karaosmanoglu adds to the sense of rejection and disappointment. He describes the failure of the city intellectuals to convey the meaning and passion of the revolution and the new Turkish nationalism to the farmers.

In 1905, Iran was rocked by its constitutional revolution. Nationalists confronted the British and the local feudal landlords, demanded a constitution that would vouchsafe them democracy and justice, and eventually agreed on a compromise. The period was rich with new kinds of writing, most of it referred to as *pishru* (progressive). These liberal and often socialist writings depict the turmoil of the period. They reacted against the purple prose and the social irrelevance of the Qajar writers. After his coup in 1921, Mohammad Reza Shah became absolute monarch of Iran. He introduced strict censorship and centralized control, but he also concerned himself with the position of women. In 1936, perhaps in response to Atatürk's recent prohibition on the wearing of the veil, the shah enforced unveiling. Some see this measure as helpful to women, whereas others recognize in it yet another violence done to women in the name of progress. To force a woman to unveil who is not ready to reveal her face is tantamount to asking her to strip publicly. Many writers have dealt with the topic.

Such legislation against veiling should be seen against the background of late-nineteenth-century debates about feminism that were going on throughout the Middle East and beyond. Claims on behalf of women's education were entering the public sphere. Recent research by feminist scholars both in the Middle East and elsewhere has revealed that it was women themselves who were the first to raise the issue of women's absence in decisionmaking positions at the national or local levels. Yet it was not until the men took up the "woman question" that it became a matter for common concern.

In 1899, the Egyptian reformer Qasim Amin (1865–1908) had published his controversial book *The Liberation of Women,* in which he called for the education of women, as the mothers of the next generation, as well as for their unveiling and greater participation in the life of the nation. Along with other modernist reformers of the period who emphasized companionate marriage and nuclear families in a world where all individuals had the right to freedom and equality, Amin was drawing attention to the fact that when half a people do not engage in the activities of the other half, then the whole suffers. This emphasis on women as the gauge of a society's progress seems to reflect James Stuart Mill's reference in 1817 to India's barbarity being demonstrated by the fact that "women were in a state of abject slavery." As employee of the East India Company, Mill clearly felt himself authorized to make such pronouncements. The Western, colonial origin of these ideas was not lost on the more conservative Middle Eastern intelligentsia.

It was not only in his native Egypt but throughout the Middle East that Amin's treatise was influential. In 1900, *The Liberation of Women* was partially translated into Persian. Its publication in Iran did not launch the kind of debate about the rights and roles of women that it had in Egypt because it fell on fallow ground (Najmabadi, 1998:100–104). In 1921, Mohammed Ali Jamalzadeh (b. 1892) had brought out his first collection of stories, titled *Once upon a Time.* The collection is as famous for its introduction, which explains the new function of literature as a mirror for the times, as it is for its satirical descriptions of Shi'ite scholars and its sympathetic portrayals of the lives of ordinary women and men (Daragahi, 1984:104–123). The following year, Morteza Moshfeq Kazemi published his two-volume work *Horrible Teheran,* which takes up the cause of women by describing the numerous abuses they routinely suffer.

Atatürk may not have been directly influenced by the Middle Eastern debates surrounding the "woman question," but his fascination with the West, where feminists were beginning to attract attention, had predisposed him to be a strong advocate of women's rights. After coming to power, he gave them the vote and placed some women in parliament. One of the women whom he supported was Halide Edip Adivar (1884–1964), an ardent revolutionary who was pictured during the occupation of Istanbul preceding the war of independence lecturing crowds of men even while veiled. Journalist, feminist activist, literary critic, and novelist, her 1926 autobiography describes her adventures with the nationalists, which included the experience of cross-dressing so as to be able to fight in the army with the Young Turks. Her best known work is *The Clown and His Daughter,* which appeared first in English in 1935 and a year later in Turkish.

During this same period, the European Zionist movement was beginning to become active as Jews emigrated from Europe to settle the land of Palestine. Zionism at that time was a socialist ideology owing more to Russian-inspired communism than to Judaism. As such it must have looked to the inhabitants of Palestine much like the *missions civilisatrices* that the French and the British had been dispatching to the Middle East since the eighteenth century. These alarming developments in the region gave rise to fledgling Islam-inspired reform movements throughout the Middle East. Their members warned against unthinking mimicry of the West and urged the virtues and relevance of Islam as nations strove to become part of the modern world.

■ The Short Story as Literary Pioneer

First the short story and later the novel provided frames within which intellectuals could address the problems of their age. The short story, said to have Middle Eastern precedents in folk literature such as *A Thousand and One Nights,* developed most rapidly as a local genre. It was well suited to the needs of writers who had urgent sociopolitical messages they wanted to convey in a succinct and persuasive manner. Quickly written and read, the short story became an important vehicle for socially engaged intellectuals to communicate with people beyond their immediate circle of friends and colleagues.

▨ Egyptian Stories

It was in Egypt that the Arabic short story first took hold, and therefore its history there can be considered to be exemplary. Lawyers like Yahya Haqqi (1905–1991) and Tawfiq al-Hakim (1898–1987), who is better known for his drama, turned some of their cases into stories that became part of a general debate about modernization. Haqqi's "The First Lesson," published in 1926, is a powerful example of naturalist criticism of the new that was often symbolized by the train. Preparing for his first day in school, the son of the station master of a remote, rural, milk-train stop, watches the Nubian station guard, a deeply spiritual man and his only friend, slip off the platform and roll under the wheels of the train. The tragedy does not interrupt the day's program. The son goes to school, sits at his new desk, and tries to fulfill the teacher's first assignment to the pupils: write an essay on the advantages of the train. Twenty-seven years later, Haqqi returned to the theme of the destructiveness of the railway in his indictment of the 1952 Free Officers' Revolution. *Good Morning!* is a novel, the only one Haqqi wrote, that contrasts the fullness of the lives of a few villagers before the introduction of the train into their lives with the pain and the suffering they experience after the station is built in their village.

Engineers and doctors also turned their professional experiences into the stuff of fiction. Whether they felt real sympathy or not is less crucial than the fact that they made the lives of the urban and rural poor available and sometimes even important for their mostly middle-class readers. Engineer Mahmud Tahir Lashin (1894–1954) wrote several stories about his professional visits to government offices, popular cafes, and also the countryside. His 1929 story "Talk of the Village," which has been described as marking the maturation of the Arabic short story (Hafez, 1992:274), confronts an urban intellectual with the reality of the romanticized village. This is no utopia but rather a place of primitive passions and traditions.

Mahmud Taymur (1894–1973), from an upper-class family of litterateurs, was drawn to the simplicity of the life of the poor but also to the injustices to which they were exposed. To write about them convincingly, he had to use their language. He is considered to be one of the pioneers in the literary usage of the colloquial. He told stories about women's abuse at the hands of unscrupulous men. He described young girls condemned to marry men older than their fathers and women paying food bills with their bodies so as to keep their families alive. The most prolific and best known of these early short story writers, Taymur kept his readers informed about the terrible lives women were leading and how the tragedy of such lives was not restricted to the individual but had implications for society as a whole.

The most diverse and complex of Arabic short story writers was Yusuf Idris (1927–1991). He was a medical doctor who had spent years practicing medicine before he turned to story writing. Like his professional forebears, he brought his experience in the clinic to his creative work. Like them also, he drew special attention to the ways in which the bad situation of women impacts everyone. His first collection of short stories, *The Cheapest Nights* (1954), deals not only with the customs and traditions but also with the diseases of the fellahin (peasants). The title story is almost a manifesto on behalf of family planning. A villager comes home one night after searching in vain for affordable entertainment, and he produces another mouth to feed! In "The Dregs of the City," Idris turns to the city to present a middle-aged, middle-class man preying on his servant, her theft of his watch, his humiliating recovery of the watch, and her consequent ejection to walk the streets as a prostitute. The storyline is not new; what is different and moving is the narration of inevitable destruction. In his many other collections of stories, as in his novels and plays, Idris examines the lives of his compatriots, dissecting those elements that lead people to destroy each other.

▪ Iranian Stories

At the end of the nineteenth century, encyclopedist Ali Akbar Dehkhoda introduced the short story to Iranian readers with the publication of some satirical articles. However, it was Jamalzadeh who turned this journalistic precedent into a local literary genre with his 1921 introduction to *Once upon a Time,* described as "a manifesto for modernist Persian prose writing" (Moayyad, 1991:31). The stories in the collection provided Iranian intellectuals with a model of how to integrate this new genre into the repertoire of a transformed national literature.

The first Iranian to succeed in writing a fully developed short story in an accessible language was Sadeq Hedayat (1903–1951). Born into the Iranian nobility, he was educated in Paris, where he was deeply engaged by surrealism. His early work described Iran's great past, whereas his later writings, which were influenced by European writers and particularly by Franz Kafka, were as dark and despairing as his life. He committed suicide in 1951. Hedayat wrote novels, critical essays, and plays, but above all short stories that portrayed with sympathy the life of the destitute in Iran's cities. He, too, used colloquial expressions, but his goal was more political than artistic: literature needed to participate in the fight against tradition and particularly religious customs as the nation strove to become part of the modern world. During the 1930s and 1940s, he published three collections, including *The Stray Dog* (1942). Through the eyes of a dog, Hedayat told a story of rejection and alienation. The use of an animal as a protagonist goes back to a strong tradition of animal fables.

Sadiq Chubak (1916–1998), a younger friend of Hedayat who is best known for his novels, and social critic Jalal Al-e Ahmad (1923–1969) elaborated what Hedayat began. It was Chubak who first experimented artistically with the use of the colloquial in formal writing. In *The Puppet Show* (1945), he strove to render the rhythm of the spoken language and not merely to include dissonant vernacular vocabulary for political effect. Like others, he was committed to describing and hoping to change the situation of women.

The son of a Muslim Shi'ite cleric, Al-e Ahmad focused on political oppression and, in the early stages of his writing career, on religious hypocrisy. The title story of his first collection, *Exchange of Visits* (1946), cynically describes a pilgrimage to a saint's tomb in Iraq. He has, however, been most closely associated with the notion of "Westoxification," the title of a book he wrote in 1962, which was used as a slogan against the shah in the 1960s. For Al-e Ahmad, as for many of his contemporaries, the greatest danger was the cultural, economic, and political subordination of countries like Iran to the West. As Tavakoli-Targhi says in an interview, Al-e Ahmad "envisaged an alternative modernity informed by Islam. This work became important for Ayatollah Khomeini and other Iranian religious scholars who viewed Islam as the foundation of Iranian cultural independence" (1999). This book may be seen as an early warning of the growing conservatism and anti-occidentalism that led to the Islamic revolution of 1978.

During the 1960s, many new short fiction writers appeared, most notably Gholam Hosayn Saedi (1935–1985). Trained as a psychiatrist and practicing in Tehran, he applied his clinical experience to his thirty volumes of stories, plays, essays, and ethnographies. Like Al-e Ahmad, he was severe in his criticism of the Westernization of Iranian society. Yet once the Islamic government was in power, he did not hesitate to criticize it in drama. His 1984 play *Othello in the Wonderland* was performed in Paris, where Saedi ran less immediate risk for his mocking portrayal of the system's obsession with covering women's bodies.

The Islamic revolution produced a new generation of writers, many of whom are women. Critics like Moayyad praise these writers, whether they called for the overthrow of the monarchy or not, for their brave stand against a corruption that had seemed endemic and unassailable for centuries. However, for some the fight became too difficult during the 1980s, and many chose exile.

▪ Turkey's Master Storyteller

One of the earliest Turkish writers of short stories was Sait Faik Aziz Abasiyanik (1906–1954). Like his counterparts in the rest of the Middle East, Abasiyanik was interested in daily life both within and outside the cities. The most prolific and admired short story writer in Turkey, as well as in Iran, where many of his works were translated into Persian, was Aziz Nesin (1915–1995), who has been called the twentieth-century Nasreddin Hoca, a witty, eloquent folk hero. Nesin wrote dozens of books, including *Elephant Hamdi* and *Madmen on the Loose*. His stories are marked by a sharp wit and concision. In "House on the Border," a Kafkaesque story about a tenant, the six thieves who prey on him, and their final forced collaboration to fight injustice, he takes on the repressive government apparatus. Nesin depicts the bumbling attempts of an alienated hero to find protection and justice from institutions that were established to protect the people but that refuse to become accountable.

Nesin's activity on behalf of the translation and publication of the controversial novel *Satanic Verses* by Salman Rushdie (b. 1947) almost cost him his life. He is one of the few Middle Eastern writers who made a handsome living from his writings; most others have had to rely on income from other professions such as journalism to allow them to write fiction. After his death, his family established the Nesin Foundation, which supports literary activity as well as social projects.

■ Women's Stories

Several women writers chose the short story as their frame for literary expression. In 1929, Egyptian Suhayr Qalamawi published a collection of short stories titled *Grandmother's Tales*. The figurative use of the "grandmother" became popular as women sought models of feminine strength and stability in a patriarchal past. The piety of the grandmother was ambivalently presented: it could be a sign of blind faith and superstition or a trace of a time when there was safety and security from outside forces threatening one's belief system. Many women have followed in Qalamawi's steps, claiming that this short story genre is perfectly suited to the life of a mother and housewife, where opportunities for concentration on a protracted plot are limited.

Three Syrian women are exemplary. Ulfa Idilbi (b. 1917) did not start publishing until the early 1950s, but she, too, described the problems women confront in a conservative society poised on the edge of change. Ghada al-Samman (b. 1940) wrote a collection of stories under the title *Your Eyes Are My Destiny* (1961), in which she explored the possibilities for women in a male-dominated world. Colette Khoury (b. 1937), more romantic but no less revolutionary, published *Days with Him* (1959), in which the heroine rebels against men's automatic reduction of women to mothers and hostesses and insists on her dignity and worth as an individual.

One of the most famous—and notorious—short stories of the Arab world is "Spaceship of Tenderness to the Moon" (1964) by Lebanese writer Layla Baalbaki (b. 1936). The story of an early morning moment in the life of a couple, it reveals their erotic love for each other and their conflict over the desire for a baby. A trial was held to assess whether or not the story was pornographic. Baalbaki was finally acquitted, but the controversy has entered the history of twentieth-century Middle Eastern literature. In most of these women's writings, the heroine is defeated by the struggle against patriarchy. Whether she gives in to a man or abandons him, the final decision brings no satisfaction. A single woman cannot defy all with whom she comes into contact when the society is not yet ready to incorporate her into its fabric.

In 1947, with the appearance of *Fire Quenched,* Simin Daneshvar (b. 1921) became the first woman in Iran to publish a collection of short stories. Farzaneh Milani has praised her for creating women who are not simply victims of an overbearing patriarchy, but rather active human beings struggling to give meaning to their lives. In the later work of women like Shahrnush Parsipur (b. 1946) and Goli Taraqqi (b. 1939), Milani recognizes Daneshvar's focus on the disappointments inherent in mostly middle-class relationships in transitional societies, where individualism is in tension with traditional values (Milani, 1992:199).

Women have written about how their domestic responsibilities restrict attention and preclude sustained invention. They have also written about wars. Emily Nasrallah (b. 1938) wrote prolifically on the devastating effects of the Lebanese civil war, particularly as it affected women's lives. Her three collections of war stories capture moments of horror and loss that other genres could not quite encompass. In Iraq during the war with Iran from 1980 to 1988, Aliya Talib and Daisy al-Amir published their daring criticisms of an autocratic regime in the succinctness of quirky tales.

■ Francophone Novels in North Africa

In the countries of North Africa that the French colonized in the nineteenth century (Algeria in 1830 and Tunisia in 1881), the first novelistic attempts appeared in French at the beginning of the twentieth century. In Tunisia, Jewish intellectuals like Jacques Victor Levi first used the novel to chronicle their daily lives. They described a multicultural society in which Arabs, Berbers, Italians, Maltese, Africans, Muslims, and Jews had lived together easily until the arrival of the colonizers. It was then that racial and religious differences began to matter. Novelists evoked the two worlds of the medina (old Arab city) and the *ville nouvelle* (new city) that accommodated the French and the constant border crossings between them. The *hammam* (Turkish bath) became the emblematic site of local authenticity and segregation.

In 1953, three years before Tunisia was to gain its independence, Albert Memmi (b. 1920) published his semiautobiographical novel. Written two years before *The Colonizer and the Colonized,* his classical study of colonial relations, *Pillar of Salt* provides a case study of the dehumanizing effects of colonial desire both on the subject as well as on the object of domination. The colonizer wants the colonized to forget who he is and to want to become like him. He fosters that desire until it nears fulfillment and then he reveals the hope to have been always empty. Benillouche, the intelligent son of a working-class family granted permission to study at a lycee, swings between his multiple and overlapping identities, at once loving and hating who he is but also the person he is becoming. This is more than self-criticism; it is refusal of self. The hero's highly conflicted relations with his father anticipate the novels of the Moroccans Driss Chraïbi (b. 1926) and Tahar Benjelloun (b. 1944) in the 1960s and 1970s, which dwell on the despotic rule of the father, transparent symbol for the patriarchal past, and the need to end it.

During the 1980s, Benjelloun wrote the two-volume novel, *Sand Child* and *Sacred Night,* that won him the Prix Goncourt, the prestigious French literary prize awarded almost exclusively to French writers from France. The novel tells the story of a father's refusal to accept the fact that his eighth child is yet another girl. He must have a son, will have a son. So he turns infant Fatima into Ahmed and produces a freak. This postmodern novel about gender construction in an Islamic patriarchy caused a scandal in Morocco. Benjelloun was accused of pandering to French voyeuristic desire for the exotic and the perverted. Some dismissed the Prix Goncourt as Benjelloun's reward for cultural betrayal.

In Algeria and Egypt, it was women who pioneered the francophone novel.[1] In the 1940s, Assia Debeche wrote about middle-class women's experiences of biculturalism: they were educated to expect opportunities for choice in love and life, but their realities often turned out to be quite different. Francophone Lebanese-Egyptian Andree Chedid (b. 1921) explored the same problem two years after the success of the Free Officers' Revolution. Her book *From Sleep Unbound* (1954) was praised, if not warmly, for its bleak depiction of the fate of a woman in a rural Coptic setting where any attempt, however slight, to improve a black destiny was greeted with shock and redoubled rejection. In the story, Samya's murder of her foul husband is as much activism as such a woman in such a context could be expected to exercise.

■ The Arabic Novel

The novel in Arabic developed a little later than the francophone novel. It was too long, too epic a form to suit the purposes of the early arabophone social and cultural reformers. More than the short story, the novel seemed an unfamiliar genre, developed as it had been for the needs and interests of the European bourgeoisie of the eighteenth and nineteenth centuries. Above all, publication was an issue. The new Arabic printing presses were given over primarily to newspapers and journals, which became the most effective outlets for works of fiction. Even today some writers continue to serialize their novels and autobiographies in these publications, which often retain the services of creative writers as though they were journalists.[2] This form of publication lends itself to the cliffhanger style familiar to European readers of nineteenth-century sociorealist fiction.

In Egypt, it was 1988 Nobel laureate Naguib Mahfouz (b. 1911) who first brought this longer genre to maturity. After publishing a few short stories in the 1930s, he recognized the benefits of a longer literary format for articulating the complexities of contemporary society. His novels from the 1940s until today provide a window on the evolving sociopolitical situation of Egypt and Egyptians in the world system.

In the 1940s, Mahfouz published two novels that revolve around events supposed to have happened during the times of the Pharaohs, focusing on the expulsion of invaders by ancient Egyptians. The allegorical nature of these

Egyptian Nobel laureate Naguib Mahfouz is best known for the sociorealist style of his novels, many of which have been translated into English.

works is transparent. This was a period of self-searching in Egypt, when local failure to act effectively in an international context was compensated for by recourse to past greatness. This turn to a past antedating the arrival of the Peninsula Arabs became a reflex in other Middle Eastern countries whose intellectuals were struggling with a crisis of identity. In Turkey, for example, just after Atatürk's death in 1938, as his successor was trying to consolidate his power in an atmosphere of uncertainty and growing repression, novelist Kemal Tahir (1910–1973) wrote *Mother State,* about the Ottoman Empire in the thirteenth and fourteenth centuries, when it was at the height of its power and glory.

Along with Turkish short story writer Sabhattin Ali (1907–1948) and Turkish novelist Orhan Kemal (1914–1970), Mahfouz pioneered sociorealism in the Middle East. *Midaq Alley* (1947), the first of Mahfouz's novels to be translated into English, reflects the concerns of other Middle Eastern writers who turned city neighborhoods into rich microcosms of their countries. The setting here is World War II Cairo, and British global dominion is quickly fading. This intricate novel was followed by Mahfouz's trilogy *Palace Walk, Palace of Desire,* and *Sugar Street* (1956–1957), which many claim won him the Nobel Prize. Although he wrote the trilogy during the Free Officers' Revolution in 1952, he did not publish it until several years later. The saga of the 'Abd al-Jawads, an upper-middle-class family, it parallels the key events of the first half of the twentieth century. The lives of three generations mirror the crises through which Egyptians were passing from World War I through independence. But once again history provides a disguise for current concerns. Mahfouz draws the reader into the inner sanctum of a traditional home, where women and men interact in a way invisible to the outsider. The reader is privileged to share the first moment of disobedience by a usually submissive wife. There is a penalty to be paid, but the die has been cast. Her children, who witnessed their mother's unwonted daring, become politically engaged. Their different avenues of activism, Muslim Brother as opposed to Communist, often produce internal clashes, but kinship ties do finally survive the stresses.

In 1959, Mahfouz published *Children of Gebelawi,* a novel that tells the story of the Abrahamic faiths and their adherents through the lives of individual members of the Gebelawi family. This book has been banned in several Muslim countries for its negative portrayal of the Prophet of Islam. But Muhammad is not the only one subjected to moral scrutiny. Mahfouz comes down hard on all the great prophets of monotheism, culminating with the prophet of the new age, Arafa, the prophet of science, spiritual skepticism, and alienation. It was this book that earned Mahfouz the 1994 knife attack by a zealous Muslim fundamentalist. Mahfouz pursued this existentialist theme throughout the 1960s, depicting hopeless characters in search of some little meaning to give to their lives.

The Six Day War of 1967 produced an intellectual crisis in the Arab world to which Mahfouz reacted very strongly, in terms of both content and form. Many readers and critics regretted the loss of the linear narrative line of his first novels, as his writing of the 1970s fragmented into the staccato of alarm and surreal confusion. In the 1980s, Mahfouz changed his style and themes again. This time he turned to the classics and wrote modern versions. He produced his own take on *A Thousand and One Nights* and also a travel narrative written in response to the famous travelogue of fourteenth-century Moroccan traveler Ibn Battutah, which Mahfouz titled *The Journey of Ibn Fattouma* (1983) in recognition of the influence.

The novel has provided many writers with the frame appropriate to contain nostalgic reflections on a world that has passed. *Fragments of Memory,* by Syrian writer Hanna Mina (b. 1924), tells the tale of a village before the onslaught of foreign values. This village is like the one Muna abandons in *September Birds* (1962), by Lebanese writer Emily Nasrallah. Like many Middle Eastern heroes, Muna is faced with the challenge of modernity, namely that the village cannot provide a sustainable future. Muna leaves for Beirut and does not know who she is, now that she is far from home.

Unlike most Arab novelists who place their stories in the city or in the village, Saudi exile Abd al-Rahman Munif (b. 1933), who now lives in Syria, has situated his novels in the desert. His magnum opus is a five-volume novel titled *Cities of Salt,* which he published throughout the 1980s. Having begun his career as a petroleum economist, he is intimately familiar with the impact of oil on the economies and lives of people living in oil-rich states. The quintet traces the transformation in the environment as well as in the consciousness of the local, mostly bedouin inhabitants after the discovery of black gold. The reader witnesses the growing brutalization of the bedouin as they recognize that in this brave new world of competition and profit, there is more to be gained by individual enterprise than by tribal solidarity. This book earned its author the displeasure of his Saudi government, which deprived him of citizenship.

■ The Iranian Novel

The Iranian novel, of which the three-volume collection *Travel Diary of Ebrahim Beg* (1890s) is said to be the first, appeared before the Arabic novel. Iranian writers, more than the Arabs, tended to work in both short story and novel genres. This was true for Hedayat, Chubak, Al-e Ahmad, and Daneshvar.

One of the best-known Iranian novels is Hedayat's *Blind Owl*, which was written by 1930 but not published until 1937 in India and until 1941 in Iran, after Reza Shah abdicated and censorship was lifted. It is a book of highly introspective notes that Hedayat wrote "for my shadow." He describes a husband tortured by his relations with a wife who gives herself easily to her many lovers but not at all to him. He becomes an opium addict, a misfit, a murderer, and a madman. The despair in this novel foreshadowed Hedayat's suicide in 1951.

Chubak wrote several novels that have been praised for their keen attention to detail. In 1963 he published his first novel, *Tongsir,* to great acclaim. It tells the story of a man from the mountains who takes revenge on those who try to defraud him. At about the same time, both Al-e Ahmad and his wife, Daneshvar, were actively and publicly engaged in the literary scene, where left-wing intellectuals struggled to resist the shah's attempts to organize and co-opt cultural, but particularly literary, production. Al-e Ahmad's novel *The School Principal* (1958), written five years after the end of the Mosaddeq regime, criticizes the Iranian system of education in place at the time. Written at a time when commitment was more important than art, its publication was a politico-literary event. The most recent influential novel was *Klidar,* which Mahmud Dowlatabadi (b. 1940) published in 1979. In ten volumes, it is a bildungsroman that tells the story of the nation.

As had been the case with the short story, Daneshvar was the first woman in Iran to write and publish a novel. *A Persian Requiem* (1969) takes place in British-occupied Shiraz toward the end of World War II. Neighbors and kin are at each other's throats, tribal leaders have revolted against the government, and Zari is at home trying to maintain stability and order. She is contrasted to a woman who writes, despite the prohibition on women's literary voices, and who struggles to hold on to her autonomy but is consequently committed to a psychiatric hospital. As can be read in women's writings everywhere, this madness is not a clinical disorder but rather represents a woman's rebellion and society's disciplining of such transgressions. The novel was a bestseller and was translated into several languages (Milani, 1992:59–61, 183).

■ The Turkish Novel

There are two novelists in Turkey who have earned international acclaim: Yashar Kemal (b. 1922) and Orhan Pamuk (b. 1948). Kemal, who has for decades been a Nobel nominee, pioneered the "village novel." Best known is his quartet titled *Memed, My Hawk,* translated into almost thirty languages, which revolves around the ultimately unsuccessful resistance of peasants against their landlords. Talat Sait Halman has described his work as "one of the truly stirring achievements in the history of Turkish literature" (1982:30).

Orhan Pamuk's first work was a family saga titled *Cevdet Bey and His Sons* (1979). Much like Mahfouz's trilogy, it followed the fortunes of three generations. This first novel did not enjoy great popularity. In fact, Pamuk did not become famous until the 1990s, when he published his controversial novel *Black Book* (1990). It is a byzantine mystery about Galip, a lawyer in Istanbul, whose wife, Ruya, and brother-in-law, Jelal, disappear one day. He keeps their disappearance a secret as he tries to follow clues. Jelal is a journalist whose complicated, sardonic articles about Islamic history, literature, and mysticism interwoven with the details of dailiness have earned him a devoted readership. Galip is jealous of Jelal's acclaim but above all of his writing skill. As his search progresses, he steps into Jelal's shoes. He moves into the journalist's abandoned apartment, wears his clothes, reads his personal writings, answers his telephone, and converses with eager fans who call with exciting material. He even imitates Jelal's style and publishes articles in his name. It is his infatuation with this mimicry that costs Jelal his life. Critics, first in Turkey and later abroad after the book was translated into several languages, were absolutely divided in their reactions. Some hailed this existential mystery novel as extraordinary and tantalizing, whereas others dismissed it. In 1997, critic Nuket Esen published the second edition of the Turkish and international articles that had appeared on the book. When Pamuk's next book, *A New Life,* was about to be published in 1995, there was so much excitement that by the end of the first day of its sale it had been reprinted several times.

■ The Israeli Novel

Unlike all other Middle Eastern literatures, which draw on deep historical pasts, Israeli literature is just sixty years old. The first Israeli novel, Moshe Shamir's (b. 1921) story *Beneath the Sun,* appeared two years after the establishment of the state in 1948. It is a highly political work that draws the profile of the new Israeli, the *sabra,* a term used to refer to those who are born on the land of Israel. The *sabra* are entirely enmeshed in the new nation's history and environment but can fall prey to unfriendly neighbors (Yudkin, 1984:42–47). The most frequently translated Israeli novelist is Amos Oz (b. 1939). After beginning his writing career with short stories, he turned to the novel. His work has been described as heavy with threat. This is particularly the case with his best-known novel, *My Michael* (1968). The heroine is obsessed by her paradoxical fear of and desire for the Arab twins she has known since she was a child. Oz's body of work plays on borders, both real and symbolic. This is significant in a country that has from the start been uncertain about and afraid for its geographical limits. Oz has situated many of his writings in the experience of the kibbutz, the communes in which many Israeli socialists lived (Yudkin, 1984:135–143, 168).

Particularly in the post-1967 period, some Palestinians within Israel wrote in Hebrew. Anton Shammas (b. 1941) wrote *Arabesques,* an autobiographical novel that has been hailed by some as a masterpiece of Hebrew prose. Yet despite the critical acclaim, the novel has not yet been accepted as part of the canon of Hebrew literature. Shammas has retrospectively described this work as his challenge to the Israeli claim that the Palestinians could be integrated as Israeli citizens. No matter how assimilated they tried to become in Israeli society, no matter how excellent the Palestinians' command of Hebrew, they could never become Israeli citizens in the full sense of the word.

■ Drama: Grafting the New onto the Old

As with the other genres coming in from Europe, Middle Eastern intellectuals sought to find indigenous precedents for the theater. Some Arabs invoked the *maqama,* a tenth-century lyrical art form that told the story of an eloquent rascal who manages to deceive all, particularly a wealthy patron. Others cited the shadow play, which had its origin in the Turkish *karagoz* of the fourteenth century. Like the *maqama,* the *karagoz* is a comedy that revolves around the adventures of the uneducated but smart *karagoz.* Although the *karagoz* does deal with daily life and the struggles of the oppressed, its inherent frivolity and unchanging characters and plots resisted the serious intent of early Middle Eastern dramaturges. According to Halman, other popular performances common in Turkey include "peasant plays, pageants, rites, processions, mock fights, festival acts . . . and *Ortaoyunu* (Turkish *commedia dell'arte*)" (1976:14).

Like the novel and the short story, drama as it is currently construed was introduced into the Middle East through translations. Major plays by William Shakespeare, Jean-Baptiste Molière, and the Russian Anton Chekhov were adapted for the Arab stage. Particularly in the torn, nostalgic works of Chekhov that described the passing of an age and the unknowability of the future, Middle Easterners could recognize the dilemmas through which their own society was passing. The theater appealed to a much wider section of the public because it did not rely on literacy, and it became very popular. It provided a context within which writers could experiment with the introduction of colloquialisms, which were anathema to the writers of prose and poetry who feared the loss of the purity of their languages. With time, successful implementation of the colloquial in conversations between illiterate characters that were often offset by the high classical language of the educated provided models for fiction writers.

In 1873, the Turk Namik Kemal (ca. 1840–1888) staged his play *Fatherland,* which was enthusiastically greeted by audiences and censured by the government of Sultan Abdulaziz. Halman claims that this play marked the beginning of "the political significance of literature in Turkish life." Atatürk saw in drama an important aspect of Westernization that he exploited by establishing the City Theater of Istanbul in 1927. Writers in other genres like Yashar Kemal, Nazim Hikmet Ran, Orhan Kemal, and Aziz Nesin experimented in theatrical writing, not always with great success. Much of the dramatic writings of the 1960s are "village dramas," which marked the first significant move away from Western influence (Halman, 1976:13, 37, 41–47).

The name that stands out above all others in the field of Arab drama is that of the Egyptian Tawfiq al-Hakim, who wrote his first plays in the early 1920s. Unlike many of his contemporaries, al-Hakim was not supportive of the burgeoning feminist movement. While others were writing of the injustices women were facing, he criticized the "new woman" who heralded moral chaos. After three years spent studying law in Paris, al-Hakim returned to Cairo in 1928. At this point, he turned to philosophical playwriting and his treatment of women mellowed, as in *Shahrazad* (1934). This change may be due to his experiences with women in Paris, about which he wrote in his autobiography.

In 1960, al-Hakim joined other writers who were criticizing the new regime, brought into power by the Free Officers' Revolution, when he published *The Sultan's Dilemma.* The sultan is a slave whose owner, the previous sultan, had died before manumitting him. He must gain his freedom and can only do so by being bought and then freed by his next owner. He is bought in auction by a woman who has heard of his dictatorial ways but discovers that he is gentle. She gives him his freedom once he has learned its real meaning. In 1964, Yusuf Idris published *Farfoors,* a play that relied on the *karagoz* genre as well as on Sufi dervish dances. He wanted to prove that drama was not new to Arabic literature and that traditional forms could hold the new politically charged content.

In the late 1960s, students throughout the Arab world turned to the theater as a sanctioned space in which to stage their sociopolitical grievances. In Syria, a group of students founded the Thorn Theater Company, which produced skits and plays of surprising daring. The screen of comedy and fiction allowed actors to convey political messages that would elsewhere be deemed sedition. Government officials and censors allowed this dangerous practice to continue, recognizing that the people needed an outlet for their frustration and anger with a repressive regime. Along with other forms of cultural production but more visibly, the theater also helped to fashion a facade of democracy for the Ba'th state.

Writers schooled in the Thorn Theater have continued to write on the razor's edge between dissidence and martyrdom. Some, like Sa'dallah Wannus (1941–1997) and Mamduh 'Adwan (b. 1941), have stayed with the stage. Wannus's first play, *An Evening's Entertainment for the Fifth of June,* came out in 1967, just a year after the Six Day War, and it has been described as the richest literary reaction to the terrible defeat. Fearless when it came to open political confrontation, Wannus criticized, even if allegorically, the current Ba'thist regime. First in 1977 with *The King Is the King* and then fifteen years later with *Historical Miniatures,* he revealed the oppressive strategies of dictatorial rule. In the more recent play, he used the relationship between four-teenth-century Mongol tyrant Tamerlane and North African historian Ibn Khaldun to criticize intellectuals for their complicity with a corrupt system. 'Adwan's play *The Ghoul* (1996) focuses on the cruelty of the last Ottoman governor to be sent to Syria. The nightmares that torment his sleep might be those of any dictator.

Other graduates of the Thorn Theater, like Durayd Lahham, have moved from the stage to television or the cinema. Paradoxically, the film industry has become the most radical of all cultural producers: it is exclusively controlled by the Ministry of Culture, yet it is engaged in stringent criticism of the government. What are the political position and ultimate fate of filmmakers like Muhammad Mallas, who are in the pay of the government but whose films, on the rare occasions when they are shown, leave their audiences breathless at their critical audacity? This is what I call commissioned criticism, because it serves to make the government look open-minded and democratic when it so wishes.

■ Poetry and the Hold of the Desert

Of all genres, the most resistant to change was poetry. The new emphasis on personal expression and free style was regarded almost as heresy. Throughout the Middle East, poetry has been and continues to be the most highly prized literary art. In the pre-Islamic period, politics and poetry had been intermeshed, and tribal leaders were expected to be accomplished poets. Islamic rulers generally continued to value the art of poetry and patronized it generously. Wherever it was composed, whether in Arabic, Turkish, or Persian, classical poetry retained elements of its origins in the desert. There were familiar tropes (figurative uses of words), images, meters, and form. Any changes had to be carefully introduced lest the innovation be considered a sign of incompetence. More formulaic even than prose literature, classical poetry did not allow for the expression of individual emotion.

The first attempts to make poetry more responsive to contemporary concerns began modestly in the mid–nineteenth century. Neoclassical poets like Turkish writer Yahya Kemal Beyatli (1884–1958) and the aristocratic Egyptians Mahmud Sami al-Barudi (1839–1904) and Ahmad Shawqi (1868–1932) were to give new life to classical motifs and language, with only slight modification in content. In general, they were formal conservatives (Somekh, 1992:40–41). The first substantive reform of poetry came from such poets as the Turk Ahmet Hasim (1885–1933), the Syrian Khalil Mutran (1872–1949), the Tunisian Abu al-Qasim al-Shabbi (1909–1934), and the Iranian Nima Yushij (1895–1959), who had been inspired by such French and English Symbolists and Romantics as Charles-Pierre Baudelaire and Alphonse-Marie-Louis de Prat Lamartine, William Wordsworth, and Percy Bysshe Shelley. Their experiments with meter, form, and language transformed poetry in the Middle East.

A revolution was in the making, but opposition to free verse remained strong. In Turkey, the Marxist Nazim Hikmet Ran (1902–1963) was the first

Syrian poet Nizar Kabbani lived from 1923 until 1998. The poem is "No. 43" from *One Hundred Love Letters.*

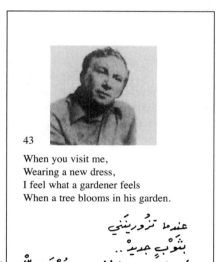

43

When you visit me,
Wearing a new dress,
I feel what a gardener feels
When a tree blooms in his garden.

عِنْدَما تَزُورِينَنِي
بِثَوْبٍ جِدِيدٍ ..
أَشْعُرُ بِما يَشْعُرُ بِهِ الْبُسْتانِيُّ
حِينَ تُزْهِرُ لَدَيْهِ شَجَرَةٌ ..

Lynne Rienner Publishers

to be recognized for his free verse. Halman relates how in 1921 Atatürk had urged the already famous poet to "write poems with a purpose" (1982:25). He did, but he had to pay for his "obedience." His outright condemnations of social and political injustices as well as his poetic calls for revolution gained such a wide following that he was made to bear responsibility for political unrest. During the late 1930s, just before Atatürk's death, he was imprisoned on the trumped-up charge of conspiracy to overthrow the regime, and his writings were banned. Upon his release, Ran fled to Moscow, where he is buried alongside such great Russian writers as Fyodor Dostoevsky. He is the most widely translated Turkish poet. His poems "Some Advice to Those Who Will Serve Time in Prison" and "Awakening" were written for those who had to undergo what he did but who were not as strong:

> I mean it's not that you can't pass
> 10 or 15 years inside,
> and more even—
> you can,
> as long as the jewel
> in the left side of your chest doesn't lose its luster.

In the Arab world and in Iran, it was women who brought to fruition what male poets had long been trying to achieve. The Iraqi Nazik al-Mala'ika (b. 1923) finally succeeded in introducing free verse into modern Arabic poetry. In 1949 she published her anthology of free verse, *Ashes and Shrapnel*. Although others before her had experimented with this new poetic form, they had had little success; critics accused them of incompetence rather than welcoming the innovation. Her work paved the way for others like Syrian Nobel nominee Adonis (Ali Ahmad Said, b. 1930) and Iraqi poet Badr Shakir al-Sayyab (1926–1964). Both of these writers gained prominence through their adoption of mythic themes of resurrection, particularly in connection with the plight of the Palestinians. In 1968, Adonis published his pathbreaking work *The Stage and the Mirrors,* which introduces a new poetic lexicon, rhythm, structure, and sensibility. His work is highly philosophical, filled with symbols, allegories, and mythical allusions. He claims that poetry should appeal to the mind, not to the emotions, and because this new poetry is a political weapon, it must be subtly wielded.

The political nature of Arab poetry and the repressiveness of several of the regimes within which these poets function has compelled some to write indirectly, obliquely, surreally, and anonymously. Arab women, particularly in more traditional countries like those of the Arabian Peninsula, have often chosen abstract symbolism to articulate emotions otherwise considered taboo. This new poetry by women like Kuwaiti princess Su'ad Mubarak al-Sabah was at first censured, even when not quite understood, because it came from the pen of a woman. In the late 1990s, however, this kind of poetry began to find a new, international audience. In March 1997 and in places as far-flung from the United Arab Emirates as Vietnam and North Carolina, newspapers carried the story of the publication of a new anthology titled *The Female Poets of the Emirates*.

In Iran, two women, Forugh Farrokhzad (1935–1967) and Simin Behbahani (b. 1927), rebelled against traditional forms and subject matter for poetry. Behbahani's first collection of poetry, *Broken String,* came out in 1951. Whereas Behbahani's rebellion took the form of neotraditionalism (Milani, 1992:235–239), Farrokhzad's method involved rejection. In 1955 she published what some considered to be a "scandalously frank" anthology titled *Captive*. But she is best known for her collection *Another Birth,* which was published in 1964. Like al-Mala'ika, she breaks with formal convention as she describes the oppressive life of a Middle Eastern woman. The personal and the political fuse in a single poetic vision.

■ Independence and Postcolonial Struggles

As previous chapters have illustrated, the second half of the twentieth century witnessed cycles of violence throughout the Middle East. There were liberation struggles followed by socialist activism followed by breakdown of law and order and widespread depression and disappointment. After independence, many wanted to reconstruct their countries and to fashion a local, "authentic" identity. Conflict and violence are so much a part of the history of the Middle East that no consideration of its literature can afford to ignore them.

Writers were concerned to play a role in the new societies that came with independence from colonial rule. Acting as conscience of the people, they set out to "revolutionize the revolution." In 1946 the Iran-Soviet Society sponsored the first congress of Iranian writers, during which the centrality of ideology to literature was announced. Seven years later, in Lebanon, the first editorial of the influential monthly periodical *Al-Adab* declared that all forms of writing must henceforth be politically engaged. The time of art for art's sake had passed, to be replaced by a revolutionary ethic in all creative activities.

■ Paying the Price

This emphasis on political commitment in literature appeared at a time when the Middle East was in the throes of revolutions and wars of liberation. Literature was to make an intervention in the political realm, to praise and promote the social good, and to criticize the retrograde. Wars of liberation from colonial rule were clearly good, but some conflicts were not so easily judged as good or bad. This was the case with the Egyptian Free Officers' Revolution of 1952. It was clearly good in that it brought back Egyptian rule after what some argued was a hiatus of millennia, namely since the Pharaohs. Others soon felt misgivings about the autocratic nature of the *nouveau regime* (new regime).

As mentioned above, Haqqi's 1954 novel *Good Morning!* openly criticized Gamal Abdul Nasser and his new regime. In the same year, another lawyer, 'Abd al-Rahman al-Sharqawi (1920–1987), published *Egyptian Earth,* which filmmaker Yusuf Shahin turned into a film titled *The Land.* It examines the impact of the revolution on the lives of the fellahin and shows the oppressiveness of the centralized authority structure that the Free Officers put in place. Again, the plot revolves around the introduction of a symbol of modernization, in this case a road, into a village that has managed to keep itself aloof from the corruption of city life. The fact that the revolution, in which so many had invested great hopes, had brought only misery to the people, was difficult for many to accept.

The intellectuals were particularly dismayed. There has been speculation that the reason Mahfouz did not publish the trilogy he had written during the early 1950s until several years later was that criticism of the new system was too patent; he must have feared punishment. Many feel ambivalence about this delay, feeling that Mahfouz should have faced the risk. In the Middle East, writers have a moral authority that is almost unimaginable in the West. They are expected to stand up for their convictions and to lead public opinion. Their boldness may earn them prison sentences, but that is as it should be. The prisoner of conscience, the intellectual who has done time, wears this experience as a badge of honor. Many prisoners of conscience in the Middle East, particularly the Communists, have written of their incarceration.

Iranian writer Buzurg Alavi (b. 1908), who had become involved in the Marxist Tudeh Party, was imprisoned in 1937. During his four years "inside," he wrote two books: *Scrap Papers from Prison* and *Fifty Three Men.* These stories about his experiences reveal the intense emotions of the prisoners but also their determination: "I gained in spirits in the prison and became better equipped for the struggle" (quoted in Alvi, 1984:283). Along the same lines, Egyptian writer Sherif Hetata (b. 1923) wrote *The Eye with an Iron Lid* (1982), an intricately told tale of its author's thirteen years behind bars first under the British and then under Nasser. His partner, Nawal El Saadawi (b. 1931), also recorded her months spent in prison under Anwar Sadat in *Memoirs from the Women's Prison* (1983). As mentioned above, Turkey's premier poet, Nazim Hikmet Ran, wrote extensively about his years "inside." The fact that these intellectuals have had such experiences and that they then publish them gives them a moral authority that others, whose writings may be just as "good," may never achieve.

▩ The Algerian War of Independence (1954–1962)

Tunisia and Morocco gained their independence from the French in 1956, but the Algerians, who had begun their anticolonial war in 1954, did not finally succeed until 1962. The war produced libraries of novels, short stories, and poetry, and even today it haunts the imagination of cultural producers, including filmmakers. Most recently, *Joseph and the Legend of the Seventh Sleeper* (1995) made the rounds of the Arab film festivals. It tells the story of a prisoner of war who escapes to find his companions. He discovers that they, like the quranic sleepers in the cave, perished in a cave with their dog. He buries his erstwhile companions and then is himself killed by traitors. The theme of the betrayal of the revolution has become common as intellectuals watch their country sink into violence, religious extremism, and isolationism.

But in the 1950s and early 1960s, hope was high. Everyone, even the women, were expected to write about the war. Women like Assia Djebar (b. 1936), who wrote *The Thirst* in 1957, about women's doomed thirst for independence, were criticized by the male literary establishment for obsession with individual problems at a time when the nation was in need of all of its citizens to be as united as possible. Later novels by Djebar are careful to place the revolution at the center of the work and to downplay the crises and disappointments in these women's lives. Although she had left the country during the early days of the liberation struggle, she published two novels on women's participation in the war, *Children of the New World* (1962) and *Naive Larks* (1967). Her description of women's mobilization, however, does not indicate any change in their consciousness about what their rights and roles in the postbellum society should be.

In contrast, male writers were writing with dread about women's growing power and influence in a society that was spinning out of control. One of the best-known novels of the war is *Nedjma* (1956), by Kateb Yacine (1929–1996). The critics have generally interpreted this story of a mysterious beauty, the four suitors to whom she is related, her legendary father, and her French mother, to be an allegory for Algeria. I have argued elsewhere that instead it narrates men's growing anxieties as they watch the emergence of the new Algerian woman out of the sea of the war (cooke, 1997:chap. 3). This thesis is more forcefully brought out in Mohamed Dib's surreal novel *Who Remembers the Sea* (1962), where the narrator loses his mind as he loses control over his wife, a guerrilla fighter. For those writers like Malek Haddad (1927–1987) who left Algeria during the war, the dread of the woman soldier is intense. It is not so surprising, then, that when the war was over, the women were quickly returned to their homes.

The story of women's disempowerment in the aftermath of the war is well known; in fact, Arab women elsewhere often refer to it as the "Algerian lesson." This lesson taught others that they must not allow society to forget women's contributions during a time of crisis and need. In the 1980s, Djebar started to bring out her quartet, which she has described as autobiographical. Each volume presents a radical revision of Algerian colonial history as seen through the eyes of women. In the second volume, *Fantasia: An Algerian Cavalcade* (1985), she links the stories of unknown nineteenth-century women resisters, omitted in the official histories and chronicles, with those of living women who had been active and then silenced during the war, and with her own story.

Djebar's quartet forms part of a national critique on the part of revolutionary women who have recognized, perhaps too late, the dangers of silence. The war of liberation was not a revolution, they claim, because its outcome did not change the material and social conditions for half the population. As long as discrimination against women continues, the expulsion of the French cannot be considered to have been a national success. The attacks in the 1990s and 2000s by Islamic fundamentalists on intellectuals, and particularly women, in the Algerian capital may be seen as the next step in the waging of a war that was not resolved in the early 1960s.

■ The Question of Palestine

Immediately after the departure of the British in 1948, Palestinians wrestled with their new loss of independence. Although most Palestinian intellectuals left in 1948, a few, like poet Mahmud Darwish (b. 1942), did stay behind what came to be called the Green Line. Darwish's family left in the first exodus and then soon stole back in. They returned after the period for registering Palestinians had passed, and so the poet's writings dwell on the lack of identity papers. His poem "Identity Card" (1965) became emblematic of the Palestinian condition.

After 1967, the Palestinians who found themselves under Israeli rule in the Gaza Strip and the West Bank began to understand why it was that those who had stayed on their land inside the Israeli borders in 1948 were not necessarily complicit, but rather might be regarded as nationalists. The importance of staying, whatever the cost, became a nationalist virtue. Emile Habibi (1921–1996) was a key figure writing inside Israel. He was the founder of the binational Israeli Communist Party and winner of both the Jerusalem Prize for Literature awarded by the Palestinian Liberation Organization and the Israel Prize. In 1974, he published *The Secret Life of Saeed, the Ill-fated Pessoptimist: A Palestinian Who Became a Citizen of Israel*. It tells the picaresque tale of a hapless Palestinian as he stumbles through life and people in Israel.

Two years later, from Nablus inside the Occupied Territories, Sahar Khalifa (b. 1941) published the first of her three novels on the experience of occupation by Israeli forces. From *Wild Thorns* (1976) to *Bab al-Saha* (1990),

Khalifa paints the canvas of possibilities for resistance. Her heroines demonstrate how some women's ways of fighting are more effective than those of the men. Mothers who give their sons and daughters stones to throw at soldiers confuse the rules of war. Are these women and their offspring civilians or militants? Can they be shot? Or must they be tolerated, their stones deflected? This ambiguity disappeared in the later stage when the women's individual acts of resistance—like the mythical hydra, when one of its heads is cut off, two will appear in its stead—were turned into a unified strategy for revolutionary action. The militarization of local oppositions was named the intifada (uprising). It is arguable that this transformation of individual Palestinian actions into a single movement was disabling for the Israelis (cooke, 1997:chap. 4).

▨ The War in Lebanon (1975–1992)

Even before civil war broke out in Lebanon in the spring of 1975, some were sensing its inevitability. This was again true before the Israeli invasion in June 1982. Both al-Samman and Etel Adnan (b. 1925) wrote works that were filled with the dread of anticipation. *Beirut 75* (1974), by al-Samman, uncannily predicts the civil war as the novel collapses into a series of nightmares. Five years later at the height of the war, she returned to the nightmare format. *Her Beirut Nightmares* (1979) takes the reader into the horror of the infamous hotels battle, which pitted opposing militias against each other for weeks in the fall of 1976. The heroine, like her author, had been caught in her villa located between the Holiday Inn, the Phoenicia, and the St. Georges hotels, and she strings together the hundreds of gruesome fantasies that haunted her during those bloody days. Many have read in Adnan's novel *Arab Apocalypse* (1980) a premonition of the Israeli invasion of 1982. The staccato poetry interrupted with symbols and figures lies splattered on the page like shrapnel exploding out of a bomb, like blood spurting out of a wound.

As happened in Iran after the Islamic revolution, chaos in Lebanon produced literature, much of it by women (Lewis and Yazdanfar, 1996:xix–xxi). The Beirut Decentrists, a school of women writing in Beirut during the war, wrote into the space of violence a script for a transformed society that would include all its members and treat them with justice (cooke, 1988). But during the civil war, they did more than that. These women writers showed how the men were responsible for creating the terrible conditions that threaten to destroy the postindependence country that was so fragile. Hanan al-Shaykh's (b. 1945) novel *The Story of Zahra* (1980) traces the growth in consciousness of a woman who had been a social misfit. As the war rages, she comes to see a role for herself, and she fights in her own limited but intense way to do something to end at least part of the madness.

The Iran-Iraq War

While the war in Lebanon was at its height, farther to the east the 1979 Islamic revolution ousted the Shah of Iran from the Peacock Throne. Saddam Hussein, the new leader of Iraq, tried to take advantage of what he had mistakenly assumed to be total disarray in neighboring Iran. The war that he launched in late 1980 as a blitzkrieg persisted for eight bloody years. Like many dictators, Hussein had an ambivalent relationship with the intellectual elite of his country. He needed them, and therefore he feared them. Throughout the war, he coerced the writers and artists who could not or did not choose to leave to glorify the war in ink and paint. The Ministry of Culture established literary series and organized festivals designed to serve the purposes of the war. Many did as they were told. Some did not. Under the watchful eye of the censor, some writers even managed to articulate criticism of a war they were being paid to praise. Using allegory and a surreal style, they published writings that vividly evoked the harrowing experiences through which the Iraqi people were forced to pass (cooke, 1997). Ironically, the Iranian government was doing exactly the same as its enemy, namely, sponsoring books of stories and autobiographies to praise the war.

The Gulf War

The Iraqi invasion of Kuwait on August 2, 1990, and the war that several Western and Arab countries under the leadership of U.S. president George H. W. Bush launched against Iraq on January 17, 1991, produced Kuwaiti and Iraqi journals, novels, and short stories that are slowly making their way into print. In *Black Barricades* (1994), Kuwait's leading woman writer, Layla al-'Uthman (b. 1951), collects stories she had written during the eight-month occupation of the capital city. The tone is one of confusion, which aptly reflects the mood of the Kuwaitis as well as of the Iraqis. The destitute, illiterate men wreaking havoc in the palaces of the Kuwaiti oil magnates may not know why they are there beyond the looting, but they do know that they do not wish to return to their home country.

Inside Iraq itself, several wrote against the brutality of the allied forces and particularly the U.S. pilots, who seemed to consider their Iraqi targets as figures no more human than characters in a Nintendo game. The Ministry of Culture has continued its publication of war stories. One of Iraq's leading women poets, Dunya Mikha'il (b. 1965), brought out her *Journal of a Wave Outside the Sea* in 1995. Far from glorifying the war as might have been expected from such a government-sponsored text, this poem depicts extreme alienation in a continuing reign of terror.

■ Emigration and Exile

There are many reasons for leaving the country of one's birth. Some, such as education and work opportunities, are voluntary; some, such as political oppression and intolerable violence, are involuntary. The travel of a young man, his head filled with dreams, to Europe; his apprenticeship for a period, usually of seven years; and his disappointed return to his native land for education and the shock of return is a topos informing many Middle Eastern works of fiction during the first part of the twentieth century. Egyptian writer Yahya Haqqi wrote the emblematic text of this "travel and return transformed" genre. His novel *Saint's Lamp* (1946) follows Isma'il from Cairo to London and then back to Cairo after seven years of training as an eye doctor. The naive young man, initiated into Western life and introduced to a different set of values by a Scottish woman, finds his native country unbearably primitive. He rejects its ways and forces Western medicine and values onto his Egyptian patients. Then he experiences a religious epiphany, which leads him to an understanding that he must resolve the tension between traditional and Western medicine. The novella was hailed as an Islamic model of how to become a Western-style scientist while nonetheless remaining a righteous Muslim.

Twenty years later, the Sudanese al-Tayyib Salih (b. 1929) developed this theme, although without the religious angle, in *Season of Migration to the North* (1966). This novel reverses the nineteenth-century colonialist's move from the metropole to the colony; Mustafa Sa'id goes north (to England) to learn but also to wreak revenge. The story of Mustafa Sa'id has often been compared to that of Othello; it has also been called the answer to Joseph Conrad's novel *Heart of Darkness* as well as to Frantz Fanon's depiction of the impotence and potential castration of the black man as he confronts the white woman (Fanon, 1967). While studying in London, Sa'id has affairs with three English women. Each ends with the woman's death, the first two in suicide, the third in a suicide-murder. Upon his return to his village in a region remote from the capital, Mustafa Sa'id is himself destroyed by his relationship with a beautiful village girl. The novel bears out Memmi's thesis of the mutually destructive effects of colonialism on both the colonizers and the colonized.

Many Middle Eastern intellectuals have chosen to leave their native lands because they can no longer live there. Sometimes the reasons are economic, sometimes political. For over a century, the Lebanese and Egyptians have left for Europe and the Americas and more recently the Turks for Germany, in search of a prosperity seemingly unavailable in the eastern Mediterranean. Citizens of repressive regimes, like the former Iraqi regime of Saddam Hussein, the Syrian Ba'thist government, and the Islamic Republic of Iran, have fled so as to find a place where they might breathe and speak freely. Many Middle Eastern intellectuals have congregated either in Paris or in London. There they have founded publishing houses and launched newspapers and magazines.

Emily Nasrallah has examined the question of emigration from a Lebanese perspective. *September Birds* (1962), a novel about a village whose vitality was being drained as the young people were lured away to the capital and to the glittering West, was supposed to have a sequel about the return of the migratory birds. The war in Lebanon forced her and others like her to understand that there was to be no return. The war turned the confusion and alienation experienced by those who were left behind into anger, for Nasrallah begins to criticize the émigrés. They should not have gone, not during the war but also not before. Looked at through the prism of war, emigration was tantamount to giving up on one's nation.

Nasrallah goes further in this later period to reveal that emigration was bad for those left behind but also bad for those who undertook it. It transpires that many who left their homes to make fame and fortune had in fact failed. They were not returning because they were ashamed that they had not realized the dream. In 1994 she published *Sleeping Embers,* a novel that seemed to bring closure to the question of emigration. Those who left should not come back because when they do, they disturb people's tranquillity by dredging up stories and pains that had been appropriately shelved.

These are difficult issues, for although emigration is chosen and exile forced, there are times when the situation in one's nation is too painful to be borne. How does one draw the line between what can and cannot be borne? After the Israeli invasion of Lebanon, some of the writers who had determined that they would not be driven from their homes started to move out. Ghada al-Samman, for instance, established herself in Paris, where she now writes about what it is like to live in a non-Arab country but to retain Arab dreams.

The various political upheavals in the Middle East have caused many to leave their homes without hope of return. We have already discussed the situation of the Palestinians who stayed on their land. There were many, however, who chose or were forced to leave. Many lived and continue to live as refugees in camps around the borders of Israel or in the neighboring countries, waiting for exile to be over and the possibility of returning to their abandoned lands.

The twentieth century has become the century of mass migration, and so the story of the displaced person has come to symbolize the dilemma of globalization: it is impossible to live at home, impossible to survive outside. Ghassan Kanafani (1936–1972) was one such refugee who went to Beirut. His 1963 novel *Men in the Sun,* which was turned into a film titled *The Dupes,* is a contemporary, visionary text that explores the possible outcome of the choice to leave one's home and to seek refuge in Arab countries. Three men entrust themselves to a Palestinian guide who has promised to drive them across the desert separating Iraq and Kuwait for an exorbitant fee. When they have almost made it, the driver is delayed at a border post. The men, who have temporarily hidden themselves in the trucks's empty water tank, suffocate in the heat. This is the story of all hosts of refugees, who soon tire of their increasingly long-term guests and end up abusing them.

Jabra Ibrahim Jabra (1919–1995), who left Palestine for Iraq and later lived throughout the region, has written several novels, all of which delve into the lives of dispersed Palestinians. Perhaps his most important work is *In Search of Walid Mas'ud* (1978), which brings together those who have chosen to write about their situation with others who have decided to fight to change it. They debate the most appropriate means to defend a cause.

After the Islamic revolution and then during the punishing war with Iraq (1980–1988), many Iranians fled the country. They are now scattered all over Europe and North America, where some are writing in the languages of their new countries, but many continue to write in Persian. The latter include Mahshid Amirshahy (b. 1937), with her books *At Home* (1986) and *Away from Home* (1998), and Goli Taraqqi, who lives in Paris. In 1992, Taraqqi published *Scattered Memories,* a collection of stories about the pains of exile. Like Nasrallah, she reveals the impoverished lives of those who had emigrated and how incapable they are of providing shelter for their stricken relatives.

Palestinian writer Ghassan Kanafani,
who was murdered in a car-bomb explosion in Beirut in 1972.

Taraqqi reminds the reader that exile means leaving the physical home where there is privacy and autonomy, but it also entails humiliation since it forces dependence on others. Shahrnush Parsipur, a highly acclaimed feminist writer whose 1989 book *Women Without Men* was banned by the Islamic Republic, is now in California, where she wrote *Tea Ceremony in the Presence of the Wolf* (1993). This collection of short stories elaborates on the sense of terrible loss and the condemnation to perpetual wandering that mark the experience of exile.

Those who write in exile often feel farther from home than the miles that mark that distance. Like the Algerians who left during the war of independence, they feel, perhaps, that they should be fighting side-by-side with those intellectuals who have chosen to stay regardless of the cost. Yet in a world whose borders are increasingly porous, where migration is a necessary part of many people's lives, a new kind of cultural nationalism is emerging that allows those who are living far from their land of birth or ancestry to retain very real ties of identity. Literary associations in the Middle East are slowly recognizing that their writers may not live in the country that they claim as their nation. Turkish novelist Habib Bektas (b. 1951) is a good example. Since 1972 he has been living and writing in Germany. In 1997, his book *The Smell of the Shadow* won the Turkish Inkilab Kitabevi Press annual prize; it was the first time this coveted prize had been awarded to a nonresident Turk. Bektas justified his Turkishness by claiming that although he may not reside in Turkey, he does live in Turkish. This adoption of the language as the nation is a strategy many writers in exile invoke.

■ The Muslim State

The Islamic revolution had been simmering in Iran long before it boiled over. Mention has already been made of Al-e Ahmad and Daneshvar, whose writings during the late 1960s seemed to be calling for reform of a society that was too much given over to the delights of the West. There is a pronounced Islamic tone in what they write. Two years before the revolution, Parsipur wrote *The Heat of the Year Zero*. The heroine's description of suffocation in the overwhelming heat of the summer and her stolen and then censured glances at men anticipated what the new regime had in store for its women.

In the early days of the revolution, the Islamic government of Iran, much like its royal predecessor, concerned itself with cultural production. Whatever was seen to be oppositional to its specifically Islamic interests was carefully censured. The case of Salman Rushdie has entered the annals of world history. Some writers complied with the government's will and wrote piously about the virtues of the revolution. Others, many of them women, protested the new restrictions, for example, A. Rahmani's "Short Hike," which acts out a tense

moment of defiance between an Islamic guard and the woman he has just reprimanded for revealing a strand of hair. Farzaneh Milani has noted that in the
short two-year period between 1983, when compulsory veiling was generally
enforced, and 1985, "126 books by or about women were published in Iran."
Restrictions had forced women to speak out (Milani, 1992:231).

As previous chapters have explored, it is not only in Iran that Muslims
have called for the establishment of an Islamic state. After the abolition of the
Ottoman caliphate in 1924 and the consequent secularization of Turkey, Muslims elsewhere in the Middle East became nervous. This was particularly true
in Egypt, where the first formal association of Muslim revolutionaries was
established in 1929. Other such groups formed, and many remain active today
in many countries of the Middle East. Their increasing prominence in public
life became a theme in literature from the 1970s on. In 1977, during a period
spent in exile in Germany, the Egyptian 'Abd al-Hakim Qasim (1935–1990)
wrote a story about the attempted conversion to Islam of a poor Coptic
umbrella maker. "Al-mahdi" explores the new animosities arising between
Christians and Muslims who had always lived together peacefully. The story
also reveals the growing chasm between young Islamists and more traditional
Muslims in rural Egypt.

The Islamists have played contradictory roles in the history and politics
of their countries. In Egypt, for instance, they helped leaders like Nasser come
to power, but they have also sought to remove such leaders. During the mid-
1960s, Nasser arrested several Muslim leaders. Their years in prison produced
several memoirs, of which arguably the most interesting is that of Zaynab al-
Ghazali (b. 1912). Since 1935, she has been the leader of the Muslim Ladies
Association, and during her tenure it has been closely associated with the
Muslim Brotherhood. In 1965, she was incarcerated for a year in the War
Prison with her male colleagues. That experience inspired her book *Days from
My Life* (1977). Less memoir than inspirational literature, this text recounts
the tortures and miracles that mark their subject as especially blessed. This
autobiography could also be read as a model for young women seeking guidance as they try to combine their scripturally defined roles as servants of God
with those as wives and mothers.

In 1981, a group of Islamists assassinated Egyptian president Anwar Sadat.
They charged him with making an unpardonable compromise in promoting the
Camp David Accords with Israel. The Islamists do not confine their targets to
political leaders, however. As seen in Algeria in the 1990s, Islamists are increasingly focusing their attention on intellectuals who are charged with secularism
and perversion of the people's morals. In 1992, Egyptian fundamentalists assassinated journalist Farag Foda for his critique of their discourse. Most annoying
to them had been his book *Before the Fall* (1992). That summer, they published
in paperback format the proceedings of a trial they had conducted, titled *Nawal
El Saadawi in the Witness Stand*. With its cover picture of a wild, white-haired

woman staring out from behind bars, the book was so widely distributed that it could be found in the streets of Cairo on the blankets of sidewalk book vendors, selling for a few piasters. These echoes of the fatwa (religious opinion) the Ayatollah Ruhollah Khomeini had pronounced on February 14, 1989, calling for Rushdie's death for his novel *Satanic Verses* were too loud to be ignored. Moral censure of literature had escalated to the sanction of deadly assaults on authors. El Saadawi, who is accustomed to threats from governments and Islamists, did not shake this threat off as idle. When the government, which had itself imprisoned her for a few months during Sadat's regime, sent guards to keep watch on her apartment, she realized that she had to leave. She went to Duke University in North Carolina in the United States, where she spent most of the following four years writing her autobiography.

Nawal El Saadawi was condemned to death because of two books. *The Fall of the Imam* (1987) is the lyrically told tale of the assassination of the highest authority in the land, a transparent reference to Sadat's assassination, and of the pursuit and execution of his assassin, who is also his illegitimate daughter, Bint Allah. *Innocence of the Devil* (1992) takes place in a psychiatric hospital, where one of the patients imagines himself to be God and another is called Eblis, the Arabic word for "Satan." In each novel, God is the main character, yet he is constantly merging into the personas of other tyrannical male authority figures.

Unlike El Saadawi's earlier fiction, in which women are confined to the role of victim, these two most recent novels explore the ways in which women brought up in monotheistic religions resist the tyranny of God. It is not so much patriarchy that is the central concern, but rather monotheism, particularly when

Mourners at the funeral for Egyptian author Farag Foda, who was assassinated in 1992.

Thomas Hartwell

it is pushed to its extreme as in the current fundamentalist phase, that exonerates men from responsibility when they brutalize women. El Saadawi depicts these men as fearing women, whom they link with the devil. It is this fear of women-devils that El Saadawi provides as key to understanding why men perpetrate violence against women and then justify their actions in religious terms. The devil, a character called Eblis, is a great friend of women, empowering them when they face injustice. He possesses their bodies so that they may have the strength to fight. Unlike God, who is constantly disguising himself, slipping into other forms, Eblis remains the same and easily recognizable. At the end, God proclaims Eblis innocent and thus destroys him and hence himself. The collapse of the God-Satan tension reveals the vanity of trying to know God through his opposite. The God who is paired with the devil is the God of organized monotheistic religions. This sacred-profane binary is only one aspect of the true God. The God who is knowable through his opposite is a tyrant who must be resisted. These two novels are open attacks on the hypocrisy and emptiness of religions when they are diverted to promoting human interests and away from meeting human needs.

■ Translation and Recognition

In conclusion, it is important to note that Middle Eastern literature is now entering the mainstream of world literature. The 1980s was the decade of translation and of international recognition for the literature of the Middle East. In 1988, Mahfouz became the second Middle Eastern writer to win the Nobel Prize for literature, having been preceded by the Israeli Shmuel Yosef Agnon (1888–1970) in 1966. In 1989, Moroccan Tahar Benjelloun won the Prix Goncourt, the first Arab to be awarded this coveted French prize. In 1997, Turk Yashar Kemal was recognized with Italy's most prestigious prize, the Nonino Literary Award.

At the same time, Arabic, Hebrew, Persian, and Turkish fiction and poetry were being translated into European languages. Previously the translation process had been idiosyncratic; random works appeared according to individual tastes of translators. By the mid-1980s, however, the translation process became more systematic, particularly with respect to Arabic works. In 1981, Palestinian poet and literary critic Salma al-Khadra' al-Jayyusi founded the Project for Translation from Arabic (PROTA) in the United States. At first, these translations found homes in marginal presses dedicated to publishing works by writers from the global South. By the late 1980s, however, major European, U.S., and even Japanese publishing houses, including some university presses that came to consider Middle Eastern literature as potential textbooks, started adopting Middle Eastern literary series as well as the works of individual authors.

The growth of the translation industry is significant for readers, who now have unprecedented access to the cultural imaginary of people they had previously known only through the stories of scholars and travelers. This is important, above all, for the writers and particularly for those who have already gained a share of recognition abroad. They are writing with the awareness that their works will be translated, that what they say about their culture is being consumed far from the local readership they had originally targeted. Writing thus entails consequences that must be anticipated. Self-criticism must become what Moroccan cultural critic 'Abdelkebir Khatibi has called "double critique." The eye turned in on the injustices of a society must simultaneously look out to discern the contours of the external enemy. Local tyrannies must be held in balance with the dangers of global hegemony, with the understanding that the one interacts with the other. This double critique changes the way people think and write, and this changed writing is cultivating new tastes and creating new markets. Middle Eastern writers of the twenty-first century are seeing their work become part of a global project in which they will play an increasingly visible role.

■ Notes

I am indebted to Guven Guzeldere for information, invaluable advice, and stimulating conversations about Turkish literature. Warm thanks to Mohamad Tavakoli-Targhi for a careful reading of the penultimate version of this chapter and for wonderful suggestions.

1. Albert Memmi notes that between 1947 and 1986, Algerian women published thirty-seven novels and short story collections (1987:6).

2. For example, Nawal El Saadawi first published her autobiography, *My Papers My Life*, in 1995 in *Al-Musawwar*, a magazine that is distributed throughout the Arab world.

■ Bibliography

Alvi, Sajida. 1984. "Buzurg Alavi's Writings from Prison (1940s)." Pp. 274–291 in Thomas M. Ricks (ed.), *Critical Perspectives on Modern Persian Literature*. Washington, D.C.: Three Continents Press.

Badawi, Mustafa M. (ed.). 1992. *Modern Arabic Literature*. Cambridge: Cambridge University Press.

cooke, miriam. 1988. *War's Other Voices: Women Writers on the Lebanese Civil War.* Cambridge: Cambridge University Press.

———. 1997. *Women and the War Story*. Berkeley: University of California Press.

Daragahi, Haideh. 1984. "The Shaping of the Modern Persian Short Story." Pp. 104–123 in Thomas M. Ricks (ed.), *Critical Perspectives on Modern Persian Literature*. Washington, D.C.: Three Continents Press.

Fanon, Frantz. 1967. *Black Skin, White Masks*. New York: Grove Press.

Hafez, Sabry. 1992. "The Modern Arabic Short Story." Pp. 270–328 in Mustafa M. Badawi (ed.), *Modern Arabic Literature*. Cambridge: Cambridge University Press.

Halman, Talat Sait (ed.). 1976. *Modern Turkish Drama. An Anthology of Plays in Translation*. Minneapolis: Bibliotheca Islamica.

———. 1982. *Contemporary Turkish Literature*. Rutherford, N.J.: Fairleigh Dickinson University Press.

Hillman, Michael. 1984. "Al-e Ahmad's Fictional Legacy." Pp. 331–342 in Thomas M. Ricks (ed.), *Critical Perspectives on Modern Persian Literature*. Washington, D.C.: Three Continents Press.

Jayyusi, Salma Khadra. 1992. "Modernist Poetry in Arabic." Pp. 132–179 in Mustafa M. Badawi (ed.), *Modern Arabic Literature*. Cambridge: Cambridge University Press.

Lewis, Franklin, and Farzin Yazdanfar. 1996. *In a Voice of Their Own: A Collection of Stories by Iranian Women Written Since the Revolution of 1979*. Costa Mesa, Calif.: Mazda.

Memmi, Albert. 1987. Introduction to *Anthologie du Roman Maghrebin*. Paris: Nathan.

Milani, Farzaneh. 1992. *Veils and Words: The Emerging Voices of Iranian Women Writers*. Syracuse, N.Y.: Syracuse University Press.

Moayyad, Heshmat (ed.). 1991. *Stories from Iran: A Chicago Anthology, 1921–1991*. Washington, D.C.: Mage.

Najmabadi, Afsaneh. 1998. "Crafting an Educated Housewife in Iran." Pp. 91–125 in Lila Abu-Lughod (ed.), *Remaking Women: Feminism and Modernity in the Middle East*. Princeton: Princeton University Press.

Ricks, Thomas M. (ed.). 1984. *Critical Perspectives on Modern Persian Literature*. Washington, D.C.: Three Continents Press.

Somekh, Sasson. 1992. "The Neo-Classical Arabic Poets." Pp. 36–81 in Mustafa M. Badawi (ed.), *Modern Arabic Literature*. Cambridge: Cambridge University Press.

Tavakoli-Targhi, Mohamad. 1990. "Refashioning Iran: Language and Culture During the Constitutional Revolution." *Iranian Studies* 23:77–101.

———. 1999. Interview by author, South Bend, Ind., February.

Yudkin, Leon I. 1984. *1948 and After: Aspects of Israeli Literature*. Manchester: University of Manchester Press.

14

Trends and Prospects

Deborah J. Gerner and Jillian Schwedler

A s this volume illustrates, the Middle East is a diverse area with significant strengths and accoplishments, as well as complex and difficult
challenges. Its long history as the crossroads for numerous ethnic and linguistic groups, the presence of oil under its desert sands, the significance of
the land for the three major monotheistic religions, the diverse forms of political structure, and the complicated foreign policy relationships within the
Middle East and between the region and the rest of the international community are among the factors that make the Middle East endlessly fascinating to
students and scholars in a variety of disciplines.

Much of what we discuss in this volume has looked backward, as we
traced the imprint of the Middle East upon the world and of the world on these
twenty-plus countries. In this final chapter, we look to the future and consider
several acute challenges facing Israel, Iran, Turkey, and the Arab world in the
twenty-first century and beyond. Among the most notable issues are those
related to the role of culture and religion in shaping society, the urgency of
economic development, the legacy of European colonialism, the desire for
increased government accountability, and demands for greater political participation.

■ Understanding the Contemporary Middle East

In introducing the region in Chapter 2, geographers Ian Manners and Barbara McKean Parmenter describe

the ways in which water links politics, economy, and religion; the ways in which cities are shaped by global practices (trading connections, colonial experiences, labor migration, flows of capital) as well as local practices and imaginings; and the ways in which species, water, people, goods, capital, and ideas move across political boundaries [and] the ways in which the past may be present in the memories of people and in the conscious and unconscious constructions of the histories of places.

Their discussion illustrates that there are a myriad of different mental maps of the Middle East, defined not only by state boundaries but by history, economic interactions, cultural patterns, and natural resources, among other attributes. All are important if we want to understand this dynamic and diverse region.

In contrast to the rich description presented by authors in this book, many Europeans and North Americans still view the Middle East as "the exotic Orient" referred to in Edward Said's famous 1979 book *Orientalism:* culturally undeveloped and unsophisticated when compared to Europe, with anachronistic and undemocratic political institutions that are inferior to those of "the West" and an incomprehensible dominant religion—Islam—along with small Christian and Jewish communities that are seen as quite dissimilar to the Christians and Jews of Europe.[1] This unfortunate attitude is heavily biased by what the Middle East is *not:* it is not Europe or the United States or Canada.

Once we move beyond analyzing the Middle East in terms of what it is not and look at what it *is,* we can recognize that these lands are full of great achievements as well as severe difficulties; in these aspects, the Middle East is not unlike other parts of the world. The region enjoys an extremely rich cultural heritage, one aspect of which miriam cooke explores in her discussion of Arabic, Turkish, Persian, and Hebrew literatures. In Chapter 13, she illustrates the myriad ways that "Middle Eastern literatures have become privileged sites for recording and engaging with sociopolitical tensions and conflicts," particularly those related to independence and postcolonial struggles.

Because of its colonial involvement and geographical proximity, the European view of the Middle East's literature, art, and philosophy had a substantial influence on the self-perception of Middle Eastern elites. Until relatively recently, most Middle Eastern intellectuals—and most of the sons of political leaders—attended universities in Europe or North America. Even within the region, Western-oriented institutions such as the American University in Cairo and the American University in Beirut educated a disproportionate number of professionals, government officials, and elites. For individuals who were not part of this privileged stratum, education was predominantly traditional, focusing on quranic learning.

In the last decades of the twentieth century, this situation began to change. Modern communication systems were installed in all but the most remote villages, modernizing governments instituted comprehensive literacy programs, and, aided by the availability of revenues from petroleum, distinctly Middle Eastern secular universities, with large student bodies drawn from both the middle and working classes, began to thrive. As seemingly mundane items such as transistor radios, cassette players, videocassette recorders, and photocopiers became more common, the various cultures of the Middle East could more easily interact without the intermediation of European interpreters. Internet cafes opened first around universities and in affluent neighborhoods, but soon spread to working-class areas where the equivalent of 50 cents buys an hour online, albeit frequently via slow connections and on outdated computers. Mobile phone use has exploded, not only in cities but also in refugee camps and poor regions where traditional land-lines are expensive or entirely unavailable. Text messaging became extremely popular several years before the service was even available in much of the United States.

The implications of new technologies and changing identities remain unclear. For instance, setting stereotypes aside, does the Middle East represent a single, distinct culture? This question is more difficult to answer, even within the Arab world (let alone the entire region), than it might at first appear. For most of the twentieth century, a pivotal region of the Middle East with a shared dominant cultural identity coincided with the centers of classical Muslim and Arab power: Cairo, Damascus, and Baghdad. Two major pan-Arab political movements, Ba'thism and Nasserism, came out of this core region. Indeed, the area still exercises a profound influence on Arab culture as a whole, although in recent years this has come more from the soap operas of Cairo's television studios and the lyrics of popular music than from the writings of intellectuals or the speeches of charismatic political leaders.

But in the late 1990s and particularly the early years of the twenty-first century, satellite television channels began to change the way Middle Easterners saw themselves as well as the world. A small number of stations provided programming of generally low quality throughout the 1990s, but a virtual revolution took place with the introduction of Qatar-based al-Jazeera, founded in 1996. Long before Western audiences became acquainted with al-Jazeera following the terrorist attacks of September 11, 2001 — largely due to the station's unparalleled coverage of events in Afghanistan — Arabic-speaking audiences throughout the region were transfixed by programming that for the first time brought meaningful political debate and reliable news coverage of international, regional, and domestic events to their television sets.

Yet as Laurie King-Irani points out in Chapter 10, the legacy of Arab nomadic peoples and their traditions continue to have "a deep imprint on Middle Eastern culture, society, and politics." The challenge is to assess the importance and changing role of such traditions within a dynamic, vibrant region. Certainly one cannot really say that the entire Middle East is part of a single cultural unit. Lisa Taraki's comment in Chapter 11 regarding the "mul-

Satellite dishes like these in the old city in Sana'a, Yemen,
began to appear atop houses in many parts of the Middle East
years before the government legalized them.

tiplicity of social, economic, political, and cultural forces and factors [that]
have shaped the statuses, experiences, and living conditions of Middle Eastern women" applies equally to Middle Eastern men. For instance, despite
sharing the Arabic language and Muslim religion with the "Arab core," the
Gulf region is distinct. The states that arose in the shadow of Ibn Saud and the
stark fundamentalism of the Wahabi movement have relatively little in common with the more cosmopolitan, urbanized populations of the eastern
Mediterranean.

Across the Gulf, Shi'i Iran stands culturally separate—as it has for three
millennia—and could logically be considered the southernmost country of
Islamic Central Asia rather than the eastern boundary of the Middle East.
Although sizable Shi'i communities exist in Yemen and Lebanon and even
constitute a majority in Iraq, Iran's distinct Indo-European language and non-
colonial experiences with foreign powers give the state an identity separate
from the Arab and even Muslim worlds. To the west and south of Egypt, the
Arab identity of the Maghreb is similarly in question. Sunni Islam and the
Arabic language are firmly in place, but the Maghreb is buffeted by conflicting cultural pressures: from nearby Europe, from indigenous Berber communities, and from sub-Saharan Africa, whose influence, particularly on the border states of Comoros, Djibouti, Mauritania, Somalia, and Sudan, has been
profound. As a nation-state established primarily by twentieth-century immi-

grants from Europe and their descendants, Israel is a cultural anomaly within the Levant.

Finally, Turkey faces a particularly difficult situation. Since the end of the Ottoman Empire, when the new Turkish republic adopted many European political and economic institutions, Turkey has tried without success to gain acceptance by Europe. Even Turkey's membership in the North Atlantic Treaty Organization (NATO) has not been sufficient to overcome European reluctance to view Turkey as an equal partner. At the same time, its Ottoman legacy complicates Turkey's relationship with the Arab states, many of which are hesitant to grant Turkey a position of influence in the region. The "Kurdish situation," that Mary Ann Tétreault discusses in Chapter 5, creates additional difficulties with neighboring Iraq and Iran. With the decline of Communist power in the Balkans and in Central Asia, Turkey now has the opportunity to provide economic leadership to weaker states that were once part of the Ottoman Empire, much as Japan has done in its economic interactions with areas that it once controlled militarily. However, such a strategy would likely pull Turkey even further from the Arab world, as would Ankara's eagerly sought membership in the European Union.

The issue of culture is related to one of the region's major quandaries: What role should religion, ideology, and "cultural morality" play in the determination of political and social policies? What is the appropriate relationship between governmental leaders and religious figures? What forms of political leadership are available to women? In many countries, a new answer has emerged in the late twentieth century: Islam, politics, and society have again become inextricably linked and now dominate nearly all discourse regarding such basic cultural values.

John Esposito, Mohammed A. Muqtedar Khan, and Jillian Schwedler explain in Chapter 12 that this widespread Islamic resurgence is a "grassroots response to multiple crises [in] a struggle for both cultural authenticity and self-determination." The central role of religion cannot be dismissed as epiphenomenal, as many believed immediately after the Islamic revolution in Iran, nor can it be pigeonholed as simply part of the "clash of civilizations," as some commentators would like (Huntington, 1993). While the Islamic resurgence is a frequent response within the Middle East to questions of morality and government, it is important to remember that some Christian and Jewish believers also have religiously based answers to these fundamental political and lifestyle concerns.

■ Economic Development

A second crucial task facing the countries of the Middle East is economic development. Extremes of poverty and wealth exist in the region—Mauritania is one of the poorest countries in the world, Kuwait one of the wealthiest—but neither extreme is typical of the area as a whole. The great majority of the population lives in countries such as Egypt, Turkey, and Iran that have a level of development similar to that found in much of Asia and Latin America.[2] These countries struggle to create a basic industrialized infrastructure (roads, bridges, airports, electrical and communications grids) while simultaneously wondering how to position themselves within a global system that has, at least for the world's wealthiest states, become postindustrial.

As in most of the developing world, such efforts are frequently complicated by accumulated debt from prior failed projects, outmoded governmental institutions, the presence of multinational corporations, and the social stress involved in adjusting to a society that is halfway between farm and factory, between the ancestral village and the "global village." The economic and political legacies of European imperialism in the Middle East have also hindered the creation of autonomous industrial programs independent of foreign assistance, external borrowing, or intervention by international organizations, a pattern that is characteristic of historically colonized states throughout the world.

In addition, as economist Elias Tuma and sociologist Valentine Moghadam discuss in Chapters 7 and 9, domestic obstacles such as burgeoning urbanization and the environmental problems that this often creates, rapid population growth relative to available resources, rising unemployment, and restrictions on economic opportunities for women have also contributed to economic stagnation and have made autonomous development an elusive goal. Finally, since independence, numerous Middle Eastern countries have had their economic development disrupted by internal civil war (e.g., Algeria, Lebanon, Somalia, Sudan, Turkey, Yemen), international war (e.g., Kuwait), or both (e.g., Egypt, Iran, Iraq, Israel, Jordan, Syria).

For all of these reasons, economic development in most of the region has proceeded in a two-steps-forward, one-step-back manner, rather than showing either the exceptional expansion of the "Asian tigers" in the 1990s or the near absence of growth found in parts of Africa. Few signs suggest that this will change anytime soon, yet addressing these development problems is key to bettering the lives of Middle Easterners. It is also essential to reduce the sense of frustration that many young people now feel when they compare their circumstances with the images of life in Los Angeles, London, and Paris that they observe on locale television as well as via satellite and the Internet. Without an improvement in economic conditions, support for political and religious fundamentalism is likely to continue.

One characteristic of some Middle Eastern economies makes them different from most other countries: the role of oil extraction. From Algeria to Yemen, petroleum has paid for many development projects. As Mary Ann Tétreault demonstrates in Chapter 8, oil wealth was a major distinguishing feature of the region for most of the twentieth century, but particularly during the 1970s and early 1980s. Yet by the end of the 1990s, partly in reponse to the economic recession in Asia, the price of oil had fallen to levels more or less comparable to those prior to the price increases of the 1970s. The decline in petroleum revenue has forced retrenchment in the oil-based economies. This may not be all bad: extravagant showcase projects have been terminated and massive weapons acquisition programs have been curtailed, for instance, and countries without large oil reserves—such as Egypt, Turkey, and Morocco— have benefited from lower energy costs.

The "oil decade" of 1973 to 1983 did leave two positive legacies. First, it led to the establishment of a large, indigenous professional class of engineers, bankers, doctors, and educators. (Ironically, because of the wide use of expatriates, these professionals are often from countries without oil wealth, notably Egypt, Jordan, and Palestine.) Second, even after taking into account failed and inappropriate projects, worthless boondoggles, and greed and corruption, oil revenues did pay for considerable basic infrastructure in much of the region. Both of these factors should facilitate further economic growth and development.

The future role of oil in the economies of the Middle East is anything but clear. For at least a decade, analysts have been predicting that the rise of an industrialized consumer culture in Asia would accelerate the demand for oil and push petroleum prices to new heights, once again providing oil-based economies (whether in the Middle East or elsewhere) with the economic power they had in the 1970s. But to date this increased demand has not materialized. Even if demand for oil does pick up, sharp price increases may be constrained by the availability of new supplies from various parts of the former Soviet Union.

■ Ethnonationalist Conflicts

Another set of issues is also related to the historical legacy of colonialism: the ethnic, religious, and territorial conflicts that occur as Middle Eastern peoples respond to situations created nearly 100 years ago and attempt to gain increased control over their political lives. In Chapter 3, historian Arthur Goldschmidt Jr. analyzes the interaction of foreign and indigenous political entities that led to the creation of states whose boundaries rarely reflect the distribution of the region's nationalities. The results have been problematic for decades and do not appear likely to be resolved in the near future.

The current circumstances of the Kurds is a key example both of this lack of correspondence between state boundaries and national groups and of the role that outside powers have played in the region. British interest in the petroleum resources of Kurdistan led to the division of the Kurdish nation among Iran, Iraq, Turkey, and Syria rather than its unification into an independent Kurdish state. While portions of Iraq's Kurds have enjoyed significant autonomy following the Gulf War of 1990, the overthrow of Saddam Hussein's regime in May 2003 is unlikely to lead to the emergence of an independent Kurdish state. One important reason is the desire of the United States to keep Iraq's boundaries intact so as not to antagonize Turkey, Syria, and Iran, and to discourage separatist movements in those countries.

In the Maghreb, Berbers are another minority attempting to preserve their distinct identity. Composing some 20 percent of the population in Algeria and 40 percent in Morocco, with significant communities also in Libya, Tunisia, and Egypt, the Berbers are a formerly nomadic people with roots in the Maghreb that date back centuries prior to the Arab invasions of the seventh century. Although the Berber populations in most of the Maghreb are integrated into the larger societies, they also struggle to maintain some 300 local Berber dialects and their cultural traditions, despite being periodically targeted by Muslim and Arab groups who object to their distinct identities.

The continuing tension between Palestinians and Israeli Jews over what was once the British mandate of Palestine is yet another example of ethnonationalist conflict. Although many view the Israeli-Arab conflict and particularly its Israeli-Palestinian dimension as intractable, peace studies scholar-activists Simona Sharoni and Mohammed Abu-Nimer provide in Chapter 6 a framework for understanding this long-standing conflict and reflect on the prospects for its resolution on terms that are both just and enduring. Like many ethnonationalist conflicts, the Israeli-Arab conflict is more appropriately described as a political conflict about not only the control of land but also about the identity of a state and the self-determination of distinct populations.

Israel's Druze community has also suffered as the boundaries of the Jewish nation-state were drawn in ways that subsumed its sizable population, which had flourished for a millennium on lands that became northern Israel just half a century ago. Unlike Palestinian citizens of Israel, the Israeli Druze—Arabs now numbering some 100,000 who practice an offshoot of the Islamic religion and speak a distinct language—have been welcomed into the Israeli army and provided many of the services afforded to Jewish Israelis but not to Palestinian Israelis. Caught in the middle of the Israeli-Palestinian conflict, the Druze have struggled to maintain their own identity while negotiating their way through the terrain of a protracted and often violent conflict.

Religious minorities struggle to exist elsewhere in the region, notably the diverse Christian minorities in Lebanon and Egypt's Coptic Christians. Muslim minority sects also struggle for survival against state repression as well as local pressures for assimilation. Significant Shi'i communities exist not only in the predominantly Sunni states of Syria, Yemen, Saudi Arabia, Lebanon, and the Arab Gulf countries, but also in predominantly Shi'i Iran. Even the majority Shi'i population of Iraq has suffered severe state repression. Unfortunately, these and other ethnonationalist conflicts in the Middle East have persisted since the end of World War I and by now defy easy solutions. They are not, however, unresolvable, although political pluralism and tolerance will likely provide more viable solutions than the fragmentation of existing states into smaller and smaller units.

■ Political Accountability

A final task facing the Middle East is the development of political systems that are supported by and accountable to the people over which they exercise governance. The wave of transitions to more democratic governance that swept across much of the world in the 1980s and 1990s did not entirely bypass the region, but neither were there the large-scale reforms that have been observed in parts of Africa and Latin America. Unless the Middle East is atypical in its political evolution, we would expect to see democratic pressures play a more prominent role in the near future. In fact, throughout most of the region, democracy and pluralism have become central to political discourse, with even authoritarian regimes describing their rule as democratic and staging less-than-meaningful elections. This trend does not suggest that the region will automatically become part of a new wave of democratization. But it does indicate that expanded political accountability is an increasingly important issue of debate as states and societies face a variety of challenges in the twenty-first century.

There are several dimensions to the challenge of increasing political accountability. First, like governments everywhere, Middle Eastern states must find a way to accommodate the demands of the professional and middle classes for greater influence and control over material and symbolic resources. One of the likely demands raised by these groups will be a substantial reduction in military expenditures. Military spending is an attractive target: the sheer amount of money involved is massive and there is widespread sentiment that those funds could perhaps be better spent on socioeconomic programs that provide greater good for society. Furthermore, because military spending occurs secretly under the guise of "national security," it is prone to both waste and corruption, neither of which has wide acceptability in the eyes of the new professional and middle classes. Finally, in many countries it is not clear who the enemy is that can justify such expenditures.

At the same time, as political scientist Deborah J. Gerner discusses in Chapter 4, the military remains a formidable force in Middle Eastern politics. Many governments have used military perks to co-opt potential opponents and secure the loyalty of ethnic minorities. The military also tends to be closely associated with internal security services, which can enable it to be tremendously disruptive in an unstable situation (as Algeria demonstrated in the 1990s). The close association of the military with an established regime—as found in Jordan, Libya, Iraq, and Yemen, among others—further complicates any serious attempt to reduce military influence.

Perhaps most important, the Middle East is currently in the midst of a significant transformation as the aging post–World War II generation of leaders are replaced by younger rulers governing increasingly younger citizenries. This, too, has implications for how the issues of leadership and political accountability might play out. In some instances, particularly simple dynastic progressions, the transitions may well be routine; thus far, the new monarchs have shown more interest in—even enthusiasm for—political reform than their predecessors, although the implementation of meaningful changes has been slow. Since the end of the 1990s, Bahrain, Syria, Jordan, and Morocco have all seen the passing of leaders who had ruled for decades and the emergence of seemingly more reform-minded sons in their stead. (Whether this pattern will continue in Oman and Saudi Arabia, two monarchies in which succession will not automatically go to a son of the current leader, remains to be seen.) In contrast, replacing long-standing personalistic leaders who have governed for decades, such as Palestinian Yasser Arafat, Yemen's Ali Abdullah Salih, and Libya's Muammar Qaddafi, is likely to be messy, notwithstanding the existence of formal institutions intended to address this situation.

The generational issue may also resolve itself relatively easily in those states that have strongly bureaucratized state structures, such as Egypt and Tunisia, and could be less pronounced in parliamentary states such as Turkey. However, generational change has had a major impact even in the most stable republic of the region, Israel. While Israel's formal institutions of governance have remained more or less intact,[3] the character of Israeli political parties has changed profoundly. Over the past decade, Israel has been transformed from a European-style system of two major parties differentiated on ideology to a situation in which the Likud and Labor Parties together control fewer than half of the seats in the Knesset and many of the successful new parties, such as Shas, are based at least in part on ethnicity.

Another aspect of political accountability has already been alluded to: the need for governments to come to terms with the many facets of political Islam. For secular elites faced with a strong Islamic challenge, options include co-optation, combat, cooperation, and coping. One of the unknown variables is whether Islam is appealing to a given population on its own merits or whether its current popularity rests primarily on its status as the most effective source of opposition to repressive and unaccountable regimes. Particularly given that most other options for protest have been cut off, political Islam provides an alternative ideology to the status quo, one that promises greater social justice.

Many analysts believe that Iran represents the latter scenario: what Khomeini initially offered was a way to get rid of the shah. Turkey, in contrast, had ample opportunities for secular (and military) opposition; nevertheless, a strong traditionalist Islamic movement has arisen there. In 2003, an Islamist-oriented party won the largest bloc and successfully formed a government that has — to the surprise of Western regimes frightened by the Iranian example — sought to maintain its relations with Western governments and to continue the push for membership in the European Union. In such cases, the support for Islamist parties may be similar to what is driving Christian fundamentalism in the United States or the Orthodox Jewish political parties in Israel: the willingness of the Islamic movement to advocate on behalf of a social agenda that the established political parties are not eager to embrace. The cases of Syria in the early 1980s and Algeria more recently suggest that the interaction of religion and state could be socially disruptive and potentially violent, although this is by no means preordained.

At the same time, the emergence of reform movements grounded in religion is a common response to modernization, not a characteristic unique to Islam or to the Middle East. Hindu fundamentalism is a similarly powerful force in contemporary India, for instance. While religious movements have at times totally transformed their societies — the Protestant Reformation in Europe is a prime example — the far more common pattern is for a religious movement to induce a series of changes and influence public political debate, then fade in influence. Previous Islamic political waves often followed this evolutionary process and it is quite possible that the current period may repeat this historical pattern.

■ Conclusion

The tasks facing the peoples and governments of the Middle East in the twenty-first century are compelling. The legacy of colonialism lingers not only in state boundaries and the structure of state institutions, but also in continued Western influence economically as well as militarily. Long-standing domestic and international conflicts create obstacles to meaningful political reform, and yet the overwhelming consensus from the people of the region is that reform is absolutely necessary. Economic reform faces the sizable challenge of increasing the overall prosperity of the region while ensuring that the new wealth does not find its way into only the hands of the entrenched elite. And identity politics could just as easily lead to greater fragmentation as it could unity and cohesion. Fortunately, the people of the Middle East — Arabs, Persians, Israelis, Kurds, Berbers, Turks, and others — bring a diverse array of skills, aspirations, and resources that will aid them in this endeavor.

■ Notes

1. In a recent book, historian R. Stephen Humphreys provides an astute description of one of the strongest steroetypes held by some in the United States:

> No creature in the American political bestiary is more enduring than the Middle East Madman. This creature takes varying forms—the ranking dictator in khaki uniform; the bearded terrorist, head wrapped in the ever-present checked kaffiyeh, bearing a thin smile and a ghostly light in his eyes; the dour yet fiery fundamentalist cleric, likewise bearded and eyes aglow, but wearing a turban and gown. But at bottom they are all alike. . . . They fill the air with terrifying threats, grotesque fabrications, and grandiose dreams of revenge and glory. Most of all they are simply out of touch with reality. They are madmen, impervious to reason and logic, utterly beyond the understanding of rational Westerns.
>
> The Middle East certainly has its full share of extravagant rhetoric and preposterous claims—though some might say the same thing about the United States—but the Middle East Madman is a mythological beast, or nearly so. When we look beyond the facade of theater and posturing, we will almost always discern a hard-headed politician who knows perfectly well how to set his goals and to craft strategies for achieving them. (1999:83)

2. A small number of countries in the region—Israel, Bahrain, and the United Arab Emirates most conspicuously—have embarked on policies designed to strategically situate themselves in a computerized, global economy. But these states, particularly the latter two, have small populations and are, arguably, more akin to Singapore or the Bahamas than to Taiwan or Mexico.

3. Israel made an institutional change in the method of electing its prime minister that coincided with the weakening of control of the major parties in the Knesset. However, decreasing the power of the Labor and Likud Parties was not the intended effect of the modification of the electoral laws, and generational politics played little role in their passage. Interestingly, a return to the earlier approach for determining the prime minister did not immediately result in a resurgence for either Labor or Likud.

■ Bibliography

Ayubi, Nazih N. 1995. *Over-Stating the Arab State: Politics and Society in the Middle East*. London: I. B. Tauris.

Baaklini, Abdo, Guilain Denoeux, and Robert Springborg. 1999. *Legislative Politics in the Arab World: The Resurgence of Democratic Institutions*. Boulder, Colo.: Lynne Rienner.

Cleveland, William L. 2000. *A History of the Modern Middle East*. 2nd ed. Boulder, Colo.: Westview Press.

Humphreys, R. Stephen. 1999. *Between Memory and Desire: The Middle East in a Troubled Age*. Berkeley: University of California Press.

Huntington, Samuel. 1993. "The Clash of Civilizations." *Foreign Affairs* 72:22–49.

Lesch, Ann M., and Dan Tschirgi. 1998. *Origins and Development of the Arab-Israeli Conflict*. Westport, Conn.: Greenwood Press.

Mallat, Chibli. 1996. *The Middle East into the Twenty-First Century: Studies on the Arab-Israeli Conflict, the Gulf Crisis, and Political Islam.* Reading, UK: Ithaca/Garnet.

Roded, Ruth, ed. 1999. *Women in Islam and the Middle East: A Reader.* London: I. B. Tauris.

Said, Edward W. 1979. *Orientalism.* New York: Vintage.

Acronyms

AHC	Arab Higher Committee for Palestine
ANAP	Anavatan Partisi (Motherland Party, Turkey)
ARAMCO	Arabian American Oil Company
ASU	Arab Socialist Union
B.C.E.	before the common era
BP	British Petroleum
C.E.	common era
CFP	French National Oil Company
CIA	Central Intelligence Agency (United States)
DFLP	Democratic Front for the Liberation of Palestine
DHS	Demographic and Health Surveys
DNA	deoxyribonucleic acid
ESCWA	Economic and Social Commission for West Asia (United Nations)
EU	European Union
FBD	father's brother's daughter
FIS	Islamic Salvation Front (Algeria)
FLN	National Liberation Front (Algeria)
GAP	Güneydocu Anadolu Projesi
GCC	Gulf Cooperation Council
GDP	gross domestic product
GNP	gross national product
Hamas	Islamic Resistance Movement
HDI	Human Development Index
ICJ	International Court of Justice
IEA	International Energy Agency

ILO	International Labour Organization
IMF	International Monetary Fund
IPC	Iraq Petroleum Company
KDP	Kurdistan Democratic Party
KOC	Kuwait Oil Company
MENA	Middle East–North Africa
MNP	Milli Nizam Partisi (National Order Party, Turkey)
MSP	Milli Selemet Partisi (National Salvation Party, Turkey)
MTI	Islamic Tendency Movement (Tunisia)
NATO	North Atlantic Treaty Organization
NDP	National Democratic Party (Egypt)
NGO	nongovernmental organization
NIOC	National Iranian Oil Company
OAPEC	Organization of Arab Petroleum Exporting Countries
OECD	Organization for Economic Cooperation and Development
OPEC	Organization of Petroleum Exporting Countries
PA	Palestinian Authority
PCP	Palestine Communist Party
PDR Yemen	People's Democratic Republic of Yemen
PFLP	Popular Front for the Liberation of Palestine
PKK	Kurdistan Workers Party
PLO	Palestine Liberation Organization
PNA	Palestinian National Authority
PPP	purchasing power parity
PROTA	Project for Translation from Arabic
PUK	Patriotic Union of Kurdistan
RP	Refah Partisi (Welfare Party, Turkey)
SAVAK	Sazman-e Ettelaat va Amniyat-e Keshvar
UAE	United Arab Emirates
UAR	United Arab Republic
UN	United Nations
UNDP	United Nations Development Programme
UNESCO	United Nations Educational, Scientific, and Cultural Organization
UNIFEM	United Nations Development Fund for Women
USAID	U.S. Agency for International Development
USFP	Socialist Union of Popular Forces (Morocco)
USSR	Union of Soviet Socialist Republics, the Soviet Union

Basic Political Data

The Basic Political Data appendix was originally compiled by David Dolson and Deborah J. Gerner and updated by Waseem El-Rayes and Deborah J. Gerner based on information from a variety of sources. Accurate data on Middle Eastern political events are often difficult to obtain and conflicting accounts and dates are common. Although we have generally used at least three different sources to corroborate each item, readers may nonetheless find discrepancies in other sources. All population figures are 2002 estimates unless otherwise noted. The United Nations Development Programme's Human Development Index (HDI) is a composite measure based on life expectancy; adult literacy; combined primary, secondary, and tertiary enrollment in school; and adjusted per capita income in each country. The HDI score can range from 0.0 to 1.0, with higher numbers reflecting greater development in terms of longevity, knowledge, and a decent standard of living; n/a indicates the data is not available.

Democratic and Popular Republic of Algeria
Capital City Algiers
Date of Independence from France July 3, 1962
Population 32,278,000
HDI Score 0.697
Rulers Since Independence
1. President Ahmed Ben Bella, 1962–June 1965
2. President Houari Boumedienne, June 1965–December 1978
3. President Benjedid Chadli, February 1979–1992
4. Five-member High Council of State, headed by Muhammed Boudiaf, fulfilled the function of the head of state until January 1994
5. President Liamine Zeroual, appointed January 30, 1994

6. President Liamine Zeroual, November 16, 1995–April 25, 1999
7. President Abdelaziz Bouteflika, elected on April 15, 1999, after all six rivals withdrew, charging electoral fraud

Kingdom of Bahrain

Capital City Manama
Date of Independence from Great Britain August 15, 1971
Population 656,000, including 228,000 non-nationals (about 35 percent)
HDI Score 0.831
Rulers Since Independence
1. Emir Isa ibn Salmon al-Khalifah, 1961–March 6, 1999
2. Emir Hamad ibn Isa al-Khalifah, March 6, 1999– (in February 2002, Bahrain became a constitutional monarchy and Hamad took the title of king)

Federal Islamic Republic of the Comoros

Capital City Moroni
Date of Independence from France July 6, 1975
Population 614,000
HDI Score 0.511
Rulers Since Independence
1. President Ahmed Abdallah, July 1975–August 1975
2. Coup led by Ali Soilih, August 1975; president, 1976–1978 (assassinated)
3. President Ahmed Abdallah, reinstated in coup by mercenaries under Robert Denard, 1978–November 27, 1989 (assassinated)
4. Robert Denard, November 27, 1989–December 15, 1989 (removed by French government)
5. Said Djohar, December 16, 1989–March 1996
6. President Mohammad Taki Abdoulkarim, March 1996–April 30, 1999
7. Coup led by Col. Assoumani Azali, April 30, 1999–

Republic of Djibouti

Capital City Djibouti
Date of Independence from France June 27, 1977
Population 473,000
HDI Score 0.445
Rulers Since Independence
1. President Hassan Gouled Aptidon, June 24, 1977; reelected June 1981, April 1987, May 1993
2. President Isma'il Omar Guelleh, elected May 8, 1999

Arab Republic of Egypt

Capital City Cairo
Date of Independence from Great Britain February 28, 1922
Population 70,712,000
HDI Score 0.642
Rulers Since Independence
1. King Fu'ad I, 1917–1936
2. King Farouk, 1936–1952 (overthrown in coup led by Col. Gamal Abdul Nasser and Abdul-al Hakim)
3. President Mohammed Neguib, June 1953–November 1954
4. Prime Minister Gamal Abdul Nasser, 1954–1956; president, 1956–1970
5. President Anwar Sadat, 1970–October 1981 (assassinated)
6. President Hosni Mubarak, October 14, 1981– ; reelected 1987, 1993, 1999

Islamic Republic of Iran

Capital City Tehran
Date of Independence Not colonized
Population 66,623,000
HDI Score 0.721
Rulers During Twentieth and Twenty-First Centuries
1. Qajar dynasty: Muzaffar al-Din, 1896–1907; Muhammad Ali, 1907–1909; Ahmad, 1909–1924
2. Pahlavi dynasty: Reza Shah, 1925–1941; Mohammad Reza Shah, 1941–1979
3. Religious leaders: Ayatollah Ruhollah Khomeini, 1979–1989; Hojatolislam Sayyed Ali Khamenei, 1989–
   Presidents: Mehdi Bazargan, 1979–1980; Abolhassan Bani-Sadr, 1980–1981; Muhammad Ali Raja'i, 1981; Sayyed Ali Khamenei, October 1981–July 1989; Hojatolislam Ali Akbar Hashemi Rafsanjani, July 1989–1997; Mohammad Khatami, 1997–

Republic of Iraq

Capital City Baghdad
Date of Independence from Great Britain October 3, 1932
Population 24,002,000
HDI Score n/a
Rulers Since Independence
1. King Faisal I, 1921–1933
2. King Ghazi ibn Faisal, 1933–1939
3. King Faisal II, 1939–July 14, 1958 (overthrown)

4. Brig. Gen. Abd al-Karim Qasim, July 14, 1958–February 1963 (overthrown)
5. National Council of Revolutionary Command led by Prime Minister Ahmad Hasan al-Bakr and President Abd al-Salaam Arif, February 1963–November 18, 1963 (overthrown)
6. President Abd al-Salaam Arif, November 1963–April 1966 (died in accident)
7. President Abd al-Rahman Arif, April 1966–July 17, 1968 (overthrown)
8. Revolutionary Command Council led by President Ahmad Hasan al-Bakr, July 17, 1968–July 16, 1979
9. President Saddam Hussein, July 16, 1979–2003 (overthrown by U.S.-led invasion)
10. Interim authority, 2003–

State of Israel

Capital City Tel Aviv or Jerusalem; contested internationally
Date of Independence from Great Britain May 15, 1948
Population 6,030,000
HDI Score 0.896
Rulers Since Independence

1. Prime Minister David Ben-Gurion, 1948–1953
2. Prime Minister Moshe Sharett, 1953–1955
3. Prime Minister David Ben-Gurion, 1955–1963
4. Prime Minister Levi Eshkol, 1963–1969
5. Prime Minister Yigal Allon (acting), 1969
6. Prime Minister Golda Meir, 1969–1974
7. Prime Minister Yitzhak Rabin, 1974–1977
8. Prime Minister Shimon Peres (acting), 1977
9. Prime Minister Menachem Begin, 1977–1983
10. Prime Minister Yitzhak Shamir, 1983–1984
11. Prime Minister Shimon Peres, 1984–1986
12. Prime Minister Yitzhak Shamir, 1986–1992
13. Prime Minister Yitzhak Rabin, 1992–1995 (assassinated)
14. Prime Minister Shimon Peres, 1995–1996
15. Prime Minister Benjamin Netanyahu, 1996–1999
16. Prime Minister Ehud Barak, 1999–2001
17. Prime Minister Ariel Sharon, March 2001–

Hashemite Kingdom of Jordan

Capital City Amman
Date of Independence from Great Britain May 25, 1946
Population 5,307,000
HDI Score 0.717
Rulers Since Independence
1. Emir then King Abdullah, 1921–July 1951 (assassinated)
2. King Talal, 1951–1953 (abdicated)
3. King Hussein I, 1953–February 7, 1999
4. King Abdullah II, February 7, 1999–

State of Kuwait

Capital City Kuwait City
Date of Independence from Great Britain June 19, 1961
Population 2,112,000, including 1,160,000 non-nationals (about 55 percent)
HDI Score 0.813
Rulers Since Independence
1. Shaikh Abdullah III al-Sabah, 1950–1965
2. Shaikh Sabah al-Salim al-Sabah, 1965–1977
3. Shaikh Jabir al-Ahmad al-Jabir al-Sabah, December 31, 1977–

Republic of Lebanon

Capital City Beirut
Date of Independence from France November 22, 1943
Population 3,678,000
HDI Score 0.755
Rulers Since Independence
1. President Bisharaal-Khuri, 1943–1952 (prime ministers: Riyad al-Solh, Sami al-Solh)
2. President Camille Chamoun, 1952–1958 (prime ministers: Abdallah al-Yafi, Sami al-Solh, Rashid Karami)
3. President Fu'ad Chehab, 1958–1964 (prime minister: Rashid Karami)
4. President Charles Hilu, 1964–1970 (prime minister: Rashid Karami)
5. President Sulayman Franjiyya, 1970–1976 (prime ministers: Rachid Anis al-Solh, Rashid Karami, Saeb Salaam)
6. President Elias Sarkis, 1976–1982 (prime minister: Salim al-Hoss)
7. President Beshir Gemayel, 1982 (assassinated)
8. President Amin Gemayel, 1982–1988 (prime ministers: Shafiq al-Wazzan, Rashid Karami, Salim al-Hoss)
9. Gen. Michel Aoun, 1988–1990 (prime minister: Salim al-Hoss)
10. President Elias Hrawi, 1990–1998 (prime ministers: Salim al-Hoss, Umar Karami, Rafiq al-Hariri)

11. President Emile Lahoud, 1998– (prime ministers: Salim al-Hoss, Rafiq al-Hariri)

Socialist People's Libyan Arab Jamahiriyah (Republic)
Capital City Tripoli
Date of Independence from Italy December 24, 1951
Population 5,369,000, including 663,000 non-nationals (about 12 percent)
HDI Score 0.773
Rulers Since Independence
1. King Idris, 1951–1969
2. Col. Muammar Mohammed Qaddafi, leader of the revolution, September 1969–

Islamic Republic of Mauritania
Capital City Nouakchott
Date of Independence from France November 28, 1960
Population 2,829,000
HDI Score 0.438
Rulers Since Independence
1. President Mokhtar Ould Daddah, 1961–July 10, 1978 (overthrown)
2. Lt. Col. Mustapha Ould Mohammed Salek, July 10, 1978–June 1979 (forced to resign)
3. Lt. Col. Mohammed Mahmoud Ould Louly, June 1979–January 4, 1980 (overthrown)
4. Lt. Col. Mohamed Khouna Ould Haidalla, January 4, 1980–December 1984 (overthrown)
5. Col. Maaouya Ould Sidi Ahmed Taya, December 1984– ; elected president in first multiparty elections, January 24, 1992; reelected December 12, 1997

Kingdom of Morocco
Capital City Rabat
Date of Independence from France March 2, 1956
Population 31,168,000
HDI Score 0.602
Rulers Since Independence
1. King Mohammed V, March 2, 1956–1961
2. King Hassan II, March 3, 1961–July 23, 1999
3. King Mohammed VI, July 23, 1999–

Sultanate of Oman

Capital City Muscat
Date of Independence Never officially a colony, but strong British influence
Population 2,713,000, including 527,000 non-nationals (about 19 percent)
HDI Score 0.751
Rulers During Twentieth and Twenty-First Centuries
  1. Sultan Faisal ibn Turki al-Said, 1888–1913
  2. Sultan Tamir ibn Faisal al-Said, 1913–1932
  3. Sultan Said ibn Tamir al-Said, 1932–1970
  4. Sultan Qaboos ibn Said al-Said, 1970–

Palestinian Territories: West Bank and Gaza Strip

Capital City Contested internationally
Date of Independence The Palestinian Authority gained control from Israel of
  most of the Gaza Strip and Jericho areas in May 1994. Subsequent agreements increased the land under Palestinian or joint Israeli-Palestinian jurisdiction. Since 2001, however, Israel has retaken control of many of these
  areas.
Population
  Gaza Strip: 1,226,000
  West Bank: 2,164,000
HDI Score n/a
Rulers Since Gaza-Jericho Agreement
  1. President Yasser Arafat, January 1996–2003
  2. President Yasser Arafat and Prime Minister Mahmoud Abbas (2003);
     President Yasser Arafat and Prime Minister Ahmad Qura'i (2003–)

State of Qatar

Capital City Doha
Date of Independence from Great Britain September 3, 1971
Population 793,000
HDI Score 0.803
Rulers Since Independence
  1. Emir Ahmad ibn Ali, 1971–1972
  2. Emir Khalifah ibn Hamad al-Thani, 1972–June 27, 1995
  3. Emir Hamad ibn Khalifah ibn Hamad al-Thani, June 27, 1995–

Kingdom of Saudi Arabia

Capital City Riyadh
Declaration of United States September 23, 1932
Population 23,513,000, including 5,361,000 non-nationals (about 23 percent)
HDI Score 0.759

Rulers Since Independence
1. King Abdul Aziz ibn Saud, 1932–1953
2. King Saud ibn Saud, 1953–1964
3. King Faisal ibn Saud, 1964–1975 (assassinated)
4. King Khalid ibn Saud, 1975–1982
5. King Fahd ibn Saud, 1982–

Somali Democratic Republic
Capital City Mogadishu
Date of Independence from Italy and Great Britain July 1, 1960
Population 7,753,000
HDI Score n/a
Rulers Since Independence
1. President Aden Abdulla Osman, 1960–1967
2. President Abdirashid Ali Shirmarke, 1967–1969 (assassinated)
3. Maj. Gen. Mohammed Siad Barre, 1969–January 27, 1991
4. No functional government, 1991–2000
5. President Abdikassim Salad Hassan, August 26, 2000– (prime minister: Hassan Abshir Farah)

Democratic Republic of Sudan
Capital City Khartoum
Date of Independence from Great Britain January 1, 1956
Population 37,090,000
HDI Score 0.499
Rulers Since Independence
1. Prime Minister Ismail al-Azhari, 1956
2. Prime Minister Abdulla Khalil, 1956–1958
3. Prime Minister Ibrahim Abboud, 1958–1964
4. Prime Minister Sir el-Khatim el-Khalifah, 1964–1965
5. Prime Minister Muhammed Ahmad Mahgoub, 1965–1966
6. Prime Minister Sayed Sadiq el-Mahdi, 1966–1967
7. Prime Minister Muhammed Ahmad Mahgoub, 1967–1969
8. Prime Minister Abubakr Awadallah, 1969
9. President Jaafar Mohammed Nimeiri, May 1969–April 1985 (overthrown)
10. Lt. Gen. Abdel Rahman Swareddahab, chairman, Transitional Military Council, April 6, 1985–1986
11. President Ahmed Ali al-Mirghani and Prime Minister Sadia al-Mahdi, 1986–June 30, 1989 (overthrown)
12. Prime Minister Omar Hassan Ahmed al-Bashir, June 30, 1989– ; appointed president October 16, 1993

Syrian Arab Republic
Capital City Damascus
Date of Independence from France April 17, 1946
Population 17,156,000
HDI Score 0.691
Rulers Since Independence
1. President Shukri al-Quwatly, 1946–1949 (overthrown)
2. Gen. Husni al-Zaim, March 1949–August 1949
3. Gen. Sami al-Hinnawi, August 1949–December 1949
4. Col. Adib Shishakli, December 1949–February 1954 (overthrown)
5. President Sabri al-Asali, 1956–1958
6. Gamal Abdul Nasser, president of United Arab Republic (Egypt and Syria), 1958–1961 (Abdul-Hakim was the Syrian supervisor during this time)
7. President Nazim al-Qudsi, 1961–1963
8. Gen. Amin al Hafiz, 1963–1966
9. President Salah al-Jadid, 1966–1970 (overthrown)
10. President Hafez al-Assad, 1970–July 17, 2000
11. President Bashar al-Assad, July 17, 2000–

Republic of Tunisia
Capital City Tunis
Date of Independence from France March 20, 1956
Population 9,380,000
HDI Score 0.722
Rulers Since Independence
1. Prime Minister Habib Bourguiba, 1956–July 1957 (becomes republic)
2. President Habib Bourguiba, July 1957–November 1987 (overthrown)
3. President Zine Abidine Ben Ali accedes to the presidency, November 1987; elected October 1999

Republic of Turkey
Capital City Ankara
Date of Independence from Ottoman Empire October 29, 1923
Population 67,309,000
HDI Score 0.742
Rulers Since Independence
1. President Mustafa Kemal (Kemal Atatürk after 1933), 1923–1938
2. President Ismet Inönü, 1938–1950
3. President Mahmud Celal Bayar, 1950–May 27, 1960 (overthrown)
4. General Cemal Gürsel, May 27, 1960–October 1961
5. President Cemal Gürsel, October 1961–1966
6. President Cevdet Sunay, 1966–1973

7. President Fahri Korutürk, 1973–September 12, 1980 (overthrown)
8. General Kenan Evren, September 12, 1980–1982
9. President Kenan Evren, 1982–October 1989
10. President Turgut Ozal, October 1989–April 1993
11. President Suleyman Demirel, April 1993–

United Arab Emirates
Capital City Abu Dhabi
Date of Independence from Great Britain December 2, 1971
Population 2,446,000, including 1,576,000 non-nationals (about 64 percent)
HDI Score 0.812
Rulers Since Independence
1. Shaikh Zayid ibn Sultan al-Nuhayyan, 1971–

Yemen Arab Republic (North Yemen), independent from Ottoman Empire in 1918
Rulers Since Independence
1. Imam Yahya, 1918–1948 (murdered in an attempted coup)
2. Imam Ahmad ibn Yahya, 1948–1962
3. Muhammad al-Badr, 1962 (overthrown after one week)
4. Brig. Gen. Abdullah Sallal, 1962–1967
5. President Abdul Rahman al-Iryani, 1967–1974
6. President Ibrahim Hamdi, 1974–1977
7. President Ahmad Hussein Ghashmi, 1977–1978 (overthrown)
8. President Ali Abdullah Salih, 1978–1990

People's Democratic Republic of Yemen (South Yemen), independent from Great Britain in 1967
Rulers Since Independence
1. President Qahtan al-Sha'bi, 1967–1969 (overthrown)
2. President Salim Rubayyi'ali, 1969–1978 (executed)
3. President Abd al-Fattah Ismaíil, 1978–1980 (resigned)
4. President Ali Nasser Muhammad, 1980–1986
5. President Haider Abu Bakr al-Attas, 1986–1990

Republic of Yemen
Capital City Sana'a
Date of Unification May 22, 1990
Population 18,701,000
HDI Score 0.479
Rulers Since Independence
1. President Ali Abdallah Salih, 1990–

■ Bibliography

Anderson, Ray R., Robert F. Siebert, and John G. Wagner. 2000. *Politics and Change in the Middle East*. 6th. ed. Englewood Cliffs, N.J.: Prentice-Hall.

Bosworth, C. E., E. Van Donzel, B. Lewis, and Ch. Pellat (eds.). 1983. *Encyclopedia of Islam*. Vol. 5. Leiden, Netherlands: E. J. Brill.

Burr, J. Millard, and Robert O. Collins. 1995. *Requiem for the Sudan War, Drought, and Disaster Relief on the Nile*. Boulder, Colo.: Westview Press.

Central Intelligence Agency. 2003. *World Factbook 2002*. http://cia.gov/cia/publications/factbook/index (accessed May 27, 2003).

Collelo, Thomas (ed.). 1988. *Syria: A Country Study*. Area Handbook Series. Washington, D.C.: Government Printing Office.

———. 1989. *Lebanon: A Country Study*. Area Handbook Series. Washington, D.C.: Government Printing Office.

Congressional Quarterly. 2000. *The Middle East*. 9th ed. Washington, D.C.: Congressional Quarterly.

Europa Publications. 2003. *The Middle East and North Africa*. 49th ed. Rochester, Kent, UK: Staples Printers Rochester Limited.

Gordon, April A., and Donald L. Gordon (eds.). 2001. *Understanding Contemporary Africa*. 3rd ed. Boulder, Colo.: Lynne Rienner.

Handloff, Robert E. (ed.). 1990. *Mauritania: A Country Study*. Area Handbook Series. Washington, D.C.: Government Printing Office.

Hiro, Dilip. 2003. *The Middle East at Your Fingertips: A Dictionary of the Middle East*. New York: Carroll & Graf.

Korbani, Agnes. 1995. *The Political Dictionary of Modern Middle East*. Lanham, Md.: University Press of America.

Legum, Colin (ed.). 1976–1998. *Middle East Contemporary Survey*. The Shiloah Center for Middle Eastern and African Studies, Tel Aviv University. Vols. 1–22. New York: Holmes and Meir.

Metz, Helen Chapin (ed.). 1989. *Libya: A Country Study*. Area Handbook Series. Washington, D.C.: Government Printing Office.

———. 1990. *Iraq: A Country Study*. Area Handbook Series. Washington, D.C.: Government Printing Office.

———. 1991. *Egypt: A Country Study*. Area Handbook Series. Washington, D.C.: Government Printing Office.

———. 1991. *Jordan: A Country Study*. Area Handbook Series. Washington, D.C.: Government Printing Office.

———. 1992. *Sudan: A Country Study*. Area Handbook Series. Washington, D.C.: Government Printing Office.

———. 1993. *Saudi Arabia: A Country Study*. Area Handbook Series. Washington, D.C.: Government Printing Office.

———. 1993. *Somalia: A Country Study*. Area Handbook Series. Washington, D.C.: Government Printing Office.

———. 1994. *Algeria: A Country Study*. Area Handbook Series. Washington, D.C.: Government Printing Office.

———. 1994. *Persian Gulf States: Country Studies*. Area Handbook Series. Washington, D.C.: Government Printing Office.

Nelson, Harold D. (ed.). 1985. *Morocco: A Country Study*. Area Handbook Series. Washington, D.C.: Government Printing Office.

———. 1986. *Tunisia: A Country Study*. Area Handbook Series. Washington, D.C.: Government Printing Office.

Simon, Reeva S., Philip Mattar, and Richard W. Bulliet (eds.). 1996. *Encyclopedia of the Modern Middle East*. 5 Vols. New York: Simon and Schuster.

Sluglett, Peter, and Marion Farouk-Sluglett (eds.). 1996. *The Times Guide to the Middle East*. London: Times Books.

UNDP (United Nations Development Programme). 2003. *Human Development Report 2003*. New York: Oxford University Press.

Wright, John W. (ed.). 2003. *The New York Times 2003 Almanac*. New York: Penguin Books.

The Contributors

Mohammed Abu-Nimer is associate professor of political science in the School of International Service at American University in Washington, D.C.

miriam cooke is professor of Asian and African languages and literature at Duke University in North Carolina.

John L. Esposito is university professor of religion and international affairs and director of the Center for Muslim-Christian Understanding at Georgetown University in Washington, D.C.

Deborah J. Gerner is professor of political science and codirector of the Center for International Political Analysis at the University of Kansas in Lawrence.

Arthur Goldschmidt Jr. is professor emeritus of Middle East history at Pennsylvania State University in University Park.

Mohammed A. Muqtedar Khan is assistant professor of political science at Adrian College in Michigan.

Laurie King-Irani is lecturer of anthropology at the University of Victoria in British Columbia.

Ian R. Manners is professor of geography at the University of Texas at Austin.

Valentine M. Moghadam is professor of sociology and director of women's studies at Illinois State University in Normal.

453

Barbara McKean Parmenter is assistant professor of architecture, community, and regional planning at the University of Texas in Austin.

Jillian Schwedler is assistant professor of government and politics at the University of Maryland in College Park.

Simona Sharoni is a member of the faculty at Evergreen State College in Olympia.

Lisa Taraki is associate professor of sociology at Birzeit University in Palestine.

Mary Ann Tétreault is distinguished professor of international affairs at Trinity University in San Antonio.

Elias H. Tuma is professor emeritus of economics at the University of California in Davis.

Index

About the Book

*U*nderstanding the Contemporary Middle East treats the crucial issues facing this complex region at the beginning of the twenty-first century. Designed as a core text for "Introduction to the Middle East" and "Middle East Politics" courses, it can also be used effectively as a supplemental reader in a wide variety of discipline-oriented curriculums. The geographical domain of the volume is the Arab world (including North Africa), Iran, Israel, and Turkey.

The authors provide up-to-date, thorough analyses of not only history, politics, and economics, but also geography, international relations, the roles of religion, class, and ethnicity, the status of women, changing demographics, and literature. Each topic is covered with reference to the latest available scholarship.

All of the chapters in this new edition have been fully revised and updated, and there is an entirely new chapter on the political economy of oil. Maps, photographs, and a table of basic political data enhance the text, which has already made its place as the best available introduction to the region.

Deborah J. Gerner is professor of political science at the University of Kansas. She is author of *One Land, Two Peoples: The Conflict Over Palestine,* as well as numerous articles dealing with the international relations and domestic politics of the Middle East. **Jillian Schwedler** is assistant professor of government and politics at the University of Maryland. Her publications include *Islamist Movements in Jordan* and *Toward Civil Society in the Middle East? A Primer.*